# File System Forensic Analysis

Brian Carrier

**Addison-Wesley**

Upper Saddle River, NJ · Boston · Indianapolis · San Francisco
New York · Toronto · Montreal · London · Munich · Paris · Madrid
Capetown · Sydney · Tokyo · Singapore · Mexico City

The publisher offers excellent discounts on this book when ordered in quantity for bulk purchases or special sales, which may include electronic versions and/or custom covers and content particular to your business, training goals, marketing focus, and branding interests. For more information, please contact:

U. S. Corporate and Government Sales
(800) 382-3419
corpsales@pearsontechgroup.com

For sales outside the U. S., please contact:

International Sales
international@pearsoned.com

Visit us on the Web: www.awprofessional.com

Library of Congress Catalog Number: 2004116962

ISBN-10: 0-32-126817-2
ISBN-13: 978-0-32-126817-4
Text printed in the United States on recycled paper at R. R. Donnelley in Crawfordsville, Indiana.
Eighth printing, February 2009

THIS BOOK IS DEDICATED TO MY GRANDPARENTS,
HENRI, GABRIELLE, ALBERT, AND RITA

# Contents

# Foreword

Computer forensics is a relatively new field, and over the years it has been called many things: "computer forensics," "digital forensics," and "media analysis" to name a few. It has only been in the past few years that we have begun to recognize that all of our digital devices leave digital breadcrumbs and that these breadcrumbs are valuable evidence in a wide range of inquiries. While criminal justice professionals were some of the first to take an interest in this digital evidence, the intelligence, information security, and civil law fields have enthusiastically adopted this new source of information.

Digital forensics has joined the mainstream. In 2003, the American Society of Crime Laboratory Directors–Laboratory Accreditation Board (ASCLD–LAB) recognized digital evidence as a full-fledged forensic discipline. Along with this acceptance came increased interest in training and education in this field. The Computer Forensic Educator's Working Group (now known as the Digital Forensic Working Group) was formed to assist educators in developing programs in this field. There are now over three-dozen colleges and universities that have, or are, developing programs in this field. More join their ranks each month.

I have had the pleasure of working with many law enforcement agencies, training organizations, colleges, and universities to develop digital forensic programs. One of the first questions that I am asked is if I can recommend a good textbook for their course or courses. There have been many books written about this field. Most take a targeted approach to a particular investigative approach, such as incident response or criminal investigation. Some tend to be how-to manuals for specific tools. It has been hard to find a book that provides a solid technical and process foundation for the field…That is, until now.

This book is the foundational book for file system analysis. It is thorough, complete, and well organized. *Brian Carrier has done what needed to be done for this field.* This book provides a solid understanding of both the structures that make up different file systems and how these structures work. Carrier has written this book in such a way that the readers can use what they know about one file system to learn another. This book will be invaluable as a textbook and as a reference and needs to be on the shelf of every digital forensic practitioner and educator. It will also provide accessible reading for those who want to understand subjects such as data recovery.

When I was first approached about writing this Foreword, I was excited! I have known Brian Carrier for a number of years and I have always been impressed with his wonderful balance of incredible technical expertise and his ability to clearly explain not just what he knows but, more importantly, what you need to know. Brian's work on Autopsy and The Sleuth Kit (TSK) has demonstrated his command of this field—his name is a household name in the digital forensic community. I have been privileged to work with Brian in his current role at Purdue University, and he is helping to do for the academic community what he did for the commercial sector: He set a high standard.

So, it is without reservation that I recommend this book to you. It will provide you with a solid foundation in digital media.

Mark M. Pollitt
President, Digital Evidence Professional Services, Inc.
Retired Director of the FBI's Regional Computer Forensic Laboratory Program

# Preface

One of the biggest challenges that I have faced over the years while developing *The Sleuth Kit* (TSK) has been finding good file and volume system (such as partition tables, RAID, and so on) documentation. It also has been challenging to explain to users why certain files cannot be recovered or what to do when a corrupt file system is encountered because there are no good references to recommend. It is easy to find resources that describe file systems at a high level, but source code is typically needed to learn the details. My goal for this book is to fill the void and describe how data are stored on disk and describe where and how digital evidence can be found.

There are two target audiences for this book. One is the experienced investigator that has learned about digital investigations from real cases and using analysis tools. The other is someone who is new to the field and is interested in learning about the general theory of an investigation and where digital evidence may exist but is not yet looking for a book that has a tutorial on how to use a specific tool.

The value of the material in this book is that it helps to provide an *education* rather than training on a specific tool. Consider some of the more formal sciences or engineering disciplines. All undergraduates are required to take a couple of semesters of physics, chemistry, or biology. These courses are not required because the students will be using all the material for the rest of their careers. In fact, software and equipment exist to perform many of the calculations students are forced to memorize. The point of the classes is to provide students with insight about how things work so that they are not constrained by their tools.

The goal of this book is to provide an investigator with an education similar to what Chemistry 101 is to a chemist in a forensics lab. The majority of digital evidence is found on a disk, and knowing how and why the evidence exists can help an investigator to better testify about it. It also will help an investigator find errors and bugs in his analysis tools because he can conduct sanity checks on the tool output.

The recent trends in digital investigations have shown that more education is needed. Forensic labs are being accredited for digital evidence, and there are debates about the required education and certification levels. Numerous universities offer courses and even Master's degrees in computer forensics. Government and university labs are conducting theoretical research in the area and focusing on future, as well as current, problems. There are also peer-reviewed journals for publishing research and investigation techniques. All these new directions require in-depth knowledge outside of a specific tool or technique.

The approach of this book is to describe the basic concepts and theory of a volume and file system and then apply it to an investigation. For each file system, this book covers analysis techniques and special considerations that the investigator should make. Scenarios are given to reinforce how the information can be used in an actual case. In addition, the data structures associated with volume and file systems are given, and disk images are analyzed by hand so that you can see where the various data are located. If you are not interested in parsing data structures, you can skip the data structure chapters. Only non-commercial tools are used so that you can download them for free and duplicate the results on your systems.

## ROADMAP

This book is organized into three parts. Part 1 provides the basic foundations, and Parts 2 and 3 provide the technical meat of the book. The book is organized so that we move up the layers of abstraction in a computer. We start by discussing hard disks and then discuss how disks are organized into partitions. After we discuss partitions, we discuss the contents of partitions, which are typically a file system.

Part 1, "Foundations," starts with Chapter 1, "Digital Investigation Foundations," and discusses the approach I take to a digital investigation. The different phases and guidelines are presented so that you know where I use the techniques described in this book. This book does not require that you use the same approach that I do. Chapter 2, "Computer Foundations," provides the computer foundations and describes data structures, data encoding, the boot process, and hard disk technology. Chapter 3, "Hard Disk Data Acquisition," provides the theory and a case study of hard disk acquisition so that we have data to analyze in Parts 2 and 3.

Part 2, "Volume Analysis," of the book is about the analysis of data structures that partition and assemble storage volumes. Chapter 4, "Volume Analysis," provides a general overview of the volume analysis techniques, and Chapter 5, "PC-based Partitions," examines the common DOS and Apple partitions. Chapter 6, "Server-based Partitions," covers the partitions found in BSD, Sun Solaris, and Itanium-based systems. Chapter 7, "Multiple Disk Volumes," covers RAID and volume spanning.

Part 3, "File System Analysis," of the book is about the analysis of data structures in a volume that are used to store and retrieve files. Chapter 8, "File System Analysis," covers the general theory of file system analysis and defines terminology for the rest of Part 3. Each file system has at least two chapters dedicated to it where the first chapter discusses the basic concepts and investigation techniques and the second chapter includes the data structures and manual analysis of example disk images. You have a choice of reading the two chapters in parallel, reading one after the other, or skipping the data structures chapter altogether.

The designs of the file systems are very different, so they are described using a general file system model. The general model organizes the data in a file system into one of five categories: file system, content, metadata, file name, and application. This general model is used to describe each of the file systems so that it is easier to compare them.

Chapters 9, "FAT Concepts and Analysis," and 10, "FAT Data Structures," detail the FAT file system, and Chapters 11, "NTFS Concepts," 12, "NTFS Analysis," and 13, "NTFS Data Structures," cover NTFS. Next, we skip to the Unix file systems with Chapters 14, "Ext2 and Ext3 Concepts and Analysis," and 15, "Ext2 and Ext3 Data Structures," on the Linux Ext2 and Ext3 file systems. Lastly, Chapters 16, "UFS1 and UFS2 Concepts and Analysis," and 17, "UFS1 and UFS2 Data Structures," examine UFS1 and UFS2, which are found in FreeBSD, NetBSD, OpenBSD, and Sun Solaris.

After Part 3 of this book, you will know where a file existed on disk and the various data structures that need to be in sync for you to view it. This book does not discuss how to analyze the file's contents.

## SCOPE OF BOOK

Now that you know what is included in this book, I will tell you what is not in this book. This book stops at the file system level and does not look at the application level. Therefore, we do not look at how to analyze various file formats. We also do not look at what files a specific OS or application creates. If you are interested in a step-by-step guide to investigating a Windows '98 computer that has been used to download suspect files, then you will be disappointed with this book. If you want a guide to investigating a compromised Linux server, then you may learn a few tricks in this book, but it is not what you are looking for. Those topics fall into the application analysis realm and require another book to do them justice. If you are interested in having more than just a step-by-step guide, then this book is probably for you.

## RESOURCES

As I mentioned in the beginning, the target audience for this book is not someone who is new to the field and looking for a book that will show the basic investigation concepts or how to use a specific tool. There are several quality books that are breadth-based, including:

Casey, Eoghan. *Digital Evidence and Computer Crime*. 2nd ed. London: Academic Press, 2004.

Kruse, Warren and Jay Heiser. *Computer Forensics*. Boston: Addison Wesley, 2002.

Mandia, Kevin, Chris Prosise, and Matt Pepe. *Incident Response and Computer Forensics*. Emeryville: McGraw Hill/Osborne, 2003.

Throughout this book, I will be using *The Sleuth Kit* (TSK) on example disk images so that both the raw data and formatted data can be shown. That is not to say that this is a tutorial on using TSK. To learn only about using TSK, the previous books or the computer forensic chapters in *Know Your Enemy*, 2nd Edition should be referred to. The appendix in this book describes TSK and Autopsy (a graphical interface for TSK). TSK and additional documentation can be downloaded from http://www.sleuthkit.org.

The URLs of other tools that are used throughout the book will be given as needed. Additional resources, links, and corrections will be available from http://www.digital-evidence.org/fsfa/.

Any corrections can be e-mailed to me at fsfa@digital-evidence.org.

# Acknowledgments

I would like to thank many people for helping me with digital forensics. First, thanks go out to those who have helped me in general over the years. My appreciation goes to Eoghan Casey, Dave Dittrich, Dan Farmer, Dan Geer, Dan Kalil, Warren Kruse, Gary Palmer, Eugene Spafford, Lance Spitzner, and Wietse Venema for various forms of guidance, knowledge, and opportunities.

I would also like to thank Cory Altheide, Eoghan Casey, Knut Eckstein, and Jim Lyle for reviewing the entire book. Special thanks go to Knut, who went through every hexdump dissection of the example disk images and verified each hexadecimal to decimal conversion (and found several typos), and to Eoghan for reminding me when the content needed more practical applications. Christopher Brown, Simson Garfinkel, Christophe Grenier, Barry Grundy, Gord Hama, Jesse Kornblum, Troy Larson, Mark Menz, Richard Russon, and Chris Sanft all reviewed and improved one or more chapters in their areas of expertise.

Many folks at Addison Wesley and Pearson helped to make this book possible. Jessica Goldstein guided and encouraged me through the process, Christy Hackerd made sure the editing and production process went smoothly, and Chanda Leary-Coutu provided her marketing expertise. Thanks to Elise Walter for her copyediting, Christal Andry for her proofreading, Eric Schroeder for his indexing, Jake McFarland for his composition work, and Chuti Prasertsith for his cover design work.

Finally, many thanks to my family and especially to my best friend (and Mrs.-to-be) Jenny, who helped me find balance in life despite the nights and weekends that I spent hunched over a keyboard (and went as far as buying me an X-Box as a distraction from data structures and abstraction layers). Also, thanks to our cat, Achoo, for reminding me each day that playing with hair elastics and laser pointers is almost as fun as playing with ones and zeros.

# PART I
## FOUNDATIONS

# Digital Investigation Foundations

I am going to assume that anyone interested in this book does not need motivation with respect to why someone would want to investigate a computer or other digital device, so I will skip the customary numbers and statistics. This book is about how you can conduct a smarter investigation, and it is about data and how they are stored. Digital investigation tools have become relatively easy to use, which is good because they reduce the time needed to conduct an investigation. However, it also means that the investigator may not fully understand the results. This could be dangerous when the investigator needs to testify about the evidence and from where it came. This book starts with the basic foundations of investigations and computers and then examines volume and file systems. There are many ways of conducting an investigation, and this chapter describes one of them. You do not need to take the same approach, but this chapter shows where I think the contents of this book fit into the bigger picture.

## DIGITAL INVESTIGATIONS AND EVIDENCE

There is an abundant number of digital forensic and investigation definitions, and this section gives the definitions that I use and a justification for them. The focus of a digital investigation is going to be some type of digital device that has been involved in an incident or crime. The digital device was either used to commit a physical crime or it executed a digital event that violated a policy or law. An example of the first case is if a suspect used the Internet to conduct research about a physical crime. Examples of the latter case are when an attacker gains unauthorized access to a computer, a user downloads contraband material, or a user sends a threatening e-mail. When the violation is detected, an investigation is started to answer questions such as why the violation occurred and who or what caused it to occur.

A *digital investigation* is a process where we develop and test hypotheses that answer questions about digital events. This is done using the scientific method where we develop a hypothesis using evidence that we find and then test the hypothesis by looking for additional evidence that shows the hypothesis is impossible. *Digital evidence* is a digital object that contains reliable information that supports or refutes a hypothesis.

Consider a server that has been compromised. We start an investigation to determine how it occurred and who did it. During the investigation, we find data that were created by events related to the incident. We recover deleted log entries from the server, find attack tools, and find numerous vulnerabilities that existed on the server. Using this data, and more, we develop hypotheses about which vulnerability the attacker used to gain access and what she did afterwards. Later, we examine the firewall configuration and logs and determine that some of the scenarios in our hypotheses are impossible because that type of network traffic could not have existed, and we do not find the necessary log entries. Therefore, we have found evidence that refutes one or more hypotheses.

In this book, I use the term *evidence* in the investigative context. Evidence has both legal and investigative uses. The definition that I previously gave was for the investigative uses of evidence, and there could be situations where not all of it can be entered into a court of law. Because the legal admissibility requirements vary by country and state and because I do not have a legal background, I am going to focus on the general concept of evidence, and you can make the adjustments needed in your jurisdiction.[1] In fact, there are no legal requirements that are specific to file systems, so the general digital investigation books listed in the Preface can provide the needed information.

So far, you may have noticed that I have not used the term "forensic" during the discussion about a digital investigation. The American Heritage Dictionary defines forensic as an adjective and "relating to the use of science or technology in the investigation and establishment of facts or evidence in a court of law" [Houghton Mifflin Company 2000]. The nature of digital evidence requires us to use technology during an investigation, so the main difference between a digital investigation and a digital forensic investigation is the introduction of legal requirements. A *digital forensic investigation* is a process that uses science and technology to analyze digital objects and that develops and tests theories, which can be entered into a court of law, to answer questions about events that

---

1. A good overview of U.S. law is *Cybercrime* [Clifford 2001].

occurred. In other words, a digital forensic investigation is a more restricted form of digital investigation. I will be using the term digital investigation in this book because the focus is on the technology and not specific legal requirements.

## DIGITAL CRIME SCENE INVESTIGATION PROCESS

There is no single way to conduct an investigation. If you ask five people to find the person who drank the last cup of coffee without starting a new pot, you will probably see five different approaches. One person may dust the pot for fingerprints, another may ask for security camera tapes of the break room, and another may look for the person with the hottest cup of coffee. As long as we find the right person and do not break any laws in the process, it does not matter which process is used, although some are more efficient than others.

The approach that I use for a digital investigation is based on the physical crime scene investigation process [Carrier and Spafford 2003]. In this case, we have a digital crime scene that includes the digital environment created by software and hardware. The process has three major phases, which are system preservation, evidence searching, and event reconstruction. These phases do not need to occur one after another, and the flow is shown in Figure 1.1.

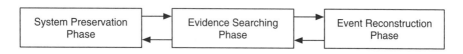

**Figure 1.1**    The three major phases of a digital crime scene investigation.

This process can be used when investigating both live and dead systems. A *live analysis* occurs when you use the operating system or other resources of the system being investigated to find evidence. A *dead analysis* occurs when you are running trusted applications in a trusted operating system to find evidence. With a live analysis, you risk getting false information because the software could maliciously hide or falsify data. A dead analysis is more ideal, but is not possible in all circumstances.

## SYSTEM PRESERVATION PHASE

The first phase in the investigation process is the *System Preservation Phase* where we try to preserve the state of the digital crime scene. The actions that are taken in this phase vary depending on the legal, business, or operational requirements of the investigation. For example, legal requirements may cause you to unplug the system and make a full copy of all data. On the other extreme could be a case involving a spyware infection or a honeypot[2] and no preservation is performed. Most investigations in a corporate or military setting that will not go to court use techniques in between these two extremes.

The purpose of this phase is to reduce the amount of evidence that may be overwritten. This process continues after data has been acquired from the system because we need to preserve the data for future analysis. In Chapter 3, "Hard Disk Data Acquisition," we will look at how to make a full copy of a hard disk, and the remainder of the book will cover how to analyze the data and search for evidence.

### Preservation Techniques

The goal of this phase is to reduce the amount of evidence that is overwritten, so we want to limit the number processes that can write to our storage devices. For a dead analysis, we will terminate all processes by turning the system off, and we will make duplicate copies of all data. As will be discussed in Chapter 3, write blockers can be used to prevent evidence from being overwritten.

For a live analysis, suspect processes can be killed or suspended. The network connection can be unplugged (plug the system into an empty hub or switch to prevent log messages about a dead link), or network filters can be applied so that the perpetrator cannot connect from a remote system and delete data. Important data should be copied from the system in case it is overwritten while searching for evidence. For example, if you are going to be reading files, then you can save the temporal data for each file so that you have a copy of the last access times before you cause them to be updated.

When important data are saved during a dead or live analysis, a cryptographic hash should be calculated to later show that the data have not changed. A cryptographic hash, such as MD5, SHA-1, and SHA-256, is a mathematical formula that generates a very big number based on input data. If any bit of the input data changes, the output number changes dramatically. (A more detailed description can be found in *Applied Cryptography*, 2nd Edition [Schneier 1995].) The algorithms are designed such that it is extremely difficult to find two inputs that generate the same output. Therefore, if the hash value of your important data changes, then you know that the data has been modified.

---

2. A honeypot is "an information resource whose value lies in unauthorized or illicit use of that resource" [Honeynet Project 2004].

## EVIDENCE SEARCHING PHASE

After we have taken steps to preserve the data we need to search them for evidence. Recall that we are looking for data that support or refute hypotheses about the incident. This process typically starts with a survey of common locations based on the type of incident, if one is known. For example, if we are investigating Web-browsing habits, we will look at the Web browser cache, history file, and bookmarks. If we are investigating a Linux intrusion, we may look for signs of a rootkit or new user accounts. As the investigation proceeds and we develop hypotheses, we will search for evidence that will refute or support them. It is important to look for evidence that refutes your hypothesis instead of only looking for evidence that supports your hypothesis.

The theory behind the searching process is fairly simple. We define the general characteristics of the object for which we are searching and then look for that object in a collection of data. For example, if we want all files with the JPG extension, we will look at each file name and identify the ones that end with the characters ".JPG." The two key steps are determining for what we are looking and where we expect to find it.

Part 2, "Volume Analysis," and Part 3, "File System Analysis," of this book are about searching for evidence in a volume and file system. In fact, the file system analysis chapters are organized so that you can focus on a specific category of data that may contain your evidence. The end of this chapter contains a summary of the popular investigation toolkits, and they all allow you to view, search, and sort the data from a suspect system so that you can find evidence.

### Search Techniques

Most searching for evidence is done in a file system and inside files. A common search technique is to search for files based on their names or patterns in their names. Another common search technique is to search for files based on a keyword in their content. We can also search for files based on their temporal data, such as the last accessed or written time.

We can search for known files by comparing the MD5 or SHA-1 hash of a file's content with a hash database such as the National Software Reference Library (NSRL) (http://www.nsrl.nist.gov). Hash databases can be used to find files that are known to be bad or good. Another common method of searching is to search for files based on signatures in their content. This allows us to find all files of a given type even if someone has changed their name.

When analyzing network data, we may search for all packets from a specific source address or all packets going to a specific port. We also may want to find packets that have a certain keyword in them.

## EVENT RECONSTRUCTION PHASE

The last phase of the investigation is to use the evidence that we found and determine what events occurred in the system. Our definition of an investigation was that we are trying to answer questions about digital events in the system. During the Evidence Searching Phase, we might have found several files that violate a corporate policy or law, but that does not answer questions about events. One of the files may have been the effect of an event that downloaded it, but we should also try to determine which application downloaded it. Is there evidence that a Web browser downloaded them, or could it be from malware? (Several cases have used malware as a defense when contraband or other digital evidence has been found [George 2004; Brenner, Carrier, and Henninger 2004].) After the digital event reconstruction phase, we may be able to correlate the digital events with physical events.

Event reconstruction requires knowledge about the applications and the OS that are installed on the system so that you can create hypotheses based on their capabilities. For example, different events can occur in Windows 95 than Windows XP, and different versions of the Mozilla web browser can cause different events. This type of analysis is out of the scope of this book, but general guidelines can be found in Casey [2004].

## GENERAL GUIDELINES

Not every investigation will use the same procedures, and there could be situations where you need to develop a new procedure. This book might be considered a little academic because it does not cover only what exists in current tools. There are some techniques that have not been implemented, so you may have to improvise to find the evidence. Here are my PICL guidelines, which will hopefully keep you out of one when you are developing new procedures. PICL stands for *preservation, isolation, correlation, and logging*.

The first guideline is *preservation* of the system being investigated. The motivation behind this guideline is that you do not want to modify any data that could have been evidence, and you do not want to be in a courtroom where the other side tries to convince the jury that you may have overwritten exculpatory evidence. This is what we saw in the Preservation Phase of the investigation process. Some examples of how the preservation guideline is implemented are

- Copy important data, put the original in a safe place, and analyze the copy so that you can restore the original if the data is modified.
- Calculate MD5 or SHA hashes of important data so that you can later prove that the data has not changed.

- Use a write-blocking device during procedures that could write to the suspect data.
- Minimize the number of files created during a live analysis because they could overwrite evidence in unallocated space.
- Be careful when opening files on the suspect system during a live analysis because you could be modifying data, such as the last access time.

The second guideline is to *isolate* the analysis environment from both the suspect data and the outside world. You want to isolate yourself from the suspect data because you do not know what it might do. Running an executable from the suspect system could delete all files on your computer, or it could communicate with a remote system. Opening an HTML file from the suspect system could cause your Web browser to execute scripts and download files from a remote server. Both of these are potentially dangerous, and caution should be taken. Isolation from the suspect data is implemented by viewing data in applications that have limited functionality or in a virtual environment, such as VMWare (`http://www.vmware.com`), that can be easily rebuilt if it is destroyed.

You should isolate yourself from the outside world so that no tampering can occur and so that you do not transmit anything that you did not want to. For example, the previous paragraph described how something as simple as an HTML page could cause you to connect to a remote server. Isolation from the outside world is typically implemented using an analysis network that is not connected to the outside world or that is connected using a firewall that allows only limited connectivity.

Note that isolation is difficult with live analysis. By definition, you are not isolated from the suspect data because you are analyzing a system using its OS, which is suspect code. Every action you take involves suspect data. Further, it is difficult to isolate the system from the outside world because that requires removing network connectivity, and live analysis typically occurs because the system must remain active.

The third guideline is to *correlate* data with other independent sources. This helps reduce the risk of forged data. For example, we will later see that timestamps can be easily changed in most systems. Therefore, if time is very important in your investigation, you should try to find log entries, network traffic, or other events that can confirm the file activity times.

The final guideline is to *log* and document your actions. This helps identify what searches you have not yet conducted and what your results were. When doing a live analysis or performing techniques that will modify data, it is important to document what you do so that you can later document what changes in the system were because of your actions.

## DATA ANALYSIS

In the previous section, I said we were going to search for digital evidence, which is a rather general statement because evidence can be found almost anywhere. In this section, I am going to narrow down the different places where we can search for digital evidence and identify which will be discussed later in this book. We will also discuss which data we can trust more than others.

## ANALYSIS TYPES

When analyzing digital data, we are looking at an object that has been designed by people. Further, the storage systems of most digital devices have been designed to be scalable and flexible, and they have a layered design. I will use this layered design to define the different analysis types [Carrier 2003a].

If we start at the bottom of the design layers, there are two independent analysis areas. One is based on storage devices and the other is based on communication devices. This book is going to focus on the analysis of storage devices, specifically non-volatile devices, such as hard disks. The analysis of communication systems, such as IP networks, is not covered in this book, but is elsewhere [Bejtlich 2005; Casey 2004; Mandia et al. 2003].

Figure 1.2 shows the different analysis areas. The bottom layer is Physical Storage Media Analysis and involves the analysis of the physical storage medium. Examples of physical store mediums include hard disks, memory chips, and CD-ROMs. Analysis of this area might involve reading magnetic data from in between tracks or other techniques that require a clean room. For this book, we are going to assume that we have a reliable method of reading data from the physical storage medium and so we have a stream 1s and 0s that were previously written to the storage device.

We now analyze the 1s and 0s from the physical medium. Memory is typically organized by processes and is out of the scope of this book. We will focus on non-volatile storage, such as hard disks and flash cards.

Storage devices that are used for non-volatile storage are typically organized into volumes. A *volume* is a collection of storage locations that a user or application can write to and read from. We will discuss volume analysis in Part 2 of the book, but there are two major concepts in this layer. One is partitioning, where we divide a single volume into multiple smaller volumes, and the other is assembly, where we combine multiple volumes into one larger volume, which may later be partitioned. Examples of this category include DOS partition tables, Apple partitions, and RAID arrays. Some media, such as floppy disks, do not have any data in this layer, and the entire disk is a volume. We will need to analyze data at the volume level to determine where the file system or other data are located and to determine where we may find hidden data.

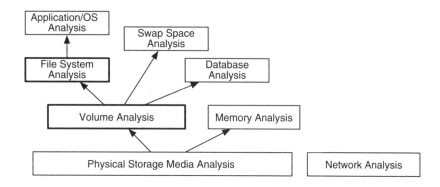

**Figure 1.2**    Layers of analysis based on the design of digital data. The bold boxes are covered in this book.

Inside each volume can be any type of data, but the most common contents are file systems. Other volumes may contain a database or be used as a temporary swap space (similar to the Windows pagefile). Part 3 of the book focuses on *file systems*, which is a collection of data structures that allow an application to create, read, and write files. We analyze a file system to find files, to recover deleted files, and to find hidden data. The result of file system analysis could be file content, data fragments, and metadata associated with files.

To understand what is inside of a file, we need to jump to the application layer. The structure of each file is based on the application or OS that created the file. For example, from the file system perspective, a Windows registry file is no different from an HTML page because they are both files. Internally, they have very different structures and different tools are needed to analyze each. Application analysis is very important, and it is here where we would analyze configuration files to determine what programs were running or to determine what a JPEG picture is of. I do not discuss application analysis in this book because it requires multiple books of its own to cover in the same detail that file systems and volumes are covered here. Refer to the general digital investigation books listed in the Preface for more information.

We can see the analysis process in Figure 1.3. This shows a disk that is analyzed to produce a stream of bytes, which are analyzed at the volume layer to produce volumes. The volumes are analyzed at the file system layer to produce a file. The file is then analyzed at the application layer.

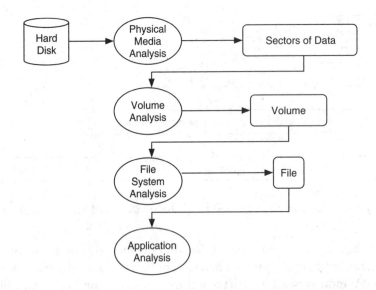

**Figure 1.3**    Process of analyzing data at the physical level to the application level.

## ESSENTIAL AND NONESSENTIAL DATA

All data in the layers previously discussed have some structure, but not all structure is necessary for the layer to serve its core purpose. For example, the purpose of the file system layer is to organize an empty volume so that we can store data and later retrieve them. The file system is required to correlate a file name with file content. Therefore, the name is essential and the on-disk location of the file content is essential. We can see this in Figure 1.4 where we have a file named miracle.txt and its content is located at address 345. If either the name or the address were incorrect or missing, then the file content could not be read. For example, if the address were set to 344, then the file would have different content.

Figure 1.4 also shows that the file has a last accessed time. This value is not essential to the purpose of the file system, and if it were changed, missing, or incorrectly set, it would not affect the process of reading or writing file content.

In this book, I introduce the concept of essential and nonessential data because we can trust essential data but we may not be able to trust nonessential data. We can trust that the file content address in a file is accurate because otherwise the person who used the system would not have been able to read the data. The last access time may or may not be accurate. The OS may not have updated it after the last access, the user may have changed the time, or the OS clock could have been off by three hours, and the wrong time was stored.

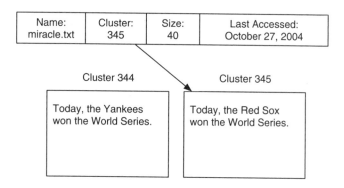

**Figure 1.4**  To find and read this file, it is essential for the name, size, and content location to be accurate, but it is not essential for the last accessed time to be accurate.

Note that just because we trust the number for the content address does not mean that we trust the actual content at that address. For example, the address value in a deleted file may be accurate, but the data unit could have been reallocated and the content at that address is for a new file. Nonessential data may be correct most of the time, but you should try to find additional data sources to support them when they are used in an incident hypothesis (i.e., the correlation in the PICL guidelines). In Parts 2 and 3 of the book, I will identify which data are essential and which are not.

## OVERVIEW OF TOOLKITS

There are many tools that can help an investigator analyze a digital system. Most tools focus on the preservation and searching phases of the investigation. For the rest of this book, I will be showing examples using *The Sleuth Kit* (TSK), which I develop and which is described later in this section. TSK is free, which means that any reader can try the examples in this book without having to spend more money.

This book is not intended to be a TSK tutorial, and not everyone wants to use Unix-based, non-commercial tools. Therefore, I am including a list of the most common analysis tools. Most of the techniques described in this book can be performed using these tools. Tools that are restricted to law enforcement are not listed here. The descriptions are not an exhaustive list of features and are based on the content of their Web site. I have not confirmed or used every feature, but each of the vendors has reviewed these descriptions.

If you are interested in a more extensive list of tools, refer to Christine Siedsma's Electronic Evidence Information site (`http://www.e-evidence.info`) or Jacco Tunnissen's Computer Forensics, Cybercrime and Steganography site (`http://www.forensics.nl`). I also maintain a list of open source forensics tools that are both commercial and non-commercial (`http://www.opensourceforensics.org`). This book helps show the theory of how a tool is analyzing a file system, but I think open source tools are useful for investigations because they allow an investigator or a trusted party to read the source code and verify how a tool has implemented the theory. This allows an investigator to better testify about the digital evidence [Carrier 2003b].

## EnCase by Guidance Software

There are no official numbers on the topic, but it is generally accepted that *EnCase* (`http://www.encase.com`) is the most widely used computer investigation software. EnCase is Windows-based and can acquire and analyze data using the local or network-based versions of the tool. EnCase can analyze many file system formats, including FAT, NTFS, HFS+, UFS, Ext2/3, Reiser, JFS, CD-ROMs, and DVDs. EnCase also supports Microsoft Windows dynamic disks and AIX LVM.

EnCase allows you to list the files and directories, recover deleted files, conduct keyword searches, view all graphic images, make timelines of file activity, and use hash databases to identify known files. It also has its own scripting language, called EnScript, which allows you to automate many tasks. Add-on modules support the decryption of NTFS encrypted files and allow you to mount the suspect data as though it were a local disk.

## Forensic Toolkit by AccessData

The *Forensic Toolkit* (FTK) is Windows-based and can acquire and analyze disk, file system, and application data (`http://www.accessdata.com`). FTK supports FAT, NTFS, and Ext2/3 file systems, but is best known for its searching abilities and application-level analysis support. FTK creates a sorted index of the words in a file system so that individual searches are much faster. FTK also has many viewers for different file formats and supports many e-mail formats.

FTK allows you to view the files and directories in the file system, recover deleted files, conduct keyword searches, view all graphic images, search on various file characteristics, and use hash databases to identify known files. AccessData also has tools for decrypting files and recovering passwords.

## ProDiscover by Technology Pathways

*ProDiscover* (http://www.techpathways.com) is a Windows-based acquisition and analysis tool that comes in both local and network-based versions. ProDiscover can analyze FAT, NTFS, Ext2/3, and UFS file systems and Windows dynamic disks. When searching, it provides the basic options to list the files and directories, recover deleted files, search for keywords, and use hash databases to identify known files. ProDiscover is available with a license that includes the source code so that an investigator or lab can verify the tool's actions.

## SMART by ASR Data

*SMART* (http://www.asrdata.com) is a Linux-based acquisition and analysis tool. Andy Rosen, who was the original developer for Expert Witness (which is now called EnCase), developed SMART. SMART takes advantage of the large number of file systems that Linux supports and can analyze FAT, NTFS, Ext2/3, UFS, HFS+, JFS, Reiser, CD-ROMs, and more. To search for evidence, it allows you to list and filter the files and directories in the image, recover deleted files, conduct keyword searches, view all graphic images, and use hash databases to identify known files.

## The Sleuth Kit / Autopsy

*The Sleuth Kit* (TSK) is a collection of Unix-based command line analysis tools, and Autopsy is a graphical interface for TSK (http://www.sleuthkit.org). The file system tools in TSK are based on *The Coroner's Toolkit* (TCT) (http://www.porcupine.org), which was written by Dan Farmer and Wietse Venema. TSK and Autopsy can analyze FAT, NTFS, Ext2/3, and UFS file systems and can list files and directories, recover deleted files, make timelines of file activity, perform keyword searches, and use hash databases. We will be using TSK throughout this book, and Appendix A, "The Sleuth Kit and Autopsy," provides a description of how it can be used.

## Summary

There is no single way to conduct an investigation, and I have given a brief overview of one approach that I take. It has only three major phases and is based on a physical crime scene investigation procedure. We have also looked at the major investigation types and a summary of the available toolkits. In the next two chapters, we will look at the computer fundamentals and how to acquire data during the Preservation Phase of an investigation.

## BIBLIOGRAPHY

Bejtlich, Richard. *The Tao of Network Security Monitoring: Beyond Intrusion Detection.* Boston: Addison Wesley, 2005.

Brenner, Susan, Brian Carrier, and Jef Henninger. "The Trojan Defense in Cybercrime Cases." *Santa Clara Computer and High Technology Law Journal*, 21(1), 2004.

Carrier, Brian. "Defining Digital Forensic Examination and Analysis Tools Using Abstraction Layers." *International Journal of Digital Evidence*, Winter 2003a. http://www.ijde.org.

Carrier, Brian. "Open Source Digital Forensic Tools: The Legal Argument." Fall 2003b. http://www.digital-evidence.org.

Carrier, Brian, and Eugene H. Spafford. "Getting Physical with the Digital Investigation Process." *International Journal of Digital Evidence*, Fall 2003. http://www.ijde.org.

Casey, Eoghan. *Digital Evidence and Computer Crime.* 2nd ed. London: Academic Press, 2004.

Clifford, Ralph, ed. *Cybercrime: The Investigation, Prosecution, and Defense of a Computer-Related Crime.* Durham: Carolina Academic Press, 2001.

George, Esther. "UK Computer Misuse Act—The Trojan Virus Defense." *Journal of Digital Investigation*, 1(2), 2004.

The Honeynet Project. *Know Your Enemy.* 2nd ed. Boston: Addison-Wesley, 2004.

Houghton Mifflin Company. *The American Heritage Dictionary.* 4th ed. Boston: Houghton Mifflin, 2000.

Mandia, Kevin, Chris Prosise, and Matt Pepe. *Incident Response and Computer Forensics.* 2nd ed. Emeryville: McGraw Hill/Osborne, 2003.

Schneier, Bruce. *Applied Cryptography.* 2nd ed. New York: Wiley Publishing, 1995.

# Computer Foundations

2

The goal of this chapter is to cover the low-level basics of how computers operate. In the following chapters of this book, we examine, in detail, how data are stored, and this chapter provides background information for those who do not have programming or operating system design experience. This chapter starts with a discussion about data and how they are organized on disk. We discuss binary versus hexadecimal values and little- and big-endian ordering. Next, we examine the boot process and code required to start a computer. Lastly, we examine hard disks and discuss their geometry, ATA commands, host protected areas, and SCSI.

## DATA ORGANIZATION

The purpose of the devices we investigate is to process digital data, so we will cover some of the basics of data in this section. We will look at binary and hexadecimal numbers, data sizes, endian ordering, and data structures. These concepts are essential to how data are stored. If you have done programming before, this should be a review.

### BINARY, DECIMAL, AND HEXADECIMAL

First, let's look at number formats. Humans are used to working with decimal numbers, but computers use binary, which means that there are only 0s and 1s. Each 0 or 1 is called a bit, and bits are organized into groups of 8 called bytes. Binary numbers are similar to decimal numbers except that decimal numbers have 10 different symbols (0 to 9) instead of only 2.

Before we dive into binary, we need to consider what a decimal number is. A decimal number is a series of symbols, and each symbol has a value. The symbol in the right-most column has a value of 1, and the next column to the left has a value of 10. Each column has a value that is 10 times as much as the previous column. For example, the second column from the right has a value of 10, the third has 100, the fourth has 1,000, and so on. Consider the decimal number 35,812. We can calculate the decimal value of this number by multiplying the symbol in each column with the column's value and adding the products. We can see this in Figure 2.1. The result is not surprising because we are converting a decimal number to its decimal value. We will use this general process, though, to determine the decimal value of non-decimal numbers.

Decimal Number: 35,812

| 10,000 | 1,000 | 100 | 10 | 1 |
|--------|-------|-----|----|----|
| 3 | 5 | 8 | 1 | 2 |

(3 x 10,000) + (5 x 1,000) + (8 x 100) + (1 x 10) + (2 x 1) = 35,812

**Figure 2.1**   The values of each symbol in a decimal number.

The right-most column is called the *least significant symbol,* and the left-most column is called the *most significant symbol.* With the number 35,812, the 3 is the most significant symbol, and the 2 is the least significant symbol.

Now let's look at binary numbers. A binary number has only two symbols (0 and 1), and each column has a decimal value that is two times as much as the previous column. Therefore, the right-most column has a decimal value of 1, the second column from the right has a decimal value of 2, the third column's decimal value is 4, the fourth column's decimal value is 8, and so on. To calculate the decimal value of a binary number, we simply add the value of each column multiplied by the value in it. We can see this in Figure 2.2 for the binary number 1001 0011. We see that its decimal value is 147.

For reference, Table 2.1 shows the decimal value of the first 16 binary numbers. It also shows the hexadecimal values, which we will examine next.

Binary Number: 1001 0011

| 128 | 64 | 32 | 16 | 8 | 4 | 2 | 1 |
|-----|----|----|----|---|---|---|---|
| 1 | 0 | 0 | 1 | 0 | 0 | 1 | 1 |

(1 x 128) + (0 x 64) + (0 x 32) + (1 x 16) + (0 x 8) + (0 x 4) + (1 x 2) + (1 x 1) = 147

**Figure 2.2**   Converting a binary number to its decimal value.

**Table 2.1**   Binary, decimal, and hexadecimal conversion table.

| Binary | Decimal | Hexadecimal |
|--------|---------|-------------|
| 0000 | 00 | 0 |
| 0001 | 01 | 1 |
| 0010 | 02 | 2 |
| 0011 | 03 | 3 |
| 0100 | 04 | 4 |
| 0101 | 05 | 5 |
| 0110 | 06 | 6 |
| 0111 | 07 | 7 |
| 1000 | 08 | 8 |
| 1001 | 09 | 9 |
| 1010 | 10 | A |
| 1011 | 11 | B |
| 1100 | 12 | C |
| 1101 | 13 | D |
| 1110 | 14 | E |
| 1111 | 15 | F |

Now let's look at a hexadecimal number, which has 16 symbols (the numbers 0 to 9 followed by the letters A to F). Refer back to Table 2.1 to see the conversion between the base hexadecimal symbols and decimal symbols. We care about hexadecimal numbers because it's easy to convert between binary and hexadecimal, and they are frequently used when looking at raw data. I will precede a hexadecimal number with '0x' to differentiate it from a decimal number.

We rarely need to convert a hexadecimal number to its decimal value by hand, but I will go through the process once. The decimal value of each column in a hexadecimal number increases by a factor of 16. Therefore, the decimal value of the first column is 1, the second column has a decimal value of 16, and the third column has a decimal value of 256. To convert, we simply add the result from multiplying the column's value with the symbol in it. Figure 2.3 shows the conversion of the hexadecimal number 0x8BE4 to a decimal number.

Hexadecimal Number: 0x8BE4

| Reference | | | | |
|---|---|---|---|---|
| 0xB = 11 | 4,096 | 256 | 16 | 1 |
| 0xE = 14 | 8 | 11 | 14 | 4 |

$$(8 \times 4{,}096) + (11 \times 256) + (14 \times 16) + (4 \times 1) = 35{,}812$$

**Figure 2.3**   Converting a hexadecimal value to its decimal value.

Lastly, let's convert between hexadecimal and binary. This is much easier because it requires only lookups. If we have a hexadecimal number and want the binary value, we look up each hexadecimal symbol in Table 2.1 and replace it with the equivalent 4 bits. Similarly, to convert a binary value to a hexadecimal value, we organize the bits into groups of 4 and then look up the equivalent hexadecimal symbol. That is all it takes. We can see this in Figure 2.4 where we convert a binary number to hexadecimal and the other way around.

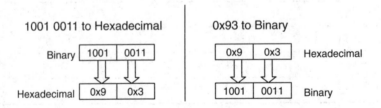

**Figure 2.4**   Converting between binary and hexadecimal requires only lookups from Table 2.1.

Sometimes, we want to know the maximum value that can be represented with a certain number of columns. We do this by raising the number of symbols in each column by the number of columns and subtract 1. We subtract 1 because we need to take the 0 value into account. For example, with a binary number we raise 2 to the number of bits in the value and subtract 1. Therefore, a 32-bit value has a maximum decimal value of

$$2^{32} - 1 = 4,294,967,295$$

Fortunately, most computers and low-level editing tools have a calculator that converts between binary, decimal, and hexadecimal, so you do not need to memorize these techniques. In this book, the on-disk data are given in hexadecimal, and I will convert the important values to decimal and provide both.

## DATA SIZES

To store digital data, we need to allocate a location on a storage device. You can think of this like the paper forms where you need to enter each character in your name and address in little boxes. The name and address fields have allocated space on the page for the characters in your name. With digital data, bytes on a disk or in memory are allocated for the bytes in a specific value.

A byte is the smallest amount of space that is typically allocated to data. A byte can hold only 256 values, so bytes are grouped together to store larger numbers. Typical sizes include 2, 4, or 8 bytes. Computers differ in how they organize multiple-byte values. Some of them use *big-endian ordering* and put the most significant byte of the number in the first storage byte, and others use *little-endian ordering* and put the least significant byte of the number in the first storage byte. Recall that the most significant byte is the byte with the most value (the left-most byte), and the least significant byte is the byte with the least value (the right-most byte).

Figure 2.5 shows a 4-byte value that is stored in both little and big endian ordering. The value has been allocated a 4-byte slot that starts in byte 80 and ends in byte 83. When we examine the disk and file system data in this book, we need to keep the endian ordering of the original system in mind. Otherwise, we will calculate the incorrect value.

IA32-based systems (i.e., Intel Pentium) and their 64-bit counterparts use the little-endian ordering, so we need to "rearrange" the bytes if we want the most significant byte to be the left-most number. Sun SPARC and Motorola PowerPC (i.e., Apple computers) systems use big-endian ordering.

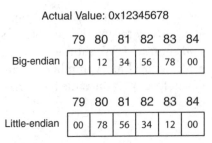

**Figure 2.5**   A 4-byte value stored in both big- and little-endian ordering.

## STRINGS AND CHARACTER ENCODING

The previous section examined how a computer stores numbers, but we must now consider how it stores letters and sentences. The most common technique is to encode the characters using ASCII or Unicode. ASCII is simpler, so we will start there. ASCII assigns a numerical value to the characters in American English. For example, the letter 'A' is equal to 0x41, and '&' is equal to 0x26. The largest defined value is 0x7E, which means that 1 byte can be used to store each character. There are many values that are defined as control characters and are not printable, such the 0x07 bell sound. Table 2.2 shows the hexadecimal number to ASCII character conversion table. A more detailed ASCII table can be found at http://www.asciitable.com/.

**Table 2.2**   Hexadecimal to ASCII conversion table.

| 00 – NULL | 10 – DLE | 20 – SPC | 30 – 0 | 40 – @ | 50 – P | 60 – ` | 70 – p |
|---|---|---|---|---|---|---|---|
| 01 – SOH | 11 – DC1 | 21 – ! | 31 – 1 | 41 – A | 51 – Q | 61 – a | 71 – q |
| 02 – STX | 12 – DC2 | 22 – " | 32 – 2 | 42 – B | 52 – R | 62 – b | 72 – r |
| 03 – ETX | 13 – DC3 | 23 – # | 33 – 3 | 43 – C | 53 – S | 63 – c | 73 – s |
| 04 – EOT | 14 – DC4 | 24 – $ | 34 – 4 | 44 – D | 54 – T | 64 – d | 74 – t |
| 05 – ENQ | 15 – NAK | 25 – % | 35 – 5 | 45 – E | 55 – U | 65 – e | 75 – u |
| 06 – ACK | 16 – SYN | 26 – & | 36 – 6 | 46 – F | 56 – V | 66 – f | 76 – v |
| 07 – BEL | 17 – ETB | 27 – ' | 37 – 7 | 47 – G | 57 – W | 67 – g | 77 – w |
| 08 – BS | 18 – CAN | 28 – ( | 38 – 8 | 48 – H | 58 – X | 68 – h | 78 – x |
| 09 – TAB | 19 – EM | 29 – ) | 39 – 9 | 49 – I | 59 – Y | 69 – i | 79 – y |

**Table 2.2**   Hexadecimal to ASCII conversion table (continued).

| | | | | | | | |
|---|---|---|---|---|---|---|---|
| 0A – LF | 1A – SUB | 2A – * | 3A – ; | 4A – J | 5A – Z | 6A – j | 7A – z |
| 0B – BT | 1B – ESC | 2B – + | 3B – ; | 4B – K | 5B – [ | 6B – k | 7B – { |
| 0C – FF | 1C – FS | 2C – , | 3C – < | 4C – L | 5C – \ | 6C – l | 7C – \| |
| 0D – CR | 1D – GS | 2D – - | 3D – = | 4D – M | 5D – ] | 6D – m | 7D – } |
| 0E – SO | 1E – RS | 2E – . | 3E – > | 4E – N | 5E – ^ | 6E – n | 7E – ~ |
| 0F – SI | 1F – US | 2F – / | 3F – ? | 4F – O | 5F – _ | 6F – o | 7F – |

To store a sentence or a word using ASCII, we need to allocate as many bytes as there are characters in the sentence or word. Each byte stores the value of a character. The endian ordering of a system does not play a role in how the characters are stored because these are separate 1-byte values. Therefore, the first character in the word or sentence is always in the first allocated byte. The series of bytes in a word or sentence is called a *string*. Many times, the string ends with the NULL symbol, which is 0x00. Figure 2.6 shows an example string stored in ASCII. The string has 10 symbols in it and is NULL terminated so it has allocated 11 bytes starting at byte 64.

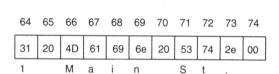

**Figure 2.6**   An address that is represented in ASCII starting at memory address 64.

ASCII is nice and simple if you use American English, but it is quite limited for the rest of the world because their native symbols cannot be represented. Unicode helps solve this problem by using more than 1 byte to store the numerical version of a symbol. (More information can be found at www.unicode.org.) The version 4.0 Unicode standard supports over 96,000 characters, which requires 4-bytes per character instead of the 1 byte that ASCII requires.

There are three ways of storing a Unicode character. The first method, UTF-32, uses a 4-byte value for each character, which might waste a lot of space. The second method, UTF-16, stores the most heavily used characters in a 2-byte value and the lesser-used characters in a 4-byte value. Therefore, on average this uses less space than UTF-32.

The third method is called UTF-8, and it uses 1, 2, or 4 bytes to store a character. Each character requires a different number of bytes, and the most frequently used bytes use only 1 byte.

UTF-8 and UTF-16 use a variable number of bytes to store each character and, therefore, make processing the data more difficult. UTF-8 is frequently used because it has the least amount of wasted space and because ASCII is a subset of it. A UTF-8 string that has only the characters in ASCII uses only 1 byte per character and has the same values as the equivalent ASCII string.

## DATA STRUCTURES

Before we can look at how data are stored in specific file systems, we need to look at the general concept of data organization. Let's return back to the previous example where we compared digital data sizes to boxes on a paper form. With a paper form, a label precedes the boxes and tells you that the boxes are for the name or address. Computers do not, generally, precede file system data with a label. Instead, they simply know that the first 32 bytes are for a person's name and the next 32 bytes are for the street name, for example.

Computers know the layout of the data because of data structures. A data structure describes how data are laid out. It works like a template or map. The data structure is broken up into fields, and each field has a size and name, although this information is not saved with the data. For example, our data structure could define the first field to be called 'number' and have a length of 2 bytes. It is used to store the house number in our address. Immediately after the 'number' field is the 'street' field and with a length of 30 bytes. We can see this layout in Table 2.3.

**Table 2.3**    A basic data structure for the house number and street name.

| Byte Range | Description |
| --- | --- |
| 0–1 | 2-byte house number |
| 2–31 | 30-byte ASCII street name |

If we want to write data to a storage device, we refer to the appropriate data structure to determine where each value should be written. For example, if we want to store the address 1 Main St., we would first break the address up into the number and name. We would write the number 1 to bytes 0 to 1 of our storage space and then write "Main St." in bytes 2 to 9 by determining what the ASCII values are for each character. The remaining bytes can be set to 0 since we do not need them. In this case, we allocated 32 bytes of storage space, and it can be any where in the device. The byte offsets are relative to the start of the space we were allocated. Keep in mind that the order of the bytes in the house number depends on the endian ordering of the computer.

When we want to read data from the storage device, we determine where the data starts and then refer to its data structure to find out where the needed values are. For example, let's read the data we just wrote. We learn where it starts in the storage device and then apply our data structure template. Here is the output of a tool that reads the raw data.

```
0000000: 0100 4d61 696e 2053 742e 0000 0000 0000  ..Main St.......
0000016: 0000 0000 0000 0000 0000 0000 0000 0000  ...............
0000032: 1900 536f 7574 6820 5374 2e00 0000 0000  ..South St......
0000048: 0000 0000 0000 0000 0000 0000 0000 0000  ...............
```

The previous output is from the xxd Unix tool and is similar to a graphical hex-editor tool. The left column is the byte offset of the row in decimal, the 8 middle columns are 16 bytes of the data in hexadecimal, and the last column is the ASCII equivalent of the data. A '.' exists where there is no printable ASCII character for the value. Remember that each hexadecimal symbol represents 4 bits, so a byte needs 2 hexadecimal symbols.

We look up the layout of our data structure and see that each address is 32 bytes, so the first address is in bytes 0 to 31. Bytes 0 to 1 should be the 2 byte number field, and bytes 2 to 31 should be the street name. Bytes 0 to 1 show us the value 0x0100. The data are from an Intel system, which is little-endian, and we will therefore have to switch the order of the 0x01 and the 0x00 to produce 0x0001. When we convert this to decimal we get the number 1.

The second field in the data structure is in bytes 2 to 31 and is an ASCII string, which is not effected by the endian ordering of the system, so we do not have to reorder the bytes. We can either convert each byte to its ASCII equivalent or, in this case, cheat and look on the right column to see "Main St.." This is the value we previously wrote. We see that another address data structure starts in byte 32 and extends until byte 63. You can process it as an exercise (it is for 25 South St).

Obviously, the data structures used by a file system will not be storing street addresses, but they rely on the same basic concepts. For example, the first sector of the file system typically contains a large data structure that has dozens of fields in it and we need to read it and know that the size of the file system is given in bytes 32 to 35. Many file systems have several large data structures that are used in multiple places.

## FLAG VALUES

There is one last data type that I want to discuss before we look at actual data structures, and it is a flag. Some data are used to identify if something exists, which can be represented with either a 1 or a 0. An example could be whether a partition is bootable or not. One method of storing this information is to allocate a full byte for it and save the 0 or 1 value. This wastes a lot of space, though, because only 1 bit is needed, yet 8 bits are allocated. A more efficient method is to pack several of these binary conditions into one value. Each bit in the value corresponds to a feature or option. These are frequently called *flags* because each bit flags whether a condition is true. To read a flag value, we need to convert the number to binary and then examine each bit. If the bit is 1, the flag is set.

Let's look at an example by making our previous street address data structure a little more complex. The original data structure had a field for the house number and a field for the street name. Now, we will add an optional 16-byte city name after the street field. Because the city name is optional, we need a flag to identify if it exists or not. The flag is in byte 31 and bit 0 is set when the city exists (i.e., 0000 0001). When the city exists, the data structure is 48 bytes instead of 32. The new data structure is shown in Table 2.4.

**Table 2.4**   A data structure with a flag value.

| Byte Range | Description |
| --- | --- |
| 0–1 | 2-byte house number |
| 2–30 | 29-byte ASCII street name |
| 31–31 | Flags |
| 32–47 | 16-byte ASCII city name (if flag is set) |

Here is sample data that was written to disk using this data structure:

```
0000000: 0100 4d61 696e 2053 742e 0000 0000 0000   ..Main St.......
0000016: 0000 0000 0000 0000 0000 0000 0000 0061   ...............a
0000032: 426f 7374 6f6e 0000 0000 0000 0000 0000   Boston..........
0000048: 1800 536f 7574 6820 5374 2e00 0000 0000   ..South St......
0000064: 0000 0000 0000 0000 0000 0000 0000 0060   ...............`
```

On the first line, we see the same data as the previous example. The address is 1 Main St, and the flag value in byte 31 has a value of 0x61. The flag is only 1 byte in size, so we do not have to worry about the endian ordering. We need to look at this value in binary, so we use the lookup table previously given in Table 2.1 and convert the values 0x6 and 0x1 to the binary value 0110 0001. We see that the least significant bit is set, which is the flag for the city. The other bits are for other flag values, such as identifying this address as a business address. Based on the flag, we know that bytes 32 to 47 contain the city name, which is "Boston." The next data structure starts at byte 48, and its flag field is in byte 79. Its value is 0x60, and the city flag is not set. Therefore, the third data structure would start at byte 80.

We will see flag values through out file system data structures. They are used to show which features are enabled, which permissions are in effect, and if the file system is in a clean state.

## BOOTING PROCESS

In the following chapters of this book, we are going to discuss where data reside on a disk and which data are essential for the operation of the computer. Many times, I will refer to boot code, which are machine instructions used by the computer when it is starting. This section describes the boot process and where boot code can be found. Many disks reserve space for boot code, but do not use it. This section will help you to identify which boot code is being used.

### CENTRAL PROCESSING UNITS AND MACHINE CODE

The heart of a modern computer is one or more *Central Processing Units* (CPU). Example CPUs are the Intel Pentium and Itanium, AMD Athlon, Motorola PowerPC, and Sun UltraSPARC. CPUs by themselves are not very useful because they do only what they are told. They are similar to a calculator. A calculator can do amazing things, but a human needs to be sitting in front of it and entering numbers.

CPUs get their instructions from memory. CPU instructions are written in machine code, which is difficult to read and not user-friendly. It is, in general, two levels below the C or Perl programming languages that many people have seen. The level in between is an assembly language, which is readable by humans but still not very user-friendly.

I will briefly describe machine code so that you know what you are looking at when you see machine code on a disk. Each machine code instruction is several bytes long, and the first couple of bytes identify the type of instruction, called the *opcode.* For example, the value 3 could be for an addition instruction. Following the opcode are the arguments to the instruction. For example, the arguments for the addition instruction would be the two numbers to add.

We do not really need much more detail than that for this book, but I will finish with a basic example. One of the machine instructions is to move values into registers of the CPU. Registers are places where CPUs store data. An assembly instruction to do this is MOV AH,00 where the value 0 is moved into the AH register. The machine code equivalent is the hexadecimal value 0xB400 where B4 is the opcode for MOV AH and 00 is the value, in hexadecimal, to move in. There are tools that will translate the machine code to the assembly code for you, but as you can see, it is not always obvious that you are looking at machine code versus some other random data.

## BOOT CODE LOCATIONS

We just discussed that the CPU is the heart of the computer and needs to be fed instructions. Therefore, to start a computer, we need to have a device that feeds the CPU instructions, also known as boot code. In most systems, this is a two-step process where the first step involves getting all the hardware up and running, and the second step involves getting the OS or other software up and running. We will briefly look into boot code because all volume and file systems have a specific location where boot code is stored, and it is not always needed.

When power is applied to a CPU, it knows to read instructions from a specific location in memory, which is typically *Read Only Memory* (ROM). The instructions in ROM force the system to probe for and configure hardware. After the hardware is configured, the CPU searches for a device that may contain additional boot code. If it finds such a device, its boot code is executed, and the code attempts to locate and load a specific operating system. The process after the bootable disk is found is platform-specific, and I will cover it in more detail in the following chapters.

As an example, though, we will take a brief look at the boot process of a Microsoft Windows system. When the system is powered on, the CPU reads instructions from the *Basic Input / Output System* (BIOS), and it searches for the hard disks, CD drives, and other hardware devices that it has been configured to support. After the hardware has been located, the BIOS examines the floppy disks, hard disks, and CDs in some configured order and looks at the first sector for boot code. The code in the first sector of a bootable disk causes the CPU to process the partition table and locate the bootable partition where the Windows operating system is located. In the first sector of the partition is more boot code, which locates and loads the actual operating system. We can see how the various components refer to each other in Figure 2.7.

In the Windows example, if the boot code on the disk were missing, the BIOS would not find a bootable device and generate an error. If the boot code on the disk could not find boot code in one of the partitions, it would generate an error. We will examine each of these boot code locations in the following chapters.

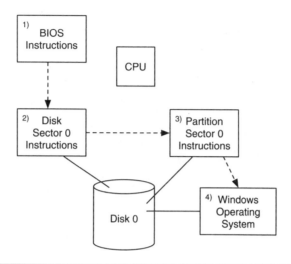

**Figure 2.7** The relationship among the various boot code locations in an IA32 system.

## HARD DISK TECHNOLOGY

If a digital investigator can learn about only one piece of hardware in a computer, hard disks are probably his best choice because they are one of the most common sources of digital evidence. This section covers hard disks basics and discusses topics that are of interest to an investigator, such as access methods, write blocking, and locations where data can be hidden. The first section is an overview of how a disk works, and the next two sections cover *AT Attachment* (ATA/IDE) disks and *Small Computer Systems Interface* (SCSI) disks, respectively.

### HARD DISK GEOMETRY AND INTERNALS

Let's start with the internals of all modern hard disks. This information is useful for a basic understanding of how data are stored and because older file systems and partitioning schemes use disk geometry and other internal values that are hidden with modern disks. Therefore, knowing about disk geometry will help you to understand some of the values in a file system. The goal of this section is not to enable you to fix hard disks. Instead, the goal is to obtain a conceptual understanding of what is going on inside.

Hard disks contain one or more circular platters that are stacked on top of each other and spin at the same time. A picture of the inside of a disk can be found in Figure 2.8. The bottom and top of each platter is coated with a magnetic media, and when the disk is manufactured, the platters are uniform and empty.

**Figure 2.8**   The inside of an ATA disk where we see the platters on the right and an arm on the left that reads from and writes to the platters.

Inside the disk is an arm that moves back and forth, and it has a head on the top and bottom of each platter that can read and write data, although only one head can read or write at a time.

A low-level format is performed on the blank platters to create data structures for tracks and sectors. A track is a circular ring that goes around the platter. It is similar to a lane on a running track so that if you go around the entire circle, you will end in the same location that you started. Each track on the hard disk is given an address from the outside inward, starting with 0. For example, if there were 10,000 tracks on each platter, the outside track of each platter would be 0, and the inside track (nearest the center of the circle) would be 9,999. Because the layout of each platter is the same and the tracks on each platter are given the same address, the term cylinder is used to describe all tracks at a given address on all platters. For example, cylinder 0 is track 0 on the bottom and top of all platters in the hard disk. The heads in the disk are given an address so that we can uniquely identify which platter and on which side of the platter we want to read from or write to.

Each track is divided into sectors, which is the smallest addressable storage unit in the hard disk and is typically 512 bytes. Each sector is given an address, starting at 1 for each track. Therefore, we can address a specific sector by using the cylinder address (C) to get the track, the head number (H) to get the platter and side, and the sector address (S) to get the sector in the track. We can see this in Figure 2.9.

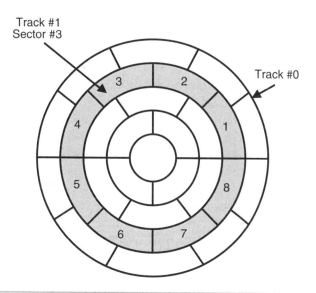

Track #1
Sector #3

Track #0

**Figure 2.9**   Disk geometry of one platter showing the track (or cylinder) and sector addresses (not even close to scale).

We will discuss in the "Types of Sector Addresses" section that the CHS address is no longer used as the primary addressing method. The *Logical Block Address* (LBA) is instead used, and it assigns sequential addresses to each sector. The LBA address may not be related to its physical location.

A sector can become defective and should therefore no longer be used to store user data. With older disks, it was the responsibility of the operating system to know where the bad sectors were and to not allocate them for files. Users could also manually tell the disk which sectors to ignore because they were bad. In fact, many file systems still provide the option to mark sectors as bad. This is typically not needed, though, because modern disks can identify a bad sector and remap the address to a good location somewhere else on the disk. The user never knows that this has happened.

The previous description of the layout is overly simplified. In reality, the disk arranges the location of the sectors to obtain the best performance. So, sectors and tracks may be offset to take advantage of the seek times and speeds of the drive. For the needs of many investigators, this simplistic view is good enough because most of us do not have clean rooms, and the equipment to locate where a specific sector is located on a platter. A more detailed discussion of drive internals can be found in *Forensic Computing* [Sammes and Jenkinson 2000].

## ATA / IDE INTERFACE

The *AT Attachment* (ATA) interface is the most popular hard disk interface. Disks that use this interface are frequently referred to as IDE disks, but IDE simply stands for *Integrated Disk Electronics* and identifies a hard disk that has the logic board built into it, which older disks did not. The actual interface that the "IDE" disks use is ATA. This section goes into some of the relevant details of the ATA specification so that we can discuss technologies, such as hardware write blockers and host protected areas.

The ATA specifications are developed by the T13 Technical Committee (`http://www.t13.org`), which is a committee for the *International Committee on Information Technology Standards* (INCITS). The final version of each specification is available for a fee, but draft versions are freely available on the INCITS Web site. For the purposes of learning about hard disks, the draft versions are sufficient.

ATA disks require a *controller*, which is built into the motherboard of modern systems. The controller issues commands to one or two ATA disks using a ribbon cable. The cable has maximum length of 18 inches and has 40 pins, but newer disks have an extra 40 wires that are not connected to any pins. The interface can be seen in Figure 2.10. The extra wires are there to prevent interference between the wires. Laptops frequently have a smaller disk and use a 44-pin interface, which includes pins for power. Adaptors can be used to convert between the two interfaces, as can be seen in Figure 2.11. There is also a 44-pin high-density interface that is used in portable devices, such as Apple iPods.

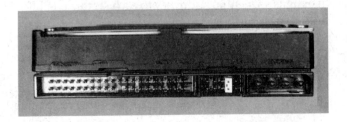

**Figure 2.10**   An ATA disk with the 40-pin connector, jumpers, and power connector.

The interface data path between the controller and disks is called a *channel*. Each channel can have two disks, and the terms "master" and "slave" were given to them, even though neither has control over the other. ATA disks can be configured as master or slave using a physical jumper on the disk. Some also can be configured to use "Cable Select," where they will be assigned as master or slave based on which plug they have on the ribbon cable. Most consumer computers have two channels and can support four ATA disks.

**Figure 2.11** A 44-pin ATA laptop drive connected to a 40-pin ATA ribbon cable using an adaptor (Photo courtesy of Eoghan Casey).

## TYPES OF SECTOR ADDRESSES

To read or write data from the disk, we need to be able to address the sectors. As we will see later in the book, a single sector will be assigned a new address each time a partition, file system, or file uses it. The address that we are referring to in this section is its physical address. The *physical address* of a sector is its address relative to the start of the physical media.

There are two different physical addressing methods. Older hard disks used the disk geometry and the CHS method, which we already discussed. Refer to Figure 2.9 for a simplistic example of how the cylinder and head addresses are organized.

The CHS addressing scheme sounds good, but it has proven to be too limiting and is not used much anymore. The original ATA specification used a 16-bit cylinder value, a 4-bit head value, and an 8-bit sector value, but the older BIOSs used a 10-bit cylinder value, 8-bit head value, and a 6-bit sector value. Therefore, to communicate with the hard disk through the BIOS, the smallest size for each value had to be used, which allowed only a 504MB disk.

To work around the 504MB limit, new BIOSes were developed that would translate the address ranges that they liked to the addresses that the ATA specification liked. For example, if the application requested data from cylinder 8, head 4, and sector 32, the BIOS might translate that and request cylinder 26, head 2, sector 32 from the disk. For translation to work, the BIOS will report a hard disk geometry that is different from what actually existed on the disk. The translation process does not work for disks that are larger than 8.1GB.

BIOSes that perform address translation are not as common anymore, but an investigator may run into difficulties if he encounters such a system. If he pulls the disk out of the system and puts it into one of his systems, the translation might not exist or might be different, and an acquisition or dead analysis cannot be performed because the wrong sectors will be returned. To solve this problem, an investigator needs to use the original system or find a similar system that performs the same translation. An investigator can determine if a system is doing translation by looking up the BIOS version on the vendors website or by looking for references in the BIOS.

To overcome the 8.1GB limit associated with translation, the CHS addresses were abandoned, and *Logical Block Addresses* (LBA) became standard. LBA uses a single number, starting at 0, to address each sector and has been supported since the first formal ATA specification. With LBA, the software does not need to know anything about the geometry; it needs to know only a single number. Support for CHS addresses was removed from the ATA specification in ATA-6.

Unfortunately, some of the file system and other data structures still use CHS addresses, so we need to be able to convert from CHS to LBA throughout this book. LBA address 0 is CHS address 0,0,1 and LBA 1 is CHS address 0,0,2. When all the sectors in the track have been used, the first sector at the next head in the same cylinder is used, which is CHS address 0,1,1. You can visualize this as filling the outer ring of the bottom platter, then moving up platters until the top platter is reached. Then, the second ring on the bottom platter is used. The conversion algorithm is

```
LBA = ((((CYLINDER * heads_per_cylinder) + HEAD) * sectors_per_track) + SECTOR - 1
```

where you replace CYLINDER, HEAD, and SECTOR with the respective CHS address values. For example, consider a disk that reported 16 heads per cylinder and 63 sectors per track. If we had a CHS address of cylinder 2, head 3, and sector 4, its conversion to LBA would be as follows:

```
2208 = (((2 * 16) + 3) * 63) + 4 - 1
```

### Interface Standards

There are a lot of interface terms in the consumer hard disk arena, which can be confusing. Some of the terms mean the same thing, where a standards committee chose one, and a hard disk company chose another. A description of the unofficial terms, such as "Enhanced IDE" and "Ultra ATA," can be found in the PC Guide's "Unofficial IDE/ATA Standards and Marketing Programs" (`http://www.pcguide.com/ref/hdd/if/ide/unstd.htm`). In general, each new standard adds a faster method of reading and writing data or fixes a size limitation of a previous standard.

Note that ATA specifications are applicable to only hard disks. Removable media, such as CD-ROMs and ZIP disks, need to use a special specification, called *AT Attachment Packet Interface* (ATAPI). ATAPI devices typically use the same cables and controller, but they require special drivers.

Here are some of the highlights of the specifications that are of interest to an investigation:

- ATA-1: Originally published in 1994. This specification had support for CHS and 28-bit LBA addresses [T13 1994].
- ATA-3: This specification was published in 1997 and added reliability and security features.*Self-Monitoring Analysis and Reporting Technology* (SMART) was introduced, which attempts to improve reliability by monitoring several parts of the disk. Passwords were also introduced in this specification [T13 1997].
- ATA / ATAPI-4: ATAPI, the specification for removable media, was integrated into the ATA specification in ATA-4, which was published in 1998. The 80-wire cable was introduced to help decrease interference. ATA-4 added the HPA, which will be discussed later [T13 1998].
- ATA / ATAPI-6: This specification was published in 2002, added 48-bit LBA addresses, removed support for CHS addresses, and added the DCO [T13 2002].
- ATA / ATAPI-7: This specification is still in draft form at the time of this writing. The drafts include serial ATA, which will be discussed later.

### Disk Commands

This section provides an overview of how the controller and hard disk communicate, which will help when we discuss hardware write protectors and the host protected area. This section does not apply to ATAPI devices, such as CD-ROMs.

The controller issues commands to the hard disk over the ribbon cable. The commands are issued to both disks on the cable, but part of the command identifies if it is for the master or slave. The controller communicates with the hard disk by writing to its registers, which are small pieces of memory. The registers work like an online order form where the controller writes data into specific registers like you would write data into specific fields of the form. When all the necessary data has been written to the registers, the controller writes to the command register, and the hard disk processes the command. This is like hitting the submit button of an HTML form. In theory, the disk should not do anything until the command register is written to.

For example, consider a case where the controller wants to read a sector of the disk. It would need to write the sector address and number of sectors to read in the appropriate registers. After the command details have been written to the registers, the controller would instruct the hard disk to perform the read action by writing to the command register.

### Hard Disk Passwords

The ATA-3 specification introduced new optional security features, including passwords that can be set through the BIOS or various software applications. If implemented, there are two passwords in hard disks, the user and the master passwords. The master password was designed so that a company administrator could gain access to the computer in case the user password was lost. If passwords are being used, there are two modes that the disk can operate in: high and maximum. In the high security mode, the user and master password can unlock the disk. In maximum-security mode, the user password can unlock the disk but the master password can unlock the disk only after the disk contents have been wiped. After a certain number of failed password attempts, the disk will freeze, and the system will need to be rebooted.

The hard disk will require the SECURITY_UNLOCK command to be executed with the correct password before many of the other ATA commands can be executed. After the correct password has been entered, the disk works normally until the disk is powered down.

Some ATA commands are still enabled on the hard disk when it is locked, so it may show up as a valid disk when inserted into a computer. However, when you try to read actual user data from a locked disk, it will either produce an error or require a password. There are several free programs on the Internet that will tell you if the disk is locked and will allow you to unlock it with the password. Two such programs are atapwd and hdunlock.[1] The password can be set through the BIOS or through various software applications. Some data-recovery companies may be able to bypass the password by opening the disk.

### Host Protected Area

The *Host Protected Area* (HPA) is a special area of the disk that can be used to save data, and a casual observer might not see it. The size of this area is configurable using ATA commands, and many disks have a size of 0 by default.

---

1. These programs are most commonly found on Web sites that document how to modify video game consoles. An example is http://www.xbox-scene.com/tools/tools.php?page=harddrive.

The HPA was added in ATA-4, and the motivation was for a location where computer vendors could store data that would not be erased when a user formats and erases the hard disk contents. The HPA is at the end of the disk and, when used, can only be accessed by reconfiguring the hard disk.

Let's go over the process in more detail using the ATA commands. Some of the commands I will use have two versions depending on the size of the disk, but we will use only one of them. There are two commands that return maximum addressable sectors values, and if a HPA exists their return values will be different. The READ_NATIVE_MAX_ ADDRESS command will return the maximum physical address, but the IDENTIFY_ DEVICE command will return only the number of sectors that a user can access. Therefore, if an HPA exists, the READ_NATIVE_MAX_ADDRESS will return the actual end of the disk and the IDENTIFY_DEVICE command will return the end of the user area (and the start of the HPA). Note that the next section will show that the READ_ NATIVE_MAX_ADDRESS is not always the last physical address of the disk.

To create an HPA, the SET_MAX_ADDRESS command is used to set the maximum address to which the user should have access. To remove an HPA, the SET_MAX_ADDRESS command must be executed again with the actual maximum size of the disk, which can be found from READ_NATIVE_MAX_ADDRESS.

For example, if the disk is 20GB, READ_NATIVE_MAX_ADDRESS will return a sector count of 20GB (41,943,040 for example). To create a 1GB host protected area, we execute SET_MAX_ADDRESS with an address of 39,845,888. Any attempt to read from or write to the final 2,097,152 sectors (1GB) will generate an error, and the IDENTIFY_DEVICE command will return a maximum address of 39,845,888. We can see this in Figure 2.12. To remove the HPA, we would execute SET_MAX_ADDRESS with the full sector count.

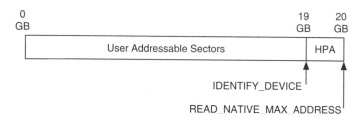

**Figure 2.12**   A 1GB Host Protected Area (HPA) in a 20GB disk.

One of the settings for the SET_MAX_ADDRESS command is a 'volatility bit' that, when set, causes the HPA to exist after the hard disk is reset or power cycled. There is also a set of locking commands in the ATA specification that prevents modifications to the maximum address until the next reset. This allows the BIOS to read or write some data in the host protected area when the system is powering up, set the host protected area so that the user cannot see the data, and then lock the area so that it cannot be changed. A password can even be used (which is a different password than is used for accessing the disk).

In summary, a hard disk may have an HPA containing system files, hidden information, or maybe both. It can be detected by comparing the output of two ATA commands. To remove it, the maximum address of the hard disk must be reset, but the volatility setting allows the change to be temporary.

### Device Configuration Overlay

In addition to data being hidden in an HPA, data can be hidden using *Device Configuration Overlay* (DCO). DCO was added to ATA-6 and allows the apparent capabilities of a hard disk to be limited. Each ATA specification has optional features that a disk may or may not implement. The computer uses the IDENTIFY_DEVICE command to determine which features a hard disk supports. A DCO can cause the IDENTIFY_DEVICE command to show that supported features are not supported and show a smaller disk size than actually exists.

Let's look at some of the DCO commands. The DEVICE_CONFIGURATION_IDENTIFY command returns the actual features and size of a disk. Therefore, we can detect a DCO by comparing the outputs of DEVICE_CONFIGURATION_IDENTIFY and IDENTIFY_DEVICE. Further, recall that the READ_NATIVE_MAX_ADDRESS command returns the size of the disk after an HPA. We can detect a DCO that hides sectors by comparing the READ_NATIVE_MAX_ADDRESS output with DEVICE_CONFIGURATION_IDENTIFY.

For example, consider a 20GB disk where a DCO has set the maximum address to 19GB. The READ_NATIVE_MAX_ADDRESS and IDENTIFY_DEVICE show that the disk is only 19GB. If a 1GB HPA is also created, the IDENTIFY_DEVICE command shows that the size of the disk is 18GB. We can see this in Figure 2.13.

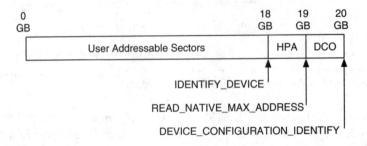

**Figure 2.13** A DCO can hide sectors at the end of the disk, in addition to sectors hidden by an HPA.

To create or change a DCO, the DEVICE_CONFIGURATION_SET command is used. To remove a DCO, the DEVICE_CONFIGURATION_RESET command is used. Unlike HPA, there is no volatile option that allows the device to change the settings for that one session. All DCO changes are permanent across resets and power cycles.

### Serial ATA

Working with ATA devices has its drawbacks. The cables are big, not flexible, and have the connectors in places that are frequently not where you want them. The hard disks also can be difficult to configure with master and slave jumpers. The cable and speed of the interface were some of the motivations behind the development of Serial ATA, which is included in the ATA-7 specification.

The interface is called serial because only one bit of information is transmitted between the controller and the disk at a time, as compared to 16 bits at a time with the original interface, or parallel ATA. The serial ATA connectors are about one-fourth the size of the parallel ATA connectors and they have only seven contacts. Each serial ATA device is connected directly to the controller, and there is no chaining of multiple devices.

Serial ATA has been designed so that a new controller can be placed in a computer, and the computer does not know the difference between the original ATA (parallel ATA) and the new serial ATA. In fact, the serial ATA controller has registers that make the computer think that it is talking to a parallel ATA disk. The host computer sees each disk that is connected to the serial ATA controller as the master disk on its own channel.

## BIOS VERSUS DIRECT ACCESS

Now that we know how the ATA hard drives work and how they are controlled, we need to discuss how software interfaces with them because this can cause problems when acquiring the contents of a disk. There are two methods that software can use to access the disk: directly through the hard disk controller or through the BIOS.

### Direct Access to Controller

We saw in a previous section that the hard disk is connected to a hard disk controller, which issues commands to the hard disk using the ribbon cable. One technique for reading and writing data is for software to communicate directly with the hard disk controller, which then communicates with the hard disk.

To communicate this way, the software needs to know how to address the controller and how to issue commands to it. For example, the software needs to know what the command code for the read operation is, and it needs to know how to identify which sectors to read. The software also will have to be able to query the hard disk for details such as type and size.

### BIOS Access to Controller

Accessing the hard disk directly is the fastest way to get data to and from the disk, but it requires the software to know quite a bit about the hardware. One of the jobs of the BIOS is to prevent software from having to know those details. The BIOS knows about the hardware, and it provides services to the software so that they can more easily communicate with hardware.

Recall from the "Boot Code Locations" section that the BIOS is used when the computer starts. The BIOS performs many tasks during the boot process, but there are two that we are interested in for this discussion. The first relevant task is that it determines the details of the currently installed disks. The second relevant task is that it loads the interrupt table, which will be used to provide services to the operating system and software.

To use the BIOS hard disk services, the software must load data, such as the sector address and sizes, into the CPU registers and execute the software interrupt command 0x13 (commonly called INT13h). The software interrupt command causes the processor to look at the interrupt table and locate the code that will process the service request. Typically, the table entry for interrupt 0x13 contains the address of the BIOS code that will use its knowledge of the hard disk to communicate with the controller. In essence, the BIOS works as a middleman between the software and the hard disk.

INT13h is actually a category of disk functions and includes functions that write to the disk, read from the disk, format tracks on the disk, and query the disk for information. The original INT13h functions for reading and writing used CHS addresses and allowed the software to access a disk that was only 8.1GB or less. To overcome this limitation, new functions were added to INT13h in the BIOS, called the "extended INT13h."

The extended INT13h functions required new BIOS code and used a 64-bit LBA address. For backward compatibility reasons, the old CHS functions remained, and software had to be rewritten to take advantage of the new LBA INT13h functions.

## SCSI DRIVES

When building a portable incident response kit, some of the more difficult decisions may include identifying what types of *Small Computer Systems Interface* (SCSI) cables, drives, and connectors should be included. This section gives an overview of SCSI, focuses on the different types, and describes how it is different from ATA. SCSI hard disks are not as common as ATA hard disks for consumer PCs, but they are standard on most servers.

Like ATA, there are many specifications of SCSI, which are published by the T10 Technical Committee for INCITS (http://www.t10.org). There are three SCSI specifications, SCSI-1, SCSI-2, and SCSI-3. SCSI-3 actually includes many smaller specifications, but covering all the details is out of the scope for this book.

### SCSI versus ATA

There are both high-level and low-level differences between SCSI and ATA. The most obvious high-level difference includes the numerous connector types. With ATA, there was only 40- and 44-pin connectors, but SCSI has many shapes and styles. The SCSI cables can be much longer than ATA cables and there can be more than two devices on the same cable. Each device on the SCSI cable needs a unique numerical ID, which can be configured with jumpers on the disk or with software. Many SCSI disks also have a jumper to make the disk read only, which provides a similar function to an ATA write blocker. ATA write blockers are external devices that block write commands, and they will be discussed in Chapter 3, "Hard Disk Data Acquisition."

The first low-level difference between ATA and SCSI is that SCSI does not have a controller. The ATA interface was designed for a single controller to tell one or two hard disks what to do. SCSI was designed as a bus where different devices communicate with each other and the devices are not limited to hard disks. With a SCSI configuration, the card that plugs into the computer is not a controller because each device on the SCSI cable is essentially an equal and can make requests of each other.

Like ATA, standard SCSI is parallel and data transfers occur in 8-bit or 16-bit chunks. Also like ATA, there is a serial version of the specification, which is the serial attached SCSI specification.

### Types of SCSI

The differences in SCSI versions boil down to how many bits are transferred at a time, the frequency of the signals on the cable (the speed of the transfer), and what types of signals are used. Older types of SCSI had a normal version and a wide version, where the normal version transferred 8 bits at a time and the wide version transferred 16-bits at a time. For example, an Ultra SCSI device performs an 8-bit transfer and a Wide Ultra SCSI device performs a 16-bit transfer. All newer systems use 16-bit transfers, and there is no need to differentiate between normal and wide.

The second difference in SCSI versions is the speed of the signals in the cable. Table 2.5 shows the names of the SCSI types, the speed, and the transfer rates for an 8-bit normal bus and a 16-bit wide bus.

**Table 2.5**   Speed differences among the different types of SCSI.

| Type | Frequency | 8-bit Transfer Rate | 16-bit (wide) Transfer Rate |
|---|---|---|---|
| SCSI (normal) | 5 MHz | 5MB/s | 10MB/s |
| Fast SCSI | 10 MHz | 10MB/s | 20MB/s |
| Ultra SCSI | 20 MHz | 20MB/s | 40MB/s |
| Ultra2 SCSI | 40 MHz | 40MB/s | 80MB/s |
| Ultra3 SCSI | 80 MHz | N/A | 160MB/s |
| Ultra160 SCSI | 80 MHz | N/A | 160MB/s |
| Ultra320 SCSI | 160 MHz | N/A | 320MB/s |

Within each of these types, there are different ways that the data are represented on the wire. The obvious method is *single ended* (SE), where a high voltage is placed on the wire if a 1 is being transmitted and no voltage is placed on the wire if a 0 is transmitted. This method runs into problems at higher speeds and with longer cables because the electric signal cannot stabilize at the high clock rate and the wires cause interference with each other.

The second method of transmitting the data is called *differential voltage*, and each bit actually requires two wires. If a 0 is being transmitted, no voltage is applied to both wires. If a 1 is being transmitted, a positive voltage is applied to one wire and the opposite voltage is applied to the second wire. When a device reads the signals from the cable, it takes the difference between the two wires. A *high voltage differential* (HVD) signal option has existed in SCSI since the first version and a *low voltage differential* (LVD) signal option uses a smaller signal, has existed since Ultra2 SCSI, and is the primary signal type for new disks. Table 2.6 shows the types of SCSI that use the different signal types.

**Table 2.6**   Signal types that can found in each type of SCSI.

| Signal Type | SCSI Types |
|---|---|
| SE | SCSI, Fast SCSI, Ultra SCSI |
| HVD | SCSI, Fast SCSI, Ultra SCSI, Ultra2 SCSI |
| LVD | Ultra2 SCSI, Ultra3 SCSI, Ultra160 SCSI, Ultra 320 SCSI |

It is very important that you do not mix different signal types. You can cause damage to your devices when you connect SE devices to HVD and some LVD devices. Some of the LVD disks are SE compatible, so they can be used in an SE environment without damage, but they will only operate at the speeds that the SE devices use. There are symbols on the SCSI devices that identify what signal type they use. Ensure that all devices have the same symbol or compatible ones. The symbols are shown in Figure 2.14.

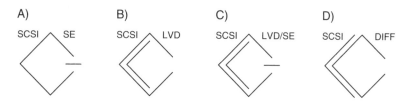

**Figure 2.14** Symbols for SCSI signal types. (A) is for SE devices, (B) is for LVD devices, (C) is for devices that are both SE and LVD compatible, and (D) is for HVD devices.

### Connector Types

There are many types of SCSI connectors, but there are only a few that are frequently encountered. In general, drives that have an 8-bit bus have a 50-pin cable, and those that have a 16-bit bus have a 68-pin cable. The high-density 68-pin adaptor is currently one of the most common, and it comes in a normal size and a very high-density size, but the normal is most common and can be seen in Figure 2.15. The 68-pin adaptor is used for both LVD and SE signals, but the physical cable for the different signal types is different. Check the writing on the cable to prevent problems.

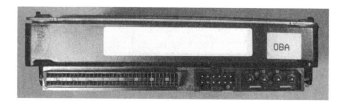

**Figure 2.15** A SCSI disk with a 68-pin connector.

A variation of the high-density 68-pin connector is the *Single Connector Attachment* (SCA) connector. The purpose of this connector is to provide power and the data wires in one connector, which makes it easier to swap drives in a server. This connector has 80 pins and includes pins for power and to configure the disk. A picture of one can be found in Figure 2.16.

**Figure 2.16**   A SCSI disk with an SCA connector.

There are many adaptors for the different SCSI connectors, and the SCSI devices are supposed to be backward compatible. However, not all adaptor and device configurations may work. If the setup does work, it will run at the speed of the slowest device. Remember to not mix any HVD devices with LVD or SE devices without the appropriate adaptors and to only mix LVD and SE devices if the LVD devices can run in SE mode.

### Size Barriers

SCSI disks do not suffer from the same size limitations as ATA disks do because the SCSI specification has always used 32-bit and 64-bit LBA addresses. Although, the size limitations of the BIOS (if you are using INT13h) or file system may be smaller that what SCSI supports, and they will be the limiting factor.

When used through the BIOS, the SCSI controller translates a CHS address to an LBA address. Different controllers can use different mapping techniques, but many of them choose one based on the geometry described by the entries in a partition table. It could be possible for an investigator to have a controller in his acquisition system that does not conduct the same mapping as the original controller, so the disk needs to be acquired using direct access and not the BIOS.

## SUMMARY

In this chapter, we have discussed the basics of data organization and storage. These are important concepts for this book because we will be looking at the data structures and storage methods that the various file systems use. Additional information about data structures can be found in C programming books. We also looked at hard disk technology, which is also important because it is where most of the evidence is found. Additional information about hard disk technology can be found in the PC Guide (http://www.pcguide.com/ref/hdd/index.htm) or in the official ATA or SCSI specifications.

# BIBLIOGRAPHY

Sammes, Tony, and Brian Jenkinson. *Forensic Computing: A Practitioner's Guide.* New York: Springer-Verlag, 2000.

T13. "Information Technology—AT Attachment Interface for Disk Drives." *X3T10, 791D Revision 4c*, 1994. http://www.t13.org/project/d0791r4c-ATA-1.pdf.

T13. "Information Technology—AT Attachment with Packet Interface—6 (ATA/ATAPI-6)." *1410D Revision 3b*, February 26, 2002. http://www.t13.org/docs2002/d1410r3b.pdf.

T13. "Information Technology—AT Attachment with Packet Interface Extension (ATA/ATAPI-4)." *1153D Revision 18*, August 19, 1998. http://www.t13.org/project/d1153r18-ATA-ATAPI-4.pdf.

T13. "Information Technology—AT Attachment-3 Interface (ATA-3)." *X3T13, 2008D Revision 7b*, January 27, 1997. http://www.t13.org/project/d2008r7b-ATA-3.pdf.

# Hard Disk Data Acquisition

The bulk of this book deals with the analysis of data found on a storage device, namely a hard disk. Data can be analyzed on a live system, but it is more common to acquire a copy of the data for a dead analysis. Acquisition typically occurs during the System Preservation phase of an investigation and is one of the most important phases in a digital forensic investigation because if data are not collected from the system, they could be lost and therefore not recognized as evidence. Further, if data are not collected properly, their value as legal evidence is diminished. This chapter shows the theory of how hard disk data can be acquired and includes a case study using the Linux dd tool.

## INTRODUCTION

We saw in Chapter 1, "Digital Investigation Foundations," that the first phase of a digital investigation is the preservation of the digital crime scene. A technique that is commonly used in the preservation of a system is to make duplicate copies of the hard disks so that they can be brought to a lab for a dead analysis. We can think of this phase the way we would think of the process of making an exact replica of a building where a physical crime occurred so that investigators can search it for evidence in a lab.

## GENERAL ACQUISITION PROCEDURE

The general, and intuitive, procedure for acquiring a storage device is to copy one byte from the original storage device (the source) to a destination storage device and repeat the process. This is analogous to copying a document by hand and reading a letter, punctuation mark, or space from the original and writing it to the duplicate. While this works, most of us do not copy documents this way because we can remember entire words, and it is more efficient to transfer one or more words at a time. Computers do the same thing and copy data from the suspect systems in chunks of data, ranging from 512 bytes to many thousands of bytes.

The chunks of data that are transferred each time are typically a multiple of 512 bytes, because that is the size of most disk sectors. If the acquisition tool encounters an error while reading data from the suspect drive, many of the tools will write zeros to the destination.

## DATA ACQUISITION LAYERS

The general theory of non-volatile data acquisition is to save every byte that we think may contain evidence. We saw in Chapter 1 that data can be interpreted at different layers; for example, the disk, volume, file, and application layers. At each layer of abstraction, data are lost. Therefore, the rule of thumb is to acquire data at the lowest layer that we think there will be evidence. For most cases, an investigator will acquire every sector of a disk, which is what we cover in this chapter. Note that when we save only the contents of each sector, we lose data that data recovery specialists may need.

To show why we typically acquire at the disk level, we will consider some scenarios. Suppose that we acquired a disk at the volume level and we made a copy of every sector in each partition. This would allow us to recover deleted files in each partition, but we would not be able to analyze the sectors that are not allocated to partitions. As we will see in Chapter 5, "PC-based Partitions," a disk that has DOS partitions may not use sectors 1 to 62, and they could contain hidden data. If we acquired at the volume level, the hidden data would be lost.

Suppose that we used a backup utility and copied only allocated files. In this case, we would not be able to recover deleted files, we might not have access to all the temporal data, and we would not be able to find data that has been hidden inside partition or file system data structures. Sometimes a backup is the only available data, and the investigator needs to make the most of it. A scenario where a backup would be critical is in a corporate environment where a server is not responding because its disks were wiped with 0s and then rebooted. The last backups of the system might provide clues about who had access to the system and whether an attacker had compromised it.

For some systems, our rule of thumb about acquiring at the level where we think there will be evidence means that we need to copy only files. Consider an intrusion investigation where there is an *Intrusion Detection System* (IDS) that contains log entries corresponding to the attack. If we do not think that the IDS was compromised, the only evidence on the system is at the file level, and we can simply copy the necessary logs and take the appropriate preservation steps. If we think that the IDS was compromised, we should acquire it at the disk level so that we can analyze all the data.

## ACQUISITION TOOL TESTING

Acquisition is a crucial part of the investigation process, and the *National Institute of Standards and Technology* (NIST) has conducted tests on common acquisition tools. The *Computer Forensic Tool Testing* (CFTT) project at NIST developed requirements and test cases for disk-imaging tools. The results and specifications can be found on their Web site (`http://www.cftt.nist.gov/disk_imaging.htm`).

## READING THE SOURCE DATA

Using the general acquisition theory that was previously described, there are two major parts of the process. First, we need to read data from a source, and then we need to write it to the destination. Because this book focuses on the analysis of volume and file system data, we are going to cover the process of acquiring at the disk level (because that is where the volume data structures are located). This section examines the issues associated with reading a disk, and the next major section examines the issues associated with writing to a destination. For this section, we assume that a typical IA32 system (such as x86/i386) is being used for the acquisition, and we will discuss how to access the data, handle errors, and reduce the risk of writing data to the suspect drive.

### DIRECT VERSUS BIOS ACCESS

As we saw in Chapter 2, "Computer Foundations," there are two methods in which the data on a disk can be accessed. In one method, the operating system or acquisition software accesses the hard disk directly, which requires that the software know the hardware details. In the second method, the operating system or acquisition software accesses the hard disk through the *Basic Input/Output System* (BIOS), which should know all the hardware details. At a casual glance, there do not seem to be many differences between these methods, and using the BIOS seems easier because it takes care of the hardware details. Unfortunately, it is not that straightforward when it comes to doing an investigation.

When the BIOS is used, there is a risk that it may return incorrect information about the disk. If the BIOS thinks that a disk is 8GB, but the disk is really 12GB, the INT13h functions will give you access to only the first 8GB. Therefore, if you are doing an acquisition of the disk, you will not copy the final 4GB. We can see this in Figure 3.1, where two applications are trying to identify the size of a disk using different methods.

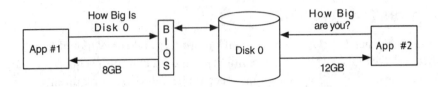

**Figure 3.1**    Two applications are trying to determine the size of a disk. The BIOS is not properly configured and says that the 12GB disk is only 8GB.

This scenario can happen in a couple of different ways. One case is when the BIOS is configured for a specific hard disk geometry that is different from the one installed. In another case, an acquisition tool uses a legacy method of requesting the size of the disk. There are two ways that an application can ask the BIOS for a disk size. One is through the original INT13h function that suffers from the 8GB limit and returns the size using the disk's geometry in CHS format. The second method is to use an extended INT13h function that returns the size in LBA format. The CFTT group at NIST had a 2GB disk and a computer where two different sizes were returned from the INT13h and the extended INT13h functions. The extended INT13h result was correct, but the legacy INT13h result was too small [U.S. Department of Justice 2003].

Occasionally, an e-mail is sent to one to the digital forensic e-mail lists from someone who acquired a disk using two different tools and got different sized images. The reason is usually because one of the tools used the BIOS and the other did not. Make sure that you know how your acquisition tools access the disk, and if the tool uses the BIOS, make sure it reports the full disk before you acquire the disk. The BIOS adds one more location where an error can be introduced into the final image, and it should be avoided if better alternatives exist.

## DEAD VERSUS LIVE ACQUISITION

An investigator has the choice of performing a dead or a live acquisition of data. A *dead acquisition* occurs when the data from a suspect system is being copied without the assistance of the suspect operating system. Historically, the term dead refers to the state of only the operating system, so a dead acquisition can use the hardware from the suspect system as long as it is booted from a trusted CD or floppy. A *live acquisition* is one where the suspect operating system is still running and being used to copy data.

The risk of conducting a live acquisition is that the attacker has modified the operating system or other software to provide false data during the acquisition. To provide an analogy to the physical world, imagine the police arriving at a crime scene where there are several people and it is unknown whether any were involved in the crime. A little while later, the police are looking for a certain object, and they ask one of these unknown people to go into one of the rooms and look for the object. The person comes back to the officer and says that he could not find the object, but should the officer trust him? Maybe this person was involved in the crime, and the object was in the room, but he destroyed it when he was sent in to look for it.

Attackers frequently install tools called rootkits into systems that they compromise, and they return false information to a user [Skoudis and Zeltser 2004]. The rootkits hide certain files in a directory or hide running processes. Typically, the attackers hide the files that they installed after compromising the system. An attacker could also modify the operating system so that it replaces data in certain sectors of the disk while it is being acquired. The resulting image might not have any evidence of the incident because it was replaced. When possible, live acquisition should be avoided so that all evidence can be reliably collected.

It is common for an investigator to boot a suspect system using a trusted DOS floppy or Linux CD that has been configured to not mount drives or modify any data. Technically, it is possible for the suspect to have modified their hardware so that it returns false data even with a trusted operating system, but that is much less likely than the operating system being tampered with.

## ERROR HANDLING

When an acquisition tool is reading data from a disk, it needs to be capable of handling errors. The errors could be caused by a physical problem where the entire drive no longer works, or the errors could be in a limited number of sectors. If only a limited number of sectors is damaged, a normal acquisition can occur, provided that the acquisition tool properly handles the errors.

The generally accepted behavior for dealing with a bad sector is to log its address and write 0s for the data that could not be read. Writing 0s keeps the other data in its correct location. If the sector were ignored instead of writing 0s, the resulting copy would be too small, and most analysis tools would not work. Figure 3.2 shows a series of values that are being acquired. Three of the values have errors and cannot be read, so 0s are written to the copy.

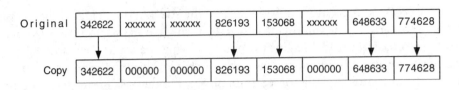

**Figure 3.2**    The original has three errors in it that have been replaced by 0s.

## HOST PROTECTED AREA

When acquiring data from an ATA disk, you should pay attention to the *Host Protected Area* (HPA) of the disk because it could contain hidden data. Unless an acquisition tool looks for an HPA, it will not be acquired. Refer to Chapter 2 for more information about HPAs.

A tool can detect an HPA by comparing the output of two ATA commands. The READ_NATIVE_MAX_ADDRESS command gives the total number of sectors on the disk, and the IDENTIFY_DEVICE returns the total number of sectors that a user can access. If an HPA exists, these two values will be different.

If you do not have access to a tool that will execute the necessary ATA commands, you may have to compare the number of sectors that are copied during an acquisition with the number of sectors that is documented on the label of the disk. Many of the current acquisition tools on the market will detect an HPA, and there are also specialized tools such as BXDR (http://www.sandersonforensics.co.uk/BXDR.htm) by Paul Sanderson, diskstat in The Sleuth Kit, DRIVEID by MyKey Technology (http://www.mykeytech.com), and hpa by Dan Mares (http://www.dmares.com/maresware/gk.htm#HPA).

If you encounter a disk with an HPA and you want to gain access to the hidden data, you will need to change the disk configuration. An HPA is removed by setting the maximum user addressable sector to be the maximum sector on the disk. This can be done using the volatility bit such that the configuration change will be lost when the hard disk is powered off. This command may be blocked by some hardware write blockers, which will be discussed later in this chapter.

The process of removing an HPA involves changing the disk configuration. There is an extremely rare possibility that the disk controller or acquisition tool has not properly implemented HPA changes, and data could be lost. Therefore, you might consider imaging the disk with the HPA before you remove it. If the removal process causes any damage, you still have the original image to analyze. We will see an example of a disk with an HPA in the dd case study later in this chapter. If you need to remove an HPA, it should be documented in your notes.

## DEVICE CONFIGURATION OVERLAY

When acquiring data from a newer ATA disk, you should look for a *Device Configuration Overlay* (DCO), which could cause the disk to look smaller than it really is. A DCO is similar to an HPA, and they can both exist at the same time. DCOs were discussed in Chapter 2.

A DCO is detected by comparing the output of two ATA commands. The READ_NATIVE_MAX_ADDRESS command returns the maximum sector of the disk that normal ATA commands have access to, and the DEVICE_CONFIGURATION_IDENTIFY command returns the actual physical number of sectors. If these are different, a DCO exists and needs to be removed if all data are going to be acquired.

To remove a DCO, the disk configuration must be changed using the DEVICE_CONFIGURATION_SET or DEVICE_CONFIGURATION_RESET commands. Both of these changes are permanent and will not be revoked at the next reset as is possible with HPA. Currently, there are few tools that detect and remove DCO. The Image MASSter Solo 2 from ICS (http://www.icsforensic.com) will copy the sectors hidden by a DCO. As with HPA, it is safest to make a copy of the drive with the DCO in place and then remove it and make a second copy. When you remove a DCO, be sure to document the process. Also test whether your hardware write blockers allow the DCO to be removed.

## HARDWARE WRITE BLOCKERS

One of the investigation guidelines that we discussed in Chapter 1 was to modify the original data as little as possible. There are many acquisition techniques that do not modify any of the original data, but mistakes can happen. Further, there are also some acquisition techniques that can modify the original data, and we may want to prevent that.

A hardware write protector is a device that sits in the connection between a computer and a storage device. It monitors the commands that are being issued and prevents the computer from writing data to the storage device. Write blockers support many storage interfaces, such as ATA, SCSI, Firewire (IEEE 1394), USB, or Serial ATA. These devices are especially important when using an operating system that could mount the original disk, such as Microsoft Windows.

We discussed ATA commands in Chapter 2 and saw that a disk should not perform any actions until its command register is written to. So, in theory, the most basic type of ATA hardware write blocker is a device that prevents the controller from writing any values to the command register that could cause data to be written to or erased from the disk. However, such a device might allow the controller to write data into other registers. This is analogous to being able to load a gun, but not being able to pull the trigger.

We can see in Figure 3.3 that read commands are passed to the disk, but write commands are not.

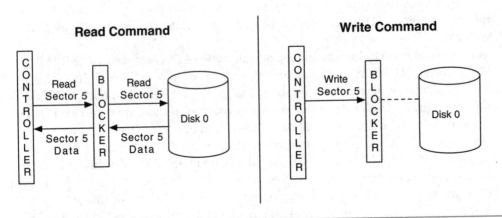

**Figure 3.3**    The read request for sector 5 is passed through the write blocker, but the write command for the same sector is blocked before it reaches the disk.

The NoWrite device by MyKey Technologies has a more advanced design and works as a state-based proxy between the controller and hard disk [MyKey Technology 2003]. It does not send any data or command to the hard disk until it knows that it is a safe command. Therefore, the command arguments are not written to the registers until the NoWrite device knows what command they are for. This makes the data transfers slower, but it is easier to show that no dangerous commands were written. Using the previous gun analogy, this process checks each bullet and allows only blanks to be loaded.

I mentioned hardware write blockers in the previous HPA and DCO sections and want to re-address those points. To remove an HPA or DCO, commands are sent to the disk. These commands modify the device and should be stopped by hardware write blockers. The NoWrite device makes an exception and allows the SET_MAX command to be executed if the volatile bit is set such that the change is not permanent. All other SET_MAX and DEVICE_CONFIGURATION commands are blocked. Other write blockers may choose to allow all these commands to pass, and others may block them all. At the time of this writing, there is little documentation on which commands are being blocked, so you should check with your vendor and conduct your own tests.

Like all investigation tools, testing of hardware write blockers is important, and the CFTT group at NIST has published a specification for hardware write blockers (http://www.cftt.nist.gov/hardware_write_block.htm). The specification classifies the ATA commands as non-modifying, modifying, and configuration. The specification states that modifying commands must be blocked and optionally return success or failure.

## SOFTWARE WRITE BLOCKERS

In addition to hardware write blockers, there are also software write blockers. At one point, most digital forensic tools were DOS-based and used the INT13h method to access a disk. Software write blockers were frequently used to prevent the disk from being modified during the acquisition and examination. In this section, we will describe how they work and what their limitations are.

The software write blockers work by modifying the interrupt table, which is used to locate the code for a given BIOS service. The interrupt table has an entry for every service that the BIOS provides, and each entry contains the address where the service code can be found. For example, the entry for INT13h will point to the code that will write or read data to or from the disk.

A software write blocker modifies the interrupt table so that the table entry for interrupt 0x13 contains the address of the write blocker code instead of the BIOS code. When the operating system calls INT13h, the write blocker code is executed and examines which function is being requested. Figure 3.4 shows an example where the software write block has been installed and blocks a write command. A write blocker allows a non-write function to execute by passing the request directly to the original INT13h BIOS code.

Software write blockers are not as effective as hardware blockers because software can still bypass the BIOS and write data directly do the controller, and the BIOS can still write data to the disk because it has direct access to the controller. In general, if you want to control access to a device, you should place the controls as close to the device as possible. The hardware write blockers are as close to the hard disk as possible, on the ribbon cable.

The CFTT group at NIST has developed requirements and has tested software write block devices. The details can be found on their Web site (http://www.cftt.nist.gov/software_write_block.htm).

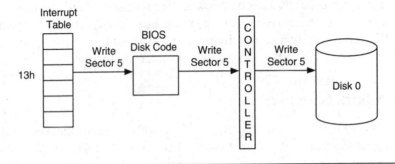

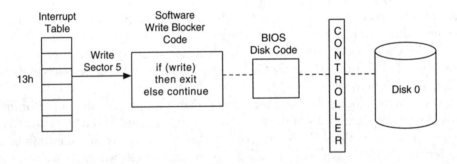

**Figure 3.4**   A BIOS interrupt table without a write block installed and with a software write block installed that prevents writes from being executed.

## WRITING THE OUTPUT DATA

After we read the data from the source disk, we need to write them somewhere. In this section, we will discuss where to save data and the various formats in which data can be saved.

### DESTINATION LOCATION

When we save the data, we can write them either directly to a disk or to a file. We will examine both options in this section.

Before there was specialized analysis software, an investigator either booted the suspect system or mounted the disks in her analysis system. She acquired the drive by copying the data directly to another disk. In other words, sector 0 of the source disk was identical to sector 0 of the destination disk. The resulting disk was frequently called a duplicate copy or a cloned copy. This method can cause problems when the destination disk is bigger than the source disk because it can be difficult to tell exactly where the copy ends. When acquiring directly to disk, it is recommended that the disk be wiped with zeros before acquisition so that unrelated data, possibly from a previous investigation, are not are not confused with data from the suspect system. A second problem with acquiring to disk is that some operating systems, such as Microsoft Windows, will try to mount any disk, and the copy could be mounted by the acquisition system and have its data changed. You also can run into difficulties if the original and destination disks have different geometries because some of the data structures rely on the geometry to describe locations.

Currently, the most common output location is to save the data to a file on a hard disk or CD-ROM. With a file, it is easy to know the boundaries of the data, and operating systems will not try to mount it automatically. The file is frequently called an *image* or a duplicate image. Many tools will allow you to break an image file into smaller pieces so that they fit onto CDs or DVDs. Some investigators will wipe the disks that store image files so that they can more easily testify that there could not have been any contamination from a previous case.

## IMAGE FILE FORMAT

If we save the data to a file, we have a choice of in what format the image will be. A *raw image* contains only the data from the source device, and it is easy to compare the image with the source data. An *embedded image* contains data from the source device and additional descriptive data about the acquisition, such as hash values, dates, and times. Some tools will create a raw image and save the additional descriptive data to a separate file. Recall that hash values, such as CRC, MD5, and SHA-1, are used to show the integrity of data. Examples of image formats can be seen in Figure 3.5.

In current implementations of acquisition tools, many of the embedded image formats are proprietary, such as those from Guidance Software's EnCase[1] and NTI's SafeBack, and some are documented, such as the format used by Technology Pathway's ProDiscover [Technology Pathways 2003]. Most analysis tools import a raw image; therefore, it is the most flexible format. The SMART tool from ASR Data and the `dcfldd/dccidd` tools acquire data in a raw format and have an external file with additional data.

---

1. A specification to the format used by Expert Witness, which is a predecessor to EnCase, can be found at `http://www.asrdata.com/SMART/whitepaper.html`.

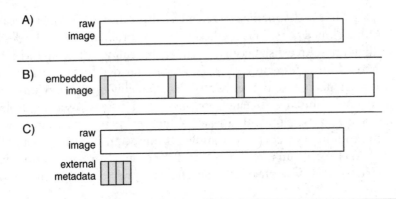

**Figure 3.5**  Examples of (A) a raw image, (B) an embedded image with meta data interleaved in the raw data, and (C) an image with the data stored in a raw format and the meta data stored in a second file.

## COMPRESSING THE IMAGE FILE

When we write the data to a file, we may have the option to compress the file so that it takes up less storage space. Compression works by storing repetitive data more efficiently. For example, if the data have 10,000 consecutive 1s, a compressed format may be able to describe that in a few hundred bits instead of 10,000 bits. If the data are random, there will be little repetition, and compression will not be as effective. If you compress data that have already been compressed, the result will not be much smaller. For example, JPEG images have compression in them, and their size does not change if they are compressed.

When an image is compressed, any analysis tool you use it with must support the compression type. This is similar to using an image format in which data are embedded. Most general types of compression require you to decompress the entire file before it can be used. Examples of this include the Winzip tools for Windows and the gzip tools in Unix. Special compression algorithms will allow you to uncompress a small part of the compressed file, and those are the ones that should be used by acquisition tools so that you do not have to uncompress the entire image.

The benefit of compression is that you can acquire a storage device to a smaller image file, although the actual amount of data saved depends on the acquired data. The negatives of compression are as follows:

- You might be limited by the number of analysis tools that support the format.
- Acquisition might take longer because the software must perform the compression.

- Analysis might be slower because the analysis tool must decompress the image when it reads data from it.

## NETWORK-BASED ACQUISITION

The basic acquisition theory also allows you to create an image file on a remote computer by using a network. In this case, data are read from the source disk, transmitted to the destination host via a network, and written to a file. This method of acquisition is convenient if you cannot get access to the suspect disk or do not have the correct adaptors or interface for the suspect disk. Many current tools support network-based acquisition of dead and live systems. Some offer encryption to provide confidentiality on the network. Compression can be useful for the transmission to reduce the amount of data sent over a slow network.

## INTEGRITY HASHES

In Chapter 1, we discussed some of the core concepts of an investigation, one of which was to calculate hash values for evidence so that we can later verify the integrity of the data. Some acquisition tools will calculate a hash while the data are being copied, and others require a separate tool. In many cases, the hashes are stored in either an embedded image or an external file with a raw image. Having the hashes embedded in the image does not provide any additional security or integrity.

It is important to note what the hashes actually do for you. Any hash that is stored with the image will not ensure that someone has not modified the data. After all, if someone modifies the image, they can also recalculate the hashes, even if they are embedded in the format. A program could be easily written to do this. To prove the integrity of an image file using a digital hash, you will need to use a cryptographic signature and a trusted time source. This requires a lot of overhead; therefore, a much easier method is to write the hash value down in your notebook. Then someone will have to modify the image, recalculate the hash, and rewrite your notebook.

While hashes are important to later prove the integrity of an image, they can also be used to show the accuracy of an acquisition process and that the acquisition process did not modify the original disk. By calculating the hash of the disk before it is acquired and comparing that value with the hash of a raw image, you can show that the raw image contains the same data that were on the original disk. Ideally, the original hash should be calculated with a tool that is independent of the acquisition tools so that any errors are not applied to both the control case and the actual image.

Note that the previous hashing process reads only the data that are available to the tool. If hardware or software problems prevent you from accessing all bytes in a disk, the hash of the disk can equal the hash of the image file even though the image file does not represent all data on the disk. For example, if the tool can read only the first 8GB of a 12GB disk, the tool will compute the hash of the first 8GB of the disk, copy the first 8GB of data, and then compute the hash of the 8GB image file.

Another consideration for hashes is how often they are calculated. Hashes are most commonly used to identify when a value in a chunk of data has been changed. If the hash shows that a value in the chunk has been changed, the chunk must not be used. Calculating hashes of smaller chunks can minimize the impact of an integrity failure. If any chunk of data fails an integrity test, then it will not be used, but the rest of the image will.

## A CASE STUDY USING DD

To illustrate the acquisition process, I will describe how we can do an acquisition with the dd tool. dd is one of the most simple and flexible acquisition tools, but it is command line-based and can be more complex to learn than other tools because each feature and option can be specified. dd comes with many of the UNIX versions and is available for Windows.[2] For this case study, we will focus on running it in Linux.

At its core, dd copies a chunk of data from one file and writes it to another. It does not care what type of data it is copying and does not know about file systems or disks, only files.

dd reads data from the input source in block-sized chunks, and the default block size is 512 bytes. It reads data from an input source, which is specified with the if= flag. If the if= flag is not given, it takes the standard input as the input source, which is typically the keyboard. dd writes the data to an output file, which is specified with the of= flag. If that is not given, the data are written to standard output, which is usually the display. As an example, to copy the contents of file1.dat, which is 1024 bytes, to file2.dat in 512-byte blocks, we use

```
# dd if=file1.dat of=file2.dat bs=512
2+0 records in
2+0 records out
```

2. George Garner's version is available at http://users.erols.com/gmgarner/forensics/, and the UnxUtils version is available at http://unxutils.sourceforge.net.

The final two lines show that two complete blocks were read from file1.dat, and two complete blocks were written to file2.dat. If a full block was not used during the last read and write, the final two lines would have ended with '+1' instead of '+0.' For example, if file1.dat were 1500 bytes instead of 1024 bytes, the following would have been seen:

```
# dd if=file1.dat of=file2.dat bs=512
2+1 records in
2+1 records out
```

Note that the resulting file will be the full 1500 bytes. dd will try to write in block-sized chunks, but if there is not enough data, it will only copy what it has.

## INPUT SOURCES

In Linux, there is a device for each storage device and partition, and it can be used as the input file. For example, the master ATA disk on the first channel is /dev/hda, and we can use that device name with the if= flag to tell dd to copy data from the disk to a file. Microsoft Windows does not have an actual device file for the hard disks, but you can use the \\.\ syntax to reference a disk, \\.\PhysicalDrive0, for example.

The default block size is 512 bytes, but we can specify anything we want using the bs= flag. We can copy 1 byte at a time, or we can copy 1GB at a time. Any value will work, but some values will give you better performance than others. Most disks read a minimum of 512 bytes at a time and can easily read more at the same time. Using a value that is too small is wasteful because the disk will need to be frequently read, and time will be wasted in the copying process. If you choose a value that is too large, you will waste time filling up the buffer in dd before the copy is performed. I have found that values in the 2KB to 8KB range work well.

Linux accesses the hard disk directly and does not use the BIOS, so we do not risk getting incorrect data from the BIOS about the size of the disk. That also means that there are not software write blockers for Linux, but you can use a hardware device if you want.

## HPA

As previously stated, dd knows about only files and therefore does not know anything about ATA HPAs. There are several methods of detecting an ATA HPA in Linux, and I will cover those here.

The scenario for this example is a 57GB disk with 120,103,200 sectors. I have placed the string "here i am" in sector 15,000, as seen here:

```
# dd if=/dev/hdb bs=512 skip=15000 count=1 | xxd
1+0 records in
1+0 records out
0000000: 6865 7265 2069 2061 6d0a 0000 0000 0000  here i am.......
```

Next, I created an HPA in the final 120,091,200 sectors. In other words, there are only 12,000 sectors that the OS or an application can access. We can see this because I can no longer see the string in sector 15,000:

```
# dd if=/dev/hdb bs=512 skip=15000 count=1 | xxd
0+0 records in
0+0 records out
```

No records were copied because it could not read the data. There are several ways of detecting an HPA in Linux. Newer versions of Linux display a message in the dmesg log. Note that this log has a limited size, and entries will be overwritten if there is an application that is writing a lot of warning or error messages. Its output for our disk is as follows:

```
# dmesg | less
[REMOVED]
hdb: Host Protected Area detected.
        current capacity is 12000 sectors (6 MB)
        native  capacity is 120103200 sectors (61492 MB)
```

Not all versions of Linux will display this message, though. Another method of detecting an HPA is using the hdparm tool that comes with Linux. It displays details about a hard disk, and we need to use the -I flag to obtain the total number of sectors. We will compare this value with the value written on the disk or from the vendor's Web site. This output will also tell us if the drive supports HPA, which older disks do not.

```
# hdparm -I /dev/hdb
[REMOVED]
        CHS current addressable sectors:     11088
        LBA     user addressable sectors:    12000
        LBA48   user addressable sectors:    12000
[REMOVED]
```

```
Commands/features:
     Enabled Supported:
       *    Host Protected Area feature set
```

In this case, the label of my drive says that it has 120,103,200 sectors; therefore, many sectors are not addressable. Lastly, you can use the diskstat tool from The Sleuth Kit. It displays the maximum native address and the maximum user address.

```
# diskstat /dev/hdb
Maximum Disk Sector: 120103199
Maximum User Sector: 11999

** HPA Detected (Sectors 12000 - 120103199) **
```

To access the data, we need to reset the maximum address. One tool that allows us to do this is setmax (http://www.win.tue.nl/~aeb/linux/setmax.c). We will run this tool and set the maximum number of sectors in the drive, which is 120,103,200 in this example. This tool modifies the configuration of your drive, and extreme care must be taken (which means you should also take good notes while you doing it). Also note that this tool sets the maximum address as nonvolatile, so the change is permanent. If you are going to use a tool like this, test it on other drives before you use it on a disk that may contain evidence.

```
# setmax --max 120103200 /dev/hdb
```

After resetting the maximum address, you can use dd to acquire the full disk. Record the location of the HPA so that you can return the disk to its original state and so that you will know where it started when you analyze the data.

## OUTPUT DESTINATIONS

The output from dd can be either a new file or another storage device. For example, the two following examples are performed in a Linux environment. The first copies the master ATA disk on the primary channel to a file, and the second example copies the master ATA disk on the primary channel to the slave ATA disk on the second channel.

```
# dd if=/dev/hda of=/mnt/hda.dd bs=2k
# dd if=/dev/hda of=/dev/hdd bs=2k
```

If you do not specify the output file, the data will be written to the display. This can be useful to calculate the MD5 hash, to extract the ASCII strings, or to send the data to a remote system using a network. For example, to hash a disk, we could use the md5sum command that comes with Linux:

```
# dd if=/dev/hda bs=2k | md5sum
```

We can also send data to a server using the netcat (http://www.atstake.com/research/tools/) or cryptcat (http://sf.net/projects/cryptcat) tools. With netcat, a trusted evidence server at IP address 10.0.0.1 would run the following to open a network port on port 7000 and save incoming data to a file:

```
# nc -l -p 7000 > disk.dd
```

The system with the source disk in it would be booted from a trusted Linux CD, and dd would be executed with the data piped to netcat, which would send data to the server at 10.0.0.1 at port 7000. The connection would close after three seconds of no activity:

```
# dd if=/dev/hda bs=2k | nc -w 3 10.0.0.1 7000
```

## ERROR HANDLING

If dd encounters an error while reading the input file, the default action is to stop copying data. If you specify the conv=noerror flag, dd will report the error and not stop. Unfortunately, this method skips the blocks with bad data, and the image will be the wrong size, and the data will be at the wrong addresses.

To maintain the addresses in the image, the sync flag should be given. The sync flag forces dd to write data in block-sized chunks, and if there is not enough data for a full block, it pads the data with 0s. Therefore, when an error is encountered, the invalid data will be replaced with 0s. The downside of always using these flag options is that the resulting image will always be a multiple of the block size, which may not be the actual size of the original storage device. For example, if I choose a block size of 4,096 bytes, but the size of my (really small) disk is 6,144 bytes, the resulting image file will be 8,192 bytes instead of 6,144 bytes. An example of using the error handling options is

```
# dd if=/dev/hda of=hda.dd bs=2k conv=noerror,sync
```

The dd_rescue tool from Kurt Garloff (http://www.garloff.de/kurt/linux/ddrescue) is similar to the original dd, but it has error handling enabled by default. If it encounters an error, it starts using a smaller block size and writes 0s to the blocks that could not be read. dd_rescue can also copy from the end of the disk toward the front, which the author claims can be useful when bad sectors exist.

## CRYPTOGRAPHIC HASHES

Normally, when you want a cryptographic hash of a file and you are using dd, you must use another utility, such as md5sum. The cryptographic hash of an image is calculated to later prove an image's integrity. Jesse Kornblum and Reid Leatzow at the U.S. Department of Defense's Cyber Crime Center created a version of dd that can calculate hashes of the data being copied. There are currently two versions of this tool. The original version is dcfldd (http://sourceforge.net/projects/biatchux/), and it can calculate only the MD5 hash. The new version is dccidd (available at http://www.dc3.gov or by sending email to dcci@dc3.gov), and it can calculate the MD5, SHA-1, and SHA-256 hashes in parallel (the change in name reflects a reorganization of the lab).

The same basic flags that we saw for dd also apply to these tools, and new flags were added for the hashes. The hashwindow= flag allows you to specify how frequently a hash should be calculated. If the value is 0, only one hash is calculated of the entire file. If a non-zero byte size is given, a hash is calculated at each point in the file, and a final hash is calculated. The hashes can be saved to an output file using the hashlog= flag. dcfldd computes only the MD5 hash, but dccidd has the hash= flag that allows you to specify which hashes should be calculated. By default, the MD5 and SHA-1 are calculated in parallel, but you can specify 'md5,' 'sha1,' or 'sha256.'

For example, if you wanted to image a Linux hard disk and calculate hashes for every 1MB you would use the following:

```
# dcfldd if=/dev/hda of=/mnt/hda.dd bs=2k hashwindow=1M hashlog=/mnt/hda.hashes
```

The hashlog has the following format:

```
0 - 1048576: 970653da48f047f3511196c8a230f64c
1048576 - 2097152: b6d81b360a5672d80c27430f39153e2c
...
103809024 - 104857600: b6d81b360a5672d80c27430f39153e2c
104857600 - 105906176: 94a171ec3908687fd1f456087576715b
Total: 28d34393f36958f8fc822ae3980f37c3
```

Each line starts with the range of bytes that the hash applies to and ends with the hash value. The last value is the hash for the entire image. The log file for `dccidd` is slightly different because it includes the SHA-1 hash, and the range field is padded with 0s. Here is the output when the hashwindow was set to 512 bytes (the SHA-1 and MD5 hashes are typically on the same line):

```
000000 - 000511:  5dbd121cad07429ed176f7fac6a133d6
09cae0d9f2a387bb3436a15aa514b16f9378efbf
000512 - 001023:  91cf74d0ee95d4b60197e4c0ca710be4
0f71d8729ad39ae094e235ab31a9855b2a5a5900
001024 - 001535:  8a0a10f43b2bcd9e1385628f7e3a8693
641b9b828e41cd391f93b5f3bfaf2d1d7b393da0
[REMOVED]
```

The Windows version `dd` from George Garner, which was previously discussed, also has built-in MD5 features. With Garner's tool, supplying the –md5sum flag calculates the MD5 hash for the file. It can also save the hash to a file using the –md5out flag.

## Summary

The hard disk is where most of the evidence is found in current investigations, which will likely be the case for many years to come, at least until all hard disks are encrypted. Acquisitions are very important in the investigation process because if they are not performed correctly, data may not exist for the investigation. This section has outlined the general theory of acquisitions and given a case studying using dd. dd is a fairly simple tool, but it is command line and can cause confusion because it has many options.

## Bibliography

MyKey Technology, Inc. "Technical White Paper: No Write Design Notes." 2003. `https://mykeytech.com/nowritepaper1.html`.

Skoudis, Ed, and Lenny Zeltser. *Malware: Fighting Malicous Code.* Upper Saddle River: Prentice Hall, 2004.

Technology Pathways, Inc. "ProDiscover Image File Forma." 2003. `https:// www.techpathways.com/uploads/ProDiscoverImageFileFormatv4.pdf`.

U.S. Department of Justice. "Test Results for Disc Imaging Tools: SafeBack 2.18." *NCJ 200032*, June 2003. `https://www.ncjrs.org/pdffiles1/nij/20032.pdf`.

# PART II
## VOLUME ANALYSIS

# Volume Analysis

This chapter begins Part 2, "Volume Analysis," of the book, and we are going to now discuss volume analysis. Volume analysis involves looking at the data structures that are involved with partitioning and assembling the bytes in storage devices so that we get volumes. Volumes are used to store file system and other structured data, which we will analyze in Part 3, "File System Analysis," of the book. This chapter takes an abstract approach to the basic concepts of volume analysis and discusses the principles that apply to all types of volume systems. The next three chapters will focus on specific types of partitioning and assembly systems.

## INTRODUCTION

Digital storage media is organized to allow efficient retrieval of data. The most common experience with a volume system occurs when installing Microsoft Windows and creating partitions on the hard disk. The installation process guides the user through the process of creating primary and logical partitions, and in the end the computer has a list of "drives" or "volumes" in which to store data. A similar process occurs when installing a UNIX operating system, and it is becoming more common in large storage environments to use volume management software to have multiple disks appear as if they comprise one large disk.

During a digital investigation, it is common to acquire an entire disk image and import the image into analysis tools. Many digital investigation tools automatically break the disk image into partitions, but sometimes they have problems. The concepts in this part of the book will help an investigator understand the details of what a tool is doing and why it is having problems if a disk has become corrupted. For example, when partitions on the disk have been deleted or modified by the suspect or the tool simply cannot locate a partition. The procedures in these chapters may also be useful when analyzing the sectors that are not allocated to a partition.

This chapter provides background theory, an overview of tools, and types of analysis techniques. The next two chapters will provide the details for several partition systems, including DOS partitions, Apple Partitions, BSD partitions, and SUN slices. The final chapter in this part of the book covers multiple disk volume systems, such as RAID and disk spanning.

## Background

### Volume Concepts

Volume systems have two central concepts to them. One is to assemble multiple storage volumes into one storage volume and the other is to partition storage volumes into independent partitions. The terms "partition" and "volume" are frequently used together, but I am going to make a distinction.

A *volume* is a collection of addressable sectors that an *Operating System* (OS) or application can use for data storage. The sectors in a volume need not be consecutive on a physical storage device; instead, they need to only give the impression that they are. A hard disk is an example of a volume that is located in consecutive sectors. A volume may also be the result of assembling and merging smaller volumes.

### General Theory of Partitions

One of the concepts in a volume system is to create partitions. A *partition* is a collection of consecutive sectors in a volume. By definition, a partition is also a volume, which is why the terms are frequently confused. I will refer to the volume in which a partition is located as the partition's parent volume. Partitions are used in many scenarios, including

- Some file systems have a maximum size that is smaller than hard disks.
- Many laptops use a special partition to store memory contents when the system is put to sleep.
- UNIX systems use different partitions for different directories to minimize the impact of file system corruption.

- IA32-based systems that have multiple operating systems, such as Microsoft Windows and Linux, may require separate partitions for each operating system.

Consider a Microsoft Windows system with one hard disk. The hard disk volume is partitioned into three smaller volumes, and each has a file system. Windows assigns the names C, D, and E to each volume. We can see this in Figure 4.1.

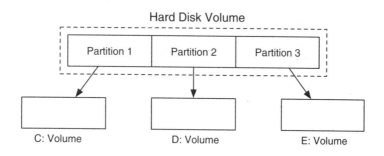

**Figure 4.1**  An example hard disk volume is organized into three partitions, which are assigned volume names.

Each operating system and hardware platform typically uses a different partitioning method. We will cover the different implementations in Chapter 5, "PC-based Partitions," and Chapter 6, "Server-based Partitions," but we will examine the basic components here. The common partition systems have one or more tables, and each table entry describes a partition. The data in the entry will have the starting sector of the partition, the ending sector of the partition (or the length), and the type of partition. Figure 4.2 shows an example table with three partitions.

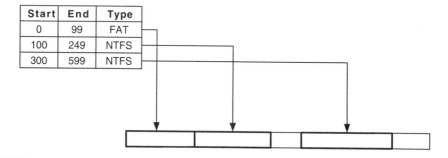

**Figure 4.2**  A basic table with entries for the start, end, and type of each partition.

The purpose of a partition system is to organize the layout of a volume; therefore, the only essential data are the starting and ending location for each partition. A partition system cannot serve its purpose if those values are corrupt or non-existent. All other fields, such as a type and description, are nonessential and could be false.

In most cases, the first and last sector of a partition does not contain anything that identifies them as the border sectors. This is similar to how most property lines are not marked. A surveyor and documents are typically needed to identify the exact property lines, and the partition data structures are the equivalent to the survey documents. When the partition system structures are missing, the partition boundaries can sometimes be guessed using knowledge of what was stored inside of the partition. This is analogous to guessing property boundaries based on the landscape.

Note that a partition system is dependent on the operating system and not the type of interface on the hard disk. Therefore, a Windows system uses the same partition system regardless if the disk uses an *AT Attachment interface* (ATA/IDE) or a *Small Computer Systems Interface* (SCSI).

## USAGE OF VOLUMES IN UNIX

UNIX systems typically do not use volumes the same way a Microsoft Windows system does. This section is intended for users who are not familiar with UNIX, and it provides a brief overview of how volumes are used in UNIX. A UNIX system administration book should be consulted for more details.

In UNIX, the user is not presented with several "drives", such as C: and D:. Instead, the user is presented with a series of directories that start at the root directory, or /. The subdirectories of / are either subdirectories in the same file system, or they are mounting points for new file systems and volumes. For example, a CD-ROM would be given the E: drive in Windows, but it may be mounted at /mnt/cdrom in Linux. This allows the user to change drives by changing directories, and in many cases the user is unaware that they have done so. Figure 4.3 shows how hard disk and CD volumes are accessed in Windows and UNIX.

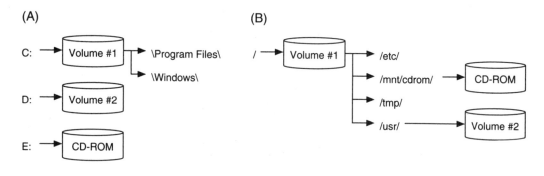

**Figure 4.3** Mount points of two volumes and a CD-ROM in (A) Microsoft Windows and (B) a typical UNIX system.

To minimize the impact of drive corruption and to improve efficiency, UNIX typically partitions each disk into several volumes. A volume for the root directory (/) stores basic information, a separate volume may exist for the user's home directories (/home/), and applications may be located in their own volume (/usr/). All systems are unique and may have a completely different volume and mounting scheme. Some systems use only one large volume for the root directory and do not segment the system.

## GENERAL THEORY OF VOLUME ASSEMBLY

Larger systems use volume assembly techniques to make multiple disks look like one. One motivation for this is to add redundancy in case a disk fails. If data are being written to more then one disk, there exists a backup copy if one disk fails. Another motivation for this is to make it easier to add more storage space. Volume spanning works by combining the total storage space of multiple volumes so that one large volume is created. Additional disks can be added to the larger volume with no impact on the existing data. We will cover these techniques in Chapter 7, "Multiple Disk Volumes."

Let's look at a quick example. Figure 4.4 shows an example of two hard disk volumes with a total of three partitions. Partition 1 is assigned a volume name of C: and a hardware device processes partitions 2 and 3. The hardware device outputs one large volume, and that is organized into two partitions, which are given volume names. Note that in this case the hardware device does not provide increased reliability, only a larger volume.

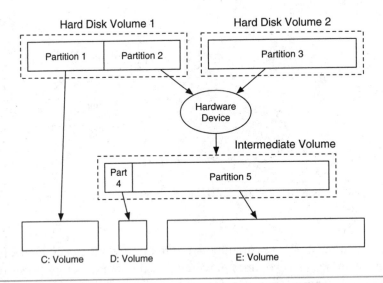

**Figure 4.4**    A volume system that merges two partitions into one volume and partitions it.

## SECTOR ADDRESSING

In Chapter 2, we discussed how to address a sector. The most common method is to use its LBA address, which is a number that starts at 0 at the first sector of the disk. This address is the *physical address* of a sector.

A volume is a collection of sectors, and we need to assign an address to each sector. A *logical volume address* is the address of a sector relative to the start of its volume. Note that because a disk is a volume, the physical address is the same as a logical volume address for the disk volume. The starting and ending locations of partitions are typically described using logical volume addresses.

When we start to talk about the contents of a partition, there is another layer of logical volume addresses. These addresses are relative to the start of the partition and not the start of the disk or parent volume. We will differentiate these by preceding the word volume with "disk" or "partition." If a sector is not allocated to a partition, it will not have a logical partition volume address. Figure 4.5 shows an example where there are two partitions and unpartitioned space in between. The first partition starts in sector 0, so the logical partition volume addresses in it are the same as the logical disk volume addresses. The second partition starts in physical sector 864 and the logical disk volume addresses of these sectors are 864 sectors larger than their logical partition volume addresses.

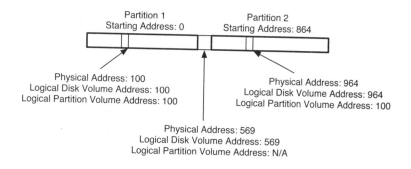

**Figure 4.5** The logical partition volume address is relative to the start of the partition while the logical disk volume address is relative to the start of the disk.

## ANALYSIS BASICS

Volume analysis occurs frequently, although many investigators may not realize it. In many cases, an investigator acquires an entire hard disk and imports the image into his analysis software to view the file system contents. To identify where the file system starts and ends, the partition tables must be analyzed.

It is also important to analyze the partition layout of the volume because not all sectors need to be assigned to a partition, and they may contain data from a previous file system or that the suspect was trying to hide. In some cases, the partition system may become corrupt or erased, and automated tools will not work.

### ANALYSIS TECHNIQUES

The basic theory of volume analysis is simple. For the partition systems, we want to locate the partition tables and process them to identify the layout. The layout information is then fed into a file system analysis tool that needs to know the offset of a partition, or it is printed to a user so she can determine what data should be analyzed. In some cases, the data in a partition or in between partitions needs to be extracted from the parent volume, which we will cover in the next section. To analyze the data inside a partition, we need to consider what type of data it is. Generally, it is a file system, and we will cover that in Part 3 of the book.

To analyze the assembly components to a volume system, we need to locate and process the data structures that describe which volumes are merged and how they are merged. As we will see in Chapter 7, there are many ways that the volumes can be merged. We will look for data that are not part of the merging process and may contain data from a previous installation or hidden data.

## CONSISTENCY CHECKS

When analyzing volume systems, it can be useful to check each partition relative to the other partitions. This can serve as a sanity check to determine where else evidence could be located besides in each partition. Most partition systems do not require the entries to be in a sorted order, so you or an analysis tool should sort them based on starting and ending location before you do these consistency checks.

The first check looks at the last partition and compares its ending location with the end of its parent volume. Ideally, it should end in the last sector of the volume. Figure 4.6(a) shows a situation where the final partition ends before the end of the volume, and there are sectors that could contain hidden or deleted data.

The next category of sanity checks compare the start and end sectors of consecutive partitions, and there are four scenarios. The first scenario, shown in Figure 4.6(b), is valid, and there are sectors in between two partitions that are not in a partition. The non-partitioned sectors could have been used to hide data and should be analyzed. The second scenario, shown in Figure 4.6(c), is what almost every system has, and the second partition starts immediately following the first.

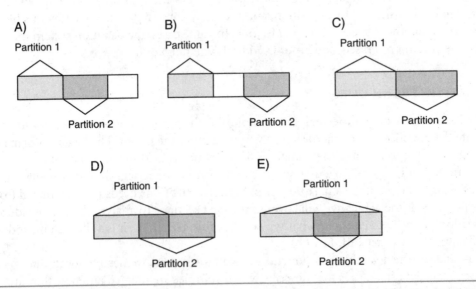

**Figure 4.6**   Five examples of how two partitions can be organized relative to each other. The first three are valid, and the last two are not.

The third scenario, shown in Figure 4.6(d), is typically invalid, and the second partition starts before the first partition ends. This creates an overlap, and in many cases this is an indication that the partition table is corrupt. To determine which, if either, partition is correct, you need to analyze the data inside each. The fourth scenario is shown in Figure 4.6(e), and it is also typically invalid. The second partition is inside the first partition, and the contents of each partition need to be analyzed to determine where the error is.

## EXTRACTING THE PARTITION CONTENTS

Some tools require a partition image as input, or we might want to extract the data in or in between partitions to a separate file. This section will show how to extract the data, and the techniques in this section apply to all partition systems. Extracting data is a simple process when the layout is known. We show how to do it with the dd tool, which we already discussed in Chapter 3, "Hard Disk Data Acquisition."

The dd tool is command line-based and takes several arguments. We will need the following to extract partition data:

- if: The disk image to read from
- of: The output file to save to
- bs: The size of the block to read each time, 512 bytes is the default
- skip: The number of blocks to skip before reading, each of size bs
- count: The number of blocks to copy from the input to the output, each of size bs

In many cases, we will want to use a 512-byte block size because that is the size of a sector. The default block size for dd is also 512 bytes, but it is always safer to specify it. We will use the skip flag to specify the starting sector where the partition begins and the count flag to specify how many sectors are in the partition.

Let's review an example of a DOS-based partition system. We used the mmls tool from The Sleuth Kit to list the contents of the partition table. We will cover the details of the output in the later sections, but we can see that there are three file system partitions.

```
# mmls -t dos disk1.dd
Units are in 512-byte sectors
      Slot   Start       End         Length      Description
00:   -----  0000000000  0000000000  0000000001  Table #0
01:   -----  0000000001  0000000062  0000000062  Unallocated
02:   00:00  0000000063  0001028159  0001028097  Win95 FAT32 (0x0B)
03:   -----  0001028160  0002570399  0001542240  Unallocated
04:   00:03  0002570400  0004209029  0001638630  OpenBSD (0xA6)
05:   00:01  0004209030  0006265349  0002056320  NTFS (0x07)
```

The mmls tool organizes the partition table entries based on their starting sector and identifies the sectors that are not allocated to a partition. The first two lines, numbered 00 and 01, are the primary partition table and the unused space between the partition table and first partition. We see from the output that line 02 is a partition with a FAT32 file system, line 04 is a partition for OpenBSD, and line 05 is a partition with an NTFS file system. We also see that line 03 is for unallocated space on the disk. A graphical representation of this data can be found in Figure 4.7.

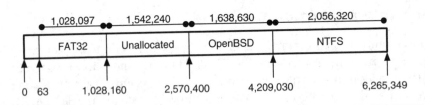

**Figure 4.7**  Layout of the example disk image.

To exact the file system partitions from the disk image, we take the starting sector and size of each partition and plug them into dd as shown here:

```
# dd if=disk1.dd of=part1.dd bs=512 skip=63 count=1028097
# dd if=disk1.dd of=part2.dd bs=512 skip=2570400 count=1638630
# dd if=disk1.dd of=part3.dd bs=512 skip=4209030 count=2056320
```

These commands take the disk1.dd file as input and save the output to files named part1.dd, part2.dd, and part3.dd. For each one, blocks of 512 bytes each are copied. The first partition is extracted by skipping 63 blocks before copying and then copying 1,028,097 blocks. In the mmls output, we saw that the partition started in sector 63, so you may be inclined to skip only 62 blocks. However, recall that the sector addresses start at 0, so we do need to skip 63. The .dd extension is used here to show that these files are raw image files that were created by a dd-like tool.

Some tools that list the layout will give the starting and ending sectors of a partition, and you will need to calculate the partition size. To do this, subtract the starting sector from the ending sector and add 1. We need to add 1 because subtracting takes the difference between two numbers, but we need to include the last number. For instance, in the previous example the size of the first partition is

```
1028159 - 63 + 1 = 1028097
```

To see the need to add 1, consider a smaller example where a partition starts in sector 2 and ends in sector 4. Its size is 3 sectors:

```
4 - 2 + 1 = 3
```

This dd process also can be used to extract the data in between partitions. For example, from the mmls output, we know that sectors 1,028,160 through 2,570,399 are unused. They can be extracted with

```
# dd if=disk1.dd of=unalloc1.dd bs=512 skip=1028160 count=1542240
```

Other low-level tools, such as hex editors, also provide the ability to save sequential sectors to a file.

## RECOVERING DELETED PARTITIONS

A common technique that is used to thwart a forensic investigation is to repartition a disk or clear the partition structures so that the original structure is gone. A similar but more innocent problem is recovering a system whose partition structures have become corrupt. Analysis becomes much more difficult in these cases, but fortunately several tools exist to help recover the partitions, and this section describes how they work.

Partition recovery tools work by assuming that a file system was located in each partition. Fortunately, many file systems start with a data structure that has a constant "magic" or signature value. For example, a FAT file system has the values 0x55 and 0xAA in bytes 510 and 511 of the first sector. The partition recovery tools search for these signature values and identify where a partition may have started.

When the search tool finds a signature, additional tests can be conducted on the range of values that are valid for a given data structure. For example, a FAT file system has a field that identifies how many sectors are in a cluster, and it must have a value that is a power of 2, such as 1, 2, 4, 8, 16, 32, 64, or 128. Any other value would indicate that the sector was not part of a FAT file system boot sector, even though it ended with 0x55AA.

The searching mechanism of each tool may vary. Some tools examine each sector and compare it to known signatures. Other tools search only cylinder boundaries because partitions are typically created on cylinder boundaries. Others may use data from the file system data structures to learn how big the file system is and jump to the end before searching for more known data structures.

An example of a Linux tool that can be used for partition recovery is gpart (http://www.stud.uni-hannover.de/user/76201/gpart/). gpart can identify a number of file system types by testing sectors and assessing which file system type is the most probable.

Its normal output is not specific enough for our needs, so the -v verbose flag must be applied. In this example, the disk had three partitions and the partition table was cleared. We run gpart on the raw disk image with the -v flag to identify the original partition locations:

```
# gpart -v disk2.dd
* Warning: strange partition table magic 0x0000.
[REMOVED]
Begin scan...
Possible partition(DOS FAT), size(800mb), offset(0mb)
   type: 006(0x06)(Primary 'big' DOS (> 32MB))
   size: 800mb #s(1638566) s(63-1638628)
   chs:  (0/1/1)-(101/254/62)d (0/1/1)-(101/254/62)r
   hex:  00 01 01 00 06 FE 3E 65 3F 00 00 00 A6 00 19 00

Possible partition(DOS FAT), size(917mb), offset(800mb)
   type: 006(0x06)(Primary 'big' DOS (> 32MB))
   size: 917mb #s(1879604) s(1638630-3518233)
   chs:  (102/0/1)-(218/254/62)d (102/0/1)-(218/254/62)r
   hex:  00 00 01 66 06 FE 3E DA E6 00 19 00 34 AE 1C 00

Possible partition(Linux ext2), size(502mb), offset(1874mb)
   type: 131(0x83)(Linux ext2 filesystem)
   size: 502mb #s(1028160) s(3839535-4867694)
   chs:  (239/0/1)-(302/254/63)d (239/0/1)-(302/254/63)r
   hex:  00 00 01 EF 83 FE 7F 2E 2F 96 3A 00 40 B0 0F 00
```

We see from the output that there were likely two FAT partitions and one Ext2 partition. The field at the end of the 'size:' line shows the location of the partition in sectors. If the -v flag were not specified, the sector location would not have been printed. A similar tool is TestDisk by Christophe Grenier (http://www.cgsecurity.org/testdisk.html). This analysis technique works only when basic wiping or partition table corruption has occurred.

## SUMMARY

All large media devices have some type of volume system and it is analyzed in every investigation, whether it is obvious or not. The volume systems exist to provide partitions or compartments in the media and the partition systems describe where each partition begins and where it ends. This chapter has given the overview of the technology, and we will next explore the details of several partition and volume creation systems.

# PC-based Partitions

The last chapter provided an overview of volume analysis and why it's important. Now we're going to leave the abstract discussion of volumes and dive into the details of the partition systems used in personal computers. In this chapter, we will look at DOS partitions, Apple partitions, and removable media. For each system, we review how it works and look at its data structure. If you are not interested in the data structure details, you can skip those sections. This chapter also covers special considerations that should be made when analyzing these systems. The next chapter will examine server-based partitioning systems.

## DOS Partitions

The most commonly encountered partition system is the DOS-style partition. DOS partitions have been used with Intel IA32 hardware (i.e., i386 / x86) for many years, yet there is no official specification. There are many Microsoft and non-Microsoft documents that discuss the partitions, but there is no standard reference.

In addition to there being no standard reference, there is also no standard name. Microsoft now calls disks using this type of partition system *Master Boot Record* (MBR) disks. This is in comparison to a *GUID Partition Table* (GPT) disk that is used with the *Extensible Firmware Interface* (EFI) and the 64-bit Intel Itanium-based systems (IA64), which are discussed in the next chapter[Microsoft 2004a]. Starting with Windows 2000, Microsoft also differentiates between basic and dynamic disks. A *basic disk* refers to either an MBR or a GPT disk, and the partitions in the disk are independent and stand-alone. Dynamic disks, which are discussed in Chapter 7, "Multiple Disk Volumes," also can be either MBR or GPT disks, and the partitions can be combined and merged to form a single, large partition. Basic disks have traditionally been associated with DOS partitions, probably because GPT disks are not yet as common. Therefore, using the current terminology, this chapter covers basic MBR disks. However, we will use the simple term DOS partitions for this book.

DOS partitions are used with Microsoft DOS, Microsoft Windows, Linux, and IA32-based FreeBSD and OpenBSD systems. DOS partitions are the most common but also the most complex partitioning system. They were originally designed in the 1980s for small systems and have been improved (i.e., hacked) to handle large modern systems. In fact, there are two different partitioning methods that are used in this system. This section will give an overview of the partitioning system, show the data structures in the system, show what tools can list the layout, and discuss investigation considerations.

## GENERAL OVERVIEW

In this section, we will examine the DOS partition concepts and boot code location. The data structures are discussed in the following section.

### Basic MBR Concepts

A disk that is organized using DOS partitions has an MBR in the first 512-byte sector. The MBR contains boot code, a partition table, and a signature value. The boot code contains the instructions that tell the computer how to process the partition table and locate the operating system. The partition table has four entries, each of which can describe a DOS partition. Each entry has the following fields:

- Starting CHS address
- Ending CHS address
- Starting LBA address
- Number of sectors in partition
- Type of partition
- Flags

Each table entry describes the layout of a partition in both CHS and LBA addresses. Recall that the CHS addresses only work for disks less than 8 GB in size, but the LBA addresses allow disks to be *terabytes* (TB) in size.

The type field in the partition identifies what type of data should exist in the partition. Common examples include FAT, NTFS, and FreeBSD. The next section has a more comprehensive list of partition types. The type value is used differently by different OSes. Linux, for example, does not care about it. You can put a FAT file system inside of a partition that has a type of NTFS, and it will mount it as FAT. Microsoft Windows, on the other hand, relies on it. Windows will not try to mount a file system in a partition if it does not support the partition type. Therefore, if a disk has a FAT file system inside a partition with a Linux file system type, the user will not see the FAT file system from within Windows. This behavior can be used to hide partitions from Windows. For example, some tools will add a bit to a partition type that Windows supports so that it will not be shown when Windows boots again.

Each entry also contains a flag field that identifies which partition is the "bootable" one. This is used to identify where the operating system is located when the computer is booting. Using the four entries in the MBR, we can describe a simple disk layout with up to four partitions. Figure 5.1 shows such a simple disk with two partitions and the MBR in the first sector.

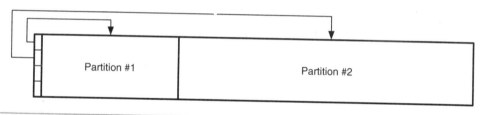

**Figure 5.1**   A basic DOS disk with two partitions and the MBR.

## Extended Partition Concepts

The MBR is a simple method of describing up to four partitions. However, many systems require more partitions than that. For example, consider a 12GB disk that the user wants to divide into six 2GB partitions because he is using multiple operating systems. We cannot describe the six partitions by using the four partition table entries.

The solution to this design problem is what makes DOS partitions so complex. The basic theory behind the solution is to use one, two, or three of the entries in the MBR for normal partitions and then create an "extended partition" that will fill up the remainder of the disk. Before we move on, some definitions may be helpful. A *primary file system partition* is a partition whose entry is in the MBR and the partition contains a file system or other structured data. A *primary extended partition* is a partition whose entry is in the

MBR, and the partition contains additional partitions. We can see this in Figure 5.2, which has three primary file system partitions and one primary extended partition.

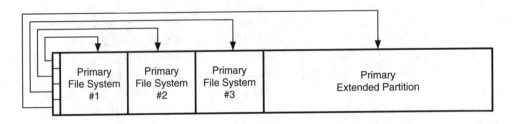

**Figure 5.2**  A DOS disk with three primary file system partitions and one primary secondary partition.

To consider what goes inside a primary extended partition, you should basically forget about everything we have discussed so far. In the MBR, we saw a central partition table that described several partitions. Here we see a linked list of partitions. The basic theory is that we are going to precede every file system partition with data that describe how big the file system partition is and where we can find the next partition. All these partitions should be located inside of the primary extended partition, which is why it must be as large as possible.

A *secondary file system partition*, also called a logical partition in Windows, is located inside the primary extended partition bounds and contains a file system or other structured data. Secondary file system partitions are equivalent to the partitions that are described in the MBR except that they are in an extended partition. A *secondary extended partition* is a partition that contains a partition table and a secondary file system partition. The secondary extended partitions wrap around the secondary file system partitions and describe where the secondary file system partition is located and where the next secondary extended partition is located.

Figure 5.3 shows an example of how secondary partitions work. Secondary Extended #1 contains a partition table that points to Secondary File System #1 and Secondary Extended #2. Secondary Extended #2 contains a partition table that points to Secondary File System #2. It also could point to another secondary extended partition, and this process could repeat until we are out of disk space.

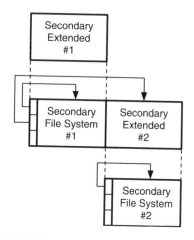

**Figure 5.3** The basic theory and layout behind the secondary extended and file system partitions.

## Putting the Concepts Together

Now let's put these two partitioning methods together. If we need one to four partitions, we can create them using only the MBR, and we do not need to worry about extended partitions. If we want more than four partitions, we must create up to three primary file system partitions in the MBR and then allocate the rest of the disk to a primary extended partition.

Inside the primary extended partition, we use the linked-list partitioning method. We can optimize the linked-list design that I described in the last section by not making the initial secondary extended partition. Instead, put a partition table at the beginning of the primary extended partition. It can describe one secondary file system and one secondary extended partition.

Consider an example. We have a 12GB disk and we want to break it up into six 2GB partitions. We create the first three 2GB partitions using the first three entries in the MBR, and the remaining 6GB is allocated to a primary extended partition, which spans from 6GB to 12GB.

We need to allocate three more partitions using the linked-list method. We use the partition table in the first sector of the primary extended partition, make a secondary file system partition that spans from 6GB to 8GB, and make a secondary extended partition that spans from 8GB to 10GB. A partition table is inside the secondary extended partition, and it has entries for a secondary file system partition that spans from 8GB to 10GB and an entry for another secondary extended partition that spans from 10GB to 12GB.

A partition table is inside the last secondary extended partition, and it has an entry for the final file system partition, which spans from 10GB to 12GB. We see this in Figure 5.4.

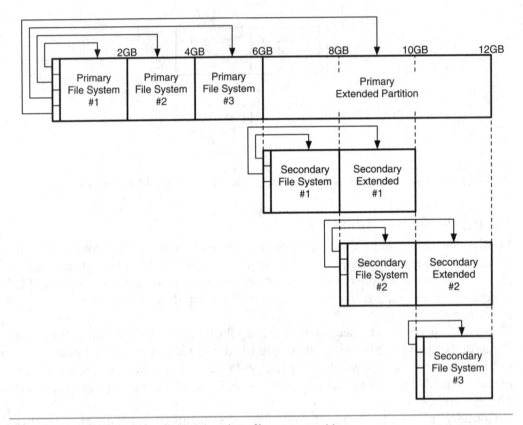

**Figure 5.4**    The layout required for a disk with six file system partitions.

As I have described it and as most documents claim, an extended partition table should have, at most, one entry for a secondary file system partition and one entry for a secondary extended partition. In practice, most operating systems will not generate an error if more than two entries are being used. In fact, in July 2003, I released a 160 MB disk image [Carrier 2003] with six 25 MB DOS partitions to the CFTT Yahoo! Groups list (http://groups.yahoo.com/group/cftt/). The image had a primary extended partition table with two secondary file system partition entries and one secondary extended partition entry. Some forensic tools properly handled the third partition entry, while others ignored it or claimed that the 25 MB partition was a 1 TB partition. This example shows how something as common as DOS partitions can cause problems with analysis tools.

Extended partitions have special types that are used in their partition table entries. To make this confusing partition scheme even more confusing, there is more than one type of extended partition, and they do not differentiate between primary and secondary extended partitions. The common types of extended partitions are "DOS Extended," "Windows 95 Extended," and "Linux Extended."

### Boot Code

The boot code in a DOS disk exists in the first 446 bytes of the first 512-byte sector, which is the MBR. The end of the sector contains the partition table. The standard Microsoft boot code processes the partition table in the MBR and identifies which partition has the bootable flag set. When it finds such a partition, it looks in the first sector of the partition and executes the code found there. The code in the start of the partition will be operating system-specific. Boot sector viruses insert themselves into the first 446 bytes of the MBR so that they are executed every time the computer is booted.

It is becoming much more common to have multiple operating systems on a computer. There are two ways to handle this. Windows handles this by having code in the bootable partition that allows a user to select which OS to load. In other words, the boot code in the MBR executes first and loads the Windows bootable code. The Windows bootable code allows a user to choose a different partition from which to boot.

The other method is to change the code in the MBR. The new MBR code presents the user with a list of options, and the user chooses which partition to boot from. This typically requires more code and uses some of the unused sectors that exist before the first partition starts.

### Summary

The DOS partition system is complex because each partition table has only four entries in it. Other partition systems discussed later in this chapter and the next have larger partition tables and are, therefore, less complex. The following high-level steps are necessary to list the layout information of a disk with DOS partitions:

1. The Master Boot Record is read from the first sector of the disk, and the four partition table entries are identified and processed.
2. When an entry for an extended partition is processed, the first sector of the extended partition is read and its partition table entries are processed in the same manner as the MBR.

3.  When an entry for a non-extended partition is processed, its starting sector and size are displayed. The ending sector address can be determined by adding the starting sector address and the size together and subtracting one.

## DATA STRUCTURES

The previous section reviewed the DOS partition system. This section provides a detailed discussion of the structures that make the system work. If you are not interested in data structures, you can skip this; however, there is an interesting example of extended partitions. This section is organized into three subsections describing the MBR, extended partitions, and show tool output from an example image.

### MBR Data Structure

DOS Partition tables exist in the MBR and in the first sector of each extended partition. Conveniently, they all use the same 512-byte structure. The first 446 bytes are reserved for assembly boot code. Code needs to exist in the MBR because it is used when the computer is started, but the extended partitions do not need it and could contain hidden data. The MBR layout in tabular form can be found in Table 5.1.

**Table 5.1**   Data structures for the DOS partition table.

| Byte Range | Description | Essential |
|---|---|---|
| 0–445 | Boot Code | No |
| 446–461 | Partition Table Entry #1 (see Table 5.2) | Yes |
| 462–477 | Partition Table Entry #2 (see Table 5.2) | Yes |
| 478–493 | Partition Table Entry #3 (see Table 5.2) | Yes |
| 494–509 | Partition Table Entry #4 (see Table 5.2) | Yes |
| 510–511 | Signature value (0xAA55) | No |

The partition table has four 16-byte entries. The entries' structures are given in Table 5.2. Note that the CHS addresses are essential for older systems that rely on them, but are not essential on newer systems.

**Table 5.2** Data structure for DOS partition entries.

| Byte Range | Description | Essential |
|---|---|---|
| 0–0 | Bootable Flag | No |
| 1–3 | Starting CHS Address | Yes |
| 4–4 | Partition Type (see Table 5.3) | No |
| 5–7 | Ending CHS Address | Yes |
| 8–11 | Starting LBA Address | Yes |
| 12–15 | Size in Sectors | Yes |

The bootable flag is not always necessary. The standard boot code for a system with only one OS looks for an entry whose flag is set to 0x80. For example, if a system has Microsoft Windows on it and the disk is partitioned into two partitions, the partition with the operating system on it (C:\windows, for example) will have the bootable flag set. On the other hand, if the boot code prompts the user to choose which partition to boot from, the bootable flag is not necessary. Although, some boot programs will set the bootable flag after the user chooses to boot that partition.

The starting and ending CHS addresses have an 8-bit head value, a 6-bit sector value, and a 10-bit cylinder value. In theory, either the CHS addresses or the LBA addresses need to be set for each partition, but not both. It is up to the OS and the code that is used to boot the system to determine which values need to be set. For example, Windows 98 and ME use the CHS addresses for partitions in the first 7.8GB of the disk, but Windows 2000 and beyond always ignore the CHS addresses [Microsoft 2003]. Some partitioning tools set both when possible for backward compatibility. The usage of these fields is application-dependent.

The partition type field identifies the file system type that should be in the partition. A list of common partition types is given in Table 5.3. A more detailed list of partition types can be found in *Partition types* [Brouwer 2004].

**Table 5.3** Some of the type values for DOS partitions.

| Type | Description |
|---|---|
| 0x00 | Empty |
| 0x01 | FAT12, CHS |
| 0x04 | FAT16, 16–32 MB, CHS |

*continues*

**Table 5.3**   Some of the type values for DOS partitions (continued).

| Type | Description |
|------|-------------|
| 0x05 | Microsoft Extended, CHS |
| 0x06 | FAT16, 32 MB–2GB, CHS |
| 0x07 | NTFS |
| 0x0b | FAT32, CHS |
| 0x0c | FAT32, LBA |
| 0x0e | FAT16, 32 MB–2GB, LBA |
| 0x0f | Microsoft Extended, LBA |
| 0x11 | Hidden FAT12, CHS |
| 0x14 | Hidden FAT16, 16–32 MB, CHS |
| 0x16 | Hidden FAT16, 32 MB–2GB, CHS |
| 0x1b | Hidden FAT32, CHS |
| 0x1c | Hidden FAT32, LBA |
| 0x1e | Hidden FAT16, 32 MB–2GB, LBA |
| 0x42 | Microsoft MBR. Dynamic Disk |
| 0x82 | Solaris x86 |
| 0x82 | Linux Swap |
| 0x83 | Linux |
| 0x84 | Hibernation |
| 0x85 | Linux Extended |
| 0x86 | NTFS Volume Set |
| 0x87 | NTFS Volume Set |
| 0xa0 | Hibernation |
| 0xa1 | Hibernation |
| 0xa5 | FreeBSD |
| 0xa6 | OpenBSD |

| Type | Description |
|------|-------------|
| 0xa8 | Mac OSX |
| 0xa9 | NetBSD |
| 0xab | Mac OSX Boot |
| 0xb7 | BSDI |
| 0xb8 | BSDI swap |
| 0xee | EFI GPT Disk |
| 0xef | EFI System Partition |
| 0xfb | Vmware File System |
| 0xfc | Vmware swap |

Notice how many partition types exist for Microsoft file systems in the 0x01 to 0x0f range. The reason is that Microsoft operating systems use the partition type to determine how to read and write data from the partition. Recall from Chapter 2, "Computer Foundations," that Windows can use either INT 13h or the extended INT 13h BIOS routines. The extended INT 13h routines are needed for accessing disks larger than 8.1GB and use LBA addressing instead of CHS. Therefore, the FAT16 0x04 and 0x0E types are the same except that the OS should use the extended routines for the latter type. Similarly, 0x0B and 0x0C types are the normal and extended versions of FAT32 and 0x05, and 0x0F types are the normal and extended for extended partitions [Microsoft 2004b]. The "hidden" versions of these partition types have a 1 instead of a 0 in the upper nibble, and various tools create them.

To illustrate the MBR and the partition tables, we will extract the sectors from an actual system and parse the structures by hand. The system is a dual boot Microsoft Windows and Linux system, and it has eight file system partitions.

The first example is from the first sector of the disk. This output is from the xxd tool in Linux, but similar data can be found using a hex editor in Windows or UNIX. The following command was used in Linux:

```
# dd if=disk3.dd bs=512 skip=0 count=1 | xxd
```

The left column is the byte offset in decimal, the middle eight columns are the data in hexadecimal format, and the final column is the data translated into ASCII. The data are from an IA32-based system, which is little-endian and stores numbers with the least significant byte at the lowest address. Therefore, the order of the bytes in the middle columns may need to be reversed. The MBR of the disk is as follows:

```
# dd if=disk3.dd bs=512 skip=0 count=1 | xxd
0000000: eb48 9010 8ed0 bc00 b0b8 0000 8ed8 8ec0  .H..............
[REMOVED]
0000384: 0048 6172 6420 4469 736b 0052 6561 6400  .Hard Disk.Read.
0000400: 2045 7272 6f72 00bb 0100 b40e cd10 ac3c   Error.........<
0000416: 0075 f4c3 0000 0000 0000 0000 0000 0000  .u..............
0000432: 0000 0000 0000 0000 0000 0000 0000 0001  ................
0000448: 0100 07fe 3f7f 3f00 0000 4160 1f00 8000  ....?.?...A`....
0000464: 0180 83fe 3f8c 8060 1f00 cd2f 0300 0000  ....?..`.../....
0000480: 018d 83fe 3fcc 4d90 2200 40b0 0f00 0000  ....?.M.".@.....
0000496: 01cd 05fe ffff 8d40 3200 79eb 9604 55aa  .......@2.y...U.
```

The first 446 bytes contain boot code. The 0xAA55 signature value can be seen in the last two bytes of the sector (although they are reversed in the output because of the endian ordering). The partition table is in bold and starts with the 0x0001 at offset 446. Each line in the output has 16 bytes, and each table entry is 16 bytes. Therefore, the second entry begins one line below the first entry with 0x8000. Using the structure previously outlined, the four partition table entries are shown in Table 5.4. The values are shown in hexadecimal format with the decimal value in parenthesis of important values.

**Table 5.4**   The contents of the primary partition table in the example disk image.

| # | Flag | Type | Starting Sector | Size |
|---|------|------|-----------------|------|
| 1 | 0x00 | 0x07 | 0x0000003f (63) | 0x001f6041 (2,056,257) |
| 2 | 0x80 | 0x83 | 0x001f6080 (2,056,320) | 0x00032fcd (208,845) |
| 3 | 0x00 | 0x83 | 0x0022904d (2,265,165) | 0x000fb040 (1,028,160) |
| 4 | 0x00 | 0x05 | 0x0032408d (3,293,325) | 0x0496eb79 (76,999,545) |

Using Table 5.4 and the partition type field in Table 5.3, we can guess what type of data are in each partition. The first partition should be for an NTFS file system (type 0x07), the second and third partitions should be for Linux file systems (0x83), and the fourth partition is an extended partition (0x05). The second entry is set to be bootable. The extended partition should have been expected because it was previously mentioned that there would be a total of eight partitions. The disk layout from this partition table is shown in Figure 5.5.

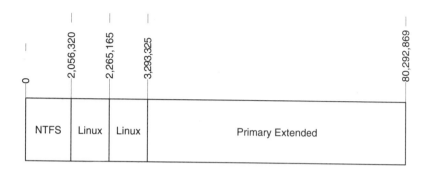

**Figure 5.5** Disk layout after processing the first partition table in example (not to scale).

## Extended Partition Data Structures

Recall that the extended partitions use the same structure in the first sector as the MBR does, but they use it to make a linked list. The partition table entries are slightly different, though, because the starting sector addresses are relative to other places on the disk besides the beginning of the disk. Furthermore, the starting sector of a secondary file system partition is relative to a different place than the starting sector of a secondary extended partition.

The starting address for a secondary file system entry is relative to the current partition table. This is intuitive because the secondary extended partitions work as wrappers around the file system partitions; therefore, they have the starting address relative to themselves. On the other hand, the starting address for a secondary extended partition entry is relative to the primary extended partition.

Let's step through the example shown in Figure 5.6. It has a primary extended partition that starts in sector 1,000 with a length of 11,000 sectors. Its partition table has two entries. The first is for a FAT file system with a starting sector of 63, which is added to the sector of the current partition table to get 1,063. The second entry is for an extended partition and its starting sector is 4,000. That is added to the start of the primary extended partition, which is sector 1,000, and we get sector 5,000.

Now let's jump ahead to that secondary extended partition (in sector 5,000). The first partition table entry is for an NTFS file system, and its starting value is 63, which is added to the address of the current partition table and to get sector 5,063. The second entry is for an extended partition, and its starting value is 6,500, which is added to the sector of the primary extended partition and to get sector 7,500.

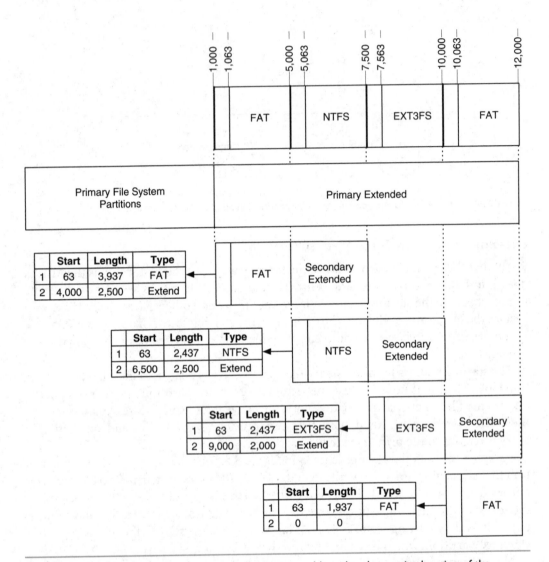

**Figure 5.6** Disk with three secondary extended partitions. Note that the starting location of the secondary extended partitions is relative to the start of the primary extended partition, sector 1000.

We'll do one more round to make sure it is clear. The next extended partition starts in sector 7,500. The first entry is for an EXT3FS file system with a starting value of 63, which is added to 7,500 to get sector 7,563. The second entry is for a secondary extended partition, and its starting value is 9,000, which is added to 1,000 to get sector 10,000.

Return to the actual system that we parsed by hand. The following are the contents of the first sector of the primary extended partition, which is located in sector 3,293,325:

```
# dd if=disk3.dd bs=512 skip=3293325 count=1 | xxd
[REMOVED]
0000432: 0000 0000 0000 0000 0000 0000 0000 0001   ...............
0000448: 01cd 83fe 7fcb 3f00 0000 0082 3e00 0000   ......?.....>...
0000464: 41cc 05fe bf0b 3f82 3e00 40b0 0f00 0000   A.....?.>.@.....
0000480: 0000 0000 0000 0000 0000 0000 0000 0000   ...............
0000496: 0000 0000 0000 0000 0000 0000 0000 55aa   .............U.
```

The four partition table entries are highlighted, and we see that the final two entries are empty. The first two partition table entries are parsed into the contents of Table 5.5 (the partition numbering is continued from Table 5.4):

**Table 5.5**  The contents of the primary extended partition table in the example disk image.

| # | Flag | Type | Starting Sector | Size |
|---|------|------|-----------------|------|
| 5 | 0x00 | 0x83 | 0x0000003f (63) | 0x003e8200 (4,096,572) |
| 6 | 0x00 | 0x05 | 0x003e823f (4,096,575) | 0x000fb040 (1,028,160) |

Entry #5 has a type for a Linux file system (0x83), so it is a secondary file system partition, and its starting sector is relative to the start of the current extended partition (sector 3,293,325).

```
3,293,325 + 63 = 3,293,388
```

Entry #6 has a type for a DOS Extended partition, so its starting sector is relative to the start of the primary extended partition, which is the current partition.

```
3,293,325 + 4,096,575  = 7,389,900
```

The disk layout, as we know it, can be found in Figure 5.7. Before we continue, note the sizes of the two partitions. In the MBR, the primary extended partition had a size of 76,999,545 sectors. In this table, the size of the next secondary extended partition is only 1,028,160 sectors. Recall that the primary extended partition has a size of all the secondary file systems and secondary extended partitions, but the secondary extended partitions have a size that is equal to the size of only the next secondary file system partition plus the size needed for a partition table.

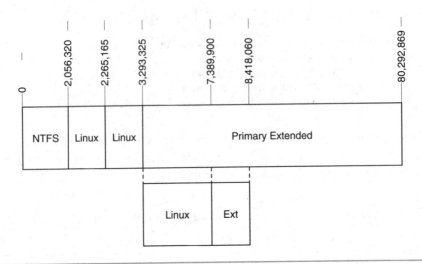

**Figure 5.7**  Disk layout after processing the second partition table (not to scale).

We can continue the example by examining the next secondary extended partition, which is located in sector 7,389,900. Its contents are shown in Table 5.6.

**Table 5.6**  The contents of the first secondary extended partition table in the example disk image.

| #  | Flag  | Type  | Starting Sector       | Size                     |
|----|-------|-------|-----------------------|--------------------------|
| 7  | 0x00  | 0x82  | 0x0000003f (63)       | 0x000fb001 (1,028,097)   |
| 8  | 0x00  | 0x05  | 0x004e327f (5,124,735)| 0x000fb040 (1,028,160)   |

Entry #7 is for a Linux swap partition, so it is a secondary file system, and its starting sector address is relative to the current extended partition, which is sector 7,389,900.

```
7,389,900 + 63 = 7,389,963
```

Entry #8 is for a DOS Extended file system, so its starting sector address is relative to the primary extended partition, which is sector 3,293,325.

3,293,325 + 5,124,735 = 8,418,060

The disk layout with the information from this partition table can be found in Figure 5.8. The full contents of the example partition table are given in the next section when we look at tools that print the partition table contents.

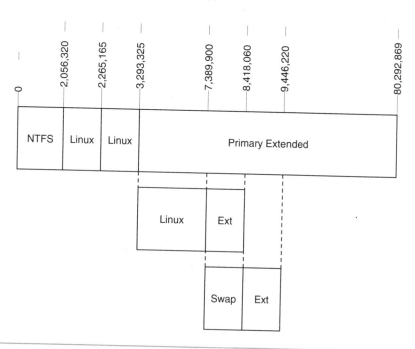

**Figure 5.8**   Disk layout after processing the third partition table (not to scale).

## Example Image Tool Output

Now that the internal structure of the partition system is known, we will show how some of the analysis tools process them. For those who actually enjoy parsing the structure by hand and never use a tool, you can skip this section. Two Linux tools will be shown here. Other Windows tools, such as full forensic analysis tools and hex editors, also perform this function.

The fdisk command comes with Linux and is different from the tool with the same name that comes with Windows. fdisk can be run on a Linux device or a disk image file generated by dd. The -1 flag forces it to list the partitions instead of going into interactive mode where the partitions could also be edited. The -u flag forces the output to be in sectors instead of cylinders. The output of the DOS Partitioned disk that we parsed by hand is as follows:

```
# fdisk -lu disk3.dd
Disk disk3.dd: 255 heads, 63 sectors, 0 cylinders
Units = sectors of 1 * 512 bytes

   Device Boot      Start         End     Blocks   Id  System
disk3.dd1               63     2056319    1028128+   7  HPFS/NTFS
disk3.dd2     *    2056320     2265164     104422+  83  Linux
disk3.dd3         2265165     3293324     514080   83  Linux
disk3.dd4         3293325    80292869   38499772+   5  Extended
disk3.dd5         3293388     7389899    2048256   83  Linux
disk3.dd6         7389963     8418059     514048+  82  Linux swap
disk3.dd7         8418123     9446219     514048+  83  Linux
disk3.dd8         9446283    17639369    4096543+   7  HPFS/NTFS
disk3.dd9        17639433    48371714   15366141   83  Linux
```

We can observe several things from this output. The output lists only the primary extended partition (disk3.dd4). The secondary extended partition in which the Linux swap partition is located is not displayed. This is acceptable for most circumstances because only the primary and secondary file system partitions are needed for an investigation, but it should be noted that you are not seeing all partition table entries.

The mmls tool in The Sleuth Kit provides slightly different information. Sectors that are unused by a partition are marked as such, the location of the partition tables is marked, and the extended partition locations are noted. Using the same disk as we used for the first fdisk example, the following is seen:

```
# mmls -t dos disk3.dd
Units are in 512-byte sectors
     Slot    Start       End         Length      Description
00:  -----   0000000000  0000000000  0000000001  Table #0
01:  -----   0000000001  0000000062  0000000062  Unallocated
02:  00:00   0000000063  0002056319  0002056257  NTFS (0x07)
03:  00:01   0002056320  0002265164  0000208845  Linux (0x83)
04:  00:02   0002265165  0003293324  0001028160  Linux (0x83)
05:  00:03   0003293325  0080292869  0076999545  DOS Extended (0x05)
06:  -----   0003293325  0003293325  0000000001  Table #1
```

```
07:    -----    0003293326    0003293387    0000000062    Unallocated
08:    01:00    0003293388    0007389899    0004096512    Linux (0x83)
09:    01:01    0007389900    0008418059    0001028160    DOS Extended (0x05)
10:    -----    0007389900    0007389900    0000000001    Table #2
11:    -----    0007389901    0007389962    0000000062    Unallocated
12:    02:00    0007389963    0008418059    0001028097    Linux Swap (0x82)
13:    02:01    0008418060    0009446219    0001028160    DOS Extended (0x05)
14:    -----    0008418060    0008418060    0000000001    Table #3
15:    -----    0008418061    0008418122    0000000062    Unallocated
16:    03:00    0008418123    0009446219    0001028097    Linux (0x83)
17:    03:01    0009446220    0017639369    0008193150    DOS Extended (0x05)
18:    -----    0009446220    0009446220    0000000001    Table #4
19:    -----    0009446221    0009446282    0000000062    Unallocated
20:    04:00    0009446283    0017639369    0008193087    NTFS (0x07)
21:    04:01    0017639370    0048371714    0030732345    DOS Extended (0x05)
22:    -----    0017639370    0017639370    0000000001    Table #5
23:    -----    0017639371    0017639432    0000000062    Unallocated
24:    05:00    0017639433    0048371714    0030732282    Linux (0x83)
```

The 'Unallocated' entries are for the space in between partitions and for the space between the end of the partition table and the beginning of the first partition. The output of mmls gives both the ending address and the size, so it can be easily used to extract the partitions with dd.

The output of mmls is sorted by the starting sector of the partition, so the first column is only a counter for each entry and has no correlation to the partition table entry. The second column shows what partition table the partition was found in and which entry in the table. The first number shows which table, 0 being the primary table and 1 being the primary extended table, and the second number shows which entry in the table. The sorted output helps to identify sectors that are not partitioned. For example, consider this image:

```
# mmls -t dos disk1.dd
Units are in 512-byte sectors
       Slot    Start         End           Length        Description
00:    -----   0000000000    0000000000    0000000001    Table #0
01:    -----   0000000001    0000000062    0000000062    Unallocated
02:    00:00   0000000063    0001028159    0001028097    Win95 FAT32 (0x0B)
03:    -----   0001028160    0002570399    0001542240    Unallocated
04:    00:03   0002570400    0004209029    0001638630    OpenBSD (0xA6)
05:    00:01   0004209030    0006265349    0002056320    NTFS (0x07)
```

In this output, we see that the NTFS partition is in a slot that is before the OpenBSD partition, but the NTFS partition starts after the OpenBSD partition. We can also see that there is no entry '00:02,' and the 1,542,240 sectors in between the FAT and OpenBSD partitions are also marked as unallocated.

## ANALYSIS CONSIDERATIONS

This section includes a few characteristics that can be taken into consideration when analyzing a DOS-based disk. The partition table and boot code require only one sector, yet 63 are typically allocated for both the MBR and extended partitions because the partitions start on a cylinder boundary. Therefore, sector 0 of the extended partition or MBR is used for code and the partition table, but sectors 1-62 may not be used. The unused area can be used by additional boot code, but it also may contain data from a previous installation, zeros, or hidden data. Windows XP does not wipe the data in the unused sectors when it partitions a disk.

As most partitions start at sector 63 (which you can use to your advantage if you are desperate to recover the contents of the first partition), the partition table is missing and the tools discussed in Chapter 4, "Volume Analysis," do not work. Try extracting data from sector 63 onward. This method includes other partitions in the image; however, you may be able to identify the actual size of the partition from file system data. The partition can be extracted with dd as follows:

```
# dd if=disk.dd bs=512 skip=63 of=part.dd
```

In theory, extended partitions should have only two entries: one secondary file system partition and another secondary extended partition. Most partitioning tools follow this theory, but it is possible to create a third entry by hand. Microsoft Windows XP and Red Hat 8.0 showed the "extra" partition when there were more than two in an extended partition, although neither OS would allow you to create such a configuration. Test your analysis tools to ensure that they are showing all of the partitions when this "invalid" configuration exists.

The value in the partition type field of the partition table is not always enforced. Windows uses this field to identify which partitions it should try to mount, but users are given access to all partitions in operating systems, such as Linux. Therefore, a user could put a FAT file system in a partition whose type is for laptop hibernation. They would not be able to mount it in Windows, but would in Linux.

Some versions of Windows only create one primary partition in the MBR and then rely on extended partitions for the remaining partitions. In other words, they do not create three primary partitions before creating an extended partition.

When parts of a partition table have become corrupt, it may be necessary to search for the extended partition tables. To find the extended partitions, a search for 0xAA55 in the last two bytes of a sector could be conducted. Note that this signature value exists at the same location in the first sector of a NTFS and FAT file system, and the remainder of the sector must be examined to determine if it is a partition table or a file system boot sector. If a sector is found to be a boot sector of a file system, a partition table may exist 63 sectors prior to it.

## SUMMARY

DOS-based partitions are the most common for current computer investigations. Unfortunately, they are also the most complex to understand because they were not originally designed for the size of modern systems. Fortunately, tools exist to easily list the layout of the disk and extract the used and unused space. Many UNIX systems that run on IA32-compatible platforms use DOS partitions in addition to their own partition systems. Therefore, every investigator needs a solid understanding of DOS partitions.

## APPLE PARTITIONS

Systems running the Apple Macintosh operating system are not as common as those running Microsoft Windows, but they have been increasing in popularity with the introduction of Mac OS X, a UNIX-based operating system. The partitions that we will describe here can be found in the latest Apple laptops and desktops running OS X, older systems that are running Macintosh 9, and even the portable iPod devices that play MP3 audio. The partition map also can be used in the disk image files that a Macintosh system uses to transmit files. The disk image file is similar to a zip file in Windows or a tar file in Unix. The files in the disk image are stored in a file system, and the file system may be in a partition.

The design of the partition system in an Apple system is a nice balance between the complexity of DOS-based partitions and the limited number of partitions that we will see in the BSD disk labels. The Apple partition can describe any number of partitions, and the data structures are in consecutive sectors of the disk. This section will give an overview of the Apple partitions, the details of the data structures, and discuss how to view the details.

## GENERAL OVERVIEW

The Apple partitions are described in the partition map structure, which is located at the beginning of the disk. The firmware contains the code that processes this structure, so the map does not contain boot code like we saw in the DOS partition table. Each entry in the partition map describes the starting sector of the partition, the size, the type, and the volume name. The data structure also contains values about data inside of the partition, such as the location of the data area and the location of any boot code.

The first entry in the partition map is typically an entry for itself, and it shows the maximum size that the partition map can be. Apple creates partitions to store hardware drivers, so the main disk for an Apple system has many partitions that contain drivers and other non-file system content. Figure 5.9 shows an example layout of an Apple disk with three file system partitions and the partition for the partition map.

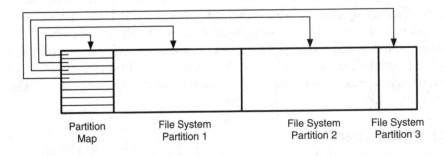

**Figure 5.9**   An Apple disk with one partition map partition and three file system partitions.

We will later see that BSD systems have a different partition structure called the disk label. Even though Mac OS X is based on a BSD kernel, it uses an Apple partition map and not a disk label.

## DATA STRUCTURES

Now that we have examined the basic concepts of an Apple partition, we can look at the data structures. As with other data structures in this book, they can be skipped if you are not interested. This section also contains the output of some analysis tools using an example disk image.

## Partition Map Entry

The Apple partition map contains several 512-byte data structures, and each partition uses one data structure. The partition map starts in the second sector of the disk and continues until all partitions have been described. The partition data structures are laid out in consecutive sectors, and each map entry has a value for the total number of partitions. The 512-byte data structure is shown in Table 5.7.

**Table 5.7**  Data structure for Apple partition entries.

| Byte Range | Description | Essential |
|---|---|---|
| 0–1 | Signature value (0x504D) | No |
| 2–3 | Reserved | No |
| 4–7 | Total Number of partitions | Yes |
| 8–11 | Starting sector of partition | Yes |
| 12–15 | Size of partition in sectors | Yes |
| 16–47 | Name of partition in ASCII | No |
| 48–79 | Type of partition in ASCII | No |
| 80–83 | Starting sector of data area in partition | No |
| 84–87 | Size of data area in sectors | No |
| 88–91 | Status of partition (see table 5-8) | No |
| 92–95 | Starting sector of boot code | No |
| 96–99 | Size of boot code in sectors | No |
| 100–103 | Address of boot loader code | No |
| 104–107 | Reserved | No |
| 108–111 | Boot code entry point | No |
| 112–115 | Reserved | No |
| 116–119 | Boot code checksum | No |
| 120–135 | Processor type | No |
| 136–511 | Reserved | No |

The type of partition is given in ASCII and not as an integer as other partition schemes use. The status values for each partition apply to both older A/UX systems and modern Macintosh systems. A/UX is an older operating system from Apple. The status value can have one of the values shown in Table 5.8 [Apple 1999].

**Table 5.8**  Status value for Apple partitions.

| Type | Description |
| --- | --- |
| 0x00000001 | Entry is valid (A/UX only) |
| 0x00000002 | Entry is allocated (A/UX only) |
| 0x00000004 | Entry in use (A/UX only) |
| 0x00000008 | Entry contains boot information (A/UX only) |
| 0x00000010 | Partition is readable (A/UX only) |
| 0x00000020 | Partition is writable (Macintosh & A/UX) |
| 0x00000040 | Boot code is position independent (A/UX only) |
| 0x00000100 | Partition contains chain-compatible driver (Macintosh only) |
| 0x00000200 | Partition contains a real driver (Macintosh only) |
| 0x00000400 | Partition contains a chain driver (Macintosh only) |
| 0x40000000 | Automatically mount at startup (Macintosh only) |
| 0x80000000 | The startup partition (Macintosh only) |

The data area fields are used for file systems that have a data area that does not start at the beginning of the disk. The boot code fields are used to locate the boot code when the system is starting.

To identify the partitions in an Apple disk, a tool (or person) reads the data structure from the second sector. It is processed to learn the total number of partitions, and then the other partition information from it is collected. The first entry is usually the entry for the partition map itself. The next sector is then read, and the process continues until all partitions have been read. Here are the contents of the first entry in the partition map:

```
# dd if=mac-disk.dd bs=512 skip=1 | xxd
0000000: 504d 0000 0000 000a 0000 0001 0000 003f  PM............?
0000016: 4170 706c 6500 0000 0000 0000 0000 0000  Apple..........
```

```
0000032: 0000 0000 0000 0000 0000 0000 0000 0000  ................
0000048: 4170 706c 655f 7061 7274 6974 696f 6e5f  Apple_partition_
0000064: 6d61 7000 0000 0000 0000 0000 0000 0000  map.............
0000080: 0000 0000 0000 003f 0000 0000 0000 0000  .......?........
0000096: 0000 0000 0000 0000 0000 0000 0000 0000  ................
[REMOVED]
```

Apple computers use Motorola PowerPC processors and, therefore, store data in big-endian ordering. As a result, we will not need to reverse the order of numbers like we did with DOS partitions. We see the signature value of 0x504d in bytes 0 to 1 and the number of partitions in bytes 4 to 7, which is 10 (0x0000000a). Bytes 8 to 11 show us that the first sector of the disk is the starting sector for this partition and that its size is 63 sectors (0x3f). The name of the partition is "Apple," and the type of partition is "Apple_partition_map." Bytes 88 to 91 show that no flags for this partition are set. Other entries in the partition map that are not for the partition map itself have status values set.

### Example Image Tool Output

You can view an Apple partition map with mmls in The Sleuth Kit. The fdisk command in Linux will not show the contents of a partition map. Here are the results from running mmls on a 20GB iBook laptop:

```
# mmls -t mac mac-disk.dd
MAC Partition Map
Units are in 512-byte sectors

      Slot    Start        End          Length       Description
00:   -----   0000000000   0000000000   0000000001   Unallocated
01:   00      0000000001   0000000063   0000000063   Apple_partition_map
02:   -----   0000000001   0000000010   0000000010   Table
03:   -----   0000000011   0000000063   0000000053   Unallocated
04:   01      0000000064   0000000117   0000000054   Apple_Driver43
05:   02      0000000118   0000000191   0000000074   Apple_Driver43
06:   03      0000000192   0000000245   0000000054   Apple_Driver_ATA
07:   04      0000000246   0000000319   0000000074   Apple_Driver_ATA
08:   05      0000000320   0000000519   0000000200   Apple_FWDriver
09:   06      0000000520   0000001031   0000000512   Apple_Driver_IOKit
10:   07      0000001032   0000001543   0000000512   Apple_Patches
11:   08      0000001544   0039070059   0039068516   Apple_HFS
12:   09      0039070060   0039070079   0000000020   Apple_Free
```

In this output, the entries are sorted by starting sector, and the second column shows in which entry in the partition map the partition was described. In this case, the entries were already in sorted order. We can see in entry 12 that Apple reports the sectors that are not currently allocated. Entries 0, 2, and 3 were added by mmls to show what space the partition map is using and which sectors are free. The drivers listed here are used by the system when it is booting.

An alternative tool that can be used on a raw disk image is the pdisk tool with the -dump flag on OS X:

```
# pdisk mac-disk.dd -dump
mac-disk.dd  map block size=512
   #:                  type name          length   base   ( size )
   1:   Apple_partition_map Apple              63 @ 1
   2:         Apple_Driver43*Macintosh        54 @ 64
   3:         Apple_Driver43*Macintosh        74 @ 118
   4:      Apple_Driver_ATA*Macintosh        54 @ 192
   5:      Apple_Driver_ATA*Macintosh        74 @ 246
   6:        Apple_FWDriver Macintosh        200 @ 320
   7:   Apple_Driver_IOKit Macintosh        512 @ 520
   8:        Apple_Patches Patch Partition   512 @ 1032
   9:           Apple_HFS untitled     39068516 @ 1544    ( 18.6G)
  10:           Apple_Free                    0+@ 39070060

Device block size=512, Number of Blocks=10053
DeviceType=0x0, DeviceId=0x0
Drivers-
1: @ 64 for 23, type=0x1
2: @ 118 for 36, type=0xffff
3: @ 192 for 21, type=0x701
4: @ 246 for 34, type=0xf8ff
```

As was mentioned in the Introduction, Apple disk image files (which are different from forensic disk image files) also can contain a partition map. A disk image file is an archive file that can save several individual files. It is similar to a zip file in Windows or a tar file in Unix. The disk image file can contain a single partition with a file system, or it can contain only a file system and no partitions. The layout of a test disk image file (files with an extension of .dmg) has the following layout:

```
# mmls -t mac test.dmg
MAC Partition Map
Units are in 512-byte sectors

     Slot    Start        End          Length       Description
00:  -----   0000000000   0000000000   0000000001   Unallocated
```

| 01: | 00 | 0000000001 | 0000000063 | 0000000063 | Apple_partition_map |
|---|---|---|---|---|---|
| 02: | ----- | 0000000001 | 0000000003 | 0000000003 | Table |
| 03: | ----- | 0000000004 | 0000000063 | 0000000060 | Unallocated |
| 04: | 01 | 0000000064 | 0000020467 | 0000020404 | Apple_HFS |
| 05: | 02 | 0000020468 | 0000020479 | 0000000012 | Apple_Free |

## ANALYSIS CONSIDERATIONS

The only unique characteristic of Apple partitions is that there are several unused fields in the data structure that could be used to hide small amounts of data. Also data could be hidden in the sectors between the last partition data structure and the end of the space allocated to the partition map. As with any partitioning scheme, anything could be in the partitions that have an official looking name or that claim to have a given type.

## SUMMARY

The Apple partition map is a fairly simple structure and is easy to understand. The data structures are all located in one place, and the maximum number of partitions is based on how the disk was originally partitioned. The mmls tool allows us to easily identify where the partitions are located if we are using a non-Apple system, and the pdisk tool can be used on an OS X system.

## REMOVABLE MEDIA

Most removable media also have partitions, but they use the same structures that hard disks use. The exception to this rule are floppy disks that are formatted for FAT12 in a Windows or UNIX system. They do not have partition tables, and each entire disk is treated like a single partition. If you image a floppy disk, you can directly analyze the image as a file system. Some of the small USB storage tokens (sometimes called 'thumb drives') do not have partitions and contain one file system, but some of them do have partitions.

Larger removable media, such as Iomega ZIP disks, do have partition tables. The partition table on a ZIP disk will depend on whether it has been formatted for a Mac or a PC. A PC-formatted disk will have a DOS-based partition table and by default will only have one partition in the fourth slot.

Flash cards, which are commonly used in digital cameras, also typically have a partition table. Many flash cards have a FAT file system and can be analyzed using normal investigation tools. Here is DOS-based partition table from a 128MB flash card:

```
# mmls -t dos camera.dd
DOS Partition Table
Units are in 512-byte sectors
      Slot    Start         End           Length        Description
00:   -----   0000000000    0000000000    0000000001    Primary Table (#0)
01:   -----   0000000001    0000000031    0000000031    Unallocated
02:   00:00   0000000032    0000251647    0000251616    DOS FAT16 (0x06)
```

Putting flash cards in a USB or Firewire reader and using dd in Linux can easily image them.

CD-ROMs are more complex because there exist many possible variations. Most CDs use the ISO 9660 format so that multiple operating systems can read the contents of the CD. The ISO 9660 naming requirements are strict, and there are extensions to ISO 9660, such as Joliet and Rock Ridge, which are more flexible. CDs are complex to describe because one CD may have data in a basic ISO 9660 format and in a Joliet format. If a CD is also an Apple hybrid disc, the data could also be in an Apple HFS+ format. The actual content of the files is only saved once, but the data are pointed to by several locations.

Recordable CDs, or CD-Rs, have a notion of a session. A CD-R can have one or more sessions on it, and the purpose of the sessions is that you can continue to add data to CD-R more than once. A new session is made each time data are burned to the CD-R. Depending on the operating system in which the CD is used, each session may show up as though it was a partition. For example, I used an Apple OS X application to create a CD with three sessions. When the CD was used in an OS X system, all three of the sessions were mounted as file systems. When the CD was used in a Linux system, the last session was the default session to be mounted, but the other two could be mounted by specifying them in the mount command. The readcd tool (http://freshmeat.net/projects/cdrecord/) can be used to determine the number of sessions on a CD. When the CD was used in a Microsoft Windows XP system, the system said it was invalid, although Smart Project's ISO Buster program (http://www.isobuster.com) in Windows could see all three sessions. Different results may occur if the multiple session CD was created from within Windows. It is important with CD-Rs to use a specialized CD analysis tool to view the contents of all sessions and not rely on the default behavior of your analysis platform.

Some CDs also contain the partition systems of the native operating system. For example, a hybrid CD is one that is in an ISO format and an Apple format. Inside the session are an Apple partition map and HFS+ file system. Standard Apple investigation techniques can be applied to these disks. For example, here is the result of running `mmls` on hybrid disk:

```
# mmls -t mac cd-slice.dd
MAC Partition Map
Units are in 512-byte sectors

      Slot    Start         End           Length        Description
00:   -----   0000000000    0000000000    0000000001    Unallocated
01:   00      0000000001    0000000002    0000000002    Apple_partition_map
02:   -----   0000000001    0000000002    0000000002    Table
03:   -----   0000000003    0000000103    0000000101    Unallocated
04:   01      0000000104    0000762559    0000762456    Apple_HFS
```

Many bootable CDs also have a native partition system. Sparc Solaris bootable CDs have a Volume Table of Contents structure in the ISO volume, and Intel bootable CDs can have a DOS-based partition table at the beginning of the CD. These structures are used after the operating system has been booted from the CD and the code required to boot the system is in the ISO format.

## BIBLIOGRAPHY

Agile Risk Management. "Linux Forensics—Week 1 (Multiple Session CDRs)." March 19, 2004. http://www.agilerm.net/linux1.html.

Apple. "File Manager Reference." March 1, 2004. http://developer.apple.com/documentation/Carbon/Reference/File_Manager/index.html.

Apple. "Inside Macintosh: Devices." July 3, 1996. http://developer.apple.com/documentation/mac/Devices/Devices-2.html.

Apple. "The Monster Disk Driver Technote." November 22, 1999. http://developer.apple.com/technotes/tn/pdf/tn1189.pdf.

Brouwer, Andries. "Minimal Partition Table Specification." September 16, 1999. http://www.win.tue.nl/~aeb/partitions/partition_tables.html.

Brouwer, Andries. "Partition Types." December 12, 2004. http://www.win.tue.nl/~aeb/partitions/partition_types.html.

Carrier, Brian. "Extended Partition Test." *Digital Forensic Tool Testing Images*, July 2003. `http://dftt.sourceforge.net/test1/index.html`.

CDRoller. *Reading Data CD*, n.d. `http://www.cdroller.com/htm/readdata.html`.

ECMA. "Volume and File Structure of CDROM for Information Interchange." *ISO Spec*, September 1998. `http://www.ecma-international.org/publications/files/ECMA-ST/Ecma-119.pdf`.

Landis, Hale. "How it Works: Master Boot Record." May 6, 2002. `http://www.ata-atapi.com/hiwmbr.htm`.

Landis, Hale. "How it Works: Partition Types." December 12, 2004. `http://www.ata-atapi.com/hiwtab.htm`.

Microsoft. "Basic Disks and Volumes Technical Reference." *Windows Server 2003 Technical Reference*, 2004. `http://www.microsoft.com`.

Microsoft. "Managing GPT Disks in Itanium-based Computers." *Windows® XP Professional Resource Kit Documentation*, 2004a. `http://www.microsoft.com`.

Microsoft. "MS-DOS Partitioning Summary." *Microsoft Knowledge Base Article 69912*, December 20, 2004b. `http://support.microsoft.com/default.aspx?scid=kb;EN-US;69912`.

Stevens, Curtis, and Stan Merkin. "El Torito: Bootable CD-ROM Format Specification 1.0." January 25, 1999. `http://www.phoenix.com/resources/specs-cdrom.pdf`.

# Server-based Partitions

6

In the last chapter we saw how personal computers partition their storage volumes, and now we are going to look at how some of the servers partition their volumes. The basic concepts of this chapter and the previous chapter are identical. In fact, they are separated only because I needed some way to break the content into medium-sized chapters, and this separation seemed as good as anything else (even though DOS and Apple partitions are also used in servers). In this chapter, we are going to look at FreeBSD, NetBSD, and OpenBSD partition systems; Sun Solaris partition systems; and GPT partitions that are found in 64-bit Intel Itanium systems.

## BSD Partitions

It is becoming more common for computer investigations to encounter BSD UNIX servers, such as FreeBSD (http://www.freebsd.org), OpenBSD (http://www.openbsd.org), and NetBSD (http://www.netbsd.org). These systems use their own partitioning system, and this section will show the details of its structures. It is more common to encounter a Linux system during an investigation, but Linux uses only the DOS-based partitions and does not have any special data structures.

Many BSD systems use IA32-based hardware (i.e., x86/i386), and they have been designed such that they can exist on the same disk as Microsoft products. Therefore, they build on the DOS partitions described in the previous chapter. A BSD system that runs on non-IA32 hardware likely does not use the DOS partitions, and they are not covered in this book.

An important concept to understand before we begin is that when an operating system is running, it can choose to what partitions it will give the user access. As will be shown, the FreeBSD operating system uses both the DOS and BSD partition systems, yet OpenBSD and NetBSD use only the BSD partition system. A basic understanding of DOS partitions is needed for this section.

## GENERAL OVERVIEW

The BSD partition system is simpler than the DOS partitions but more limited than the Apple partition map. There is only one sector that contains the needed data, and it is located inside a DOS partition, as shown in Figure 6.1. It is inside a DOS partition so that the system can also have Windows on the same disk and give the user a choice of which operating system to load. The DOS partition table will have an entry for a partition with a FreeBSD, OpenBSD, or NetBSD type—0xa5, 0xa6, and 0xa9, respectively. The BSD partition will be one of the primary DOS partitions.

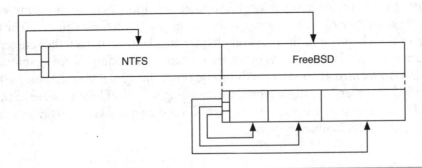

**Figure 6.1**   A disk with two DOS partitions and three BSD partitions inside the FreeBSD-type DOS partition.

If we wanted to be very strict with our terminology, we would say that the BSD partitions are located inside a volume created by a DOS partition. As discussed in Chapter 4, "Volume Analysis," this is an example where we are partitioning a volume that was created from a partition.

The central data structure is the disk label. It is at least 276 bytes in size and is located in the second sector of the BSD partition. For some non-IA32 systems, it may be in the first sector and have an offset. FreeBSD, OpenBSD, and NetBSD use the same structure, but the implementation is slightly different. Therefore, the general theory will be described here, and specific details are given in later sections.

The disk label structure contains hardware specifications of the disk and a partition table for eight or sixteen BSD partitions. Unlike Apple partitions, the partition table is a fixed size, and unlike DOS partitions, there is only one partition table. Each entry in the BSD partition table has the following fields:

- Starting sector of the BSD partition
- Size of the BSD partition
- Partition type
- Size of the UFS file system fragment
- Number of UFS file system fragments per block
- Number of cylinders per UFS Cylinder group

The starting sector address is given relative to the start of the disk, not the disk label or DOS partition. The partition type field identifies the file system type that should be in the BSD partition, such as UFS, swap space, FAT, and unused. The last three values are used only when the partition contains a UFS file system. The UFS file system is described in Chapter 16, "UFS1 and UFS2 Concepts and Analysis," and Chapter 17, "UFS1 and UFS2 Data Structures."

The basic theory of BSD partitions is simple. The one structure is read, and the list of partitions can be easily processed. The challenge to an investigator, though, is to know to what partitions the user had access. For example, if it was a dual boot system, the investigator must know if the user had access to the Windows partition as well as the BSD partitions. FreeBSD handles this differently from OpenBSD and NetBSD. I will discuss how each OS uses the data in the disk label, even though this may be considered application-level analysis.

### FreeBSD Overview

FreeBSD gives the user access to all DOS and BSD partitions on the disk. FreeBSD uses the term "slice" to refer to each DOS partition and uses the term "partition" to refer to the BSD partitions. Therefore, if a system has both Windows and FreeBSD installed on it, the user would have access to the Windows slices when running FreeBSD.

The disk label structure in FreeBSD is used to organize the sectors in only the FreeBSD DOS partition. This may sound obvious, but it is one of the ways in which the OpenBSD implementation is different from the FreeBSD implementation. If we refer to Figure 6.2, the disk label describes three partitions inside the FreeBSD type DOS partition but it does not need to describe the NTFS type partition.

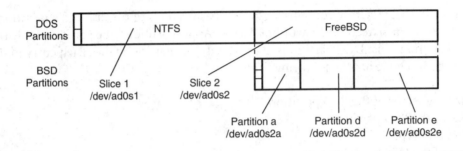

**Figure 6.2**    FreeBSD Disk with device names added.

FreeBSD, like other UNIX flavors, assigns a special device file to each partition and slice. The file is named according to its DOS partition number and its BSD partition number. The base name for the primary ATA disk is /dev/ad0. Each slice, also called a DOS partition, adds the letter 's' and the slice number to the base name. For example, the first slice is /dev/ad0s1 and the second slice is /dev/ad0s2. Any slice that has a FreeBSD partition type is processed for the disk label structure. The partitions in the slice are given letters based on their entries in the disk label partition table. For example, if the second DOS partition was FreeBSD, the first BSD partition would be /dev/ad0s2a, and the second BSD partition would be /dev/ad0s2b. A second set of devices that does not include the slice number may also be made for the BSD partitions. For example, /dev/ad0a would be a shortcut to the /dev/ad0s2a partition if the FreeBSD partition was DOS partition 2.

Some of the BSD partitions have special meaning. The 'a' partition is usually for the root partition, which is where the boot code is located. The 'b' partition is usually for the swap space of the system, the 'c' partition is usually for the entire slice, and the partitions starting at 'd' can be anything. The term 'usually' is used because that is how many of the BSD partitioning tools will create the partitions, but any user can edit the disk label partition table with a hex editor and modify the entries.

In summary, a FreeBSD system provides access to all DOS partitions and BSD partitions. An investigator must analyze each of the DOS partitions and BSD partitions in the disk label to fully analyze the system.

### NetBSD and OpenBSD Overview

OpenBSD and NetBSD give a user access to only the entries in the BSD disk label structure. Unlike the FreeBSD disk label, the OpenBSD and NetBSD disk label structure can describe partitions anywhere on the disk. In other words, the disk label can describe partitions that are outside the bounds of the DOS partition in which it is located. For the rest of this chapter, I will refer to OpenBSD only, but I really mean both OpenBSD and NetBSD. The OpenBSD code split from the NetBSD code years ago.

After the OpenBSD kernel is loaded, the DOS partitions are ignored. The DOS partitions are only used to locate the start of the OpenBSD partition. Therefore, if a system has both Windows and OpenBSD on it and users had access to a FAT partition from OpenBSD, the FAT partition would be in both the DOS partition table and the BSD disk label. We can see this in Figure 6.3 where we have the same DOS partitions as in Figure 6.2. In this case, though, we need to have an additional entry in the disk label so that we can access the NTFS type DOS partition.

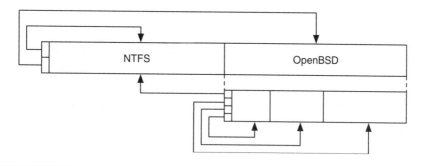

**Figure 6.3**  A disk with two DOS partitions and an OpenBSD disk label that describes three partitions inside the OpenBSD type DOS partition and the entire NTFS partition.

OpenBSD uses file names that are similar to the ones that FreeBSD uses for partition devices. The base name for the primary ATA device is /dev/wd0. There is no notion of slices, and the BSD partitions are named with letters. Therefore, the first BSD partition is /dev/wd0a and the second is /dev/wd0b. Like FreeBSD, the first partition is usually for the root partition and the second partition is for swap space. The third partition, /dev/wd0c in our example, is the device for the entire disk. Recall that the third partition for FreeBSD was for only the slice, or DOS partition.

In summary, an OpenBSD system provides access to only the partitions described in the OpenBSD disk label. An analysis of an OpenBSD system should focus on the partitions that are listed in the disk label.

### Boot Code

The boot code for a BSD system surrounds the disk label structure, which is located in sector 1 of the volume. Sector 0 of the volume contains boot code, and it is executed when the boot code in the MBR finds the bootable BSD-type partition. Not all the boot code can fit in sector 0, so it jumps to sector 2, and boot code can exist until the file system data starts, which is typically in sector 16.

## DATA STRUCTURES

This section will describe the BSD disk label data structure and parse example disk images from FreeBSD and OpenBSD systems. The output from running analysis tools on the example disk images is also given.

### Disk Label Data Structure

We will now look at the details of the disk label data structure. If you are not interested in this, you can skip ahead and look at the tool output when we list the contents of our example disk images. I will first describe the BSD disk label structure and then examine the FreeBSD and OpenBSD implementation details. The disk label has the layout given in Table 6.1. Note that the data marked as non-essential could be essential for other disk operations, but are not essential for determining the layout of the disk.

Table 6.1   Data structure for the BSD disk label.

| Byte Range | Description | Essential |
|---|---|---|
| 0–3 | Signature value (0x82564557) | No |
| 4–5 | Drive type | No |
| 6–7 | Drive subtype | No |
| 8–23 | Drive type name | No |
| 24–39 | Pack identifier name | No |
| 40–43 | Size of a sector in bytes | Yes |
| 44–47 | Number of sectors per track | No |
| 48–51 | Number of tracks per cylinder | No |
| 52–55 | Number of cylinders per unit | No |
| 56–59 | Number of sectors per cylinder | No |
| 60–63 | Number of sectors per unit | No |
| 64–65 | Number of spare sectors per track | No |

| Byte Range | Description | Essential |
|---|---|---|
| 66–67 | Number of spare sectors per cylinder | No |
| 68–71 | Number of alternate cylinders per unit | No |
| 72–73 | Rotational speed of disk | No |
| 74–75 | Hardware sector interleave | No |
| 76–77 | Track skew | No |
| 78–79 | Cylinder skew | No |
| 80–83 | Head switch time in microseconds | No |
| 84–87 | Track-to-track seek time in microseconds | No |
| 88–91 | Flags | No |
| 92–111 | Drive specific information | No |
| 112–131 | Reserved | No |
| 132–135 | Signature value (0x82564557) | No |
| 136–137 | Checksum | No |
| 138–139 | Number of partitions | Yes |
| 140–143 | Size of boot area | No |
| 144–147 | Maximum size of file system boot super block | No |
| 148–163 | BSD Partition #1 (see Table 6.2) | Yes |
| 164–179 | BSD Partition #2 (see Table 6.2) | Yes |
| 180–195 | BSD Partition #3 (see Table 6.2) | Yes |
| 196–211 | BSD Partition #4 (see Table 6.2) | Yes |
| 212–227 | BSD Partition #5 (see Table 6.2) | Yes |
| 228–243 | BSD Partition #6 (see Table 6.2) | Yes |
| 244–259 | BSD Partition #7 (see Table 6.2) | Yes |
| 260–275 | BSD Partition #8 (see Table 6.2) | Yes |
| 276–291 | BSD Partition #9 (see Table 6.2) | Yes |

*continues*

**Table 6.1**    Continued

| Byte Range | Description | Essential |
|---|---|---|
| 292–307 | BSD Partition #10 (see Table 6.2) | Yes |
| 308–323 | BSD Partition #11 (see Table 6.2) | Yes |
| 324–339 | BSD Partition #12 (see Table 6.2) | Yes |
| 340–355 | BSD Partition #13 (see Table 6.2) | Yes |
| 356–371 | BSD Partition #14 (see Table 6.2) | Yes |
| 372–387 | BSD Partition #15 (see Table 6.2) | Yes |
| 388–403 | BSD Partition #16 (see Table 6.2) | Yes |
| 404–511 | Unused | No |

The 16-byte BSD partition table entries have the layout given in Table 6.2.

**Table 6.2**    Data structure for BSD disk label entry.

| Byte Range | Description | Essential |
|---|---|---|
| 0–3 | Size of BSD partition in sectors | Yes |
| 4–7 | Starting sector of BSD partition | Yes |
| 8–11 | File system fragment size | No |
| 12–12 | File system type (see Table 6.3) | No |
| 13–13 | File system fragments per block | No |
| 14–15 | File system cylinders per group | No |

The file system type field identifies the type of file system that could be located in the BSD partition. The type values shown in Table 6.3 are defined.

**Table 6.3**    BSD partition type values.

| Type | Description |
|---|---|
| 0 | Unused Slot |
| 1 | Swap space |

| Type | Description |
|------|-------------|
| 2 | Version 6 |
| 3 | Version 7 |
| 4 | System V |
| 5 | 4.1BSD |
| 6 | Eighth edition |
| 7 | 4.2BSD fast file system (FFS) |
| 8 | MSDOS file system (FAT) |
| 9 | 4.4BSD log-structured file system (4.4LFS) |
| 10 | In use, but unknown or unsupported |
| 11 | OS/2 HPFS |
| 12 | CD-ROM (ISO9660) |
| 13 | Bootstrap |
| 14 | Vinum drive |

The most common file system for FreeBSD and OpenBSD is the 4.2BSD *fast file system* (FFS). The system will also have at least one swap partition. An NTFS partition will typically have an 'in use, but unknown' type.

We can now look at an example system that has both FreeBSD and OpenBSD on it. The DOS partition table has the following contents:

```
# mmls -t dos bsd-disk.dd
Units are in 512-byte sectors

      Slot    Start         End          Length        Description
00:   -----   0000000000    0000000000   0000000001    Primary Table (#0)
01:   -----   0000000001    0000000062   0000000062    Unallocated
02:   00:00   0000000063    0002056319   0002056257    Win95 FAT32 (0x0B)
03:   00:01   0002056320    0008209214   0006152895    OpenBSD (0xA6)
04:   00:02   0008209215    0019999727   0011790513    FreeBSD (0xA5)
```

We can see that the disk has a 1GB FAT partition, a 3GB OpenBSD partition, and a 6GB FreeBSD partition. Inside each of the OpenBSD and FreeBSD partitions are disk label structures that describe additional partitions. The next two sections will look at the two BSD partitions.

### OpenBSD Example Image

We will first extract and parse the OpenBSD disk label. The partition starts in sector 2,056,320, and the disk label is located in the second sector.

```
# dd if=bsd-disk.dd skip=2056321 bs=512 count=1 | xxd
0000000: 5745 5682 0500 0000 4553 4449 2f49 4445   WEV.....ESDI/IDE
0000016: 2064 6973 6b00 0000 4d61 7874 6f72 2039    disk...Maxtor 9
0000032: 3130 3234 4434 2020 0002 0000 3f00 0000   1024D4  ....?...
0000048: 1000 0000 ff3f 0000 f003 0000 f02b 3101   .....?.......+1.
0000064: 0000 0000 0000 0000 100e 0100 0000 0000   ................
[REMOVED - ZEROS]
0000128: 0000 0000 5745 5682 b65e 1000 0020 0000   ....WEV..^... ..
0000144: 0000 0100 501f 0300 8060 1f00 0004 0000   ....P....`......
0000160: 0708 1000 e061 0900 d07f 2200 0004 0000   .....a....".....
0000176: 0108 1000 f02b 3101 0000 0000 0000 0000   .....+1.........
0000192: 0000 0000 501f 0300 b0e1 2b00 0004 0000   ....P.....+.....
0000208: 0708 1000 8056 0200 0001 2f00 0004 0000   .....V..../.....
0000224: 0708 1000 0000 0000 0000 0000 0000 0000   ................
0000240: 0000 0000 3f4b 3c00 00f8 4000 0004 0000   ....?K<...@.....
0000256: 0708 1000 80a0 0f00 8057 3100 0004 0000   .........W1.....
0000272: 0708 1000 4160 1f00 3f00 0000 0000 0000   ....A`..?.......
0000288: 0800 0000 9dae b300 3f43 7d00 0000 0000   ........?C}.....
0000304: 0a00 0000 0000 0000 0000 0000 0000 0000   ................
0000320: 0000 0000 0000 0000 0000 0000 0000 0000   ................
0000336: 0000 0000 0000 0000 0000 0000 0000 0000   ................
0000352: 0000 0000 0000 0000 0000 0000 0000 0000   ................
0000368: 0000 0000 0000 0000 0000 0000 0000 0000   ................
0000384: 0000 0000 0000 0000 0000 0000 0000 0000   ................
0000400: 0000 0000 0000 0000 0000 0000 0000 0000   ................
[REMOVED]
```

We can see the two signature values, 0x82564557, at bytes 0 to 3 and 132 to 135. After the second signature value, bytes 138 to 139 show that there are 16 (0x0010) partition table entries. The partition table starts on the next line in byte 148 and continues for 16 16-byte structures to end at 403. Entries 11 to 16 are not used and contain 0s. The remainder of the sector is not used by the disk label structure.

The sixteen partition table entries can be parsed into the data shown in Table 6.4, where the decimal value is given in parentheses.

**Table 6.4**    The contents of the BSD disk label structure in our example OpenBSD disk image.

|    | Start | Size | Type |
|----|-------|------|------|
| 1  | 0x001f6080 (2,056,320) | 0x00031f50 (204,624) | 0x07 (7) |
| 2  | 0x00227fd0 (2,260,944) | 0x000961e0 (614,880) | 0x01 (1) |
| 3  | 0x00000000 (0) | 0x01312bf0 (19,999,728) | 0x00 (0) |
| 4  | 0x002be1b0 (2,875,824) | 0x00031f50 (204,624) | 0x07 (7) |
| 5  | 0x002f0100 (3,080,448) | 0x00025680 (153,216) | 0x07 (7) |
| 6  | 0x00000000 (0) | 0x00000000 (0) | 0x00 (0) |
| 7  | 0x0040f800 (4,257,792) | 0x003c4b3f (3,951,423) | 0x07 (7) |
| 8  | 0x00315780 (3,233,664) | 0x000fa080 (1,024,128) | 0x07 (7) |
| 9  | 0x0000003f (63) | 0x001f6041 (2,056,257) | 0x08 (8) |
| 10 | 0x007d433f (8,209,215) | 0x00b3ae9d (11,775,645) | 0x0a (10) |

Before we look at this in detail, we will review the special BSD partitions. The first partition is for the root partition, and it contains the boot code. The second partition is for the swap space, the third partition is for the entire disk, and partitions four and up are for any BSD partition.

Our example image follows these guidelines, and the first partition begins at the start of the DOS partition, which is sector 2,056,320. The second partition has a type value of 1, which translates to swap space. The third partition begins in sector 0 and has the size of the entire disk. Partitions 4, 5, 7 and 8 have a 4.2BSD FFS type and the starting sector of the partitions increase until partition 9. Partition 9 has a starting sector of 63, and its type is for a FAT file system. This partition is the BSD disk label entry for the FAT partition that is described in the first entry of the DOS partition table. Partition 10 has an unknown type value and is the BSD disk label entry for the FreeBSD partition that is the third entry in the DOS partition table that we previously saw. Because partition 9 is labeled as 'i,' the user could access the FAT partition with device /dev/wd0i. Remember that OpenBSD ignores the DOS partition table contents after it is loaded.

Table 6.5 shows to which partitions the user would have access from within this OpenBSD system.

**Table 6.5**   A summary of the file systems the OpenBSD system could access.

| Device | Description | Mounting Point | Starting sector | Ending Sector |
|---|---|---|---|---|
| /dev/wd0a | 4.2FFS BSD | / | 2,056,320 | 2,260,943 |
| /dev/wd0b | swap | N/A | 2260944 | 2875823 |
| /dev/wd0c | entire disk | N/A | 0 | 19999727 |
| /dev/wd0d | 4.2FFS BSD | /tmp/ | 2875824 | 3080447 |
| /dev/wd0e | 4.2FFS BSD | /home/ | 3080448 | 3233663 |
| /dev/wd0g | 4.2FFS BSD | /var/ | 4257792 | 820921 |
| /dev/wd0h | 4.2FFS BSD | /usr/ | 3233664 | 4257791 |
| /dev/wd0i | FAT | user's discretion | 63 | 2056319 |
| /dev/wd0j | FreeBSD Partition | N/A | 8209215 | 19984859 |

Note that the FreeBSD partition cannot be mounted because its disk label must be first read to identify the file system locations. We can see the same data from the disk label using the mmls tool and supplying the bsd type. The offset of the BSD partition must be given using the -o flag because we have a disk image.

```
# mmls -t bsd -o 20563210 bsd-disk.dd
BSD Disk Label
Units are in 512-byte sectors

      Slot    Start        End          Length       Description
00:   02      0000000000   0019999727   0019999728   Unused (0x00)
01:   08      0000000063   0002056319   0002056257   MSDOS (0x08)
02:   00      0002056320   0002260943   0000204624   4.2BSD (0x07)
03:   01      0002260944   0002875823   0000614880   Swap (0x01)
04:   03      0002875824   0003080447   0000204624   4.2BSD (0x07)
05:   04      0003080448   0003233663   0000153216   4.2BSD (0x07)
06:   07      0003233664   0004257791   0001024128   4.2BSD (0x07)
07:   06      0004257792   0008209214   0003951423   4.2BSD (0x07)
08:   09      0008209215   0019984859   0011775645   Unknown (0x0A)
```

Remember that mmls will sort the output based on the starting sector of the partition, so the FAT partition is located at the beginning of the output even though it was the eighth entry in the partition table. The 'slot' column shows where the partition was actually described.

## FreeBSD Example Image

Now let's look at the FreeBSD partition in our example image. The partition starts in sector 8,209,215, and the disk label is in the second sector.

```
# dd if=bsd-disk.dd skip=8209216 bs=512 count=1 | xxd
0000000: 5745 5682 0500 0000 6164 3073 3300 0000  WEV.....ad0s3...
0000016: 0000 0000 0000 0000 0000 0000 0000 0000  ................
0000032: 0000 0000 0000 0000 0002 0000 3f00 0000  ............?...
0000048: 1000 0000 814d 0000 f003 0000 f02b 3101  .....M.......+1.
0000064: 0000 0000 0000 0000 100e 0100 0000 0000  ................
[REMOVED - ZEROS]
0000128: 0000 0000 5745 5682 b9ab 0800 0020 0000  ....WEV...... ..
0000144: 0000 0000 0000 0800 3f43 7d00 0008 0000  ........?C}.....
0000160: 0708 0880 a073 1700 3f43 8500 0000 0000  .....s..?C......
0000176: 0100 0000 b1e8 b300 3f43 7d00 0000 0000  .......?C}.....
0000192: 0000 0000 0000 0800 dfb6 9c00 0008 0000  ................
0000208: 0708 0880 0000 0800 dfb6 a400 0008 0000  ................
0000224: 0708 0880 1175 8400 dfb6 ac00 0008 0000  .....u..........
0000240: 0708 886f 0000 0000 0000 0000 0000 0000  ...o............
0000256: 0000 0000 0000 0000 0000 0000 0000 0000  ................
0000272: 0000 0000 eb0e 4254 5801 0180 f60f 8007  ......BTX.......
0000288: 0020 0000 fa31 c08e d0bc 0018 8ec0 8ed8  . ...1..........
0000304: 666a 0266 9dbf 001e b900 3957 f3ab 5fbe  fj.f......9W.._.
0000320: e296 ac98 91e3 1dac 92ad 93ad b608 d1eb  ................
0000336: 730b 8905 8875 0288 5505 83c0 048d 7d08  s....u..U.....}.
0000352: e2ec ebde c645 0518 c645 0810 c645 0d1e  .....E...E...E..
0000368: c645 6668 bb20 28e8 bb00 0f01 1ed6 960f  .Efh. (.........
0000384: 0116 d096 0f20 c066 83c8 010f 22c0 ea7f  ..... .f...."...
0000400: 9008 0031 c9b1 108e d1b1 380f 00d9 ba00  ...1......8.....
0000416: a000 0036 0fb7 0513 0400 00c1 e00a 2d00  ...6..........-.
0000432: 1000 0029 d0b1 3351 5068 0202 0000 6a2b  ...)..3QPh....j+
0000448: ff35 0c90 0000 5151 5151 52b1 076a 00e2  .5....QQQQR..j..
0000464: fc61 071f 0fa1 0fa9 cffa bc00 1800 000f  .a..............
0000480: 20c0 25ff ffff 7f0f 22c0 31c9 0f22 d90f  .%.....".1..."..
0000496: 0115 d096 0000 66ea e890 1800 b120 8ed1  .....f...... ..
```

We can see from the value in bytes 138 to 139 that there are eight partitions. The eight partition table entries are in bytes 148 to 275 and can be parsed into the fields shown in Table 6.6, where the decimal values are given in parentheses.

**Table 6.6**   The contents of the BSD disk label in our FreeBSD example disk image.

|   | Start | Size | Type |
|---|-------|------|------|
| 1 | 0x007d433f (8,209,215) | 0x00080000 (524,288) | 0x07 (7) |
| 2 | 0x0085433f (8,733,503) | 0x001773a0 (1,536,928) | 0x01 (1) |
| 3 | 0x007d433f (8,209,215) | 0x00b3e8b1 (11,790,513) | 0x00 (0) |
| 4 | 0x009cb6df (10,270,431) | 0x00080000 (524,288) | 0x07 (7) |
| 5 | 0x00a4b6df (10,794,719) | 0x00080000 (524,288) | 0x07 (7) |
| 6 | 0x00acb6df (11,319,007) | 0x00847511 (8,680,721) | 0x07 (7) |
| 7 | 0x00000000 (0) | 0x00000000 (0) | 0x00 (0) |
| 8 | 0x00000000 (0) | 0x00000000 (0) | 0x00 (0) |

We see that the first BSD partition has the same starting sector as the DOS partition in which the disk label is located, and it has a 4.2BSD FFS type. The second entry is for swap space, and the third entry is for only the sectors in the DOS partition. Entries 4, 5, and 6 are FFS file system partitions. To summarize, the device name and location of each partition that a FreeBSD user would have access to is given in Table 6.7.

**Table 6.7**   A summary of the file systems the FreeBSD system could access.

| Device | Description | Mounting Point | Starting sector | Ending Sector |
|--------|-------------|----------------|-----------------|---------------|
| /dev/ad0s1 | FAT DOS partition | User's discretion | 63 | 2056319 |
| /dev/ad0s2 | OpenBSD DOS partition | N/A | 2056320 | 8209214 |
| /dev/ad0s3a | 4.2BSD FFS partition | / | 8209215 | 8733502 |
| /dev/ad0s3b | swap | N/A | 8733503 | 10270430 |
| /dev/ad0s3c | Entire FreeBSD DOS partition | N/A | 8209215 | 19999727 |
| /dev/ad0s3d | 4.2BSD FFS partition | /tmp | 10270431 | 10794718 |
| /dev/ad0s3e | 4.2BSD FFS partition | /var | 10794719 | 11319006 |
| /dev/ad0s3f | 4.2BSD FFS partition | /usr | 11319007 | 19999727 |

The mmls tool from The Sleuth Kit can be used to list the disk label contents. The output for our example image is as follows:

```
# mmls  -t bsd -o 82092165 bsd-disk.dd
BSD Disk Label
Units are in 512-byte sectors

      Slot    Start        End          Length       Description
00:   -----   0000000000   0008209214   0008209215   Unallocated
01:   00      0008209215   0008733502   0000524288   4.2BSD (0x07)
02:   02      0008209215   0019999727   0011790513   Unused (0x00)
03:   01      0008733503   0010270430   0001536928   Swap (0x01)
04:   03      0010270431   0010794718   0000524288   4.2BSD (0x07)
05:   04      0010794719   0011319006   0000524288   4.2BSD (0x07)
06:   05      0011319007   0019999727   0008680721   4.2BSD (0x07)
```

Note that the space allocated to the FAT and OpenBSD partition is marked as 'Unallocated' because there are disk label entries for that space. The DOS partition table is needed to carve that data into partitions.

## ANALYSIS CONSIDERATIONS

Each BSD partition in the disk label structure has a type field, but it is not enforced. It is actually enforced less with the BSD systems than with Microsoft Windows because Windows uses the type field to determine if the partition should get a drive letter or not. With a BSD system, a device is created for every disk label entry, so the partitions can be mounted as any type. Therefore, verify that the partition doesn't have a known file system even when the type identifies it as an old UNIX format because it could actually be a common file system, such as FAT.

The disk label structure is, at most, 404 bytes. For disk labels with only eight entries in them, the disk label structure is only 276 bytes. Therefore, the rest of the 512-byte sector can be used to hide data, although not a lot of it. If the DOS partition table is corrupt and the location of the BSD-type partition cannot be determined, a search for the 0x82564557 signature value can be performed. The signature value should exist at byte 0 and byte 132 of the disk label structure.

With a FreeBSD system, remember that the user had access to both the DOS partitions and the BSD partitions. Therefore, the investigation must include the analysis of all DOS partitions and the BSD partitions. Note that the system may not have support for NTFS, so the user would not have been able to mount an NTFS partition if one exists.

With an OpenBSD system, remember that the user had access to only the partitions in the disk label. Because OpenBSD ignores the DOS partition table when it starts, it can be useful to compare the contents of the DOS partition table with the BSD disk label. Look for BSD and DOS partitions that overlap and where gaps may exist. Figure 6.4 shows two interesting examples of BSD partitions. One of the BSD partitions is contained inside the NTFS-type DOS partition. If the NTFS partition has an NTFS file system inside it, this is an unlikely scenario and should be investigated. The figure also shows a BSD partition that exists in space that is unallocated to a DOS partition. This is not a good practice from a systems administration point of view because another program may allocate the space to a DOS partition and overwrite the BSD data, but it is possible.

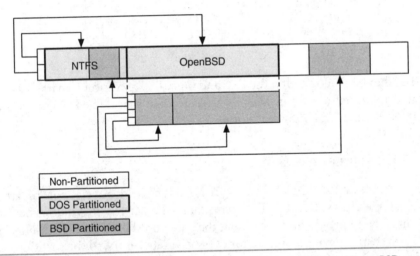

**Figure 6.4**    A disk with two BSD partitions inside the OpenBSD type DOS partition, a BSD partition inside the NTFS-type DOS partition, and a BSD partition that is not part of a DOS partition.

## SUMMARY

BSD partitions are described in a simple disk label structure. A difficulty for an investigator is to identify all the data that the user had access to on the suspect system. BSD systems are frequently used as servers and are involved with criminal and corporate investigations. A thorough understanding of BSD partitions will provide more comprehensive investigations.

# SUN SOLARIS SLICES

The Solaris operating system from Sun Microsystems is used in large servers and desktop systems. It uses two different types of partitioning systems depending on the size of the disk and the version of Solaris. Solaris 9 introduced support for file systems larger than 1-terrabyte and uses EFI partition tables because they have a 64-bit address field [Sun 2003]. EFI partitions are described in the next section.

All other versions of Solaris use data structures that are similar to the BSD disk label that we just looked at. In fact, the primary data structure is also called a disk label, although the actual layout of the structure is different. This may not be surprising considering that the layout is even different for Sparc-based Solaris and i386-based Solaris. To make things confusing and difficult to remember, the names of the Solaris data structures are the same as the BSD ones, but the names of the media compartments are different. Solaris uses the term "slice" for each of its partitions. For simplicity, I will use the term "Solaris partition" in this section, but keep in mind that other books will likely use the proper term. I will break this discussion into three sections and first discuss the general characteristics of the Solaris architecture, then the Sparc data structure specifics, and finally the i386 data structure specifics.

## GENERAL OVERVIEW

When you install Solaris, a disk label structure is created on the disk. The exact location is based on the hardware platform so that will be discussed more in later sections. The disk label has a maximum number of partitions that it can describe, and the maximum is eight for Sparc systems and 16 for i386.

Each partition in the disk label is described with its starting location, size, a set of flags, and a type. The flags tell you if the partition is read only and if it cannot be mounted, such as the swap space. In the other partition systems that we have seen in this book, the type field was used to describe the file system type, but in Solaris it typically describes the mounting point of the partition. For example, some types specify the home, usr, or var partitions, and others specify the swap space or unassigned. A full listing of types is given in the "Data Structures" section.

Solaris uses a cryptic, but scalable, naming convention for the partitions. When you are in a Solaris environment, the block devices can be found in the /dev/dsk/ directory, and the raw devices can be found in the /dev/rdsk/ directory. Within those directories, the Solaris partitions (or slices) have names such as cWtXdYsZ in a Sparc system and cWdYsZ in an i386 system. In the name, the W is replaced by the controller number, X is replaced by the physical bus target number (SCSI ID), Y is replaced by the drive number on the bus, and Z is replaced by the slice number on the drive. For example, if your Sparc system has only one controller, the disk is SCSI ID 6, and you want slice 5, you would access the raw device at /dev/rdsk/c0t6d0s5.

With Solaris, it is common for a partition to have a location in the disk label table that is based on its mounting point. This is not a requirement, but a disk that has the operating system on it will typically use the naming convention given in Table 6.8.

**Table 6.8**  The typical partition that is created in each table entry.

| Table Entry | Description |
| --- | --- |
| 0 | /root/partition—The operating system and kernel |
| 1 | Swap space |
| 2 | The entire disk, including the disk label and all partitions |
| 3 | /export/ partition |
| 4 | /export/swap/ partition |
| 5 | /opt/ partition |
| 6 | /usr/ partition |
| 7 | /home/ partition |

Additional disks that are added to the system may only have one partition on them, and that partition may use partitions entry 5, 6, or 7.

## SPARC DATA STRUCTURES

On a Sparc system, the disk label structure is created in the first sector of the disk, sector 0. Sectors 1–15 contain the "bootblock," which is the boot code for the system, and sectors 16 and above are partitioned to store file systems and swap space. Solaris uses a UFS file system, and we will see in Chapter 16 that the file system starts in sector 16. We can see the layout of an example Sparc disk in Figure 6.5.

The layout of the disk label can be confusing because the layout information for the Solaris partitions is not in one location. There are two data structures within the disk label structure that hold the partition data. The VTOC structure contains the number of partitions and the type, permissions, and timestamps for each, but the starting location and size of each partition is stored in the disk map structure. The contents of the Sparc disk label are given in Table 6.9.

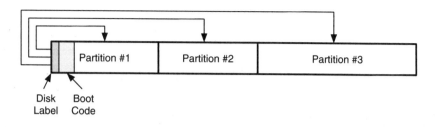

**Figure 6.5** The layout of a Sun Sparc disk where the disk label and boot code are located in the first partition.

**Table 6.9** Data structure for the Sun Sparc disk label.

| Byte Range | Description | Essential |
|---|---|---|
| 0–127 | ASCII Label | No |
| 128–261 | Sparc VTOC (see Table 6.10) | Yes |
| 262–263 | Sectors to skip, writing | No |
| 264–265 | Sectors to skip, reading | No |
| 266–419 | Reserved | No |
| 420–421 | Disk speed | No |
| 422–423 | Number of physical cylinders | No |
| 424–425 | Alternates per cylinder | No |
| 426–429 | Reserved | No |
| 430–431 | Interleave | No |
| 432–433 | Number of data cylinders | No |
| 434–435 | Number of alternate cylinders | No |
| 436–437 | Number of heads | Yes |
| 438–439 | Number of sectors per track | Yes |
| 440–443 | Reserved | No |
| 444–451 | Partition #1 disk map (see Table 6.13) | Yes |
| 452–459 | Partition #2 disk map (see Table 6.13) | Yes |

*continues*

**Table 6.9**   Continued

| Byte Range | Description | Essential |
| --- | --- | --- |
| 460–467 | Partition #3 disk map (see Table 6.13) | Yes |
| 468–475 | Partition #4 disk map (see Table 6.13) | Yes |
| 476–483 | Partition #5 disk map (see Table 6.13) | Yes |
| 484–491 | Partition #6 disk map (see Table 6.13) | Yes |
| 492–499 | Partition #7 disk map (see Table 6.13) | Yes |
| 500–507 | Partition #8 disk map (see Table 6.13) | Yes |
| 508–509 | Signature Value (0xDABE) | No |
| 510–511 | Checksum | No |

The VTOC can be found in bytes 128 to 261. This structure tells you how many partitions there are (bytes 12–13) and the flags, type, and a timestamp for each partition. The VTOC has the fields given in Table 6.10.

**Table 6.10**   Data structure for the VTOC in Sun Sparc disk labels.

| Byte Range | Description | Essential |
| --- | --- | --- |
| 0–3 | Version (0x01) | No |
| 4–11 | Volume Name | No |
| 12–13 | Number of Partitions | Yes |
| 14–15 | Partition #1 type (see Table 6.11) | No |
| 16–17 | Partition #1 flags (see Table 6.12) | No |
| 18–19 | Partition #2 type (see Table 6.11) | No |
| 20–21 | Partition #2 flags (see Table 6.12) | No |
| 22–23 | Partition #3 type (see Table 6.11) | No |
| 24–25 | Partition #3 flags (see Table 6.12) | No |
| 26–27 | Partition #4 type (see Table 6.11) | No |
| 28–29 | Partition #4 flags (see Table 6.12) | No |

| Byte Range | Description | Essential |
|---|---|---|
| 30–31 | Partition #5 type (see Table 6.11) | No |
| 32–33 | Partition #5 flags (see Table 6.12) | No |
| 34–35 | Partition #6 type (see Table 6.11) | No |
| 36–37 | Partition #6 flags (see Table 6.12) | No |
| 38–39 | Partition #7 type (see Table 6.11) | No |
| 40–41 | Partition #7 flags (see Table 6.12) | No |
| 42–43 | Partition #8 type (see Table 6.11) | No |
| 44–45 | Partition #8 flags (see Table 6.12) | No |
| 46–57 | Boot info | No |
| 58–59 | Reserved | No |
| 60–63 | Signature Value (0x600DDEEE) | No |
| 64–101 | Reserved | No |
| 102–105 | Partition #1 timestamp | No |
| 106–109 | Partition #2 timestamp | No |
| 110–113 | Partition #3 timestamp | No |
| 114–117 | Partition #4 timestamp | No |
| 118–121 | Partition #5 timestamp | No |
| 122–125 | Partition #6 timestamp | No |
| 126–129 | Partition #7 timestamp | No |
| 130–133 | Partition #8 timestamp | No |

The type field for each of the partitions in the VTOC specifies what the partition is used for and where it should be mounted. The operating system will use a different configuration file, though, when it comes time to actually mount the file systems. So just because the type is set for the /usr/ partition does not mean that it will be mounted as /usr/. The Solaris disk label structure does not specify the file system type for each partition, as other partition systems do. The partition type can have the values given in Table 6.11.

**Table 6.11**    Type values for each Sun partition (used for both Sparc and i386).

| Value | Description |
| --- | --- |
| 0 | Unassigned |
| 1 | partition /boot/ |
| 2 | / partition |
| 3 | Swap |
| 4 | /usr/ partition |
| 5 | The entire disk |
| 6 | /stand/ partition |
| 7 | /var/ partition |
| 8 | /home/ partition |
| 9 | Alternate sector partition |
| 10 | cachefs partition |

Each partition also has a flags field, and it can have the values given in Table 6.12 (or none of them):

**Table 6.12**    Flag values of each Sun partition (used for both Sparc and i386).

| Value | Description |
| --- | --- |
| 1 | The partition cannot be mounted |
| 128 | The partition is read-only |

The previous information is useful, but the most important part of the disk label, for this discussion, is the location of the partitions. The disk map structures, not the VTOC, contain the starting cylinder and size of each partition. The disk map structures are located at the end of the disk label structure and have the fields given in Table 6.13.

**Table 6.13**  Data structure for the Sun Sparc disk label disk map.

| Byte Range | Description | Essential |
|---|---|---|
| 0–3 | Starting Cylinder | Yes |
| 4–7 | Size | Yes |

We care about the starting sector and not the cylinder, so we will need to convert this value—it is actually quite simple. Recall that cylinder address X is the collection of tracks at address X on each platter in a disk. To convert the cylinder address to a sector address, we multiply the cylinder value with the number of sectors per track and the number of heads (which can both be found in the disk label structure).

For example, consider a disk with 15 heads and 63 sectors per track. If the starting cylinder were 1,112, then we would calculate

```
63 * 15 * 1,112 = 1,050,840
```

Therefore, we would use sector 1,050,840 to extract the data and examine the data with our tools that support the LBA addressing scheme.

Let's get our hands dirty with some data structures and a hex editor. The following is the first sector of a Solaris Sparc hard disk:

```
# dd if=sparc-disk.dd bs=512 count=1 | xxd
0000000: 4d61 7874 6f72 2038 3532 3530 4136 2063  Maxtor 85250A6 c
0000016: 796c 2031 3038 3534 2061 6c74 2032 2068  yl 10854 alt 2 h
0000032: 6420 3135 2073 6563 2036 3300 0000 0000  d 15 sec 63.....
0000048: 0000 0000 0000 0000 0000 0000 0000 0000  ................
[REMOVED - ZEROS]
0000128: 0000 0001 0000 0000 0000 0000 0008 0002  ................
0000144: 0000 0003 0001 0005 0000 0000 0000 0000  ................
0000160: 0000 0007 0000 0004 0000 0008 0000 0000  ................
0000176: 0000 0000 0000 0000 0000 600d deee  ............`...
[REMOVED - ZEROS]
0000416: 0000 0000 1518 2a68 0000 0000 0000 0001  ......*h........
0000432: 2a66 0002 000f 003f 0000 0000 0000 0826  *f.....?.......&
0000448: 0020 b06b 0000 0000 0010 0176 0000 0000  . .k.......v....
0000464: 009c 8286 0000 0000 0000 0000 0000 0000  ................
0000480: 0000 0000 0000 0609 0007 cd0d 0000 1101  ................
0000496: 005d bdd5 0000 0458 0006 3e61 dabe 1ffe  .].....X..>a....
```

A Sparc system uses big-endian ordering, and therefore you do not need to reverse the numbers. The first eight lines show the 128-byte ASCII label, which describes the type of hard disk. The VTOC starts at 128 and bytes 140 to 141 show that there are 8 partitions in the structure. From bytes 142 to 173 we can see the 2-byte type and 2-byte flag fields for each partition. For example, the first partition has its type value in bytes 142 to 143 and it is 2, which is the / partition. Its flag value is in bytes 144 to 145, and it is 0. Bytes 146 to 147 show that the second partition has a type of 3 (swap space) and bytes 148 to 149 show that its flag is 1 (not mountable).

Bytes 436 to 437 show us that there are 15 (0x0f) heads and bytes 438 to 439 show that there are 63 (0x3f) sectors per track. We will need this to convert the cylinder addresses.

The layout information starts at byte 444, and the starting cylinder and size are both 4-byte values. The first partition has a starting cylinder of 2,086 (0x00000826) and a size of 2,142,315 (0x0020b06b) sectors. Recall that this partition had a type for the / partition. To calculate the starting sector, we multiply

```
15 * 63 * 2,086 = 1,971,270
```

This partition is in the first slot, and therefore it would be "slice 0" for the disk, even though it starts thousands of sectors into the disk. The next partition is described in bytes 452 to 459, and its starting cylinder is 0 with a size of 1,048,950 (0x00100176) sectors. This is the swap space for the system and it is "slice 1." The third partition entry, "slice 2," is usually for the entire disk, and it is located in bytes 460 to 467. Its starting cylinder is 0 and size is 10,257,030 (0x009c8286) sectors.

The Sparc disk label can be viewed with several tools, but not all are useful during an investigation. The format and prtvtoc commands in Solaris can be run only on a device, not on a disk image file. The fdisk command in Linux can be used to list the partitions from a Sparc disk image though. You also can use the mmls tool in The Sleuth Kit with the -t sun flag. Running mmls on the example image gives:

```
# mmls -t sun sparc-disk.dd
Sun VTOC
Units are in 512-byte sectors

     Slot    Start         End           Length        Description
00:  01      0000000000    0001048949    0001048950    swap (0x03)
01:  02      0000000000    0010257029    0010257030    backup (0x05)
02:  07      0001050840    0001460024    0000409185    /home/ (0x08)
03:  05      0001460025    0001971269    0000511245    /var/ (0x07)
04:  00      0001971270    0004113584    0002142315    / (0x02)
05:  06      0004113585    0010257029    0006143445    /usr/ (0x04)
```

## i386 DATA STRUCTURES

When Solaris is installed on an i386 system, one or more DOS-based partitions must be first created. A typical installation will create a boot partition (DOS partition type 0xBE) and a partition with the file systems (DOS partition type 0x82). The boot partition contains the boot code needed to start the system and does not contain an actual file system. The disk label structure is located in the second sector of the file system DOS partition (type 0x82) and it describes the layout of the Sun partitions inside of that DOS partition. All Sun partitions must start after the start of the DOS partition. We can see this in Figure 6.6, where there is a disk with three DOS partitions, and the final one contains a disk label and three Sun partitions.

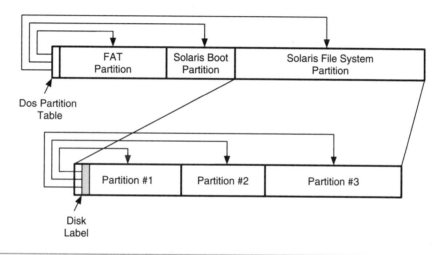

**Figure 6.6** An i386 Sun disk with three DOS partitions. The final one contains a disk label and three Sun partitions.

The disk label structure is 512 bytes in size and is better organized than the Sparc version because all the partition information is in one location. Another benefit of the i386 version is that the information is stored by using LBA addresses and not CHS. Other than those differences, the two structures are very similar. The first 456 bytes of the disk label are called the *Volume Table of Contents* (VTOC), and this is where the partitions, disk label, sector size, and number of partitions is located. The disk label data structure is given in Table 6.14.

**Table 6.14**   Data structure for the Sun i386 disk label.

| Byte Range | Description | Essential |
| --- | --- | --- |
| 0–11 | Bootinfo | No |
| 12–15 | Signature Value (0x600DDEEE) | No |
| 16–19 | Version | No |
| 20–27 | Volume Name | No |
| 28–29 | Sector size | Yes |
| 30–31 | Number of Partitions | Yes |
| 32–71 | Reserved | No |
| 72–83 | Partition #1 (see Table 6.15) | Yes |
| 84–95 | Partition #2 (see Table 6.15) | Yes |
| 96–107 | Partition #3 (see Table 6-15) | Yes |
| 108–119 | Partition #4 (see Table 6.15) | Yes |
| 120–131 | Partition #5 (see Table 6.15) | Yes |
| 132–143 | Partition #6 (see Table 6.15) | Yes |
| 144–155 | Partition #7 (see Table 6.15) | Yes |
| 156–167 | Partition #8 (see Table 6.15) | Yes |
| 168–179 | Partition #9 (see Table 6.15) | Yes |
| 180–191 | Partition #10 (see Table 6.15) | Yes |
| 192–203 | Partition #11 (see Table 6.15) | Yes |
| 204–215 | Partition #12 (see Table 6.15) | Yes |
| 216–227 | Partition #13 (see Table 6.15) | Yes |
| 228–239 | Partition #14 (see Table 6.15) | Yes |
| 240–251 | Partition #15 (see Table 6.15) | Yes |
| 252–263 | Partition #16 (see Table 6.15) | Yes |
| 264–327 | Timestamps (not used) | No |
| 328–455 | Volume Label | No |

| Byte Range | Description | Essential |
|---|---|---|
| 456–507 | Hardware Details | No |
| 508–509 | Signature Value (0xDABE) | No |
| 510–511 | Checksum | No |

Each of the 16 partition entries has the data structure given in Table 6.15.

**Table 6.15**  Data structure for the Sun i386 disk label partition entry.

| Byte Range | Description | Essential |
|---|---|---|
| 0–1 | Partition Type (see Table 6.11) | No |
| 2–3 | Flag (see Table 6.12) | No |
| 4–7 | Starting Sector | Yes |
| 8–11 | Size in Sectors | Yes |

The type and flag fields use the same values that were described in the preceding section on Sparc data structures. To identify the partitions that an i386 Solaris system has, the partition entries in the VTOC are examined, and the layout is determined using the starting sector and the size. The starting sector is relative to the DOS-based partition (the one with type 0x82). In our example disk image, the DOS partition with the disk label starts in sector 22,496. Therefore, the disk label is located in 22,497, shown here:

```
# dd if=i386-disk.dd bs=512 skip=22497 | xxd
0000000: 0000 0000 0000 0000 0000 0000 eede 0d60  ...............'
0000016: 0100 0000 0000 0000 0000 0000 0002 1000  ................
0000032: 0000 0000 0000 0000 0000 0000 0000 0000  ................
0000048: 0000 0000 0000 0000 0000 0000 0000 0000  ................
0000064: 0000 0000 0000 0000 0200 0000 c00e 1000  ................
0000080: 0082 3e00 0300 0100 d00b 0000 f002 1000  ..>.............
0000096: 0500 0000 0000 0000 309a 7001 0000 0000  ........0.p.....
0000112: 0000 0000 0000 0000 0000 0000 0000 0000  ................
0000128: 0000 0000 0400 0000 c090 4e00 2000 fa00  ..........N. ...
0000144: 0000 0000 0000 0000 0000 0000 0800 0000  ................
0000160: e090 4801 0041 1f00 0100 0100 0000 0000  ..H..A..........
0000176: f003 0000 0900 0100 f003 0000 e007 0000  ................
[REMOVED - ZEROS]
0000320: 0000 0000 0000 0000 4445 4641 554c 5420  ........DEFAULT
```

```
0000336: 6379 6c20 3233 3936 3420 616c 7420 3220   cyl 23964 alt 2
0000352: 6864 2031 3620 7365 6320 3633 0000 0000   hd 16 sec 63....
[REMOVED - ZEROS]
0000448: 0000 0000 0000 0000 9e5d 0000 9c5d 0000   .........]...]..
0000464: 0200 0000 1000 0000 3f00 0000 0100 0000   ........?.......
0000480: 0000 100e 0000 0000 0000 0000 0000 0000   ...............
0000496: 0000 0000 0000 0000 0000 0000 beda a24a   ...............]
```

This is from an i386 system, which means that the values are stored in little-endian ordering. At offset 30 we see that there are 16 (0x10) partitions in the table. The first partition entry begins at offset 72 and ends at offset 83. Bytes 72 to 73 show us that it has a type of 0x02, which is the root partition. The starting sector is given in bytes 76 to 79 and we see 1,052,352 (0x00100EC0). Bytes 80 to 83 give the partition size and we see 4,096,512 (0x003e8200). There are 10 partitions being used in this disk label, and the last one is located at bytes 180 to 191. The timestamps are all zero, and the volume name is "DEFAULT" with the disk geometry information.

For an i386 disk image, you can use any DOS-partition tool to list where the boot partition and file systems partitions are located. Here is the output from running mmls on an i386 Solaris disk:

```
# mmls -t dos i386-disk.dd
DOS Partition Table
Units are in 512-byte sector
      Slot  Start       End         Length      Description
00:   ----- 0000000000  0000000000  0000000001  Primary Table (#0)
01:   ----- 0000000001  0000001007  0000001007  Unallocated
02:   00:00 0000001008  0000022175  0000021168  Solaris 8 Boot (0xBE)
03:   ----- 0000022176  0000022495  0000000320  Unallocated
04:   00:01 0000022496  0024180911  0024158416  Linux Swap / Solaris x86 (0x82)
```

Recall that the 0xBE type partition contains the boot code and does not contain a file system. The file systems and disk label structure are located in the 0x82-type partition. You can get the same output using the fdisk tool in Linux, but fdisk will not list the Solaris partitions in the disk label. To view the file systems, you can either extract the partition that starts at 22,496 or simply call mmls with the -o flag to set the offset.

```
# mmls -t sun -o 22496 disk8.dd
Sun VTOC
Units are in 512-byte sectors
      Slot  Start       End         Length      Description
00:   02    0000000000  0024156719  0024156720  backup (0x05)
01:   08    0000000000  0000001007  0000001008  boot (0x01)
```

| 02: | 09 | 0000001008 | 0000003023 | 0000002016 | alt sector (0x09) |
|-----|----|------------|------------|------------|-------------------|
| 03: | 01 | 0000003024 | 0001052351 | 0001049328 | swap (0x03) |
| 04: | 00 | 0001052352 | 0005148863 | 0004096512 | / (0x02) |
| 05: | 05 | 0005148864 | 0021532895 | 0016384032 | /usr/ (0x04) |
| 06: | 07 | 0021532896 | 0023581151 | 0002048256 | /home/ (0x08) |

Recall that these addresses are relative to the start of the DOS partition, so you will have to add 22,496 to any of the starting sector addresses when you extract them with dd. I have found that when you boot Linux with an i386 Solaris disk as one of the slave disks, Linux makes devices for only the first eight of the Solaris partitions. Devices are not created for any of the partitions after the first eight.

## ANALYSIS CONSIDERATIONS

The special considerations for a Solaris investigation are the same ones that other partition systems have. There are some unused values in the disk label structure, and they could be used to store data, although there is not much unused space.

As with other partition systems, the 'type' field in the partition description is not enforced. Just because the disk label structure says that the partition is for the /var/ partition or swap space does not mean that it is. As always, look at the disk for unused space.

If the location of the disk label cannot be determined, a search can be performed using the signature values. The signature value of 0x600DDEEE exists inside the disk label, and 0xDABE exists in bytes 508 to 509.

## SUMMARY

Solaris systems are common in corporate settings and will be investigated for intrusions and cases of fraud. This section has shown how Solaris organizes its disks and how the layout can be listed and extracted. The disk label structure is fairly simple, and it can be read with the fdisk or mmls tools.

# GPT PARTITIONS

Systems with 64-bit Intel Itanium processors (IA64) do not have a BIOS like IA32 systems do. Instead, they have an *Extensible Firmware Interface* (EFI). EFI (available at http://www.intel.com/technology/efi) is also used by non-Intel platforms, such as Sun Sparc systems. The EFI uses a partition system called the *GUID Partition Table* (GPT) that can support up to 128 partitions and uses 64-bit LBA addresses. Backup copies of the important data structures are maintained in case of failure. At the time of this writing, GPT disks are found in high-end servers and not in typical desktop systems.

## GENERAL OVERVIEW

A GPT disk has five major areas to it, as shown in Figure 6.7. The first area is the *Protective MBR*, and it starts in the first sector of the disk and contains a DOS partition table with one entry. The single entry is for a partition with a type of 0xEE that spans the entire disk. This partition exists so that legacy computers can recognize the disk as being used and do not try to format it. EFI does not actually use the partition, though.

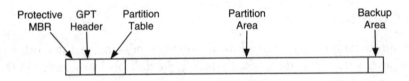

**Figure 6.7**    A GPT disk has five areas in its layout.

The second part of the GPT disk starts in sector 1 and contains the GPT header. The header defines the size and location of the partition table, which are fixed when the GPT disk is created. Windows limits the number of entries in the partition table to 128 [Microsoft 2004]. The header also contains a checksum of the header and the partition table so that errors or modifications can be detected.

The third section contains the partition table. Each entry in the partition table contains a starting and ending address, a type value, a name, attribute flags, and a GUID value. The 128-bit GUID is supposed to be unique for that system and is set when the partition table is created.

The fourth section of the disk is the partition area. The partition area is the largest area and contains the sectors that will be allocated to partitions. The starting and ending sectors for this area are defined in the GPT header. The final section of the disk contains a backup copy of the GPT header and partition table. It is located in the sector following the partition area.

## DATA STRUCTURES

The first area of a GPT disk uses a standard DOS partition table, which we previously examined. A GPT disk has a DOS partition table with one entry that spans the entire disk. An example is shown here:

```
# mmls -t dos gpt-disk.dd
DOS Partition Table
Units are in 512-byte sectors
      Slot    Start        End          Length       Description
00:  -----    0000000000   0000000000   0000000001   Primary Table (#0)
01:  00:00    0000000001   0120103199   0120103199   GPT Safety Partition (0xEE)
```

Following the DOS partition table, sector 1 contains the GPT header. The GPT header describes the layout of the disk. Its data structure is given in Table 6.16.

**Table 6.16**  Data structure for the GPT header.

| Byte Range | Description | Essential |
| --- | --- | --- |
| 0–7 | Signature value ("EFI PART") | No |
| 8–11 | Version | Yes |
| 12–15 | Size of GPT header in bytes | Yes |
| 16–19 | CRC32 checksum of GPT header | No |
| 20–23 | Reserved | No |
| 24–31 | LBA of current GPT header structure | No |
| 32–39 | LBA of the other GPT header structure | No |
| 40–47 | LBA of start of partition area | Yes |
| 48–55 | LBA of end of partition area | No |
| 56–71 | Disk GUID | No |
| 72–79 | LBA of the start of the partition table | Yes |
| 80–83 | Number of entries in partition table | Yes |
| 84–87 | Size of each entry in partition table | Yes |
| 88–91 | CRC32 checksum of partition table | No |
| 92–End of Sector | Reserved | No |

Using these values, we can determine the layout of the disk including the locations of the partition table, partition area, and backup copies of the GPT header and partition table.

The GPT header for an example disk image is shown here:

```
# dd if=gpt-disk.dd bs=512 skip=1 count=1 | xxd
0000000: 4546 4920 5041 5254 0000 0100 5c00 0000   EFI PART....\...
0000016: 8061 a3b0 0000 0000 0100 0000 0000 0000   .a..............
0000032: 1fa1 2807 0000 0000 2200 0000 0000 0000   ..(.....".......
0000048: fea0 2807 0000 0000 7e5e 4da1 1102 5049   ..(.....~^M...PI
0000064: ab2a 79a6 3ea6 3859 0200 0000 0000 0000   .*y.>.8Y........
0000080: 8000 0000 8000 0000 69a5 7180 0000 0000   ........i.q.....
0000096: 0000 0000 0000 0000 0000 0000 0000 0000   ................
[REMOVED]
```

We can see the signature value in the first 8 bytes and bytes 12 to 15 show us that the size of the GPT header is 96 bytes (0x5c). Bytes 32 to 39 show that the backup copy of the header is located in sector 120,103,199 (0x0728a1af). Note that this is the same sector that we saw as the last sector of the DOS protection partition. Bytes 40 to 47 show that the partition area starts in sector 34 (0x22) and ends in sector 120,103,166 (0x0728a0fe). Bytes 72 to 79 show that the partition table starts in sector 2, and bytes 80 to 83 show that there are 128 (0x80) entries in the table. Bytes 84 to 87 show that each entry is 128 (0x80) bytes, which means that 32 sectors are needed.

Using the information from the GPT header, we can locate the start and end of the partition table and the size of each entry. Each table entry has the fields in Table 6.17.

**Table 6.17**   Data structure for each GPT partition table entry.

| Byte Range | Description | Essential |
| --- | --- | --- |
| 0–15 | Partition type GUID | No |
| 16–31 | Unique partition GUID | No |
| 32–39 | Starting LBA of partition | Yes |
| 40–47 | Ending LBA of partition | Yes |
| 48–55 | Partition attributes | No |
| 56–127 | Partition name in Unicode | No |

The 128-bit type value identifies the contents of the partition. With a GPT disk, partitions are used to hold both system information and file systems. For example, every computer that uses EFI must have an EFI System Partition that contains the files needed to start the system's hardware and software. The vendors assign the type values; unfortunately, there is currently no central list of values that are being used. The Intel specification defines the partition types given in Table 6.18.

**Table 6.18**  GPT partition types defined by Intel.

| GUID Type Value | Description |
| --- | --- |
| 00000000-0000-0000-0000-000000000000 | Unallocated entry |
| C12A7328-F81F-11D2-BA4B-00A0C93EC93B | EFI system partition |
| 024DEE41-33E7-11d3-9D69-0008C781F39F | Partition with DOS partition table inside |

Microsoft has defined some of the type values that it uses, and they are given in Table 6.19.

**Table 6.19**  GPT partition types that Microsoft has defined.

| GUID Type Value | Description |
| --- | --- |
| E3C9E316-0B5C-4DB8-817D-f92DF00215AE | Microsoft Reserved Partition (MRP) |
| EBD0A0A2-B9E5-4433-87C0-68B6B72699C7 | Primary partition (basic disk) |
| 5808C8AA-7E8F-42E0-85D2-E1E90434CFB3 | LDM metadata partition (dynamic disk) |
| AF9B60A0-1431-4F62-BC68-3311714A69AD | LDM data partition (dynamic disk) |

Windows uses a "Reserved Partition" to store temporary files and data. A "Primary Partition" is a basic partition and a file system is located inside of it. Primary partitions are similar to the primary partitions that we saw with DOS partitions. The "LDM Metadata Partition" and "LDM Data Partition" are used for Microsoft dynamic disks, which are described in the next chapter. Dynamic disks are used to merge the data from multiple disks into one volume.

The 64-bit attribute field is divided into three parts. The lowest bit is set to 1 when the system cannot function without this partition. This is used to determine if a user is allowed to delete a partition. Bits 1 to 47 are undefined and bits 48–63 can store any data that the specific partition type wants. Each partition type can use these values as they like.

Here are the contents of a partition table entry from our very basic system:

```
# dd if=gpt-disk.dd bs=512 skip=34 | dd bs=128 skip=3 count=1 | xxd
0000000: 16e3 c9e3 5c0b b84d 817d f92d f002 15ae  ....\..M.}.-....
0000016: 2640 69eb 2f99 1942 afc0 d673 7c0b 8ae4  &@i./..B...s|...
0000032: 2200 0000 0000 0000 0080 3e00 0000 0000  ".........>.....
0000048: 0000 0000 0000 0000 0000 ffff ffff ffff  ...............
0000064: ffff ffff ffff ffff ffff ffff ffff ffff  ...............
[REMOVED]
```

The top line is bytes 0 to 15, and we see the Partition type GUID and the Partition GUID is given on the second line in bytes 16 to 31. The starting address of the partition is in bytes 32 to 39, and we see that it is sector 32 (0x0022). The ending address of the partition is given in bytes 40 to 47 and it is 4,096,000 (0x003E8000).

We can see the output of running `mmls` on this image here:

```
# mmls -t gpt gpt-disk.dd
GUID Partition Table
Units are in 512-byte sectors

      Slot    Start         End           Length        Description
00:   -----   0000000000    0000000000    0000000001    Safety Table
01:   -----   0000000001    0000000001    0000000001    GPT Header
02:   -----   0000000002    0000000033    0000000032    Partition Table
03:   00      0000000034    0004096000    0004095967
04:   01      0004096001    0012288000    0008192000
```

At the end of the disk are the backup copies of the GPT header and partition table. They are in reverse order: The GPT header is in the last sector, and the partition table is before it. In our example image, the backup GPT header is in sector 120,103,199.

## ANALYSIS CONSIDERATIONS

At the time of this writing, GPT disks are rare, and most investigation tools do not advertise whether or not they support them. Linux can be used to breakup a GPT disk into partitions so that other file system analysis tools can be used. The Sleuth Kit also supports GPT partitions if you need to break the disk up.

GPT disks have a backup copy of the partition table so data can be more easily recovered if the original table becomes corrupt. The unused portions of sector 0, sector 1, and any of the unused partition entries could be used to hide data.

## SUMMARY

As of the writing of this book, GPT partitions are not frequently encountered during investigations, and not all forensic analysis tools support them. In the future, this will surely not be the case as more systems use 64-bit hardware. GPT partitions are much more flexible and simple than the DOS partitions.

## BIBLIOGRAPHY

FreeBSD Documentation Project. "FreeBSD Handbook." 2005. http://www.freebsd.org.

Holland, Nick, ed. "OpenBSD Installation Guide." January 2005. http://www.openbsd.org/faq/faq4.html.

Intel. *Extensible Firmware Interface, Version 1.10*, December 1, 2002. http://developer.intel.com/technology/efi/.

Marshall Kirk McKusick, Keith Bostic, Michael Karels, John Quaterman. *The Design and Implementation of the 4.4 BSD Operating System*. Boston: Addison Wesley, 1996.

Marshall Kirk McKusick, George V. Neville-Neil. *The Design and Implementation of the FreeBSD Operating System*. Boston: Addison Wesley, 2005.

Mauro, Jim, and Richard McDougall. *Solaris Internals: Core Kernel Architecture*. Upper Saddle River: Sun Microsystems Press, 2001.

Microsoft. "Disk Sectors on GPT Disks." *Windows® XP Professional Resource Kit Documentation*, 2004. http://www.microsoft.com/resources/documentation/Windows/XP/all/reskit/en-us/Default.asp?url=/resources/documentation/Windows/XP/all/reskit/en-us/prkd_tro_zkfe.asp.

Sun. "Solaris 9 System Administration Guide: Basic Administration. Chapter 31." May 2002. http://docs.sun.com/db/doc/806-4073/6jd67r9fn?a=view.

Sun. "System Administration Guide: Basic Administration. Chapter 32: Managing Disks." April 2003. http://docsun.cites.uiuc.edu/sun_docs/C/solaris_9/SUNWaadm/SYSADV1/p117.html.

Winsor, Janice. *Solaris System Administrator's Guide*. 3rd edition. Palo Alto: Sun Microsystems Press, 2000.

# Multiple Disk Volumes

In many critical servers, multiple disks are used for performance, reliability, or scalability. The disks are merged and processed so that they look normal but they are not. This chapter covers RAID and disk spanning systems, both of which can be difficult to investigate. There can be many challenges when investigating a system that uses a multiple disk volume, and not all the problems have been solved. This chapter explains the technology behind both of these volume systems and then provides some suggestions for analyzing or acquiring the data. Of any chapter in this book, this will likely become outdated the most quickly because new technology is being developed to create new types of storage systems and because new analysis techniques will be developed to help fill the void in this area. The first part of this chapter examines RAID systems, which provide redundancy, and the second part of the chapter examines disk spanning, which creates larger volumes.

## RAID

RAID stands for *Redundant Arrays of Inexpensive Disks* and is commonly used in high-performance systems or in critical systems. RAID was first proposed in the late 1980s as a method of using inexpensive disks to achieve performance and storage capacities similar to the expensive high-performance disks [Patterson, et al. 1988]. The main theory behind RAID is to use multiple disks instead of one in order to provide redundancy and improve disk performance. A hardware controller or software driver merges the multiple disks together, and the computer sees a large single volume.

RAID used to be found only in high-end servers but is now becoming more common on desktop systems. Microsoft Windows NT, 2000, and XP have the option to provide the user with some level of RAID. In this section, we will first describe the technology involved with RAID systems, and then we will discuss how to acquire or analyze a RAID system. A RAID volume can be partitioned using any of the methods shown in Chapter 5, "PC-based Partitions," and Chapter 6, "Server-based Partitions."

## RAID LEVELS

There are multiple levels of RAID, and each level provides a different amount of reliability and performance improvements. In this section, we will cover how six of the different RAID levels work. A *RAID volume* is the volume created by the hardware or software that combines the hard disks.

RAID *Level 0* volumes use two or more disks, and the data is striped across the disks in block-size chunks. When data are striped, consecutive blocks of the RAID volume are mapped to blocks on alternate disks. For example, if there are two disks, RAID block 0 is block 0 on disk 1, RAID block 1 is block 0 on disk 2, RAID block 2 is block 1 on disk 1, and RAID block 3 is block 1 on disk 2. This can be seen in Figure 7.1 where 'D0,' 'D1,' 'D2,' and 'D3' are blocks of data. A system would use this level of RAID for performance reasons and not redundancy because only one copy of the data exists.

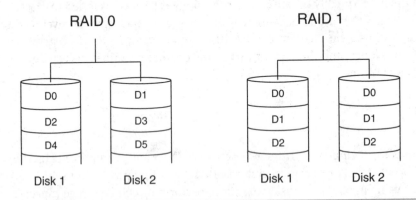

**Figure 7.1**   A RAID Level 0 volume with two disks and data striped across them in block-sized chunks and a RAID Level 1 volume with two disks and data mirrored between them.

RAID *Level 1* volumes use two or more disks and mirror the data. When data are written to one disk, they are also written to the other disk, and both disks contain the same allocated data. The two disks may contain different data in the sectors that are not used in the RAID volume. If there is a disk failure, the other disk can be used for recovery. For example, if we have two disks in a RAID Level 1 volume, RAID block 0 is block 0 on both disks 1 and 2, RAID block 1 is block 1 on both disks 1 and 2, etc. This also can be seen in Figure 7.1.

RAID *Level 2* volumes are rare and use error-correcting codes to fix any incorrect data when it is read from the disks. The data are striped across many disks using bit-sized chunks, and additional disks contain the error-correcting code values.

RAID *Level 3* volumes require at least three disks and have a dedicated parity disk. The parity disk is used to recognize errors in the other two disks or to recreate the contents of a disk if it fails. An inefficient example of parity is traditional addition. If I have two values, 3 and 4, I can add them and my parity is 7. If at any time the two values do not add to 7, I know that there is an error. If one of the values is lost, I can recover it by subtracting the value that still exists from 7.

With RAID Level 3, the data are broken up into byte-sized chunks and striped, or alternated, across the data disks. A dedicated parity disk contains the values needed to duplicate the data to rebuild any data that is lost when one of the disks fails. This level is similar to what we saw with Level 0, except that the striping size is much smaller (bytes instead of blocks) and there is a dedicated parity disk. An example with two data disks and one parity disk can be found in Figure 7.2.

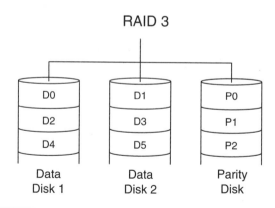

**Figure 7.2**   A RAID Level 3 volume with two data disks and one parity disk.

A common method of calculating the parity information is by using the "exclusive or" (XOR) operation. The XOR operator takes two one-bit inputs and generates a one-bit output using the rules found in Table 7.1. The XOR of two values larger than one bit can be calculated by independently applying the XOR rules to each set of bits.

**Table 7.1**    Rules for the XOR operation.

| Input 1 | Input 2 | Output |
| --- | --- | --- |
| 0 | 0 | 0 |
| 0 | 1 | 1 |
| 1 | 0 | 1 |
| 1 | 1 | 0 |

The XOR operator is useful because if you know any of the two of the input or output values, you can calculate the third value. This is similar to adding two numbers and then subtracting one to get the original. For example, let there be three data disks and one parity disk. The data disks have the values: 1011 0010, 1100 1111, and 1000 0001. The parity for these values would be calculated as follows:

```
(1011 0010 XOR 1100 1111) XOR 1000 0001
(0111 1101) XOR 1000 0001
1111 1100
```

The byte 1111 1100 would be written to the parity disk. If the second disk failed, its byte could be created as follows:

```
1111 1100 XOR (1011 0010 XOR 1000 0001)
1111 1100 XOR (0011 0011)
1100 1111
```

We have easily reconstructed the byte for the second disk.

RAID *Level 4* volumes are similar to Level 3, except that the data is striped in block-sized chunks instead of byte-sized chunks. Level 4 uses two or more data disks and a dedicated parity disk, so its architecture is the same as shown in Figure 7.2.

RAID *Level 5* volumes are similar to Level 4, but they remove the bottleneck associated with the parity disk. In Level 5, there is no dedicated parity disk, and all the disks contain both data and parity values on an alternating basis. For example, if there are three disks, RAID block 0 is block 0 of disk 1, RAID block 1 is in block 0 of disk 2, and the corresponding parity block is block 0 of disk 3. The next parity block will be block 1 of disk 2 and will contain the XOR of block 1 of disks 1 and 3. This can be seen in Figure 7.3.

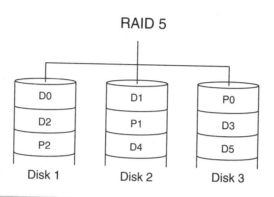

**Figure 7.3** A RAID Level 5 volume with three disks and distributed parity data.

Level 5 is one of the more common forms of RAID and requires at least three disks. There are many other RAID levels that are not very common. They combine multiple RAID levels and make analysis even harder.

## HARDWARE RAID

One method of creating a RAID volume is to use special hardware. This section will examine how this is done and how to acquire such a system.

### Background

A hardware RAID implementation can come in two major forms: as a special controller that plugs into one of the buses or as a device that plugs into a normal disk controller, such as ATA, SCSI, or Firewire. In either case, the hard disks plug into a special piece of hardware and, in general, the computer sees only the RAID volume and not the individual disks. Figure 7.4 shows the connections between the disks, controller, and volume.

If a special RAID controller is being used, the computer probes for the controller when booting. With many IA32 systems, the BIOS for the RAID controller displays messages on the screen, and the user can enter a setup screen to configure the controller and disks. The OS needs hardware drivers for the RAID controller. Disks that are created with one controller typically cannot be used with another controller. If a special device is being used that goes in between the normal disk controller and the hard disks, no special drivers are needed.

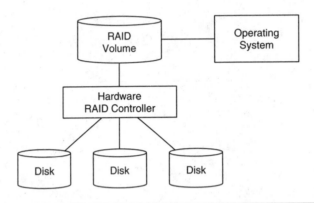

**Figure 7.4**    A hardware controller makes the disks look like one for the OS.

## Acquisition and Analysis

There are many types of RAID hardware implementations, so we will only provide some basic guidelines here. To analyze the RAID volume, it is easiest to acquire the final RAID volume as though it were a normal single disk and use the typical file system and partition analysis tools. One method of performing this is to boot the suspect system with a bootable Linux, or similar, CD that has drivers for the RAID controller. You can then use dd, or a similar command, to acquire the final RAID volume. Note that some RAID volumes are very large; therefore, you will need a large amount of disk space on which to store the image (or maybe your own RAID volume).

Different bootable Linux CDs have drivers for different RAID controllers, so check your favorite CDs and make a list of which controllers they support. You may need to make your own CD or bring several CDs with you so that you are prepared.

If you do not have the needed drivers for the RAID controller for an onsite acquisition, the individual disks and controller should be taken back to the lab. Not much has been published about the layout of data on the individual disks, so it could be difficult to merge the disks without the controller.

The RAID volume may not use all sectors on a disk and it is possible that the unused sectors contain hidden data. Therefore, acquiring the contents of each disk in addition to the RAID volume is the safest, although not always the easiest, solution. If you do not know the layout of the data, it could be difficult to identify the unused sectors of the disk. If you have specific keywords for which you are looking, the individual disks can be searched, in addition to searching the RAID volume.

## Software RAID

RAID volumes also can be implemented in software. This section will examine how this is done and how to acquire a software RAID volume.

### Background

With a software RAID, the operating system has special drivers that merge the individual disks. In this scenario, the OS sees the individual disks, but may show only the RAID volume to the user. The individual disks can typically be accessed through raw devices in UNIX system or through device objects in Microsoft Windows. Most operating systems now offer some levels of RAID, including Microsoft Windows NT, 2000, and XP; Apple OS X; Linux; Sun Solaris; HP-UX; and IBM AIX. Software RAID is not as efficient as hardware RAID because the CPU must be used to calculate the parity bits and split the data. We can see the connections in Figure 7.5.

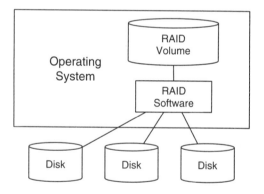

**Figure 7.5** With software RAID, the OS merges the disks and it has access to each disk.

In Windows 2000 and XP, the *Logical Disk Manager* (LDM) controls the RAID volumes. The LDM requires that disks be formatted as dynamic disks, which are different from the DOS-based partitions that we previously saw in Chapter 5, "PC-Based Partitions." The LDM can create RAID level 0 (striping), RAID level 1 (mirroring), and RAID level 5 (striping with parity) volumes, although RAID levels 1 and 5 are available only with the server version of Windows. A dynamic disk can be used for more than one

RAID volume, but that is unlikely if the system is using RAID for performance or redundancy reasons. All configuration information for the Windows RAID volume is stored on the disks and not on the local system. We will discuss LDM in much more detail later in the chapter when we discuss disk spanning.

In Linux, RAID is achieved with the *multiple device* (MD) kernel driver. The disks in a Linux RAID do not have to be formatted in any special way and can be normal DOS-partitioned disks. The configuration information is stored on the local system in a configuration file, /etc/raidtab by default. The resulting RAID volume gets a new device that can be mounted as a normal disk. The MD driver supports RAID Level 0 (striping), RAID Level 1 (mirroring), and RAID Level 5 (striping with parity). There is an optional "persistent superblock" option that places configuration information on the disk so that it can be used in other systems besides the original system (which makes offsite analysis easier).

### Acquisition and Analysis

Analysis and acquisition of software RAID is similar to a hardware RAID. Based on current technology, the easiest scenario is to acquire the RAID volume so that the normal file system tools can be used. Unlike hardware RAID, there are some analysis tools that can merge the individual disks together.

With software RAID, you may not need the original software to recreate the RAID volume. For example, Linux has support for *Windows Logical Disk Management* (LDM) and may be able to properly merge the Windows disks. Not all Linux kernels ship with LDM enabled, but you can enable it by recompiling the kernel. If you are using Microsoft Windows to create the RAID volume, apply hardware write blockers to prevent overwriting data.

Let's look at a Windows LDM example with Linux. When you boot a Linux kernel with support for LDM, a device is created for each of the partitions in the RAID. You have to edit the /etc/raidtab file so that it describes the RAID setup and partitions. For example, the following is a configuration file for a Windows LDM RAID Level 0 (striping) with two partitions (/dev/hdb1 and /dev/hdd1) using 64KB blocks:

```
# cat /etc/raidtab
raiddev /dev/md0
        raid-level              0
        nr-raid-disks           2
        nr-spare-disks          0
        persistent-superblock 0
        chunk-size              64k
        device                  /dev/hdb1
```

```
raid-disk           0
device              /dev/hdd1
raid-disk           1
```

Using this configuration file, the device /dev/md0 could be mounted read-only or imaged using dd. Test the process before an incident happens and make backup copies of real disks during an incident. We will cover the process of using Linux with Windows LDM in more detail in the "Disk Spanning" section. A similar process is used for making a Linux MD software RAID on the acquisition system. If you can copy the raidtab file from the original system, its contents can be used as a base to make the RAID volume on the acquisition system.

EnCase from Guidance Software and ProDiscover from Technology Pathways can import the disks from a Windows RAID volume and analyze them as though they were a single volume. This is actually the better long-term method of analyzing the data because it provides access to data that may be hidden in the individual disks and would not be acquired by collecting only the RAID volume. There is always a risk, though, of using software, in either Linux or third-party tools, that does not use an official specification because it could have errors and not produce an accurate version of the original RAID volume.

## GENERAL ANALYSIS COMMENTS

Investigating a system with a RAID volume can be difficult because they are not frequently encountered and not every implementation is the same. Be very careful when trying different acquisition techniques that you do not modify the original disks in the process. Use hardware write-blockers or the read-only jumper on the individual hard disks to prevent modifications. It may also be useful to make images of the individual disks before you make an image of the full RAID volume. The individual disk images may contain hidden data that are not in the final RAID volume. No cases involving hidden RAID data have been published, but it could be possible depending on whom you are investigating. It is also possible that the entire disk is not being used for the RAID. Some RAID systems use only part of the hard disk so that it is easier to replace the disk if it fails. For example, only 40GB of each individual disk in the RAID volume could be used, regardless if each individual disk is 40GB or 80GB. The unused area may contain data from a previous usage or be used to hide data.

## SUMMARY

This section has given an overview of RAID. RAID is common in high-end servers and is becoming more common in desktop systems that need performance or large amounts of disk space. The low-level details were not given because they vary by implementation and there is no single standard. More details will be given later in the "Disk Spanning" section because many systems incorporate software RAID in their volume management support.

The key concept for investigations is to practice acquiring RAID systems. If possible, it is easiest to acquire the full RAID volume at the scene and then perform analysis using standard tools. The problems with this approach are that it requires a very large disk to save the data to, and there could be data on the individual disks that are not shown in the final RAID volume. Therefore, it is safest to always acquire the individual disks as well.

## DISK SPANNING

Disk spanning makes multiple disks appear to be one large disk. Disk spanning is frequently discussed with RAID because many software RAID solutions also provide disk spanning, but disk spanning offers no redundancy or performance benefits. It is used to create large storage systems, and some versions allow you to add disks and dynamically increase the size of the file system.

Many operating systems now include disk spanning, and in this section we cover the software solutions that come with Microsoft Windows and Linux. Other systems, such as Sun Solaris, IBM AIX, and Apple OSX, come with their own versions of disk spanning, but they are not covered here. The first part of this section covers the basic concepts and provides some general definitions that are used in all implementations. Then we cover the Windows and Linux systems. This section, like the previous RAID section, does not provide answers to every problem that you may encounter because not all the answers are known. This section describes how disk spanning works so that you can have a better understanding about why tools may not exist that meet all your needs.

### OVERVIEW

The main theory behind disk spanning is similar to using a three-ring binder for taking notes instead of a spiral notebook. When you use all the pages in the spiral notebook, you must buy a new one and carry both of them around. When you use all the pages in the three-ring binder, you can add more pages to the end of it and even use a larger binder if needed. With disk spanning, the storage space from new disks is appended to the end of the existing storage space. Figure 7.6 shows an example where there are two disks being used for spanning, and each disk holds 100 data blocks. Blocks 0 to 99 are written to disk 1, and blocks 100 to 199 are written to disk 2.

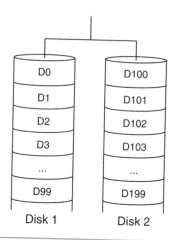

**Figure 7.6** Disk spanning with 100 units on the first disk and 100 units on the second disk.

A *logical volume* is the output of the disk-spanning software. The logical volume is made up of multiple physical disks or partitions that are sequentially merged together. Many systems also have *disk groups*, which are groups of physical disks, and only disks in the same group can be combined to make a logical volume. Figure 7.7 shows the relationship between the levels of abstraction. It contains three physical disks that are grouped into one disk group. The disks are spanned to form two logical volumes.

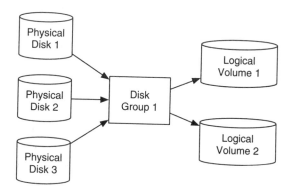

**Figure 7.7** Terms and relationships for disk-spanning systems.

## Linux MD

There are two methods of disk spanning in Linux. The MD driver, which we previously saw with RAID systems, also can perform basic disk spanning, and there is also the more advanced system called the Logical Volume Manager (LVM). Both systems come with major Linux distributions, and this section examines MD devices. We are covering Linux before Windows because the Linux drivers can be used to analyze a Windows system.

### Background

The MD driver uses normal DOS-based partitions and groups them together to form a RAID or disk-spanning volume. Each disk can have multiple partitions and each can be used in a different RAID or logical volume. There is no notion of disk groups in this model. There is a configuration file, /etc/raidtab, that lists which partitions go in which order, and the volume cannot be mounted unless it is configured in this file. The configuration file has the same layout as was described in the previous RAID section except that the 'raid-level' setting is set to 'linear.' An example configuration file for a logical volume with two partitions (/dev/hdb1 and /dev/hdd1) is

```
# cat /etc/raidtab
raiddev /dev/md0
        raid-level        linear
        nr-raid-disks     2
        nr-spare-disks    0
        persistent-superblock    1
        chunk-size        4k
        device            /dev/hdb1
        raid-disk         0
        device            /dev/hdd1
        raid-disk         1
```

This kernel reads the configuration file and creates a device, /dev/md0, that can be mounted and used as a single volume, but it really combines the storage space of /dev/hdb1 and /dev/hdd1.

If the 'persistent-superblock' value is set to 0, then the only configuration data for the device is in the /etc/raidtab file. If the value is set to 1, each disk or partition contains configuration data at the end of it that allows the auto-detect feature of Linux to automatically create the MD device. For the auto-detect process to work with Linux, the DOS partition that it is located in must have a partition type of 0xfd. You can see if the device was created during the boot by looking at the /var/log/messages log file. The auto-detect process occurs when the 'md' kernel module is loaded.

If the disks or partitions contain the persistent superblock, they have a 1024-byte structure that is broken up into sections. The first section contains settings about the resulting disk spanning or RAID volume, such as versions, the number of disks, creation time, and identifiers. The second section contains general information, such as the last update time, a counter, the state of the volume, and the number of working and failed disks. The remaining sections contain information about each of the disks in the volume, including the major and minor numbers of the device, the role of the device in the volume, and the disk's state. As we will see in the analysis section, a typical Linux system updates the values in the superblock when it boots, even if the volume is never mounted. Using the superblock, the kernel can determine if the disks have been removed from the system and placed in a different order.

### Acquisition and Analysis

To analyze the data on a MD volume, your best bet is to acquire the volume as a single drive or partition and use standard analysis tools. The easiest scenario is if the volume has a persistent superblock. Otherwise, you will have to create the /etc/raidtab file on your acquisition system. If you need to create the raidtab file, then you should try to access the /etc/ directory on the original and use it as a base.

After the configuration file has been created, the MD device can be created using the raidstart command. That makes a device in the /dev/ directory based on the name given in the configuration file, and the volume can be acquired with dd or a similar tool. After the acquisition, the raidstop command needs to be executed to stop the MD device. If there is a persistent superblock, be aware that some of the values in the superblock are updated when you make a new raid device with raidstart. Ensure that you have backup images of the disks and try ATA or SCSI write blockers if you have them.

If the partition type for each of the DOS partitions in the volume is set to 0xfd, the persistent superblock exists, and the system is set to autodetect MD devices—a device will be created during startup. As with executing raidstart, this process updates the 'last update' time, the counter, and the corresponding checksum value in the superblock. This occurs even when the MD volume is not mounted!

If you place the disks into a system in a different order and location from where they originally were, the superblock will be rewritten. This happens even if the volume is not mounted, so care must be taken to reduce the changes to each disk. Furthermore, I have experienced problems when I had only one of two disks in the analysis system when I booted. The counter on that disk increased, but when I booted next with both disks, Linux would not create the MD device because they had different counter values.

I have also found that when dealing with MD disks, it is best to get into the habit of not keeping a `raidtab` file. It can be very dangerous because if you shut the system down and put new disks in there, Linux will try and process them as a volume. You might consider modifying your shutdown scripts to copy the raidtab file to another name so that it does not exist for the next power on.

Bootable Linux CDs can be used to acquire MD volumes, and some autodetect the volume while others do not and require that you make an `/etc/raidtab` file. If you can boot from a CD and create the MD device, acquire that as normal. Otherwise, acquire each disk and document which places they were in so that you minimize any modifications to the disk by putting them in a different order. I have not been able to recreate MD volumes by using a raw image of the original partitions or loopback devices. Therefore, you may need to restore the images to a disk and extract the data from the disks in the lab.

## LINUX LVM

The second method of disk spanning in Linux is with LVM. This section describes the design of LVM and acquisition techniques.

### Background

LVM has a more advanced architecture than MD and uses the notion of disk groups, which it calls *volume groups*. DOS partitions that are used with LVM have a partition type of 0x8e. The disks or partitions in the volume group are divided into *physical extents*, which are equal-sized containers and typically have a size that is several MBs. Each system can have one or more volume groups and each volume group has a subdirectory in the `/dev/` directory.

A logical volume is made up of *logical extents*, which have the same size as the physical extents, and there is a mapping between each logical extent and physical extent. We can see this in Figure 7.8, where a logical volume is created from three sets of physical extents from two physical disks.

Logical volumes can be implemented by either concatenating the available physical extents or by using striping (where consecutive logical extents are on different disks). A 2GB concatenated volume may have its first 1.5GB from disk 1 and the last 500MB from disk 2. On the other hand, if the volume is striped, it may use two 1GB disks where the first 1MB is from disk 1, the second 1MB from disk 2, the third 1MB from disk 1, and so on. The logical volumes are given a device file in the volume group subdirectory in `/dev/`.

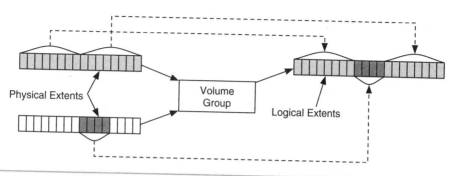

**Figure 7.8**   LVM organizes physical disks into physical extents that are mapped to logical extents in the logical volume.

The configuration data for a logical volume are stored on both the local system and the disks. The local configuration files are stored in the /etc/lvmtab file and the /etc/lvmtab.d/ directory. The configuration files are in a binary format and are updated with the LVM utilities, such as vgimport, vgscan, and vgchange. The on-disk structure is located at the beginning of the disk and contains information about the disk, the volume group of which the disk is a member, and the logical volumes that the volume group has. None of the fields in the structure is for a time value, so the structure is not updated when the logical volume is created as occurs with MD devices.

### Acquisition and Analysis

The analysis of an LVM system can be more automated than that of MD devices. The steps that I will describe here are from my experience with current versions of LVM, and I have verified them with LVM developers.[1] LVM has the vgexport and vgimport utilities that are supposed to be used when moving disks between systems, but I have found that they are not needed for acquiring the disks. The vgexport utility removes the local configuration files for the volume and writes the word "-EXPORT" in the volume group name on the disk. This step is not needed for an investigation when removing the disks from the suspect system.

To analyze a LVM volume, you can either remove the disks from the system and place them in a trusted Linux system or boot the suspect system from a bootable Linux CD with LVM support. As we discussed with MD, it is safest to have your systems configured to not automatically mount and configure logical volumes. When the analysis system is running, execute the vgscan command to scan the devices for logical volumes. This

---

1. Email communication with Heinz Mauelshagen and A. J. Lewis. November 17, 2003.

automatically creates the /etc/lvmtab file and configuration files in the /etc/lvmtab.d/ directory. After the configuration files have been created, the vgchange -a y command is needed to activate the volumes that were found in the scan. With LVM, the location and master or slave configuration of the disks is not important. When the volume has become active, you can dd it from the volume device in /dev/. In my experience, using the vgscan and vgchange commands does not change the MD5 value of the disks. The command sequence can be found here where the system was booted from The Penguin Sleuth Kit (note that the Penguin Sleuth Kit is not related to The Sleuth Kit analysis tools). The Penguin Sleuth Kit is available at http://www.linux-forensics.com.

```
# vgscan
vgscan -- reading all physical volumes (this may take a while...)
vgscan -- found inactive volume group "vg_big2"
vgscan -- "/etc/lvmtab" and "/etc/lvmtab.d" successfully created
vgscan -- WARNING: This program does not do a VGDA backup of your volume group

# vgchange -a y
vgchange -- volume group "vg_big2" successfully activated
```

Note that this behavior could change in future versions of LVM, so test your procedures before you perform these actions on a real system and make disk backups before merging the volumes.

## MICROSOFT WINDOWS LDM

Microsoft has included support for disk spanning since Windows NT. This section will describe the design of Windows LDM and acquisition techniques.

### Dynamic Disks

LDM is responsible for managing the logical volumes in Windows 2000 and XP. LDM supports simple volumes that are similar to basic partitions, disk spanning, RAID Level 0 (splitting), RAID Level 1 (mirroring), and RAID Level 5. The RAID capabilities were briefly discussed earlier in the chapter and they will be discussed in more detail here.

Basic disks are those that we saw in Chapters 5 and 6. These disks have a DOS or GPT partition table, and each partition is self-contained. Basic disks cannot be used with LDM. A *dynamic disk* has additional data structures to make partitions that can be used to make logical volumes. We will now discuss dynamic disks in more detail.

A dynamic disk has two important areas. The *LDM partition area* consumes most of the disk, and it is where dynamic partitions are allocated. The last 1MB of the dynamic disk is allocated to the LDM database. The LDM database contains entries to describe how the partition area is organized and how logical volumes should be created.

Each dynamic disk in an IA32 system has a DOS-based partition table in the first sector so that legacy systems will know that the disk is being used. The partition table has only one entry, and it spans the entire disk with a partition type of 0x42. The LDM partition area and database are located inside this DOS partition, as shown in Figure 7.9. We can see the partition table here using mmls from The Sleuth Kit:

```
# mmls -t dos vdisk.dd
DOS Partition Table  .
Units are in 512-byte sectors
      Slot    Start        End         Length      Description
00:   -----   0000000000   0000000000  0000000001  Primary Table (#0)
01:   -----   0000000001   0000000062  0000000062  Unallocated
02:   00:00   0000000063   0120101939  0120101877  Win LVM / Secure FS (0x42)
```

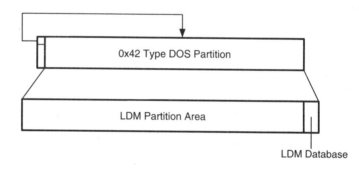

**Figure 7.9**  The layout of a dynamic disk in an IA32 system where the LDM data structures are inside a DOS partition.

Each dynamic disk in an IA64 (Intel Itanium, and so on) system has GPT partitions for the partition area and LDM database. There are specific partition types for these partitions and a partition is created for each.

Windows supports only one disk group, so all dynamic disks are automatically assigned to it. The partition area of each dynamic disk can be partitioned into dynamic partitions. Dynamic partitions from one or more disks are grouped to make logical volumes. We can see this relationship in Figure 7.10. It is important in this section to distinguish between the terms that Microsoft uses for dynamic disks versus DOS partitions. With DOS partitions, Microsoft considers logical volumes to be partitions that are inside an extended partition, whereas with dynamic disks all partitions that can contain a file system or other data are called logical volumes.

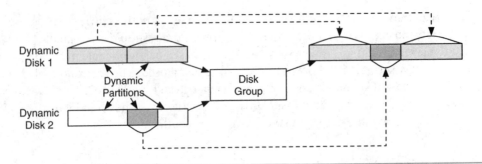

**Figure 7.10**    A LDM logical volume is made up of dynamic partitions from a disk group.

### The LDM Database

The LDM database is where the dynamic partitions are defined and where the rules for creating the logical volumes can be found. Microsoft has not published the exact layout and structures of the LDM database, but groups on the Internet have identified some of the internal data structures (one of the groups, Linux NTFS, is available at `http://linux-ntfs.sourceforge.net`). From the published Microsoft references [Soloman and Russinovich 2000], we know that the LDM database has four major sections. The *Private Header* is similar to the boot sector of a file system. It describes the unique characteristics of the disk and the logical volume. This structure contains a unique ID for the disk (its Windows Globally Unique Identifier (GUID)) and the name of the disk group. Windows has only one disk group, which is based on the name of your computer. The *Table of Contents* section is next, and its size is 16 sectors. According to Solomon and Russinovich, it "contains information regarding the databases' layout," which refers to the next section of the LDM,
the database.

The *database* area has entries to describe disks, partitions, components, and volumes. A *disk entry* exists for each dynamic disk, which could be a DOS or GPT disk. The *partition entries* are used to describe how the dynamic disks are partitioned. The *component entries* are used to describe how the partitions should be merged. Each of the partition entries points to the component entry that it uses. Component entries exist for spanning, splitting, and mirroring. Lastly, the *volume entries* are used to describe a logical volume, which is the result of applying the component type to the partitions.

I'll give an example using two dynamic disks. We have a logical volume, and the first part of the volume is from a 15MB partition on disk 1, the second part is from a 10MB partition on disk 2, and the final part is from a 20MB partition on disk 1. Obviously, these sizes are much smaller than we would ever encounter in the real world. This is the same basic layout that was shown in Figure 7.10. The dmdiag.exe tool from Microsoft (available at http://www.microsoft.com/window2000/techinfo/reskit/tools/existing/dmdiag-o.asp) displays the entries in the database and the relevant output is as follows:

```
Disk:     Disk1 rid=0.1027 updated=0.1122
assoc:    diskid=6a565b54-b83a-4ebb-95eb-842ede926e88
flags:

Disk:     Disk2 rid=0.1063 updated=0.1112
assoc:    diskid=533fe4ab-0409-4ea6-98b3-9648bbc3bd12
flags:
```

The previous two records are the disk entries for the two physical disks. Disk1 has an ID of 0.1027, and Disk2 has an ID of 0.1063.

```
Group:    hashDg1 rid=0.1025 update=0.1028
id:       dgid=d4f40362-7794-429a-a6ad-a6dfc0553cee
diskset:  id=00000000-0000-0000-0000-000000000000
copies:   nconfig=all nlog=all
minors:   >= 0
```

The previous record is a disk group entry and shows that the disk group is named with the computer name, hash.

```
Subdisk:  Disk1-01 rid=0.1109 updated=0.1112
info:     disk=0.1027 offset=0 len=30720 hidden=0
assoc:    plex=0.1107 (column=0 offset=0)

Subdisk:  Disk1-02 rid=0.1121 updated=0.1122
info:     disk=0.1027 offset=30720 len=40960 hidden=0
assoc:    plex=0.1107 (column=0 offset=51200)
```

The previous two entries are partition entries for the physical disk named Disk1 (ID: 0.1027). They both have a 'plex' value of 0.1107, which refers to the component entry that is used to make the logical volume. The first entry, ID 0.1109, is for the 15MB partition and has a sector offset of 0 and a length of 30,720 sectors. The second entry, ID 0.1121, is for the 20MB partition and has an offset of sector 30,720 with a length of 40,960 sectors.

```
Subdisk:   Disk2-01 rid=0.1111 updated=0.1112
info:      disk=0.1063 offset=0 len=20480 hidden=0
assoc:     plex=0.1107 (column=0 offset=30720)
```

The previous entry is a dynamic partition entry on Disk2 (ID: 0.1063). It is a partition with ID 0.1111 with an offset of 0 sectors and a length of 20,480 sectors. We can see the relationship between the physical disk and dynamic partition entries in Figure 7.11. The direction of the arrow shows that the dynamic partition entries contain a pointer to the physical disk.

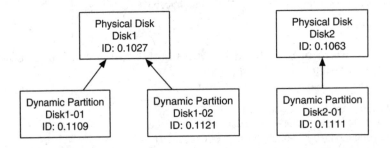

**Figure 7.11**   Relationship between the physical disk and dynamic partition entries in the LDM database.

```
Plex:      Volume1-01 rid=0.1107 update=0.1124
type:      layout=CONCAT
state:     state=ACTIVE
assoc:     vol=0.1105
```

The previous record is a disk-spanning (CONCAT) component entry that describes how the dynamic partitions should be combined to create a logical volume. We can see that it has an ID of 0.1107, which we saw in each of the partition entries. We also see that it is associated with Volume ID 0.1105, which is shown next.

```
Volume:    Volume1 rid=0.1105 update=0.1124 mountname=F:
info:      len=92160 guid=e40794d0-6e3c-4788-af3d-ff49d2ce769d
type:      parttype=7 usetype=gen
state:     state=ACTIVE
policies:  read=SELECT
flags:     writeback
```

Lastly, we see the previous record, which is for a volume entry for the logical volume. Its mounting point is F:\, and its length is 92,160 sectors. We see that it has an ID of

0.1105 and a name of 'Volume1.' The relationship of these records can be seen in Figure 7.12. Note that all disks in the disk group contain the same database entries.

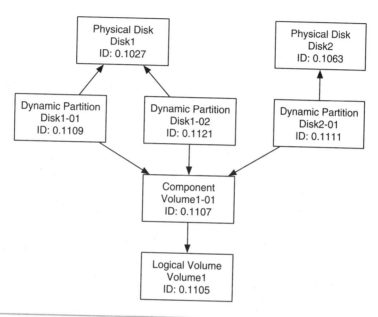

**Figure 7.12** Relationship between the entries in the LDM database. The arrow direction shows which objects have pointers to other objects.

We can see the final layout and organization of the logical volume in Figure 7.13. Notice that the order of the dynamic partitions is not consecutive in the logical volume.

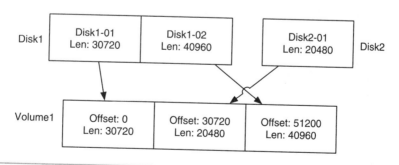

**Figure 7.13** Layout of example LDM disk with two physical disks, three dynamic partitions, and one logical volume.

The final section of the LDM database is the *Transactional Log*, and it is a log of modifications to the LDM. In case of power failure or crash, this is used to put the disk in a safe state.

## Acquisition and Analysis

Analysis of any logical volume is difficult, especially when it is implemented in software, and it is not trivial to recreate the volume in a read-only fashion. As previously mentioned in the "RAID" section, the analysis of the system is easiest when the logical volume is acquired and standard analysis tools are used. However, this is not always possible within Windows because it attempts to mount the disks when it boots. Acquiring a mounted file system can result in a corrupt image, and the mounting may modify data. There is also a risk when moving LDM disk groups between computers. Windows supports only one disk group at a time, and any dynamic disks are added to the local group, if one exists [Microsoft 2003]. Therefore, if dynamic disks from a suspect system are imported into an analysis system that uses dynamic disks, the suspect disks are added to the local disk group, and this requires the OS to write new data to the LDM database.

The Linux kernel comes with support for LDM disk spanning, although it is not always enabled by default. You may need to recompile the kernel if your distribution has not enabled it. If your kernel supports LDM, Linux will read the database and create devices for each of the dynamic partitions in each dynamic disk. For example, if we booted Linux with the two disks from the previous example, we could have had /dev/hdb1, /dev/hdb2, and /dev/hdd1 devices. We would then have to create an /etc/raidtab file to describe the layout so that the MD kernel driver could make a single device for them. If /dev/hdb1 had the first partition, /dev/hdd1 had the second, and /dev/hdb2 had the third, the following would be the raidtab file:

```
raiddev /dev/md0
        raid-level        linear
        nr-raid-disks     3
        nr-spare-disks    0
        persistent-superblock   0
        chunk-size        4k
        device            /dev/hdb1
        raid-disk         0
        device            /dev/hdd1
        raid-disk         1
        device            /dev/hdb2
        raid-disk         2
```

In the case of a 'linear' RAID volume, the chunk-size can be any size, but it must exist. EnCase by Guidance Software and ProDiscover from Technology Pathways can import the individual images from a Windows logical volume and merge them together.

If only disk spanning is used, you can manually extract the partitions and put them together manually from the disk images. We saw the layout details in the dmdiag.exe output, but that tool can only examine the disks from within Windows and needs to have the disks mounted. Therefore, we will use a different tool from Linux. The Linux NTFS group has developed the ldminfo tool (http://linux-ntfs.sourceforge.net/status.html#ldmtools) and it examines the LDM database entries of a Windows dynamic disk and displays them in detail when the --dump flag is given. It can be run on any of the raw devices or disk images in the volume span because all disks contain the same database entries. The output contains all the same detailed info as dmdiag.exe did, but we will only focus on the volume layout information from the example we previously used:

```
# ldminfo --dump disk1.dd
...
VOLUME DEFINITIONS:
Volume1 Size: 0x00016800 (45 MB)
Disk1-01    VolumeOffset: 0x00000000 Offset: 0x00000000 Length: 0x00007800
Disk2-01    VolumeOffset: 0x00007800 Offset: 0x00000000 Length: 0x00005000
Disk1-02    VolumeOffset: 0x0000C800 Offset: 0x00007800 Length: 0x0000A000
```

This output shows us that there are three partitions in the volume from two disks. We can easily re-create the disk because it is using spanning and not splitting. We previously saw from the output of mmls on the disk image that the partition area begins in sector 63. Therefore, we need to add 63 to the disk offset values that we see in the ldminfo output because those values are relative to the start of the partition area. The first partition is extracted by extracting 30,720 sectors (0x7800) from the partition area of the first disk:

```
# dd if=disk1.dd skip=63 count=30720 > span.dd
```

The second part of the disk span is from the first part of the second disk. We will append this data to the end of the data from the first disk. Therefore, we will extract the first 20,480 sectors (0x5000) from the partition area of the second disk:

```
# dd if=disk2.dd skip=63 count=20480 >> span.dd
```

The final part of the disk span comes from the partition area of the first disk. It will be appended to the end of what we extracted from the second disk. It starts in sector 30,720 (0x7800) of the partition area; therefore, it is sector 30,783 relative to the start of the disk, and its length is 40,960 sectors.

```
# dd if=disk1.dd skip=30783 count=40960 >> span.dd
```

We can now process the span.dd image as a normal file system image. If you have LDM support from the kernel, then I would recommend that you try that before doing it by hand. Also note that most third-party support drivers and tools for LDM have not been developed from a detailed specification from Microsoft and, therefore, may not be correct.

## BIBLIOGRAPHY

Lewis, A.J. "The LVM HOWTO." *The Linux Documentation Project*, 2002-2004. http://tldp.org/HOWTO/LVM-HOWTO/.

Microsoft. "Description of Disk Groups in Windows Disk Management." *Microsoft Knowledge Base Article 222189*, November 21, 2003. http://support.microsoft.com/kb/222189.

Microsoft. *Microsoft Windows XP Professional Resource Kit Documentation*, 2004. http://www.microsoft.com/resources/documentation/Windows/XP/all/reskit/en-us/prork_overview.asp.

Ostergaard, Jakob. "The Software-RAID HOWTO." *The Linux Documentation Project*, June 3, 2004. http://www.tldp.org/HOWTO/Software-RAID-HOWTO.html.

Patterson, David A., Garth Gibson, and Randy H. Katz. "A Case for Redundant Arrays of Inexpensive Disks (RAID)." *ACM SIGMOD International Conference on Management of Data*, June 1988.

PC Guide. "Redundant Arrays of Inexpensive Disks." April 17, 2001. http://www.pcguide.com/ref/hdd/perf/raid/index.htm.

Solomon, David, and Mark Russinovich. *Inside Microsoft Windows 2000*. 3rd ed. Redmond: Microsoft Press, 2000.

Sourceforge.net. "LDM Documentation." *Linux NTFS Project*, 2002. http://linux-ntfs.sourceforge.net/ldm/index.html.

# PART III
## FILE SYSTEM ANALYSIS

# File System Analysis

File system analysis examines data in a volume (i.e., a partition or disk) and interprets them as a file system. There are many end results from this process, but examples include listing the files in a directory, recovering deleted content, and viewing the contents of a sector. Recall that analyzing the contents of a file is application-level analysis and is not covered in this book. In this chapter, we look at the general design of file systems and different analysis techniques. This chapter approaches the topic in an abstract fashion and is not limited to how a specific tool analyzes a file system. Instead, we discuss the analysis in general terms. The remaining nine chapters discuss how specific file systems are designed and what is unique about them with respect to digital investigations.

## WHAT IS A FILE SYSTEM?

The motivation behind a file system is fairly simple: computers need a method for the long-term storage and retrieval of data. File systems provide a mechanism for users to store data in a hierarchy of files and directories. A file system consists of structural and user data that are organized such that the computer knows where to find them. In most cases, the file system is independent from any specific computer.

For an analogy, consider a series of filing cabinets in a doctor's office . The fictitious *National Association of Medical Record Filing Procedures* (NAMRFP) could specify that all patient records must be organized into filing cabinets and sorted by the last name of the patient. The tag that is used to identify the record must be typed in English and have the last name followed by the first name. Any person trained in this procedure would be able to file and retrieve patient records at an office that uses the procedure. It doesn't matter if the office has 100 patients and one filing cabinet or 100,000 patients and 25 filing cabinets. All that matters is that the person recognizes what a filing cabinet is, knows how to open it, and knows how to read and create the tags. If that person visited an office that used the *National Association of Medial Record Stacking Procedures* method where all records were stacked in a corner, his filing cabinet training would be useless and he would not be able to find the needed records.

File systems are similar to these record-storing procedures. File systems have specific procedures and structures that can be used to store one file on a floppy disk or tens of thousands of files in a storage array. Each file system instance has a unique size, but its underlying structure allows any computer that supports the type of file system to process it.

Some data needs internal structure and organization inside the file. This is not unlike physical documents needing structure in the form of sections and chapters. The internal structure of a file is application dependent and outside the scope of this book. This book is concerned about the procedures and techniques needed to obtain the data inside of a file or the data that are not allocated to any file.

## DATA CATEGORIES

As we examine each of the different file system types in this part of the book, it will be useful to have a basic reference model so that the different file systems can be more easily compared. Having such a reference model also makes it easier to determine where your evidence may be located. For example, a reference model makes it easier to compare the difference between FAT and Ext3 file systems. For this basic model, we will use five categories: file system, content, metadata, file name, and application. All data in a file system belong to one of the categories based on the role they play in the file system. We will use these categories throughout this book when describing file systems, although some file systems, namely FAT, cannot be applied to this model as easily as others can. The tools in *The Sleuth Kit* (TSK) are based on these same categories.

The *file system* category contains the general file system information. All file systems have a general structure to them, but each instance of a file system is unique because it has a unique size and can be tuned for performance. Data in the file system category may tell you where to find certain data structures and how big a data unit is. You can think of data in this category as a map for this specific file system.

The *content* category contains the data that comprise the actual content of a file, which is the reason we have file systems in the first place. Most of the data in a file system belong to this category, and it is typically organized into a collection of standard-sized containers. Each file system assigns a different name to the containers, such as clusters and blocks, and I will use the general term *data units* until we discuss specific file systems.

The *metadata* category contains the data that describe a file; they are data that describe data. This category contains information, such as where the file content is stored, how big the file is, the times and dates when the file was last read from or written to, and access control information. Note that this category does not contain the content of the file, and it may not contain the name of the file. Examples of data structures in this category include FAT directory entries, *NTFS Master File Table* (MFT) entries, and UFS and Ext3 inode structures.

The *file name* category, or human interface category, contains the data that assign a name to each file. In most file systems, these data are located in the contents of a directory and are a list of file names with the corresponding metadata address. The file name category is similar to a host name in a network. Network devices communicate with each other using IP addresses, which are difficult for people to remember. When a user enters the host name of a remote computer, the local computer must translate the name to an IP address before communication can start.

The *application* category contains data that provide special features. These data are not needed during the process of reading or writing a file and, in many cases, do not need to be included in the file system specification. These data are included in the specification because it may be more efficient to implement them in the file system instead of in a normal file. Examples of data in this category include user quota statistics and file system journals. These data can be useful during an investigation, but because they are not needed to write and read a file, they could be more easily forged than other data.

We can see the relationship between the five categories in Figure 8.1.

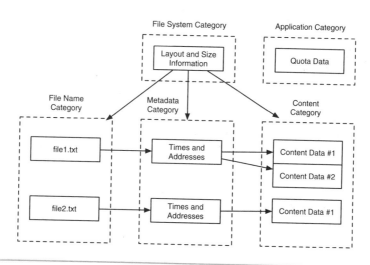

**Figure 8.1**  Interaction between the five data categories.

## ESSENTIAL AND NON-ESSENTIAL DATA

In Chapter 1, "Digital Investigation Foundations," we discussed the difference between essential and non-essential data, and I will quickly review it again. *Essential file system data* are those that are needed to save and retrieve files. Examples of this type of data include the addresses where the file content is stored, the name of a file, and the pointer from a name to a metadata structure. *Non-essential file system data* are those that are there for convenience but not needed for the basic functionality of saving and retrieving files. Access times and permissions are examples of this type of data.

Why is it important to differentiate between essential and non-essential data? It is important because we have to trust the essential data, but we do not have to trust the non-essential data. For example, all file systems have some value that points to where the file content is stored. This value is essential because it needs to be true. If it is false, the user will not be able to read the file. On the other hand, a time value or a User ID is not essential because it does not need to be true. If the time value is never updated, it will not affect the user when she tries to read from or write to the file. Therefore, we should trust the essential data more than the non-essential data because it is required and it is needed for the file system to save and restore files.

Some OSes may require a certain value to be set, but that does not mean it is essential. For example, a very strict (and fictitious) OS might not mount a file system that has any files with a last access time that is set in the future. Another OS may not have a problem with the times and will mount the file system and save data to it. Microsoft Windows requires that all FAT file systems start with a certain set of values even though they are used only when the file system is bootable. Linux, on the other hand, has no requirements for those values.

When viewed this way, it becomes apparent that knowing the OS that wrote to the file system is just as important as knowing the type of file system. When discussing file recovery, it is not enough to ask how to recover a file from a FAT file system. Instead, ask how to recover a file that was deleted in Windows 98 on a FAT file system. Many OSes implement FAT file systems, and each can delete a file using different techniques. For example, most OSes do the minimal amount of work needed to delete a file, but there could be others that erase all data associated with the file. In both cases, the end result is a valid FAT file system.

In this book, we will focus on the essential data. When available, I will describe application-specific, non-essential information. However, it is important for an investigator to verify and test the application-specific behavior in the context of a specific incident.

## ANALYSIS BY CATEGORY

The remainder of this chapter and book use the five data categories to describe analysis techniques. In Chapter 1, we saw that we look for evidence by identifying the properties that it should have and where we expect to find it. Based on where we expect to find the evidence, we can identify the appropriate data category and analysis techniques to search for it. For example, if we are searching for files with the "JPG" extension, we will focus on file name category analysis techniques. If we are searching for a file with a certain value in it, we will use the metadata category analysis techniques because that category contains the data unit addresses.

Many forensic analysis tools integrate analysis techniques from several categories; therefore, the individual descriptions in this book may seem awkward. Each of the techniques is separated to show all steps that are going on "under the hood" of the analysis tool and to show where faults may occur. The techniques presented here are not specific to any analysis tools. For many of the techniques, I have listed the tool from TSK that performs it, and Appendix A, "The Sleuth Kit and Autopsy," can be referred to for more details.

## FILE SYSTEM CATEGORY

The file system category contains the general data that identify how this file system is unique and where other important data are located. In many cases, most of these data are located in a standard data structure in the first sectors of the file system, similar to having a map in the lobby of a building. With this information, the locations of other data, which may vary depending on the size of the file system, can be found.

Analysis of data in the file system category is required for all types of file system analysis because it is during this phase that you will find the location of the data structures in the other categories. Therefore, if any of this data becomes corrupt or is lost, additional analysis is more difficult because you have to find backup copies or guess what the values were. In addition to general layout information, analysis of this category might also show the version of file system, the application that created the file system, the creation date, and the file system label. There is little data in this category that a typical user would be able to set or view without the help of a hex editor. In many cases, the non-layout data in this category is considered non-essential data and may not be accurate.

## ANALYSIS TECHNIQUES

Data in this category are typically single and independent values; therefore, there is not much that can be done with them except to display them to the investigator or use them in a tool. If you are recovering data by hand, the layout information might be useful. If you are trying to determine on which computer a file system was created, a volume ID or version might be useful. The data structures in this category frequently have unused values and storage locations that could be used to hide small amounts of data. A consistency check in this category is to compare the size of the file system with the size of the volume in which it is located. If the volume is larger, the sectors after the file system are called *volume slack* and could be used to hide data.

TSK has a tool called `fsstat` that displays the file system category data for a file system. The amount of information in the output is different for each file system type, as will be shown in the following chapters.

## CONTENT CATEGORY

The content category includes the storage locations that are allocated to files and directories so that they can save data. The data in this category are typically organized into equal sized groups, which I am calling data units even though each file system has a unique name for them, such as cluster or block. A data unit is either in an allocated or unallocated state. There is typically some type of data structure that keeps track of the allocation status of each data unit.

When a new file is created or an existing file is made larger, the OS searches for an unallocated data unit and allocates it to a file. The different search strategies will be discussed in the following "Allocation Strategies" section. When a file is deleted, the data units that were allocated to the file are set to the unallocated state and can be allocated to new files. Most OSes do not wipe the contents of the data unit when it is unallocated, although some "secure delete" tools and OSes provide that ability.

Analysis of the content category is conducted to recover deleted data and conduct low-level searches. There are a lot of data in this category; therefore, it is typically not analyzed by hand. As a reference, if an investigator could examine a 512-byte sector in five seconds, she could examine a 40GB drive in 388 days if she searched for 12 hours per day.

### GENERAL INFORMATION

In this section, we will look at how to address data units, how data units are allocated, and how file systems handle damaged data units.

## Logical File System Address

A sector can have multiple addresses, each from a different perspective. In our discussion of acquisition techniques, we saw that every sector has an address relative to the start of the storage media, which is its physical address. Volume systems create volumes and assign logical volume addresses that are relative to the start of the volume.

File systems use the logical volume addresses but also assign *logical file system addresses* because they group consecutive sectors to form a data unit. In most file systems, every sector in the volume is assigned a logical file system address. An example of a file system that does not assign a logical file system address to every sector is FAT.

Figure 8.2 shows a volume with 17 sectors and their logical volume addresses. Below them are the logical file system addresses. This fictitious file system created data units that were each two sectors, and the file system did not assign addresses until sector 4. This very small file system ends in sector 15, and sector 16 is volume slack.

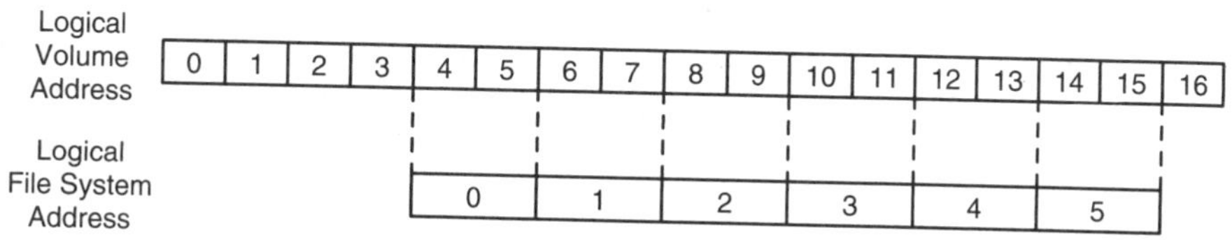

**Figure 8.2**  An example volume where the file system has assigned addresses to sectors in groups of two and has not assigned addresses to some sectors.

## Allocation Strategies

An OS can use different strategies for allocating data units. Typically, an OS allocates consecutive data units, but that is not always possible. When a file does not have consecutive data units, it is called *fragmented*.

A *first available* strategy searches for an available data unit starting with the first data unit in the file system. After a data unit has been allocated using the first available strategy and a second data unit is needed, the search starts again at the beginning of the file system. This type of strategy can easily produce fragmented files because the file is not allocated as a whole. For example, consider a theater that uses a first available strategy to assign seats. If a group of four wanted tickets to a show, the box office would start with the front row and scan for available seats. They may get all four seats together or two people may get seats in front and the other two in the back. If someone returns a ticket while the search is underway, the third person may end up getting a seat closer to the front than the first two people did. In the example shown in Figure 8.3, data unit 1 would be allocated next using a first available strategy. An OS that uses first available overwrites deleted data at the beginning of the file system more quickly than other algorithms will. Therefore, if you encounter a system using this algorithm, you will probably have better luck recovering deleted content from the end of the file system.

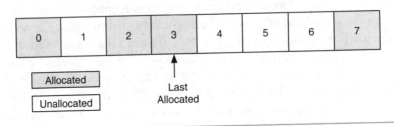

**Figure 8.3**   Example allocation status of 8 data units.

A similar strategy is *next available*, which starts its search with the data unit that was most recently allocated instead of at the beginning. For example, if data unit 3 in Figure 8.3 is allocated, the next search starts at data unit 4 instead of 0. In our theater example, we would start the search from the last seat that was sold instead of starting in the front row. With this algorithm, if a ticket at the front of the theater was returned while the search was underway, it would not be sold until the search reached the last seat. This algorithm is more balanced for data recovery because the data units at the beginning of the file system are not reallocated until the data units at the end have been reallocated.

Another strategy is *best fit*, which searches for consecutive data units that fit the needed amount of data. This works well if it is known how many data units a file will need, but when a file increases in size, the new data units will likely be allocated somewhere else and the file can still become fragmented. If the algorithm cannot find a location for all the data, a first or next available strategy may be used. This is the algorithm that typically occurs when assigning seats in a theater. The empty seats are scanned until enough free consecutive seats can be found for the group. In our Figure 8.3 example, if we had a two-data unit file, it would be allocated to data units 4 and 5 and not split up between 1 and 4.

Each OS can choose an allocation strategy for a file system. Some file systems specify what strategy should be used, but there is no way to enforce it. You should test an implementation of the file system before assuming that it uses the strategy in the specification.

In addition to testing the operating system to determine its allocation strategy, you should also consider the application that creates the content. For example, when updating an existing file some applications open the original file, update it, and save the new data over the original data. Another application might make a second copy of the original file, update the second copy, and then rename the copy so it overwrites the original.

In this case, the file is located in new data units because it is part of a new file. This behavior should not be confused with the allocation strategy of the OS because the OS did not force new data units to be allocated.

### Damaged Data Units

Many file systems have the ability to mark a data unit as damaged. This was needed with older hard disks that did not have the capability to handle errors. The operating system would detect that a data unit was bad and mark it as such so that it would not be allocated to a file. Now, modern hard disks can detect a bad sector and replace it with a spare, so the file system functionality is not needed.

It is easy to hide data using the file system functionality, if it exists. Many consistency-checking tools will not verify a data unit that the file system reports as being damaged is actually damaged. Therefore, a user could manually add a data unit to the damaged list and place data in it. Most acquisition tools report bad sectors, so that report can be compared the damaged list to identify sectors that may have been manually added to hide data.

## ANALYSIS TECHNIQUES

Now that we have looked at the basic concepts of data in the content category, we will look at how to analyze the data. This section covers different analysis techniques that can be used when searching for evidence.

### Data Unit Viewing

Data unit viewing is a technique used when the investigator knows the address where evidence may be located, such as one allocated to a specific file or one that has special meaning. For example, in many FAT32 file systems, sector 3 is not used by the file system and is all zeros, but data could be hidden there, and viewing the contents of sector 3 shows the investigator if there are non-zero data.

The theory behind this type of analysis is simple. The investigator enters the logical file system address of the data unit and a tool calculates the byte or sector address of the data unit. The tool then seeks to that location and reads the data. For example, consider a file system where data unit 0 starts at byte offset 0 and each data unit is 2,048 bytes. The byte offset of data unit 10 is 20,480 bytes, which we can see in Figure 8.4.

There are many tools, such as hex editors and investigation tools, which perform this function. In TSK, the dcat tool allows you to view a specific data unit and displays it in raw or hexadecimal format.

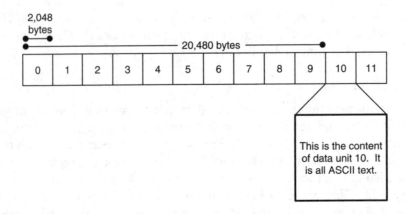

**Figure 8.4**   Graphical representation where we view the contents of data unit 10.

## Logical File System-Level Searching

In the previous technique, we knew *where* evidence could be, but we may not have known *what* the evidence would be. In this technique, we know what content the evidence should have, but we do not know where it is. A logical file system search looks in each data unit for a specific phrase or value. For example, you may want to search for the phrase "forensics" or a specific file header value. We can see this in Figure 8.5 where we are looking at each data unit for the string "forensics."

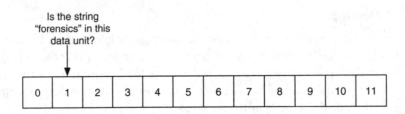

**Figure 8.5**   A logical file system search looks in each data unit for a known value.

This search technique has historically been called a physical search because it used the physical ordering of the sectors, but I do not feel this is accurate. This was accurate when a single disk was being analyzed, but this is not true for systems that use disk spanning and RAID. For those systems, the order of the sectors is not the physical order, and a more precise name should be used.

Unfortunately, files do not always allocate consecutive data units, and if the value you are searching for is located in two non-consecutive data units of a fragmented file, a logical file system search will not find it. We will see in the "Logical File Searching" section that a logical file search will find this value. Many forensic tools offer the capability to do both logical volume and logical file searches. To determine what search techniques your analysis tool uses, you can use some of the keyword search test images at the Digital Forensic Tool Testing (DFTT) site [Carrier 2004] that I maintain.

If we return to the theater analogy from the "Allocation Strategies" section, we may want to search for a specific family. A logical file system search of the theater for the family would start in the front row and examine each group of four consecutive people. If the family did not have consecutive seats, this search would fail. The search could be repeated by searching for only one person in the family, but that would probably result in many false hits from people who look similar.

### Data Unit Allocation Status

If we do not know the exact location of the evidence, but we know that it is unallocated, we can focus our attention there. Some tools can extract all unallocated data units from the file system image to a separate file, and others can restrict their analysis to only the unallocated areas. If you extract only the unallocated data, the output will be a collection of raw data with no file system structure, so you cannot use it in any file system analysis tools.

We can see this in Figure 8.6 where the bitmap for the first 12 data units are shown. A bitmap is a data structure that has a bit for each data unit. If the bit is 1, the data unit is allocated, and if it is 0, it is not. If we were going to extract the unallocated data units, we would extract units 2, 6, 7, and 11.

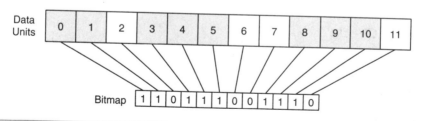

**Figure 8.6**  To extract the unallocated data units, we examine the allocation bitmap and extract the data units that have a given value.

Many digital forensic analysis tools allow you extract the unallocated space of a file system, although the definition of unallocated space may vary. I have observed that some tools consider any data not allocated to a file to be unallocated data, including the data in the file system and metadata categories. Alternatively, some tools recover deleted files and consider the data units of the deleted files to be allocated, even though they are technically unallocated. Do you know what your analysis tool considers unallocated data?

In TSK, you can use the dls tool to extract the unallocated data to a file. After you find interesting data, you might want to know which data unit in the file system it was in, and you can use the dcalc tool to determine that. TSK considers unallocated data to be the data units in the content category that have an allocation status set to unallocated. If there are data units that are used by the file system and do not have an allocation status, they are considered allocated.

### Data Unit Allocation Order

I previously discussed some of the strategies an OS can use when it allocates data units. The strategy that is used is, in general, OS dependent; therefore, it is in the realm of application-level analysis. For example, Windows ME could use a different allocation strategy for a FAT file system than Windows 2000, yet they both still produce a valid FAT file system.

If the relative allocation order of two or more data units is important, you can consider using the allocation strategies of the OS to help determine this. This is very difficult because it requires you to determine the strategy used by the OS, and you will need to examine each of the scenarios that could have caused the data unit's status. This involves application-level information and is out of the scope of this book. This technique is used during event reconstruction, which occurs after we have already recognized the data units as evidence.

### Consistency Checks

Consistency checks are an important analysis technique for every data category. They allow us to determine if the file system is in a suspicious state. One consistency check in the content category uses data from the metadata category and verifies that every allocated data unit has exactly one allocated metadata entry pointing to it. This is done to prevent a user from manually setting the allocation status to a data unit without having a name for the data. Allocated data units that do not have a corresponding metadata structure are called *orphan data units*. We see this in Figure 8.7 where data units 2 and 8 are allocated. Data unit 2 does not have a metadata entry pointing to it; therefore, it is an orphan. Data unit 8 has two metadata entries pointing to it, which is not allowed by most file systems.

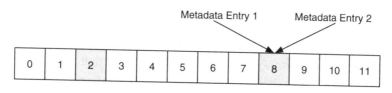

**Figure 8.7** A consistency check should verify that all data units have one and only one metadata entry pointing to them.

Another check examines each of the data units that are listed as damaged. If you have an image of the hard disk and it contains damaged sectors, many of the acquisition tools will fill in the damaged data with zeros. Therefore, any data unit that is in the damaged list should have zeros in it (if your acquisition tool fills in zeros for bad data). Any non-zero data should be examined because it could be data that was hidden by the user.

## WIPING TECHNIQUES

Now that we have discussed how we would analyze data in this category, we will discuss how a user could make your life harder. Most wiping, or "secure delete," tools operate in the content category and write zeros or random data to the data units that a file allocated or to all unused data units.

Secure deletion is becoming more common and a standard feature on some operating systems. Wiping tools that are built into the OS are the most effective at wiping all data. The third-party applications frequently rely on the OS to act in a certain way; therefore, they may not be as effective. For example, many years ago there was a Linux-based tool that wrote zeros to the data unit before it was unallocated, but the OS did not immediately write the zeros to disk. Later, the OS would notice that the data unit had been unallocated, and it did not bother writing the zeros to disk. Similarly, many tools assume that when it writes data to an existing file that the OS will use the same data units. An OS could choose to allocate new data units, and, in that case, the file content will still exist.

Detection of wiping tools in this category can be difficult. Obviously, if all unallocated data units contain zeros or random values, you may suspect a wiping tool. If the tool writes random values or makes copies of other existing data units, detection is virtually impossible without application-level evidence that a tool was used. Of course, if you find a wiping tool on the system, you should check whether it was used and what its last access time was. You may also find temporary copies of the file if each file had to be explicitly wiped.

## METADATA CATEGORY

The metadata category is where the descriptive data reside. Here we can find, for example, the last accessed time and the addresses of the data units that a file has allocated. Few tools explicitly identify metadata analysis; instead, it is typically merged with file name category analysis. We separate them, though, in this book to show where the data are coming from and why some deleted files cannot be recovered.

Many metadata structures are stored in a fixed or dynamic-length table, and each entry has an address. When a file is deleted, the metadata entry is set to the unallocated state, and the OS may wipe some of the values in the entry.

Analysis is conducted in the metadata category to determine more details about a specific file or to search for a file that meets certain requirements. This category tends to have more non-essential data than other categories. For example, the last accessed or written times may not be accurate or the OS may not have enforced the access control settings on a file; therefore, an investigator cannot conclude that a user did or did not have read access to a file. Additional evidence is needed to support the non-essential data in this category.

### GENERAL INFORMATION

In this section, we will look at the basic concepts of the metadata category. We will look at another addressing scheme, slack space, deleted file recovery, compressed files, and encrypted files.

### Logical File Address

We previously looked at how a data unit had a logical file system address. A data unit that is allocated to a file also has a logical file address. A data unit's *logical file address* is relative to the start of the file to which it is allocated. For example, if a file allocated two data units, the first data unit would have a logical file address of 0, and the second would have a logical file address of 1. The name or metadata address for the file is needed to make a unique logical file address. We can see this in Figure 8.8, which expands on a previous example. It shows two files that have allocated five data units. Note that logical file system address 1 is not allocated; therefore, it does not have a logical file address.

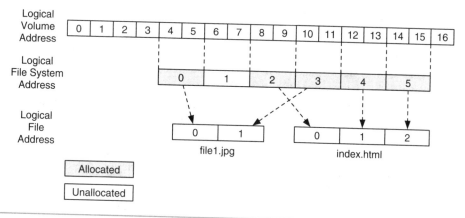

**Figure 8.8**  Two files have allocated five data units, and logical file addresses have been assigned to the data units.

## Slack Space

Slack space is one of the buzzwords of digital forensics that most people have heard at one time or another. Slack space occurs when the size of a file is not a multiple of a data unit size. A file must allocate a full data unit, even if it needs only a small part of it, and the unused bytes in the last data unit are called *slack space*. For example, if a file is 100 bytes, it needs to allocate a full 2,048-byte data unit, and the final 1,948 bytes would be slack space.

Slack space is interesting because computers are lazy. Some of them do not wipe the unused bytes, so the slack space contains data from previous files or from memory. By the design of most computers, there are two interesting areas of slack space. The first area is located in between the end of the file and the end of the sector in which the file ends. The second area is located in the sectors that contain no file content. There are two distinct areas because hard disks are block-based and can be written to in only 512-byte sector-sized chunks. In the previous example, the OS cannot write only 100 bytes to the disk, it must write 512 bytes. Therefore, it needs to pad the 100 bytes with 412 bytes of data. This is similar to shipping an item and having only one size of a box. The smaller the item is, the more packing material will be needed so that the box is full.

The first area of slack space is interesting because the OS determines what to pad the file content with. The obvious method is to fill in the sector with zeros, and that is what most OSes do. This is like filling a box with white packing paper. Some older OSes, namely DOS and early Windows, fill the remainder of the sector with data from memory. This is similar to filling a box with copies of your financial statements. This area of slack space was called RAM slack [NTI 2004], and it is now typically filled with zeros. RAM slack from memory could reveal passwords and other data that was not supposed to be written to disk.

The second area of slack space is the remaining unused sectors in the data unit. This area is interesting because some OSes wipe the sectors and others ignore them. If ignored, the sectors will contain data from the file that previously allocated them.

Consider an NTFS file system with a 2048-byte cluster and 512-byte sectors. Our file is 612 bytes, so it uses the entire first sector and 100 bytes of the second sector in the cluster. The remaining 412 bytes of the second sector are padded with data of the OSes choice. The third and fourth sectors may be wiped with zeros by the OS, or they might not be touched and might keep the data from a deleted file. We can see this in Figure 8.9, where the grayed areas are the file content and the white space is the slack space.

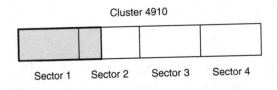

Cluster 4910

Sector 1    Sector 2    Sector 3    Sector 4

**Figure 8.9**    Slack space of a 612-byte file in a 4096-byte cluster.

A common analogy for slack space is VHS videotape [Kruse 2003]. One night you record a 60-minute episode of the latest criminal investigation TV show. Eventually, you get around to watching the show, and then you rewind the tape. Later in the week, you tape a 30-minute TV program. At this point, the tape is "allocated" to the 30-minute TV show, but there are still 30 minutes of the previous show at the end of the tape.

All file systems have slack space because all file systems allocate data in multiple-byte chunks instead of in individual bytes. Slack space is interesting because of the OS and what it writes, not because of the file system. It is important to note that slack space is considered allocated data. It may contain data from a previously deleted file, but it is currently allocated to a file. If you extract the unallocated data from a file system, it should not include the slack space of a file.

## Metadata-based File Recovery

In some cases, you might want to search for evidence in deleted files. There are two major methods for recovering deleted files: metadata-based and application-based. We will discuss application-based analysis techniques at the end of this chapter and will discuss metadata-based here. Metadata-based recovery works when metadata from the deleted file still exists. If the metadata was wiped or if the metadata structure was reallocated to a new file, you will need to rely on application-based techniques.

After you find the metadata structure for the file, recovery is easy. It is no different from reading the contents of an allocated file. For example, Figure 8.10(A) shows an example where the unallocated metadata entry still has its data unit addresses, and we can easily read the contents. On the other hand, Figure 8.10(B) shows an example where the OS has cleared the addresses when the file was deleted. We will discuss specific recovery techniques in the following file system chapters.

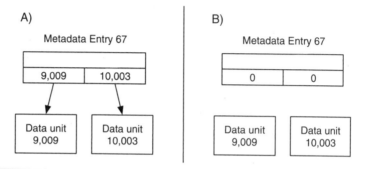

**Figure 8.10**   Two scenarios where in (A) the data unit pointers are not wiped when the entry is unallocated and in (B) they are wiped.

We need to be careful when doing metadata-based recovery because the metadata structures and the data units can become out of sync because the data units are allocated to new files. Consider the example given in Figure 8.10. The contents of data unit 9,009 would be overwritten if they were allocated by metadata entry 70, even though entry 67 still points to them. When we try to recover the contents of metadata 67, we will get data from the file using metadata entry 70.

This is similar to linking a person with a hotel room in which they stayed. After the person checks out, there may still be a record that he stayed in room 427, but the state of the room from that point on may have nothing to do with him.

When recovering deleted files, it can be difficult to detect when a data unit has been reallocated. Let's consider a sequence of allocations and deletions to reinforce this point. Metadata entry 100 allocates data unit 1,000 and saves data to it. The file for entry 100 is then deleted, and both entry 100 and data unit 1,000 are unallocated. A new file is created in metadata entry 200, and it reallocates data unit 1,000. Later, that file is also deleted. If we analyzed this system, we would find two unallocated metadata entries that have the same data unit address. We can see this in Figure 8.11(A).

We need to determine which of the entries allocated the file most recently. One method of doing this is to use the time information from each entry (or other external data), but we may not be able to trust it. Another method is to use the file type, if the metadata records that information. For example, metadata entry 200 could have been for a directory, so we could analyze the content of data unit 1,000 to see if it has the format of a directory.

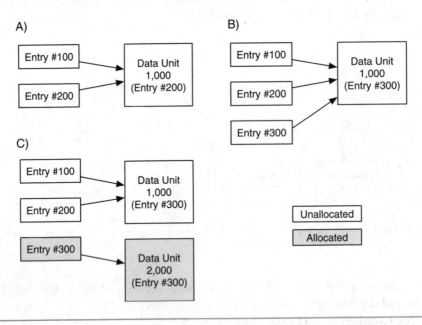

**Figure 8.11**   The sequence of states where files are allocated and deleted and in (C) it is not clear from where the data in data unit 1,000 came.

Even if we can determine that entry 200 allocated the data unit after entry 100, we do not know if entry 200 was the last entry to allocate it. To show this, consider entry 300 allocating data unit 1,000 after it was unallocated by entry 200. That file is then deleted, and we see the result in Figure 8.11(B), where there are three unallocated entries that have the same data unit address.

Next, a new file was created and entry 300 was reallocated for it with a new data unit, data unit 2,000. If we analyzed the system in this state, we would not find any evidence that entry 300 allocated data unit 1,000, even though the content in the data unit is from entry 300. We would only find evidence that entries 100 and 200 allocated it. This is shown in Figure 8.11(C).

The point of this example is that even if an unallocated metadata structure still contains the data unit addresses, it is very difficult to determine if the content in the data unit corresponds to that file or a file that was created after the metadata structure was unallocated. You can verify that a recovery was accurate by trying to open it up in the application that you think created it. If a new file allocated one of the data units in the deleted file and wrote data to it, the internal structure of the file may be corrupt and a viewer cannot open it.

Many tools offer some form of file recovery. There is unfortunately very little published in terms of the procedures used to perform recovery when metadata is missing, so you should test and compare your tools. There are some recovery test images on the *Digital Forensic Tool Testing* (DFTT) site to help you with this.

### Compressed and Sparse Files

Some file systems allow data to be stored in a compressed format so that they occupy fewer data units on the disk. For files, compression can occur in at least three levels. At the highest level is when data inside a file format are compressed. A JPEG file is an example of this where the data that stores the image information are compressed, but the file header is not. The next level is when an external program compresses an entire file and creates a new file.[1] The compressed file must be uncompressed to another file before it can be used.

The last and lowest level of compression is when the file system compresses the data. In this case, an application that writes the file does not know that the file is being compressed. There are two basic compression techniques used by file systems. The most intuitive technique is to use the same compression techniques that are used on files and apply them to the file's data units. The second technique is to not allocate a physical data unit if it is going to be filled with all zeros. Files that skip data units filled with zeros are called *sparse files*, and an example can be seen in Figure 8.12. There are several ways that this can be implemented, for example, the *Unix File System* (UFS) writes a 0 to the field that usually stores the address of a block. No file can allocate block 0, so the OS knows that this means a block of all 0s.

Compressed files can present a challenge for an investigation because the investigation tool must support the compression algorithm. Further, some forms of keyword searching and file recovery are ineffective because they examine the compressed data instead of the uncompressed data.

---

1. Examples of external compression programs include WinZip, www.winzip.com, and gzip, http://www.gnu.org/software/gzip/gzip.html.

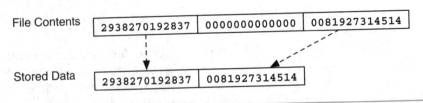

**Figure 8.12**  A file stored in a sparse format where the data unit of zeros is not written.

## Encrypted Files

File content can be stored in an encrypted form to protect it against unauthorized access. Encryption can be applied by the application that creates the file, by an external application that reads an unencrypted file and creates an encrypted file,[2] or by the OS when it creates the file. Before a file is written to disk, the OS encrypts the file and saves the cipher text to the data units. The non-content data, such as the file name and last access time, are typically not encrypted. The application that wrote the data does not know the file is encrypted on the disk. Another method of encrypting file content is to encrypt an entire volume.[3] In this case, all data in the file system are encrypted and not only the content. In general, the volume that contains the OS is not entirely encrypted.

Encrypted data can present a challenge to an investigator because most of the files are inaccessible if she does not know the encryption key or password. It is even worse if the encryption technique is not known. Some tools exist to guess every key or password combination, called a brute force attack, but those are not useful if the algorithm is not known. If only select files and directories were being encrypted, copies of the unencrypted data may be found in temporary files or in unallocated space [Casey 2002; Wolfe 2004].

## ANALYSIS TECHNIQUES

We now look at how to analyze data in the metadata category. We will use the metadata to view file contents, search for values, and locate deleted files.

---

2. Common examples of this include PGP, www.pgp.com, and GPG, www.gpg.org.

3. Examples of this include PGP Disk, www.pgp.com, Macintosh encrypted disk images, www.apple.com, and Linux AES encrypted loopback images.

## Metadata Lookup

In many cases, we analyze metadata because we found the name of a file that points to a specific metadata structure and we want to learn more about the file. We, therefore, need to locate the metadata and process its data structure. For example, if we are looking through the directory contents and find a file named "badstuff.txt," we might want to know what its contents are and when it was created. Most tools automatically perform this lookup when listing the file names in a directory and allow you to sort the output based on the metadata values.

The exact procedures for this technique are file system-dependent because the metadata could be located in various places in the file system. In TSK, the istat tool shows you the values from the metadata data structure. We see this in Figure 8.13, where our sample file system has metadata structures located in data unit 371. Our tool reads the data unit and shows the contents of two metadata entries. One of the entries is a deleted file and the other is an allocated directory.

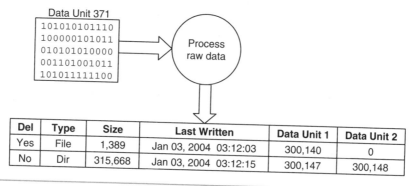

| Del | Type | Size | Last Written | Data Unit 1 | Data Unit 2 |
|-----|------|------|--------------|-------------|-------------|
| Yes | File | 1,389 | Jan 03, 2004  03:12:03 | 300,140 | 0 |
| No | Dir | 315,668 | Jan 03, 2004  03:12:15 | 300,147 | 300,148 |

**Figure 8.13**  Process for viewing the contents of a metadata entry.

## Logical File Viewing

After we look up the metadata for a file, we can view the file contents by reading the data units allocated to the file. We do this when we are searching for evidence in the content of a file. For example, after we have determined the data unit addresses for our "badstuff.dat" file, now we want to look at the actual contents.

This process occurs in both the metadata and content categories. We use the metadata lookup technique to find the data units allocated to the file and then use the content-viewing technique to find the actual content. We can see this in Figure 8.14 where the data units allocated to metadata entries 1 and 2 are listed. Many graphical tools combine this procedure with listing file names. When you select a file, the tool will lookup the data units listed in the file's metadata.

During this process, we need to keep slack space in mind because the file may not be using the entire final data unit. We can calculate how much of the final data is being used by dividing the size of the file by the size of each data unit.

In TSK, the icat tool allows you to view the contents of the data units that are allocated to a metadata structure. If the -s flag is given, the slack space is shown and the -r flag attempts to recover deleted files.

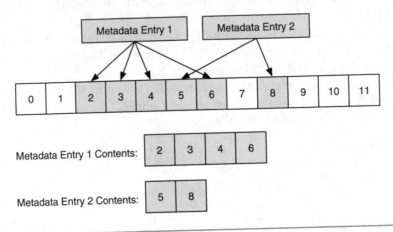

**Figure 8.14**   We can combine the information from the metadata entries and the data units to view the file content.

## Logical File Searching

The previous technique assumed that you had a specific file and wanted to look at its contents. Many times, this is not the case, and we are trying to find a file based on its content. For example, we want all files with the term "forensics" in it. That is when we use a logical file search. This search uses the same techniques we saw for the logical file viewing technique, but we search the data for a specific value instead of viewing it.

This process may sound very similar to the logical file system search. It is, except that now we are searching the data units in the order that they are used by files and not by their order in the volume. We can see this in Figure 8.15 where we have two metadata entries and the data units that they have allocated. In this case, we search data units 2, 3, 4, and 6 as a set. The benefit of this search over a logical file system search is that values that cross-fragmented data units or sectors will be found. For example, in this case we are looking for the term "forensics," and it starts in data unit 4 and ends in data unit 6. We would not find it in the previous logical file system search because it is not contained in consecutive data units. A variation of this search is to search for a file with a specific MD5 or SHA-1 cryptographic hash.

Keep in mind that only allocated data units have logical file addresses. Therefore, you should conduct a logical volume search of the unallocated data units for the same value. For example, a logical file search of the setup in Figure 8.15 would not have looked at data units 0 and 1, so we should do a second search that includes 0, 1, 7, 9, 10, 11, and so on.

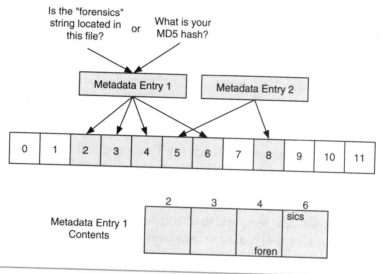

**Figure 8.15**   A logical file search looks into the data units allocated to a metadata entry.

It is important to know whether your analysis tool includes the slack space of a file in a logical file search because some do and some do not. You can use the keyword search test images on DFTT to determine whether your favorite tool includes the slack space.

## Unallocated Metadata Analysis

If you are searching for deleted content, you should not limit yourself to only the deleted file names that are shown in a directory listing. We will see some examples in the "File Name Category" section, but it is possible for the name of a deleted file to be reused before the metadata structure is. Therefore, your evidence could be sitting in an unallocated metadata entry and you cannot see it because it no longer has a name. Most analysis tools will list the unallocated entries for you to search or view. In TSK, the i1s tool can list the unallocated data structures.

## Metadata Attribute Searching and Sorting

It is also common to search for files based on one of their metadata values. For example, maybe you have an *Intrusion Detection System* (IDS) alert and want to find all files that were created within a two-minute window around the time of the alert. Or, maybe you are investigating a user and want to find all files to which he can write. In general, we may need to search for a metadata value at some point during an investigation. I will look at some of the examples in this section.

File times can be easily changed on any system, but they can also provide many clues. For example, if we have a hypothesis that an attacker gained access to the computer at 8:13 p.m. and installed attack tools, we can test the hypothesis by searching for all files created between time 8:13 p.m. and 8:23 p.m. If we do not find any files of interest in that time span, but we do find some attack tools that were created at a different time, the times are incorrect, our hypothesis is incorrect, or both.

Temporal data also can be used when you are faced with a computer that you know little about. The temporal data show what files were recently accessed and created. That information can give you hints about how the computer was used.

Some tools create a timeline of the file activity. In many timelines, each file has as many entries in the timeline as it has temporal values. For example, if it has a last accessed, last written, and last modified entry, it will have three entries in the timeline. The first entry in the timeline is the file with the oldest temporal data, and the last entry is the file with the most recent temporal data. You can scan through it for evidence of events. In TSK, the `mactime` tool is used to make timelines of file activity. An example of the `mactime` output for the `C:\Windows` directory is shown here:

```
Wed Aug 11 2004 19:31:58    34528 .a. /system32/ntio804.sys
                            35392 .a. /system32/ntio412.sys

[REMOVED]
Wed Aug 11 2004 19:33:27     2048 mac /bootstat.dat
                            1024 mac /system32/config/default.LOG
                            1024 mac /system32/config/software.LOG
Wed Aug 11 2004 19:33:28   262144 ma. /system32/config/SECURITY
                          262144 ma. /system32/config/default
```

In the previous output, we can see the file activity at each second. The first column has the date stamp, the second column is the file size, and the third column shows if this entry is for a content modification (m-time), content access (a-time), or metadata change (c-time). The last column gives the file name and the actual output contains much more information, but it is too wide for the book.

Note that you should understand how a file system stores its time stamps before trying to correlate file times and log entries from multiple computers. Some time stamps are stored in UTC, which means that you will need to know the time zone offset where the computer was located to determine the actual time value. For example, if I access a file at 2:00 p.m. in Boston, MA, the OS will record that I accessed it at 7:00 p.m. UTC because Boston is five hours behind UTC. When an investigator analyzes the file, they need to convert the 7:00 p.m. time to the actual local time. Other file systems store the time with respect to the local time zone and would store 2:00 p.m. in the previous example. Daylight savings also introduces problems with some tools.

You might also want to search for files to which a given user had write access. This shows which files a suspect could have created, if we assume that the OS enforced the permissions and the suspect did not have administrator rights. You also can search for the owner ID, if it exists. These can be used when you are investigating a specific user.

If we previously conducted a logical file system search and found interesting data in one of the data units, we might want to search the metadata entries for the data unit address. This might show which file allocated the data unit, and we could then find the other data units that are part of the same file. An example of this can be found in Figure 8.16 where we have found evidence in data unit 34. We search the metadata and find that structure 107 has allocated it, as well as data units 33 and 36. If the OS does not wipe the address values when a file is deleted, then this process also can identify unallocated metadata structure. The ifind tool in TSK will do this for you.

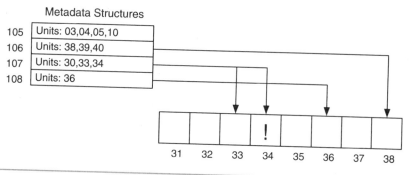

**Figure 8.16**   It can be useful to search the metadata structures to find one that has allocated a given data unit.

## Data Structure Allocation Order

If you need to know the relative allocation times of two entries, you may be able to use the allocation strategy of the OS to determine it. This is very OS dependent and difficult. Metadata entries are typically allocated using a first available or next available strategy. A full discussion of this analysis technique is out of the scope of this book because it is application dependent.

## Consistency Checks

A consistency check with the metadata may reveal attempts to hide data or may reveal that the file system image has some internal errors that will prevent you from seeing accurate information. The only data that we can draw conclusions about in a consistency check is the essential data, which includes the data unit addresses, the size, and the allocation status of each metadata entry.

One check that can be performed is to examine each allocated entry and verify that the data units allocated to it are also allocated. It should be verified that the number of data units allocated is consistent with the size of the file. Most file systems do not allocate more data units than are needed. In the "Content Category Consistency Check" section, we discussed verifying that every allocated data unit was pointed to by exactly one allocated metadata entry.

You also should verify that entries for special types of files do not have data units allocated to them. For example, some file systems can have special files called sockets that are used by processes to communicate with each other, and they do not allocate data units.

Another consistency check uses information from the file name category of data and verifies that every allocated directory entry has an allocated name that points to it. Checks also can be performed on the ranges of dates or other non-essential data, but a more precise check cannot generally be applied.

## Wiping Techniques

Metadata can be wiped when a file is deleted to make it more difficult to recover the files. The times, size, and data unit addresses can be wiped with zeros or random data. An investigator may be able to detect wiping by finding a zeroed or otherwise invalid entry in between two valid entries. A more intelligent wiping tool would fill the values in with valid data that has no correlation to the original file. A more extreme version of a metadata wiping tool would shift the remaining entries so that there would be no unused entry. This, however, would be very time intensive.

# FILE NAME CATEGORY

The file name category includes the names of files, and it allows the user to refer to a file by its name instead of its metadata address. At its core, this category of data includes only a file's name and its metadata address. Some file systems may also include file type information or temporal information, but that is not standard.

An important part of file name analysis is to determine where the root directory is located because we need it to find a file when its full path is given. The root directory is the base directory. For example, in Windows C:\ is the root directory of the C: drive. Each file system has its own way of defining the location of the root directory.

## GENERAL INFORMATION

In this section, we look at the general concepts of the file name category. The file name category is relatively simple and we need to look only at name-based file recovery.

### File Name-based File Recovery

We saw in the "Metadata Category" section that deleted files can be recovered using their metadata. With file name-based recovery, we use a deleted file name and its corresponding metadata address to recover the file content using metadata-based recovery. In other words, the hard stuff is done at the metadata layer, and all we are doing in this layer is identifying the metadata entries on which to focus.

We can see this in Figure 8.17 where we have two file names and three metadata entries. The favorites.txt file is deleted, and its name points to an unallocated metadata entry. We can try to recover its contents using the metadata-based recovery techniques. Note that the content from metadata entry 2 also can be recovered, but it no longer has a name. This section covers some of the issues associated with recovering files based on their names.

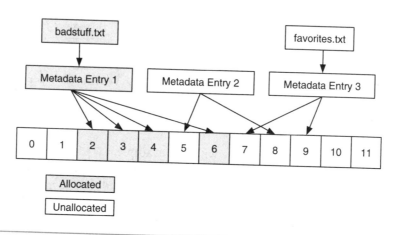

**Figure 8.17**  We can recover files based on their unallocated name, but we still rely on metadata-based recovery techniques.

In the "Metadata-based Recovery" section, I gave several examples of how recovery was complicated because the data units were reallocated before the metadata was and they became out of sync. Now I am going to expand on those examples to show how file names and metadata can become out of sync.

Consider a file that had a file name structure with the name `file1.dat` in it and it pointed to metadata entry 100, which is shown in Figure 8.18(A). That file was deleted and both the file name and metadata structures were unallocated, but the pointer in the file name data structure was not wiped. A new file named `file2.dat` was created in a new file name structure, and it reallocated metadata entry 100 as shown in Figure 8.18(B). Later, the `file2.dat` was deleted and both the file name and metadata structures were unallocated as shown in Figure 8.18(C). If we were to examine the system in this state, we would find two unallocated file names pointing to the same metadata entry. We would not know if the content pointed to by metadata entry 100 was for `file1.dat` or `file2.dat`.

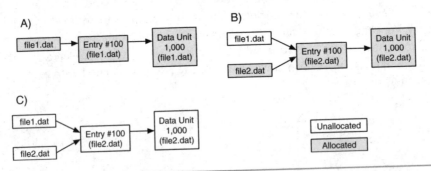

**Figure 8.18**   The sequence of states after file allocation and deletion where in (C) there are two deleted file names that point to the same metadata structure, and it is unknown to which the content corresponds.

To add more confusion, let's continue with this example. `file3.dat` is created in a new name structure, a new metadata entry 200, and data unit 1,000 from the previous example. This is shown in Figure 8.19(A). `file3.dat` is deleted and the file name structure is reallocated to the `file4.dat` file (which we do not care about). Next, the `file5.dat` file is created and it reallocates metadata entry 100 and data unit 1,000, as shown in Figure 8.19(C). `file5.dat`, is also deleted. Finally, `file6.dat` is created and it reallocates the same file name entry as `file5.dat`, and it uses a new metadata entry 300 and new data unit 2,000, which is shown in Figure 8.19(C).

Now let's assume that we are investigating the system in this state. We are faced with the following problems:

- Data unit 1,000 has two metadata entries pointing to it, and we aren't sure which one was the last one or if there were other metadata entries that pointed to it at one time that have since been reallocated.
- Metadata entry 100 has two file names pointing to it and we aren't sure which one was the last one or if there were other names that were pointing to it that have since been reallocated. In this case, file5.dat was the last to allocate it, but it no longer exists.
- Metadata entry 200 has no file names pointing to it, so we don't know the name of any files that allocated it.

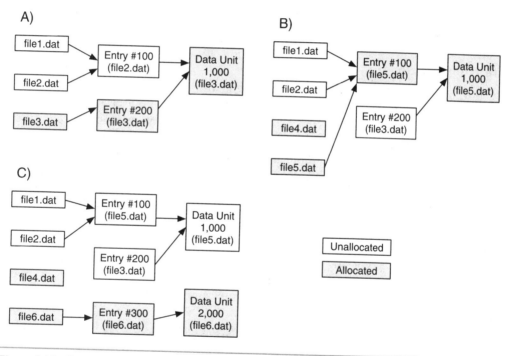

**Figure 8.19**   The sequence of states where files are allocated and deleted and in (C) there are several pointers that are out of sync.

There are several ways that these problems affect the investigator. Consider an analysis tool that lists the files in a directory and lists the associated time values next to the name. The time information and content for file1.dat and file2.dat will be incorrect because the data actually corresponds to the file5.dat file, for which the name no longer exists. The values associated with metadata entry 200 will not be seen from the file listings because there is no file name associated with it. This type of situation illustrates why I have separated the file name and metadata categories in this discussion because it can be misleading to think they are more closely linked.

In summary, when examining deleted files from the file name perspective, keep in mind that the metadata and data units could have been reallocated to a new file. Also remember that you will need to examine the unallocated metadata structures to find ones that no longer have names pointing to them.

## ANALYSIS TECHNIQUES

This section looks at the analysis techniques that can be performed with data from the file name category.

### File Name Listing

The purpose of the file name category is to assign names to files; therefore, it should not be surprising that one of the most common investigation techniques is to list the names of the files and directories. We do this when we are searching for evidence based on the name, path, or extension of a file. After a file has been recognized, we can use its metadata address to get more information. Variations on this technique will sort the files based on a file extensions so that files of the same reported type can be grouped.

Many file systems do not clear the file name of a deleted file, so deleted file names can also be shown in the listing. In some cases, though, the metadata address is cleared when a file is deleted, and you will not be able to obtain more information.

The basic theory behind this technique is to first locate the root directory of the file system. This process is typically the same as we previously saw for the logical file viewing technique in the "Metadata Category" section. The layout of the root directory is stored in a metadata entry, and we need to locate the entry and the data units that the directory has allocated.

After we locate the directory contents, we process them and obtain a list of files and corresponding metadata addresses. If a user wants to view the contents of a file that is listed, then we can use the logical file viewing technique using the metadata address listed. If a user wants to list the contents of a different directory, we load and process the contents of the directory. In either case, this process is based on logical file viewing.

Most analysis tools offer this technique, and many merge the data from the file name category with the data from the metadata category so that you can also see, for example, the dates and times associated with the file name in one view. Figure 8.20 shows an example of this analysis process where we process data unit 401 and find two names. We are interested in the `favorites.txt` file and notice that its metadata is in entry 3. Our file system stores that metadata structure in data unit 200, so we process the relevant data from that data unit and get the size and content addresses for the file.

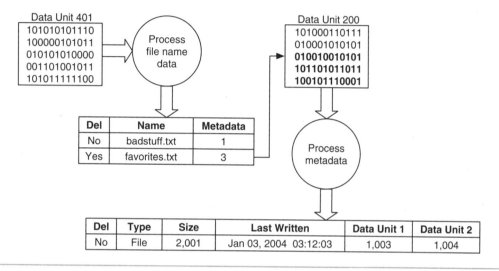

**Figure 8.20** We view file names by processing a data unit and listing the names and sometimes the metadata associated with it.

Most tools offer this analysis capability. In TSK, the `fls` tool lists the allocated and deleted file names.

### File Name Searching

Listing the file names works well if we know for what file we are looking, but that is not always the case. If we don't know the full file name, we can search for the part that we do know. For example, we may know its extension, or we may know its file name but not its full path. A search will show a series of files that meet the search pattern. In Figure 8.20, if we did a name search for `.txt`, the tool would examine each entry and report both `badstuff.txt` and `favorites.txt`. Note that searching by extension does not necessarily return files of a given type because the extension may have been changed to hide the file. Application-level analysis techniques that rely on the file structure can be used to find all files of a given type.

The process required to search for a name is similar to what we saw for file name listing. We load and process the contents of a directory. We compare each entry in the directory with the target pattern. When we find a directory, we might search it as well if we are doing a recursive search.

Another search in this category is to search for the name of the file that has allocated a given metadata entry. This is needed when you find evidence in a data unit and then search for the metadata structure that allocated it. After you find the metadata structure, you need to search the file names for the full name of the file that allocated the evidence. The ffind tool in TSK will do this.

### Data Structure Allocation Order

As we already discussed with content and metadata, the allocation order of file name structures can be used to find the relative creation time of two names. As was previously stated, this is OS dependent and out of the scope of this book.

### Consistency Checks

Consistency checks for the file name data include verifying that all allocated names point to allocated metadata structures. It is valid for some file systems to have multiple file names for the same file, and many of them implement this functionality by having more than one file name entry with the same metadata address.

## WIPING TECHNIQUES

A wiping tool in this category clears the name and metadata address from the structure. One wiping technique might write over the values in the file name structure, so the analysis will show that an entry existed but the data are no longer valid. For example, the file name setuplog.txt could be replaced with abcdefgh.123. With some OSes, this is difficult because the OS will place the new name at the end of a list, using a next available strategy.

Another technique for wiping file names is to reorganize the list of names so that one of the existing file names overwrites the deleted file name. This is much more complex than the first method and much more effective as a hiding technique because the investigator may never know that anything is out of the ordinary in this directory.

# APPLICATION CATEGORY

Some file systems contain data that belongs in the application category. These data are not essential to the file system, and they typically exist as special file system data instead of inside a normal file because it is more efficient. This section covers one of the most common application category features, which is called *journaling*.

Technically, any file that an OS or an application creates could be designed as a feature in a file system. For example, Acme Software could decide that its OS would be faster if an area of the file system were reserved for an address book. Instead of saving names and addresses in a file, they would be saved to a special section of the volume. This might cause a performance improvement, but it is not essential for the file system.

## FILE SYSTEM JOURNALS

As any computer user knows, it is not uncommon for a computer to halt and crash. If the OS was writing data to the disk or if it was waiting to write some data to disk when the crash occurred, the file system could be in an inconsistent state. There could be an allocated metadata structure with allocated data units, but no pointers between them and no file name pointing to the metadata structure.

To find the inconsistencies, an OS runs a program that scans the file system and looks for missing pointers and other signs of corruption. This can take a very long time for large file systems. To make the scanning program's job easier, some file systems implement a journal. Before any metadata changes are made to the file system, an entry is made in the journal that describes the changes that will occur. After the changes are made, another entry is made in the journal to show that the changes occurred. If the system crashes, the scanning program reads the journal and locates the entries that were not completed. The program then either completes the changes or rolls them back to the original state.

Many file systems now support journaling because it saves time when booting large systems. The journal is in the application category because it is not needed for the file system to operate. It exists to make the consistency checking faster.

File system journals may turn out to be useful in investigations, although to date they have not been fully utilized. A journal shows which file system events recently occurred, and this could help with event reconstruction of a recent incident. Most forensic tools do not process the contents of a file system journal. TSK has tools called `jls` and `jcat` that list the contents of some journals.

## APPLICATION-LEVEL SEARCH TECHNIQUES

I said in the beginning of this book that I was going to focus primarily on the volume and file system layers of the analysis model. This is one of the sections where I will move into the application layer and discuss a couple of techniques that can be used to recover deleted files and to organize allocated files for analysis. These are file system-independent; therefore, they will not be discussed again in the subsequent chapters.

Both of these techniques rely on the fact that many files have structure to them, including a signature value that is unique to that type of file. The signature can be used to determine the type of an unknown file. The `file` command comes with many Unix systems and has a database of signatures that it uses to identify the structure of an unknown file (`ftp://ftp.astron.com/pub/file/`).

## APPLICATION-BASED FILE RECOVERY (DATA CARVING)

Data carving is a process where a chunk of data is searched for signatures that correspond to the start and end of known file types. The result of this analysis process is a collection of files that contain one of the signatures. This is commonly performed on the unallocated space of a file system and allows the investigator to recover files that have no metadata structures pointing to them. For example, a JPEG picture has standard header and footer values. An investigator may want to recover deleted pictures, so she would extract the unallocated space and run a carving tool that looked for the JPEG header and extract the data in between the header and footer.

An example tool that performs this is `foremost`, (`http://foremost.sourceforge.net`) which was developed by Special Agents Kris Kendall and Jesse Kornblum of the United States Air Force Office of Special Investigations. `foremost` analyzes a raw file system or disk image based on the contents of a configuration file, which has an entry for each signature. The signature contains the known header value, the maximum size of the file, whether the header value is case sensitive, the typical extension of the file type, and an optional footer value. An example can be seen here for a JPEG:

```
jpg      y      200000  \xff\xd8        \xff\xd9
```

This shows that the typical extension is 'jpg,' the header and footer are case sensitive, the header is 0xffd8, and the footer is 0xffd9. The maximum size of the file is 200,000 bytes, and if the footer is not found after reading this amount of data, the carving will stop for that file. In Figure 8.21 we can see an example set of data where the JPEG header is found in the first two bytes of sector 902 and the footer value is found in the middle of sector 905. The contents of sectors 902, 903, 904, and the beginning of sector 905 would be extracted as a JPEG picture.

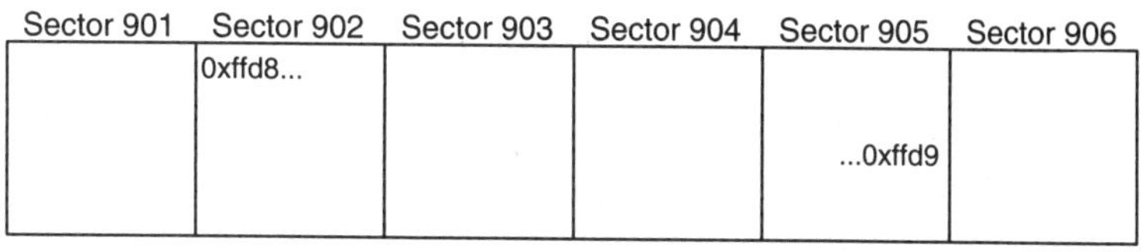

| Sector 901 | Sector 902 | Sector 903 | Sector 904 | Sector 905 | Sector 906 |
|---|---|---|---|---|---|
|  | 0xffd8... |  |  |  |  |
|  |  |  |  | ...0xffd9 |  |

**Figure 8.21**    Blocks of raw data that can be carved to find a JPEG picture in sectors 902 to 905.

A similar tool is `lazarus` (available in The Coroner's Toolkit at `http://www.porcupine.org/forensics/tct.html`) by Dan Farmer, which examines each sector in a raw image and executes the `file` command on it. Groups of consecutive sectors that have the same type are created. The end result is a list with an entry for each sector and its type. This is basically a method of sorting the data units by using their content. This is an interesting concept, but the implementation is in Perl and can be slow.

## FILE TYPE SORTING

File type can also be used to organize the files in a file system. If the investigation is looking for a specific type of data, an investigator can sort the files based on their content structure. An example technique would be to execute the `file` command on each file and group similar file types together. This would group all pictures together and all executables together. Many forensics tools have this feature, but it is not always clear if they are sorting based on file name extension or by file signature. The `sorter` tool in TSK sorts files based on their file signature.

## SPECIFIC FILE SYSTEMS

The remaining chapters in this book will examine how FAT, NTFS, Ext2/Ext3, and UFS store data and will apply the five categories to them. For latter reference, Table 8.1 contains the names of the data structures in each data category for the file systems in this book.

**Table 8.1**   The data structures in each data category for the file systems in this book.

| | File System | Content | Metadata | File Name | Application |
|---|---|---|---|---|---|
| ExtX | Superblock, group descriptor | Blocks, block bitmap | Inodes, inode bitmap, extended attributes | Directory entries | Journal |
| FAT | Boot sector, FSINFO | Clusters, FAT | Directory entries, FAT | Directory entries | N/A |
| NTFS | $Boot, $Volume, $AttrDef | Clusters, $Bitmap | $MFT, $MFTMirr, $STANDARD_ INFORMATION, $DATA, $ATTRIBUTE_ LIST, $SECURITY_ DESCRIPTOR | $FILE_NAME, $IDX_ROOT, $IDX_ ALLLOCATION, $BITMAP | Disk Quota, Journal, Change Journal |
| UFS | Superblock, group descriptor | Blocks, fragments, block bitmap, fragment bitmap | Inodes, inode bitmap, extended attributes | Directory entries | N/A |

There are other file systems not included in this book, but which you may encounter. HFS+ is the default file system of Apple computers. Apple has published the data structures and details of the file system [Apple 2004]. ReiserFS is one of the Linux file systems, and it is the default file system on some distributions, such as SUSE [Reiser 2003]. The standard ReiserFS documents do not provide much data structure details, but Florian Bucholz [2003] and Gerson Kurz [2003] have documented them. The Journaled File System (JFS) for Linux is from IBM, and it is another file system that is used by Linux systems. Note that this is different from the JFS file system that IBM has developed for its AIX systems. IBM has documented the file system layout and structure [IBM 2004].

## SUMMARY

File system analysis is used to produce most of the evidence in current digital investigations. In this chapter, we introduced categories of data in a file system so that we can have a consistent framework when discussing specific file systems. We also discussed analysis techniques for each category of data (in a rather academic way). Table 8.2 provides a summary of the analysis techniques that can be used based on what type of data you are search for.

**Table 8.2**  The search methods and locations, depending on what evidence you are looking for.

| Analysis Needs | Data Category | Search Technique |
|---|---|---|
| A file based on its name, extension, or directory | File name | File name search or listing directory contents |
| An allocated or unallocated file based on its time values | File name and metadata | Metadata attribute searching |
| An allocated file based on a value in its content | File name (using metadata and content) | Logical file search |
| An allocated file based on its SHA-1 hash value | File name (using metadata and content) | Logical file search with hashes |
| An allocated file or an unallocated data unit based on a value in its content | File name (using metadata and content) | Logical file search with metadata-based file recovery and logical file system search |
| An unallocated file based on its application type | Application and content | Application-based file recovery (data carving) of unallocated data units |
| Unallocated data based on its content (and not its application type) | Content | Logical file system search |

# BIBLIOGRAPHY

Apple. "Technical Note TN1150—HFS Plus Volume Format." March 2004. `http://developer.apple.com/technotes/tn/tn1150.html`.

Buchholz, Florian. "The Structure of the Reiser File System." August 17, 2003. `http://www.cerias.purdue.edu/homes/florian/reiser/reiserfs.php`.

Carrier, Brian. "Digital Forensic Tool Testing Images." 2004. `http://dftt.sourceforge.net`.

Casey, Eoghan. "Practical Approaches to Recovering Encrypted Digital Evidence." *International Journal of Digital Evidence*, 1(3), 2002. `http://www.ijde.org`.

IBM. "Journaled File System Technology for Linux." 2004. `http://www.ibm.com/developerworks/oss/jfs/`.

Kruse, Warren. "Computer Forensics Primer." CSI 30th Annual Computer Security Conference, November 3, 2003. `http://csiannual.com/classes/j1.pdf`.

Kurz, Gerson. "ReiserFS Docs." 2003. http://p-nand-q.com/download/rfstool/reiserfs_docs.html.

NTI Dictionary. "File Slack Defined." January 6, 2004. http://www.forensics-intl.com/def6.html.

Reiser, Hans. "Reiser4." 2003. http://www.namesys.com.

Wolfe, Hank. "Penetrating Encrypted Evidence." *Journal of Digital Investigation,* 1(2), 2004.

# FAT Concepts and Analysis

The *File Allocation Table* (FAT) file system is one of the most simple file systems found in common operating systems. FAT is the primary file system of the Microsoft DOS and Windows 9x operating systems, but the NT, 2000, and XP line has defaulted to the New Technologies File System (NTFS), which is discussed later in the book. FAT is supported by all Windows and most Unix operating systems and will be encountered by investigators for years to come, even if it is not the default file system of desktop Windows systems. FAT is frequently found in compact flash cards for digital cameras and USB "thumb drives." Many people are familiar with the basic concepts of the FAT file system but may not be aware of data hiding locations, addressing issues, and its more subtle behaviors. The goal of this chapter is to provide the general concepts and analysis techniques associated with FAT by using the five-category model. Chapter 10, "FAT Data Structures," discusses the low-level data structures. You can choose to read the two chapters in parallel, read them in sequential order, or skip the data structures chapter all together.

## INTRODUCTION

One of the reasons the FAT file system is considered simple is because it has a small number of data structure types. Unfortunately, it also means that there have been some modifications over the years to give it new features (although they are not quite as confusing as those done to DOS partitions are). The FAT file system does not clearly follow the five-category model that was previously described; therefore, the following sections may seem awkward (in fact, trying to explain the file system in this way makes it more complex than it needs to be). There are two important data structures in FAT (the File Allocation Table and directory entries) that serve multiple purposes and belong to multiple categories of the model. For these data structures, part of the data structure will be explained in one section, and the rest of it will be explained in another section. They are described in more detail in the next chapter. It is important to describe the FAT file system using the categories so that it is easier to compare it with more advanced file systems that more clearly follow the model. The FAT file system does not contain any data that falls into the application category.

The basic concept of a FAT file system is that each file and directory is allocated a data structure, called a directory entry, that contains the file name, size, starting address of the file content, and other metadata. File and directory content is stored in data units called clusters. If a file or directory has allocated more than one cluster, the other clusters are found by using a structure that is called the FAT. The FAT structure is used to identify the next cluster in a file, and it is also used to identify the allocation status of clusters. Therefore it is used in both the content and metadata categories. There are three different versions of FAT: FAT12, FAT16, and FAT32. The major difference among them is the size of the entries in the FAT structure. The relationships between these data structures will be examined in more detail, but we can see this relationship in Figure 9.1.

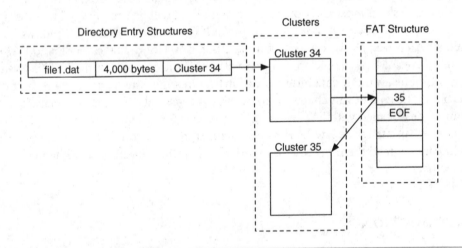

**Figure 9.1**  Relationship between the directory entry structures, clusters, and FAT structure.

The layout of the FAT file system has three physical sections to it, which can be seen in Figure 9.2. The first section is the *reserved area*, and it includes data in the file system category. In FAT12 and FAT16 this area is typically only 1 sector in size, but the size is defined in the boot sector. The second section is the *FAT area*, and it contains the primary and backup FAT structures. It starts in the sector following the reserved area, and its size is calculated based on the number and size of FAT structures. The third section is the *data area*, and it contains the clusters that will be allocated to store file and directory content.

**Figure 9.2**  Physical layout of a FAT file system.

## FILE SYSTEM CATEGORY

The data in the file system category describe the general file system, and they are used to find the other important data structures. This section describes the general concepts about where FAT stores the data in this category and how we can analyze the data.

### General Concepts

In a FAT file system, the file system category of data can be found in the *boot sector* data structure. The boot sector is located in the first sector of the volume, and it is part of the reserved area of the file system. Microsoft refers to some of the data in the first sector as belonging to the *BIOS Parameter Block* (BPB), but for simplicity I'll use the term *boot sector*.

The boot sector contains data that belong to all categories in the model, so I will wait until we get to each of those categories to describe those values. There is no field that identifies the file system as FAT12, FAT16, or FAT32. The type can be determined only by performing calculations from the boot sector data. I will show that calculation at the end of the chapter because it relies on concepts that have not yet been discussed.

A FAT32 file system boot sector contains additional data, including the sector address of a backup copy of the boot sector and a major and minor version number. The backup copy of the boot sector can be used if the version in sector 0 becomes corrupt, and the

Microsoft documentation says that it should always be in sector 6 so that tools can automatically find it if the default copy goes bad. The data structure for the boot sector is discussed in Chapter 10.

FAT32 file systems also have an FSINFO data structure that contains information about the location of the next available cluster and the total amount of free clusters. The data are not guaranteed to be accurate, and are there only as a guide for the operating system. Its data structure is described in the next chapter.

### Essential Boot Sector Data

One of the first things we need to know when analyzing a FAT file system is the location of the three physical layout areas. The reserved area starts in sector 0 of the file system, and its size is given in the boot sector. For FAT12/16 the reserved area is typically only 1 sector, but FAT32 will typically reserve many sectors.

The FAT area contains one or more FAT structures, and it begins in the sector after the reserved area. Its size is calculated by multiplying the number of FAT structures by the size of each FAT; both of these values are given in the boot sector.

The data area contains the clusters that will store file and directory contents and begins in the sector after the FAT area. Its size is calculated by subtracting the starting sector address of the data area from the total number of sectors in the file system, which is specified in the boot sector. The data area is organized into clusters, and the number of sectors per cluster is given in the boot sector.

The layout of the data area is slightly different in FAT12/16 and FAT32. In FAT12/16 the beginning of the data area is reserved for the root directory, but in FAT32 the root directory can be anywhere in the data area (although it is rare for it to not be in the beginning of the data area). The dynamic size and location of the root directory allows FAT32 to adapt to bad sectors in the beginning of the data area and allows the directory to grow as large as it needs to. The FAT12/16 root directory has a fixed size that is given in the boot sector. The starting address for the FAT32 root directory is given in the boot sector, and the FAT structure is used to determine its size. Figure 9.3 shows how the various boot sector values are used to determine the layout of FAT12/16 and FAT32 file systems.

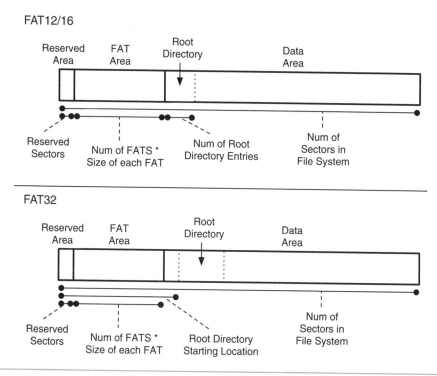

**Figure 9.3** FAT file system layout and data from the boot sector that is used to calculate the locations and sizes.

## Non-essential Boot Sector Data

In addition to the layout information, the boot sector contains many non-essential values. The non-essential values are those that are not needed for the file system to save and retrieve files, and they are there for convenience and may not be correct. One such value is an eight-character string called the *OEM name* that may correspond to what tool was used to make the file system, but it is an optional value. For example, a Windows 95 system sets it to "MSWIN4.0," a Windows 98 system sets it to MSWIN4.1, and a Windows XP or 2000 system sets it to "MSDOS5.0." I found that the Linux mkfs.msdos sets it to mkdosfs, some USB tokens have random values, and some compact flash cards in digital cameras have names that resemble the camera model. Anyone with a hex editor can change this value, but it may help you to determine what type of computer formatted a floppy. Some versions of Windows require that this value be set.

FAT file systems have a 4-byte volume serial number that is, according to the Microsoft specification, determined at file system creation time by using the current time, although the operating system that creates the file system can choose any value. My testing has shown different behavior with different versions of Windows. I tested a Windows 98 system, and it had the behavior reported by Craig Wilson [Wilson 2003], where the serial number is the result of adding the date and time fields in a specific order. This calculation is described in the "Boot Sector" section of Chapter 10. Windows XP did not create volume serial numbers using the same algorithm. Windows uses this value with removable media to determine when a disk has been changed.

There is also an eight-character type string that contains "FAT12," "FAT16," "FAT32," or "FAT." Most tools that create a FAT file system will set this string properly, but it does not need to be correct. The only way to determine the actual type is by calculating some numbers, which we will do later. The last identifying label is an eleven-character volume label string that the user can specify when he creates the file system. The volume label is also saved in the root directory of the file system, and I have observed that when a label is added in XP, the label is written to only the root directory and not the boot sector.

### Boot Code

The boot code for a FAT file system is intertwined with file system data structures [Microsoft 2003e]. This is unlike the Unix file system, which has completely separate boot code. The first three bytes of the boot sector contain a jump instruction in machine code that causes the CPU to jump past the configuration data to the rest of the boot code. As you can see from the data structure in the next chapter, the boot sector is 512 bytes, and bytes 62 to 509 in FAT12/16 and bytes 90 to 509 in FAT32 are not used. These bytes contain the boot code, and FAT32 can use the sectors following the boot sector for additional boot code.

It is common for FAT file systems to have boot code even though they are not bootable file systems. The boot code displays a message to show that another disk is needed to boot the system. The FAT boot code is called from the boot code in the MBR of the disk, and the FAT boot code locates and loads the appropriate OS files.

### Example Image

I will be using data from an example FAT32 image throughout this section. *The Sleuth Kit* (TSK) has a tool called `fsstat` that displays much of the data in the file system category of data. Here is the output from running `fsstat` on our example image:

```
# fsstat -f fat fat-4.dd
FILE SYSTEM INFORMATION
-------------------------------------------
```

```
File System Type: FAT
OEM Name: MSDOS5.0
Volume ID: 0x4c194603
Volume Label (Boot Sector): NO NAME
Volume Label (Root Directory): FAT DISK
File System Type Label: FAT32

Backup Boot Sector Location: 6
FS Info Sector Location: 1
Next Free Sector (FS Info): 1778
Free Sector Count (FS Info): 203836
Sectors before file system: 100800

File System Layout (in sectors)
Total Range: 0 - 205631
* Reserved: 0 - 37
** Boot Sector: 0
** FS Info Sector: 1
** Backup Boot Sector: 6
* FAT 0: 38 - 834
* FAT 1: 835 - 1631
* Data Area: 1632 - 205631
** Cluster Area: 1632 - 205631
*** Root Directory: 1632 - 1635

CONTENT-DATA INFORMATION
---------------------------------------------
Sector Size: 512
Cluster Size: 1024
Total Cluster Range: 2 - 102001
[REMOVED]
```

We can see from the previous output that there are 38 reserved sectors until the first FAT. In the reserved area are a backup boot sector and a FSINFO data structure. There are two FAT structures, and they span from sectors 38 to 834 and 835 to 1,631. The data area starts in sector 1,632, and it has clusters that are 1,024 bytes in size.

## ANALYSIS TECHNIQUES

The purpose of analyzing the file system category of data is to determine the file system layout and configuration details so that more specific analysis techniques can be conducted. In the process we also may find evidence that is specific to the case. For example, we may find which OS formatted the disk or hidden data.

To determine the configuration of a FAT file system, we need to locate and process the boot sector, whose data structure is given in Chapter 10. Processing the boot sector is simple because it is located in the first sector of the file system and has basic fields. There are two versions of the boot sector, but both are clearly documented. Using the information from the boot sector, we can calculate the locations of the reserved area, the FAT area, and the data area.

The FAT32 FSINFO data structure might also provide some clues about recent activity, and its location is given in the boot sector. It is typically located in sector 1 of the file system. Backup copies of both data structures also exist in FAT32.

## ANALYSIS CONSIDERATIONS

As we have seen, the data in this category provides structural data about the file system, and there is little data that the user has control over. Therefore, you will not likely find many smoking guns here. There are no values that show when or where the file system was created, but the OEM label and volume label, which are nonessential, may give some clues because different tools have different default values. We will later see that there is a special file that has a name equal to the volume label, and it might contain the file system creation time.

There are several places that are not used by the file system, and they could contain data that has been hidden by the user. For example, there are over 450 bytes of data between the end of the boot sector data and the final signature. Windows generally uses this space to store boot code for the system, but it is not needed for non-bootable file systems.

FAT32 file systems typically allocate many sectors to the reserved area, but only a few are used for the primary boot sector, the backup boot sector, and the FSINFO data structure. Therefore, these could contain hidden data. In addition, the FAT32 FSINFO data structure has hundreds of unused bytes. The OS generally wipes the sectors in the reserved area when it creates the file system.

There also could be hidden data between the end of the file system and the end of the volume. Compare the number of sectors in the file system, which is given in the boot sector, with the number of sectors that are in the volume to find volume slack. Note that it is relatively easy for someone to create volume slack because they need to modify only the total number of sectors value in the boot sector.

FAT32 file systems have a backup boot sector, and it should be located in sector 6. The primary and backup copies could be compared to identify inconsistencies. If the primary copy is corrupt, the backup should be examined. If the user modified any of the labels or other values in the primary boot sector by using a hex editor, the backup copy might contain the original data.

## ANALYSIS SCENARIO

During a raid on a suspect's house, a hard disk is found in a drawer. During the acquisition process, we realize that the first 32 sectors of the disk are damaged and cannot be read. The suspect probably put the drive in the drawer after it failed and used a new drive, but we want to examine it for evidence. The suspect's computer was running Windows ME and, therefore, using a FAT file system. This scenario shows how we can find the file systems even though the partition table does not exist.

To find the start of a FAT file system, we will search for the signature values of 0x55 and 0xAA in the final two bytes of the boot sector. We should expect a considerable number of false hits by doing only this search. If a disk contained random data, we would expect, on average, to find this signature every 65,536 (i.e., $2^{16}$) sectors. We can reduce the number of false hits by using a larger signature or by using other data. This scenario shows how the latter method works well with FAT32 because there is a pattern of these signatures in the reserved area of the file system. Of course, automated tools can do this for us more quickly, but we are going to do it by hand.

We will use the sigfind tool from TSK to look for the signature. Any tool that searches for hexadecimal values should work. The sigfind tool prints the sector in which the signature was found and gives the distance since the previous hit. Here is the output, along with commentary:

```
# sigfind -o 510 55AA disk-9.dd
Block size: 512  Offset: 510
Block: 63 (-)
Block: 64 (+1)
Block: 65 (+1)
Block: 69 (+4)
Block: 70 (+1)
Block: 71 (+1)
Block: 75 (+4)
Block: 128504 (+128429)
Block: 293258 (+164754)
[REMOVED]
```

The first hit for the signature is in sector 63, which makes sense because the first partition typically starts in sector 63. We read the sector and apply the boot sector data structure. We learn that it has a backup boot sector in sector 6 and FSINFO in sector 1 of the file system. We also learn that there are 20,482,812 sectors in the file system. The FSINFO data structure has the same signature as the boot sector, so sector 64 is also a hit.

Similarly, sectors 69 and 70 are hits because they are the backup copies of the boot sector and FSINFO, which are located six sectors from the original. Blocks 65 and 71 are all zeros except for their signatures. The hit in block 128,504 is a false hit and is random data when we view it. Therefore, based on the location of the boot sector and the relative location of the backup copies, we can assume that there is a FAT file system from disk sector 63 to 20,482,874. We will now view more of the sigfind output:

```
[REMOVED]
Block: 20112453 (+27031)
Block: 20482875 (+370422)
Block: 20482938 (+63)
Block: 20482939 (+1)
Block: 20482940 (+1)
Block: 20482944 (+4)
Block: 20482945 (+1)
Block: 20482946 (+1)
Block: 20482950 (+4)
Block: 20513168 (+30218)
```

In the output that I removed, there were many false hits, and the output shown has sector 20,482,875 with a hit. That sector follows the end of the previous file system, which ended in 20,482,874. The sequence of hits following 20,482,875 is different from what we previously saw, though, because the next hit is 63 sectors away, and then there are several that are close together. We view sector 20,482,875 to see if it is a false hit:

```
# dd if=disk-9.dd bs=512 skip=20482875 count=1 | xxd
0000000: 088c 039a 5f78 7694 8f45 bf49 e396 00c0  ...._xv..E.I....
0000016: 889d ddc0 6d36 60df 485d adf7 46d1 3224  ....m6`.H]..F.2$
0000032: 3829 95cd ad28 d2a2 dc89 f357 d921 cfde  8)...(.....W.!..
0000048: df8e 1fd3 303e 8619 641e 9c2f 95b4 d836  ....0>..d../...6
[REMOVED]
0000416: 3607 e7be 1177 db5f 11c9 fba1 c913 1a3d  6....w._........=
0000432: da81 143d 00c7 7083 9d42 330c 0287 0001  ...=..p..B3.....
0000448: c1ff 0bfe ffff 3f00 0000 fc8a 3801 0000  .......?.....8...
0000464: c1ff 05fe ffff 3b8b 3801 7616 7102 0000  .......;.8.v.q...
0000480: 0000 0000 0000 0000 0000 0000 0000 0000  ................
0000496: 0000 0000 0000 0000 0000 0000 0000 55aa  ..............U.
```

It could be easy to pass this off as a false hit, but notice the last four lines in the output and think back to Chapter 5, "PC-based Partitions," when we discussed DOS partitions. This sector contains an extended partition table, and the partition table starts at byte 446. DOS partition tables use the same signature value as FAT boot sectors. If we were to process the two non-zero entries in the table, we would learn that there is a FAT32 partition from sector 20,482,938 to 40,965,749 and an extended partition from sector 40,965,750 to 81,931,499. This confirms our `sigfind` output because we had a hit in sector 20,482,938 and hits 1, 6, and 7 sectors after that for the FSINFO data structure and backup copies. A graphical representation of this example can be found in Figure 9.4. It shows the two file systems we found and the locations of the various false hits and extended partition tables.

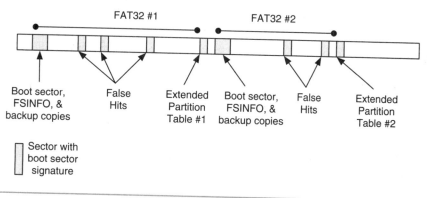

**Figure 9.4**   Results from searching for the FAT boot sector signature on a disk with no partition table.

In this example, we have shown how we can find a FAT32 file system if the boot sector exists. A search for only the 2-byte signature generates many false hits, but FAT32 makes it a little easier because we expect to find hits 1, 6, and 7 sectors away from the FSINFO data structure and backup copies. FAT12/16 is more difficult because there are no backup structures, but all we need to do is find the first hit. We can start by looking in sector 63. After we find a file system, we can use the file system length to skip ahead and start searching from there. We also can use any DOS extended partition table structures to help find file systems.

## CONTENT CATEGORY

The content category includes the data that comprise file or directory content. A FAT file system uses the term cluster for its data units. A *cluster* is a group of consecutive sectors, and the number of sectors must be a power of 2, such as 1, 2, 4, 8, 16, 32, or 64. According to the Microsoft specification, the maximum cluster size is 32KB. Each cluster is given an address, and the address of the first cluster is 2. In other words, there are no clusters that have an address of 0 or 1. The clusters are all located in the data area region of the file system, which is the last of the three areas.

### Finding the First Cluster

Finding the location of the first cluster, which is cluster 2, is harder than it sounds because it is not at the beginning of the file system; it is in the data area. The reserved and FAT areas, which occur before the data area, do not use cluster addresses. The FAT file system is an example where not every logical volume address has a logical file system address. As we will see in Chapter 11, this was changed in NTFS where the first cluster is also the first sector of the file system.

The procedure for finding the sector address of cluster 2 is different for FAT12/16 and FAT32. Cluster 2 in a FAT32 file system starts with the first sector of the data area. For example, consider a file system with 2,048-byte clusters and a data area that starts in sector 1,224. The sector address of cluster 2 will be sector 1,224, and the sector address of cluster 3 will be 1,228. We can see this in the bottom of Figure 9.5.

With a FAT12 and FAT16 file system, the first sectors of the data area are for the root directory, which is allocated when the file system is created and has a fixed size. The number of root directory entries is given in the boot sector, and cluster 2 starts in the next sector. For example, consider a FAT16 file system with 32 sectors allocated for the root directory. If the data area starts in sector 1,224, the root directory spans from sectors 1,224 to 1,255. If we had 2048-byte clusters, cluster 2 would start in sector 1,256 and cluster 3 would start in sector 1,260. We can see this in the top of Figure 9.5.

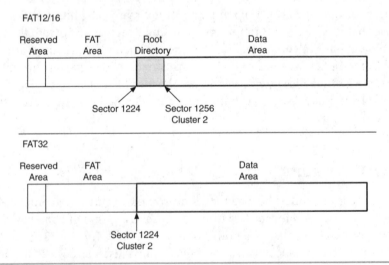

**Figure 9.5**   In a FAT12/16 file system, cluster 2 follows the root directory, and in a FAT32 file system, cluster 2 is the first sector of the data area.

## Cluster and Sector Addresses

As we just discussed, the cluster addresses do not start until the data area. Therefore, to address the data in the reserved and FAT areas, we have to either use two different addressing schemes or use the lowest common denominator, which is the sector address (the logical volume address). Using the sector address for everything is relatively simple and is what all tools and operating systems internally use because they need to know where the data is located relative to the start of the volume. Some tools, including TSK, show all addresses to the user in sector addresses so that only one addressing scheme is needed.

To convert between cluster and sector addresses, we need to know the sector address of cluster 2, and we need to know how many sectors there are per cluster. The basic algorithm for calculating the sector address of cluster C is

```
(C - 2) * (# of sectors per cluster) + (sector of cluster 2)
```

To reverse the process and translate a sector S to a cluster, the following is used:

```
( (S - sector of cluster 2) / (# of sectors per cluster) ) + 2
```

## Cluster Allocation Status

Now that we know where to find the clusters, we need to determine which ones are allocated. The allocation status of a cluster is determined using the FAT structure. There are typically two copies of the FAT, and the first one starts after the reserved area of the file system. The FAT is discussed in more detail in Chapter 10, but I will provide the needed details here.

The FAT is used for many purposes, but the basic concept is that it has one entry for every cluster in the file system. For example, table entry 481 corresponds to cluster 481. Each table entry is a single number whose maximum value depends on the FAT version. FAT12 file systems have a 12-bit table entry, FAT16 file systems have a 16-bit table entry, and FAT32 file systems have a 32-bit table entry (although only 28 of the bits are used).

If the table entry is 0, the cluster is not allocated to a file. If the table entry is 0xff7 for FAT12, 0xfff7 for FAT16, or 0x0fff fff7 for FAT32, the cluster has been marked as damaged and should not be allocated. All other values mean that the cluster is allocated, and the meaning of the value will be discussed later in the "Metadata Category" section.

## ALLOCATION ALGORITHMS

The OS gets to choose which allocation algorithm it uses when it allocates the clusters. I tested Windows 98 and Windows XP systems, and it appeared that a next available algorithm was being used in both. The next available algorithm searches for the first available cluster starting from the previously allocated cluster. For example, if cluster 65 is allocated to a new file and then cluster 62 is unallocated, the next search will start at cluster 66 and will not immediately reallocate cluster 62. We can see this in Figure 9.6. There are many factors that could affect the allocation of clusters, and it is difficult to identify the exact algorithms used.

To find an unallocated cluster that it can allocate, the OS scans the FAT for an entry that has a 0 in it. Recall that a FAT32 file system has the FSINFO data structure in the reserved area that identifies the next free cluster so that can be used as a guide by the operating system. To change a cluster to unallocated status, the corresponding entries in the FAT structures are located and set to 0. Most operating systems do not clear the cluster contents when it is unallocated unless they implement a secure wiping feature.

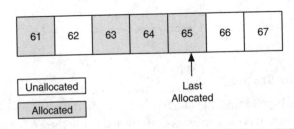

**Figure 9.6** The search for an unallocated cluster starts from the last allocated cluster, not the start of the file system.

## ANALYSIS TECHNIQUES

Analysis of the content category is performed to locate a specific data unit, determine its allocation status, and do something with the content. Locating a specific data unit in FAT is more complex than with other file systems because cluster addresses do not start at the beginning of the file system. When we are trying to locate a data unit prior to the start of the data area, we need to use sector addresses. For the data units in the data area, we can use either sector or cluster addresses.

The allocation status of each cluster can be determined by looking at the cluster's entry in the FAT. Entries with a zero value are unallocated and non-zero entries are allocated. If we wanted to extract the contents of all unallocated clusters, we would read the

FAT and extract each cluster with a zero in the table. The data units prior to the data area are not listed in the FAT; therefore, they do not have an official allocation state, although most are used by the file system. Test your tools to determine whether they consider any data prior to the data area to be unallocated.

## ANALYSIS CONSIDERATIONS

With a FAT file system, the clusters marked as bad should be examined because many disks handle bad sectors at the hardware level, and the operating system does not see them. Bad data units should be examined with any type of file system, but Microsoft notes that some copyright applications store data in FAT clusters that are marked as bad, so the ScanDisk tool in Windows will not verify that sectors marked as bad are indeed bad [Microsoft 2004b]. Some versions of the format command in Windows will preserve the bad status of a cluster when they reformat a file system [Microsoft 2003c].

The size of the data area may not be a multiple of the cluster size, so there could be a few sectors at the end of the data area that are not part of a cluster. These could be used to hide data or could contain data from a previous file system. Figure 9.7 shows an example of this where there is an odd number of sectors in the data area and each cluster includes 2 sectors. The final sector is gray and does not have a cluster address.

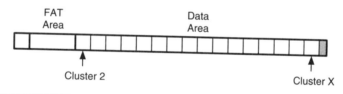

**Figure 9.7** The final sectors in the Data Area may not fit into a full cluster and, therefore, could contain hidden data or data from a previous file system.

To determine if there are unused sectors, subtract the sector address of cluster 2 from the total number of sectors and divide by the number of sectors in a cluster. If there is a remainder from the division, there are unused sectors:

```
(Total number of sectors - Sector address of cluster 2) / (Number of sectors per
cluster)
```

Data also could be hidden between the end of the last valid entry in the primary FAT structure and the start of the backup copy and between the end of the last entry in the backup FAT and the start of the data area. To calculate how much unused space there is, we need to compare the size of each FAT, which is given in the boot sector, with the size needed for the number of clusters in the file system. For example, in the FAT32 file system that was previously analyzed using fsstat, we saw that it had 797 sectors allocated to each FAT. Each table entry in the FAT32 file system is four bytes and, therefore, 128 entries exist in each 512-byte sector. Each table has room for

```
797 sectors * 128 (entries / sector) = 102,016 entries
```

The fsstat output also shows that there were 102,002 clusters, so there are 14 unused table entries for a total size of 64 bytes.

Not every sector in the volume is assigned a cluster address, so the results from doing a logical volume search versus a logical file system search may be different. Test your tools to see if they search the boot sector and FAT areas. An easy way to test this is to search for the phrase "FAT" and see if it finds the boot sector (first verify that your boot sector has the string in it, though).

## ANALYSIS SCENARIO

We have a FAT16 file system and need to locate the first sector of cluster 812. All we have is a hex editor that does not know about the FAT file system.

Our first step is to view the boot sector, which is located in sector 0 of the file system. We process it and learn that that there are six reserved sectors, two FATs, and each FAT is 249 sectors. Each cluster is 32 sectors, and there are 512 directory entries in the root directory.

Now we need to do some math. The first FAT starts in sector 6 and ends in sector 254. The second FAT starts in sector 255 and ends in 503. Next is the root directory. There are 512 entries in the root directory and (as we will later see) each entry is 32 bytes, so the directory needs 16,384 bytes, which comprise 32 sectors. Therefore, the root directory will be in sectors 504 to 535, and the data area will begin in sector 536.

The first cluster in the data area has an address of 2. We are looking for cluster 812, which is the 810th cluster in the data area, and each cluster is 32 sectors. Therefore, cluster 812 is 25,920 sectors from the start of the data area. Finally, we add the data area starting address and determine that cluster 812 starts in sector 26,456 and extends to sector 26,487. We see this layout in Figure 9.8.

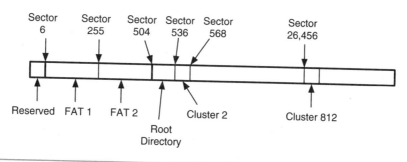

**Figure 9.8** Layout of our scenario example where we are looking for cluster 812.

## METADATA CATEGORY

The metadata category includes the data that describe a file or directory, including the locations where the content is stored, dates and times, and permissions. We will use this category of data to obtain additional information about a file or to identify suspect files. In a FAT file system, this information is stored in a directory entry structure. The FAT structure also is used to store metadata information about the layout of a file or directory.

### Directory Entries

The *directory entry* is a data structure that is allocated for every file and directory. It is 32 bytes in size and contains the file's attributes, size, starting cluster, and dates and times. The directory entry plays a role in both the metadata and file name category because the name of the file is located in this structure. Directory entries can exist anywhere in the data area because they are stored in the clusters allocated to a directory. In the FAT file system, a directory is considered a special type of file. The directory entry data structure is described in detail in Chapter 10.

When a new file or directory is created, a directory entry in the parent directory is allocated for it. Because each directory entry is a fixed size, we can imagine the contents of a directory to be a table of directory entries. Directory entries are not given unique numerical addresses, like clusters are. Instead, the only standard way to address a directory entry is to use the full name of the file or directory that allocated it. We will discuss this more in the "Directory Entry Addresses" section.

The directory entry structure has an attributes field, and there are seven file attributes that can be set for each file. However, the OS (or your analysis tool) might ignore some of them. I will cover the essential attributes first—these attributes cannot be ignored because they affect the way that the directory entry must be processed. The *directory* attribute is used to identify the directory entries that are for directories. The clusters allocated to a directory entry should contain more directory entries. The *long file name* attribute identifies a special type of entry that has a different layout. It will be discussed in detail in the "File Name" section. The final essential attribute is for the *volume label*, and only one directory entry, by specification, should have this attribute set. I have observed that with Windows XP, the volume label a user specifies is saved in this location and not in the boot sector. If none of these attributes are set, the entry is for a normal file.

There are four non-essential attributes that can be set for each file or directory. The impact of these being set depends on how the OS wants to enforce them. The *read only* attribute should prevent a file from being written to, but I found that directories in Windows XP and 98 can have new files created in them when they are set to read only. The *hidden* attribute may cause files and directories to not be listed, but there is typically a setting in the OS that causes them to be shown. The *system* attribute should identify a file as a system file, and Windows typically sets the *archive* attribute when a file is created or written to. The purpose of this attribute is that a backup utility can identify which files have changed since the last backup.

Each directory entry has three times in it: created, last accessed, and last written. One of the strange traits of FAT is that each of these times has a widely different granularity. The created timestamp is optional and accurate to a tenth of a second; the access time-stamp is also optional and accurate to the day; and the written timestamp is required by the specification and accurate to two seconds. There are no specifications for which operations cause each time to be updated, so each OS that uses FAT has its own policy with respect to when it updates the times. The Windows 95+ and NT+ lines update all times, but DOS and Windows 3.1 update only the last modified times. The times are stored with respect to the local time zone, which means that you do not have to convert the time based on where the computer was located.

The allocation status of a directory entry is determined by using the first byte. With an allocated entry, the first byte stores the first character in the file name, but it is replaced with 0xe5 when the entry becomes unallocated. This is why FAT recovery tools require you to enter the first letter of the file name.

### Cluster Chains

The directory entry contains the starting cluster of the file, and the FAT structure is used to find the remaining clusters in the file. Previously I noted that if a FAT entry is non-zero, its cluster is allocated. The non-zero entry contains the address of the next cluster in the file, an end of file marker, or a value to show that the cluster has bad sectors. To find the next cluster in a file, you simply look at the cluster's entry in the FAT and deter-mine if it is the last cluster in the file or if there is another one. The FAT data structure layout and values are discussed in more detail in Chapter 10.

Using the FAT to find cluster addresses is analogous to a treasure hunt. You are given clues about the location of the first site. When you get to the first site, you find a treasure and directions to the second site. This process repeats until you find the final site.

For example, consider a file that is located in clusters 40, 41, and 45. If we wanted to read the contents of this file, we would first examine the starting cluster field in the directory entry, which should have a value of 40. The size of the file will show that more than one cluster is needed for the file, so the FAT entry for cluster 40 is referred to. The entry contains the value 41, which means that cluster 41 is the second cluster in the file. The file size shows that one more cluster is needed, and we examine the FAT entry for cluster 41 to find the value of 45. The FAT entry for cluster 45 contains the *End of File* (EOF) marker because it is the final cluster in the file. The sequence of clusters is sometimes called a *cluster chain*, and we can see an example cluster chain in Figure 9.9.

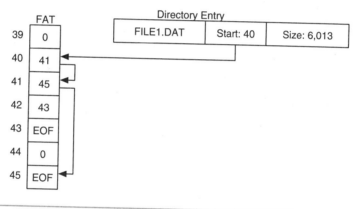

**Figure 9.9**   A FAT showing a cluster chain from cluster 40 to 41 to 45.

The maximum size of a FAT file system is based on the size of the FAT entries. Each entry has a maximum address that it can store for the next cluster in the chain. Therefore, there is a maximum cluster address. The FAT32 file system uses only 28-bits of the 32-bit entry, so it can describe only 268,435,456 clusters (actually, the maximum is a little less because there are some reserved values for EOF and bad clusters).

## Directories

When a new directory is created, a cluster is allocated to it and wiped with 0s. The size field in the directory entry is not used, and should always be 0. The only way to determine the size of the directory is to use the starting cluster from the directory entry and follow the cluster chain in the FAT structure until the end of file marker is found.

The first two directory entries in a directory are for the . and .. directories. People who use the command line are used to these names because the . name is used to address the current directory, and .. is used to address the parent directory. These entries are actual directory entries with the directory attribute set, but Windows does not seem to update the values after they are created. The written, accessed, and created times seem to reflect the time that the directory was created. This behavior could be used to verify the creation date on a directory because it should be the same value as the . and .. entries. We cannot confirm the last written date of the directory, though, because the . and .. entries are not updated for every directory modification. We can see this situation in Figure 9.10 where the dir1 created time is different from the . and .. entries. The user could have done this to hide some activity, or an application on the system may have modified it.

Cluster 110

| Name | Created | Cluster |
|------|---------|---------|
| dir2 | 3/30/04 01:29:01 | 128 |
| dir1 | 4/03/04 11:47:40 | 196 |
| file8.dat | 3/30/04 20:41:12 | 112 |

Cluster 196

| Name | Created | Cluster |
|------|---------|---------|
| . | 4/1/04 09:27:00 | 196 |
| .. | 4/1/04 09:27:00 | 110 |
| file1.dat | 4/3/04 12:58:23 | 297 |

**Figure 9.10**   The created time in the directory entry for the directory does not match the '.' and '..' entries.

## Directory Entry Addresses

As I previously mentioned, the only standard way to address a directory entry is to use the full name of the file or directory that allocated it. There are at least two problems with this, and they are addressed in this section.

Consider a scenario where we want to find all allocated directory entry structures. To do this, we start in the root directory and recursively look in each of the allocated directories. For each directory, we examine each 32-byte structure and skip over the unallocated ones. The address of each structure is the name of the directory that we are currently looking at plus the name of the file.

This works great for normal file system usage, but investigators also want to find unallocated directory entries. This is where we find our first problem. The first letter of the name is deleted when the directory entry is unallocated. If a directory had two files A-1.DAT and B-1.DAT that were deleted, both entries would have the same name in them, _-1.DAT. Therefore, we have a unique naming conflict.

The second problem occurs when a directory is deleted and its entry is reallocated. In this case, there is no longer a pointer to the files and directories in the deleted directory, so they have no address. Consider Figure 9.11(A), where a directory entry for a directory points to cluster 210. That directory is deleted, and the directory entry is later reallocated, and it now points to cluster 400, as shown in Figure 9.11(B). The unallocated directory entries in cluster 210 still exist, but we cannot find them by simply following the directory tree, and if we do find them, we do not have an address for them. These are called orphan files.

To find orphan files, we need to examine every sector of the data area. There is no standard method of doing this, but one method is to examine the first 32-bytes of each sector, not cluster, and compare it to the fields in a directory entry. If they are in a valid range, the rest of the sector should be processed. By searching each sector, you may find entries in the slack space of clusters that have been allocated to other files. A similar technique is to search the first 32 bytes of each cluster to find the . and .. entries that are the first two entries in every directory (we will show an example of this later). This technique will only find the first cluster of a directory and not any of its fragments.

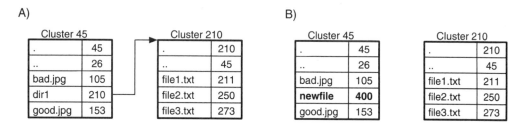

**Figure 9.11** A) shows an allocated directory and its contents. B) shows the state when the directory is deleted and the parent directory's directory entry is reallocated.

One way to solve these problems is to use a different addressing method. For example, TSK uses a method that is also used by several Unix systems where it assumes that every cluster and sector could be allocated by a directory. Therefore, we can imagine that every sector is divided into 32-byte entries that could store a directory entry, and we assign a unique address to each entry. Therefore, the first 32-byte entry of the first sector in the data area would have an address of 0, and the second entry would have an address of 1.

This works, but there is a slight problem. Every directory and file will have a numerical address except for the root directory. Recall that the location and size of the root directory is given in the boot sector and not in a directory entry. The fix that TSK uses is to assign the root directory with an address of 2 (because that is what other Unix-based file systems use) and assign the first entry in the first sector an address of 3. We can see this in Figure 9.12 where sectors 520 and 1,376 are expanded to show the entry addresses inside them. Each 512-byte sector can store 16 directory entry structures, so sector 520 will have entries 3 to 18.

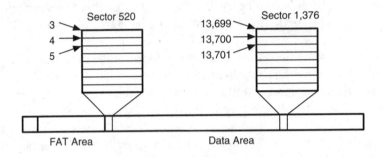

**Figure 9.12**   Addresses that are assigned to directory entries based on the sector and location in the sector.

## Example Image

To show the data that exists for a typical FAT file, the output from istat is given here for a file in our example image. The directory entry for this file is analyzed in Chapter 10, but here is the formatted output:

```
# istat -f fat fat-4.dd 4
Directory Entry: 4
Allocated
File Attributes: File, Archive
Size: 8689
Name: RESUME-1.RTF

Directory Entry Times:
Written:        Wed Mar 24 06:26:20 2004
Accessed:       Thu Apr  8 00:00:00 2004
Created:        Tue Feb 10 15:49:40 2004

Sectors:
1646 1647 1648 1649 1650 1651 1652 1653
1654 1655 1656 1657 1658 1659 1660 1661
1662 1663
```

We see that this file has allocated 18 sectors, which is equivalent to nine clusters in this file system. The created, last written, and last accessed dates and times also are given, as are the attributes for the file. Because the file name is stored in the directory entry, we know the name of the file given only its address, but we do not know its full path.

## ALLOCATION ALGORITHMS

In the metadata category, there are two general types of data that are allocated. The directory entries need to be allocated for new files and directories, and the temporal information for each file and directory needs to be updated. As with most allocation strategies, the actual behavior is OS-dependent and cannot be enforced by the file system data structures. A specific OS should be tested before conclusions are drawn based on the allocation algorithms. I will give my observations from Windows 98 and XP.

### Directory Entry Allocation

Windows 98 uses a first-available allocation strategy and starts its search for an unallocated directory entry from the beginning of the directory. Windows XP uses a next-available allocation method and starts its search for an unallocated directory entry from the last allocated directory entry. Windows XP restarts its scan from the beginning of the directory when it gets to the end of the cluster chain. When Windows 98 or XP cannot find an unallocated directory entry, a new cluster is allocated.

The difference in the allocation methods can be seen in Figure 9.13, where entry 3 was unallocated after entry 4 was allocated. When the next entry is allocated, Windows 98 starts from the beginning of the cluster and allocates directory entry 3. Windows XP starts at entry 4 and allocates entry 5.

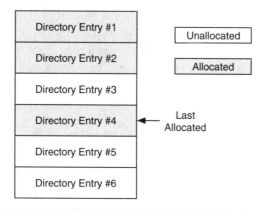

**Figure 9.13**   Directory entry 4 was just allocated. Windows 98 allocates entry 3 next, but Windows XP allocates entry 5 next.

233

When a file is renamed in Windows, a new entry is made for the new name, and the entry for the old name is unallocated. A similar behavior also can be seen when a new file or directory is created in Windows by using the right mouse button and choosing 'New.' This results in an entry for the default name, New Text Document.txt, for example, which is unallocated when the user enters a more unique name.

An interesting behavior of Windows XP is that when a file is created from a Windows application, two entries are created. The first entry has all the values except the size and the starting cluster. This entry becomes unallocated, and a second entry is created with the size and starting cluster. This occurs when saving from within an application, but not from the command line, drag and dropping, or using the 'New' menu option.

When a file is deleted, the first byte of the directory entry is set to 0xe5. Windows does not change any other values in the directory entry, but other OSes might. The clusters that were allocated for the file are unallocated by setting their corresponding entries in the FAT structure to 0. Fortunately, Windows keeps the starting cluster of the cluster chain in the directory entry so some file recovery can be performed until the clusters are allocated to new files and overwritten.

### Time Value Updating

There are three time values in a directory entry: last accessed, last written, and created. There are few requirements in the FAT specification, but Microsoft Knowledge Base article 299648 describes the behavior in Windows [Microsoft 2003d]. The time values are non-essential and could be false.

The created time is set when Windows allocates a new directory entry for a *new* file. The "new file" part is important because if the OS allocates a new directory entry for an existing file, even if original location was on a different disk, the original creation time is kept. For example, if a file is renamed or is moved to another directory or disk, the creation time from the original entry is written to the new entry. There is one known exception to this rule, and it is if the move is done from the command line of a 2000/XP system to a different volume. In this case, the created time is set to the time of the move. If a file is copied, a new file is being created, and a new creation time is written to the new entry. The creation time corresponds to the time when the first directory entry was allocated for the file, regardless of the original location (unless the file was moved to a new file system by using the command line).

The written time is set when Windows writes new file content. The write time is content-based and not directory entry-based and follows data as it is copied around. If files are moved or copied in Windows, the new directory entry has the written time from the original file. Changing the attributes or name of a file does not result in an update to this time. Windows updates this time when an application writes content to the file, even if the application is doing an automatic save and no content has changed.

In summary, if you move a file in Windows, the resulting file will have the original written and original creation time unless the move is to a different volume and the command line is used. If you copy a file, the resulting file will have the original written time and a new creation time. This can be confusing because the creation date is after the written time. If you create a new file from an application in Windows, it is common for the written time to be a little later than the creation time.

The last accessed date, which is only accurate to the day, is updated the most frequently. Anytime the file is opened, the date is updated. When you right-click on the file to see its properties, its access date is updated. If you move a file to a new volume, the access date on the new file is updated because Windows had to read the original content before it could write it to the new volume. If you move a file within the same volume, though, the access date will not change because the new file is using the same clusters. If you copy or move a file, the access date on both the source and destination is updated. The one exception to this simple rule is that under Windows XP, the access date is not updated when the file is copied or when the "copy" menu features are used. Alternatively, Windows 98 does update the access time of the source file when the destination file was created. Some versions of Windows can be configured to not update the last access date.

For directories, I observed that the dates were set when the directory was created and were not updated much after that. Even when new clusters were allocated for the directory or new files were created in the directory, the written times were not updated.

## ANALYSIS TECHNIQUES

The reason for analyzing the metadata category of data is to determine more details about a file or directory. To do this in FAT, we must locate a specific directory entry, process its contents, and determine where the file or directory content is stored. Locating all entries in FAT is difficult because only allocated directory entries have a full address, which is their path and file name. We will see an example of this in the "Scenarios" section. Unallocated entries might not have full addresses; therefore, a tool-specific addressing scheme will likely be used.

After a directory entry has been located, it is relatively straightforward to process it. To identify all clusters that a file has allocated, we use the starting cluster from the directory entry and the FAT structure to locate the other clusters.

## ANALYSIS CONSIDERATIONS

When analyzing the metadata from a FAT file system, there are some special considerations that should be taken into account. These considerations have to deal with the directory entry time values, allocation routines, and consistency checks.

One consideration, which can work to the benefit of the investigator, is that times are stored without respect to time zone, so it does not matter what time zone your analysis system is set to. This also makes dealing with daylight savings easier because you don't need to figure out whether you need to add or subtract an hour based on what month it is.

Another consideration is that the last accessed and the created dates and times are optional by specification and might be 0. Like the times on most file systems, it is easy to change the times on a file. In fact, there is a Microsoft document that tells developers to save the access time of a file before opening it so that it can be restored if the application was not able to read it [Microsoft 2003a]. Additional application-level data should be used to confirm temporal data. Further, the time updating is not even consistent within Microsoft platforms.

Windows sets the last written time to the last time that the data content itself was changed on the local system. Copying a file can result in a creation time that corresponds to the time that the copy occurred and a written date that corresponds to the last written date of the original location. This type of scenario is fairly common and not necessarily a sign of tampering. The resolution of the last access date is only accurate to the day, so it does not help much when trying to reconstruct the events on a system.

The allocation routines for new directory entries in an XP system allow you to see the names of deleted files for longer than would be expected because a first available algorithm is not used. In reality, this may not allow you to recover any more files than if a first available algorithm had been used because the clusters of the file will be reallocated just as quickly. Therefore, you might not recover the original file content even if you can see the name.

The DEFRAG utility that comes with Windows compacts directories and removes unused directory entries. It also moves the file content around to make it more contiguous. Therefore, recovery after running DEFRAG is difficult because the directory entries of the deleted files are gone and the clusters have been moved around.

The content of slack space is OS-dependent, but Microsoft Windows' systems have not added non-zero RAM slack to a file for several years. The unused sectors in the last cluster of a file allocated by Windows typically contain deleted data. It is entirely within the FAT specification for an operating system to clear all sectors when it allocates a cluster to a file, but this is rare.

Microsoft Windows does not show any data after it finds a directory entry with all zeros. Therefore, it is relatively easy for someone to create a directory with only a few files and then use the rest of the directory space for hiding data. The allocated size of a directory should be compared to the number of allocated files. A logical file system search should find any data that is hidden in these locations.

While doing research for this book, I found some interesting things about directory entries with the volume label attribute, and they can be used to hide data and provide some clues. The access and created times in the volume label entry are frequently set to 0, but the last written time is usually set by Windows to the current time when the file system is created. So you may be able to get some information about when the file system was created, although this value can of course be modified.

With Windows XP, a volume label directory entry can be used to hide data. It is, after all, a normal directory entry and has fields to store the starting cluster of a cluster chain. If you manually edit the starting cluster field to contain the address of an unused cluster and then go to the FAT and manually edit it to create a cluster chain, the ScanDisk program in Windows XP will not raise any warnings or errors. The cluster chain will stay allocated. Typically, if a directory entry is not referencing a cluster chain, the ScanDisk program will place it in a lost clusters directory. The ScanDisk program in Windows 98 will detect that clusters have been allocated to the volume label and remove them.

Another interesting behavior of Windows XP and the volume label attribute is that you can have as many entries as you want and in any location. The specification for one entry in the root directory is not enforced. Therefore, you can have multiple entries in multiple directories that are flagged as volume labels and hiding data. The ScanDisk program in Windows 98 detects this and alerts the user. This process is currently manual, but tools could be developed in the future to do this. I have a test image on the *Digital Forensic Tool Testing* (DFTT) site for FAT volume labels [Carrier 2004b].

## ANALYSIS SCENARIOS

### File System Creation Date

We encounter a FAT file system with only a few files and directories in it. This could be because the file system was not used much, because it was recently formatted, or because there is data being hidden from the investigator. We can test the second hypothesis by looking at the times of the directory entry with the volume label attribute set in the root directory. Our analysis tool lists the directory entry as a normal file, and we see that it was formatted two weeks before the disk was acquired. This explains why there are few file names listed, but there could still be hidden data and data from the previous file system. The next scenario will look for data from the previous file system.

### Searching for Deleted Directories

We have a FAT file system and want to recover deleted directories. This scenario can occur during a normal investigation where we want to find deleted files or when a FAT file system has been recently formatted and we want to find the directories from before the format. For this example, we are going to extract the unallocated space and then search for the signature associated with the . directory entry that starts a directory.

I am going to do this in TSK, but you can use any tool that allows you to search only unallocated space and that allows you to search for a hexadecimal value. With TSK, we must extract the unallocated space using dls.

```
# dls —f fat fat-10.dd > fat-10.dls
```

We are going to search for the first four bytes of a directory, which corresponds to the ASCII values for ".   " (a period and three spaces). This is 0x2e202020 in hexadecimal. We search our unallocated space for this signature using sigfind.

```
# sigfind —b 512 2e202020 fat-10.dls
Block size: 512  Offset: 0
Block: 180 (-)
Block: 2004 (+1824)
Block: 3092 (+1088)
Block: 3188 (+96)
Block: 19028 (+15840)
[REMOVED]
```

We view the contents of sector 180 in the fat-10.dls image (not the original file system image). It has the following contents:

```
# dd if=fat-10.dls skip=180 count=1 | xxd
0000000: 2e20 2020 2020 2020 2020 2010 0037 5daf   .            ..7].
0000016: 3c23 3c23 0000 5daf 3c23 4f19 0000 0000   <#<#..].<#0.....
0000032: 2e2e 2020 2020 2020 2020 2010 0037 5daf   ..           ..7].
0000048: 3c23 3c23 0000 5daf 3c23 dc0d 0000 0000   <#<#..].<#......
0000064: e549 4c45 312e 4441 5420 2020 0000 0000   .ILE1.DAT   ....
0000080: 7521 7521 0000 0000 7521 5619 00d0 0000   u!u!....u!V.....
[REMOVED]
```

Each directory entry is 32 bytes, and there are three entries shown here. The first two are for the . and .. entries. If we interpret the first two entries, we see that the . entry points to cluster 6,479 (0x194f) and the .. entry points to cluster 3,548 (0x0ddc). The third entry is for a file, and it starts in cluster 6,486 (0x1956) with a size of 53,248 (0xd000) bytes. File recovery can be performed on this file now that we know its starting address and size.

The steps that were performed in this scenario are shown in Figure 9.14. We extracted the unallocated space and then searched for clusters that start with a . directory entry.

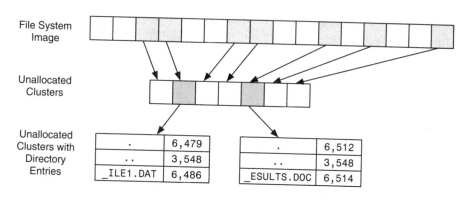

**Figure 9.14**  Process used to find deleted directories based on the directory entry structure.

## FILE NAME CATEGORY

Typically, analysis in the file name category allows us to map a file name with a metadata structure. FAT does not separate the file name address and metadata address, so we will not be doing that here. In fact, we already saw the basics of file and directory names in the "Metadata Category" section because the file name is used as a metadata address. To recap, the directory entry data structure contains the name of a file using the 8.3 naming convention, where the name of the file has eight characters and the extension has three characters. In this section we focus on how FAT handles long file names.

If a file is given a name that is longer than eight characters or if the name has special values, a *long file name* (LFN) type of directory entry is added. Files with an LFN also have a normal, *short file name* (SFN), directory entry. The SFN entry is needed because LFN entries do not contain any of the time, size, or starting cluster information. They contain only the file name. The LFN data structure is discussed in detail in Chapter 10. When an LFN entry becomes unallocated, the first byte in the data structure is set to 0xe5.

The SFN and LFN data structures have an attribute field in the same location, and the LFN entries use a special attribute value. The remaining bytes in the entry are used to store 13 Unicode characters encoded in UTF-16, which are 2 bytes each. If a file name needs more than 13 characters, additional LFN entries are used. All LFN entries precede the SFN entry in the directory and contain a checksum that can be used to correlate the

LFN entries with the SFN entry. The LFN entries are also in reverse order so that the first part of the file name is closest to the SFN entry.

Figure 9.15 shows a list of directory entries that exist in our example image. The directory entries are parsed by hand in Chapter 10, but overall, there are two allocated files in this directory, and one has a long file name. It has two LFN directory entries preceding its SFN entry, and the entries have the My Long File Name.rtf name in backwards order. Notice that the checksum values are the same for each entry, which is calculated based on the SFN.

```
Atr: File   Name: RESUME-1.RTF Cluster: 9
Atr: LFN    Seq: 2  CSum: 0xdf   Name: Name.rtf
Atr: LFN    Seq: 1  CSum: 0xdf   Name: My Long File
Atr: File   Name: MYLONG~1.RTF Cluster: 26
Atr: File   Name: _ILE6.TXT Cluster: 48
```

**Figure 9.15**   Directory entries from the example image where there are three files, and one file has a long file name and another has been deleted.

Here is the output from running the fls tool on this directory in our example file system image:

```
# fls -f fat fat-2.dd
r/r   3: FAT DISK      (Volume Label Entry)
r/r   4: RESUME-1.RTF
r/r   7: My Long File Name.rtf (MYLONG~1.RTF)
r/r * 8: _ile6.txt
```

We can see the LFN on the third line and the deleted file on the fourth output line. Recall that the metadata addresses are assigned based on the directory entry slot. There is an address gap between RESUME-1.RTF and My Long File Name.rtf because of the LFN entries in slots 5 and 6.

LFN entries have Unicode characters, which allow them to have international characters in addition to the American English characters in ASCII. Prior to the introduction of the LFN entries, the international community was able to create file names with their native symbols by using *code pages*. ASCII uses only the first 128 values out of a total 256. Code pages use the additional 128 entries and assign characters to them. The SFN entry may contain values from a code page instead of normal ASCII. A listing of code pages can be found at Microsoft [Microsoft 2004a].

## ALLOCATION ALGORITHMS

The file names are stored in the same data structures as the metadata, so the allocation algorithms for the file name category are the same as for the metadata category. The one difference is that the LFN entries must come before the SFN, so the OS will look for enough room for all entries. Therefore, when using a first available strategy, the OS will skip over entries that do not have other unallocated entries around them.

The deletion routines are the same as were previously discussed in the "Metadata Category" section, specifically that the first byte of the entry is replaced with 0xe5. With an SFN entry, this will overwrite the first character of the name and an LFN directory entry will have its sequence number overwritten. Typically, when we recover deleted files we need to supply the first character of the short name, but if the file also has a long name, we can use its first character. When a directory is deleted, the entries inside it may or may not be changed.

## ANALYSIS TECHNIQUES

Analysis of the file name category is performed to find a specific file name. To do this in FAT, we first locate the root directory, which varies depending on the version of FAT. With FAT12/16, the root directory starts in the sector following the FAT area, and its size is given in the boot sector. With FAT32, the starting cluster address of the root directory is given in the boot sector, and the FAT structure is used to determine its layout.

We process the contents of a directory by stepping through each 32-byte directory entry structure. If the attribute for the structure is set for an LFN entry, its contents are stored and the next entry is examined. This storage process repeats until we find an entry that is not an LFN and whose checksum matches that of the long name entries. The allocation status of an entry is determined using the first byte, which works like a flag.

When we find a file or directory of interest, we will likely want to find its corresponding metadata. This is very easy with FAT because all the metadata for a file is located in the directory entry. This means that the metadata associated with a file name will not become out of sync after the file is deleted. The metadata associated with an unallocated file name will be accurate until both are overwritten.

## ANALYSIS CONSIDERATIONS

Because the file name and metadata are in the same data structure, we will always have a name for unallocated entries that we find. If LFNs are used, the entire long name can be recovered, although we may lose part of the name when the first byte is changed to 0xe5.

I observed with a Windows XP system that the scandisk tool for FAT file systems is not very exhaustive. I was able to create LFN entries that did not correspond to any SFN entries, and no error was given. This allowed me to save small amounts of data and not raise any alarms, and the data would not be shown when the directory contents were listed. Depending on how the keyword search of an analysis tool is done, the values hidden in the LFN entries may not be found.

As mentioned in the "Metadata Category" section, an attacker may also be able to hide data at the end of a directory. Some OSes will stop processing directory entries after finding one that is all zeros. Data could be hidden after that all zero entry, although another implementation of FAT could skip over that zero entry and continue to process entries until the end of the directory.

If you are using the keyword search mechanism of a search tool to look for a file name, make sure that you use the Unicode version of long file names. The SFN is stored in ASCII, but the LFN entries are in Unicode. You also will have to keep in mind that the entire name might not be stored sequentially, and it might be broken up into smaller pieces in multiple parts of multiple LFN entries (see the scenario in the next section).

## ANALYSIS SCENARIOS

To illustrate some of the analysis techniques, this section contains two scenarios. One is about searching for a file name, and the other is about the relative ordering of directory entries.

### File Name Searching

Suppose that we want to find all references to a file named TheStuff.dat. We are interested in both allocated and deleted instances of this file. How do we do this if our analysis tool does allow us to search for file names?

If we do a keyword search of the file system for the name, we might find the content of files that reference our file. However, we won't find the file itself because the name is stored in an LFN entry and the SFN entry has a modified version of the name. Therefore, we can either search for "THESTUF~1DAT" in ASCII or modify our search for the long name entry.

If we want to find the long version of the name, we need to split the name up into chunks. Each long name entry can hold 13 characters and is broken up into chunks of five, six, and two characters. Therefore, our long entry will be broken up into "TheSt," "uff.da," and "t" in Unicode. To reduce the number of false positives, we should search for the longest string, which is "uff.da." A graphical representation of the directory entries for this file is shown in Figure 9.16.

Directory Entries for the file "TheStuff.dat"

**Figure 9.16**    Performing an ASCII or Unicode keyword search for a file name may not find its directory entry as shown here.

## Directory Entry Ordering

While investigating a system, we find a directory full of contraband graphic images, and we want to determine how they got there.[1] For example, were they downloaded individually or copied from a CD? We notice that the directory entries in the directory are in alphabetical order, and we find this strange because Windows does not typically create directory entries in a sorted order. There are also no unallocated entries in the directory.

We develop several hypotheses about this directory, including

- It was copied or moved to this location, and the new entries were created in alphabetical order.
- It was created by opening a ZIP file, and the unzip program created them in alphabetical order.
- The user downloaded each of these files in alphabetical order because that is the way they were listed on the remote server.

To test the first scenario, we can look at the created and last written times of the files. Files that are the result of a copy will have a created time that is more recent than its last written time. In this case, all the files have a created time that is equal to the last written time, so copying does not seem likely if we can trust the temporal data.

To test if the directory was moved, we set up a system that is similar to the one being investigated and conduct some tests. We create a directory with the same names as those we are investigating and create them in a non-alphabetical order. To test the moving hypothesis, we set the sorting option in the file manager to sort by name and then move the files by dragging and dropping. This results in a directory with entries that are almost in alphabetical order, but not quite. The entries are sorted more than they were in the original location, but not fully sorted. We repeat the tests by using different window sorting options, but still do not get the desired effect. We do find that if each file was moved individually in the sorted order, the new directory is sorted.

---

1. Thanks to Eoghan Casey for suggesting the basic concept of this example.

The second scenario was that the files were created from opening a ZIP file. We run more tests by creating a ZIP file that contains the files in question and then extracting them to a new directory. We find that the files are extracted from the ZIP file in the order that they were added to the ZIP file. Therefore, if they were added in alphabetical order, they would be created in that order. We also notice that the resulting files have the same created and written times and they are equal to the original last written time of the file. Therefore, we do not find any basic evidence to show that this scenario could not have occurred.

The last scenario was that the files were created from downloading them in the sorted order. We run tests and find that this could occur, but the time values raise doubts about this scenario. The created and written times of the different files are days and sometimes months apart. Therefore, the user would have had to download these files in the sorted order over the course of months. This could be a reasonable situation if the files were released on a periodic basis and the naming convention of the files was based on when they were released.

From our three scenarios, we conclude that the last two are the most likely. We will investigate both of these scenarios in more detail to find supporting evidence. For example, we can search for ZIP files or evidence of long-term downloading of these files. There are probably many other scenarios that could have caused this situation, and this is not meant to be an exhaustive set of tests. The results could vary by OS and ZIP versions.

## THE BIG PICTURE

So far, we have seen the details of the FAT file system organized by the data categories. This is not always the most intuitive way to think about the file system, so I will summarize with some examples of how a file is created and deleted.

### FILE ALLOCATION EXAMPLE

To review how a file is created in a FAT file system, we will step through the process to create the dir1\file1.dat file. In this example, the dir1 directory already exists, the cluster size is 4,096 bytes, and the file size is 6,000 bytes.

1. We read the boot sector from sector 0 of the volume and locate the FAT structures, data area, and root directory.
2. We need to find the dir1 directory, so we process each directory entry in the root directory and look for one that has dir1 as its name and the directory attribute set. We find the entry, and it has a starting cluster of 90.

3. We read the contents of dir1's starting cluster, cluster 90, and process each directory entry in it until we find one that is unallocated.

4. We find an available entry and set its allocation status by writing the name file1.txt. The size and current time are also written to the appropriate fields.

5. We need to allocate clusters for the content, so we search the FAT structure. We allocate cluster 200 for the file by setting its entry to the EOF value.

6. We write the address of cluster 200 in the starting cluster field of the directory entry. The first 4,096 bytes of the file content are written to the cluster. There are 1,904 bytes left, so a second cluster is needed.

7. We search the FAT structure for another cluster and allocate cluster 201.

8. The FAT entry for the first cluster, cluster 200, is changed so that it contains 201. The last 1,904 bytes of the file are written to cluster 201.

We can see the state of the file system after the file creation in Figure 9.17.

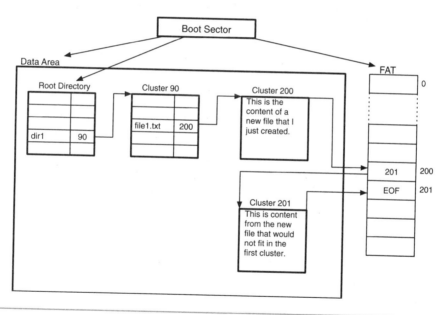

**Figure 9.17** File system state after allocating the 'dir1\file1.txt' file.

## FILE DELETION EXAMPLE

We now repeat the previous example, but we are going to delete the `dir1\file1.txt` file.

1. We read the boot sector from sector 0 of the volume and locate the FAT structures, data area, and root directory.
2. We locate the `dir1` directory by processing each directory entry in the root directory and looking for one that has `dir1` as its name and that has the directory attribute set.
3. We process the contents of `dir1`'s starting cluster, cluster 90, to find a directory entry that has the name `file1.txt`. We find that it has a starting cluster of 200.
4. We use the FAT structure to determine the cluster chain for the file. In this case, the file has allocated clusters 200 and 201.
5. We set the FAT entries for clusters 200 and 201 to 0.
6. We unallocated the directory entry for `file1.txt` by changing the first byte to 0xe5.

This final state can be seen in Figure 9.18 where the pointers that have been cleared have dashed lines and the first letter of the file name is missing.

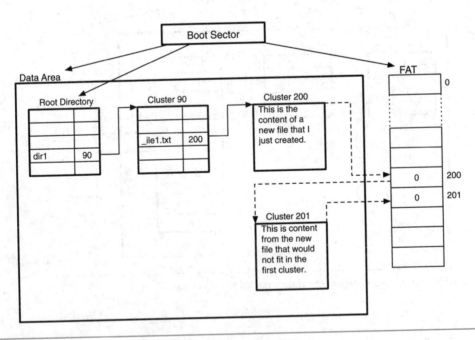

**Figure 9.18**  File system state after deleting the 'dir1\file1.txt' file.

## OTHER TOPICS

There are a few topics that do not apply to any specific category, and they are discussed in this final section. We discuss file recovery techniques and what should be performed during a file system consistency check. We also examine how to determine the file system type based on the number of clusters in the file system.

### FILE RECOVERY

Tools have existed for file recovery from a FAT file system since the early DOS days, but there is little documented theory on how it should be done. Recall that when a file is deleted from within Windows, the directory entry is marked as unused and the FAT entries for the clusters are set to 0. We saw an example diagram of this in Figure 9.18. To recover the file, we have the starting location and the size of the file. We have no information about the remaining clusters in the file.

We can try to recover the file data by reading the data from the known starting cluster. A recovery tool (or person) has two options when it comes to choosing the remaining clusters to read. It can blindly read the amount of data needed for the file size and ignore the allocation status of the data, or it can read only from the unallocated clusters.

The second option will succeed more often than the first option because it will recover some fragmented files. To explain the differences I will use Figure 9.19, which shows six clusters from a file system and three different scenarios. The file is 7,094 bytes in size and each cluster is 2,048 bytes, so we know it allocated four clusters. We also know that the starting cluster of the file was cluster 56. The light gray clusters represent the actual location of the file content for each scenario.

Figure 9.19(A) shows the scenario where the four clusters of the file are consecutive. In this scenario, both options will correctly recover clusters 56 to 59. Figure 9.19(B) shows the scenario where the file was fragmented into three chunks and the clusters in between the fragments, clusters 57 and 60, are still allocated to another file when the recovery takes place. In this scenario, option 1 will recover clusters 56 to 59 and incorrectly include the contents of cluster 57. Option 2 will correctly recover clusters 56, 58, 59, and 61. Figure 9.19(C) shows the scenario where the file allocated the same fragments as Figure 9.19(B), but the clusters in between the fragments are not allocated when the recovery takes place. In this scenario, both options will incorrectly recover clusters 56 to 59 like they did in the first scenario. There are other scenarios that could occur during file recovery, but they involve part of the file being overwritten, in which case no technique will accurately recover the data. Therefore, recovery option 2, where the allocation status of clusters is considered, can recover deleted files from more scenarios than option 1. Eoghan Casey performed some file recovery tests with WinHex and EnCase and found that WinHex version 11.25 used the first option and EnCase version 4 used the second option [Casey 2004].

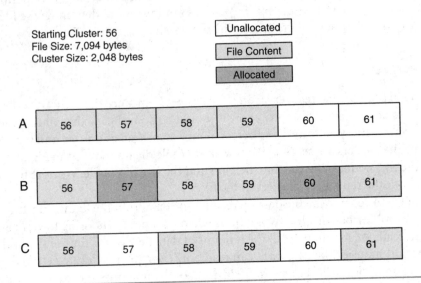

**Figure 9.19**   Three example scenarios for discussing file recovery.

A final note on recovery is that multiple cluster directories are likely to be fragmented. This is because the second cluster is only allocated when it is needed and it is highly unlikely that the next consecutive cluster will be available (because that cluster was probably allocated to one of the files in the directory). Therefore, directories are harder to recover, unless the directory is the result of a copy or the file system has been recently defragmented. When a directory is copied and its size is known, then consecutive clusters could be allocated for it.

If a user frequently runs defragmenting software on her file system, recovery of the files deleted after the last defragmenting will be easier because more of the files will be in consecutive clusters. On the other hand, files that were deleted prior to the defragmenting will be very difficult to recover because the clusters could have been reallocated.

I have created a FAT file recovery test image, and it is on the DFTT site [Carrier 2004a]. The test image has several deleted files and directories that you can use to test your recovery tools.

## DETERMINING THE TYPE

In the beginning of this chapter, I mentioned that there is no single field that identifies a FAT file system as FAT12, FAT16, or FAT32. Now that we have discussed all the areas and concepts for a FAT file system, I'll cover the methods for calculating the type.

The official method determines the type based on the number of clusters in the file system. To get the number of clusters, we need to determine how many sectors there are in the data area and then divide that number by the number of sectors per cluster.

For FAT12 and FAT16, the root directory takes the first sectors of the data area, and cluster 2 starts after it. For FAT32, the root directory is dynamic, and cluster 2 starts at the beginning of the data area. There is a value in the boot sector that identifies how many entries there are in the root directory, and for FAT32 this value is 0. We can calculate the number of sectors in the root directory by multiplying the number of entries by 32 bytes (the size of each directory entry), dividing by the number of bytes per sector, and rounding up (if needed):

```
((NUM_ENTRIES * 32) + (BYTES_PER_SECTOR - 1)) / (BYTES_PER_SECTOR)
```

The previous calculation will be zero for FAT32. We determine the number of sectors that are allocated to clusters by taking the total number of sectors in the file system and subtracting the size of the reserved area, the size of the FAT area, and the size of the root directory. In other words, we are subtracting the sector address of cluster 2 from the total number of sectors.

```
TOTAL_SECTORS - RESERVED_SIZE - NUM_FAT * FAT_SIZE - ROOTDIR_SIZE
```

Lastly, we divide the number of sectors in the data area by the number of sectors in a cluster. If this value is less than 4,085, the file system should be FAT12; if the value is 4,085 or greater and less than 65,525, the file system should be FAT16, and any size greater than or equal to 65,525 should be FAT32. These values correspond to the maximum number of clusters that a FAT can store. Recall that there are 8 reserved values for end of file, 1 for bad clusters, and the unused entries in slots 0 and 1.

When formatting a volume in Windows, you are typically given a choice if you want FAT16 or FAT32. Windows will chose the cluster size such that the resulting number of clusters will fall into the previous range. For example, a 4-kilobyte cluster could be used if you format a file system as FAT16, and a 2-kilobyte cluster could be used if you format it as FAT32.

## CONSISTENCY CHECK

When investigating a file system, it is useful to perform some consistency checks to identify corrupt file systems and hidden data. For the boot sector and other data structures in the reserved area of a FAT file system, a consistency check should verify that the defined values are in the appropriate range, and it should examine the unused locations for non-zero values. For example, there are many sectors in the reserved area that are not used in every file system. If a backup boot sector is available for a FAT32 file system, a consistency check should compare the two and report any differences.

The backup and primary FATs should be compared to verify that they have the same values. Each entry that is marked as bad should be examined because most hard disks fix errors before the operating system notices them. Floppy disks may have valid bad sectors, though. The space between the FAT entry for the last cluster and the end of the sector allocated to the FAT should be examined for each FAT because this space is not used by the file system and could contain hidden data. Space between the end of the last cluster and the end of the file system might exist that does not have a cluster address.

The root directory and its subdirectories should be examined, and each cluster chain in the FAT should be checked to make sure that an allocated directory entry points to the start of it. The reverse check also should be done to make sure that allocated directory entries point to allocated clusters. If multiple directory entries point to a cluster chain, Microsoft recommends that both files be copied to a new location and the original versions deleted [Microsoft 2003b]. The length of the cluster chain should be the number of clusters needed for the size of the file.

Any directory entries that are marked as volume labels should not have a starting cluster, and there should only be one volume label entry in the file system. The checksums for the allocated LFN directory entries should be examined and compared to the allocated SFN entry. If a corresponding SFN entry cannot be found, the LFN entries should be examined. This could be a result of a file system crash, using an OS that doesn't support long file names, or they could contain hidden data. Any directory entries in a directory that are all zeros or random data and have allocated entries before and after it could be the result of a wiping tool. Also check if there are any directory entries after a null entry. Some OSes will not show entries after a null entry.

## SUMMARY

FAT file systems have relatively few data structures but present challenges with respect to file recovery and temporal-based auditing. The data structures for the file system are well defined in the specification, but guidelines for allocation and the updating of times are not. Furthermore, there are many systems that use the FAT file system, and each may choose different algorithms. It is a good idea to test and observe the allocation algorithms for the types of systems that you are examining. If you have not been reading Chapter 10 along with this chapter, then I recommend you read the next chapter if you are interested in the layout of the data on disk.

FAT file systems will be around for some time to come and are well suited for an investigator to examine by hand. Many hex editors offer support for FAT file systems and allow you to examine each of the data structures. Unfortunately, a suspect can use those same hex editors to modify the file system contents.

After reading this chapter, you may be questioning the five-category data model, but it should be more intuitive from here on.

# BIBLIOGRAPHY

Bates, Jim. "File Deletion in MS FAT Systems." September 23, 2002. http://www.computer-investigations.com/arts/tech02.html.

Brouwer, Andries. "The FAT File System." September 20, 2002. http://www.win.tue.nl/~aeb/linux/fs/fat/fat.html.

Carrier, Brian. "FAT Undelete Test #1." *Digital Forensic Tool Testing*, February 2004a. http://dftt.sourceforge.net/.

Carrier, Brian. "FAT Volume Label Test #1." *Digital Forensic Tool Testing*, August 2004b. http://dftt.sourceforge.net/.

Casey, Eoghan. "Tool Review—WinHex." *Journal of Digital Investigation*, 1(2), 2004.

Landis, Hale, "How It Works: DOS Floppy Disk Boot Sector." May 6, 2002. http://www.ata-atapi.com/hiwdos.htm.

Microsoft. "FAT: General Overview of On-Disk Format." *FAT32 File System Specification, Version 1.03*, December 6, 2000. http://www.microsoft.com/whdc/system/platform/firmware/fatgen.mspx.

Microsoft. "Last Access Date." *MSDN Library*, February 2003a. http://msdn.microsoft.com/library/en-us/win9x/lfn_5mg5.asp?frame=true.

Microsoft. "How to Fix Cross-linked Files." *Microsoft Knowledge Base Article—83140*, May 10, 2003b. http://support.microsoft.com/default.aspx?scid=kb;en-us;83140.

Microsoft. "MS-DOS FORMAT Does Not Preserve Clusters Marked Bad." *Knowledge Base Article—103548*, May 6, 2003c. http://support.microsoft.com/default.aspx?scid=kb;en-us;103548.

Microsoft. "Description of NTFS Date and Time Stamps for Files and Folders." *Microsoft Knowledge Base Article 299648*, July 3, 2003d. http://support.microsoft.com/default.aspx?scid=kb;en-us;299648.

Microsoft. "Detailed Explanation of FAT Boot Sector." *Microsoft Knowledge Base Article Q140418*, December 6, 2003e. http://support.microsoft.com/kb/q140418/.

Microsoft. "Encodings and Code Pages." *Global Development and Computing Portal*, 2004a. http://www.microsoft.com/globaldev/getWR/steps/wrg_codepage.mspx.

Microsoft. "How to Cause ScanDisk for Windows to Retest Bad Clusters." *Microsoft Knowledge Base Article—127055*, December 16, 2004b. http://support.microsoft.com/default.aspx?scid=kb;en-us;127055.

Microsoft. "Windows 2000 Server Operations Guide (Part 1)." n.d. http://www.microsoft.com/resources/documentation/windows/2000/server/reskit/en-us/serverop/part1/sopch01.mspx.

Wilson, Craig. "Volume Serial Numbers & Format Verification Date/Time." *Digital Detective White Paper*, October 2003. http://www.digital-detective.co.uk/documents/Volume%20Serial%20Numbers.pdf.

# FAT Data Structures 10

In the previous chapter, we examined the basic concepts of a FAT file system and how to analyze it. Now we are going to get more detailed and examine the data structures that make up FAT. This chapter will ignore the five-category model and instead focus on each individual data structure. This makes it easier to understand FAT because many of the data structures are in more than one category. I assume that you have already read Chapter 9, "FAT Concepts and Analysis," or that you are reading it in parallel. All the hexdumps and data shown in this chapter correspond to the data that were analyzed in Chapter 9 using tools from *The Sleuth Kit* (TSK).

## BOOT SECTOR

The boot sector is located in the first sector of FAT file system and contains the bulk of the file system category of data. FAT12/16 and FAT32 have different versions of the boot sector, but they both have the same initial 36 bytes. The data structure for the first 36 bytes is given in Table 10.1, and the data structures for the remaining bytes are given in Tables 10.2 and 10.3.

**Table 10.1**    Data structure for the first 36 bytes of the FAT boot sector.

| Byte Range | Description | Essential |
|---|---|---|
| 0–2 | Assembly instruction to jump to boot code. | No (unless it is a bootable file system) |
| 3–10 | OEM Name in ASCII. | No |
| 11–12 | Bytes per sector. Allowed values include 512, 1024, 2048, and 4096. | Yes |
| 13–13 | Sectors per cluster (data unit). Allowed values are powers of 2, but the cluster size must be 32KB or smaller. | Yes |
| 14–15 | Size in sectors of the reserved area. | Yes |
| 16–16 | Number of FATs. Typically two for redundancy, but according to Microsoft it can be one for some small storage devices. | Yes |
| 17–18 | Maximum number of files in the root directory for FAT12 and FAT16. This is 0 for FAT32 and typically 512 for FAT16. | Yes |
| 19–20 | 16-bit value of number of sectors in file system. If the number of sectors is larger than can be represented in this 2-byte value, a 4-byte value exists later in the data structure and this should be 0. | Yes |
| 21–21 | Media type. According to the Microsoft documentation, 0xf8 should be used for fixed disks and 0xf0 for removable. | No |
| 22–23 | 16-bit size in sectors of each FAT for FAT12 and FAT16. For FAT32, this field is 0. | Yes |
| 24–25 | Sectors per track of storage device. | No |
| 26–27 | Number of heads in storage device. | No |
| 28–31 | Number of sectors before the start of partition.[1] | No |
| 32–35 | 32-bit value of number of sectors in file system. Either this value or the 16-bit value above must be 0. | Yes |

---

1. My testing has shown that for file systems in an extended partition, Windows sets this value based on the beginning of the extended partition, not the beginning of the disk.

The first value in the boot sector, bytes 0 to 2, is a boot code instruction tells the computer where to find the code needed to boot the operating system. If the file system is not used to boot the computer, the value is not needed. You could use this value to identify what boot code is used. Note that DOS and Windows require that the value be set on non-bootable file systems, but other OSes, such a Linux, do not.

The media type value is used to identify if the file system is on fixed or removable media, but Microsoft Windows does not use it. A second copy of the media type exists in the file allocation table, and it is the one that Windows uses [Microsoft 2001]. The concepts of the other fields were discussed in Chapter 9.

From bytes 36 onward, FAT12 and FAT16 have a different layout than FAT32. The one value that they both have in common is the signature 0x55 in byte 510 and 0xAA in byte 511. Note that this is the same signature at the same location that the DOS partition table uses in its first sector (you'll also see it again in the first NTFS sector). The data structure values for the rest of the FAT12 and FAT16 boot sector are given in Table 10.2.

**Table 10.2** Data structure for the remainder of the FAT12/16 boot sector.

| Byte Range | Description | Essential |
|---|---|---|
| 0–35 | See Table 10.1. | Yes |
| 36–36 | BIOS INT13h drive number. | No |
| 37–37 | Not used. | No |
| 38–38 | Extended boot signature to identify if the next three values are valid. The signature is 0x29. | No |
| 39–42 | Volume serial number, which some versions of Windows will calculate based on the creation date and time. | No |
| 43–53 | Volume label in ASCII. The user chooses this value when creating the file system. | No |
| 54–61 | File system type label in ASCII. Standard values include "FAT," "FAT12," and "FAT16," but nothing is required. | No |
| 62–509 | Not used. | No |
| 510–511 | Signature value (0xAA55). | No |

The data structure for the rest of the FAT32 boot sector is given in Table 10.3.

**Table 10.3**   Data structure for the remainder of the FAT32 boot sector.

| Byte Range | Description | Essential |
|---|---|---|
| 0–35 | See Table 10.1. | Yes |
| 36–39 | 32-bit size in sectors of one FAT. | Yes |
| 40–41 | Defines how multiple FAT structures are written to. If bit 7 is 1, only one of the FAT structures is active and its index is described in bits 0–3. Otherwise, all FAT structures are mirrors of each other. | Yes |
| 42–43 | The major and minor version number. | Yes |
| 44–47 | Cluster where root directory can be found. | Yes |
| 48–49 | Sector where FSINFO structure can be found. | No |
| 50–51 | Sector where backup copy of boot sector is located (default is 6). | No |
| 52–63 | Reserved. | No |
| 64–64 | BIOS INT13h drive number. | No |
| 65–65 | Not used. | No |
| 66–66 | Extended boot signature to identify if the next three values are valid. The signature is 0x29. | No |
| 67–70 | Volume serial number, which some versions of Windows will calculate based on the creation date and time. | No |
| 71–81 | Volume label in ASCII. The user chooses this value when creating the file system. | No |
| 82–89 | File system type label in ASCII. Standard values include "FAT32," but nothing is required. | No |
| 90–509 | Not used. | No |
| 510–511 | Signature value (0xAA55). | No |

The difference between the FAT12/16 and FAT32 boot sector is that the FAT32 sector includes data to make the file system more scalable and flexible. There can be different policies for how the FAT structures are written to and a backup copy of the boot sector exists. There is also a version field, but there seems to be only one version used by Microsoft at the time of this writing.

The data between bytes 62 to 509 in a FAT12/16 file system, and bytes 90 to 509 in a FAT32 file system do not have a specified purpose, but are typically used to store boot code and error messages. Here is a hex dump of the first sector of a FAT32 file system from a Windows XP system:

```
# dcat -f fat fat-4.dd 0 | xxd
0000000: eb58 904d 5344 4f53 352e 3000 0202 2600  .X.MSDOS5.0...&.
0000016: 0200 0000 00f8 0000 3f00 4000 c089 0100  ........?.@.....
0000032: 4023 0300 1d03 0000 0000 0000 0200 0000  @#..............
0000048: 0100 0600 0000 0000 0000 0000 0000 0000  ................
0000064: 8000 2903 4619 4c4e 4f20 4e41 4d45 2020  ..).F.LNO NAME
0000080: 2020 4641 5433 3220 2020 33c9 8ed1 bcf4     FAT32   3.....
0000096: 7b8e c18e d9bd 007c 884e 028a 5640 b408  {......|.N..V@..
0000112: cd13 7305 b9ff ff8a f166 0fb6 c640 660f  ..s......f...@f.
0000128: b6d1 80e2 3ff7 e286 cdc0 ed06 4166 0fb7  ....?.......Af..
[REMOVED]
0000416: 0000 0000 0000 0000 0000 0000 0d0a 5265  ..............Re
0000432: 6d6f 7665 2064 6973 6b73 206f 7220 6f74  move disks or ot
0000448: 6865 7220 6d65 6469 612e ff0d 0a44 6973  her media....Dis
0000464: 6b20 6572 726f 72ff 0d0a 5072 6573 7320  k error...Press
0000480: 616e 7920 6b65 7920 746f 2072 6573 7461  any key to resta
0000496: 7274 0d0a 0000 0000 00ac cbd8 0000 55aa  rt...........U.
```

The first line shows us that the OEM name is "MSDOS5.0," which may have been generated by a Windows 2000 or XP system. The data is written in little endian ordering, so the data structure fields that are numbers will appear in reverse order and strings will appear in the expected order. Bytes 11 to 12 show us that each sector is 512 bytes, (0x0200) and byte 13 shows us that the size of each cluster in the data area is 2 sectors, which is 1024 bytes. Bytes 14 to 15 show us that there are 38 (0x0026) sectors in the reserved area, so we know that the FAT area will start in sector 38, and byte 16 shows that there are two FAT structures. Bytes 19 to 20 contain the 16-bit file system size value and it is 0, which means that the 32-bit field in bytes 32 to 35 must be used. This field shows us that the size of the file system is 205,632 (0x00032340) sectors. Bytes 28 to 31 show that there are 100,800 (0x0001 89c0) sectors before the start of this file system, which may have been allocated to a small partition. For example, this could be a dual boot system, or there could be a hibernation partition for a laptop. The partition table should be analyzed for more information.

This image is FAT32, so we need to apply the appropriate data structure from now on. Bytes 36 to 39 show that the size of each FAT structure is 797 (0x0000 031d) sectors, and because we know there will be two FAT structures, the total size of the FAT area will be 1,594 sectors. Bytes 48 to 49 show that the FSINFO information is located in sector 1, and bytes 50 to 51 show that the backup copy of the boot sector is in sector 6.

The volume serial number is located in bytes 67 to 70, and its value is 0x4c194603. The volume label is in bytes 71 to 81 and has the value "NO NAME" (plus four spaces). We will see later that the real label is stored in another location in the file system. The type label is in bytes 82 to 89, and it is "FAT32" (plus three spaces) for this system. Bytes 90 to 509 are not used by the file system, but we can see data here that is used if the system tries to boot from this file system. Bytes 510 and 511 have the signature 0xAA55 value. The output from running the fsstat tool from TSK on this image was given in Chapter 9.

As mentioned in Chapter 9, some versions of Windows will assign the volume serial number using the file system creation date and time values. I found that Windows 98 does this, but that Windows XP does not. The calculation is broken up into the upper 16 bits and the lower 16 bits [Wilson 2003]. With the exception of the year, each field in the date is converted to a 1-byte hexadecimal value and placed in its location in the equation. The year gets a 2-byte hexadecimal value. Figure 10.1 shows the process. The upper 16 bits are the result of adding the hours, minutes, and year. The lower 16 bits are the result of adding the month, day, seconds, and tens of seconds. The sample file system image we looked at is from a Windows XP system and it does not use this calculation.

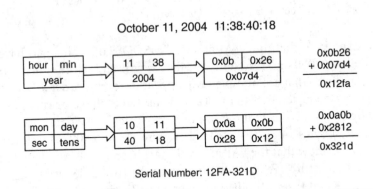

**Figure 10.1**   Process for calculating the volume serial number from the creation date and time.

# FAT32 FSINFO

A FAT32 file system has a FSINFO data structure that includes hints about where the operating system can allocate new clusters. Its location is given in the boot sector, and its layout is given in Table 10.4.

**Table 10.4** Data structure for the FAT32 FSINFO sector.

| Byte Range | Description | Essential |
|---|---|---|
| 0–3 | Signature (0x41615252) | No |
| 4–483 | Not used | No |
| 484–487 | Signature (0x61417272) | No |
| 488–491 | Number of free clusters | No |
| 492–495 | Next free cluster | No |
| 496–507 | Not used | No |
| 508–511 | Signature (0xAA550000) | No |

None of these values is required. They are there as a suggestion for the OS, but it is valid for them to not be updated. Here we see the contents of sector 1 from the file system we previously examined. The byte offsets are given relative to the start of this sector.

```
# dcat -f fat fat-4.dd 1 | xxd
0000000: 5252 6141 0000 0000 0000 0000 0000 0000   RRaA...........
0000016: 0000 0000 0000 0000 0000 0000 0000 0000   ...............
[REMOVED]
0000464: 0000 0000 0000 0000 0000 0000 0000 0000   ...............
0000480: 0000 0000 7272 4161 1e8e 0100 4b00 0000   ....rrAa....K...
0000496: 0000 0000 0000 0000 0000 0000 0000 55aa   .............U.
```

We see the signatures at bytes 0 to 3, 484 to 487, and 508 to 511. The number of free clusters is in bytes 488 to 491, and this file system has 101,918 (0x0001 8e1e) free clusters. Note that this value is in clusters and not sectors. The next free cluster is located in bytes 492 to 495, and we see that it is cluster 75 (0x0000 004b).

# FAT

The FAT is crucial to a FAT file system and has two purposes. It is used to determine the allocation status of a cluster and to find the next allocated cluster in a file or directory. This section covers how we find the FAT and what it looks like.

There are typically two FATs in a FAT file system, but the exact number is given in the boot sector. The first FAT starts after the reserved sectors, the size of which is given in the boot sector. The total size of each FAT is also given in the boot sector, and the second FAT, if it exists, starts in the sector following the end of the first.

The table consists of equal-sized entries and has no header or footer values. The size of each entry depends on the file system version. FAT12 has 12-bit entries, FAT16 has 16-bit entries, and FAT32 has 32-bit entries. The entries are addressed starting with 0, and each entry corresponds to the cluster with the same address.

If a cluster is not allocated, its entry will have a 0 in it. If a cluster is allocated, its entry will be non-zero and will contain the address of the next cluster in the file or directory. If it is the last cluster in a file or directory, its entry will have an end-of-file marker, which is any value greater than 0xff8 for FAT12, 0xfff8 for FAT16 and 0x0fff fff8 for FAT32. If an entry has a value of 0xff7 for FAT12, 0xfff7 for FAT16, or 0x0fff fff7 for FAT32, the cluster has been marked as damaged and should not be allocated.

Recall that the first addressable cluster in the file system is #2. Therefore, entries 0 and 1 in the FAT structure are not needed. Entry 0 typically stores a copy of the media type, and entry 1 typically stores the dirty status of the file system. There is also a storage value for the media type in the boot sector, but as previously noted, Windows might not use it and could use the value in FAT entry 0 instead. The dirty status can be used to identify a file system that was not unmounted properly (improper shutdown) or that hardware surface errors were encountered. Both of these values are non-essential and may not be accurate.

To examine FAT structure of our sample image we view sector 38, which is the first sector following the reserved area:

```
# dcat -f fat fat-4.dd 38 | xxd
[REMOVED]
0000288: 4900 0000 4a00 0000 4c00 0000 0000 0000   I...J...L.......
0000304: 4d00 0000 ffff ff0f 4f00 0000 ffff ff0f   M.......O.......
0000320: 5100 0000 5200 0000 ffff ff0f ffff ff0f   Q...R...........
0000336: ffff ff0f 0000 0000 0000 0000 0000 0000   ................
0000352: 0000 0000 0000 0000 0000 0000 0000 0000   ................
```

This output is from a FAT32 file system, so each entry is 4 bytes (two columns) and the first entry shown has a value of 73 (0x0000 0049). Its actual location in the FAT structure is at byte offset 288, and we can divide it by four (the number of bytes per entry) to determine that it is entry 72. We know that this entry is allocated because it is non-zero and the next cluster in the file is cluster 73.

We can see that the entry at bytes 300 to 303 and the entries at bytes 340 onwards are all 0, which means that the clusters corresponding to those entries are not allocated. In this example, the bytes at 300 to 303 are for cluster 75, and the bytes at 340 are for cluster 85 and onwards. There is an example in the directory entry section that shows how to follow a cluster chain in the FAT.

We can see the allocation status of a cluster using tools from TSK, but we will have to translate sectors and clusters. In this example file system, the sector of cluster 2 is 1,632 and each cluster is 2 sectors. We can translate cluster 75 to a sector by using

```
(Cluster 75 - Cluster 2) * 2 (Sectors per Cluster) + Sector 1,632 = Sector 1,778
```

The dstat tool in TSK will show us the allocation status and cluster address of any sector. When we run it on sector 1,778 we get

```
# dstat -f fat fat-4.dd 1778
Sector: 1778
Not Allocated
Cluster: 75
```

## DIRECTORY ENTRIES

The FAT directory entry contains the name and metadata for a file or directory. One of these entries is allocated for every file and directory, and they are located in the clusters allocated to the file's parent directory. This data structure supports a name that has only 8 characters in the name and 3 characters in the extension. If the file has a more complex name, there will be a long file name directory entry in addition to a directory entry. The long file name version is discussed in the next section of this chapter. The basic directory entry structure has the fields given in Table 10.5.

**Table 10.5**  Data structure for a basic FAT directory entry.

| Byte Range | Description | Essential |
|---|---|---|
| 0–0 | First character of file name in ASCII and allocation status (0xe5 or 0x00 if unallocated) | Yes |
| 1–10 | Characters 2 to 11 of file name in ASCII | Yes |
| 11–11 | File Attributes (see Table 10.6) | Yes |
| 12–12 | Reserved | No |
| 13–13 | Created time (tenths of second) | No |
| 14–15 | Created time (hours, minutes, seconds) | No |
| 16–17 | Created day | No |
| 18–19 | Accessed day | No |
| 20–21 | High 2 bytes of first cluster address (0 for FAT12 and FAT16) | Yes |
| 22–23 | Written time (hours, minutes, seconds) | No |
| 24–25 | Written day | No |
| 26–27 | Low 2 bytes of first cluster address | Yes |
| 28–31 | Size of file (0 for directories) | Yes |

The first byte of the data structure works as the allocation status, and if it is set to 0xe5 or 0x00, the directory entry is unallocated. Otherwise, the byte is used to store the first character of the file name. The name is typically in ASCII, but could also use one of the Microsoft code pages if the name uses non-ASCII symbols [Microsoft 2004]. If the file name has the value 0xe5 in that byte, 0x05 should be used instead. If the name does not have 8 characters in its name, unused bytes are typically filled in with the ASCII value for a space, which is 0x20.

The file size field is 4 bytes and, therefore, the maximum file size is 4GB. Directories will have a size of 0 and the FAT structure must be used to determine the number of clusters allocated to it. The attributes field can have one or more of the bits in Table 10.6 set.

**Table 10.6**   Flag values for the directory entry attributes field.

| Flag Value (in bits) | Description | Essential |
|---|---|---|
| 0000 0001 (0x01) | Read only | No |
| 0000 0010 (0x02) | Hidden file | No |
| 0000 0100 (0x04) | System file | No |
| 0000 1000 (0x08) | Volume label | Yes |
| 0000 1111 (0x0f) | Long file name | Yes |
| 0001 0000 (0x10) | Directory | Yes |
| 0010 0000 (0x20) | Archive | No |

The upper two bits of the attribute byte are reserved. Directory entries that have the long file name attribute set have a different structure because they are storing the long name for a file, and they will be described in the next section. Notice that the long file name attribute is a bit-wise combination of the first four attributes. Microsoft found that older OSes would ignore directory entries with all the bits set and would not complain about the different layout.

The date portion of each timestamp is a 16-bit value that has three parts, which are shown in Figure 10.2(A). The lower 5 bits are for the day of the month, and the valid values are 1 to 31. Bits 5 to 8 are for the month, and the valid values are 1 to 12. Bits 9 to 15 are for the year, and the value is added to 1980. The valid range is from 0 to 127, which gives a year range of 1980 to 2107. A conversion of the date April 1, 2005 to its hexadecimal format can be found in Figure 10.2(B).

The time value is also a 16-bit value and also has three parts. The lower 5 bits are for the second, and it uses two-second intervals. The valid range of this value is 0 to 29, which allows a second range of 0 to 58 in two-second intervals. The next 6 bits are for the minute and have a valid range of 0 to 59. The last 5 bits are for the hour and have a valid range of 0 to 23. This can be seen in Figure 10.3(A). An example of converting the time 10:31:44 a.m. to the FAT format can be found in Figure 10.3(B).

Fortunately, there are many tools that will convert these values for you so that you do not have do always do it by hand.[1] Many hex editors will show the date if you highlight the value and have the correct options set. As we will see in the later chapters, this method of saving the time is much different from other file systems, which save the time as the number of seconds since a given time.

---

1. An example is "Decode from Digital Detective" (https://www.digital-detective.co.uk).

A)

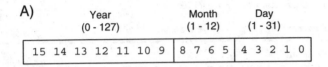

B)

Start: April 1, 2005

| Normal | Decimal | Hex | Binary |
|--------|---------|------|----------|
| 1 | 1 | 0x01 | 0 0001 |
| April | 4 | 0x04 | 0100 |
| 2005 | 25 | 0x19 | 001 1001 |

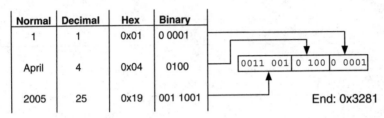

End: 0x3281

**Figure 10.2**   Breakdown of the date value and the conversion of April 1, 2005 to its FAT date format.

A)

Hour (0 - 23)    Minute (0 - 59)    Second (0 - 29)

| 15 14 13 12 11 | 10 9 8 7 6 5 | 4 3 2 1 0 |

B)

Start: 10:31:44 AM

| Normal | Decimal | Hex | Binary |
|--------|---------|--------|----------|
| 44 | 22 | 0x16 | 1 0110 |
| 31 | 31 | 0x01f | 01 1111 |
| 10 | 10 | 0x0a | 0 1010 |

0101 0 011 111 1 0110

End: 0x53f6

**Figure 10.3**  Breakdown of the time value and the conversion of 10:31:44 a.m. to its FAT time format.

Let's look at the raw contents of two directory entries from the root directory. The starting location of the root directory in a FAT32 file system is given in the boot sector.

```
# dcat -f fat fat-4.dd 1632 | xxd
0000000: 4641 5420 4449 534b 2020 2008 0000 0000  FAT DISK   .....
0000016: 0000 0000 0000 874d 252b 0000 0000 0000  .......M%+......
0000032: 5245 5355 4d45 2d31 5254 4620 00a3 347e  RESUME-1RTF ..4~
0000048: 4a30 8830 0000 4a33 7830 0900 f121 0000  .0.0.....0...!..
```

The first two lines show a directory entry with the attribute at byte 11 set to the binary value 0000 1000 (0x08), which is for a volume label. We can also see that the write time and date are set at bytes 22 to 25 on line 2. The write time on a volume label may contain the date when the file system was created. Note that the volume label in the boot sector was set to "NO NAME."

The third and fourth lines are for a second directory entry, and we see that the name of this file is "RESUME-1.RTF." The attribute value at byte 43 is 0000 0010 (0x20), which means that only the archive attribute bit is set. Byte 45 shows the tenths of a second for the create time, which is 163 (0xa3). Bytes 46 to 47 have the created time, 0x7e34, which is 15:49:40. The created day is in bytes 48 to 49 and has a value of 0x304a, which is February 10, 2004. The rest of the times are left as an exercise, if you are really bored.

We can see from bytes 52 to 53 and 58 to 59 that the starting cluster is 9 (0x0000 0009), and bytes 60 to 63 show that the file size is 8,689 (0x0000 21f1) bytes. To determine all the clusters in this file, we will need to refer to the FAT. Cluster 9 has a 36-byte offset into the FAT32 structure, and we previously calculated that the primary FAT structure starts in sector 38. Its contents are shown here:

```
# dcat -f fat fat-4.dd 38 | xxd
[REMOVED]
0000032: ffff ff0f 0a00 0000 0b00 0000 0c00 0000  ...............
0000048: 0d00 0000 0e00 0000 0f00 0000 1000 0000  ...............
0000064: 1100 0000 ffff ff0f 1300 0000 1400 0000  ...............
```

The table entry for cluster 9 is located in bytes 36 to 39, and we see that the value is 10 (0x0000 000a), which means that cluster 10 is the next cluster in the chain. The table entry for cluster 10 is in bytes 40 to 43, and we see that the value is 11 (0x0000 000b). We can see that consecutive clusters were allocated to this file until we get to entry 17 at bytes 68 to 71, which has an end-of-file marker (0x0fff ffff). We can verify that we have the correct number of clusters by comparing the file size with the allocated space. The file has allocated 9 1,024-byte clusters, so there are 9,216 bytes of storage space for the 8,689-byte file.

We can now view some of this same data with TSK. Remember that TSK uses sector addresses instead of cluster addresses. To convert cluster 9 to its sector address, we need the sector address of cluster 2, which is 1,632:

```
(Cluster 9 - Cluster 2) * 2 (Sectors per Cluster) + Sector 1,632 = Sector 1,646
```

The fsstat tool in TSK dumps the contents of the FAT structures. We previously saw part of the fsstat output when discussing the file system category of data, but the FAT contents were removed. Here is that output:

```
# fsstat -f fat fat-4.dd
[REMOVED]
1642-1645 (4) -> EOF
1646-1663 (18) -> EOF
1664-1681 (18) -> EOF
[REMOVED]
```

Here the output shows us the cluster chain for RESUME-1.RTF from sectors 1646 to 1663 and the End of File. Each cluster was 2 sectors in size, so we can see in the parentheses that there are 18 sectors in the cluster chain.

The istat tool in TSK shows the details of a directory entry and its output for this entry is given next. Using the metadata-addressing scheme of TSK, the RESUME-1.RTF file is the second entry in the root directory, which means that it has an address of 4.

```
# istat -f fat fat-4.dd 4
Directory Entry: 4
Allocated
File Attributes: File, Archive
Size: 8689
Name: RESUME-1.RTF

Directory Entry Times:
Written:        Wed Mar 24 06:26:20 2004
Accessed:       Thu Apr  8 00:00:00 2004
Created:        Tue Feb 10 15:49:40 2004

Sectors:
1646 1647 1648 1649 1650 1651 1652 1653
1654 1655 1656 1657 1658 1659 1660 1661
1662 1663
```

# LONG FILE NAME DIRECTORY ENTRIES

The standard directory entry can support names with only 8 characters in the name and 3 characters in the extension. Longer names or names that use special characters require *long file name* (LFN) directory entries. A file will have a normal entry in addition to any LFN entries, and the LFN entries will precede the normal entry. The LFN version of the directory entry has the fields shown in Table 10.7.

**Table 10.7** Data structure for an LFN FAT directory entry.

| Byte Range | Description | Essential |
|---|---|---|
| 0–0 | Sequence number (ORed with 0x40) and allocation status (0xe5 if unallocated) | Yes |
| 1–10 | File name characters 1–5 (Unicode) | Yes |
| 11–11 | File attributes (0x0f) | Yes |
| 12–12 | Reserved | No |
| 13–13 | Checksum | Yes |
| 14–25 | File name characters 6–11 (Unicode) | Yes |
| 26–27 | Reserved | No |
| 28–31 | File name characters 12–13 (Unicode) | Yes |

The sequence number field is a counter for each entry needed to store the file name, and the first entry has a value of 1. The sequence number increases for each LFN entry until the final entry, which is a bitwise OR with the value 0x40. When two values are bitwise ORed together, the result has a 1 wherever any of the two inputs had a 1.

The LFN entries for a file are listed before the short name entry and are in reverse order. Therefore, the first entry that you will find in the directory will be the last LFN entry for the file and will have the largest sequence value. Unused characters are padded with 0xff, and the name should be NULL-terminated if there is room.

The file attributes of a LFN entry must be 0x0F. The checksum is calculated using the short name of the file, and it should be the same for each of the LFN entries for the file. If the checksum in a LFN entry does not match its corresponding short name, an OS that does not support long file names could have been used and made the directory corrupt. The checksum algorithm iterates over each letter in the name, and at each step it rotates the current checksum by one bit to the right and then adds the ASCII value of the next letter. The C code for it is

```
c = 0;
for (i = 0; i < 11; i++) {
    // Rotate c to the right
    c = ((c & 0x01) ? 0x80 : 0) + (c >> 1);
    // Add ASCII character from name
    c = c + shortname[i];
}
```

Let's look at the two LFN and one normal entry for a file in the root directory of our test image:

```
# dcat -f fat fat-4.dd 1632 | xxd
[REMOVED]
0000064: 424e 0061 006d 0065 002e 000f 00df 7200   BN.a.m.e......r.
0000080: 7400 6600 0000 ffff ffff 0000 ffff ffff   t.f.............
0000096: 014d 0079 0020 004c 006f 000f 00df 6e00   .M.y. .L.o....n.
0000112: 6700 2000 4600 6900 6c00 0000 6500 2000   g. .F.i.l...e. .
0000128: 4d59 4c4f 4e47 7e31 5254 4620 00a3 347e   MYLONG~1RTF ..4~
0000144: 4a30 8830 0000 4a33 7830 1a00 8f13 0000   J0.0..J3x0......
```

The first entry is in the first two lines, and we see that byte 75 is set to 0x0f, so we know it is a LFN entry. The sequence number is in byte 64, and it is 0x42. If we remove the OR of 0x40 for the end marker, we get 0x02 and see that there will be two LFN entries. The checksum in byte 77 gives a value of 0xdf, which we can later verify when we find the short name. The first five characters in this entry (although not the first characters in the name) are in bytes 65 to 74 and give 'Name.' The second section of characters in bytes 78 to 89 gives 'rtf.' The rest of the values are set to 0xffff. The final section of characters in bytes 92 to 95 is also set to 0xffff. Therefore, we know that the end of the long name is 'Name.rtf.'

The second entry, starting at byte 96, also has its LFN attribute set, and its sequence number is 1. It has the same checksum as the first entry, 0xdf. The characters in this entry give us 'My Lo,' 'ng Fil,' and 'e.' The sequence number of this entry is 1, so we know it is the last one we will find. We can append the characters of the two entries to get 'My Long File Name.rtf.' The short version of this name can be found in the third entry, which is a normal directory entry and has the name 'MYLONG~1.RTF.'

We can now verify the checksum, but first we need to know the ASCII values for the characters in binary. These are given in Table 10.8.

**Table 10.8**  ASCII values for the characters in our example LFN.

| Character | Hex | Binary |
|-----------|------|-----------|
| M | 0x4d | 0100 1101 |
| Y | 0x59 | 0101 1001 |
| L | 0x4c | 0100 1100 |
| O | 0x4f | 0100 1111 |
| N | 0x4e | 0100 1110 |
| G | 0x47 | 0100 0111 |
| ~ | 0x7e | 0111 1110 |
| 1 | 0x31 | 0011 0001 |
| R | 0x52 | 0101 0010 |
| T | 0x54 | 0101 0100 |
| F | 0x46 | 0100 0110 |

For clarity, we will do this whole thing in binary instead of constantly translating. The first step is to assign our variable 'check' to the value of the first letter of the name, 'M.'

```
check = 0100 1101
```

For the remaining 10 rounds, we rotate the current checksum to the right by one bit and then add the next letter. The next two steps will shift our current value and add 'Y.'

```
check = 1010 0110
check = 1010 0110 + 0101 1001 = 1111 1111
```

We rotate (with no effect because it is all 1s) and add 'L.'

```
check = 1111 1111
check = 1111 1111 + 0100 1100 = 0100 1011
```

We rotate and add 'O.'

```
check = 1010 0101
check = 1010 0101 + 0100 1111 = 1111 0100
```

From now on, I'll leave out the rotate line and show only the addition. The next step is to rotate and add 'N.'

```
check = 0111 1010 + 0100 1110 = 1100 1000
```

We rotate and add 'G.'

```
check = 0110 0100 + 0100 0111 = 1010 1011
```

We rotate and add '~.'

```
check = 1101 0101 + 0111 1110 = 0101 0011
```

We rotate and add '1.'

```
check = 1010 1001 + 0011 0001 = 1101 1010
```

We rotate and add 'R.'

```
check = 0110 1101 + 0101 0010 = 1011 1111
```

We rotate and add 'T.'

```
check = 1101 1111 + 0101 0100 = 0011 0011
```

Finally, we rotate and add 'F.'

```
check = 1001 1001 + 0100 0110 = 1101 1111 = 0xdf
```

Hopefully, you will never have to do this by hand, but now you can at least say that you have seen it before. The final value of 0xdf is the same that we saw in each of the LFN entries.

As an example output of processing this directory entry, we can look at the `fls` tool from TSK. `fls` prints the LFN and puts the short name in parentheses, as shown here:

```
# fls -f fat fat-2.dd
r/r    3: FAT DISK      (Volume Label Entry)
r/r    4: RESUME-1.RTF
r/r    7: My Long File Name.rtf (MYLONG~1.RTF)
r/r *  8: _ile6.txt
```

The first two lines of the output show the volume label and short file name directory entries that we saw in the "Directory Entries" section. The third line shows the long name that we recently dissected and shows the name of a deleted file, _ile6.txt. The star in front of the name shows that it is deleted and the first letter is missing because the first letter of the name is used to set the unallocated status. The number before the name shows the address of the directory entry where the details can be found.

## SUMMARY

FAT has simplicity because of its small number of data structures. The boot sector and FAT are crucial to analyzing the file system in an automated way, and the directory entries are crucial to recovering deleted files without application-level techniques.

## BIBLIOGRAPHY

Microsoft. "ScanDisk May Not Fix the Media Descriptor Byte." *Knowledge Base Article—158869*, July 28, 2001. http://support.microsoft.com/default.aspx?scid=kb;en-us;158869.

Microsoft. "Encodings and Code Pages." *Global Development and Computing Portal*, 2004. http://www.microsoft.com/globaldev/getWR/steps/wrg_codepage.mspx.

Wilson, Craig. "Volume Serial Numbers & Format Verification Date/Time." *Digital Detective White Paper*, October 2003. http://www.digital-detective.co.uk/documents/Volume%20Serial%20Numbers.pdf.

See also the Bibliography section of Chapter 9.

# NTFS Concepts

The *New Technologies File System* (NTFS) was designed by Microsoft and is the default file system for Microsoft Windows NT, Windows 2000, Windows XP, and Windows Server. At the time of this writing, Microsoft has discontinued the sale of the Windows 98 and ME lines, and the home version of Windows XP is standard among new consumer systems. FAT will still exist in mobile and small storage devices, but NTFS will likely be the most common file system for Windows investigations. NTFS is a much more complex file system than FAT because it has many features and is very scalable. Because of the complexity of NTFS, we will need three chapters to discuss it. This chapter discusses the core concepts of NTFS that apply to all the five categories in our model. Chapter 12, "NTFS Analysis," discusses the analysis of NTFS and uses the five-category model to show where we can find evidence. Chapter 13, "NTFS Data Structures," shows the data structures associated with NTFS.

## INTRODUCTION

NTFS was designed for reliability, security, and support for large storage devices. Scalability is provided by the use of generic data structures that wrap around data structures with specific content. This is a scalable design because the internal data structure can change over time as new demands are placed on the file system, and the general wrapper can remain constant. One example of a generic wrapper is that every byte of data in an NTFS file system is allocated to a file. We will be discussing the concept of an NTFS file in this chapter.

NTFS is a complex file system and, unfortunately, there is no published specification from Microsoft that describes the on-disk layout. High-level descriptions of the file system components have been published, but low-level details are sparse. Fortunately, other groups have published what they think the on-disk data structures are [Linux NTFS 2004], and those are included in this book and we use them to dissect a disk by hand. It should be stressed, though, that it is unknown if the data structures presented here are exactly what exists on-disk.

NTFS is standard in many Windows systems and becoming common in most of the free Unix distributions. The combination of no official specification and one dominant application that creates the file system makes it difficult to differentiate between the application-specific properties and the general properties of the file system. For example, there are other methods that could be used to initialize a file system that Microsoft does not use, and it is not clear if they should be considered "valid NTFS" file systems. Microsoft has made changes to the file system with each new release of Windows, and I have noted the differences here.

## EVERYTHING IS A FILE

One of the most important concepts in understanding the design of NTFS is that important data are allocated to files. This includes the basic file system administrative data that are typically hidden by other file systems. In fact, the files that contain the administrative data can be located anywhere in the volume, like a normal file can. Therefore, an NTFS file system does not have a specific layout like other file systems do. The entire file system is considered a data area, and any sector can be allocated to a file. The only consistent layout is that the first sectors of the volume contain the boot sector and boot code.

## MFT CONCEPTS

The Master File Table (MFT) is the heart of NTFS because it contains the information about all files and directories. Every file and directory has at least one entry in the table, and the entries by themselves are very simple. They are 1 KB in size, but only the first 42 bytes have a defined purpose. The remaining bytes store attributes, which are small data structures that have a very specific purpose. For example, one attribute is used to store the file's name, and another is used to store the file's content. Figure 11.1 shows the basic layout of an MFT entry where there is some header information and three attributes.

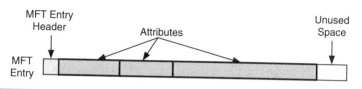

**Figure 11.1** An MFT entry has a small header, and the rest of it is used to store different types of attributes. This entry has three attributes.

Microsoft calls each entry in the table a *file record*, but I think calling each entry an *MFT entry* is simpler and results in fewer terms to remember. Each entry is given an address based on its location in the table, starting with 0. To date, all entries have been 1,024 bytes in size, but the exact size is defined in the boot sector.

Like everything in NTFS, the MFT is a file. What makes this confusing is that the MFT has an entry for itself. The first entry in the table is named $MFT, and it describes the on-disk location of the MFT. In fact, it is the only place where the location of the MFT is described; therefore, you need to process it to determine the layout and size of the MFT. The starting location of the MFT is given in the boot sector, which is always located in the first sector of the file system. We can see this in Figure 11.2 where the boot sector is used to find the first MFT entry, which shows that the MFT is fragmented and goes from clusters 32 to 34 and 56 to 58. Like FAT, NTFS uses clusters, which are groups of consecutive sectors.

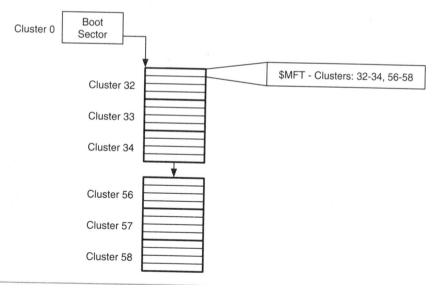

**Figure 11.2** The relationship between the boot sector and $MFT with respect to determining the layout of the MFT.

In Microsoft's implementation of NTFS, the MFT starts as small as possible and expands when more entries are needed. In theory, an OS could create a fixed number of entries when the file system is created, but the dynamic nature of Microsoft's implementation allows it to easily make the file system larger when more space is added from volume spanning. Microsoft does not delete MFT entries after they have been created.

## MFT ENTRY CONTENTS

The size of each MFT entry is defined in the boot sector, but all versions from Microsoft have used a size of 1,024 bytes. The first 42 bytes of the data structure contain 12 fields, and the remaining 982 bytes are unstructured and can be filled with attributes. You can think of an MFT entry as a large box that is used to store your possessions. On the outside of the box is basic information, such as your name and address. The basic information is equivalent to an MFT entry's fixed fields. The inside of the box is initially empty, but it can be used to store anything as long as it is in a container that is smaller than the box. This is similar to how an MFT entry has no internal structure and it contains several attributes that contain specific information.

The first field in each MFT entry is the signature, and a standard entry will have the ASCII string "FILE." If an error is found in the entry, it may have the string "BAAD." There is also a flag field that identifies if the entry is being used and if the entry is for a directory. The allocation status of an MFT entry also can be determined from the $BITMAP attribute in the $MFT file, which is shown in Chapter 13.

If a file cannot fit its attributes into one entry, it can use multiple entries. When this occurs, the first entry is called the base file record, or base MFT entry, and each of the subsequent entries contains the address of the base entry in one of its fixed fields.

Chapter 13 shows the data structure for an MFT entry and dissects our example file system image.

## MFT ENTRY ADDRESSES

Each MFT entry is sequentially addressed using a 48-bit value, and the first entry has an address of 0. The maximum MFT address changes as the MFT grows and is determined by dividing the size of $MFT by the size of each entry. Microsoft calls this sequential address the *file number*.

Every MFT entry also has a 16-bit sequence number that is incremented when the entry is allocated. For example, consider MFT entry 313 with a sequence number of 1. The file that allocated entry 313 is deleted, and the entry is reallocated to a new file. When the entry is reallocated, it has a new sequence number of 2. The MFT entry and sequence number are combined, with the sequence number in the upper 16-bits, to form a 64-bit *file reference* address, as is shown in Figure 11.3.

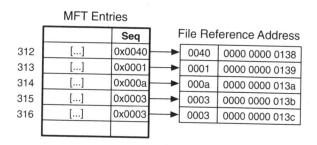

**Figure 11.3**    Example of the MFT entry address and sequence number combining to form a file reference address.

NTFS uses the file reference address to refer to MFT entries because the sequence number makes it easier to determine when the file system is in a corrupt state. For example, if the system crashes at some point while the various data structures for a file are being allocated, the sequence number can determine whether a data structure contains an MFT entry address because the previous file used it or because it is part of the new file. We also can use it when recovering deleted content. For example, if we have an unallocated data structure with a file reference number in it, we can determine if the MFT entry has been reallocated since this data structure used it. The sequence number can be useful during an investigation, but in this chapter I will primarily refer to the file number, or MFT entry address, for simplicity.

## FILE SYSTEM METADATA FILES

Because every byte in the volume is allocated to a file, there must exist files that store the file system's administrative data. Microsoft calls these files metadata files, but this may cause confusion because we also refer to file metadata. I will refer to these special files as *file system metadata files*.

Microsoft reserves the first 16 MFT entries for file system metadata files.[2] The reserved entries that are not used are in an allocated state and have only basic and generic

---

2. Microsoft documentation says it reserves only the first 16 entries, but in practice the first entry that is allocated to a user file or directory is entry 24. Entries 17 to 23 are sometimes used as overflow when the reserved entries are not enough.

information. Every file system metadata file is listed in the root directory, although they are typically hidden from most users. The name of each file system metadata file begins with a "$," and the first letter is capitalized. We will cover each of the file system metadata files in Chapter 12, but they are listed in Table 11.1 as an easy reference.

**Table 11.1**   The standard NTFS file system metadata files.

| Entry | File Name | Description |
| --- | --- | --- |
| 0 | $MFT | The entry for the MFT itself. |
| 1 | $MFTMirr | Contains a backup of the first entries in the MFT. See the "File System Category" section in Chapter 12. |
| 2 | $LogFile | Contains the journal that records the metadata transactions. See the "Application Category" section in Chapter 12. |
| 3 | $Volume | Contains the volume information such as the label, identifier, and version. See the "File System Category" section in Chapter 12. |
| 4 | $AttrDef | Contains the attribute information, such as the identifier values, name, and sizes. See the "File System Category" section in Chapter 12. |
| 5 | . | Contains the root directory of the file system. See the "File Name Category" section in Chapter 12. |
| 6 | $Bitmap | Contains the allocation status of each cluster in the file system. See the "Content Category" section in Chapter 12. |
| 7 | $Boot | Contains the boot sector and boot code for the file system. See the "File System Category" section in Chapter 12. |
| 8 | $BadClus | Contains the clusters that have bad sectors. See the "Content Category" section in Chapter 12. |
| 9 | $Secure | Contains information about the security and access control for the files (Windows 2000 and XP version only). See the "Metadata Category" section in Chapter 12. |
| 10 | $Upcase | Contains the uppercase version of every Unicode character. |
| 11 | $Extend | A directory that contains files for optional extensions. Microsoft does not typically place the files in this directory into the reserved MFT entries. |

# MFT Entry Attribute Concepts

An MFT entry has little internal structure and most of it is used to store *attributes*, which are data structures that store a specific type of data. There are many types of attributes, and each has its own internal structure. For example, there are attributes for a file's name, date and time, and even its contents. This is one of the ways that NTFS is very different from other file systems. Most file systems exist to read and write file content, but NTFS exists to read and write attributes, one of which happens to contain file content.

Consider the previous analogy that described an MFT entry as a large box that is initially empty. Attributes are similar to smaller boxes inside the larger box where the smaller boxes can be any shape that most efficiently stores the object. For example, a hat can be stored in a short-round box, and a poster can be stored in a long-round box.

While each type of attribute stores a different type of data, all attributes have two parts: the header and the content. Figure 11.4 shows an MFT entry with four header and content pairs. The header is generic and standard to all attributes. The content is specific to the type of attribute and can be any size. If we think of our boxes analogy, there is always the same basic information on the outside of each small box, but the shape of each box may be different.

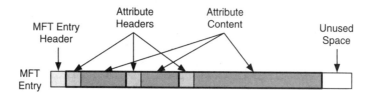

**Figure 11.4**  Our example MFT entry with the header and content locations specified.

## Attribute Headers

The attribute header identifies the type of attribute, its size, and its name. It also has flags to identify if the value is compressed or encrypted. The attribute type is a numerical identifier based on the data type and we will discuss the default attribute types in the "Standard Attribute Types" section. An MFT entry can have multiple attributes of the same type.

Some of the attributes can be assigned a name and it is stored in UTF-16 Unicode in the attribute header. An attribute also has an identifier value assigned to it that is unique to that MFT entry. If an entry has more than one attribute of the same type, this identifier can be used to differentiate between them. The attribute header data structure is given in the "Attribute Header" section of Chapter 13.

## ATTRIBUTE CONTENT

The content of the attribute can have any format and any size. For example, one of the attributes is used to store the content for a file, so it could be several MB or GB in size. It is not practical to store this amount of data in an MFT entry, which is only 1,024 bytes.

To solve this problem, NTFS provides two locations where attribute content can be stored. A *resident* attribute stores its content in the MFT entry with the attribute header. This works for only small attributes. A *non-resident* attribute stores its content in an external cluster in the file system. The header of the attribute identifies if the attribute is resident or non-resident. If an attribute is resident, the content will immediately follow the header. If the attribute is non-resident, the header will give the cluster addresses. In Figure 11.5 we see the example MFT entry that we saw previously, but now its third attribute is too large to fit in the MFT, and it has allocated cluster 829.

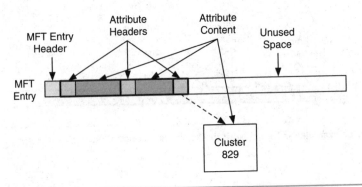

**Figure 11.5**   Our example MFT entry where the third attribute has become too large and became non-resident.

Non-resident attributes are stored in *cluster runs*, which are consecutive clusters, and the run is documented using the starting cluster address and run length. For example, if an attribute has allocated clusters 48, 49, 50, 51, and 52, it has a run that starts in cluster 48 with a length of 5. If the attribute also allocated clusters 80 and 81, it has a second run that starts in cluster 80 with a length of 2. A third run could start at cluster 56 and have a length of 4. We can see this in Figure 11.6.

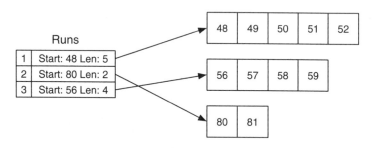

**Figure 11.6**   Example runlist with three runs of allocated clusters.

Throughout this book, we have differentiated between the different types of addresses. For example, we defined the logical file system address as the address assigned to file system data units and the logical file address as relative to the start of a file. NTFS uses different terms for these addresses. The *Logical Cluster Number* (LCN) is the same as the logical file system address, and the *Virtual Cluster Number* (VCN) is the same as a logical file address.

NTFS uses VCN-to-LCN mappings to describe the non-resident attribute runs. If we return to our previous example, this attribute's run shows that VCN addresses 0 to 4 map to LCN addresses 48 to 52, VCN addresses 5 to 6 map to LCN addresses 80 to 81, and VCN addresses 7 to 10 map to LCN addresses 56 to 59. The runlist data structure is given in the "Attribute Header" section of Chapter 13.

## STANDARD ATTRIBUTE TYPES

So far we have been speaking in general terms about attribute types. Now we are going to look at the basics of some of the standard attributes. Many of these will be discussed in detail in Chapter 12.

As was previously mentioned, a number is defined for each type of attribute, and Microsoft sorts the attributes in an entry using this number. The standard attributes have a default type value assigned to them, but we will later see that it can be redefined in the $AttrDef file system metadata file. In addition to a number, each attribute type has a name, and it has all capital letters and starts with "$." Some of the default attribute types and their identifiers are given in Table 11.2. Not all these attribute types and identifiers will exist for every file. In addition to the more detailed descriptions in Chapter 12, the data structures for many are given in Chapter 13.

**Table 11.2**   List of default MFT entry attribute types.

| Type Identifier | Name | Description |
| --- | --- | --- |
| 16 | $STANDARD_INFORMATION | General information, such as flags; the last accessed, written, and created times; and the owner and security ID. |
| 32 | $ATTRIBUTE_LIST | List where other attributes for file can be found. |
| 48 | $FILE_NAME | File name, in Unicode, and the last accessed, written, and created times. |
| 64 | $VOLUME_VERSION | Volume information. Exists only in version 1.2 (Windows NT). |
| 64 | $OBJECT_ID | A 16-byte unique identifier for the file or directory. Exists only in versions 3.0+ and after (Windows 2000+). |
| 80 | $SECURITY_DESCRIPTOR | The access control and security properties of the file. |
| 96 | $VOLUME_NAME | Volume name. |
| 112 | $VOLUME_INFORMATION | File system version and other flags. |
| 128 | $DATA | File contents. |
| 144 | $INDEX_ROOT | Root node of an index tree. |
| 160 | $INDEX_ALLOCATION | Nodes of an index tree rooted in $INDEX_ROOT attribute. |
| 176 | $BITMAP | A bitmap for the $MFT file and for indexes. |
| 192 | $SYMBOLIC_LINK | Soft link information. Exists only in version 1.2 (Windows NT). |
| 192 | $REPARSE_POINT | Contains data about a reparse point, which is used as a soft link in version 3.0+ (Windows 2000+). |
| 208 | $EA_INFORMATION | Used for backward compatibility with OS/2 applications (HPFS). |
| 224 | $EA | Used for backward compatibility with OS/2 applications (HPFS). |
| 256 | $LOGGED_UTILITY_STREAM | Contains keys and information about encrypted attributes in version 3.0+ (Windows 2000+). |

Nearly every allocated MFT entry has a $FILE_NAME and a $STANDARD_INFORMATION type attribute. The one exception is non-base MFT entries, which are discussed next. The $FILE_NAME attribute contains the file name, size, and temporal information. The $STANDARD_INFORMATION attribute contains temporal, ownership, and security information. The latter attribute exists for every file and directory because it contains the data needed to enforce data security and quotas. In an abstract sense, there is no essential data in this attribute, but the application-level features of the file system require it to be there. Both of these attributes are always resident.

Every file has a $DATA attribute, which contains the file content. If the content is over roughly 700 bytes in size, it becomes non-resident and is saved in external clusters. When a file has more than one $DATA attribute, the additional attributes are sometimes referred to as *alternate data streams* (ADS). The default $DATA attribute that is created when a file is created does not have a name associated with it, but additional $DATA attributes must have one. Note that the attribute name is different from the type name. For example, $DATA is the name of the attribute type, and the attribute's name could be "fred." Some tools, including *The Sleuth Kit* (TSK), will assign the name "$Data" to the default $DATA attribute.

Every directory has an $INDEX_ROOT attribute that contains information about the files and subdirectories that are located in it. If the directory is large, $INDEX_ALLOCATION and $BITMAP attributes are also used to store information. To make things confusing, it is possible for a directory to have a $DATA attribute in addition to the $INDEX_ROOT attribute. In other words, a directory can store both file content and a list of its files and subdirectories. The $DATA attribute can store any content that an application or user wants to store there. The $INDEX_ROOT and $INDEX_ALLOCATION attributes for a directory typically have the name "$I30."

Figure 11.7 shows the example MFT entry that we previously used, and its attributes have been given names and types. It has the three standard file attributes. In this example, all the attributes are resident.

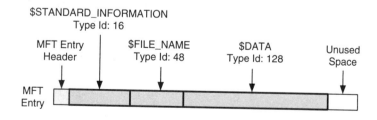

**Figure 11.7**   Our example MFT entry where the type names and identifiers have been added to the attributes.

## OTHER ATTRIBUTE CONCEPTS

The previous section looked at the basic concepts that apply to all NTFS attributes. Although not every attribute is basic, and this section looks at the more advanced concepts. In particular, we look at what happens when a file has too many attributes and we look at ways that the contents of an attribute can be compressed and encrypted.

### BASE MFT ENTRIES

A file can have up to 65,536 attributes (because of the 16-bit identifier), so it may need more than one MFT entry to store all the attribute headers (even non-resident attributes need their header to be in the MTF entry). When additional MFT entries are allocated to a file, the original MFT entry becomes the *base MFT entry*. The non-base entries will have the base entry's address in one of their MFT entry fields.

The base MFT entry will have an $ATTRIBUTE_LIST type attribute that contains a list with each of the file's attributes and the MFT address in which it can be found. The non-base MFT entries do not have the $FILE_NAME and $STANDARD_INFORMATION attributes in them. We will examine the $ATTRIBUTE_LIST attribute in the "Metadata Category" section of Chapter 12.

### SPARSE ATTRIBUTES

NTFS can reduce the space needed by a file by saving some of the non-resident $DATA attribute values as sparse. A sparse attribute is one where clusters that contain all zeros are not written to disk. Instead, a special run is created for the zero clusters. Typically, a run contains the starting cluster location and the size, but a sparse run contains only the size and not a starting location. There is also a flag that indicates if an attribute is sparse.

For example, consider a file that should occupy 12 clusters. The first five clusters are non-zero, the next three clusters contain zeros, and the last four clusters are non-zero. When stored as a normal attribute, one run of length 12 may be created for the file, as shown in Figure 11.8(A). When stored as a sparse attribute, three runs are created and only nine clusters are allocated, which can be seen in Figure 11.8(B).

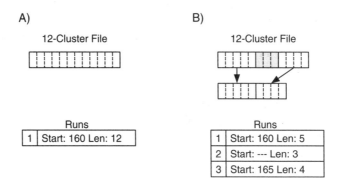

**Figure 11.8**  A 12-cluster file that is stored in A) normal layout and B) sparse layout with a sparse run of three clusters.

## COMPRESSED ATTRIBUTES

NTFS allows attributes to be written in a compressed format, although the actual algorithm is not given. Note that this is a file system-level compression and not an external application-level compression that can be achieved by using zip or gzip. Microsoft says that only the $DATA attribute should be compressed, and only when it is non-resident. NTFS uses both sparse runs and compressed data to reduce the amount of space needed. The attribute header flag identifies whether it is compressed, and the flags in the $STANDARD_INFORMATION and $FILE_NAME attribute also show if the file contains compressed attributes.

Before the attribute contents are compressed, the data are broken up into equal sized chunks called *compression units*. The size of the compression unit is given in the attribute header. There are three situations that can occur with each compression unit:

1. All the clusters contain zeros, in which case a run of sparse data is made for the size of the compression unit and no disk space is allocated.
2. When compressed, the resulting data needs the same number of clusters for storage (i.e., the data did not compress much). In this case, the compression unit is not compressed, and a run is made for the original data.
3. When compressed, the resulting data uses fewer clusters. In this case, the data is compressed and stored in a run on the disk. A sparse run follows the compressed run to make the total run length equal to the number of clusters in a compression unit.

Let's look at a simple example to examine each of these scenarios. Assume that the compression unit size is 16 clusters and we have a $DATA attribute that is 64 clusters in length, as shown in Figure 11.9. We divide the content into four compression units and examine each. The first unit compresses to 16 clusters, so it is not compressed. The second unit is all zeros, so a sparse run of 16 clusters is made for it, and no clusters are allocated. The third unit compresses to 10 clusters, so the compressed data is written to disk in a run of 10 clusters, and a sparse run of six clusters is added to account for the compressed data. The final unit compresses to 16 clusters, so it is not compressed and a run of 16 clusters is created.

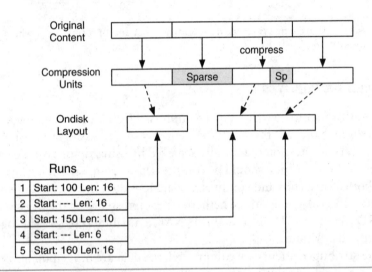

**Figure 11.9**   An attribute with two compression units that do not compress, one unit that is sparse, and one unit that compresses to 10 clusters.

When the OS, or forensics tool, reads this attribute, it sees that the compression flag is set and organizes the runs into compression unit-sized chunks. The first run is the same size as a compression unit, so we know it is not compressed. The second run is the same size as a compression unit, and it is sparse, so we know that there are 16 clusters of zeros. The third and fourth runs combine to make a compression unit, and we see that it is only 10 clusters and needs to be uncompressed. The final run is a compression unit and it is not compressed.

The last example was too simple, so I will present the more challenging file shown in Figure 11.10. The reason this is more complex is because the layout is not initially organized using compression units. To process this file, we need to first organize all the data in the six runs and then organize the data into compression units of 16 clusters. After merging the fragmented runs, we see that there is one run of content, one sparse run, more content, and another sparse run. The merged data are organized into compression units, and we see that the first two units have no sparse runs and are not compressed. The third and fifth units have a sparse run and are compressed. The fourth unit is sparse, and the corresponding data are all zeros.

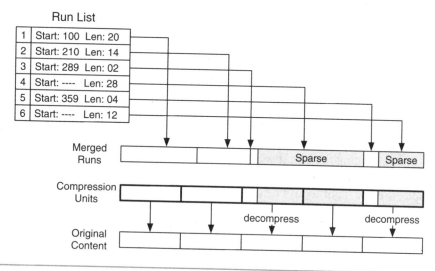

**Figure 11.10**  A compressed attribute with fragmented runs that do not lie on compression unit boundaries.

## ENCRYPTED ATTRIBUTES

NTFS provides the capability for attribute contents to be encrypted. This section gives an overview of how it is done and what exists on disk. In theory, any attribute could be encrypted, but Windows allows only $DATA attributes to be encrypted. When an attribute is encrypted, only the content is encrypted and the attribute header is not. A $LOGGED_UTILITY_STREAM attribute is created for the file, and it contains the keys needed to decrypt the data.

In Windows, a user can choose to encrypt a specific file or a directory. An encrypted directory does not have any encrypted data, but any file or directory that is created in the directory will be encrypted. An encrypted file or directory has a special flag set in the $STANDARD_INFORMATION attribute, and each attribute that is encrypted will have a special flag set in its attribute header.

## Cryptography Basics

Before we get into how cryptography is implemented in NTFS, I will give a brief overview of basic cryptographic concepts. Encryption is a process that uses a cryptographic algorithm and a key to transform plaintext data to ciphertext data. Decryption is a process that uses a crypgraphic algorithm and a key to transform ciphertext data to plaintext data. If someone is shown the ciphertext data, they should not be able to determine the plaintext data without knowing the key.

There are two categories of cryptographic algorithms: symmetric and asymmetric. A *symmetric algorithm* uses the same key to encrypt and decrypt data. For example, the key "spot" could be used to encrypt the plaintext into ciphertext, and the same key could be used to decrypt the ciphertext into plaintext. Symmetric encryption is very fast, but it is difficult when sharing the ciphertext data. If we encrypt a file with symmetric encryption and want multiple people to access it, we need to either encrypt it with a key that everyone knows or make a copy of the file for each user and encrypt each with a key that is unique to that user. If we use one key for everyone, it is difficult to revoke access from a user without changing the key. If we encrypt it for every user, we waste a lot of space.

*Asymmetric encryption* uses one key for encryption and a different key for decryption. For example, the key "spot" could be used to encrypt the plaintext into ciphertext, and the key "felix" could be used to decrypt the ciphertext. The most common use of asymmetric encryption is where one of the keys is made public, such as "spot," and the other is kept private, such as "felix." Anyone can encrypt data with the public key, but it can be decrypted with only the private key. Obviously, a real situation would use keys that are much longer than "spot" and "felix." In fact, they are typically over 1,024-bits long.

## NTFS Implementation

When an NTFS $DATA attribute is encrypted, its contents are encrypted with a symmetric algorithm called DESX. One random key is generated for each MFT entry with encrypted data, and it is called the *file encryption key* (FEK). If there are multiple $DATA attributes in the MFT entry, they are all encrypted with the same FEK.

The FEK is stored in an encrypted state in the $LOGGED_UTILITY_STREAM attribute. The attribute contains a list of *data decryption fields* (DDF) and *data recovery fields* (DRF). A DDF is created for every user who has access to the file, and it contains the user's *Security ID* (SID), encryption information, and the FEK encrypted with the user's public key. A data recovery field is created for each method of data recovery, and it contains the FEK encrypted with a data recovery public key that is used when an administrator, or other authorized user, needs access to the data. We can see this process in Figure 11.11.

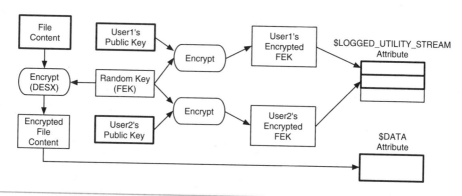

**Figure 11.11** Encryption process starting with file content and public keys and ending with encrypted content and encrypted keys.

To decrypt a $DATA attribute, the $LOGGED_UTILITY_STREAM attribute is processed and the user's DDF entry is located. The user's private key is used to decrypt the FEK, and the FEK is used to decrypt the $DATA attribute. When access is revoked from a user, her key is removed from the list. A user's private key is stored in the Windows registry and encrypted with a symmetric algorithm that uses her login password as the key. Therefore, the user's password and the registry are needed to decrypt any encrypted files that are encountered during an investigation. This process is shown in Figure 11.12.

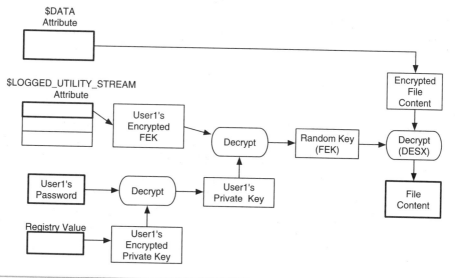

**Figure 11.12** Decryption process starting with encrypted content, keys, and a user password, and ending with the decrypted content.

Several security tools can perform a brute force attack against a user's login password, and this can be used to decrypt the data. Unencrypted copies of file content might also exist in unallocated space if only some directories and files were encrypted. In fact, there is a small flaw in the NTFS design because it creates a temporary file named EFS0.TMP and it contains the plaintext version of the file being encrypted. After the OS finishes encrypting the original file, it deletes the temporary file, but the contents are not wiped. Therefore, a plaintext version of the file exists, and recovery tools might be able to recover the file if its MFT entry has not been reallocated. The swap space or page file might also provide copies of unencrypted data. It has been reported that if the administrator, domain controller, or other account that is configured as the recovery agent is compromised, any file can be decrypted because that account has access to all files [Microsoft 1999].

## INDEXES

NTFS uses index data structures in many situations, and this section describes them. An *index* in NTFS is a collection of attributes that is stored in a sorted order. The most common usage of an index is in a directory because directories contain $FILE_NAME attributes.

Prior to version 3.0 of NTFS (which came with Windows 2000), only the $FILE_NAME attribute was in an index, but now there are several other uses of indexes and they contain different attributes. For example, security information is stored in an index, as is quota information. This section shows what an index looks like and how it is implemented.

## B-TREES

An NTFS index sorts attributes into a tree, specifically a B-tree. A tree is a group of data structures called nodes that are linked together such that there is a head node and it branches out to the other nodes. Consider Figure 11.13(A), where we see node A on top and it links to nodes B and C. Node B links to node D and E. A parent node is one that links to other nodes, and a child node is one that is linked to. For example, A is a parent node to B and C, which are children of A. A leaf node is one that has no links from it. Nodes C, D, and E are leaves. The example shown is a binary tree because there are a maximum of two children per node.

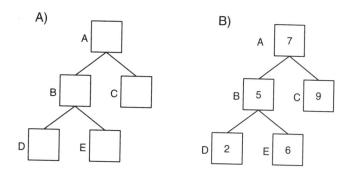

**Figure 11.13** Examples of A) a tree with 5 nodes and B) the same tree that is sorted by the node values.

Trees are useful because they can be used to easily sort and find data. Figure 11.13(B) shows the same tree as we saw on the left side, but now with values that are assigned to each node. If we are trying to look up a value, we compare it to the root node. If the root node is larger, we go to the child on the left. If the root node is smaller, we go to the child on the right. For example, if we want to find the value 6, we compare it to the root value, which is 7. The node is larger, so we go to the left-hand child and compare its value, which is 5. This node is smaller, so we go to the right-hand child and compare its value, which is 6. We have found our value with only three comparisons. We could have found the value 9 in only two comparisons instead of five if the values were in a list.

NTFS uses B-trees, which are similar to the binary tree we just saw, but there can be more than two children per node. Typically, the number of children that a node has is based on how many values each node can store. For example, in the binary tree we stored one value in each node and had two children. If we can store five values in each node, we can have six children. There are many variations of B-trees, and there are more rules than I will describe here because the purpose of this section is to describe their concepts, not to describe how you can create a B-tree.

Figure 11.14 shows a B-tree with names as values instead of numbers. Node A contains three values and four children. If we were looking for the file ggg.txt, we would look at the values in the root node and determine that the name alphabetically falls in between eee.txt and lll.txt. Therefore, we process node C and look at its values. We find the file name in that node.

Now let's make this complex by looking at how values are added and deleted. This is an important concept because it explains why deleted file names are difficult to find in NTFS. Let us assume that we can fit only three file names per node, and the file jjj.txt is added. That sounds easy, but as we will see it results in two nodes being deleted and five new nodes being created. When we locate where jjj.txt should fit, we identify that it should be at the end of node C, following the iii.txt name. The top of Figure 11.15 shows this situation, but unfortunately, there are now four names in this node, and it can fit only three. Therefore, we break node C in half, move ggg.txt up a level, and create nodes F and G with the resulting names from node C. This is shown at the bottom of Figure 11.15.

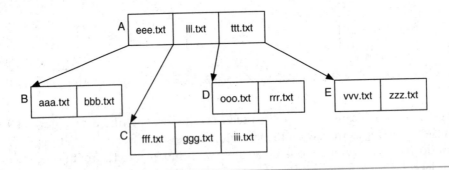

**Figure 11.14**   A B-tree with file names as values.

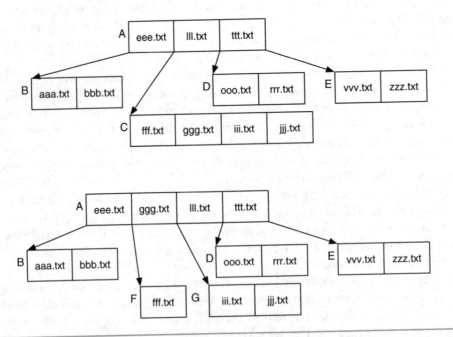

**Figure 11.15**   The top tree shows 'jjj.txt' added to node C, and the bottom tree is the result of removing node C because each node can have only three names.

Unfortunately, node A now has four values in it. So we divide it in half and move ggg.txt to the top-most node. The final result can be found in Figure 11.16. Adding one file results in removing nodes A and C and adding nodes F, G, H, I, and J. Any remnant data in nodes A and C from previously deleted files may now be gone.

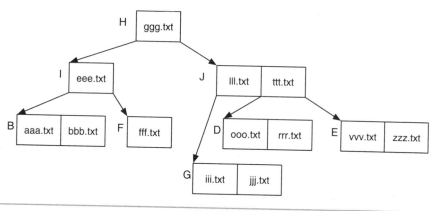

**Figure 11.16**   The final state from adding the 'jjj.txt' file.

Now delete the zzz.txt file. This action removes the name from node E and does not require any other changes. Depending on the implementation, the details of zzz.txt file may still exist in the node and could be recovered.

To make things more difficult, consider if fff.txt was deleted. Node F becomes empty, and we need to fill it in. We move eee.txt from node I to node F and move bbb.txt from node B to node I. This creates a tree that is still balanced where all leaves are the same distance from node H. The resulting state is found in Figure 11.17.

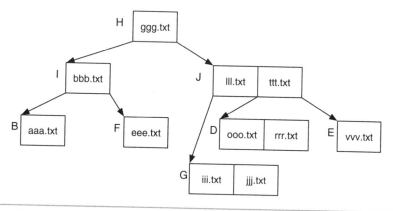

**Figure 11.17**   Tree after deleting the 'zzz.txt' file and the 'fff.txt' file.

Node B will contain bbb.txt in its unallocated space because bbb.txt was moved to node I. Our analysis tool might show that the bbb.txt file was deleted, but it really wasn't. It was simply moved because fff.txt was deleted.

The point of walking through the process of adding and deleting values from the tree was to show how complex the process could be. With file systems, such as FAT, that use a list of names in a directory, it is easy to describe why a deleted name does or does not exist, but with trees it is very difficult to predict the end result.

## NTFS INDEX ATTRIBUTES

Now that we have described the general concept of B-trees, we need to describe how they are implemented in NTFS to create indexes. Each entry in the tree uses a data structure called an *index entry* to store the values in each node. There are many types of index entries, but they all have the same standard header fields, which are given in Chapter 13. For example, a directory index entry contains a few header values and a $FILE_NAME attribute. The index entries are organized into nodes of the tree and stored in a list. An empty entry is used to signal the end of the list. Figure 11.18 shows an example of a node in a directory index with four $FILE_NAME index entries.

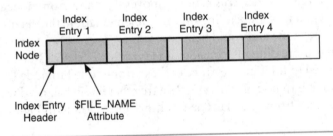

**Figure 11.18**   A node in an NTFS directory index tree with four index entries.

The index nodes can be stored in two types of MFT entry attributes. The $INDEX_ROOT attribute is always resident and can store only one node that contains a small number of index entries. The $INDEX_ROOT attribute is always the root of the index tree.

Larger indexes allocate a non-resident $INDEX_ALLOCATION attribute, which can contain as many nodes as needed. The content of this attribute is a large buffer that contains one or more index records. An *index record* has a static size, typically 4,096 bytes, and it contains a list of index entries. Each index record is given an address, starting with 0. We can see this in Figure 11.19 where we have an $INDEX_ROOT attribute with three index entries and a non-resident $INDEX_ALLOCATION attribute that has allocated cluster 713, and it uses three index records.

An $INDEX_ALLOCATION attribute can have allocated space that is not being used for index records. The $BITMAP attribute is used to manage the allocation status of the index records. If a new node needs to be allocated for the tree, $BITMAP is used to find an available index record; otherwise, more space is added. Each index is given a name and the $INDEX_ROOT, $INDEX_ALLOCATION, and $BITMAP attributes for the index are all assigned the same name in their attribute header.

Each index entry has a flag that shows if it has any children nodes. If there are children nodes, their index record addresses are given in the index entry. The index entries in a node are in a sorted order, and if the value you are looking for is smaller than the index entry and the index entry has a child, you look at its child. If you get to the empty entry at the end of the list, you look at its child.

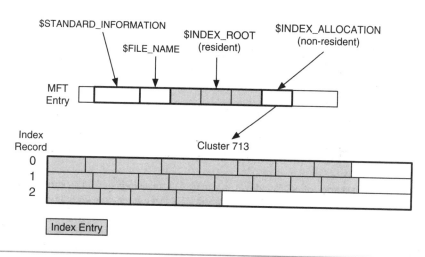

**Figure 11.19**   This directory has three index entries in its resident $INDEX_ROOT attribute and three index records in its non-resident $INDEX_ALLOCATION attribute.

Let us go over some examples. Consider an index with three entries that fit into $INDEX_ROOT. In this case, only a $INDEX_ROOT is allocated, and it contains three index entry data structures and the empty entry at the end of the list. This can be seen in Figure 11.20(A). Now consider an index with 15 entries, which do not fit into an $INDEX_ROOT but fit into an $INDEX_ALLOCATION attribute with one index record. It can be seen in Figure 11.20(B). After we fill up the index entries in the index record, we need to add a new level, and we create a three-node tree. This scenario is shown in Figure 11.20(C). This has one value in the root node and two children nodes. Each child node is located in a separate index record in the same $INDEX_ALLOCA-TION attribute, and it is pointed to by the entries in the $INDEX_ROOT node.

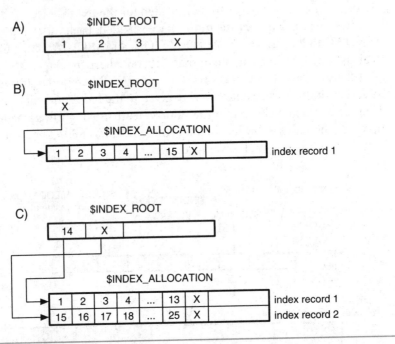

**Figure 11.20**   Three scenarios of NTFS indexes, including A) a small index of three entries, B) a larger index with two nodes and 15 entries, and C) a three-node tree with 25 entries.

## ANALYSIS TOOLS

All the tools mentioned in Chapter 1 support NTFS images, and they may give different amounts of access to individual attributes. If you are interested in viewing the different attributes you have on a Windows system, you can use the nfi.exe tool from Microsoft [Microsoft 2000]. It displays the MFT contents of a live system, including the attribute names and the cluster addresses. This is not useful for a forensic investigation because the system must be live, but it is useful for learning about NTFS. The NTFSInfo tool [Russinovich 1997] from Mark Russinovich provides similar information about a live system.

TSK allows you to view the contents of any attribute. To make the examples in the next two chapters more clear, I will describe the syntax needed to view the different attributes. Recall that each attribute has a type value and each attribute in an MFT entry is assigned a unique identifier. With these two values, we can display any attribute.

Instead of specifying only the metadata address, we will give icat the address and the attribute type. If there is more than one attribute of that type, we will give the unique identifier. For example, if we are examining MFT entry 34, we can see its $FILE_NAME attribute (type 48) by specifying '34-48.' If we want to view its $DATA attribute (type 128), we specify '34-128.' If there are multiple $DATA attributes, we also specify the unique attribute identifier. If the attribute we want has an ID of 3, we specify '34-128-3.'

The istat tool in TSK lists all the attributes for a file. Here is the output that shows the attributes for an MFT entry:

```
[REMOVED]
Type: $STANDARD_INFORMATION (16-0)   Name: N/A   Resident   size: 72
Type: $FILE_NAME (48-2)   Name: N/A   Resident   size: 84
Type: $OBJECT_ID (64-8)   Name: N/A   Resident   size: 16
Type: $DATA (128-3)   Name: $Data   Non-Resident, Encrypted   size: 4294
94843 94844 94845 94846 94847 94848 102873 102874
102875
Type: $DATA (128-5)   Name: ADS   Non-Resident, Encrypted   size: 4294
102879 102880 102881 102882 102883 102884 102885 102886
102887
Type: $LOGGED_UTILITY_STREAM (256-7)   Name: $EFS   Non-Resident   size: 552
102892 102893
```

## SUMMARY

Everything important in NTFS is associated with a file or an index. In this chapter, we have looked at the core NTFS concepts, which are MFT entries, attributes, and indexes. Using these basic concepts, we can now examine the specific attributes and analysis categories in Chapter 12.

## BIBLIOGRAPHY

Cooperstein, Jeffrey, and Richter, Jeffrey. "Keeping an Eye on Your NTFS Drives: The Windows 2000 Change Journal Explained." *Microsoft Systems Journal*, September 1999. http://www.microsoft.com/msj/0999/journal/journal.aspx.

Cooperstein, Jeffrey, and Richter, Jeffrey. "Keeping an Eye on Your NTFS Drives, Part II: Building a Change Journal Application." *Microsoft Systems Journal*, October 1999. http://www.microsoft.com/msj/1099/journal2/journal2.aspx.

Linux NTFS Project. *NTFS Documentation*. 1996-2004. http://linux-ntfs. sourceforge.net/ntfs/index.html.

Microsoft. "Analysis of Reported Vulnerability in the Windows 2000 Encrypting File System (EFS)." 1999. http://www.microsoft.com/technet/security/news/ analefs.mspx.

Microsoft. "Description of NTFS Date and Time Stamps for Files and Folders." *Microsoft Knowledge Base Article 299648*, 2003. http://support.microsoft.com/ default.aspx?scid=kb;en-us;299648.

Microsoft. "INFO: Understanding Encrypted Directories." *Knowledge Base Article 248723*, 2003. http://support.microsoft.com/default.aspx?scid=kb;en-us; 248723&sd=tech.

Microsoft. "Overview of FAT, HPFS, and NTFS File Systems." *Knowledge Base Article 100108*, 2003. http://support.microsoft.com/default.aspx?scid=kb;EN-US;100108.

Microsoft. "Windows NT 4.0 and Windows 2000 OEM Support Tools." February 2, 2000. http://www.microsoft.com/downloads/details.aspx?FamilyId=82D6AB58-890C-405F-B532-B751D9217CA4&displaylang=en.

Microsoft. "Windows Server 2003 Technical Reference." *Storage Technologies Collection Section*, 2004. http://www.microsoft.com/resources/documentation/WindowsServ/ 2003/all/techref/en-us/Default.asp?url=/resources/documentation/windowsServ/ 2003/all/techref/en-us/W2K3TR_ntfs_intro.asp.

Microsoft. "Windows XP Professional Resource Kit Documentation." *Chapter 13—File Systems*, 2004. http://www.microsoft.com/resources/documentation/Windows/XP/all/ reskit/en-us/Default.asp?url=/resources/documentation/Windows/XP/all/reskit/ en-us/prork_overview.asp.

Microsoft MSDN Library. "Change Journals." 2004. http://msdn.microsoft.com/ library/default.asp?url=/library/en-us/fileio/base/change_journals.asp.

Microsoft TechNet. "Encrypting File System in Windows XP and Windows Server 2003." 2002. http://www.microsoft.com/technet/prodtechnol/winxppro/deploy/ cryptfs.mspx#XSLTsection122121120120.

Russinovich, Mark. "Inside Encrypting File System." *Part 1, Windows and .Net Magazine Network*, June 1999. `http://www.winntmag.com/Articles/Print.cfm?ArticleID=5387`.

Russinovich, Mark. "Inside Encrypting File System." *Part 2, Windows and .Net Magazine Network*, July 1999. `http://www.winntmag.com/Articles/Print.cfm?ArticleID=5592`.

Russinovich, Mark. "Inside Win2K NTFS." *Part 1, Windows and .Net Magazine Network*, November 2000. `http://www.winnetmag.com/Articles/Print.cfm?ArticleID=15719`.

Russinovich, Mark. "Inside Win2K NTFS." *Part 2, Windows and .Net Magazine Network*, Winter 2000. `http://www.winnetmag.com/Articles/Print.cfm?ArticleID=15900`.

Russinovich, Mark. "NTFSInfo." 1997. `http://www.sysinternals.com/ntw2k/source/ntfsinfo.shtml`

Solomon, David, and Mark Russinovich. *Inside Windows 2000*. 3rd ed. Redmond: Microsoft Press, 2000.

# NTFS Analysis

This is the second NTFS chapter, and we will now start to discuss analysis techniques and considerations using the five-category model presented in Chapter 8, "File System Analysis." NTFS is much different from other file systems, so we covered the core NTFS concepts in the previous chapter before diving into this material. If you are not familiar with NTFS and skipped Chapter 11, I recommend returning to it before starting this chapter. Chapter 13, "NTFS Data Structures," covers the data structures for NTFS. Most of this book has been organized so that you can read the file system analysis and data structure chapters in parallel. This is more difficult with NTFS because everything is a file, and it is difficult to show the file system metadata files in the file system category before we look at attributes in the metadata category. Therefore, it will be the least confusing if you read this chapter before starting Chapter 13.

## FILE SYSTEM CATEGORY

The file system category of data includes the data that describe the general file system, and the data do not typically correspond to a specific user file. NTFS stores these data in file system metadata files, which have file names in the root directory. With the exception of the boot code, the on-disk location of these data could be anywhere in the file system.

One interesting characteristic of these files is that they have date and time stamps associated with them because they are similar to normal files. The date and time stamps are, in my experience, set to the time that the file system was created, which may be useful in some investigations. This section examines each of the file system metadata files, and Chapter 13 will show their data structures.

## $MFT FILE OVERVIEW

One of the most important file system metadata files is the $MFT file because it contains the *Master File Table* (MFT), which has an entry for every file and directory. Therefore, we need it to find other files. The starting address of the MFT is given in the boot sector, which is described later in this section. The layout of the MFT is determined by processing entry 0 in the MFT.

The first MFT entry is named $MFT and its $DATA attribute contains the clusters used by the MFT. Refer to Chapter 11, "NTFS Concepts," for a description of MFT entries. The $MFT file also has a $BITMAP attribute, which is used to manage the allocation status of the MFT entries. The $MFT file also has the standard $FILE_NAME and $STANDARD_INFORMATION attributes, which are described in the "Metadata Category" section.

In Windows, the $MFT file starts as small as possible and grows larger as more files and directories are created. The $MFT file can become fragmented, but some space is reserved for its expansion, as will be discussed in the "File System Layout" section within the "Content Category" section.

For the file system metadata files, I will give the details from our example file system image using the istat tool from *The Sleuth Kit* (TSK). We will see the full output of istat at the end of the "Metadata Category" section, and only the relevant data will be shown here.

```
# istat -f ntfs ntfs1.dd 0
[REMOVED]
$STANDARD_INFORMATION Attribute Values:
Flags: Hidden, System
Owner ID: 0      Security ID: 256
Created:        Thu Jun 26 10:17:57 2003
File Modified:  Thu Jun 26 10:17:57 2003
MFT Modified:   Thu Jun 26 10:17:57 2003
Accessed:       Thu Jun 26 10:17:57 2003
[REMOVED]
Attributes:
Type: $STANDARD_INFORMATION (16-0)   Name: N/A   Resident    size: 72
Type: $FILE_NAME (48-3)    Name: N/A   Resident    size: 74
Type: $DATA (128-1)   Name: $Data   Non-Resident    size: 8634368
342709 342710 342711 342712 342713 342714 342715 342716
342717 342718 342719 342720 342721 342722 342723 342724
[REMOVED]
443956 443957 443958 443959 443960 443961 443962 443963
Type: $BITMAP (176-5)    Name: N/A   Non-Resident    size: 1056
342708 414477 414478 414479
```

The temporal data for $MFT is typically the date that the file system was created, and it is not updated. We can see that the file has the standard $STANDARD_INFORMATION and $FILE_NAME attributes, an 8-MB $DATA attribute, and a $BITMAP attribute.

## $MFTMIRR FILE OVERVIEW

In the last section, I stated that the $MFT file is very important because it is used to find all other files. Therefore, it has the potential of being a single point of failure if the pointer in the boot sector or the $MFT entry is corrupt. To fix this problem, there exists a backup copy of the important MFT entries that can be used during recovery. MFT entry 1 is for the $MFTMirr file, which has a non-resident attribute that contains a backup copy of the first MFT entries.

The $DATA attribute of the $MFTMirr file allocates clusters in the middle of the file system and saves copies of at least the first four MFT entries, which are for $MFT, $MFTMirr, $LogFile, and $Volume. If there are problems determining the layout of the MFT, a recovery tool can use the volume size to calculate where the middle sector of the file system is located and read the backup data. Each MFT entry has a signature that can be used to verify that it is an MFT entry.

With these four backup entries, the recovery tool can determine the MFT layout and size, the location of the $LogFile so that the file system can be recovered, and the version and status information from the $Volume attributes.

The details of the $MFTMirr file from our example image are shown here:

```
# istat -f ntfs ntfs1.dd 1
  [REMOVED]
Attributes:
Type: $STANDARD_INFORMATION (16-0)   Name: N/A   Resident    size: 72
Type: $FILE_NAME (48-2)   Name: N/A   Resident   size: 82
Type: $DATA (128-1)   Name: $Data   Non-Resident   size: 4096
514064 514065 514066 514067
```

Our example image has 1,028,128 clusters in it, and the $DATA attribute for $MFTMirr starts in the middle cluster. The temporal data was removed from this output, but it had the same values that were shown for $MFT.

## $BOOT FILE OVERVIEW

The $Boot file system metadata file is located in MFT entry 7 and contains the boot sector of the file system. This is the only file system metadata file that has a static location. Its $DATA attribute is always located in the first sector of the file system because it is needed to boot the system. Microsoft typically allocates the first 16 sectors of the file system to $Boot, but I have found that only the first half has non-zero data.

The NTFS *boot sector* is very similar to the FAT boot sector, and they share many fields. They even share the 0xAA55 signature, which means that you might find an NTFS boot sector when searching for lost FAT boot sectors (and vice versa). The boot sector gives you basic size information about the size of each cluster, the number of sectors in the file system, the starting cluster address of the MFT, and the size of each MFT entry. The boot sector also gives a serial number for the file system.

The remainder of the sectors allocated to the $Boot file's $DATA attribute are used for boot code. The boot code is essential only on bootable file systems and locates the files needed to load the operating system. The details of the boot sector are given in Chapter 13.

A backup copy of the boot sector exists in either the last sector of the volume or in the middle of the volume [Microsoft 2003]. My survey of Windows NT 4.0, 2000, and XP volumes had the backup copy in the last sector. I found that the total number of sectors in the file system was less than the total number of sectors in the volume, so the backup copy of the boot sector did not have to be allocated to a specific file. For example, in our example file system image, the volume has 2,056,257 sectors, and the boot sector reports 2,056,256 sectors in the file system. The final sector in the volume that is not allocated to the file system contains the backup copy of the boot sector.

To show the attribute details of what a $Boot file looks like, the output from running istat on our example image is shown here:

```
# istat -f ntfs ntfs1.dd 7
  [REMOVED]
Attributes:
Type: $STANDARD_INFORMATION (16-0)   Name: N/A   Resident    size: 48
Type: $FILE_NAME (48-2)    Name: N/A    Resident   size: 76
Type: $SECURITY_DESCRIPTOR (80-3)   Name: N/A   Resident    size: 104
Type: $DATA (128-1)    Name: $Data   Non-Resident    size: 8192
0 1 2 3 4 5 6 7
```

The bottom lines show us that it has four attributes, including the $DATA attribute that is 8 KB in size and has allocated clusters 0 to 7. The temporal data was removed from the output, but it was the same that we saw for $MFT and $MFTMirr.

## $VOLUME FILE OVERVIEW

The $Volume file system metadata file is located in MFT entry 3 and contains the volume label and other version information. It has two unique attributes that no other file is supposed to have. The $VOLUME_NAME attribute contains the Unicode name of the volume, and the $VOLUME_INFORMATION attribute contains the NTFS version and dirty status. In addition to these attributes, the file typically has a $DATA attribute, but I have found that it has a size of 0 bytes. The details of the $VOLUME_NAME and $VOLUME_INFORMATION attributes are given in Chapter 13.

The NTFS file system has had minor changes for each new major release of Windows, and the version number can be found in this file. Windows NT 4.0 had version 1.2, Windows 2000 had version 3.0, and Windows XP had version 3.1. The differences among versions are minor, and the same general data structures apply to all of them.

The attribute details of the $Volume file in our example image are shown here:

```
# istat -f ntfs ntfs1.dd 3
[REMOVED]
Attributes:
Type: $STANDARD_INFORMATION (16-0)   Name: N/A   Resident   size: 48
Type: $FILE_NAME (48-1)   Name: N/A   Resident   size: 80
Type: $OBJECT_ID (64-6)   Name: N/A   Resident   size: 16
Type: $SECURITY_DESCRIPTOR (80-2)   Name: N/A   Resident   size: 104
Type: $VOLUME_NAME (96-4)   Name: N/A   Resident   size: 22
Type: $VOLUME_INFORMATION (112-5)   Name: N/A   Resident   size: 12
Type: $DATA (128-3)   Name: $Data   Resident   size: 0
```

The $VOLUME_NAME and $VOLUME_INFORMATION are unique to this MFT entry, and they contain the data in which we are interested. Note that the $DATA attribute exists, but it has a size of 0. The temporal data were removed from the output, but they were the same values that were seen in the previous file system metadata files.

## $ATTRDEF FILE OVERVIEW

Another general file system category of data includes the $AttrDef file system metadata file, which is MFT entry 4. The $DATA attribute of this file defines the names and type identifiers for each type of attribute. There are a few circular logic issues with NTFS, and this is one of them. How are you supposed to read the $DATA attribute of the $AttrDef file to learn what the type identifier for a $DATA is? Fortunately, there are default values for the attributes, which we saw in Chapter 11.

This file allows each file system to have unique attributes for its files and allows each file system to redefine the identifier for standard attributes. The details of the $AttrDef file in our example image are as follows:

```
# istat -f ntfs ntfs1.dd 4
[REMOVED]
Attributes:
Type: $STANDARD_INFORMATION (16-0)   Name: N/A  Resident   size: 48
Type: $FILE_NAME (48-2)   Name: N/A   Resident   size: 82
Type: $SECURITY_DESCRIPTOR (80-3)   Name: N/A   Resident    size: 104
Type: $DATA (128-4)   Name: $Data   Non-Resident   size: 2560
342701 342702 342703
```

Notice that its $DATA attribute is over 2 KB. The temporal data was removed, but they were the same as what we have seen in the other file system metadata files.

## EXAMPLE IMAGE

I have shown some of the file details from our example image, and now I will give the output from running fsstat on it. We will be using this data in later examples. To find out where this data came from on-disk, refer to Chapter 13.

```
# fsstat -f ntfs ntfs1.dd
FILE SYSTEM INFORMATION
--------------------------------------------
File System Type: NTFS
Volume Serial Number: 0450228450227C94
OEM Name: NTFS
Volume Name: NTFS Disk 2
Version: Windows XP

META-DATA INFORMATION
--------------------------------------------
First Cluster of MFT: 342709
First Cluster of MFT Mirror: 514064
Size of MFT Entries: 1024 bytes
Size of Index Records: 4096 bytes
Range: 0 - 8431
Root Directory: 5

CONTENT-DATA INFORMATION
--------------------------------------------
```

```
Sector Size: 512
Cluster Size: 1024
Total Cluster Range: 0 - 1028127
Total Sector Range: 0 - 2056255

$AttrDef Attribute Values:
$STANDARD_INFORMATION (16)    Size: 48-72    Flags: Resident
$ATTRIBUTE_LIST (32)    Size: No Limit    Flags: Non-resident
$FILE_NAME (48)    Size: 68-578    Flags: Resident,Index
$OBJECT_ID (64)    Size: 0-256    Flags: Resident
$SECURITY_DESCRIPTOR (80)    Size: No Limit    Flags: Non-resident
$VOLUME_NAME (96)    Size: 2-256    Flags: Resident
$VOLUME_INFORMATION (112)    Size: 12-12    Flags: Resident
$DATA (128)    Size: No Limit    Flags:
$INDEX_ROOT (144)    Size: No Limit    Flags: Resident
$INDEX_ALLOCATION (160)    Size: No Limit    Flags: Non-resident
$BITMAP (176)    Size: No Limit    Flags: Non-resident
$REPARSE_POINT (192)    Size: 0-16384    Flags: Non-resident
$EA_INFORMATION (208)    Size: 8-8    Flags: Resident
$EA (224)    Size: 0-65536    Flags:
$LOGGED_UTILITY_STREAM (256)    Size: 0-65536    Flags: Non-resident
```

## ANALYSIS TECHNIQUES

We analyze the file system category of data so that we can determine the configuration and layout of the file system. With an NTFS file system, the first step is to process the boot sector in the first sector of the file system, which is part of the $Boot file. The boot sector will identify the starting location of the MFT and the size of each MFT entry. Using that information, we can process the first entry in the MFT, which is for the $MFT file. This will tell us where the rest of the MFT is located. If any data are corrupt and we know the size of the volume, we can calculate the middle sector of the file system to find backup copies of the first MFT entries that are stored in $MFTMirr.

After we have determined the layout of the MFT, we locate and process the $Volume and $AttrDef file system metadata files. These files tell us the version of the file system, the volume label, and special attribute definitions.

## ANALYSIS CONSIDERATIONS

There are not many user-specified data in the file system category. The boot sector is the easiest to locate and contains only the basic layout information. The remaining data are located in one of the MFT entries, which are not easy to locate by hand using only a hex editor. The boot sector has many values that are not used by NTFS, but Microsoft says some must be 0. I have found that Windows XP will not mount file systems that have non-zero values in those fields.

Small amounts of data could be hidden in the boot sector, but more space is available at the end of the $Boot file after the boot code. I have observed that there are several unused sectors in there. The number of sectors in the file system should be compared with the size of the volume to determine if there is volume slack or unused space after the file system. Recall that the backup copy of the boot sector is frequently located in a sector after the end of the file system but before the end of the volume.

The temporal data associated with the file system metadata files typically correspond to when the file system was created. This could help during an investigation when you need to determine when a disk was formatted. For example, if you were expecting to find more files on a disk, you can check the date it was formatted to see how long the file system has been used.

The $MFT file can be any size and will not decrease in size from within Windows. The end of the file could be used to hide data, although this is risky because the data could be overwritten by normal activity. For example, someone could create a large number of files and force the MFT to get very large. The files are then deleted, and there are many unused entries that could be used to hide data.

It also might be useful to identify the attributes for each of the file system's metadata files. It could be possible for someone to allocate additional attributes to the files to hide data.

## ANALYSIS SCENARIO

During an investigation, we encounter a disk and acquire it. Unfortunately, there are many bad sectors in it including the first sector (where the partition table is located) and sector 63 (where the first partition typically starts). Therefore, we need to determine if a partition started at sector 63 and determine its type and size. The disk came from a Windows XP system, and we think it used an NTFS file system. Our disk image is a raw image, and 0s were written to the bad sectors.

Our first search is for the signature value in the boot sector, which is the value 0xAA55 in the last two bytes of the sector. Using this search, we hope to find either the first sector of the NTFS file system or the sector after the end of the file system, which is where the backup copy is located. We use the sigfind tool for this search, but you can use any tool that allows you to search for a hexadecimal value.

```
# sigfind -o 510 -l AA55 disk5.dd
Block size: 512  Offset: 510
```

```
Block: 210809 (-)
Block: 210810 (+1)
Block: 210811 (+1)
Block: 210812 (+1)
Block: 210813 (+1)
Block: 210814 (+1)
Block: 210815 (+1)
Block: 210816 (+1)
Block: 318170 (+107354)
Block: 339533 (+21363)
Block: 718513 (+378980)
[REMOVED]
```

These results show a series of hits that are very close together, starting at sector 210,809. This is not what we would expect from finding the boot sector at the start of the file system because the boot code should follow it, not more copies. This is also not the expected layout from partition tables, which have the same signature.

We look at one of the copies to see if it is a false hit.

```
# dd if=disk5.dd skip=210809 count=1 | xxd
0000000: eb3c 904d 5357 494e 342e 3100 0208 0100   .<.MSWIN4.1.....
0000016: 0200 0203 51f8 0800 1100 0400 0100 0000   ....Q...........
0000032: 0000 0000 8000 2900 0000 004e 4f20 4e41   ......)....NO NA
0000048: 4d45 2020 2020 4641 5431 3220 2020 33c9   ME    FAT12    3.
[REMOVED]
```

This is not what we expect from an NTFS file system, and it actually looks like a boot sector from a FAT12 file system. We look at the hit in the next sector:

```
# dd if=disk5.dd skip=210810 count=1 | xxd
0000000: eb58 904d 5357 494e 342e 3100 0202 0800   .X.MSWIN4.1.....
0000016: 0100 0400 00f8 0000 1100 0400 0100 0000   ...............
0000032: 0000 2000 e01f 0000 0000 0000 0000 0000   .. ............
0000048: 0100 0600 0000 0000 0000 0000 0000 0000   ................
0000064: 8000 2900 0000 004e 4f20 4e41 4d45 2020   ..)....NO NAME
0000080: 2020 4641 5433 3220 2020 33c9 8ed1 bcf4    FAT32    3.....
[REMOVED]
```

This is the basic template for a FAT32 file system boot sector. The hit at 210,811 is the basic template for the FSINFO FAT data structure with no values. These do not seem to apply to our search for an NTFS boot sector, so we make a note to look at this again and move on.

To reduce the number of false positives, we search for the string "NTFS" starting in byte 3 of a sector, which is part of the OEM field. We will compare those search results with the previous hits to narrow ones that could be from our file system. Note that the "NTFS" value is not an essential value in the NTFS boot sector, so it might not be there. "NTFS" in hexadecimal is 0x4e544653, and some tools can find sectors that have both signatures in a sector.

```
# sigfind -o 3 4e544653 disk5.dd
```

This produces fewer hits, and when the two results are compared we find that sectors 1,075,545; 1,075,561; and 2,056,319 occur in both results. We view the contents of sector 1,075,545, and it looks valid, but its value for the total number of sectors is 0. The same situation exists in sector 1,075,561, so these are not useful and not likely to be from a real file system.

The hit in sector 2,056,319 has more non-zero values than the previous two hits. It has a cluster size of 1,024 bytes; the number of sectors is 2,056,256; and the starting MFT cluster is 342,709. If this boot sector is legitimate, there are two scenarios for it. One is that it is located in the first sector of the file system, and the second is that it is located in the sector following the end of the file system. We notice that the reported number of sectors in the file system is 63 sectors smaller than the address of where we found the boot sector. Therefore, this could be the backup boot sector for a file system that started in sector 63.

We can check this theory by looking for the MFT. The boot sector reported that the starting cluster for the MFT was cluster 342,709, which is sector 685,418 of the file system and sector 685,481 of the disk. Each MFT entry starts with the signature string "FILE," and we see the signature:

```
# dd if=disk5.dd skip=685481 count=1 | xxd
0000000: 4649 4c45 3000 0300 4ba7 6401 0000 0000  FILE0...K.d.....
[REMOVED]
```

To show that this is indeed the first entry in the MFT, we move back two sectors (because each MFT entry is 1,024 bytes) and show that it does not start with "FILE":

```
# dd if=disk5.dd skip=685479 count=1 | xxd
0000000: ffff 00ff ffff ffff ffff ffff ffff ffff  ................
[REMOVED]
```

We are now convinced that there could have been an NTFS file system that started in sector 63 and had a size of 2,056,256 sectors. We make a copy of our disk image and copy the boot sector backup to sector 63. To import the file system into our normal analysis tool, we can either extract the 2,056,256 sectors of the file system from the disk image or we can create a basic partition table in sector 0 of the disk image with a partition from sector 63 to 2,056,318.

# CONTENT CATEGORY

## CLUSTERS

An NTFS file is a collection of attributes, some of which are resident and store the content in the MFT entry and others are non-resident and store the content in clusters. A *cluster* is a group of consecutive sectors, and the number of sectors per cluster is a power of 2 (i.e., 1, 2, 4, 8, 16).

Each cluster has an address, starting with 0. Cluster 0 starts with the first sector of the file system, which is much less confusing than the way it was calculated with FAT. To convert a cluster address to a sector address, we multiply it by the number of sectors in a cluster:

```
SECTOR = CLUSTER * sectors_per_cluster
```

NTFS does not have strict layout requirements, and any cluster can be allocated to any file or attribute, with the exception of $Boot always allocating the first cluster. Microsoft has some general layout strategies, and they will be discussed in the "Allocation Algorithm" section. If the size of the volume is not a multiple of the cluster size, some of the sectors at the end of the disk will not be part of a cluster. The total size of this area will be less than a cluster.

## $BITMAP FILE OVERVIEW

The allocation status of a cluster is determined using the $Bitmap file system metadata file, which is in MFT entry 6. This file has a $DATA attribute that has one bit for every cluster in the file system; for example, bit 0 corresponds to cluster 0, and bit 1 corresponds to cluster 1. If the bit is set to 1, the cluster is allocated; if it is set to 0, it is not. Refer to the "$Bitmap File" section of Chapter 13 for details on how the bitmap is laid out and an example dissection.

The details of the $Bitmap file in our example file system image are shown here:

```
# istat -f ntfs ntfs1.dd 6
[REMOVED]
Attributes:
Type: $STANDARD_INFORMATION (16-0)   Name: N/A   Resident   size: 72
Type: $FILE_NAME (48-2)   Name: N/A   Resident   size: 80
Type: $DATA (128-1)   Name: $Data   Non-Resident   size: 128520
514113 514114 514115 514116 514117 514118 514119 514120
514121 514122 514123 514124 514125 514126 514127 514128
[REMOVED]
```

We can see that the $Bitmap file has the standard attributes for a file, and its temporal data was the same that we saw for the file system metadata files previously analyzed.

## $BADCLUS FILE OVERVIEW

NTFS keeps track of the damaged clusters by allocating them to a $DATA attribute of the $BadClus file system metadata file, which is in MFT entry 8. The $DATA attribute, named $Bad, is a sparse file, and when a cluster is reported to be bad, it is added to the attribute. Recall from Chapter 11 that a sparse file is one that saves space by not allocating a cluster if it is going to be filled with zeros. The reported size of the $Bad attribute is equal to the total size of the file system, but it initially does not have any clusters allocated to it. Windows adds clusters to the $Bad attribute when it finds bad clusters, but many hard disks will find a bad sector before the file system does.

The details of the $BadClus file in our example file system image are shown here:

```
# istat -f ntfs ntfs1.dd 8
[REMOVED]
Attributes:
Type: $STANDARD_INFORMATION (16-0)   Name: N/A   Resident   size: 72
Type: $FILE_NAME (48-3)   Name: N/A   Resident   size: 82
Type: $DATA (128-2)   Name: $Data   Resident   size: 0
Type: $DATA (128-1)   Name: $Bad   Non-Resident   size: 1052803072
```

Notice that the file has two $DATA attributes, and the default one, $Data, is resident with a size of 0. The $DATA attributed named $Bad is non-resident and has a size of 1,052,803,072 bytes, but no cluster addresses are shown because this file system has no bad clusters. The size of the attribute is the same as the file system size, which we saw in the fsstat output.

## ALLOCATION ALGORITHMS

This section documents my observations of the strategy that Windows XP uses when it allocates new NTFS clusters. As with other file systems, an allocation strategy is OS-dependent, and different implementations of NTFS may use different strategies. I have observed that Windows XP uses the best-fit algorithm. The best-fit algorithm is when the data is placed in a location that will most efficiently use the available space, even if it is not the first or next available. Therefore, if a small amount of data is being written, it will be placed in clusters that are part of a small group of unallocated clusters instead of in a large group where larger files could be stored. For example, Figure 12.1 shows a scenario where we need to allocate 10 clusters for a file. There are three chunks of unallocated clusters. The first chunk is from cluster 100 to 199, the second is from cluster 280 to 319, and the third is from cluster 370 to 549. The best-fit algorithm would allocate clusters 280 to 289 for the new file because that is in the smallest available group of clusters that the file can fit.

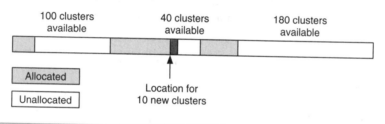

**Figure 12.1**  The best fit algorithm will place 10 new clusters in the smallest space that will fit them.

## FILE SYSTEM LAYOUT

The NTFS file system does not have strict layout requirements, but Windows formats the file system using some general guidelines. The layout is different for most versions of NTFS, but there are some basic concepts.

One basic concept for all versions of NTFS is the MFT Zone. Windows creates the MFT as small as possible and expands it only when more entries are needed. Therefore, there is a risk that it could easily become fragmented if the space after the MFT is allocated to a file. To prevent this, Microsoft reserves part of the file system for the MFT. The *MFT Zone* is a collection of consecutive clusters that are not used to store file or directory content unless the rest of the disk is full. By default, Microsoft allocates 12.5% of the file system to the MFT. If the rest of the file system fills up, the MFT Zone will be used.

All versions of NTFS and Windows allocate the first clusters to the $Boot file. Windows NT and 2000 allocated its file system metadata files right after the $Boot file and in the middle of the file system. For example, if a file system had a 1 KB cluster size, the first eight clusters would be allocated to the $Boot file, and the clusters for the $MFT file may start in cluster 16 or 32. The MFT Zone would extend for the next 12.5% of the file system. The middle cluster in the file system would be allocated to the $MFTMirr file and the remainder of the file system metadata files, such as $LogFile, $Root, $Bitmap, and $Upcase, would follow. One difference that I observed between Windows NT and 2000 is that NT places the $AttrDef file in the latter part of the file system, but Windows 2000 places it before the $MFT file.

I found that Windows XP moves some of the data to the one-third point in the file system. The $LogFile, $AttrDef, $MFT, and $Secure files allocated clusters at one-third of the way through the file system. The other file system metadata files were located one-half of the way through the file system. Only the $Boot file is located in the first few clusters of the file system. All the clusters in between the file system metadata files can be allocated to user files and directories. Figure 12.2 shows the locations where different file system metadata files are located when formatted by Windows 2000 or XP.

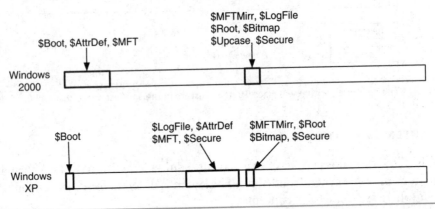

**Figure 12.2**  File system metadata layout for a file system formatted by Windows 2000 and Windows XP.

## ANALYSIS TECHNIQUES

Analysis of the content category involves locating a specific cluster, determining its allocation status, and processing the content in some fashion. Finding a specific cluster is easy because the first cluster is at the start of the file system, and the cluster size is given in the first sector.

The allocation status of a cluster is determined by locating the $Bitmap file and processing its $DATA attribute. Each bit in the attribute corresponds to a cluster in the file system.

A common analysis technique is to extract the unallocated space of a file system. We do this with NTFS by examining the $Bitmap file, and the contents of each cluster with a 0 bit would be extracted. All NTFS file system administrative data are located in a file, so none of it should be considered unallocated data during this process.

## ANALYSIS CONSIDERATIONS

There are no unique considerations that must be made when analyzing the content category of NTFS versus other file systems. The cluster addresses start with the first cluster, so only one addressing scheme is needed. Microsoft typically allocates only the needed number of sectors to the file system, so there should not be any sectors at the end of the file system without a cluster address. On the other hand, this means that there could be sectors after the file system and before the end of the volume that could have hidden data.

When doing keyword searches, there is no difference between a logical volume search and a logical file system search because every sector used by the file system is allocated to a cluster. Because all data in the file system category is allocated to a file, it should be clear which clusters are allocated and which are not. Recall that with FAT, it is not obvious if a tool will treat the FAT area and reserved areas as allocated or not.

As with all modern systems, you should check the clusters that are marked as bad by the file system because many disks will remap bad sectors before the file system notices that they are indeed bad.

## ANALYSIS SCENARIO

In this example, we are going to locate cluster 9,900,009. The first step is to determine the cluster size. We read the first sector of the file system and determine that each sector is 512 bytes and each cluster is eight sectors, which is 4,096 bytes.

Cluster 0 in NTFS starts with sector 0. Therefore, we can calculate the sector address of our cluster by multiplying it by the number of sectors per cluster. When we do this, we get sector 792,00,072. To get the byte location, we multiply the sector address by 512 and get byte 40,550,436,864. Compare this process to how many steps it took in FAT to find the byte or sector location of a cluster.

## METADATA CATEGORY

The metadata category includes data that describes a file or directory. All metadata is stored in one of the attributes, so we will now look at details of the file attributes. To review, a typical file has a $STANDARD_INFORMATION, a $FILE_NAME, and a $DATA attribute. The attributes that are used by directories and indexes are discussed in the "File Name Category" section. Figure 12.3 shows a typical file that has the standard attributes. The data structures for the attributes are given in Chapter 13.

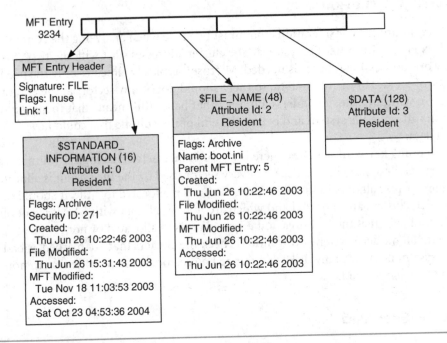

**Figure 12.3** A basic file with the three standard attributes.

## $STANDARD_INFORMATION ATTRIBUTE

The $STANDARD_INFORMATION attribute exists for all files and directories and contains the core metadata. It is here that you find the primary, but not exclusive, set of time and date stamps, and you also find ownership, security, and quota information. Nothing in this attribute is essential to storing files, but many of the application-level features that Microsoft provides depend on it.

The default type ID for this attribute is 16, and it has a static size of 72 bytes in the Windows 2000 and XP versions and 48 bytes in the Windows NT version. Microsoft sorts the attributes in an MFT entry, and this one is always first in the entry because it has the lowest type ID.

There are four date and timestamps in this attribute. NTFS date and time stamps are 64-bit values that represent the number of one-hundred nanoseconds since January 1, 1601 UTC [Microsoft 2004], which is useful if you need to investigate a computer that was used during the eighteenth century. As a reference to the size of this number, the value for January 1, 1970 UTC is 116,444,736,000,000,000 hundred nanoseconds. Needless to say, I am not going to provide a method for converting this time to a human readable time because most calculators cannot handle such a number, but most hex editors or other tools can.[1] The four time values in this attribute are as follows:

**Creation Time:** The time that the file was created.

**Modified Time:** The time that the content of the $DATA or $INDEX attributes was last modified.

**MFT Modified Time:** The time that the metadata of the file was last modified. Note that this value is not shown in Windows when you select the properties of a file.

**Accessed Time:** The time that the content of the file was last accessed.

The attribute also contains a flag for general properties of the file, such as read only, system or archive. This properties value also tells you if the file is compressed, sparse, or encrypted. This value will not identify if an entry is for a file or a directory, but the flags in the MFT entry headers will show that.

In the 3.0+ versions of NTFS (Windows 2000 and XP), this attribute contains four additional values used for security information and application-level features. One of the new values is the owner identity, which corresponds to the owner of the file and is an index into the quota data that stores how much data a user has been using. The attribute also has a value for how many bytes were added to the user's quota because of this file. The Security ID value is used as an index for the $Secure file and is used to determine the access control rules that apply to this file. The $Secure file will be discussed later in the "Metadata Category" section. If change journaling is being used, this attribute contains the *update sequence number* (USN) for the last record that was created for this file. Change journaling will be discussed later in the "Application Category" section, but it is a file that contains a list of files that have been changed and is used to quickly identify the files that have changed in a certain time frame instead of looking at each file individually.

---

1. An example is Decode from Digital Detective (http://www.digital-detective.co.uk).

In summary, this attribute contains many interesting pieces of metadata, but none are essential for the file system. The primary time and date information and other identifiers are stored here, but it is up to the OS when the times are updated and whether they will use the identifiers. Note that this attribute exists for all files and directories, but it may not exist in non-base MFT entries.

## $FILE_NAME ATTRIBUTE

Every file and directory has at least one $FILE_NAME attribute in its MFT entry. In addition, every file and directory has at least one other instance of a $FILE_NAME attribute in the index of its parent directory, although the two instances do not necessarily contain the same data. The $FILE_NAME attribute in the parent directory will be discussed later in the "File Name Category" section. This section focuses only on the one in the MFT entry. The attribute has a type identifier of 48 and a variable length, which depends on the length of the file name. The base length is 66 bytes plus the name.

The $FILE_NAME attribute contains the name of the file encoded in UTF-16 Unicode. The name must be in a specific name space, such as the 8.3 DOS format, Win32 format, or POSIX. Windows typically forces a file to have a name in the 8.3 DOS name space, so some files have $FILE_NAME attributes for both the real file name and the DOS version, but this behavior can be disabled. Each name space has different restrictions on what they consider valid characters.

The $FILE_NAME attribute contains the file reference for the parent directory, which is actually one of the most useful values in the attribute when it is located in an MFT entry. This allows a tool to more easily identify the full path of a random MFT entry.

This attribute also contains a set of the four temporal values that were previously described in the "$STANDARD_INFORMATION Attribute" section. Windows does not typically update this set of temporal values like it does with those in the $STANDARD_INFORMATION attribute, and they frequently correspond to when the file was created, moved, or renamed.

The $FILE_NAME attribute has fields for the actual and the allocated size of the file, but I have found that these values are 0 for user files and directories in Windows. Lastly, this attribute contains a flags field that can identify if an entry is for a directory, read-only, a system file, compressed, encrypted, and so on. The same flags that were used in $STANDARD_INFORMATION are included here.

In summary, this attribute contains many values that are duplicated with $STAN-DARD_INFORMATION. The new values are the name of the file and the address of the parent directory, which can be used to determine the full path.

## $DATA ATTRIBUTE

The $DATA attribute is used to store any form of data—it has no format or defined values. Its attribute type identifier is 128, and it can be any size, including 0 bytes. One $DATA attribute is allocated for each file, and it does not have a name. Some tools, including *The Sleuth Kit* (TSK) will assign it the name $Data. Additional $DATA attributes can be allocated to an MFT entry, but they must have names.

There are many uses for additional $DATA attributes. In Windows, a user can enter "Summary" information for a file when she right clicks it, and the information is stored in a $DATA attribute. Some anti-virus and backup software will create a $DATA attribute on files that it has processed. Directories can even have a $DATA attribute in addition to their index attributes. Additional $DATA attributes can also be used to hide data. The additional $DATA attributes are not shown when the contents of a directory are listed; so special tools are needed to locate them. Most forensic tools will show the additional $DATA attributes, which are also called *alternate data streams* (ADS).

It is easy for a user to create an ADS because all he needs is a command prompt. He can save data to an ADS by appending a colon and the attribute name to the end of the file name. For example, to create a $DATA attribute named foo on the file.txt file, the following would be used:

```
C:\> echo "Hello There" > file.txt:foo
```

Recall from Chapter 11 that the $DATA attribute can be encrypted to prevent unauthorized access to the data or compressed to save space. When any of these options are used, the attribute header will have the corresponding flag set. When encryption is being used, the $LOGGED_UTILITY_STREAM also will exist to store the encryption key. Figure 12.4 shows a file that has two $DATA attributes that are encrypted. When multiple $DATA attributes exist, both use the same encryption key.

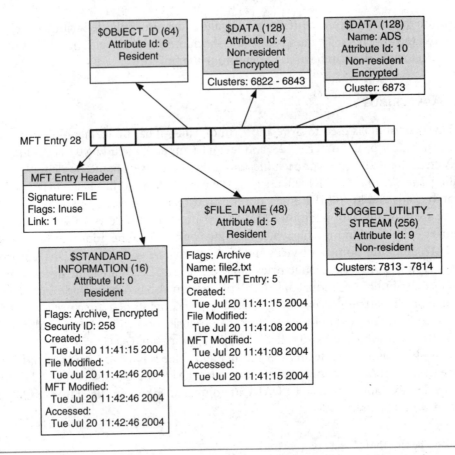

**Figure 12.4**    A file with two $DATA attributes that are encrypted.

## $ATTRIBUTE_LIST ATTRIBUTE

The $ATTRIBUTE_LIST attribute is used when a file or directory needs more than one MFT entry to store all its attributes. A file or directory can have up to 65,536 attributes, and they may not all fit in one MFT entry. At a minimum, we need to store the header of each attribute in an MFT entry. The content can be non-resident, but sometimes we need multiple MFT entries to store the headers. This is common if a non-resident attribute becomes fragmented and its runlist becomes long.

The $ATTRIBUTE_LIST attribute has a small type identifier of 32, which is the second smallest type. Therefore, it is always going to be in the base MFT entry. It contains a list of all of the file's attributes, except itself. Each entry in the list contains the attribute type and the MFT entry address of where it is located. The non-base MFT entries will have the address of the base entry in their MFT entry header.

To make things more complex, it is possible for an attribute to become very fragmented and require multiple MFT entries just to save the runlist, which typically occurs only with $DATA attributes. When this happens, each non-base MFT entry will have a normal $DATA attribute, but it will identify where it fits in the file. The attribute header has a field that shows the starting *Virtual Cluster Number* (VCN) of the run, which is the logical file address. For example, let there be a file that needs two MFT entries to store the runlist for its $DATA attribute. The first entry can fit runs for the first 500 MB of the attribute, and the second entry contains the rest of the runs. The attribute header in the second entry will identify that its runs start at the 500 MB point in the full $DATA attribute.

Consider Figure 12.5. Here we see the base entry in MFT, entry 37. The base entry contains the $STANDARD_INFORMATION attribute and $ATTRIBUTE_LIST attribute, which has five entries in its list. The first entry is for the $STANDARD_INFORMATION attribute, which we already processed. The second entry is for the $FILE_NAME attribute, and it is located in entry 48. The third and fourth list entries are for the same $DATA attribute, and the fifth entry is for a different $DATA attribute. You can tell which $DATA attribute each entry is for by looking at the ID field. The first 284 MB of the first $DATA attribute are described in entry 48 and the rest of the attribute is described in entry 49.

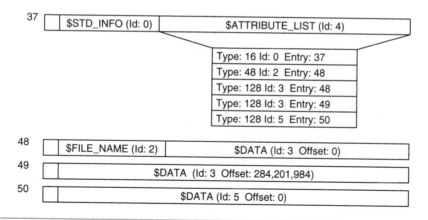

**Figure 12.5**   An attribute list with five entries. This file needed three additional MFT entries, and one of the $DATA attributes needed two entries for its run lists.

## $SECURITY_DESCRIPTOR ATTRIBUTE

The $SECURITY_DESCRIPTOR attribute is primarily found in file systems from Windows NT because NTFS version 3.0 and beyond have this attribute for backward compatibility only. Windows uses *security descriptors* to describe the access control policy that should be applied to a file or directory. Older versions of NTFS store a file's security descriptor in the $SECURITY_DESCRIPTOR attribute, which has a type identifier of 80. The newer versions of NTFS store the security descriptors in a single file because many files have the same security descriptor, and it is a waste of space to store one for each file.

### $SECURE FILE

As mentioned in the previous section, security descriptors are used to define the access control policy for a file or directory. In versions 3.0+ of NTFS, the security descriptors are stored in the $Secure file system metadata file, which is located in MFT entry 9.

The $STANDARD_INFORMATION attribute of every file and directory contains an identifier, called the *Security ID*, and it is used as an index to the $Secure file so that the appropriate descriptor can be found. Note that these 32-bit Security IDs are different from the Windows *Security Identifiers* (SID) that are assigned to users. The Security ID is unique to only the file system, whereas the SIDs are globally unique.

The $Secure file contains two indexes ($SDH and $SII) and one $DATA attribute ($SDS). The $DATA attribute contains the actual security descriptors, and the two indexes are used to reference the descriptors. The $SII index is sorted by the Security ID, which is located in the $STANDARD_INFORMATION attribute of each file. The $SII index is used to locate the security descriptor for a file when its Security ID is known. Alternatively, the $SDH index is sorted by a hash of the security descriptor. The OS uses this index when a new security descriptor is applied to a file or directory. If the hash of the new descriptor cannot be found, a new descriptor and Security ID are created and added to both indices.

Here we see the output of istat on the $Secure file on a small system:

```
# istat -f ntfs ntfs2.dd 9
[REMOVED]
Attributes:
Type: $STANDARD_INFORMATION (16-0)   Name: N/A   Resident   size: 72
Type: $FILE_NAME (48-7)   Name: N/A   Resident   size: 80
Type: $DATA (128-8)   Name: $SDS   Non-Resident   size: 266188
10016 10017 10018 10019 10020 10021 10022 10023
10024 10025 10026 10027 10028 10029 10030 10031
10032 10033 10034 10035 10036 10037 10038 10039
```

```
[REMOVED]
Type: $INDEX_ROOT (144-11)    Name: $SDH    Resident    size: 56
Type: $INDEX_ROOT (144-14)    Name: $SII    Resident    size: 56
Type: $INDEX_ALLOCATION (160-9)    Name: $SDH    Non-Resident    size: 4096
8185 8186 8187 8188 8189 8190 8191 8192
Type: $INDEX_ALLOCATION (160-12)    Name: $SII    Non-Resident    size: 4096
8196 8197 8198 8199 8200 8201 8202 8203
Type: $BITMAP (176-10)    Name: $SDH    Resident    size: 8
Type: $BITMAP (176-13)    Name: $SII    Resident    size: 8
```

We can see in this output that there is a 200KB $DATA attribute with copies of the security descriptors and two indexes named $SDH and $SII.

## EXAMPLE IMAGE

To close this section, I will give the output of istat on a typical file. In this case, it is the C:\boot.ini file of a system. The output is broken up so that it can be more easily described.

```
# istat -f ntfs ntfs1.dd 3234
MFT Entry Header Values:
Entry: 3234        Sequence: 1
$LogFile Sequence Number: 103605752
Allocated File
Links: 1
```

This part of the output shows the data in the MFT entry header, and we see that its sequence is 1, which means it is the first file to allocate this entry. We also see the *$LogFile Sequence Number* (LSN), which corresponds to when the file was last changed. The file system journal log uses this value.

```
$STANDARD_INFORMATION Attribute Values:
Flags: Hidden, System, Not Content Indexed
Owner ID: 256        Security ID: 271
Quota Charged: 1024
Last User Journal Update Sequence Number: 4372416
Created:        Thu Jun 26 10:22:46 2003
File Modified:  Thu Jun 26 15:31:43 2003
MFT Modified:   Tue Nov 18 11:03:53 2003
Accessed:       Sat Jul 24 04:53:36 2004
```

Here we see the data from the $STANDARD_INFORMATION attribute, including the flag values and owner information. The Security ID is given so we can look the data up in the $Secure index. We also see the Last User Journal Update number, which is updated when file is changed. This value is used by the change journal, which is described in the "Application Category" section.

```
$FILE_NAME Attribute Values:
Flags: Archive
Name: boot.ini
Parent MFT Entry: 5      Sequence: 5
Allocated Size: 0        Actual Size: 0
Created:           Thu Jun 26 10:22:46 2003
File Modified:     Thu Jun 26 10:22:46 2003
MFT Modified:      Thu Jun 26 10:22:46 2003
Accessed:          Thu Jun 26 10:22:46 2003
```

Here are the data from $FILE_NAME. Notice that the time values are different from those in $STANDARD_INFORMATION, and that the size values are 0 bytes. We also see that the parent directory is MFT entry 5, which is the root directory.

```
Attributes:
Type: $STANDARD_INFORMATION (16-0)   Name: N/A   Resident   size: 72
Type: $FILE_NAME (48-2)    Name: N/A   Resident   size: 82
Type: $DATA (128-3)    Name: $Data   Resident   size: 194
```

In the final part of the output, we see all the file's attributes. It has a resident $DATA attribute with a size of 194 bytes. The type identifier and attribute identifier are given after the type name.

## ALLOCATION ALGORITHMS

We will now look at the metadata allocation algorithms. As with every other discussion of allocation algorithms, they are application-specific rather than file-system specific. There are three strategies that we can discuss with metadata: The first two are how MFT entries and attributes are allocated, and the third is about temporal value updating.

### MFT Entry and Attribute Allocation

The first allocation strategy that we will consider is the allocation of MFT entries. I have found that Windows allocates MFT entries on a first-available basis starting with entry

24. Entries 0 to 15 are reserved and set to an allocated state even if they are not being used, and 16 to 23 are not typically allocated. User files start at entry 24, and the size of the table increases as needed. When the entry is no longer being used, no data are changed except for the flag that identifies it as being used. Therefore, the temporal and runlist information can be recovered. When an entry is allocated, it is wiped, and the values from the previous file are deleted. Therefore, there will not be slack data from a previous file in an MFT entry.

The second discussion about allocation involves allocating space for attributes in the MFT entry. Microsoft sorts the entries based on the attribute type and packs them in one after another. If the $DATA attribute at the end of the entry is resident and its size is decreased, its old contents can be found at the end of the entry (minus the end marker of 0xffffffff). When an attribute grows from a resident attribute to a non-resident attribute, the content in the MFT entry exists until it is overwritten by other attributes.

### Time Value Updating

The final discussion of allocation involves when the temporal values are updated. We saw that temporal data are stored in both $STANDARD_INFORMATION and $FILE_NAME. When you select the properties of a file in Windows, you are seeing the times from the $STANDARD_INFORMATION attribute, and only three of the four times are shown. I will outline my test results for the times in $STANDARD_INFORMATION and when they were updated. The $FILE_NAME values are updated when the file is created and moved, but I have not found conclusive results for when they are updated.

Time updating for NTFS in Windows is similar to that in FAT file systems. The creation time is set for a *new* file. If you create a new file from scratch or if you copy a file, the new file's creation time is set to the current time. If you move a file, even if the move is to a different volume, the creation time from the original file remains.

The last modified time is set when the value of any $DATA, $INDEX_ROOT, or $INDEX_ALLOCATION attributes are modified. If you move or copy a file, the content is not changing and the new file has the original modified time. If a file has multiple $DATA attributes, this time is also updated when the non-default attribute is modified. If you change the attributes or the name of a file, this value should remain the same.

The MFT modified time is set when any of the attributes are changed, and I also have observed that it is set when an application opens a file but does not modify the content. When a file is renamed or moved in the same volume, this value is updated because the $FILE_NAME attribute changes. If the file is moved to a different volume, this value does not seem to change. Note that this value is not shown to a user when they view the properties of a file in Windows, but many forensic tools show it to you.

The last access time is set when the metadata or content is viewed. If a user views the properties of a file, this is updated. If the file is opened, this is updated. When a file is copied or moved, the access time on the original file is updated to reflect that it was read. For efficiency, Windows does not immediately update the last access time on the disk. It keeps the correct version in memory, but it might not be written to disk for up to an hour. Further, there is an option in Windows to disable the updating of the last access time.

To summarize, when a file is created from scratch, all $STANDARD_INFORMATION and $FILE_NAME values are set to the current time. When a file is copied, the last accessed time on the original file is updated and the new file has updated access times and creation times. The MFT modified and file modified times are set to the original values. This means that the creation time will be later than the modification times. When a file is moved in the same volume, the access time and MFT modified times are changed. When a file is moved to a different volume, the access time is updated, but the MFT is not modified. When a file is deleted, the times are not updated by default. In some cases, I have observed that the last access time was updated, but I could not find a pattern.

A similar behavior occurs for directories. When files are created or deleted, the contents of the directory changes and the modification times are updated to the current time. When the contents of a directory are listed, the access time is updated. When a directory is copied, all four of its times are updated to reflect the time of the copy. When a directory is moved in the same volume, the same MFT entry is used and only the MFT modified and accessed times are updated. When moved to a different volume, all four of the times are updated to the time of the move.

## ANALYSIS TECHNIQUES

The metadata category of data is analyzed to learn more about a specific file or directory. This process involves locating an MFT entry and processing its contents. To locate a specific MFT entry, we need to first locate the MFT using the starting address in the boot sector. The first MFT entry describes the cluster layout of rest of the table. Each entry in the table is the same size and we can seek to the specific table entry.

After the table location has been determined, we process its attributes. A file or directory might have needed multiple MFT entries for its attributes, and the $ATTRIBUTE_LIST attribute lists the additional entry addresses, which also need to be processed. To process an MFT entry, we first process its header and then locate the first attribute. We process the first attribute by reading its header, determining its type, and processing the content appropriately. The location of the second attribute is determined from the length of the first attribute, and we repeat this procedure until all attributes have been processed. Figure 12.6 shows an example of this where the attribute lengths are given. After the last attribute, the 0xffffffff value exists.

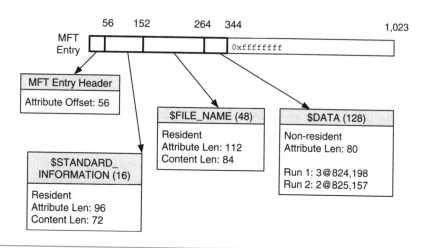

**Figure 12.6**   The MFT entry for a basic file with the attributes lengths given to show how an entry is processed.

The core metadata can be found in the $STANDARD_INFORMATION attribute, and the $DATA attribute(s) has the file content. For example, if we wanted to learn the temporal or ownership information about a file, we would check $STANDARD_INFORMATION. If we wanted to learn about the content of a file, we would check the $DATA attribute. The $FILE_NAME attribute is useful when we want to verify the creation date of the file and when we want to determine the parent directory of the file.

The allocation status of an MFT entry is determined by both a flag in the MFT entry and a bitmap in $MFT. The content of an attribute can be found either inside the MFT entry or in a cluster run. Attributes that are resident have a content offset and size value in the header. Non-resident attributes have a runlist in the header that describes the starting cluster and number of clusters in each run.

It is sometimes useful to search for the unallocated MFT entries. We do this by determining the layout of the MFT and then examining each entry. If the entry's "in use" flag is not set, it should be processed for information about the file that previously allocated it. The attributes should still exist in the entry.

If there are problems locating $MFT and $MFTMirr, we can search the file system for clusters that start with the "FILE" ASCII signature. Unfortunately, there is not an easy way to determine which MFT entry it corresponds to if the MFT was fragmented.

## ANALYSIS CONSIDERATIONS

Any file or directory may have multiple $DATA attributes in addition to its standard one. The extra attributes could have been used to hide data because they are not shown in Windows, or they could be used for a legitimate purpose. Some of the NTFS test images I have at the *Digital Forensic Tool Testing* (DFTT) [Carrier 2003] site have multiple $DATA attributes, and you can use them in your tools to check if all attributes are shown. You also can use this test image to determine if your tools will search the attributes during a keyword search.

Another data-hiding location is in the unused part of an MFT entry or even an attribute. Both of these locations would be difficult to hide data in, though, because of the dynamic nature of NTFS. If the end of an MFT entry is used, any attributes that are added or changed by the OS could overwrite the data. For example, an administrative program could create additional $DATA attributes when it scans or backs up the file, and this could overwrite the hidden data.

With NTFS, it is easy to find the unallocated MFT entries because they are all allocated in a single table. This is unlike a FAT file system where the metadata could be located anywhere in the file system. When we find an unallocated MFT entry of interest, the $FILE_NAME attribute gives us its original name and the MFT entry address of the parent directory. This helps to put context around a file. For example, we could search for all MFT entries that were created in a given time range. This search might find unallocated entries and knowing the full path would be more useful than only its entry address.

The content associated with deleted files can be more easily recovered with NTFS. If the file's $DATA attribute was resident, it will still exist in the MFT entry and we do not have to worry about the clusters being allocated to a different file. Therefore, if we find the MFT entry we will have found the content. Unfortunately, if a file is larger than 700 bytes, it typically becomes non-resident. Most files that have evidence are larger than 700 bytes.

If the file's $DATA attribute was non-resident, we need to worry about the content being out of sync like we do with any other file system. The clusters could have been allocated to a new file before we investigate the system. One benefit of NTFS is that the location of the non-resident runs is saved in the MFT entries, and Windows does not clear them when the file is deleted.

If all attributes for a file cannot fit into a single MFT entry, recovery becomes more challenging. In this case, we need to check if the other entries were reallocated since the file was deleted. For example, if a file needed two MFT entries to store its attribute information, the non-base entry could be reallocated before the base is. In many cases, it will be obvious that this occurred because the entry that was a non-base entry will either be a base entry or it will point to a different non-base entry. This can also cause problems when the $DATA attribute is described in multiple MFT entries. When one or more of the entries are reallocated, we will not be able to recover the entire attribute.

We can see these three scenarios in Figure 12.7. Entry 90 shows a resident attribute, and the content is overwritten when the MFT entry is allocated. Entry 91 shows a non-resident attribute, and we can recover the content using application-level techniques if the MFT entry is reallocated before the clusters are. Entries 92 is the base entry for entry 93, and the $DATA attribute is very fragmented and described in both entries. If any one of these entries is reallocated, the $DATA attribute cannot be recovered.

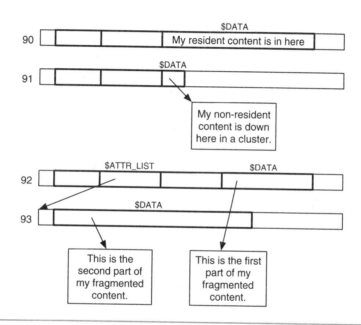

**Figure 12.7**   The locations where the $DATA content can be stored so that we can discuss what happens when MFT entries are reallocated.

When it comes to reallocation of MFT entries in Windows, the unallocated entries with a small address are going to be reused before larger addressed entries will. So, it is harder to recover files that have smaller MFT addresses. If the $DATA attribute for a file was resident and the MFT entry is reallocated, the data are lost. With non-resident files, even if the MFT entry is reallocated, application-level recovery techniques can be used to recover the file.

Windows writes 0s to the unused bytes in the last sector of a file but does not wipe the unused sectors. Therefore, data from deleted files can typically be found at the end of a file in the slack space.

The time values for a file are not updated when the file is deleted, so we may not be able to tell when a file was deleted. The $FILE_NAME attribute contains a set of temporal values, and they are set when the file or directory is created or moved. These can be used to detect when someone may have tried to modify the creation time in $STANDARD_INFORMATION. The time value is stored with respect to UTC, so an analysis tool must convert the time to the time zone where the computer was originally located. This makes it easier to correlate the time values in logs and other systems.

Encrypted and compressed attributes can present a challenge to an investigation. If the user's password is not known, the unallocated space on the disk needs to be searched for decrypted copies of the encrypted files. Many forensic tools now support compressed and encrypted files. Compressed files might not have slack space, and application-level recovery techniques will not work on deleted data that was stored in a compressed format. Also test search features on your analysis tools to verify that they search inside compressed files.

## ANALYSIS SCENARIO

During an investigation of a Windows 2000 system, we find that one of the volumes was formatted a day before the disk was acquired. We determine this based on the temporal data associated with the file system metadata files. The file system has no files or directories in the root directory, but we want to recover some of the files from the previous file system.

When a file system is formatted, a new MFT is created with the minimal number of MFT entries. Therefore, the MFT entries from the previous file system should still exist in the unallocated clusters of the new file system. If we find the entries, we can use them to recover their original attribute contents.

The first step is to extract the unallocated space of the file system so that we can search it. If your search tool allows you to search only unallocated space, you do not need this step. We will use dls from TSK for this:

```
# dls -f ntfs ntfs9.dd > ntfs9.dls
```

Now we will search for the old MFT entries. Each MFT entry starts with the ASCII signature "FILE." We can do this search with a normal text-searching tool like grep or we can use sigfind again. We will use sigfind because it allows us to limit hits to those that are at an offset of 0 bytes from the start of the sector. We convert "FILE" in ASCII to hexadecimal and get 0x46494c45.

```
# sigfind -o 0 46494c45 ntfs9.dls
```

This produces several hits, including one in sector 412. To show what we do with the results, I am going to step through the basic analysis of it. If you are interested in the NTFS data structures, you should return to this example after reading the next chapter. The contents of sector 412 are the following (the different parts of the data structure have been broken up):

```
# dd if=ntfs9.dls skip=412 count=2 | xxd
0000000: 4649 4c45 3000 0300 b6e5 1000 0000 0000  FILE0..........
0000016: 0100 0100 3800 0100 0003 0000 0004 0000  ....8..........
0000032: 0000 0000 0000 0000 0400 0000 4800 0000  ...........H...
0000048: 0500 6661 0000 0000                       ..fa....
```

This is the MFT entry header, and the flag in bytes 22 to 23 show that this entry was allocated (0x0001 in little-endian ordering) before it was formatted, and bytes 20 to 21 show that the first attribute starts at byte offset 56 (0x0038). The header of the first attribute is shown here:

```
0000048:                  1000 0000 6000 0000       ....`...
0000064: 0000 0000 0000 0000 4800 0000 1800 0000  ........H.......
[REMOVED]
0000144: b049 0000 0000 0000                       .I......
```

This first attribute is for the $STANDARD_INFORMATION attribute (0x0010), and its length is 96 bytes (0x0060). We could analyze this attribute for the temporal information it contains. Next, we advance ahead 96 more bytes from byte 56 to byte 152:

```
0000144:                  3000 0000 7000 0000       0...p...
0000160: 0000 0000 0000 0200 5800 0000 1800 0100  ........X.......
0000176: 0500 0000 0000 0500 d064 f7b9 eb69 c401  .........d...i..
[REMOVED]
0000240: 0b03 6c00 6500 7400 7400 6500 7200 3100  ..l.e.t.t.e.r.1.
0000256: 2e00 7400 7800 7400                       ..t.x.t.
```

The second attribute is for the $FILE_NAME attribute (0x0030), and its length is 112 bytes (0x0070). We also see that the parent directory of this file was MFT entry 5, which is the root directory. The name of the file is given, and it is "letter1.txt." Next, we advance ahead 112 bytes from our starting location of byte 152 and get to byte 264:

```
0000256:                      4000 0000 2800 0000      @...(...
0000272: 0000 0000 0000 0300 1000 0000 1800 0000      ..............
0000288: 6dd4 12e6 d9d5 d811 a5c7 00b0 d01d e93f      m.............?
```

The third attribute is an $OBJECT_ID attribute (0x0040), and its length is 40 bytes (0x28). We advance to the next attribute at byte 304:

```
0000304: 8000 0000 c801 0000 0000 1800 0000 0100      ..............
0000320: ae01 0000 1800 0000 4865 6c6c 6f20 4d72      ........Hello Mr
0000336: 204a 6f6e 6573 2c0a 5765 2073 6861 6c6c       Jones,.We shall
[REMOVED]
```

This last attribute is a $DATA attribute (0x0080), and its length is 456 bytes (0x01c8). The content of the attribute starts at byte 328 and starts with "Hello Mr. Jones." The entire letter is in the MFT entry because it is in a resident attribute. Had it been non-resident, we would have had to parse the run list and locate the clusters in the file system image. This entry had the layout shown in Figure 12.8.

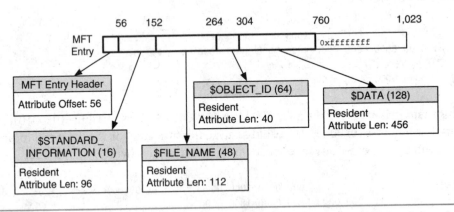

**Figure 12.8**  The layout of the MFT entry we found in unallocated space because of a recent formatting.

In this scenario, we looked for evidence of files prior to a volume being formatted. We searched for the "FILE" signature that exists for MFT entries and then parsed one by hand. The individual data structures for each attribute are parsed in more detail in the next chapter.

# FILE NAME CATEGORY

The file name category includes the data that are used to link a file's name with its contents. So far, we have looked at how NTFS stores data and what metadata is recorded, but now we need to examine how to correlate a name with the file. NTFS uses indexes, which were discussed in Chapter 11, to organize directory contents. An NTFS index is a collection of data structures that are sorted by some key. The tree contains one or more nodes, which are stored in $INDEX_ROOT and $INDEX_ALLOCATION attributes. The $INDEX_ROOT attribute is always the root of the tree, and the $INDEX_ ALLOCATION contains index records that are used to store other nodes. The $BITMAP attribute is used to manage the allocation status of the index records. Each node in the tree contains a list of index entries.

## DIRECTORY INDEXES

An NTFS directory has a normal MFT entry with a special flag set in its header and in its $STANDARD_INFORMATION and $FILE_NAME attributes. The index entries in a directory index contain a file reference address and a $FILE_NAME attribute. Recall that the $FILE_NAME attribute contains the file's name, temporal information, size, and basic flags. Windows updates the temporal and size information so that it is accurate. If Windows is configured to require a DOS name space name, multiple $FILE_NAME attributes for the same file exist in the index. The $INDEX_ROOT, $INDEX_ALLOCA-TION, and $BITMAP attributes are all assigned the name $I30. These data structures were described in Chapter 11, and the data structures are given in Chapter 13.

Figure 12.9 shows a simple two-level directory structure where the root node is in the $INDEX_ROOT attribute, and there are two index records in the $INDEX_ ALLOCATION attribute. The entries in index record 0 have names less than hhh.txt, and the entries in index record 1 have names greater than hhh.txt. Notice that the eeeeeeeeeee.txt file is not in the DOS name space, and there is a second entry for it.

When a file is added to or deleted from a directory, the tree is reorganized so that everything is in sorted order. This may result in the entries in the index records being moved around and overwriting data from deleted files. Each node in the tree has a header value that identifies where the last allocated entry is. In Figure 12.9, there are entries for the ccc.txt file in the $INDEX_ROOT and qqq.txt file in index record 1 that are in the unallocated space. The qqq.txt file is a deleted file, but ccc.txt is not deleted, it is in index record 0. See the "Indexes" section in Chapter 11 for examples of why this occurs.

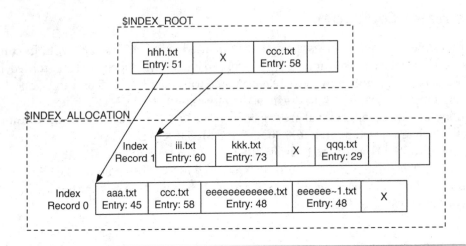

**Figure 12.9**    A basic directory tree with two levels.

## ROOT DIRECTORY

With any file system, it is crucial for you to know where the root directory is located if you want to find a file based on its full path. The NTFS root directory is always located in MFT entry 5; "." is its name. It will have the standard $INDEX_ROOT, $INDEX_ ALLOCATION, and $BITMAP attributes. All the file system metadata files are located in this directory (even though they are hidden from most users).

## LINKS TO FILES AND DIRECTORIES

NTFS allows a file to have more than one name, which occurs when a *hard link* is created. A hard link does not look any different from the original file name and is allocated an entry in its parent directory index that points to the same MFT entry as the original name. The link count in the MFT entry header is incremented by one when a hard link is created, and the entry will not be unallocated until its link count has become zero. In other words, if the original file name is deleted but a hard link still exists, the file will not be deleted. An MFT entry will have one $FILE_NAME attribute for each of its hard link names. Hard links can be created within only the same volume.

NTFS v3.0+ has a feature called reparse points that can be used to link files, directories, and volumes. A reparse point is a special file or directory that contains information about what it links to. Reparse points can link to files and directories on the same volume, on other volumes, or on remote servers. Reparse points also can be used to mount a volume on a directory instead of mounting it at a drive letter such as 'E:\.' A *symbolic link* is a reparse point that links two files, a *junction* is one that links two directories, and a *mount point* is one that links a directory with a volume. The Windows Remote Storage Server feature of Windows uses reparse points to describe the server location of a file or directory.

Reparse points are special files, and they have a flag set in their $STANDARD_INFORMATION and $FILE_NAME attributes. They also have a $REPARSE_POINT attribute that contains information about where the target file or directory is. The data structure for the $REPARSE_POINT attribute is discussed in Chapter 13.

NTFS keeps track of the reparse point locations using an index in the \$Extend\$Reparse file system metadata file. The index is sorted by the file reference of the reparse point, but it does not contain the target location.

In addition to the $Reparse file, NTFS keeps track of mount points in a $DATA attribute in the root directory, MFT entry 5. The $DATA attribute, named $MountMgrRemoteDatabase, contains a list of the target volumes that are pointed to by mount points. This $DATA attribute is created only when a mount point exists in the file system.

## OBJECT IDENTIFIERS

NTFS version 3.0+ allows a second method for addressing files and directories instead of using a typical directory and file name or the MFT entry address. An application or the OS can assign a unique 128-bit object identifier to the file, and it can be used to refer to the file even when its name has been changed or it is moved to a different volume. Microsoft products use object IDs when they embed files inside of other files. The embedded file will be referred to by its object ID so that it can be found even if it has been moved.

A file or directory that has an object ID assigned to it has an $OBJECT_ID attribute that contains the object ID and may contain information about the original domain and volume on which it was created. If you want to find a file based on its object ID, you can refer to the \$Extend\$ObjId index. This index contains an entry for every assigned object ID in the file system and gives the file reference address for it.

This method of addressing can affect an investigator because he may need to locate a file given its object ID. At the moment, I do not know of any tools that allow the investigator to search for files based on the object ID.

## ALLOCATION ALGORITHMS

NTFS indexes use B-trees, which means that there are not first or next available strategies for allocating data structures. Although, there are variations on how a B-tree can be implemented when it needs to add and remove entries. The basic idea is to determine where in the tree the file belongs and add it. If the node has too many entries, it is broken up and a new level is created. This process repeats until the tree is in a valid state. When deleting a file, its entry is removed from the tree, and the remaining entries in that node are moved over. If a node has too few entries, it tries to borrow entries for other nodes so that the tree stays balanced.

A small directory will have one node, and it will be allocated to the $INDEX_ROOT attribute. When the entries no longer fit in there, the OS will move the entries to an index record in an $INDEX_ALLOCATION attribute. At this point, there is still only one node in the B-tree, and $INDEX_ROOT has no entries besides the empty entry that points to the child node. When the index record fills up, a second will be allocated, and the $INDEX_ROOT attribute will be used as the root node. Its children will be the two index records. When these index records are filled, a third will be allocated, and the root will have three children.

In the systems I have seen, the temporal and size values in the $FILE_NAME attribute are updated at the same rate as the values in the $STANDARD_INFORMATION attribute in the file's MFT entry. Refer to the "Allocation Algorithms" section within the "Metadata Category" section for more details.

## ANALYSIS TECHNIQUES

File name category analysis is conducted to locate files and directories based on their names. This process involves locating the directories, processing the contents, and locating the metadata associated with a file.

As was shown in this section and in the previous chapter, analysis of NTFS file names and indexes is a complex process. The first step is to locate the root directory, which is in MFT entry 5. To process a directory, we examine the contents of the $INDEX_ROOT and $INDEX_ALLOCATION attributes and process the index entries. These attributes contain lists called index records that correspond to nodes in a tree. Each index record contains one or more index entries. An index record also may contain unallocated index entries, and the record header identifies where the last allocated entry is located. The allocation status of the index records can be determined using the directory's $BITMAP attribute. Allocated files may have unallocated index entries in addition to their allocated entries because directories are stored in B-trees and must be re-sorted when files are added and deleted.

A file name may correspond to a reparse point, which is a pointer or mount point. The target of the reparse point is defined in the MFT entry's $REPARSE_POINT attribute. Microsoft has defined some types of reparse points, but others can be application-specific. With Microsoft reparse points, the target location can be easily read because it is in Unicode.

## ANALYSIS CONSIDERATIONS

Unallocated file names can be misleading in NTFS. When files are added and deleted from a directory, the tree is re-sorted, and entries are moved to different nodes and different locations within a node. This causes data from deleted files to exist in the unallocated space of a tree node and data from deleted files to be overwritten. The unallocated space of some indexes may contain multiple copies of data for the same file. To determine if a file has truly been deleted, the rest of the index entries must be searched for a copy of the file name in allocated space.

When the name of a deleted file is found, there are several benefits over other file systems. The sequence number in the file reference can show if the MFT entry has been reallocated since the file was deleted. If it has, the MFT entry data might not be for this file name. With other file systems, we have to guess if they are still in sync. Another benefit is that the $FILE_NAME attribute exists in the index and contains a full set of time values and flags. Therefore, even if the MFT entry has been reallocated and the data from the file overwritten, we still have basic information.

When trying to determine which deleted files exist in a directory, an analysis tool should check two locations. The first is the unallocated areas of each node in the directory index tree. The second location is in the unallocated MFT entries. If a file name was erased from the index but its MFT entry still exists, we can identify that it was part of the directory by looking at its parent directory MFT address in the $FILE_NAME attribute. Verify if your analysis tool uses both procedures when it shows deleted file names in a directory.

## ANALYSIS SCENARIO

Your lab is looking to upgrade its file system analysis tools, and it is your job to test the tools being considered. During your next investigation, you decide to use the Digital Investigator 4000 (DI4K) and confirm the findings with your current tool, the FSAnalyzer 1000 (FSA1K). The computer being analyzed has an NTFS file system, and you find a directory with many pieces of evidence. You decide to compare the directory contents between the two tools and find several differences, which are

1. The deleted file aaa.txt is not shown in the DI4K output, but it is in the FSA1K output.
2. The date and time stamps for the mmm.txt file are different in the two outputs. The DI4K times are earlier than those printed by FSA1K.
3. The deleted file www.txt is shown in the DI4K output, but it is not in the FSA1K output.

There are no differences in the outputs for the allocated files. To get to the bottom of this, you open up a hex editor and start parsing the directory index. After processing the $INDEX_ROOT and $INDEX_ALLOCATION attributes by hand, you find that the index has the structure shown in Figure 12.10 (A).

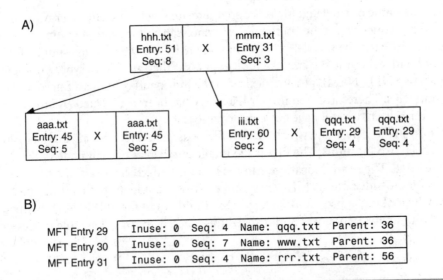

**Figure 12.10**   The directory that caused different tool outputs had the layout shown in (A), and the relevant MFT entries are given in (B).

Using this layout, you can see why the first problem occurred. The FSA1K printed the aaa.txt file as deleted even though the file is allocated. The unallocated entry was likely created after another file was deleted, and the aaa.txt entry moved over in the node. The newer DI4K probably looked for the allocated aaa.txt entry and did not print the unallocated entry.

The second problem was regarding the time stamps on the mmm.txt file. You see the index entry in the root of the index and that its metadata is in MFT entry 31, which is shown in Figure 12.10(B). You process the $STANDARD_INFORMATION attribute for MFT entry 31 and find the times that the FSA1K was showing. You also process the times in the $FILE_NAME attribute in the index entry and find the times that DI4K was showing. To find out which is more accurate, you compare the sequence numbers in the index entry and in the MFT entry. You find that the index entry has a sequence number of 3 and the MFT entry has a sequence number of 4. Therefore, the MFT entry was reallocated after the mmm.txt file was deleted, and the DI4K tool saw this and showed the dates from the $FILE_NAME index entry.

The third problem was regarding a new www.txt file, but you do not see that in the index. You remember reading about deleted orphan NTFS files, which occur because the deleted name was overwritten in the index. You search the MFT entries for one that has the name www.txt by doing a logical file system search for "www.txt" in Unicode. This process finds MFT entry 30, which has a parent directory of entry 36, which is the entry of the directory we were analyzing. Therefore, you conclude that the new DI4K searches for orphan files in addition to showing only the unallocated entries that are in the index.

In your test report, you document the differences you found. Neither tool was generating false data, but the DI4K was generating data that was more accurate.

## APPLICATION CATEGORY

NTFS is a unique file system in that it provides support for many application-level features. These are features that do not need to be included in a file system but that allow the operating system or applications to run more efficiently. It also means that none of these features is essential with respect to a file system's purpose of saving and retrieving files. In fact, a user or application can disable some of them. In this section, we will discuss disk quotas, logging (or file system journaling), and change journaling. The data structures for these are given in Chapter 13. In this section, we will refer to the data being essential if they are required for the application-level goal of the feature and not if they are required for storing data.

### DISK QUOTAS

NTFS includes support for disk space quotas. Quotas can be setup by an administrator to limit the amount of space that each user allocates. Part of the quota information is stored as file system data and other data is stored in application-level files, such as the Windows registry. In versions of NTFS prior to 3.0, there existed a \$Quota file system metadata file in MFT entry 9, but in versions 3.0+ the same file exists in the \$Extend directory and it can be in any MFT entry.

The $Quota file uses two indexes to manage the quota information. One index is named $O, and it correlates an SID with an owner ID (note that this is the typical Windows SID and not the ID we saw with security descriptors). The second index is named $Q and it correlates an owner ID with the details of how many bytes have been charged to the user's quota and how many bytes he is allowed.

### Analysis Considerations

The quota is considered non-essential because an operating system does not need to use the quota information when it uses the file system. For example, another OS could mount an NTFS file system and not update the quota when a user creates a file. The quota could be useful during a forensic analysis when trying to determine which users have stored large amounts of data. For example, if you find a system with multiple accounts and a large amount of pirated movies, you can use the quota files to determine which user created them. You can get the same information from looking at the $STANDARD_INFORMATION attribute of each file. The quota system is not turned on by default, so this data does not exist for most systems.

## LOGGING—FILE SYSTEM JOURNALING

To improve the reliability of a file system, Microsoft added journaling to NTFS. They call the feature logging, but it is typically called journaling in other files systems. Recall from Chapter 8 that a file system journal allows an operating system to more quickly bring a file system to a clean state. The file system typically becomes corrupt if the system crashes while data were being written to the file system. The journal records information about any metadata updates before they happen and then records when the updates have been performed. If the system crashes before the journal records that the update has been performed, the OS can quickly change the system back to a known state.

The NTFS log journal file is located in MFT entry 2, which is named $LogFile. This MFT entry does not have any special attributes, and the log data is stored in the $DATA attribute. I have found that the log file is around one or two percent of the total size of the file system. Little is known about the exact contents of the log, but Microsoft has published some high-level information in their resource guides and in the *Inside Windows 2000* book.

The log file has two major sections to it: the restart area and the logging area. As shown in Figure 12.11, the restart area contains two copies of a data structure that help the OS determine what transactions need to be examined when a cleanup is performed.

It contains a pointer into the logging area for the last transaction that was known to be successful.

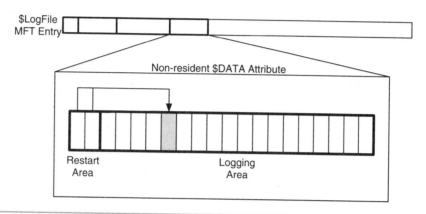

**Figure 12.11**   Layout of the $LogFile $DATA attribute that contains the NTFS journal.

The logging area contains a series of records. Each record has a *logical sequence number* (LSN), which is a unique 64-bit value. The LSNs are allocated in an increasing order. The logging area has a finite size, and when there is no more space at the end of the file for a new record, the record is placed at the beginning of the file. In this scenario, the record at the start of the log file will have a LSN that is larger than the record at the end of the file. In other words, the LSN is assigned to a record based on when the record was created, not on where the record is located. The records that are no longer needed are overwritten when the log cycles.

There are multiple types of records, but Microsoft describes only two of them. The update record is the most common and is used to describe a file system transaction before it occurs. It is also used when the file system transaction has been performed. Many transactions require more than one record because they are broken up into smaller operations, and each operation has an update record. Example file system transactions include

- Creating a new file or directory
- Changing the content of a file or directory
- Renaming a file or directory
- Changing any of the data stored in the MFT entry of a file or directory (user ID, security settings, and so on)

Each update record has two major fields in addition to its LSN value. One of the fields contains information about what the operation is going to do, and it is called the redo field. The other field contains the opposite information and shows how to undo this operation. These records are created before the file system transaction is performed. After the file system transaction is performed, another update record is created that shows that the transaction was completed. This is called a commit record.

The second type of record is a checkpoint record. The checkpoint record identifies where in the log file the OS should start from if it needs to verify the file system. Windows creates one of these records every five seconds, and its LSN value is stored in the restart area of the log file.

To verify the file system, an OS locates the last checkpoint record and identifies the transactions that were started. If the transaction completed and a commit record exists, the OS can use the content in the redo field to ensure that the data were updated on the disk and not lost in a cache. If the transaction did not complete and no commit record can be found, the OS uses the content in the undo field to ensure that the data are brought back to the state before the transaction started.

For example, consider Figure 12.12. We see a pointer from the restart area to the location of the last checkpoint record. We scan from there and see two transactions. Transaction 1 has a commit record, so we use the 'redo' to ensure that the disk is correct. Transaction 2 does not have a commit record, so we use the 'undo' to ensure that none of the proposed changes exist.

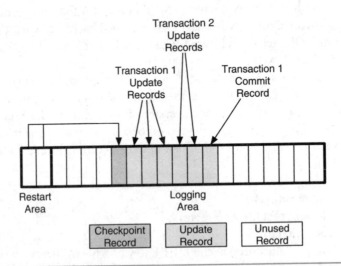

**Figure 12.12**    An example $LogFile with two transactions after the last checkpoint record. One of the transactions did not commit.

The log does not contain user data that is non-resident and stored in a cluster, so it cannot be used for file recovery. It does store the content of resident attributes, so it can be used to recover recent changes. At the time of this writing, I am not aware of any forensic tools that can take advantage of the data in the log file because not all the data structures are known. You may find some small amounts of data, however, by viewing the ASCII or Unicode strings in the file, as I show in the "$LogFile File" section of Chapter 13.

In the header of each MFT entry, there is a value with the last LSN for the file. It is shown in the istat output in the previous examples. This could be used to determine the order in which two files were changed.

### Analysis Considerations

The journal could provide information about recent changes to the file system, but it is not known how long the entries exist before they are overwritten and, worst of all, it is not known how the file is organized. Therefore, you may be able to find evidence, but it may be difficult to explain. The LSN value that is given in the MFT entry header of a file could be used to reconstruct the order in which files were edited. The larger the number, the more recently it was edited.

## CHANGE JOURNAL

The change journal is a file that records when changes are made to files and directories. It can exist in versions 3.0+ of NTFS and can be used by an application to determine which files have changed in a certain time span. Typically, to determine which files changed, an application would have to examine each file and directory in the file system and compare them to a baseline. This takes a while on large file systems, so the change log journal makes this process much easier because it lists the files that have had changes.

In Windows, any application can turn the change journal feature on and off. By default, it is turned off. The journal has a 64-bit number assigned to it and changes each time the journal is enabled or disabled. An application can use this number to determine whether the journal might have missed some changes because of being disabled. When the journal is disabled, Windows purges the file and deletes the file in Windows 2000 and XP.

The change journal is stored in the \$Extend\$UsrJrnl file. This file is not typically allocated one of the reserved MFT entries, and it has two $DATA attributes. One is named $Max and contains basic information about the journal. The other is named $J and contains the actual journal as a list of varying sized records. Each record contains a file name, the time of change, and the type of change. The length of a record is based on the length of the file name. Each record has an *Update Sequence Number* (USN), which is 64-bits in size. The USN is used to index the records in the journal, and it is stored in the $STANDARD_INFORMATION attribute of the file that was modified. The USN corresponds to the byte offset in the journal, so it is easy to find a record given its USN (because each record has a different size). The record does not include which data changed, just the type of change that occurred.

Windows has a maximum size that it allocates for the journal. If the journal reaches that size, Windows turns the file into a sparse file and continues to append data to the end of the file. When it allocates a new cluster at the end of the file, it removes the first cluster and makes it sparse. So the file looks like it is getting bigger, but it always has the same number of allocated clusters. The USN numbers are, therefore, always increasing because they correspond to the byte offset from the start of the file.

### Analysis Considerations

It is not clear how much information can be gathered from this file because there is no guarantee that it will be enabled. Further, when it is disabled, Windows deletes its contents, and any application can disable it. If, for a second, we consider that it was enabled and that we could trust its contents, this could be useful for reconstructing the events that recently occurred. A file saves only the last modified or created time, but this file could show many occurrences of changes, although the exact changes would not be known.

## THE BIG PICTURE

After a chapter full of different data structures and complex interactions, let us go over some of the steps that may occur when a file is allocated and deleted. This will hopefully help to bring it all together. Note that the order of these steps may not be what actually occurs.

### FILE ALLOCATION EXAMPLE

We will create the file \dir1\file1.dat and assume that the dir1 directory already exists in the root directory. The size of the file is 4,000 bytes and each cluster is 2,048 bytes.

1. We read the first sector of the file system and the boot sector is processed to determine the cluster size, starting address of the MFT, and the size of each MFT entry.

2. We read the first entry from the MFT, which is the $MFT file, and it is processed to determine the layout of the rest of the MFT, which is in the $DATA attribute.

3. We first allocate an MFT entry for the new file. To find an unused entry, we process the $BITMAP attribute of the $MFT file. The first free entry, entry 304, is allocated to the new file and the corresponding bit is set to a 1.

4. We initialize MFT entry 304 by seeking to its location in the MFT and clearing its contents. The $STANDARD_INFORMATION and $FILE_NAME attributes are created, and the times are set to the current time. The in-use flag is set in the MFT entry header.

5. We next need to allocate two clusters for the file by using the $DATA attribute of the $Bitmap file, which is MFT entry 6. This file needs two clusters, so two consecutive clusters, clusters 692 and 693, are found using the best-fit algorithm. The corresponding bits for the clusters are set to 1. The file content is written to the clusters and the $DATA attribute is updated with the cluster addresses. The MFT entry is modified and file modified times are updated.

6. Our next step is to add a file name entry for it. The root directory, in MFT entry 5, is processed to locate dir1. We read the $INDEX_ROOT and $INDEX_ALLOCATION attributes and traverse the sorted tree. The dir1 index entry is found, and its MFT entry address is 200. The last accessed time of the directory is updated.

7. We seek to MFT entry 200 and process its $INDEX_ROOT attribute to find the location where file1.dat should go. A new index entry is created for it, and the tree is resorted. This might result in index entries around in the node. The new index entry has the MFT entry 304 in its file reference address, and the times and flags are set appropriately. The last written, modified, and accessed times are updated for the directory.

8. In each of the previous steps, entries could have been made to the file system journal in $LogFile and to the change journal in \$Extend\$UsrJrnl. If quotas were being enforced, the new file size would be added to the user's quota in \$Extend\$Quota.

We can see the relationship among the components and the final state in Figure 12.13.

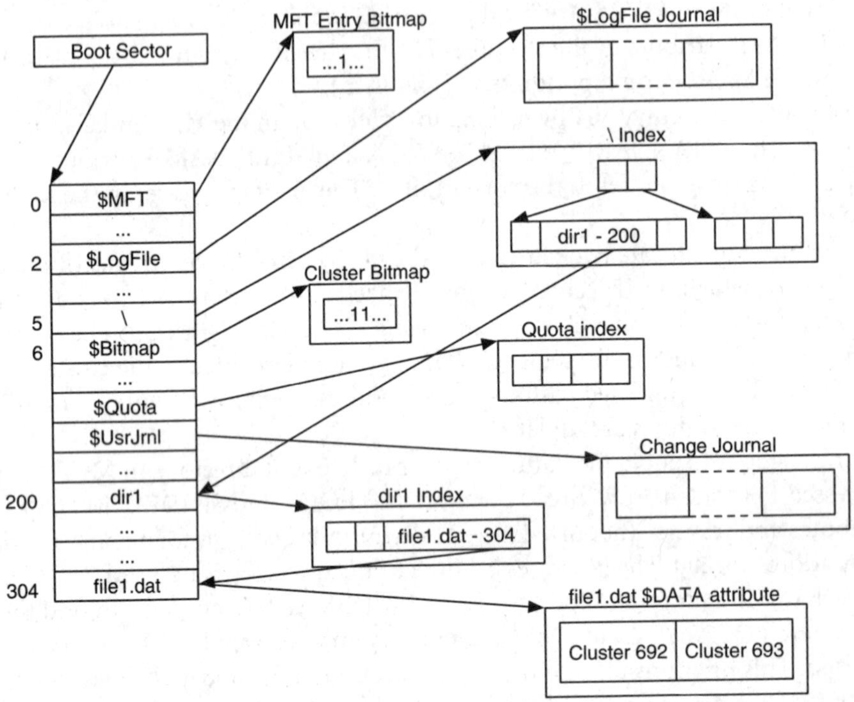

**Figure 12.13**   Final state after adding the '\dir1\file1.dat' file.

## FILE DELETION EXAMPLE

Now we will show what occurs when the \dir1\file1.dat file is deleted.

1. We read the first sector of the file system, and the boot sector is processed to determine the cluster size, starting address of the MFT, and the size of each MFT entry.
2. We read the first entry from the MFT, which is the $MFT file, and it is processed to determine the layout of the rest of the MFT, which is in the $DATA attribute.
3. We need to find the dir1 directory, so we process MFT entry 5, the root directory, and traverse the index in the $INDEX_ROOT and $INDEX_ALLOCATION attributes. We find the dir1 entry, and its MFT entry address is 200. The last accessed time of the directory is updated.
4. We process the $INDEX_ROOT attribute of MFT entry 200 and search for the file1.dat entry. The MFT address for the file is found to be entry 304.

5. We remove the entry from the index, and entries in the node are moved and over-write the original entry. The last written, modified, and accessed times for the directory are updated.
6. We unallocate MFT entry 304 by cleaning the in-use flag. We also process the $DATA attribute of the `$Bitmap` file and set the bitmap to 0 for this entry.
7. The non-resident attributes for MFT entry 304 are processed, and the corresponding clusters are set to an unallocated state in the bitmap of the `\$Bitmap` file. In this case, we unallocate clusters 692 and 693.
8. In each of the previous steps, entries could have been made to the file system journal in `$LogFile` and the change journal in `\$Extend\$UsrJrnl`. If quotas were being enforced, the file size would be subtracted from the user's quota in `\$Extend\$Quota`.

The final state can be seen in Figure 12.14. Notice that when a file is deleted in NTFS, Windows does not clear any of the pointers. So, the link between the MFT entry and the cluster still exists, and the link between the file name and MFT entry would have existed if the entry had not been lost because of resorting.

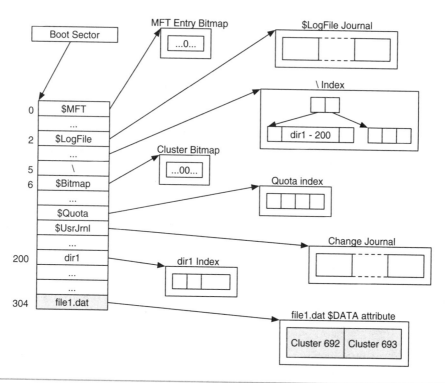

**Figure 12.14** Final state after deleting the 'dir1\file1.dat' file. The grayed boxes are unallocated.

347

## OTHER TOPICS

This section discusses a couple of topics that do not apply to a specific data category. We discuss deleted file recovery and file system consistency checks.

### FILE RECOVERY

Recovering deleted files in NTFS is easier than in most file systems. When a file is deleted, the name is removed from the parent directory index, the MFT entry is unallocated, and the clusters are unallocated. Microsoft does not clear any of the pointers, although they could in the future if they wanted to.

The big disadvantage of NTFS is that when the file name is removed from the parent directory index, the index is re-sorted and the name information could be lost. Therefore, you may not see the name of the deleted file in its original directory. This disadvantage is offset, though, because the MFT entries are found in one table, so all unallocated entries can be easily found. Further, each entry has the $FILE_NAME attribute with the file reference address of the parent directory. Therefore, when an unallocated entry is found, we can typically determine its entire path, unless any of the parent directories have been reallocated to a new file or directory.

Another consideration when recovering deleted NTFS files is to look for additional $DATA attributes. You can test your NTFS recovery tools using a test image from the DFTT site [Carrier 2004]. This image contains deleted files with multiple $DATA attributes that do not have an index entry pointing to them.

To recover all deleted files in NTFS, the MFT should be examined for unallocated entries. When they are found, the name can be determined using the $FILE_NAME attribute and the parent directory file reference. The cluster pointers should still exist, and the data can be recovered if it has not been overwritten. Recovery is possible even if the file was very fragmented. If the attribute value was resident, the data will not be overwritten until the MFT entry is reallocated. If the file needed more than one MFT entry to store its attributes, the other MFT entries may be needed for the recovery. Windows uses a first-available allocation strategy for MFT entries, so the low-numbered MFT entries could be allocated more frequently than the high numbered entries.

When recovering files or examining deleted content, the file system log or change journal could be useful for recent deletions. The change journal is not always enabled, but it shows when the file was deleted and when it was last edited.

## CONSISTENCY CHECK

Consistency checks are used in an investigation to identify corrupt images or to detect tampering. This section covers some of the checks that can be performed on an NTFS file system image. The first check is the boot sector. An NTFS boot sector has little data in it, but Microsoft enforces that some of the unused values should be zero. I have found that there are frequently many unused clusters after the boot code in the $Boot file. As with other file systems, the clusters that have been marked as bad in the $BadClus file should be examined because many hard disks fix the bad clusters before the file system recognizes them.

The $MFT file, the file for the MFT itself, only grows in size with Windows. An advanced attacker could try to make the table very long and hide data at the end of it, but they risk having the data overwritten when new files are created. The first 16 MFT entries are reserved, and several are not currently used. Metadata structures that are reserved and unused have historically been used with other file systems to hide data, and the same could occur with an NTFS file system.

Each cluster that is allocated must be part of a cluster run to a file. Every allocated NTFS cluster is part of a file or directory, and a consistency check should verify that. Each allocated MFT entry must have its inuse flag and its bit in the $BITMAP attribute set. Each allocated MFT entry also must have a directory index entry for each of its file names. Even file system metadata files have a name in the root directory.

For each directory index entry and MFT entry, there are so many flags and options for each entry that it is not worth giving a list of every flag to check. One of the difficulties with NTFS is that it is very flexible and can support many options. Without an official specification, which value combinations are valid and which are invalid is unknown.

## SUMMARY

If you have made it this far, you have probably realized that NTFS is a very complex and powerful file system. When we examined a FAT file system, it was complex because it was not originally designed to scale to today's data sizes or needs. With NTFS, it is complex because it has been designed to handle today's needs and many future needs. NTFS also incorporates many application-level features into itself, and that adds complexity.

At the time of this writing, NTFS is becoming the dominant Windows file system. Home users are installing XP and formatting their disks as NTFS instead of FAT. NTFS helps investigators because it is easier to recover deleted files and because the different journals, if enabled, might cause a history of events to exist. On the other hand, its complexity may make it more challenging for an investigator to describe where evidence was found.

## BIBLIOGRAPHY

Carrier, Brian. "NTFS Keyword Search Test #1." *Digital Forensic Tool Testing*, October 2003. `http://dftt.sourceforge.net`.

Carrier, Brian. "NTFS Undelete (and leap year) Test #1." *Digital Forensic Tool Testing*, February 2004. `http://dftt.sourceforge.net`.

Microsoft. "Recovering NTFS Boot Sector on NTFS Partitions." *Knowledge Base Article 153973*, 2003. `http://support.microsoft.com/default.aspx?scid=kb;EN-US;q153973`.

Microsoft MSDN Library. "FILETIME." 2004. `http://msdn.microsoft.com/library/en-us/sysinfo/base/filetime_str.asp`.

See also the Bibliography section of Chapter 11.

# NTFS Data Structures

This is the third and final chapter devoted to NTFS, and here we will examine its data structures. The previous two chapters examined the basic concepts of NTFS and how to analyze it. For many, the information covered thus far is sufficient, but others of us want to know more about what is going on. This chapter is organized so that we cover the data structures of the basic elements first and then examine the specific attributes and index types. Lastly, the file system metadata files are covered. Unlike the other file system chapters, this one was written so that it should be read after Chapter 11, "NTFS Concepts," and Chapter 12, "NTFS Analysis." The first part of the chapter can be read in parallel with Chapter 11, but the latter parts should be read after finishing Chapter 12 and having an understanding of the various attributes. Before we begin, remember that there is no official published specification of NTFS. The data structures presented here are from the Linux NTFS group, and as we will see, they match what exists on disk. There could be additional flag values and subtle details, however, that are not known.

## BASIC CONCEPTS

In this section, we examine the basic NTFS data structure concepts. In the first subsection, we examine a design feature of large data structures that makes them more reliable. Next, we discuss the data structure for an MFT entry and an attribute header.

## FIXUP VALUES

Before we look at any specific NTFS data structure, we need to discuss a storage technique that is used for increased reliability. NTFS incorporates fixup values into data structures that are over one sector in length. With *fixup values,* the last two bytes of each sector in large data structures are replaced with a signature value when the data structure is written to disk. The signature is later used to verify the integrity of the data by verifying that all sectors have the same signature. Note that fixups are used only in data structures and not in sectors that contain file content.

The data structures that use fixups have header fields that identify the current 16-bit signature value and an array that contains the original values. When the data structure is written to disk, the signature value is incremented by one, the last two bytes of each sector are copied to the array, and the signature value is written to the last two bytes of each sector. When reading the data structure, the OS should verify that the last two bytes of each sector are equal to the signature value, and the original values are then replaced from the array. Figure 13.1 shows a data structure with its real values and then the version that is written to disk. In the second data structure, the last two bytes of each sector have been replaced with 0x0001.

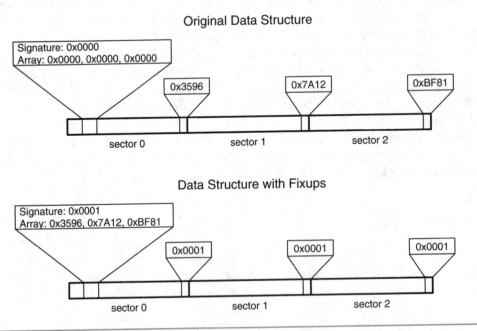

**Figure 13.1**   A multi-sector data structure with its original values and then with the fixups applied to the last two bytes of each sector.

Fixups are used to detect damaged sectors and corrupt data structures. If only one sector of a multi-sector data structure was written, the fixup will be different from the signature, and the OS will know that the data are corrupt. When we dissect our example file system, we will need to first replace the signature values.

## MFT ENTRIES (FILE RECORDS)

As already discussed in Chapters 11 and 12, the *Master File Table* (MFT) is the heart of NTFS and has an entry for every file and directory. MFT entries are a fixed size and contain only a few fields. To date, the entries have been 1,024 bytes in size, but the size is defined in the boot sector. Each MFT entry uses fixup values, so the on-disk version of the data structure has the last two bytes of each sector replaced by a fixup value. Refer to the previous section for an explanation of fixup values. The data structure fields for an MFT entry are given in Table 13.1.

**Table 13.1** Data structure for a basic MFT entry.

| Byte Range | Description | Essential |
|---|---|---|
| 0–3 | Signature ("FILE") | No |
| 4–5 | Offset to fixup array | Yes |
| 6–7 | Number of entries in fixup array | Yes |
| 8–15 | $LogFile Sequence Number (LSN) | No |
| 16–17 | Sequence value | No |
| 18–19 | Link count | No |
| 20–21 | Offset to first attribute | Yes |
| 22–23 | Flags (in-use and directory) | Yes |
| 24–27 | Used size of MFT entry | Yes |
| 28–31 | Allocated size of MFT entry | Yes |
| 32–39 | File reference to base record | No |
| 40–41 | Next attribute id | No |
| 42–1023 | Attributes and fixup values | Yes |

The standard signature value is "FILE," but some entries will also have "BAAD" if chkdsk found an error in it. The next two fields are for the fixup values, and the array is typically stored after byte 42. The offset values are relative to the start of the entry.

The LSN is used for the file system log (or journal), which was discussed in the "Application Category" section of Chapter 12. The log records when metadata updates are made to the file system so that a corrupt file system can be more quickly fixed.

The sequence value is incremented when the entry is either allocated or unallocated, determined by the OS. The link count shows how many directories have entries for this MFT entry. If hard links were created for the file, this number is incremented by one for each link.

We find the first attribute for the file using the offset value, which is relative to the start of the entry. All other attributes follow the first one, and we find them by advancing ahead using the size field in the attribute header. The end of file marker 0xffffffff exists after the last attribute. If a file needs more than one MFT entry, the additional ones will have the file reference of the base entry in their MFT entry.

The flags field has only two values. The 0x01 bit is set when the entry is in use, and 0x02 is set when the entry is for a directory.

Let us take a look at a raw MFT entry. To view the table, we will use icat from *The Sleuth Kit* (TSK) and view the $DATA attribute for the $MFT file, which is entry 0. Remember that we can specify any attribute in TSK by adding the attribute type ID following the MFT entry address. In this case, the $DATA attribute has a type of 128.

```
# icat -f ntfs ntfs1.dd 0-128 | xxd
0000000: 4649 4c45 3000 0300 4ba7 6401 0000 0000  FILE0...K.d.....
0000016: 0100 0100 3800 0100 b801 0000 0004 0000  ....8...........
0000032: 0000 0000 0000 0000 0600 0000 0000 0000  ................
0000048: 5800 0000 0000 0000 1000 0000 6000 0000  X...........`...
[REMOVED]
0000496: 3101 b43a 0500 0000 ffff ffff 0000 5800  1..:..........X.
0000512: 0000 0000 0000 0000 0000 0000 0000 0000  ................
[REMOVED]
0001008: 0000 0000 0000 0000 0000 0000 0000 5800  ..............X.
```

This output is in little-endian ordering, so we need to reverse the order of the numbers. We see the "FILE" signature, and bytes 4 and 5 show that the fixup array is located 48 bytes (0x0030) into the MFT entry. Bytes 6 to 7 show us that the array has three values in it. Bytes 16 to 17 show that the sequence value for this MFT entry is 1, which means that this is the first time this entry has been used. Bytes 18 to 19 show that the link count is 1, so we know it has only one name. Bytes 20 to 21 show that the first attribute is located at byte offset 56 (0x0038).

The flags in bytes 22 to 23 show that this entry is in use (0x0001). The base entry values in bytes 32 to 39 are 0, which shows that this is a base entry, and bytes 40 to 41 show that the next attribute ID to be assigned is 6. Therefore, we should expect that there are attributes with IDs 1 to 5.

The fixup array starts at byte 48. The first two bytes show the signature value, which is 0x0058. The next two-byte values are the original values that should be used to replace the signature value. We look at the last two bytes of each sector, bytes 510 to 511 and 1022 to 1023, and see that each has 0x0058. To process the entry, we replace those values with 0x0000, which are the values in the fixup array. Following the fixup array, the first attribute begins in byte 56. This file's attributes end at byte 504 with the end of file marker 0xffff ffff. The rest of the attribute entry is 0s.

If you want to view any MFT entry with TSK, you can use dd along with icat to skip ahead to the correct location. You can do this by setting the block size to 1024, which is the size of each MFT entry. For example, to see entry 1234 you would use

```
# icat -f ntfs ntfs1.dd 0 | dd bs=1024 skip=1234 count=1 | xxd
```

## ATTRIBUTE HEADER

An MFT entry is filled with attributes, and each attribute has the same header data structure, which we will now examine. As a reminder, Figure 13.2 shows a diagram of a typical file and the header locations. The data structure is slightly different for resident and non-resident attributes because non-resident attributes need to store the run information.

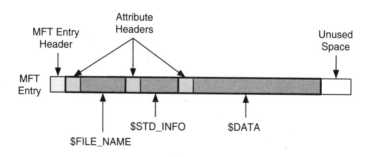

**Figure 13.2** A typical file with the different header locations.

The first 16 bytes are the same for both types of attributes and contain the fields given in Table 13.2.

**Table 13.2** Data structure for the first 16 bytes of an attribute.

| Byte Range | Description | Essential |
|---|---|---|
| 0–3 | Attribute type identifier | Yes |
| 4–7 | Length of attribute | Yes |
| 8–8 | Non-resident flag | Yes |
| 9–9 | Length of name | Yes |
| 10–11 | Offset to name | Yes |
| 12–13 | Flags | Yes |
| 14–15 | Attribute identifier | Yes |

These values give the basic information about the attribute, including its type, size, and name location. The size is used to find the next attribute in the MFT entry, and if it is the last, 0xffff ffff will exist after it. The non-resident flag is set to 1 when the attribute is non-resident. The flag's value identifies if the attribute is compressed (0x0001), encrypted (0x4000), or sparse (0x8000). The attribute identifier is the number that is unique to this attribute for this MFT entry. The offset to the name is relative to the start of the attribute. A resident attribute has the fields shown in Table 13.3.

**Table 13.3** Data structure for a resident attribute.

| Byte Range | Description | Essential |
|---|---|---|
| 0 - 15 | General header (see Table 13.2) | Yes |
| 16–19 | Size of content | Yes |
| 20–21 | Offset to content | Yes |

These values simply give the size and location (relative to the start of the attribute) of the attribute content, also called a *stream*. Let us look at an example. When we previously dissected the MFT entry, we saw that attributes started in byte 56. I've taken the attribute from there and reset the offset numbers on the side of the output so that the attribute header offsets can be more easily determined.

```
0000000: 1000 0000 6000 0000 0000 1800 0000 0000    ....`...........
0000016: 4800 0000 1800 0000 305a 7a1f f63b c301    H.......0Zz..;..
```

This output shows the attribute type in the first four bytes as 16 (0x10), which is for $STANDARD_INFORMATION. Bytes 4 to 7 show that it has a size of 96 bytes (0x60). Byte 8 shows that this is a resident attribute (0x00), and byte 9 shows that it does not have a name (0x00). The flags and id values are set to 0 in bytes 12 to 13 and 14 to 15. Bytes 16 to 19 show that the attribute is 72 bytes (0x48) long, and bytes 20 and 21 show that it starts 24 bytes (0x18) from the start of the attribute. A quick sanity check shows that the 24 byte offset and 72 byte attribute length equal a total of 96 bytes, which is the reported length of the attribute.

Non-resident attributes have a different data structure because they need to be able to describe an arbitrary number of cluster runs. The attribute has the fields given in Table 13.4.

**Table 13.4**  Data structure for a non-resident attribute.

| Byte Range | Description | Essential |
|---|---|---|
| 0–15 | General header (see Table 13.2) | Yes |
| 16–23 | Starting Virtual Cluster Number (VCN) of the runlist | Yes |
| 24–31 | Ending VCN of the runlist | Yes |
| 32–33 | Offset to the runlist | Yes |
| 34–35 | Compression unit size | Yes |
| 36–39 | Unused | No |
| 40–47 | Allocated size of attribute content | No |
| 48–55 | Actual size of attribute content | Yes |
| 56–63 | Initialized size of attribute content | No |

Recall that VCN is a different name for the logical file addresses that we defined in Chapter 8, "File System Analysis." The starting and ending VCN numbers are used when multiple MFT entries are needed to describe a single attribute. For example, if a $DATA attribute was very fragmented and its runs could not fit into a single MFT entry, it would allocate a second MFT entry. The second entry would contain a $DATA attribute with a starting VCN equal to the VCN after the ending VCN of the first entry. We will see an example of this in the "$ATTRIBUTE_LIST" section. The compression unit size value was described in Chapter 11 and is needed only for compressed attributes.

The offset to the data runlist is given relative to the start of the attribute. The format of a runlist is very efficient and slightly confusing. It has a variable length, but must be at least one byte. The first byte of the data structure is organized into the upper 4 bits and lower 4 bits (also known as nibbles). The four least significant bits contain the number of bytes in the run length field, which follows the header byte. The four most significant bits contain the number of bytes in the run offset field, which follows the length field. We can see an example of this in Figure 13.3. The first byte shows that the run length field is 1 byte and that the run offset field is 2 bytes.

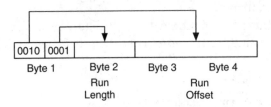

Byte 1    Byte 2    Byte 3    Byte 4
          Run                 Run
          Length              Offset

**Figure 13.3**   The first byte in the run shows that the length field is 1 byte, and the offset field is 2 bytes.

The values are in cluster-sized units, and the offset field is a signed value that is relative to the previous offset. For example, the offset of the first run in the attribute will be relative to the start of the file system, and the second run offset will be relative to the previous offset. A negative number will have its most significant bit set to 1, and if you are going to plug the value into a calculator to convert the value, you must add as many 1s as needed to make a full 32 or 64 bit number. For example, if the value is 0xf1, you need to enter 0xfffffff1 into a converter.

To look at a non-resident attribute, we return to the entry we previously analyzed and advance further in to look at the $DATA attribute. The attribute contents are shown here, and the offset values are relative to the start of the attribute:

```
0000000: 8000 0000 6000 0000 0100 4000 0000 0100   ....`.....@.....
0000016: 0000 0000 0000 0000 ef20 0000 0000 0000   ......... ......
0000032: 4000 0000 0000 0000 00c0 8300 0000 0000   @...............
0000048: 00c0 8300 0000 0000 00c0 8300 0000 0000   ................
0000064: 32c0 1eb5 3a05 2170 1b1f 2290 015f 7e31   2...:.!p..".._~1
0000080: 2076 ed00 2110 8700 00b0 6e82 4844 7e82    v..!.....n.HD~.
```

The first four bytes show that the attribute has a type of 128 (0x80), and the second set of four bytes show that its total size is 96 bytes (0x60). Byte 8 is 1, which shows that this is a non-resident attribute, and byte 9 is 0, which shows that the length of the attribute name is 0, and therefore this is the default $DATA attribute and not an ADS. The flags in bytes 12 to 13 are 0, which means that the attribute is not encrypted or compressed.

The non-resident information starts at byte 16, and bytes 16 to 23 show that the starting VCN for this set of runs is 0. The ending VCN for this set of runs is in bytes 24 to 31, and they are set to 8,431 (0x20ef). Bytes 32 to 33 show that the offset of the runlist is 64 bytes (0x0040) from the start. Bytes 40 to 47, 48 to 55, and 56 to 63 are for the allocated, actual, and initialized amount of space, and they are all set to the same value of 8,634,368 bytes (0x0083c000).

At byte 64, we finally get to the runlist. I will copy the relevant output again:

```
0000064: 32c0 1eb5 3a05 2170 1b1f
```

Recall that the first byte is organized into the upper and lower 4 bits, which show how large each of the other fields are. The lower 4 bits of byte 64 show that there are two bytes in the field for the run length and the upper 4 bits show that there are three bytes in the offset field. To determine the length of the run, we examine bytes 65 to 66, which give us 7,872 clusters (0x1ec0). The next three bytes, bytes 67 to 69, are used for the offset, which is cluster 342,709 (0x053ab5). Therefore, the first run starts at cluster 342,709 and extends for 7,872 clusters.

The data structure for the next run starts after the previous one, which is byte 70. There we see that the length field is 1 byte, and the offset field is 2 bytes. The length value is in byte 71, which is 112 (0x70). The offset value is in bytes 72 to 73, which is 7,963 (0x1f1b). The offset is signed and relative to the previous offset, so we add 7,963 to 342,709 and get 350,672. Therefore, the second run starts at cluster 350,672 and extends for 112 clusters. I will leave the rest of the runlist for you to decode.

## STANDARD FILE ATTRIBUTES

The previous section outlined how we process an MFT entry and the attribute headers. Each attribute header points to a resident or non-resident location where the attribute content can be found. This section explains how we process each of the different attribute content types.

### $STANDARD_INFORMATION Attribute

The $STANDARD_INFORMATION attribute, which has a type identifier of 16, is always resident and contains the basic metadata for a file or directory. It exists in every file and directory and is typically the first attribute because it has the lowest type identifier. It has the (non-essential) fields given in Table 13.5.

**Table 13.5**   Data structure for the $STANDARD_INFORMATION attribute.

| Byte Range | Description | Essential |
|---|---|---|
| 0–7 | Creation time | No |
| 8–15 | File altered time | No |
| 16–23 | MFT altered time | No |
| 24–31 | File accessed time | No |
| 32–35 | Flags (see Table 13.6) | No |
| 36–39 | Maximum number of versions | No |
| 40–43 | Version number | No |
| 44–47 | Class ID | No |
| 48–51 | Owner ID (version 3.0+) | No |
| 52–55 | Security ID (version 3.0+) | No |
| 56–63 | Quota Charged (version 3.0+) | No |
| 64–71 | Update Sequence Number (USN) (version 3.0+) | No |

The four time values are stored as the number of one hundred nanoseconds since January 1, 1601 UTC. The same time fields also exist in the $FILE_NAME attribute, but these are the ones that Windows displays when you view the properties of a file, and these are the ones that are updated. The ID values are used for either application-level features or security. The Security ID value is the index to the $Secure file, not the Windows SID value. The flag values are given in Table 13.6.

**Table 13.6**   Flag values for the $STANDARD_INFORMATION attribute.

| Flag Value | Description | Essential |
|---|---|---|
| 0x0001 | Read Only | No |
| 0x0002 | Hidden | No |
| 0x0004 | System | No |

| Flag Value | Description | Essential |
|---|---|---|
| 0x0020 | Archive | No |
| 0x0040 | Device | No |
| 0x0080 | Normal | No |
| 0x0100 | Temporary | No |
| 0x0200 | Sparse file | No |
| 0x0400 | Reparse point | No |
| 0x0800 | Compressed | No |
| 0x1000 | Offline | No |
| 0x2000 | Content is not being indexed for faster searches | No |
| 0x4000 | Encrypted | No |

Many of these flags are the same as were seen with FAT, and a description of them can be found there. The flags for encrypted and sparse attributes are also given in the attribute headers, so I consider them to not be essential in this location. This is debatable, though, because another person could claim that this flag is essential and the MFT entry header values are not essential.

Let us take a look at a $STANDARD_INFORMATION attribute. We can view the attribute by using icat and specifying the attribute type. This removes the standard header for us automatically and gives us only the content. The contents of the attribute for the $MFT file are

```
# icat -f ntfs ntfs1.dd 0-16 | xxd
0000000: 305a 7a1f f63b c301 305a 7a1f f63b c301  0Zz..;..0Zz..;..
0000016: 305a 7a1f f63b c301 305a 7a1f f63b c301  0Zz..;..0Zz..;..
0000032: 0600 0000 0000 0000 0000 0000 0000 0000  ................
0000048: 0000 0000 0001 0000 0000 0000 0000 0000  ................
0000064: 0000 0000 0000 0000                      ........
```

The first eight bytes show the creation time, which is the same for each of the four time fields. Bytes 32 to 35 give the flag value, which is 0x00000060, and includes bits for hidden and system, which is expected for a file system metadata file. Bytes 36 to 39 and 40 to 43 show that file versions are not being used, and 44 to 47 show that the class ID is 0. The owner ID in bytes 48 to 51 is 0, and the security ID in bytes 52 to 55 is 1. The rest of the values are 0, which is not surprising for $MFT because it is not typically applied to any user's quota, and most systems do not have change journaling enabled, so the USN would not be assigned.

## $FILE_NAME ATTRIBUTE

The $FILE_NAME attribute, which has a type identifier of 48, is used for two purposes. It is placed in an MFT entry to store the file's name and parent directory information, and it is used in a directory index. When it is used in an MFT entry, it does not contain any essential information, but it does when it is used in a directory index.

For a standard file or directory, this will be the second attribute and is always resident. If a file requires multiple MFT entries, the $ATTRIBUTE_LIST attribute will occur between the $STANDARD_INFORMATION attribute and this attribute. The $FILE_NAME attribute has the fields given in Table 13.7.

Table 13.7   Data structure for the $FILE_NAME attribute.

| Byte Range | Description | Essential |
|------------|-------------|-----------|
| 0–7 | File reference of parent directory | No |
| 8–15 | File creation time | No |
| 16–23 | File modification time | No |
| 24–31 | MFT modification time | No |
| 32–39 | File access time | No |
| 40–47 | Allocated size of file | No |
| 48–55 | Real size of file | No |
| 56–59 | Flags (see Table 13.6) | No |
| 60–63 | Reparse value | No |
| 64–64 | Length of name | Yes / No |
| 65–65 | Namespace (see Table 13.8) | Yes / No |
| 66 + | Name | Yes / No |

The final three name fields are essential when this attribute is used in the directory index, but not when it is used in the MFT entry for a file. The flag field uses the same values as $STANDARD_INFORMATION does, and they were previously listed.

The namespace byte identifies what rules the name follows. Its values are given in Table 13.8.

**Table 13.8** Values for the $FILE_NAME name space field.

| Name space value | Description |
| --- | --- |
| 0 | POSIX: The name is case sensitive and allows all Unicode characters except for '/' and NULL. |
| 1 | Win32: The name is case insensitive and allows most Unicode characters except for special values such as '/', '\', ':', '>', '<', and '?'. |
| 2 | DOS: The name is case insensitive, upper case, and no special characters. The name must have eight or fewer characters in the name and three or less in the extension. |
| 3 | Win32 & DOS: Used when the original name already fits in the DOS namespace and two names are not needed. |

To view a $FILE_NAME attribute, we will look at $MFT again and specify the attribute type 48:

```
# icat -f ntfs ntfs1.dd 0-48 | xxd
0000000: 0500 0000 0000 0500 305a 7a1f f63b c301   ........0Zz..;..
0000016: 305a 7a1f f63b c301 305a 7a1f f63b c301   0Zz..;..0Zz..;..
0000032: 305a 7a1f f63b c301 0040 0000 0000 0000   0Zz..;...@......
0000048: 0040 0000 0000 0000 0600 0000 0000 0000   .@..............
0000064: 0403 2400 4d00 4600 5400                  ..$.M.F.T.
```

The first eight bytes are for a file reference, so the upper two bytes are the sequence number and the lower six bytes are the MFT entry. Therefore, the parent directory is MFT entry 5, and its sequence is 5, which is the entry for the root directory. The next eight bytes are for the creation time and are the same value as the other three time values in the attribute.

Bytes 40 to 47 and 48 to 55 show the allocated and actual sizes of the file, respectively. Both of these values are set to 16,384 bytes (0x4000). In reality, the $DATA attribute for this file is 8,634,368 bytes, so this is clearly not accurate. Many files have these sizes set to 0, but it is accurate when this attribute is used in a directory index.

The flag values at bytes 56 and 57 are set to 0x0006, which are the hidden and system flags. These were the same flags we saw in $STANDARD_INFORMATION. Byte 64 shows that the name is 4 letters long, and byte 65 shows it is in name space 3, which is both DOS and Win32 compliant. The name is in UTF-16 Unicode and can be seen starting in byte 66. The name is $MFT.

As a final example, consider a file with two $FILE_NAME attributes because Windows required that a DOS name exist. This file has $FILE_NAME attributes for both a DOS name space and a Win32 name space. We will not dissect them in detail, but the output is shown here:

```
# icat -f ntfs ntfs1.dd 5009-48-2 | xxd
0000000: 3920 0000 0000 0300 00b6 89a9 086a c401   9 ...........j..
0000016: 00b6 89a9 086a c401 00b6 89a9 086a c401   .....j.......j..
0000032: 00b6 89a9 086a c401 0000 0000 0000 0000   .....j..........
0000048: 0000 0000 0000 0000 2020 0000 0000 0000   ........  ......
0000064: 0b01 3500 3700 3300 3900 3800 3400 3000   ..5.7.3.9.8.4.0.
0000080: 3800 6400 3000 3100                       8.d.0.1.
```

Notice that byte 65 shows the name space as 1, which is Win32. The name in this entry is "57398408d01." Now, we will look at the next $FILE_NAME attribute, which has the same type identifier of 48, but its attribute identifier is 3:

```
# icat -f ntfs ntfs1.dd 5009-48-3 | xxd
0000000: 3920 0000 0000 0300 00b6 89a9 086a c401   9 ...........j..
0000016: 00b6 89a9 086a c401 00b6 89a9 086a c401   .....j.......j..
0000032: 00b6 89a9 086a c401 0000 0000 0000 0000   .....j..........
0000048: 0000 0000 0000 0000 2020 0000 0000 0000   ........  ......
0000064: 0802 3500 3700 3300 3900 3800 3400 7e00   ..5.7.3.9.8.4.~.
0000080: 3100                                      1.
```

This attribute has a name space in byte 65 of 2, which is DOS. The name in this entry is "573984~1."

## $DATA ATTRIBUTE

The $DATA attribute is the simplest to understand because it has no native structure. After the header, there is only raw content that corresponds to the contents of a file. It has a type identifier of 128 and has no minimum or maximum sizes. If the content is over 700 bytes, it will probably be a non-resident attribute. For most files, this is the last attribute in the MFT entry. Note that directories can have $DATA attributes in addition to their index attributes.

## $ATTRIBUTE_LIST ATTRIBUTE

An $ATTRIBUTE_LIST attribute exists in an MFT entry to show where other attributes can be located. It is used for files that have attribute headers that will not fit into one MFT entry and contains a list with an entry for every attribute in the file or directory. The attribute has a type identifier of 32 and each list entry has the fields in Table 13.9.

**Table 13.9** Data structure for the list entries in the $ATTRIBUTE_LIST attribute.

| Byte Range | Description | Essential |
|---|---|---|
| 0–3 | Attribute type | Yes |
| 4–5 | Length of this entry | Yes |
| 6–6 | Length of name | Yes |
| 7–7 | Offset to name (relative to start of this entry) | Yes |
| 8–15 | Starting VCN in attribute | Yes |
| 16–23 | File reference where attribute is located | Yes |
| 24–24 | Attribute ID | Yes |

The starting VCN value is used when multiple MFT entries are needed to describe a single attribute. When that occurs, the additional entries will have non-zero starting VCN values. The attribute header should also show that it has a non-zero starting VCN.

Let us take a look at a file with an $ATTRIBUTE_LIST attribute.

```
# icat -f ntfs ntfs1.dd 5009-32 | xxd
0000000: 1000 0000 2000 001a 0000 0000 0000 0000  .... ...........
0000016: 9113 0000 0000 0800 0000 0000 0000 0000  ................
0000032: 3000 0000 2000 001a 0000 0000 0000 0000  0... ...........
0000048: 9113 0000 0000 0800 0300 0000 0006 0000  ................
0000064: 3000 0000 2000 001a 0000 0000 0000 0000  0... ...........
0000080: 9113 0000 0000 0800 0200 0200 502d 40bc  ...........P-@.
0000096: 8000 0000 2000 001a 0000 0000 0000 0000  .... ...........
0000112: 3713 0000 0000 1200 0000 0000 1000 0000  7...............
0000128: 8000 0000 2000 001a 2014 0000 0000 0000  .... ... .......
0000144: ad13 0000 0000 0800 0000 0000 0000 0000  ................
```

The first four bytes show the type of the first entry, which is 16 (0x10) and therefore the $STANDARD_INFORMATION attribute. Bytes 4 to 5 show that the length of this list entry is 32 bytes (0x0020) and bytes 16 to 21 show that the attribute is located in MFT entry 5,009 (0x1391), which is the one that we are currently looking at.

The next two entries start at bytes 32 and 64 and are for $FILE_NAME attributes, which have a type identifier of 48 (0x30). Both of those attributes are also located in the current MFT entry.

Byte 96 is where the first entry for the $DATA attribute begins. Bytes 104 to 111 show that this $DATA attribute is for VCN 0 of the attribute, and bytes 112 to 117 show that the attribute is located in MFT entry 4,919 (0x1337). A second entry for the $DATA attribute begins at byte 128. We can tell they are part of the same $DATA attribute because the ID value in both data structures is equal to 0. Bytes 136 to 143 show us that the second entry has a starting VCN of 5,152 (0x1420). In other words, the $DATA attribute in the first entry had enough space in the MFT entry to describe the first 5,152 clusters. The rest of the cluster runs are stored in a $DATA attribute in MFT entry 5,037 (0x13ad), which we can see in bytes 144 to 149.

Figure 13.4 shows a summary of this file. It has one $STANDARD_INFORMATION and two $FILE_NAME attributes in the base MFT entry 5,009, and the headers for the $DATA attribute are located in entries 4,919 and 5,037.

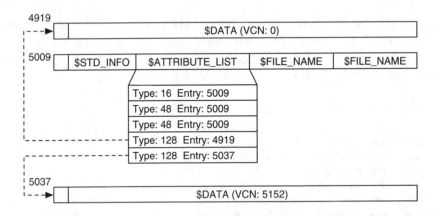

**Figure 13.4** Layout of attribute list entries for sample image.

Recall from Chapter 12 that the non-base MFT entries will not have the standard $FILE_NAME and $STANDARD_INFORMATION attributes. We can verify this by looking at one of the entries in this example. The output from running istat on the non-base entry 4919 is as follows:

```
# istat -f ntfs ntfs1.dd 4919
MFT Entry Header Values:
Entry: 4919        Sequence: 18
Base File Record: 5009
$LogFile Sequence Number: 66117460
Allocated File
Links: 0
[REMOVED]
Attributes:
Type: $DATA (128-0)   Name: $Data   Non-Resident   size: 5787792
929409 929410 929411 929412 929413 929414 929415 929416
[REMOVED]
```

This MFT entry has only a $DATA attribute, and we can see that the header shows the base record to be entry 5,009. The link count is 0 because there are no names pointing to it.

## $OBJECT_ID ATTRIBUTE

The $OBJECT_ID attribute has a type identifier of 64 and stores a file's 128-bit global object identifier that can be used to address the file instead of its name. This allows a file to be found even when its name is changed. The \$Extend\$ObjId index is sorted by the object IDs of files and contains the file reference address where each file can be found. The attribute has only four fields, and typically only the first one is defined. The fields are given in Table 13.10.

**Table 13.10**  Data structure for the $OBJECT_ID attribute.

| Byte Range | Description | Essential |
|---|---|---|
| 0–15 | Object ID | Yes |
| 16–31 | Birth volume ID | No |
| 32–47 | Birth object ID | No |
| 48–63 | Birth domain ID | No |

Many files that have an object ID assigned have only the first value, and the attribute size is 16 bytes. The $Volume file frequently contains an $OBJECT_ID attribute, and it is shown here:

```
# icat -f ntfs img.dd 3-64 | xxd
0000000: fe24 b024 e292 fe47 95ac e507 4bf5 6782   .$.$...G....K.g.
```

## $REPARSE_POINT ATTRIBUTE

The $REPARSE_POINT attribute has an attribute identifier of 192, and it is used for files that are reparse points. Reparse points are used for symbolic links, junctions, and mount points for volumes. Microsoft defines some $REPARSE_POINT attribute contents, but application-specific ones also can be developed. The contents of a junction and mount point have the structure shown in Table 13.11.

**Table 13.11**   Data structure for the junction and mount point $REPARSE_POINT attributes.

| Byte Range | Description | Essential |
|---|---|---|
| 0–3 | Reparse type flags | Yes |
| 4–5 | Size of reparse data | Yes |
| 6–7 | Unused | No |
| 8–9 | Offset to target name (relative to byte 16) | Yes |
| 10–11 | Length of target name | Yes |
| 12–13 | Offset to print name of target (relative to byte 16) | Yes |
| 14–15 | Length of print name | Yes |

The type flags for a junction or mount point will have the 0xa0000000 flag set. Here we see a reparse point that links to c:\windows:

```
# icat -f ntfs ntfs2.dd 167-192 | xxd
0000000: 0300 00a0 2800 0000 0000 1c00 1e00 0000   ....(...........
0000016: 5c00 3f00 3f00 5c00 6300 3a00 5c00 7700   \.?.?.\.c.:.\.w.
0000032: 6900 6e00 6400 6f00 7700 7300 0000 1200   i.n.d.o.w.s.....
```

Byte 8 to 9 show that the offset to the target name is 0 bytes, so it starts at byte 16. Its length is given in bytes 10 to 11, and we see that it is 28 bytes (0x1c). In Unicode, we see the name of the target as "\??\c:\windows."

## INDEX ATTRIBUTES AND DATA STRUCTURES

The previous sections covered the attributes and concepts that apply to all files. This section focuses on the data structures and attributes that are specific to indexes. Recall that the basic concept behind indexes is that there is a data structure that is in a sorted tree. The tree has one or more nodes, and each node has one or more index entries. The root of the tree is located in the $INDEX_ROOT attribute, and the other nodes are located in index records in the $INDEX_ALLOCATION attribute. The $BITMAP attribute is used to manage the allocation status of the index records.

In this section, we start on the outside and work in. We will start with the attributes and then describe the data structures that are common to both of them.

### $INDEX_ROOT ATTRIBUTE

The $INDEX_ROOT attribute is always resident and has a type identifier of 144. It is always the root of the index tree and can store only a small list of index entries. The $INDEX_ROOT attribute has a 16-byte header, which is followed by the node header and a list of index entries. This can be seen in Figure 13.5. The node header will be described in the "Index Node Header Data Structure" section and the index entries will be described in the "Generic Index Entry Data Structure" section. Here we will focus on the $INDEX_ROOT header.

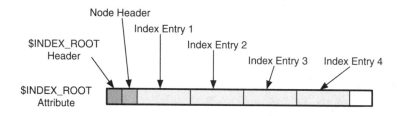

**Figure 13.5**    The internal layout of an $INDEX_ROOT attribute with its header, a node header, and index entries.

The $INDEX_ROOT header has the values given in Table 13.12 and starts at byte 0 of the attribute content.

**Table 13.12**   Data structure for the $INDEX_ROOT attribute header.

| Byte Range | Description | Essential |
|---|---|---|
| 0–3 | Type of attribute in index (0 if entry does not use an attribute) | Yes |
| 4–7 | Collation sorting rule | Yes |
| 8–11 | Size of each index record in bytes | Yes |
| 12–12 | Size of each index record in clusters | Yes |
| 13–15 | Unused | No |
| 16+ | Node header (see Table 13.14) | Yes |

This data structure identifies the type of attribute that the index entries will contain, how they are sorted, and the size of each index record in the $INDEX_ALLOCATION attribute. The value in bytes 8 to 11 are the size in bytes, and the value in byte 12 is either the number of clusters or the logarithm of the size. The "$Boot File" section describes this encoding method in more detail. Note that the size of the index record was also given in the boot sector.

To look at the contents of an $INDEX_ROOT attribute, we use icat and supply the 144 type:

```
# icat -f ntfs ntfs1.dd 7774-144 | xxd
0000000: 3000 0000 0100 0000 0010 0000 0400 0000 0..............
0000016: 1000 0000 a000 0000 a000 0000 0100 0000 ...............
[REMOVED]
```

Bytes 0 to 3 show that the attribute in the index is for the attribute type 48 (0x30), which is the $FILE_NAME attribute, and bytes 8 to 11 show that each index record will be 4,096 bytes.

## $INDEX_ALLOCATION ATTRIBUTE

Large directories cannot fit all their index entries into the resident $INDEX_ROOT attribute, so they need a non-resident $INDEX_ALLOCATION attribute. The $INDEX_ALLOCATION attribute is filled with index records. An *index record* has a static size and contains one node in the sorted tree. The index record size is defined in the $INDEX_ROOT attribute header and in the boot sector, but the typical size is 4,096 bytes. The $INDEX_ALLOCATION attribute has type identifier of 160 and should not exist without an $INDEX_ROOT attribute.

Each index record starts with a special header data structure, which is followed by a node header and a list of index entries. The node header and index entries are the same data structures that are used in the $INDEX_ROOT attribute. The first index record starts at byte 0 of the attribute. We can see this in Figure 13.6, which has two index records in the $INDEX_ALLOCATION attribute.

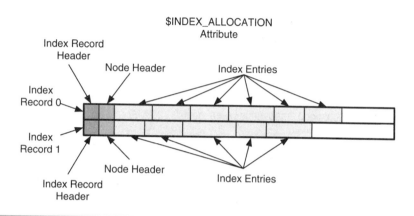

**Figure 13.6**   The internal layout of an $INDEX_ALLOCATION attribute with its record headers, node headers, and index entries.

The index record header has the values given in Table 13.13.

**Table 13.13**   Data structure for the index record header.

| Byte Range | Description | Essential |
|---|---|---|
| 0–3 | Signature value ("INDX") | No |
| 4–5 | Offset to fixup array | Yes |
| 6–7 | Number of entries in fixup array | Yes |
| 8–15 | $LogFile Sequence Number (LSN) | No |
| 16–23 | The VCN of this record in the full index stream | Yes |
| 24+ | Node header (see Table 13.14) | Yes |

The first four fields are almost identical to the fields for an MFT entry, but the signature is different. Refer to the beginning of this chapter for the discussion of fixup arrays.

The VCN value in bytes 16 to 23 identifies where this record fits into the tree. The $INDEX_ALLOCATION attribute is filled with index records, which could be out of order. The VCN value in the header identifies where this index record fits into the larger buffer. When an index entry points to its child node, it uses the VCN address in the node's index record header.

Let's look at the contents of the $INDEX_ALLOCATION attribute from the same directory whose $INDEX_ROOT attribute was examined:

```
# icat -f ntfs ntfs1.dd 7774-160 | xxd
0000000: 494e 4458 2800 0900 4760 2103 0000 0000  INDX(...G`!.....
0000016: 0000 0000 0000 0000 2800 0000 f808 0000  ........(.......
[REMOVED]
```

We can see the signature value "INDX" in the first line, and bytes 4 to 5 and 6 to 7 show the fixup record values. Bytes 16 to 23 show that this index record is VCN 0 buffer. The node header starts at byte 24. The $INDEX_ALLOCATION attribute is 8,192 bytes in size, so there is room for another index record. It starts at byte 4,096:

```
[REMOVED]
0004096: 494e 4458 2800 0900 ed5d 2103 0000 0000  INDX(....]!.....
0004112: 0400 0000 0000 0000 2800 0000 6807 0000  ........(...h...
0004128: e80f 0000 0000 0000 3b00 0500 6900 c401  ........;...i...
[REMOVED]
```

We see the "INDX" signature and bytes 4,112 to 4,119 show us that this is VCN 4 (each cluster in this file system is 1,024 bytes). We will return to this example after discussing the node header and index entries.

## $BITMAP ATTRIBUTE

In the previous section, we saw an $INDEX_ALLOCATION attribute with two 4,096-byte index records. It is possible for some of the index records to not be in use. The $BITMAP attribute is used to keep track of which index records in the $INDEX_ALLOCATION attribute are allocated to an index record. Typically, Windows allocates index records only when needed, but a directory may have unneeded records after deleting many files or because each cluster is larger than one index record. Note that this attribute was also used by $MFT to keep track of which MFT entries were allocated.

The $BITMAP attribute has a type identifier of 176 and is organized by bytes, and each bit corresponds to an index record. We can view the $BITMAP attribute for the previous directory by using icat:

```
# icat -f ntfs ntfs1.dd 7774-176 | xxd
0000000: 0300 0000 0000 0000                        ........
```

We can see the value 0x03 in byte 0, which is 0000 0011 in binary. Therefore, index records 0 and 1 are allocated.

## INDEX NODE HEADER DATA STRUCTURE

So far, we have seen the $INDEX_ROOT and $INDEX_ALLOCATION attributes, and they both have some header data that is followed by the node header and a list of index entries. In this section, we describe the node header data structure. This header occurs in the $INDEX_ROOT and in each index record data structure and is used to show where the list of index entries starts and ends. The header has the fields given in Table 13.14.

**Table 13.14**  Data structure for the index node header.

| Byte Range | Description | Essential |
|---|---|---|
| 0–3 | Offset to start of index entry list (relative to start of the node header) | Yes |
| 4–7 | Offset to end of used portion of index entry list (relative to start of the node header) | Yes |
| 8–11 | Offset to end of allocated index entry list buffer (relative to start of the node header) | Yes |
| 12–15 | Flags | No |

The index entries for an $INDEX_ROOT node will start immediately after the node header, but the index entries in an index buffer may not because of the fixup values. When we are looking for remnant data from deleted index entries, we will examine the data in between the end of the used portion of the buffer and the end of the allocated buffer.

The flags field has only one flag, and the 0x01 flag is set when there are children nodes that are pointed to by the entries in this list. This same flag exists in each index entry.

Let us look at the previous attributes that were dissected. The $INDEX_ROOT attribute had the following data:

```
# icat -f ntfs ntfs1.dd 7774-144 | xxd
0000000: 3000 0000 0100 0000 0010 0000 0400 0000  0..............
0000016: 1000 0000 a000 0000 a000 0000 0100 0000  ..............
[REMOVED]
```

The node header starts at byte 16, and bytes 16 to 19 show that the list starts 16 bytes (0x10) away, which is byte 32, and ends 160 bytes (0xa0) away, which is byte 176. In this case, the allocated space and used space are the same because they are from an $INDEX_ROOT attribute, which is resident and must be as small as possible. Byte 28 has the 0x01 flag set, so there are children nodes to this node (which are located in $INDEX_ALLOCATION).

Now let us look at the $INDEX_ALLOCATION attribute again:

```
# icat -f ntfs ntfs1.dd 7774-160 | xxd
0000000: 494e 4458 2800 0900 4760 2103 0000 0000  INDX(...G`!.....
0000016: 0000 0000 0000 0000 2800 0000 f808 0000  ........(......
0000032: e80f 0000 0000 0000 2100 0000 0600 0000  ........!.......
[REMOVED]
```

The first 24 bytes are for the index record header, and the node header starts after that. Bytes 24 to 27 show that the index entry list starts at byte offset 40 (0x28). Note that this is relative to the start of the node header, so we need to add 24 to it, which gives us 64. This is a case where the index entry list does not immediately follow the index entry list header because the fixup record array is in between the index entry list header and the actual list. Recall that bytes 4 to 5 of the index record header show that the fixup array is located at offset 40 (0x28).

Bytes 28 to 31 show that the offset to the end of the last list entry is 2,296 bytes (0x08f8), and bytes 32 to 35 show that the offset to the end of the allocated list buffer is 4,072 bytes (0x0fe8). Therefore, there are 1,776 bytes of unused space in the buffer that may contain data from files with names stored in those node entries. Bytes 36 to 39 show that the flag value is 0, so there are no children nodes to this node.

## GENERIC INDEX ENTRY DATA STRUCTURE

So far, we have discussed the general concepts of NTFS indexes, and the only thing missing is the discussion of index entries. From this point on, the data structures will be specific to the type of index, but there is a general structure to all index entry data structures, which I will describe in this section.

The standard fields for an index entry are given in Table 13.15.

**Table 13.15**  Data structure for a generic index entry.

| Byte Range | Description |
|---|---|
| 0–7 | Undefined |
| 8–9 | Length of this entry |
| 10–11 | Length of content |
| 12–15 | Flags (see Table 13.16) |
| 16+ | Content |
| Last 8 bytes of entry, starting on an 8-byte boundary | VCN of child node in $INDEX_ALLOCATION (field exists only if flag is set) |

The first eight bytes are used to store data that is specific to the index entry. Bytes 8 to 9 define how big the index entry is, and 10 to 11 give the length of the index entry content, which starts in byte 16. The content can be any data. The flags field has the values given in Table 13.16.

**Table 13.16**  Flag values for the index entry flag field.

| Value | Description |
|---|---|
| 0x01 | Child node exists |
| 0x02 | Last entry in list |

When an index entry has a child node, the 0x01 flag will be set, and the VCN address of the child node will be found in the last eight bytes of the index entry. Recall that each index record has a VCN. The 0x02 flag is set when this is the final entry in the list.

## DIRECTORY INDEX ENTRY DATA STRUCTURE

A directory index, which is used for file names, has a specific index entry data structure. It uses the basic template, as outlined in the previous section, and includes a file reference address and a $FILE_NAME attribute. Each index entry has the fields given in Table 13.17.

**Table 13.17**   Data structure for directory index entry.

| Byte Range | Description | Essential |
|---|---|---|
| 0–7 | MFT file reference for file name | Yes |
| 8–9 | Length of this entry | Yes |
| 10–11 | Length of $FILE_NAME attribute | No |
| 12–15 | Flags (see Table 13.16) | Yes |
| 16+ | $FILE_NAME Attribute (if length is > 0) | Yes |
| Last 8 bytes of entry, starting on an 8-byte boundary | VCN of child node in $INDEX_ALLOCATION (field exists only if flag is set) | Yes |

The file reference value points to the MFT entry to which this index entry corresponds. The two flag values apply to this entry, which is 0x01 if there is a child node and 0x02 if this is the last entry in the list.

Now let us look at the rest of the $INDEX_ROOT and $INDEX_ALLOCATION attributes that we have already partially dissected. The contents of the $INDEX_ROOT attribute are shown here:

```
# icat -f ntfs ntfs1.dd 7774-144 | xxd
0000000: 3000 0000 0100 0000 0010 0000 0400 0000   0..............
0000016: 1000 0000 a000 0000 a000 0000 0100 0000   ...............
0000032: c51e 0000 0000 0500 7800 5a00 0100 0000   ........x.Z.....
0000048: 5e1e 0000 0000 0300 e03d ca37 5029 c401   ^........=.7P)..
0000064: 004c c506 0202 c401 e09a 2a36 5029 c401   .L........*6P)..
0000080: d0e4 22b5 096a c401 0004 0000 0000 0000   .."..j..........
0000096: 7003 0000 0000 0000 2120 0000 0000 0000   p.......! ......
0000112: 0c02 4d00 4100 5300 5400 4500 5200 7e00   ..M.A.S.T.E.R.~.
0000128: 3100 2e00 5400 5800 5400 0000 0000 0300   1...T.X.T.......
0000144: 0000 0000 0000 0000 0000 0000 0000 0000   ...............
0000160: 1800 0000 0300 0000 0400 0000 0000 0000   ...............
[REMOVED]
```

We already processed the first 32 bytes because the first 16 bytes were the $INDEX_ROOT header, and the second 16 bytes were the node header. Bytes 32 to 37 show that this entry is for MFT entry 7,877 (0x1ec5). Bytes 40 to 45 show that the size of the index entry is 120 bytes (0x78), so it will end in byte 152 in our output. Bytes 26 to 27 show that the size of the attribute is 90 bytes (0x5a). The flag at byte 28 shows that there is a child node whose address will be given in the final eight bytes of the entry, which we expected because the flag in the node header showed that there was a child.

The $FILE_NAME attribute is located in bytes 48 to 137 and bytes 144 to 151 are the final bytes in the index entry and contain the VCN of the child node, which is cluster 0. We can see the name "MASTER~1.TXT" as the name of the file. Bytes 152 to 175 contain an empty index entry and the flag at byte 164 is 3, which shows that it is the end of the list and that it contains a child. Bytes 168 to 175 contain the address of the child node, which is VCN 4. These are the two index records we saw in the $INDEX_ALLOCATION attribute. Figure 13.7 shows the graphical layout of this attribute.

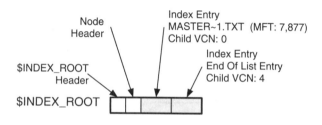

**Figure 13.7** Layout of the $INDEX_ROOT attribute in our example directory.

The same process can be repeated for each of the index records in the $INDEX_ALLOCATION attribute. Instead, we will look at some interesting data that occurs well after the node header. We previously saw that the index entries in index record 0 ended at offset 2,296, but that there were another 1,776 bytes allocated to the node. Therefore, there could be deleted file name information. We can seek through the unused area and look for valid index entries. Byte offset 2,400 has the following:

```
0002400: be1e 0000 0000 0600 6800 5400 0000 0000  ........h.T.....
0002416: 5e1e 0000 0000 0300 908b bf37 5029 c401  ^.........7P)..
0002432: 004c c506 0202 c401 e09a 2a36 5029 c401  .L........*6P)..
0002448: 30a7 6410 9c4a c401 003c 0000 0000 0000  0.d..J...<.....
0002464: 003a 0000 0000 0000 2120 0000 0000 0000  .:.......! .....
0002480: 0903 7000 7300 6100 7000 6900 2e00 6400  ..p.s.a.p.i...d.
0002496: 6c00 6c00 6500 0000 2513 0000 0000 0b00  l.l.e...%.......
```

This is an index entry for the file in MFT entry 7,870 (0x1ebe), and the name of the file is psapi.dll. Due to the nature of how indexes are re-sorted, we cannot tell if this file was deleted or if was moved to a different entry location because another file was added or deleted. We can tell only after looking at all the other index entries. TSK displays all entries and leaves it up to the user to identify why it is unallocated. Autopsy will filter the TSK output, though, and show only unique names.

Figure 13.8 shows the relationship between the index entries in $INDEX_ROOT and the index records in $INDEX_ALLOCATION. We can see that the root node of the index had two entries. Any file with a name less than MASTER~1.TXT could be found in the index record at VCN 0, and any with a name greater than it could be found in the index record at VCN 4. The index record at VCN 0 had unallocated space at the end of it, and we were able to find the data for the file psapi.dll. Notice that this name is greater than MASTER~1.TXT, so when it was saved to this node, there was likely a different entry in the root node.

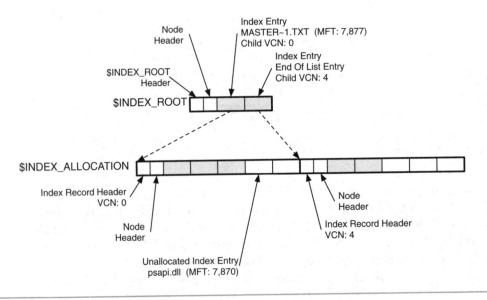

**Figure 13.8**   Layout of the index entries in the dissection examples.

## FILE SYSTEM METADATA FILES

Now that we have looked at the various attributes that a file and index can have, we will look at the file system metadata files. Most of these use the normal file attributes, but a couple of them have their own attributes. Those attributes are described in the following sections.

## $MFT FILE

The $MFT file is located in MFT entry 0 and was already discussed in the beginning of this chapter because it is crucial to every file in the file system. The istat output for the $MFT file in our example image was given in Chapter 12. It has the standard attributes, and the $DATA attribute is the MFT.

The one unique attribute of $MFT is a $BITMAP attribute, which is used to manage the allocation status of MFT entries. It is organized by bytes, and when a bit is set to 1 the entry is allocated. Otherwise, when the bit is 0 the entry is not allocated. We can view the $BITMAP attribute using icat and specifying the attribute type of 176.

```
# icat -f ntfs ntfs1.dd 0-176 | xxd
0000000: ffff 00ff ffff ffff ffff ffff ffff ffff  ...............
0000016: ffff ffff ffff ffff ffff ffff ffff ffff  ...............
[REMOVED]
```

We see here that most of the bits are set to 1 except in byte 2. This byte corresponds to MFT entries 16 to 23.

## $BOOT FILE

The $Boot file is located in MFT entry 7 and contains the boot sector and boot code in its $DATA attribute. This attribute always starts in sector 0, and the boot sector data structure is located there. The other sectors are used for boot code. The boot sector has the fields shown in Table 13.18.

Table 13.18   Data structure for the boot sector.

| Byte Range | Description | Essential |
| --- | --- | --- |
| 0–2 | Assembly instruction to jump to boot code | No (unless it is the bootable file system) |
| 3–10 | OEM Name | No |
| 11–12 | Bytes per sector | Yes |
| 13–13 | Sectors per cluster | Yes |
| 14–15 | Reserved sectors (Microsoft says it must be 0) | No |

*continues*

**Table 13.18**  Data structure for the boot sector (Continued).

| Byte Range | Description | Essential |
|---|---|---|
| 16–20 | Unused (Microsoft says it must be 0) | No |
| 21–21 | Media descriptor | No |
| 22–23 | Unused (Microsoft says it must be 0) | No |
| 24–31 | Unused (Microsoft says it is not checked) | No |
| 32–35 | Unused (Microsoft says it must be 0) | No |
| 36–39 | Unused (Microsoft says it is not checked) | No |
| 40–47 | Total sectors in file system | Yes |
| 48–55 | Starting cluster address of MFT | Yes |
| 56–63 | Starting cluster address of MFT Mirror $DATA attribute | No |
| 64–64 | Size of file record (MFT entry) | Yes |
| 65–67 | Unused | No |
| 68–68 | Size of index record | Yes |
| 69–71 | Unused | No |
| 72–79 | Serial number | No |
| 80–83 | Unused | No |
| 84–509 | Boot code | No |
| 510–511 | Signature (0xaa55) | No |

The fields that are not used correspond to *BIOS Parameter Block* (BPB) fields in the FAT boot sector. The Microsoft document identifies that some of them must be 0 for the file system to be mounted, but these are still considered nonessential values because they are not necessary for the file system to function, and Microsoft could decide to not check the values. I verified that Windows XP does not mount the disk if the values are non-zero.

The important values in the boot sector are the size of each sector and cluster. Without these, we will not be able to identify the location of anything. The next important value is the starting location of the MFT and the size of each MFT entry. To date, MFT entries have always been 1,024 bytes, but this field exists so that the size can be easily changed in the future. Also notice that the address of the $DATA attribute of $MFTMirr is given. This allows a recovery tool to determine where the backup copy of the $MFT entry is so that the location of the MFT can be determined.

The fields that show the MFT entry and index record sizes have a special format. If the value is larger than 0, it represents the number of clusters that are used for each data structure. If the value is less than 0, it represents the log base-2 of the number of bytes in each data structure. To calculate the number of bytes, take the absolute value of the negative number (i.e., the positive value) and raise the number two to that that power. For example, if the value is −10, the size of the data structure is $2^{10} = 1024$ bytes. This occurs when the size of a cluster is larger than a single MFT entry or index record.

Let us dissect a boot sector. We saw the istat output for the $Boot file in Chapter 12, and now we can use icat to view the $DATA attribute (type 128).

```
# icat -f ntfs ntfs1.dd 7-128 | xxd
0000000: eb52 904e 5446 5320 2020 2000 0202 0000   .R.NTFS    .....
0000016: 0000 0000 00f8 0000 3f00 ff00 3f00 0000   ........?...?...
0000032: 0000 0000 8000 8000 4060 1f00 0000 0000   ........@`......
0000048: b53a 0500 0000 0000 10d8 0700 0000 0000   .:..............
0000064: 0100 0000 0400 0000 947c 2250 8422 5004   .........|"P."P.
0000080: 0000 0000 fa33 c08e d0bc 007c fbb8 c007   .....3.....|....
0000096: 8ed8 e816 00b8 000d 8ec0 33db c606 0e00   ..........3.....
[REMOVED]
0000448: 6d70 7265 7373 6564 000d 0a50 7265 7373   mpressed...Press
0000464: 2043 7472 6c2b 416c 742b 4465 6c20 746f    Ctrl+Alt+Del to
0000480: 2072 6573 7461 7274 0d0a 0000 0000 0000    restart........
0000496: 0000 0000 0000 0000 83a0 b3c9 0000 55aa   .............U.
[REMOVED]
```

On the first line we see the OEM name, which is "NTFS," followed by some ASCII spaces (0x20). This is the standard name that Windows assigns. Bytes 11 and 12 show us the number of bytes in each sector, which is 512 (0x0200). Byte 13 shows that there are two sectors per cluster, so each cluster is 1,024 bytes. Bytes 40 to 47 show that the total number of sectors in the file system is 2,056,256 (0x001f6040), which means that the file system is 1GB in size. Bytes 48 to 55 show the starting cluster of the MFT to be 342,709 (0x00053ab5) and bytes 56 to 63 show the starting cluster of the $DATA attribute of the MFT mirror to be 514,064 (0x0007d810).

Byte 64 shows the size of each MFT entry. Recall that the encoding of this value depends on whether it is positive or negative. In this case, it is 1, so it represents the number of clusters in the MFT entry, which is 1,024 bytes. Byte 68 is the size of each index record, which is used for directories. This value is 4, so there are four clusters per index record.

Bytes 72 to 79 show the serial number of the file system, which is 0x04502284 50227C94. The remainder of the bytes contains boot code and bytes 510 and 511 have the 0xAA55 signature, which is the same as we saw for FAT.

## $ATTRDEF FILE

The $AttrDef file system metadata file is MFT entry number 4 and defines the file system attribute names and identifiers. The $DATA attribute for this file contains a list of entries, which have the fields shown in Table 13.19.

**Table 13.19**   Data structure for the $AttrDef entries.

| Byte Range | Description | Essential |
|---|---|---|
| 0–127 | Name of attribute | Yes |
| 128–131 | Type identifier | Yes |
| 132–135 | Display rule | No |
| 136–139 | Collation rule | No |
| 140–143 | Flags (see Table 13.20) | Yes |
| 144–151 | Minimum size | No |
| 152–159 | Maximum size | No |

If the attribute does not have any size limits, the minimum size will be 0, and the maximum size will be 0xffffffffffffffff. The flag field can have the values shown in Figure 13.20 set.

**Table 13.20**   Flag values for the $AttrDef entry flag field.

| Value | Description |
|---|---|
| 0x02 | Attribute can be used in an index |
| 0x04 | Attribute is always resident |
| 0x08 | Attribute can be non-resident |

The collation rule is used when the attribute is in an index. It determines how it should be sorted. The $DATA attribute of the $AttrDef file in our example image has the following contents:

```
# icat -f ntfs ntfs1.dd 4-128 | xxd
0000000: 2400 5300 5400 4100 4e00 4400 4100 5200  $.S.T.A.N.D.A.R.
0000016: 4400 5f00 4900 4e00 4600 4f00 5200 4d00  D._.I.N.F.O.R.M.
0000032: 4100 5400 4900 4f00 4e00 0000 0000 0000  A.T.I.O.N.......
0000048: 0000 0000 0000 0000 0000 0000 0000 0000  ................
0000064: 0000 0000 0000 0000 0000 0000 0000 0000  ................
0000080: 0000 0000 0000 0000 0000 0000 0000 0000  ................
0000096: 0000 0000 0000 0000 0000 0000 0000 0000  ................
0000112: 0000 0000 0000 0000 0000 0000 0000 0000  ................
0000128: 1000 0000 0000 0000 0000 0000 4000 0000  ............@...
0000144: 3000 0000 0000 0000 4800 0000 0000 0000  0.......H.......
[REMOVED]
```

We can see that the first attribute definition is for the $STANDARD_INFORMATION attribute. At bytes 128 to 131 we see the type of this attribute is 16 (0x10). The flags in bytes 140 to 143 show that this entry is always resident. Bytes 144 to 151 show that the minimum size of this attribute is 48 bytes (0x30), and the maximum size is 72 bytes (0x48).

## $BITMAP FILE

The $Bitmap file, which is located in MFT entry 6, has a $DATA attribute that is used to manage the allocation status of clusters. The bitmap data are organized into 1-byte values, and the least significant bit of each byte corresponds to the cluster that follows the cluster that the most significant bit of the previous byte corresponds to.

For example, consider two bytes with the binary values 00000001 and 00000011. The first byte has a 1 in the least significant bit, which corresponds to cluster 0. The next seven bits in the byte (going backwards from right to left) are all 0, so we know that clusters 1 to 7 are not allocated. The second byte has the two least significant bits set to 1, which corresponds to clusters 8 and 9. As you can see, you read this by looking at the least significant bit, moving backwards from right to left, and then going to the next byte to the right.

To determine the allocation status of a given cluster, we need to determine in which byte of the bitmap it is located. This is done by dividing the cluster address by 8 and ignoring the remainder. For example, cluster 5 would be in byte 0 of the bitmap, and cluster 18 would be in byte 2 of the bitmap. To find the bit in the byte that corresponds to the cluster, we examine the remainder. For example, when we divided 5 by 8, we had a remainder of 5, and when we divided 18 by 8 we had a remainder of 2. See Figure 13.9 for an illustrated example of calculating the location of cluster 5 and 74 in the bitmap.

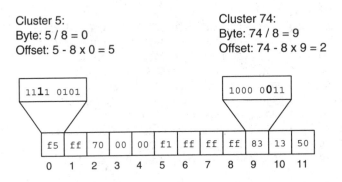

**Figure 13.9**    Example of finding the allocation status of clusters 5 and 74 in the bitmap.

With knowledge about how the bits are organized in the bitmap, let us return to our example file system. We can examine the contents of the $DATA attribute using icat:

```
# icat -f ntfs ntfs1.dd 6-128 | xxd
0000000: ffff ffff ffff ffff ffff ff3f 0000 0000   ...........?....
0000016: 0000 f0ff ffff ffff ffff ffff ffff ffff   ................
0000032: ffff ffff ffff ffff ffff ffff ffff ffff   ................
0000048: ffff ffff ffff ffff 0300 0000 ffff ffff   ................
0000064: ffff ffff ffff ffff ffff ffff ffff ffff   ................
0000080: ffff ffff ffff ffff ffff ffff ffff ffff   ................
[REMOVED]
```

We see here that the initial bits are all 1s, which makes sense because the boot sector is located in the first 8 KB of the file system, so we expect those to be allocated. In byte 11 of the output, we see the value 0x3f, which is 00111111 in binary. This byte corresponds to clusters 88 to 95 of the file system, and the six least significant bits are set to 1, which means that they are allocated. The seventh and eighth bits are set to 0, which correspond to clusters 94 and 95. We also can see that the next six bytes are all zero, so all the clusters for those bits are unallocated. In byte 18 we see the value 0xf0, which is 1111 0000 in binary.

## $VOLUME FILE

The $Volume file is in MFT entry 3, and it has two unique attributes. They are described in this section.

### $VOLUME_NAME Attribute

The $VOLUME_NAME attribute has a type identifier of 96 and is supposed to be allocated to only the $Volume file. It contains the name of the volume in UTF-16 Unicode and nothing else. Its contents from our example image are shown here:

```
# icat -f ntfs ntfs1.dd 3-96 | xxd
0000000: 4e00 5400 4600 5300 2000 4400 6900 7300   N.T.F.S. .D.i.s.
0000016: 6b00 2000 3200                            k. .2.
```

We see that the volume name for this file system is "NTFS Disk 2."

### $VOLUME_INFORMATION Attribute

The second attribute that is unique to the $Volume file is the $VOLUME_INFORMATION attribute, which has a type identifier of 112. This attribute contains the version of the file system. It has the fields given in Table 13.21.

**Table 13.21**  Data structure for the $VOLUME_INFORMATION attribute.

| Byte Range | Description | Essential |
|---|---|---|
| 0–7 | Unused | No |
| 8–8 | Major version | Yes |
| 9–9 | Minor version | Yes |
| 10–11 | Flags (see Table 13.22) | No |

Windows NT used a major version of 1 and a minor version of 2. Windows 2000 used a major version of 3 and a minor version of 0. Windows XP used a major version of 3 and a minor version of 1. The flags shown in Table 13.22 apply to this data structure.

**Table 13.22**   Flag values for the $VOLUME_INFORMATION flags field.

| Flag | Description |
|------|-------------|
| 0x0001 | Dirty |
| 0x0002 | Resize $LogFile (file system journal) |
| 0x0004 | Upgrade volume next time |
| 0x0008 | Mounted in NT |
| 0x0010 | Deleting change journal |
| 0x0020 | Repair object IDs |
| 0x8000 | Modified by chkdsk |

The $VOLUME_INFORMATION attribute in our example file system has the following contents:

```
# icat -f ntfs ntfs1.dd 3-112 | xxd
0000000: 0000 0000 0000 0000 0301 0000          ............
```

Byte 8 and 9 show us that this file system is version 3.1, which is XP. The flags are set to 0.

## $OBJID FILE

As we saw in Chapter 12, a file can be addressed using its object ID instead of its name. This allows a file to be renamed but still be found. The \$Extend\$ObjId file has an index named $O that correlates a file's object ID to its MFT entry. The $ObjId file is not typically located in a reserved MFT entry.

The index will have the typical $INDEX_ROOT and $INDEX_ALLOCATION attributes, and its index entries will have the fields given in Table 13.23.

**Table 13.23**   Data structure for the $ObjId index entries.

| Byte Range | Description | Essential |
|------------|-------------|-----------|
| 0–1 | Offset to file information | Yes |
| 2–3 | Size of file information | Yes |

| Byte Range | Description | Essential |
|---|---|---|
| 4–7 | Unused | No |
| 8–9 | Size of index entry | Yes |
| 10–11 | Size of object ID (16-bytes) | Yes |
| 12–15 | Flags (see Table 13.16) | Yes |
| 16–31 | Object ID | Yes |
| 32–39 | File reference | Yes |
| 40–55 | Birth volume ID | No |
| 56–71 | Birth object ID | No |
| 72–87 | Birth domain ID | No |

The flags field has the standard values of 0x01 when child nodes exist and 0x02 when it is the last entry in the index entry list. Here are some index entries from an $INDEX_ROOT attribute, with the node header removed:

```
0000000: 2000 3800 0000 0000 5800 1000 0000 0000    .8.....X.......
0000016: fe24 b024 e292 fe47 95ac e507 4bf5 6782    .$.$...G....K.g.
0000032: 0300 0000 0000 0300 0000 0000 0000 0000    ...............
0000048: 0000 0000 0000 0000 0000 0000 0000 0000    ...............
0000064: 0000 0000 0000 0000 0000 0000 0000 0000    ...............
0000080: 0000 0000 0000 0000 2000 3800 0000 0000    ........ .8.....
0000096: 5800 1000 0000 0000 a162 3d5e cdda d811    X........b=^....
0000112: 883c 00b0 d01d e93f a400 0000 0000 0100    .<.....?........
0000128: fe24 b024 e292 fe47 95ac e507 4bf5 6782    .$.$...G....K.g.
0000144: a162 3d5e cdda d811 883c 00b0 d01d e93f    .b=^.....<.....?
0000160: 0000 0000 0000 0000 0000 0000 0000 0000    ...............
```

We see from byte 8 that the entry is 88 bytes (0x58) long, and bytes 16 to 31 show the 16-byte object id. Bytes 32 to 37 show the MFT entry address for this object ID, which is 3. This is the index entry for the $OBJECT_ID attribute that was dissected in the "$OBJECT_ID Attribute" section. The rest of the ID fields are 0 for this entry, and the next entry begins at byte 88.

## $QUOTA FILE

The \$Extend\$Quota file is used by the user quota feature. It is not located in a reserved MFT entry. It contains two indexes that both use the standard $INDEX_ROOT and $INDEX_ALLOCATION attributes to store their index entries. The $O index correlates a SID to an owner ID, and the $Q index correlates an owner ID to quota information. The index entry for the $O index has the fields given in Table 13.24.

**Table 13.24** Data structure for the $O index entries in $Quota.

| Byte Range | Description | Essential |
|---|---|---|
| 0–1 | Offset to owner ID (OFF) | Yes |
| 2–3 | Length of owner ID | Yes |
| 4–7 | Unused | No |
| 8–9 | Size of index entry | Yes |
| 10–11 | Size of SID (L) | Yes |
| 12–15 | Flags (see Table 13.16) | Yes |
| 16–(16+L-1) | SID | Yes |
| OFF+ | Owner ID | Yes |

The flag values for this index entry are the same as we saw for file names. 0x01 is set when there is a child node, and 0x02 is set when it is the last entry in the list. If a child exists, the last 8 bytes will be used for the VCN of the child.

Here is the first index entry in the $O index:

```
0000000: 1c00 0400 0000 0000 2000 0c00 0000 0000    ........ ........
0000016: 0101 0000 0000 0005 1200 0000 0401 0000    ................
0000032: 1c00 0400 0000 0000 2000 0c00 0000 0000    ........ ........
0000048: 0101 0000 0000 0005 1300 0000 0301 0000    ................
[REMOVED]
```

Bytes 0 to 1 show that the owner ID is located at offset 28 (0x1c) from the start of the entry, and bytes 2 to 3 show that the owner ID is four bytes long. Bytes 8 to 9 show that the index entry is 32 bytes (0x20) long, and bytes 10 to 11 show that the SID is 12 bytes (0x0c). Bytes 16 to 27 contain the SID, and bytes 28 to 31 contain the owner ID, which is

260 (0x0104). The second entry in the list starts at byte 32, and its owner ID is found in bytes 60 to 63, which is 259 (0x0103).

The $Q index maps an owner ID to the owner's quota information. Its index entry has the values shown in Table 13.25.

**Table 13.25**  Data structure for the $Q index entries in $Quota.

| Byte Range | Description | Essential |
|---|---|---|
| 0–1 | Offset to quota information | Yes |
| 2–3 | Size of quota information | Yes |
| 4–7 | Unused | No |
| 8–9 | Size of index entry | Yes |
| 10–11 | Size of owner ID (4 bytes) | Yes |
| 12–15 | Flags (see Table 13.16) | Yes |
| 16–19 | Owner ID | Yes |
| 20–23 | Version | No |
| 24–27 | Quota flags (see Table 13.26) | Yes |
| 28–35 | Bytes charged to user | Yes |
| 36–43 | Time of last charge | No |
| 44–51 | Threshold value (a soft limit) | Yes |
| 52–59 | Hard limit value | Yes |
| 60–67 | Exceeded time | Yes |
| 68–79 | SID | Yes |

The index entry flags are the standard flags of 0x01, if there is a child node and 0x02 if this is the last entry in the list. The quota flags have the values shown in Table 13.26.

**Table 13.26**  Flag values for the $Q index entry flags field.

| Flag | Description |
| --- | --- |
| 0x00000001 | Default limits being used |
| 0x00000002 | Limit reached |
| 0x00000004 | ID deleted |
| 0x00000010 | Tracking data usage |
| 0x00000020 | Enforcing data usage |
| 0x00000040 | Usage tracking requested |
| 0x00000080 | Create log when threshold is met |
| 0x00000100 | Create log when limit is met |
| 0x00000200 | Out of date |
| 0x00000400 | Corrupt |
| 0x00000800 | Pending deletes |

Here is an index entry from the same image that we used for the $0 index. This came from the $INDEX_ALLOCATION attribute, and the header data has been removed. This actually comes from inside the entry list and corresponds to the owner IDs shown in the previous example.

```
0000000: 1400 3c00 0000 0000 5000 0400 0000 0000   ..<.....P.......
0000016: 0301 0000 0200 0000 0100 0000 0028 0500   .............(..
0000032: 0000 0000 401b 7c3c 7751 c401 ffff ffff   ....@.|<wQ......
0000048: ffff ffff ffff ffff ffff ffff 0000 0000   ................
0000064: 0000 0000 0101 0000 0000 0005 1300 0000   ................
0000080: 1400 3c00 0000 0000 5000 0400 0000 0000   ..<.....P.......
0000096: 0401 0000 0200 0000 0100 0000 0094 6602   ..............f.
0000112: 0000 0000 90fe 8bdf d769 c401 ffff ffff   .........i......
0000128: ffff ffff ffff ffff ffff ffff 0000 0000   ................
0000144: 0000 0000 0101 0000 0000 0005 1200 0000   ................
```

Byes 0 to 1 show that the offset to the quota information is 20 bytes (0x14), and bytes 2 to 3 show that there are 60 bytes of quota information. Bytes 16 to 19 show that this is for owner ID 259 (0x0103), which is the second entry we saw in the $0 index. Bytes 24 to 27 have the quota flags, and we see that this user has the default limits. Bytes 28 to 35 show that this user has only 337,920 bytes (0x052800) charged to her account. The next entry is also included if you would like to parse it.

## $LogFile File

The $LogFile is in MFT entry 2 and is used as the NTFS journal. It has the standard file attributes and stores the log data in the $DATA attribute. Unfortunately, the exact data structure details are not known. We will take a peak at the contents, though, to get a rough idea about what is in there.

The log is organized into 4,096 byte pages. The first two are for the restart area, and they have the signature "RSTR" in their first four pages of each page:

```
# icat -f ntfs ntfs1.dd 2 | xxd | grep RSTR
0000000: 5253 5452 1e00 0900 0000 0000 0000 0000  RSTR...........
0004096: 5253 5452 1e00 0900 0000 0000 0000 0000  RSTR...........
```

Many of the other values in this data structure are zero, and the only string is "NTFS" in Unicode. After the second restart data structure at byte offset 8192 are the records, and each of them starts with the signature "RCRD":

```
# icat -f ntfs ntfs1.dd 2 | xxd | grep RCRD
0008192: 5243 5244 2800 0900 0050 2500 0000 0000  RCRD(....P%.....
0012288: 5243 5244 2800 0900 0050 2500 0000 0000  RCRD(....P%.....
[REMOVED]
```

It is not directly obvious what the values in the record are for. To show that resident data attributes can be found in the log file, I created a file called C:\log-test.txt with the ASCII string "My new file, can you see it?" In the log file we see the following:

```
2215936: 5243 5244 2800 0900 f93b 9403 0000 0000  RCRD(....;......
[REMOVED]
2217312: 3801 1800 0000 0000 ec12 0000 0000 0000  8..............
2217328: a14d 0500 0000 0000 4d79 206e 6577 2066  .M......My new f
2217344: 696c 652c 2063 616e 2079 6f75 2073 6565  ile, can you see
2217360: 2069 743f 0000 0000 0000 0000 0000 0000   it?...........
2217376: 0000 0000 0000 0000 0000 0000 0000 0000  ..............
[REMOVED]
2217808: 0003 0000 0094 7c22 5010 0000 004e 5446  ......|"P....NTF
2217824: 5320 4469 736b 2032 0043 3a5c 6c6f 672d  S Disk 2.C:\log-
2217840: 7465 7374 2e74 7874 0000 1500 2e00 2e00  test.txt........
```

```
2217856:  5c00 2e00 2e00 5c00 2e00 2e00 5c00 6c00    \.....\.....\.l.
2217872:  6f00 6700 2d00 7400 6500 7300 7400 2e00    o.g.-.t.e.s.t...
2217888:  7400 7800 7400 0300 4300 3a00 5c00 6000    t.x.t...C.:.\.`.
```

We can see the text of the file is located inside of a record. Later in the record we can also see the name of the file and the name of the disk "NTFS Disk 2." After the file was saved, I modified the string to also include "This is my update.." That data was located later in the log file:

```
2248704:  5243 5244 2800 0900 f24b 9403 0000 0000    RCRD(....K......
[REMOVED]
2250800:  ec12 0000 0000 0000 a14d 0500 0000 0000    .........M......
2250816:  2020 5468 6973 2069 7320 6d79 2075 7064      This is my upd
2250832:  6174 652e 0000 0000 0000 0000 0000 0000    ate.............
2250848:  0000 0000 0000 0000 0000 0000 0000 0000    ................
```

This record contains only the new content and does not contain the path name of the file being updated. There is probably a reference in this record that points to another record that identifies the file name.

## $UsrJrnl File

The change journal falls into the application category and records when changes are made to files. The changes are recorded in the $DATA attribute named $J of the \$Extend\$UsrJrnl file, which is not located in a reserved MFT entry. The $J $DATA attribute is sparse, and it contains a list of different sized data structures, called change journal entries. There is also a $DATA attribute named $Max that contains information about the maximum settings for the user journal.

As we discussed in Chapter 12, this data are non-essential with respect to the file system goals of storing and retrieving data. Therefore, the 'Essential' column in this table refers to whether the data are essential for the goal of providing a log of file changes. The data structure for the entries in $J has the fields given in Table 13.27.

Table 13.27   Data structure for the $J attribute entries in $UsrJrnl.

| Byte Range | Description | Essential |
|---|---|---|
| 0–3 | Size of this journal entry | Yes |
| 4–5 | Major version | Yes |

| Byte Range | Description | Essential |
|---|---|---|
| 6–7 | Minor version | Yes |
| 8–15 | File reference of file that caused this entry | Yes |
| 16–23 | Parent directory file reference for file that caused this entry | No |
| 24–31 | USN for entry | Yes |
| 32–39 | Timestamp | Yes |
| 40–43 | Flags for type of change (see Table 13.28) | Yes |
| 44–47 | Source information | No |
| 48–51 | Security ID (SID) | No |
| 52–55 | File attributes | No |
| 56–57 | Size of file name | Yes |
| 58+ | File name | Yes |

Bytes 40 to 43 contain the reason for the change journal entry. This field is a set of flags, and there could be more than one reason that the entry was created. The values given in Table 13.28 are defined.

**Table 13.28**  Values for the change type field in $J entries.

| Value | Description |
|---|---|
| 0x00000001 | The default $DATA attribute was overwritten |
| 0x00000002 | The default $DATA attribute was extended |
| 0x00000004 | The default $DATA attribute was truncated |
| 0x00000010 | A named $DATA attribute was overwritten |
| 0x00000020 | A named $DATA attribute was extended |
| 0x00000040 | A named $DATA attribute was truncated |
| 0x00000100 | The file or directory was created |

*continues*

**Table 13.28**  Values for the change type field in $J entries (Continued).

| Value | Description |
|---|---|
| 0x00000200 | The file or directory was deleted |
| 0x00000400 | The extended attributes of the file were changed |
| 0x00000800 | The security descriptor was changed |
| 0x00001000 | The name changed—change journal entry has old name |
| 0x00002000 | The name changed—change journal entry has new name |
| 0x00004000 | Content indexed status changed |
| 0x00008000 | Changed basic file or directory attributes |
| 0x00010000 | A hard link was created or deleted |
| 0x00020000 | Compression status changed |
| 0x00040000 | Encryption status changed |
| 0x00080000 | Object ID changed |
| 0x00100000 | Reparse point value changed |
| 0x00200000 | A named $DATA attribute was created, deleted, or changed |
| 0x80000000 | The file or directory was closed |

The source value in bytes 44–47 is typically 0, but can be non-zero if the OS caused the entry to be made and not a user. Let us take a look at a small change journal. To find the MFT entry for the journal, we examine the contents of the \$Extend file system metadata directory, which is MFT entry 11.

```
# fls -f ntfs ntfs3.dd 11
r/r 25-144-2:   $ObjId:$O
r/r 24-144-3:   $Quota:$O
r/r 24-144-2:   $Quota:$Q
r/r 26-144-2:   $Reparse:$R
r/r 27-128-3:   $UsnJrnl:$J
r/r 27-128-4:   $UsnJrnl:$Max
```

We see that it is MFT entry 27. We display the $J attribute contents with icat:

```
# icat -f ntfs ntfs3.dd 27-128-3 | xxd
0000000: 5000 0000 0200 0000 1c00 0000 0000 0100   P..............
0000016: 0500 0000 0000 0500 0000 0000 0000 0000   ...............
0000032: 3000 e2b9 eb69 c401 0001 0000 0000 0000   0....i..........
0000048: 0201 0000 2000 0000 1400 3c00 6600 6900   .... .....<.f.i.
0000064: 6c00 6500 2d00 3000 2e00 7400 7800 7400   l.e.-.0...t.x.t.
```

The first four bytes show us that this change journal entry is 80 bytes, and bytes 8 to 13 show us that the entry is for MFT entry 28 (0x1c). Bytes 24 to 31 show us that this entry has a USN of 0, and bytes 40 to 43 show the reason flags as 0x00000001, which is for the overwriting of the default $DATA attribute. Lastly, we see that this entry is for the file file-0.txt.

The $Max attribute contains the general change journal administrative information. It has the fields given in Table 13.29.

**Table 13.29** Data structure for the $Max attribute of $UsrJrnl.

| Byte Range | Description | Essential |
|---|---|---|
| 0–7 | Maximum size | Yes |
| 8–15 | Allocation size | Yes |
| 16–23 | USN ID | Yes |
| 24–31 | Lowest USN | Yes |

This information will likely not help during an investigation, but the contents of the $Max attribute are given for completeness:

```
# icat -f ntfs ntfs3.dd 27-128-4 | xxd
0000000: 0000 8000 0000 0000 0000 1000 0000 0000   ...............
0000016: 4057 7491 eb69 c401 0000 0000 0000 0000   @Wt..i.........
```

# SUMMARY

There are a lot of data structures in NTFS and many pointers, which makes it difficult to do any manual analysis. In this chapter, we have examined the common data structures that are known. It should be reinforced that these are not from an official specification, but they have been shown to be reliable. There could be values or flag options that have not yet been seen.

## BIBLIOGRAPHY

Linux NTFS Project. *NTFS Documentation*, 1996-2004. `http://linux-ntfs.`
`sourceforge.net/ntfs/index.html`.

Solomon, David and Mark Russinovich. *Inside Windows 2000*. 3rd ed. Redmond: Microsoft Press, 2000.

See also the Bibliography section of Chapter 11.

# Ext2 and Ext3 Concepts and Analysis

The Ext2 and Ext3 file systems, which I will lump into the term ExtX from now on, are the default file systems for many distributions of the Linux operating system. Ext3 is the newer version of Ext2 and adds file system journaling, but the basic Ext2 construction remains the same. ExtX are based on the *UNIX File System* (UFS). ExtX removed many of the components of UFS that are no longer needed, so it is easier to understand and explain and will be covered first. Unlike other operating systems, Linux supports a large number of file systems, and each distribution can choose which file system will be the default. At the time of this writing, Ext3 is the default file system of most distributions, but the Reiser file system is also popular, and its design is nothing like ExtX. This chapter examines how ExtX works, and Chapter 15, "Ext2 and Ext3 Data Structures," examines what the data structures look like. You can read this chapter and the next in parallel or in series.

## INTRODUCTION

ExtX takes its design from UFS, which was designed to be fast and reliable. Copies of important data structures are stored throughout the file system, and all data associated with a file are localized so that the hard disk heads do not need to travel much when reading them. The layout of the file system starts with an optional reserved area, and the remainder of the file system is divided into sections, which are called block groups. All block groups, except for the last, contain the same number of blocks, which are used to store file names, metadata, and file content. If we return to our analogy from Chapter 8,

"File System Analysis," about the allocation of seats in a theater, block groups are like sections in a theater. Each section is numbered, and all sections have the same number of seats.

The basic layout information of ExtX is stored in the superblock data structure, which is at the beginning of the file system. File content is stored in blocks, which are groups of consecutive sectors. The metadata for each file and directory are stored in a data structure called an inode, which has a fixed size and is located in an inode table. There is one inode table in each block group. The name of a file is stored in a directory entry structure, which is located in the blocks allocated to the file's parent directory. Directory entry structures are simple data structures that contain the name of the file and a pointer to the file's inode entry. The relationship between the directory entry, inode, and blocks can be seen in Figure 14.1.

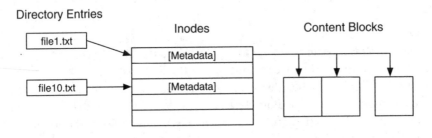

**Figure 14.1** Relationship between ExtX directory entries, inodes, and data blocks that are used to store file content.

ExtX has optional features that are organized into three categories based on what the operating system should do if it encounters a file system with a feature that it does not support. The first category is the *compatible features*, and if the OS does not support one of these features, it can still mount the file system and continue as normal. Examples of this include allocation methods, the existence of a file system journal, and extended attributes. There are also *incompatible features*, and if an OS encounters one of these, it should not mount the file system. An example of this includes compression. Lastly, a feature can be a *read only compatible feature*. When an OS encounters one of these features that it does not support, the file system should be mounted as read only. Examples of this include large file support and using B-trees to sort directories instead of an unsorted list.

ExtX has many experimental components and features that have not been implemented into the major distributions of Linux. That is not to say that the computer you are investigating does not have the features installed. With Linux, the local administrator can add any kernel features that she wants to, so we cannot make assumptions about the OS. If you are investigating a Linux system that was used as a corporate server, it might have a more standard build. On the other hand, if you are investigating a Linux system that was the desktop system of a person suspected of breaking into other systems, it might have some experimental features. Examining the kernel and what modifications were made falls into the application analysis arena and is out of the scope of this book. The flags that identify which features are being used may show you that the file system has experimental features that are not described in this book.

In the rest of this chapter, we will examine the five-category data model with respect to Ext2 and Ext3. Each section will discuss the basic properties of the category and then the details of ExtX. The more stable features will be discussed, but keep in mind that they could change and be out of date by the time you are reading this.

## FILE SYSTEM CATEGORY

The file system category of data is where the general data about a file system are located. This section looks at where this category of data is located and then looks at how to analyze the data.

### OVERVIEW

In ExtX, there are two data structures that store data in the file system category: the superblock and the group descriptor. The *superblock* is located in the beginning of the file system and contains the basic size and configuration information. It is similar to the boot sector data structures in an NTFS or FAT file system. As previously mentioned, the file system is organized into block groups and each group has a *group descriptor* data structure that describes the layout of the group. The group descriptors are located in the group descriptor table, which is located in the block after superblock. Backup copies of the superblock and group descriptor tables exist throughout the file system in case the primary copies are damaged.

### Superblock

The ExtX superblock is located 1,024 bytes from the start of the file system and is 1,024 bytes in size, although most of the bytes are not used. This data structure contains only configuration values and no boot code. Backup copies of the superblock are typically stored in the first block of each block group.

The superblock contains basic information, such as the block size, the total number of blocks, the number of blocks per block group, and the number of reserved blocks before the first block group. The superblock also contains the total number of inodes and the number of inodes per block group. Nonessential data in the superblock includes the volume name, the last write time, the last mount time, and the path where the file system was last mounted. There are also values that identify if the file system is clean or if a consistency check needs to be run on it. The superblock also keeps some bookkeeping data about the total number of free inodes and blocks. These are used when new inodes and blocks are allocated.

To determine the file system layout, we first use the block size and number of blocks to calculate the file system size. If this value is less than the volume size, there could be hidden data following the file system, which is called volume slack. The first block group is located in the block following the reserved area. Figure 14.2 shows which values are used to determine the layout. Note that the last group in this figure does not have the same number of blocks as the first four.

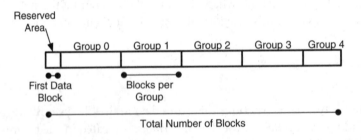

**Figure 14.2**  Layout of ExtX with five block groups.

The superblock defines what features the file system has enabled. Recall from the "Introduction" section that there are three categories of features: compatible, incompatible, and read only compatible. For simplicity, the details of each feature will be discussed in their respective section of this chapter. Here I will only discuss the read only compatible feature called "sparse superblock." When the sparse superblock feature is used, only some block groups contain backup copies of the superblock and the group descriptor table. In a sample file system, I found that groups 1, 3, 5, 7, and 9 had backup copies, and the next copies did not occur until groups 25 and 27. When an ExtX file system is created in Linux, the sparse superblock feature is enabled by default. This feature should not have an effect on an investigation except that you should not assume that every group has reserved space for a superblock backup.

With Linux, the volume label in the superblock can be used to identify the file system. For example, the default way to refer to a file system in Unix is to use its device name, /dev/hda5 for example. Another way of referring to it is by its volume label and the system configuration files may refer to the label instead of the device name. For example, the /etc/fstab in Linux lists the file systems that should be mounted and it could refer to the /dev/hda4 device as "LABEL=rootfs" if the volume label is rootfs.[1]

For the data structure layout and an example of a superblock, refer to the next chapter. The output from running fsstat on the file system will be shown later in this section.

### Block Group Descriptor Tables

In the block following the superblock is the group descriptor table, which contains a *group descriptor* data structure for every block group in the file system. Backup copies of the table exist in each of the block groups, unless the sparse superblock feature is enabled. In addition to file content, block groups contain administrative data, such as superblocks, group descriptor tables, inode tables, inode bitmaps, and block bitmaps. The group descriptor describes where these data can be found. The basic layout of a block group is shown in Figure 14.3.

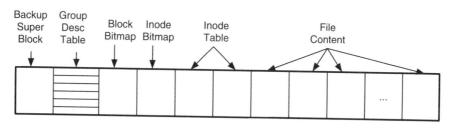

**Figure 14.3**    Layout of a sample block group

The block bitmap manages the allocation status of the blocks in the group, and its starting block address is given in the group descriptor. Its size in bytes can be calculated by dividing the number of blocks in the group by eight. When Linux creates a file system, it defines the number of blocks per group to be equal to the number of bits in a block. Therefore, the block bitmap will require exactly one block.

---

1. While this configuration can be useful for normal systems, it can be dangerous for a forensic analysis system because if a suspect drive is placed in the system and it has the same labels as the analysis drive, it could be mounted by the OS. You should make sure that your analysis and acquisition systems are configured to use device names and not volume labels.

The inode bitmap manages the allocation status of the inodes in the group, and its starting block address is also given in the group descriptor. Its size in bytes can be calculated by dividing the number of inodes per group by eight. In general, there are fewer inodes than blocks per group, but a user can choose these values when they create the file system. Lastly, the starting block address of the inode table is given in the group descriptor, and its size is calculated by multiplying the number of inodes per group by the size of each inode, which is 128 bytes.

The group descriptor also contains the number of free blocks and inodes in the block group. The superblock contains the total number of free blocks and inodes in all groups. The group descriptor data structure is given in Chapter 15.

## Boot Code

If an ExtX file system contains the OS kernel, it may have boot code. All other non-boot file systems should not have boot code. When boot code exists, it will be in the 1,024 bytes before the superblock (i.e., the first two sectors). The boot code will be executed after control is passed to it from the boot code in the *Master Boot Record* (MBR) in sector 0 of the disk. The ExtX boot code typically knows which blocks have been allocated to the kernel and will load it into memory.

Many Linux systems do not have boot code in the file system with the kernel. Instead, there is a *boot loader* in the MBR, and it knows in which blocks the kernel is located. In that case, the code in the MBR will load the kernel, and no additional boot code in the file system is needed.

## Example Image

We will be using an example image in this chapter, and this section contains the output of running fsstat from *The Sleuth Kit* (TSK) on that image. We will use some of these values in later examples. This is the same image that is manually parsed in the next chapter.

```
# fsstat -f linux-ext3 ext3.dd
FILE SYSTEM INFORMATION
--------------------------------------------
File System Type: Ext3
Volume Name:
Volume ID: e4636f48c4ec85946e489517a5067a07

Last Written at: Wed Aug  4 09:41:13 2004
Last Checked at: Thu Jun 12 10:35:54 2003

Last Mounted at: Wed Aug  4 09:41:13 2004
```

Unmounted properly
Last mounted on:

Source OS: Linux
Dynamic Structure
Compat Features: Journal,
InCompat Features: Filetype, Needs Recovery,
Read Only Compat Features: Sparse Super, Has Large Files,

Journal ID: 00
Journal Inode: 8

METADATA INFORMATION
--------------------------------------------
Inode Range: 1 - 1921984
Root Directory: 2
Free Inodes: 1917115

CONTENT INFORMATION
--------------------------------------------
Block Range: 0 - 3841534
Block Size: 4096
Free Blocks: 663631

BLOCK GROUP INFORMATION
--------------------------------------------
Number of Block Groups: 118
Inodes per group: 16288
Blocks per group: 32768

Group: 0:
  Inode Range: 1 - 16288
  Block Range: 0 - 32767
  Layout:
    Super Block: 0 - 0
    Group Descriptor Table: 1 - 1
    Data bitmap: 2 - 2
    Inode bitmap: 3 - 3
    Inode Table: 4 - 512
    Data Blocks: 513 - 32767
  Free Inodes: 16245 (99%)
  Free Blocks: 0 (0%)
  Total Directories: 11

```
Group: 1:
  Inode Range: 16289 - 32576
  Block Range: 32768 - 65535
[REMOVED]
```

The output shows the general data from the superblock, such as the total number of inodes and blocks and the block sizes. The layout details for each block group are also given, and those for group 0 are shown. We can see the block and inode range for group 0 and the locations of the bitmaps and inode table. The feature flags and temporal information also are shown.

## ANALYSIS TECHNIQUES

Analysis of the file system category of data involves processing key data structures so that the layout of the file system can be determined, which leads to more advanced and fruitful analysis techniques. With ExtX, the first step is to locate the superblock, which is easy because it is always located at an offset of 1,024 bytes from the start of the file system. After the superblock has been located, it is straightforward to process it. This structure is essential to an investigation because it gives the size and locations for key data structures. If it is corrupt, many backup copies should exist. The features flags will identify if this file system has any unique features that are not supported by the analysis tool or OS. The size of the file system can be calculated using the block size and the number of blocks in the file system.

In the block following the superblock, the group descriptor table can be found. This contains an entry for each group and is used to locate the data structures that will determine the allocation status of blocks and inodes. Backup copies of this also can be found in each group that has a superblock. Using the superblock and group descriptors, we can locate all of the data structures that are used by files and directories.

## ANALYSIS CONSIDERATIONS

Like every other file system, this category contains essential information that describes the layout of the file system, but it does not contain many values that are supplied by the user and contain evidence of an event. There is a lot of unused space in the superblock and it could be used to hide data. After reading Chapter 15 and the UFS chapters, you will see that the ExtX superblock is much cleaner than the UFS superblock, and this makes it easier to detect values that are being used to hide data. The 1,024 bytes before the start of the superblock are reserved for boot code, but they may not be needed and might contain hidden data. Also compare the file system size with the volume size to determine if there could be unused sectors after the file system.

The group descriptor table has entries that efficiently use the data allocated to them, but there could be unused space at the end of the table. That should be checked, including the backup copies, for hidden data.

If the superblock cannot be found or it is corrupt, a search can be conducted for the backup copies. One search method is to look for the data structure's signature value, which is 0xef53 in bytes 56 to 57. You also can try to determine the block group boundaries using the expected block size and the fact that the size of a block group is frequently based on how many bits there are in one block. Therefore, if you multiply the block size by eight and add one, then you should find a backup copy in that sector. For example, if the file system had a block size of 1,024 bytes, then each block group should have 8,192 blocks, and the backup superblock should be in block 8,192 (if there are no reserved blocks). Backup copies of the data structure could be used to detect any manual modifications.

## ANALYSIS SCENARIO

Consider a scenario where you encounter a system that has no partition table. In Chapter 4, "Volume Analysis," we saw an example where gpart was used to find file systems when the partition table was missing or corrupt. Here we will do what a gpart-like tool may do.

We think that our disk was used as a Linux system, so we search for an ExtX file system. The computer also could have used Reiser or another file system, so we should not limit our searches to only ExtX. Also remember that many Linux systems will frequently use multiple file systems and partitions on the same disk. It is not uncommon for the first file system to be fairly small because it is used for only the boot code and the kernel.

The ExtX superblock has the signature value 0xef53 in bytes 56 to 57. We will search for that value to try and locate the start of the file system. We should expect to find many false hits during this search because it is a short signature. To determine if a hit is false, we can check other values that should be in the superblock to make sure they are valid (for example is the block size reasonable). We also can use the fact that backup copies exist in each block group, so when we find an actual ExtX superblock, we should see a series of equally spaced hits. Further, the block groups are typically based on the size of a block so the distance between the superblocks should be 8,192, 16,384, or 32,768 if the default creation procedure was used. We also will need to keep in mind that the sparse superblock feature could be in use, and we will not see a backup copy in every block group.

You can search for the signature in any tool that allows hexadecimal values to be searched for. Note that a tool like grep will not work in this case because it supports only ASCII values. For this example, we will use the sigfind tool from TSK. The hex signature is stored on the disk in little-endian ordering, so you may need to configure your tool appropriately or reverse the order of the signature when you input it (i.e. use 0x53ef). The output from sigfind is shown here (split up by my commentary):

```
# sigfind -o 56 -1 ef53 disk-8.dd
Block size: 512 Offset: 56
Block: 298661 (-)
Block: 315677 (+17016)
Block: 353313 (+37636)
Block: 377550 (+24237)
```

The sigfind tool prints the sector where the signature was found and the distance from the previous hit. These distances are not powers of two, and they are not consistently spaced. Therefore we will not bother with them until later (an automated tool would probably examine them, though). We do, however, have some interesting data later in the output.

```
[REMOVED]
Block: 2056322 (+274327)
Block: 2072706 (+16384)
Block: 2105474 (+32768)
Block: 2138242 (+32768)
Block: 2171010 (+32768)
Block: 2203778 (+32768)
```

Notice that the last four entries are all the same distance apart, and the entry before those is 16,384 sectors away from the previous hit. All these distances are what we would expect between block groups. Therefore our initial hypothesis is that the first superblock is in sector 2,056,322, and backup copies exist in sectors 2,072,706, 2,105,474 and so on. There are probably 16,384 sectors per block group, and the sparse superblock feature is being used so that not all groups have a superblock.

To test this hypothesis, we extract 1,024 bytes starting at sector 2,056,322. We apply the superblock data structure and examine the various values. We see that the block size is 1,024 bytes and that the sparse superblock feature is enabled. There are a total of 104,422 blocks in the file system and 8,192 blocks per group. Therefore, the backup copy of the superblock should be 16,384 sectors away (because there are two sectors per block), which is what we saw.

The final test is to determine if the superblock in sector 2,056,322 is the first one of the file system or if it is a backup copy. The superblock has a field that identifies which block group it is part of, and it has a value of 0. Similarly, the superblock in sector 2,072,706 has a value of 1. Therefore, we can assume that the file system starts in sector 2,056,320 (2 before the superblock) and that it extends until sector 2,265,164.

Note that you may be inclined to simply compare the different superblocks to determine which are the same so that you can group them as backup copies. Unfortunately, this will not work because the backup copies are not updated as frequently as the primary copy. The primary copy contains temporal data and dirty status flags, and those values are not updated on backup copies. Further, there is the value that shows which block group the superblock is in, so no two backup copies should be identical.

The previous example was very clean and nice because it was for the /boot partition, which does not have many updates. The next set of hits is not as clean, though. Notice that the next hit is two sectors after where we calculated the previous file system should end.

```
Block: 2265167 (+61389)
Block: 2265733 (+566)
Block: 2265985 (+252)
Block: 2266183 (+198)
Block: 2266357 (+174)
Block: 2266457 (+100)
[REMOVED]
```

Based on the location of sector 2,265,167 relative to the end of the previous partition, we would think that this could be the start of a new file system. On the other hand, the hits that follow it are not spaced as though they were backup copies, and there are over 200 of these entries, many having only 20 sectors in between them. So we may be inclined to ignore these hits. Let's skip a couple of hundred entries and move on.

```
[REMOVED]
Block: 2278273 (+2800)
Block: 2281551 (+3278)
Block: 2282617 (+1066)
Block: 2314319 (+31702)
Block: 2347087 (+32768)
Block: 2379855 (+32768)
Block: 2412623 (+32768)
```

Now we see hits that have spacing that is expected for backup copies. When we examine the contents of sector 2,314,319 we see that it is Ext3 with a 1,024-byte block size and 8,192 blocks per group. We also notice that it reports to be from block group 3. Therefore, block group 0 must have started 49,152 sectors ago, which is sector 2,265,167 and the one that comes right after the end of the previous file system.

The reason that we had hundreds of hits for the superblock signature was because there were copies of the primary superblock inside the file system journal file, which is located at the beginning of the file system. We will see at the end of the chapter that Ext3 will record all superblock updates and the first two hundred superblocks were copies that were saved to the journal. We can see this scenario in Figure 14.4. It shows some false hits at the start and end of the disk. We also see a lot of sectors that have the signature value in the start of the second file system, which is where the journal is located.

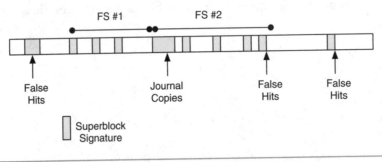

**Figure 14.4**   Hits where the superblock signature was found, including many hits in the journal.

In this scenario, we were able to use the magic value in the superblock to find the locations of ExtX in a disk. The extra copies of the superblock in the file system journal makes this process more tedious to find the start of the file system, but it means that there are more backup copies in case there is major disk failure.

## CONTENT CATEGORY

The content category of data includes file and directory contents. This section describes the ExtX content category of data and how to analyze it.

## OVERVIEW

ExtX uses blocks as its data unit and a *block* is a group of consecutive sectors. It is similar to a cluster in FAT or NTFS. This section describes block sizes and addresses as well as how to determine their allocation status.

### Blocks

An ExtX block can be 1,024; 2,048; or 4,096 bytes, and the size is given in the superblock. If you are reading this chapter in parallel with Chapter 15, you might have noticed references to fragments. UFS, on which ExtX is based, breaks a block into fragments. The Linux code for ExtX does not support this, although there is a field in the superblock that can be used to document the fragment size. As there are no major systems that support fragments, it is unknown how they should be handled, so this book assumes that the fragment size is the same as a block size.

All blocks are given an address, starting with 0, and block 0 is located in the first sector of the file system. All blocks belong to a block group, except in cases where the superblock has defined a reserved area at the beginning of the file system. In that case, the reserved blocks do not belong to a group, and group 0 starts immediately following the reserved blocks. To determine the group to which a block belongs, we use the following calculation (using the number of blocks per group, which is given in the superblock):

```
group = (block - FIRST_DATA_BLOCK) / BLOCKS_PER_GROUP
```

For example, if there is no reserved area and there are 32,768 blocks per group, block 60,000 would be part of group 1.

### Allocation Status

The allocation status of a block is determined by the group's block bitmap, the location of which is given in the group descriptor. The block bitmap will have a full block allocated to it, and each bit corresponds to a block in the group. To determine which bit corresponds to a given block, we need to first determine the block's address relative to the start of the group. This can be thought of as the block's *logical group address*. The calculation for determining the first block in a group is a variation of the previous one.

```
first_block = group * BLOCKS_PER_GROUP + FIRST_DATA_BLOCK
```

Next, we subtract the block's address from the address of the first block in the group. For example, the base for group 1 in our example is 32,768, so block 60,000 is at a bit offset of 27,232. It would, therefore, be in byte 3,404 of the bitmap. An example of an ExtX bitmap is given in the next chapter.

The tools that Linux uses to create the file system will create the block group sizes such that the block bitmap needs only one block. Therefore, all file systems with a 4,096-byte block will, by default, have 32,768 blocks per group. The user can override this value when the file system is created, and other applications could use a different algorithm.

Unlike NTFS, not every allocated block is allocated to a file. There are many allocated blocks that contain administrative file system data and are not allocated to a file. Examples include the superblocks, group descriptor tables, the bitmaps for the blocks and inodes, and the inode tables.

The dstat tool in TSK will show the allocation status of a block and the block group to which it belongs. An example from our image is shown here:

```
# dstat -f linux-ext3 ext3.dd 14380
Block: 14380
Allocated
Group: 0
```

We see that block 14,380 is located in block group 0 and that it is allocated. This block will be allocated by the inode in our example in the "Metadata" section.

## ALLOCATION ALGORITHMS

With Linux, allocation of blocks is done on a group basis, but other OSes could choose a different method. When a block is allocated to an inode, Linux will use a first-available strategy and try to allocate a block in the same group as the inode. The goal of this is to reduce the amount of movement that a disk head has to make when it reads the file. If an existing file is being made larger, Linux will first try a next-available strategy and look at the blocks after the end of the current file. There is a compatible file system feature that will preallocate blocks for directories so that they will not become fragmented when they need additional blocks.

If there is no more space in the group, a block in a different group will be used. Note that this is application-specific, and not every OS uses this technique for allocation. For example, an OS could just as easily ignore groups and use a first available algorithm that starts at the beginning of the file system instead of at the beginning of a specific block group.

ExtX will typically prevent a user from allocating every block in the file system. The superblock has a value that defines how many blocks should be reserved for a specific user, typically the root user. When the number of available blocks drops to the minimum value, normal users are no longer allowed to create files, but the administrator can still login to clean the system. This is application-specific, though, and not all OSes may enforce this policy.

When Linux writes data to a block, it zeros out the unused bytes. Therefore, there should not be any data in the slack space of the last file block.

## ANALYSIS TECHNIQUES

When analyzing the content category of ExtX, we need to be able to locate any block, read its contents, and determine its allocation status. Locating a given block is easy because the first block starts in the first sector of the file system, and the block size is given in the superblock.

Determining the allocation status of any block is a three-step process. First, we must determine to which block group the block belongs. Next, we locate the group's entry in the group descriptor table and determine where its block bitmap is stored. Lastly, we process the block bitmap and examine the bit associated with the block in question. If the bit is set, then the block is allocated.

If we wanted to extract all unallocated blocks from the file system, we would sequentially go through each entry in the group descriptor table. For each entry we would load the block bitmap and search it for 0s. Any block whose bit is a 0 would be extracted. For ExtX, the superblocks, group descriptors, inode tables, and bitmaps are all allocated data even though they are not allocated to a file. If there are reserved sectors at the beginning of the file system, it is less clear what their allocation status should be because there is no bitmap entry for them. This will likely be tool-dependent.

## ANALYSIS CONSIDERATIONS

The allocation algorithms of the ExtX file systems might help when it comes to recovering deleted content. If the OS allocated blocks in the same group as the inode, searches can generally be restricted to the group instead of to the entire file system. For example, if you are looking for a file that had a keyword in it and you know of which group the file was a member, the group can be searched for evidence. This is much faster than searching the entire file system. This should not be the only method of searching, though, because other copies of the file may exist in other groups and the OS might not have allocated blocks in the same group as the inode. The group location can be determined using the output of fsstat in TSK, as we previously saw, and other tools may give the same information.

The time it takes to have deleted data overwritten will be different with ExtX than with NTFS or FAT. Data in groups that already have a lot of data and little activity will not be overwritten as fast as data in groups that have a lot of write activity. With NTFS and FAT, any cluster had the same chances of being over written; whereas in ExtX it depends on in which group a block is located.

## ANALYSIS SCENARIO

Consider a scenario where we need to read the contents of the last block in the file system because that is where a rootkit saves its password (I am actually not aware of a rootkit that does this, but we will ignore that). This process requires us to determine the block size and the number of blocks in the file system. Both of these are in the superblock. The trick is that we have only a hex editor that works in 512-byte sectors.

We read the superblock, which is in sector 2 of the file system. The block size is located in bytes 24 to 27, which have the value 2. The block size is stored as the number of bit places that we need to shift the number 1024 (0x0400), and our file system requires us to shift it twice to the left. Shifting it once gives 2048 (0x0800), and shifting it a second time gives 4096 (0x1000). If you did not follow that, remember that 0x4 is 0100 in binary, and 0x8 is 1000 in binary. When we shifted 0x400 by 1 to the left, the bit in 0x4 moved to form 0x8.

Next, we need to determine the last block in the file system. This is stored in bytes 4 to 7 and requires no fancy calculations. There are 512,064 blocks in the file system, which means that we need to seek ahead 512,063 blocks, and each block is 4,096 bytes, or eight sectors. Therefore, we need to view sectors 4,096,504 to 4,096,511 in our hex editor.

In this scenario, we performed the basic process of locating where a specific block is located. Most analysis tools will do this for you, but it is a common process, and it is useful to know what needs to occur.

## METADATA CATEGORY

The metadata category includes the data that describe a file or directory. This section describes where the data are stored and how to analyze them.

## OVERVIEW

In ExtX, a file's primary metadata is stored in an inode data structure. Additional metadata may be stored in extended attributes. We will discuss each of these data structures in this section.

### Inodes

All ExtX inodes are the same size, which can be defined in the superblock. One inode is allocated to every file and directory, and each inode has an address, starting with 1. A set of inodes, whose size is given in the superblock, is assigned to each block group. The inodes in each group are stored in a table, whose location is given in the group descriptor. Given an inode address, its group can be determined with the following calculation:

```
group = (inode - 1) / INODES_PER_GROUP
```

Inodes 1 to 10 are typically reserved and should be in an allocated state. The superblock has the value of the first non-reserved inode. Of the reserved inodes, only number 2 has a specific function, and it is used for the root directory. Inode 1 keeps track of bad blocks, but it does not have any special status in the Linux kernel. The journal typically uses inode 8, but this can be redefined in the superblock. The first user file is typically allocated in inode 11, and this is frequently used for the lost+found directory. File system consistency checkers use the lost+found directory, and any inode that is allocated but does not have a file name pointing to it is added to this directory with a new name.

Each inode has a static number of fields, and additional information might be stored in extended attributes and indirect block pointers, which will be discussed later in this section. The allocation status of an inode is determined using the inode bitmap, whose location is given in the group descriptor.

An inode contains the file's size, ownership, and temporal information. The size value in newer versions of ExtX is 64 bits, but older versions had only 32 bits and therefore could not handle files over 4GB. Newer versions utilize an unused field for the upper 32 bits of the size value and set a read-only compatible feature flag when a large file exists.

"Ownership" information is stored using the user and group ID. In Unix, every user is assigned a user ID, and the /etc/passwd file is used to translate the user ID to a user name. Similarly, the /etc/groups file is used to translate the group ID to a group name. Note that the user ID in the inode does not necessarily mean that the user created the file. The user and group IDs in the inode can be changed at any time using the chown

and `chgrp` commands. Also note that a user name does not have to exist in /etc/
password for every user ID. The standard system tools will simply show the ID if it
cannot translate it to a name.

For temporal information, the inode contains times for the last access, modification,
change, and deletion. The times are stored as the number of seconds since January 1,
1970 UTC. The last modified, accessed, and changed times also exist in UFS and are frequently referred to as MAC times. The last accessed time, or A-time, corresponds to the
time that the file content was last accessed. The last modified time, or M-time, corresponds to the time that the file content was last modified, and the last changed time, or
C-time, corresponds to when the file metadata was last changed. When a file is created,
all three values are typically set to the current time. The deletion, or D-time, corresponds
to when the file was deleted. In Linux and other Unix systems, it is fairly easy to assign an
arbitrary M- and A-time to a file using the `touch` command. The `touch` command allows
a user to assign any value to the M- and A-time, but the C-time is updated during
the process.

The type of the file is stored in the mode field, which also contains basic permission
values. Everything is a file in Unix, and therefore there are many file types. A normal file
that a user creates is called a regular file, and a directory is, intuitively, called a directory.
Beyond that, the names become less intuitive to non-Unix people, and the "files" do not
allocate any blocks. The files are simply there as a name for programs to use when referring to hardware devices or other communication services.

Hardware devices are assigned one or more file names, and each will have a file type
of a block or a character device. A *block device* is used for devices that operate on only
block-sized chunks of data, such as hard disks, for example. As we saw in Chapter 2,
"Computer Foundations," to read any data from a hard disk, you need to read at least
512 bytes. If an application reads less than a sector from a block device, then the OS will
read the needed sectors and return only what the application requested. On the other
hand, a *character device*, also called a raw device, is used for devices that do not need to
operate in blocks, such as keyboards. A block device typically also has a character device
created for it, but an error is generated if it is used to read and write data using non-
block sized chunks. The inode space that usually stores information about what blocks
has been allocated to a file are used to store device identifier information.

Other file types are used to send data between processes. A *FIFO*, also called a named
pipe, provides one-way data transmission between two or more processes. A process can
open the file and receive data that has been written to it by another process. The data is
stored in kernel memory and not on disk. If two-way communication is needed between
processes, a Unix socket is used. A *Unix socket* is a file that processes open using special
functions, and it allows bi-directional communication. As with named pipes, the data is

not written to disk. The last type of file is a symbolic link, which is a soft link. Symbolic links will be discussed more in the "File Name Category" section, but they provide a shortcut to another file or directory.

In addition to the file type, the mode field contains basic permissions. These permissions allow read, write, and execute commands for the owner, group, or all users. For example, if the permissions allow group read access and deny access to all other users, only users in the group whose ID is stored in the inode can read the file. The group members can be determined using the /etc/groups file. This is of course, nonessential data because an OS might not enforce the permissions.

Lastly, the mode field identifies special properties that a file or directory may have. If the "sticky bit" is set on an executable file, then some of the process data will remain in memory after the process ends. When it is set on a directory, only the owner of a file can delete the directory contents. When the *set user ID* (SUID) and *set group ID* (SGID) bits are set for an executable, the process takes on the user and group identifies from the file instead of the user that actually started the process. This allows a non-privileged user to execute specific programs as a privileged user. When the SGID bit is set on a directory, all files in the directory are assigned the same group ID as the directory.

Each inode contains a link count value that is equal to the number of file names that point to the inode. When this value equals 0 and no process has the file open, the inode will be unallocated. When the value equals 0 and a process does have it open, it becomes an orphan inode and will be deleted when the process closes it. The inode also has a generation ID value, which is used by the *Network File System* (NFS) to determine when a new file has been allocated. When the inode is allocated to a new file, this value changes and allows the server to know that a new file exists. This is similar to the sequence number we saw in NTFS. Linux assigns this value with an event counter, and it could potentially be used to determine the order of file allocation.

For the data structure layout and an example of an inode, refer to the next chapter.

### Block Pointers

ExtX, like UFS, was designed for efficiency of small files. Therefore, each inode can store the addresses of the first 12 blocks that a file has allocated. These are called direct pointers. If a file needs more than 12 blocks, a block is allocated to store the remaining addresses. The pointer to the block is called an indirect block pointer. The addresses in the block are all four bytes, and the total number in each block is based on the block size. The indirect block pointer is stored in the inode.

If a file has more blocks than can fit in the 12 direct pointers and the indirect block, a double indirect block is used. A double indirect block is when the inode points to a block that contains a list of single indirect block pointers, each of which point to blocks that contain a list of direct pointers. Lastly, if a file needs still more space, it can use a triple indirect block pointer. A triple indirect block contains addresses of double indirect blocks, which contain addresses of single indirect blocks. The graphical representation of each of these types of data structures can be found in Figure 14.5. Each inode contains 12 direct pointers, one single indirect pointer, one double indirect block pointer, and one triple indirect pointer.

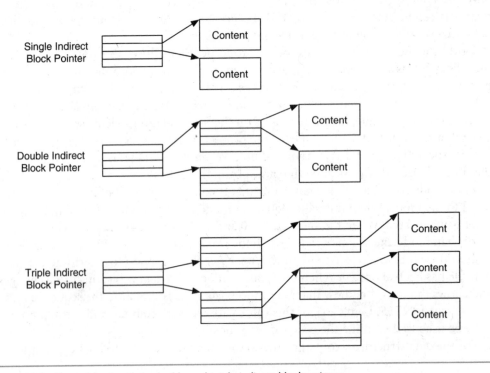

**Figure 14.5** Examples of a single, double, and triple indirect block pointer.

ExtX allows a file to have sparse blocks. Sparse blocks exist when the original block was either undefined or all zeros. Undefined blocks exist because the program that created the file forced the file to be a specific size but never wrote data to some parts. Instead of allocating a block of all 0s, the OS will place the address 0 in the block pointer. Analysis tools and the OS should process this as a block of all 0s.

### Attributes

Each inode has attributes, which are described in the flags field, but they may not be actually supported by the current OS. Some of the attributes are experimental, and others are no longer supported by Linux. The supported attributes include one that does not update the A-time of files and directories. Another is used to identify files that should be written to disk as soon as its data changes instead of being cached. Two attributes are for security, and one makes files append only so that data cannot be removed from them, and the other makes files immutable so that data cannot be added or changed. Lastly, the dump attribute identifies files that should not be saved when the dump command is used to backup files.

The attributes that are not generally supported at the time of this writing include secure deletion, compression, and undelete. Secure deletion would wipe the blocks associated with a file, and undelete would make a backup copy of the file when it was deleted so that it could be recovered. Linux kernels that have been built with experimental patches could use some of these attributes.

In addition to the attributes just described, a file also may have extended attributes. With Linux, extended attributes can be used only when the file system has been mounted with the user_xattr option and when the kernel has support for them, which was added in version 2.4. You can check if the file system was, by default, mounted with the user_xattr option by looking in the /etc/fstab file. If a file system has extended attributes, a compatible feature flag should be set.

An extended attribute is a list of name and value pairs. A user can create any pair, such as "user.source = http://www.digital-evidence.org," using the setfattr command. In this case, user is the name space, and there are also trusted and security name spaces. The extended attributes are stored in a block that has been allocated to the file. If more than one file has the same extended attributes, they will share the same block. The block lists all of the name and value pairs. The 2.6 Linux kernel requires that the extended attributes be stored in one block.

One of the ways that the OS uses the extended attributes is for POSIX *access control lists* (ACL). ACLs are a more advanced method of restricting access to a file than what normally exists with ExtX. With an ACL, selected users can be allowed access instead of having to use Unix groups. The ACL information is stored in an extended attribute. With Linux, a user sets the ACL with the setfacl command, and the file system needs to be mounted with the acl option. The data structures and an example of extended attributes can be found in the next chapter.

## Example Image

To show sample data that can come from a file, I have included the output from running istat on a file in our example file system image. This inode is processed in the next chapter, but here is the nicely formatted summary:

```
# istat -f linux-ext3 ext3.dd 16
inode: 16
Allocated
Group: 0
Generation Id: 199922874
uid / gid: 500 / 500
mode: -rw-r--r--
size: 10240000
num of links: 1

Inode Times:
Accessed:        Fri Aug  1 06:32:13 2003
File Modified:   Fri Aug  1 06:24:01 2003
Inode Modified:  Fri Aug  1 06:25:58 2003

Direct Blocks:
14380 14381 14382 14383 14384 14385 14386 14387
14388 14389 14390 14391 14393 14394 14395 14396
[REMOVED]
16880 16881 16882 16883

Indirect Blocks:
14392 15417 15418 16443
```

We can see that the file is 10 MB, and it required four indirect block pointers to point to all the allocated blocks. This output shows us the permissions and file type as well as the MAC times.

## ALLOCATION ALGORITHMS

This section discusses my observations and the Linux kernel source code with respect to how ExtX metadata is allocated. Another OS or a custom Linux kernel could use different allocation algorithms. These results are from a standard Fedora Core 2 system.

### Inode Allocation

When a new inode is needed for a file or directory, the first consideration that Linux makes is the block group in which the inode should exist. If the inode is for a non-directory, Linux allocates an inode in the same block group as the parent directory. This helps to ensure that all information for a directory is in the same general area. If the group has no free inodes or free blocks, a search is performed for another group. Linux uses a quadratic hash to select a random group. The quadratic hash process selects groups by starting with the current block group and adding powers of 2 to it (1, 2, 4, 8, 16, etc.). If the selected group has a free inode, it is used. If the process fails to find a group with a free inode, a linear search is done starting with the current group. Both processes use a first available search to find an available inode.

If the inode is for a directory, the goal is to place it in a group that has not been used much. This helps ensure that all groups are equally used. The first part of this search process is to calculate the average number of free inodes and free blocks per group. This is calculated by using the total number of free inodes and blocks, which are stored in the superblock. Linux then searches each of the groups, starting with 0, and uses the first one whose free inode and block counts are less than the averages. If no group is found with both values that are less than average, the group with the smallest number of directories and largest number of free inodes is used. Both of these values are stored in the group descriptors.

When an inode is allocated, its contents are cleared, and the M-time, A-time, and C-time are set to the current time. The D-time is set to 0. The link count, which identifies how many file names are pointing to the inode is set to 1 for the file name. Directories will have a link count of 2 because of the '.' entry inside of the directory. Linux also assigns the generation field with the current value of a counter.

When a file is deleted in Linux, the link value in the inode is decremented by one. If the link count becomes zero, then it is unallocated. If a process still has the file open, then it becomes an *orphan file* and it is added to a list in the superblock. When the process closes the file or when the system is rebooted, the inode will be deallocated.

Ext2 and Ext3 handle file deletion differently. Ext3 sets the file size to 0 and wipes the block pointers in the inode and in the indirect blocks. Ext2, on the other hand, does not wipe these values, which makes file recovery easier. The M-time, C-time, and D-time are also updated to reflect the time of deletion. If the file was deleted because it was moved to a different volume, its A-time also will be set to when the content was read. This could help to distinguish between a delete and a move.

### Time Value Updating

ExtX inodes have four temporal values, and we also need to discuss when they are updated. In my testing, Linux updates the A-time when the content of the file or directory is read. For a file, this occurs when a process reads the contents, when the file is copied, and when the file is moved to a new volume. If the move is to the same volume, the content does not move, and therefore this time does not change. For a directory, the

A-time is updated when a directory listing is done on its contents or when a file or subdirectory is opened. As we will later see, the contents of a directory's blocks are the names of the files in the directory.

The M-time corresponds to the last file modification, and the time is updated when the content of a file or directory changes. For files, this occurs when any of the file content changes. For directories, this occurs when a file is created or deleted inside of it. When a file is moved, the M-time on the destination file is the same as the original because the file content did not change during the move. When a file is copied, the M-time on the destination file is updated to reflect the current time because it is considered new file content. Note that when a file is moved to a network attached drive, the M-time on the destination file might have an updated time because the network server considers it a new file.

The C-time corresponds to the last inode change, and this occurs when the metadata for a file or directory changes. This can occur when a file or directory is created and when the permissions or ownership of a file are changed. It also occurs when the content of a file or directory changes. If a file is moved then the C-time of the file will be updated. The D-time corresponds to when a file was deleted, and it is set only when a file has been deleted. It is cleared when the inode is allocated. Many deleted files have the M- and C-times equal to the D-time.

In summary, when a file is created then the file's M-, A-, and C-times are updated to the time of creation, the D-time is set to 0, and the parent directory's M- and C-times are updated. When a file is copied the original file and parent directory have an updated A-time; the destination file has new M-, A-, and C-times; and the destination parent directory has new M- and C-times. When a file is moved, the parent directory of the original file has updated M-, A-, and C-times, the parent directory of the destination file has updated M- and C-times, and the destination file has the same M- and A-times as the original and an updated C-time. If the move is inside of the same volume, the same inode will be used, but if the move is to a new volume, the source inode will be unallocated and the M-, A-, C-, and D-times will be updated.

## ANALYSIS TECHNIQUES

Analysis of the metadata category of data involves locating and processing the data structures that store file and directory metadata so that we can collect more details about a given file. With ExtX, this involves locating and processing the inode data structures. To locate a specific inode, we need to first determine which block group it is part of. Next, we process the group descriptor for that group and locate the group's inode table. Lastly, we identify which entry in the table is for our inode and process it.

With the exception of the indirect block pointers and extended attributes, the inode data structure is self-contained and stores all the metadata. To identify the blocks that are allocated to a file or directory, we read the 12 direct block pointers. If the file has more blocks allocated, then we process the single, double, and triple indirect block pointers, which point to blocks that contain a list of block addresses where content is stored. If the block pointer has an address of 0, the file is sparse, and a block was not allocated for that part of the file because it would have been filled with 0s.

To determine the allocation status of an inode, we examine the inode bitmap for the group. The address of the bitmap is given in the group descriptor. If the corresponding bit is a 1, the inode is allocated.

It is sometimes useful to examine the unallocated inode entries because they contain temporal data about when the file was deleted. With an Ext3 file system, deleted file names will point to their inode entries, but Ext2 deletes the link. Even with Ext3, the file names may be overwritten before the inode data is. Therefore, in both cases we need to examine each unallocated inode entry to find data about all deleted files. We can typically determine if an unallocated inode entry has been used if some of its values are non-zero.

The extended attributes could contain important data associated with the file. We locate them by using the pointer in the inode and processing the associated block. The block has a collection of name and value pairs that can be assigned by a user.

## ANALYSIS CONSIDERATIONS

The allocation strategies that are used by UFS-based file systems might allow an unallocated inode entry to exist for a longer amount of time if it is in a group with little activity. The M-, C-, and D-time values also may show when the file was deleted.

In Linux, and most Unix systems, a user can easily set the M- and A-times by using the touch command, so finding independent sources of temporal information, such as logs or network packets, can be useful when assessing the reliability of the times on an allocated file. Also the time values are stored with respect to UTC, so your analysis tool needs to know the time zone where the computer was located so that the time values that it shows are accurate.

Slack space is an operating system-dependent feature, but Linux will write 0s to the unused bytes of a block. Therefore, data from deleted files will exist only in unallocated blocks. You can check if your search tools will look at the slack space of an Ext3 file system by using the test images from the *Digital Forensic Tool Testing* (DFTT) site [Carrier 2003].

Unfortunately, the file size and allocated blocks will probably be wiped from unallocated inode entries, so file recovery will need to rely on application level techniques. Further, the indirect block pointers could be located in between the blocks with content, so carving tools should not, when possible, include the indirect block pointers in the final file. You may be able to identify indirect block pointers because they contain a list of 4-byte addresses that could have increasing or similar values. An investigator can use the allocation strategy to her benefit when carving data because she can carve only the unallocated data from a specific block group instead of the full file system if she is targeting a specific file or directory.

If you encounter an ExtX with a deleted file whose size and block pointers were not wiped, special considerations must be made with respect to indirect block pointers. If the indirect block pointers point to blocks that have been reallocated, the block contents may no longer contain a list of block addresses, or the address may be for a different file.

The extended attributes of a file also should be examined for possible evidence. Test if your analysis tools include those values during a keyword search. These are similar to alternate data streams in NTFS, but their size is much smaller.

One file-hiding method is to have a process open a file for reading or writing and then delete the file name. In this case, the link count of the inode is 0, but it is not unallocated. When this occurs, the kernel should add the orphan inode to a list in the superblock, and it should be examined during an investigation. With TSK, you can find these files by looking at the `fsstat` output.

## ANALYSIS SCENARIO

While investigating a Linux incident, a directory with a suspicious name is found, and we are trying to determine which user account created the files inside of it. A file's inode contains the User ID of the owner, and we use the `/etc/passwd` file to correlate the ID with an actual name.

As we are translating some of the User ID values, we find some that do not exist in the password file. There are two scenarios that cause this. One is when a user account was created during the incident, the files were created, and then the account was deleted. The second scenario is when the files came from an archive file, such as `tar`, and it saved the User ID from the computer where the archive file was created. Therefore, there was never a user with that ID on the computer being investigated.

We test the first theory by searching the unallocated blocks of the file system that contains the `/etc/` directory for a deleted copy of the password file. For our search term, we copy a string from the current file. This could result in us finding a version of the file with the new user account. This search is unsuccessful.

To test the second theory, we search the system for tar files that may contain the files in question. For an actual system where the second scenario occurred, refer to the Forensic Challenge [Honeynet Project 2001] that was released by the Honeynet Project in 2001. The challenge is of a compromised Linux system, and it contains files with User IDs that are not in the password file. When a timeline of the system is created in TSK, we get the following values:

```
[REMOVED]
Wed Nov 08 2000 08:51:56
..c -/-rwxr-xr-x 1010      users     /usr/man/.Ci/ /Anap
..c -/-rwxr-xr-x 1010      users     /usr/man/.Ci/bx
Wed Nov 08 2000 08:52:09
m.c l/lrwxrwxrwx root       root      /.bash_history -> /dev/null
m.c l/lrwxrwxrwx root       root      /root/.bash_history -> /dev/null
[REMOVED]
```

The two files in /usr/man/.Ci have a changed time of 08:51:56, and their User ID is 1010. Normally, the timeline tool translates the ID to the user name, as you can see in the bottom two entries where the User ID of 0 is translated to root. The search of our system finds a tar file that contains the suspicious directory. The User ID of a file can be changed using the chown command, and even if the ID exists in the password file, there is no proof that it is the user who created the file. If we want to know who created the suspicious named directory, we should examine the permissions of its parent directory. In this case, the parent directory is /usr/local/, and it is owned by root, and only it has write permissions. This is a common setup, so we will assume that the attacker did not change the permissions after he created the directory. This means that the attacker likely had access to the root account.

## FILE NAME CATEGORY

The file name category of data includes the data structures that store the name of each file and directory. This section describes where the data are stored and how to analyze them.

### OVERVIEW

ExtX has several methods for assigning names to a file or directory, and this section examines three of them. The first subsection looks at directory entries, which are the basic data structure used to assign names. We next look at hard and soft links and then hash trees.

## Directory Entries

An ExtX directory is just like a regular file except that it has a special type value in its inode. Directories allocate blocks that will contain a list of directory entry data structures. A *directory entry* is a simple data structure that contains the file name and the inode address where the file's metadata can be found. The size of the directory corresponds to the number of blocks that it has allocated and is irrelevant to how many files actually exist.

Every directory starts off with directory entries for the '.' and '..' directories, which are for the current and parent directory. Following them are entries for every file and subdirectory in the directory. The root directory is always located in inode 2.

A directory entry has a dynamic length because the file name can be anywhere from 1 to 255 characters long. Therefore, the data structure has a field that identifies how long the name is and where the next directory entry can be found. The length of the entry is rounded up to a multiple of four. We can see this in Figure 14.6(A), where we have three files in a directory. The first two entries are for '.' and '..' and the last entry points to the end of the allocated block. The space after the c.txt file is unused.

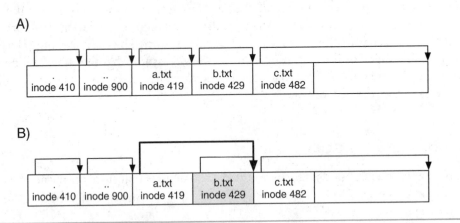

**Figure 14.6**   Directory entries contain the file name and inode. They also contain a pointer to the next entry. Unused entries are skipped over by increasing the pointer of the previous entry.

When a file or directory is deleted, its name needs to be modified so that the OS does not print it. The OS hides a directory entry by increasing the record length of the previous directory entry so that it points to the entry after the one being hidden. We can see this in Figure 14.6(B) where the `b.txt` file was deleted and the pointer in `a.txt` was incremented to point to `c.txt`. A directory listing would skip over it, but the data still exists.

When a new entry is created, the OS examines each existing entry and compares its record length with the name length. Each directory entry has eight bytes of static fields in addition to the name, so the minimum record length can be determined by adding eight to the name length and rounding up to a multiple of four. If the record length of an entry is larger than it needs to be and the difference is more than the size of the entry being added, the entry is placed in the unused space. For example, consider a new directory that has only a '.' and '..' entries in a 4,096-byte block. There will be two entries with the values given in Table 14.1.

**Table 14.1**   Directory entry values for a new directory.

| Name | Name Length | Record Length |
|------|-------------|---------------|
| . | 1 | 12 |
| .. | 2 | 4,084 |

The final '..' entry has a record length of 4,084 bytes because it needs to point to the end of the block, but it needs only 12 bytes. Therefore, the new entry will be added 12 bytes after the start of the '..' entry, and the record length of the new entry will point to the end of the block. The new entries would have the fields given in Table 14.2.

**Table 14.2**   Directory entry values after creating a new file.

| Name | Name Length | Record Length |
|------|-------------|---------------|
| . | 1 | 12 |
| .. | 2 | 12 |
| File1.dat | 8 | 4,072 |

There are actually two versions of directory entry structures. An older version has only the name, inode address, and length values. The updated version uses one of the bytes in the file name length field and uses it to store the file type, such as file, directory, or character device. We will later see how this can be used to detect when an inode has been reallocated since a file name was deleted. The data structures of both types of directory entries are given in the next chapter.

Here is the output of running fls on a directory in our file system image. It shows one deleted file, the file with the "*" before it. The first column shows the file type according to the directory entry and then according to the inode. Notice that the types for the deleted file are still the same, which means that the inode may not have been reallocated yet.

```
# fls -f linux-ext3 -a ext3.dd 69457
d/d 69457:          .
d/d 53248:          ..
r/r 69458:          abcdefg.txt
r/r * 69459:        file two.dat
d/d 69460:          subdir1
r/r 69461:          RSTUVWXY
```

### Links and Mount Points

ExtX provides both hard and soft links so that users can define multiple names for a file or directory. A hard link is an additional name for a file or directory in the same file system. After a hard link is created, you will not be able to tell if it is the original name or a link. To make a hard link, the OS allocates a new directory entry and points it to the original inode. The link count in the inode is incremented by one to account for the new name. A file will not be deleted until all its hard links are deleted.

Note that the '.' and '..' entries in each directory are hard links to the current and parent directory. Therefore, the link count for a directory is equal to at least two plus the number of subdirectories it has.

Soft links are also a second name for a file or directory, but they can span different file systems. The OS creates a soft link using a symbolic link, which is a special type of file. The full path of the destination file or directory is stored in either blocks allocated to the file or in the inode if the path is less than 60 characters long. The next chapter shows example data structures that contain symbolic links.

We can see an example of hard and soft links in Figure 14.7. Part A shows a hard link named hardlink.txt that points to the file1.txt file. Part B shows a soft link to the same file, but this time there is another level of indirection. softlink.txt has its own inode that contains the path of the file. Notice that in Part B both inodes have a link count of one. In reality, the symbolic link would store the /file1.txt address in its block pointers because the path is shorter than 60 characters.

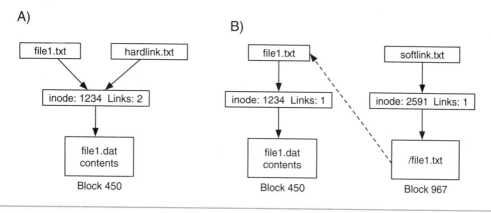

**Figure 14.7** An example of A) a hard link and B) a soft link to the 'file1.txt' file.

In Unix, directories can be used for both storing files and volume mount points, as we discussed in Chapter 4. Consider a directory dir1 that is in a file system named FS1. If file system FS2 is mounted on the dir1 directory, when a user changes into that directory and lists the contents, the files from FS2 are shown. Even if the dir1 directory has its own files in FS1, they will not be shown when FS2 is mounted on it. We can see this in Figure 14.8, where part A shows the three pictures in dir1 and part B shows that dir1 now contains the three files in the root directory of volume FS2.

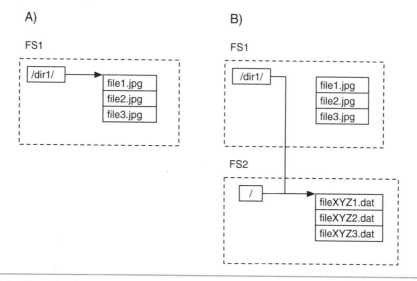

**Figure 14.8** Example where a directory in FS1 contains three files, but when FS2 is mounted on the directory, they are not seen.

For investigators, this means that you need to know where file systems were mounted. If you are looking for a specific file, you might need to reference several file systems before you find the file because different directories could have been on different volumes. Many current post-mortem investigation tools do not show volumes at their mount point, and therefore you will need to determine which volume should be there. On the plus side, because the tools do not show volumes at their mount points, you can see the directory contents of the mount points. One hiding technique is to create files in a directory and then mount a volume on the directory so that a casual observer would not notice them.

## Hash Trees

When the file system is created, the user can choose to use a hash tree to organize the files instead of the unsorted list that I just described. If a file system is using hash trees, then a compatible feature flag will be set in the superblock. The hash trees still use directory entry data structures, but they are in a sorted order.

The hash trees in ExtX are similar to the B-trees that were discussed in Chapter 11, "NTFS Concepts," so refer to that section for an overview of how trees are used in a directory. The major difference between hash and B-trees is that hash trees sort the files based on a hash of the file name and not based on the name itself. Note that there is also experimental support for B-Trees in ExtX that are like the NTFS B-Trees, but we do not discuss them in this chapter because they are not yet standard.

If a directory is using a hash tree, it will have multiple blocks and each will be a node in the tree. Each node contains the files whose hash value is in a given range. The first block of the directory is the root node, and it contains the '.' and '..' directory entries. The rest of the first block contains node descriptors, which contain a hash value and a block address. The OS uses the node descriptors to determine to which block it should jump for a given hash value.

We can see this in Figure 14.9 where we have several files in two leaves. The first block contains the header and node descriptors, and the second and third blocks contain the file directory entries. An OS that did not know about hash trees would process the entries in all the blocks without knowing that they were in a sorted order.

There can be up to three layers of nodes in a hash index tree. The data structures for the node descriptors and an actual directory are given in Chapter 15.

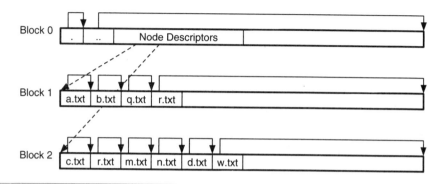

Block 0

. | .. | Node Descriptors

Block 1

a.txt | b.txt | q.txt | r.txt

Block 2

c.txt | r.txt | m.txt | n.txt | d.txt | w.txt

**Figure 14.9**   A directory with hash trees and two leaves. The tree uses directory entries so it can be processed as a normal directory.

## ALLOCATION ALGORITHMS

When a new file name is created, Linux uses a first-available strategy. The OS starts at the beginning of the directory and examines each directory entry. Using the name length, it calculates how long the entry needs to be. It compares that with the actual record length. If they are different, it assumes that either it is at the end of a block or that the record length was increased to cover a deleted entry. In either case, the OS tries to add the name in the unused area. If no unused areas exist that are large enough for the name, then the name is appended to the list. New blocks are added as needed, and they are wiped before use. Linux will not allow an entry to cross a block boundary. Other OSes could choose a different strategy. If hash trees are being used, the file is added to the block that corresponds to the file's hash value.

When a file is deleted, the record length of the previous entry is incremented so that it points to the entry after the one being deleted. That is the only action that places the entry in an unallocated status. Linux will clear the inode pointer in an Ext2 file system, but not an Ext3 file system. Unused entries are not rearranged to compress the size of a directory.

## ANALYSIS TECHNIQUES

Analysis of the file name category of data involves listing the names in a directory so that we can find a specific files or files that have a given pattern. The first step in this process is to locate the root directory, which is easy in ExtX because it is always located in inode 2. Directories are similar to files, except that they have a special type set in their inode. After locating the directory content, we process it as a sequence of directory entry data structures. To examine only the allocated names, we process a directory entry structure, jump ahead by its reported size, and process the next entry. This process repeats until the end of the block.

If we want to view unallocated file names as well, we ignore the reported size of the entry and calculate how long the entry should be and advance to that point. For example, if the last character of a name is in byte 34, we advance to byte 36. After we advance to the boundary, we apply the directory entry data structure and perform sanity checks to determine if the data could have been for a directory entry. If it is, it is processed, and if not, we advance four more bytes and test that location. This process eventually brings us to where the previous directory entry would have pointed us.

Figure 14.10 shows an example where we have two unallocated directory entries in between two allocated entries. There is unused space between each of the directory entries, so simply advancing to the next 4-byte boundary after each entry would not find the names.

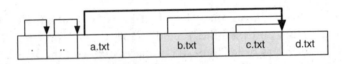

**Figure 14.10**   A list of directory entries where two unallocated names are in between two allocated names, and we must advance through the unused space to find the unallocated names.

The allocation status of a directory entry structure is determined based on whether it is pointed to by an allocated entry. The first two entries in each directory will always be allocated because they are for the '.' and '..' entries. When we find a file in which we are interested, we can look up its metadata using the inode address.

In some cases, we might want to search the file system for blocks that were previously used by a directory. To do so, we should examine the first 24 bytes of each block to determine if the '.' and '..' entries exist. If so, this block was the first block in a directory. Linux always allocates directory entries on block boundaries, so a more general search would examine the first bytes for any file name, not only '..'.

It might be possible to infer about the order in which files were deleted by using the pointer values. Figure 14.11 shows the six possible combinations of how three consecutive files could be deleted. The top of the figure gives the starting state where there are four allocated directory entries. The number below each block is the "address" of the entry, which is there to make it easier to describe each scenario. Each shaded block is an unallocated entry, and the number corresponds to the order in which it was deleted. For example, in the (A) scenario entry 1 was deleted first, and the length of entry 0 was increased to point entry 2. Entry 2 was then deleted, and the length of entry 0 was increased to point to entry 3. Lastly, entry 3 was deleted, and the length of entry 0 was increased to point to the entry after 3. The state shown (A) is unique among the other combinations of how those files can be deleted.

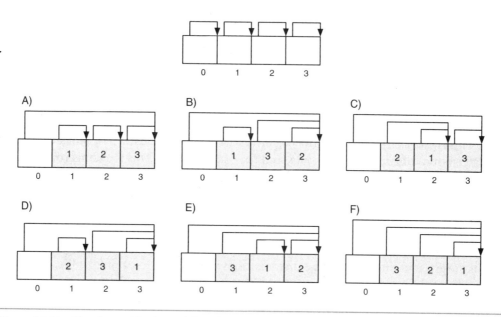

**Figure 14.11**    The six combinations of the relative order that three consecutive directory entries could be unallocated. Only the 1-3-2 and 2-3-1 sequences have the same final state.

If we look at the final states of the six scenarios, only (B) and (D) are the same. In both of these scenarios, we can still determine that the middle file was the last to be deleted. We will see an example of this analysis procedure in the following scenario section.

## ANALYSIS CONSIDERATIONS

Deleted file names are easy to locate in ExtX, and the Ext3 inode number is not cleared by Linux, so you might also be able to obtain temporal information about when the file name was deleted. In Linux, the directory entry structure will remain in the unallocated state until a new file is created whose name is the same length or smaller. Therefore, a file with a short name might not have its directory entry overwritten as quickly as a file whose name is long. Other OSes could use different allocation methods or even compact the directories to make them smaller. The `fsck` tool in Linux can repackage directories to make them smaller and remove the unused space.

When a deleted file name is found, care must be taken when analyzing it. If the file's inode has been reallocated, the metadata is no longer relevant to the deleted name. There is no easy method for determining if an inode has been reallocated since the file name was deleted. One method is to use the file type value in the directory entry and compare it with the type in the inode. If the directory entry type is for a directory and the inode has a regular file, it is likely that the inode has been reallocated. This is why the `fls` output in TSK gives both the directory entry and inode types.

It could be possible for data to be hidden in directory entry structures. The space between the last directory entry and the end of the block is unused and could contain data. This is especially true when the hash trees are used because the first block contains a small amount of administrative data, and the rest is unused. This is a dangerous hiding technique, though, because the OS could overwrite it when a new file name is created.

## ANALYSIS SCENARIOS

To show how we can use the low-level details of ExtX directory entries, two example scenarios are given in this section. The first identifies the original location of a file, and the second identifies a possible order in which files were deleted.

### Source of a Moved File

While investigating a Linux system that has been compromised, we come across a file called `snifferlog-1.dat` that contains network packets. The other files in the directory have names similar to `log-001.dat` and do not contain network data. The listing is shown here:

```
# fls -f linux-ext3 ext3-8.dd 1840555
r/r 1840556:    log-001.dat
r/r 1840560:    log-002.dat
r/r 1840566:    log-003.dat
r/r 1840569:    log-004.dat
r/r 32579:      snifferlog-1.dat
r/r 1840579:    log-005.dat
r/r 1840585:    log-006.dat
```

To find the executable that could have created this file, we search for the full path of the file. Executable files sometimes contain the names of the files that they open, but our search is unsuccessful. It is trivial for an executable to obfuscate the names of the files that it opens. We are about to move on to another part of the system when we notice the odd sequence of inode addresses in the listing.

The parent directory and the log files all have inode addresses around 1,840,500, but the snifferlog-1.dat file has an address of 32,579. We know from the allocation strategy of Linux that files are typically allocated an inode in the same block group as the parent directory. Therefore, snifferlog-1.dat was either originally allocated to a different parent directory and moved to its current location, or it was created in the current directory but the block group was full.

We look at the fsstat output and determine that the log directory is in block group 113, which has 99% of its inodes and 48% of its blocks free. Therefore, it is unlikely that it was full when the file was created unless there were a lot of files that were deleted since then.

```
Group: 113:
  Inode Range: 1840545 - 1856832
  Block Range: 3702784 - 3735551
  Free Inodes: 16271 (99%)
  Free Blocks: 15728 (48%)
```

We now investigate the sniffer log inode, which is 32,579, in more detail and determine that it belongs to block group 2.

```
Group: 2:
  Inode Range: 32577 - 48864
  Block Range: 65536 - 98303
  Free Inodes: 16268 (99%)
  Free Blocks: 0 (0%)
```

One theory is that it was created in a directory in block group 2 and moved to the directory in block group 113. Therefore, we will look for directories in block group 2 that could have been the parent directory for snifferlog-1.dat. We will do this with the ils tool in TSK. ils lists details about inodes in a given range, and we will supply the range of the block group and filter out all non-directory entries. The -m flag is given so that the mode will be converted to a human readable format, and the -a flag is given to list only allocated inode entries. We also use grep to filter out all entries that are not directories (it is using the fifth column).

```
# ils -f linux-ext3 -m -a ext3-8.dd 32577-48864 | grep "|d"
<ext3-8.dd-alive-32577>|0|32577|16893|drwxrwxr-x|4|500|500|0|4096|
<ext3-8.dd-alive-32655>|0|32655|16893|drwxrwxr-x|2|500|500|0|4096|
<ext3-8.dd-alive-32660>|0|32660|16877|drwxr-xr-x|2|500|500|0|4096|
```

The first column is a fake name for each entry where it is "dead" if the entry is unallocated and "alive" if the entry is allocated. The third column is the inode address. This output is normally processed using the mactime tool to make timelines, so it is not user friendly.

We view the three allocated directories using fls. The directory at inode 32577 is the most promising.

```
# fls -f linux-ext3 ext3-8.dd 32577
r/r 32578:   only_live_twice.mp3
r/r 32582:   goldfinger.mp3
r/r 32580:   lic_to_kill.mp3
r/r 32581:   diamonds_forever.mp3
```

This might look like an innocent directory of James Bond MP3 files, but notice that the inode numbers and what we know about inode and directory entry allocation. Inodes are allocated on a first-available basis in the block group. The inode address of our sniffer log was 32,579, which could have been allocated in between only_live_twice.mp3 and lic_to_kill.mp3. Also notice that goldfinger.mp3 has a larger inode than the other files, and it is in the middle of the directory. Further, the name goldfinger.mp3 is 14 characters long, and the name snifferlog-1.dat is 16 characters long, which means that they can use the same sized directory entry.

When we examine each of these files, we notice that only_live_twice.mp3 is an executable, and the other files are network sniffer logs in the same format as snifferlog-1.dat. Also the network packets in only_live_twice.mp3 have timestamps before the packets in snifferlog-1.dat, and the timestamps in lic_to_kill.mp3 are after the snifferlog-1.dat times.

Using this information, our theory is that snifferlog-1.dat file was created after the only_live_twice.mp3 file, and then lic_to_kill.mp3 was created. Some time after the diamonds_forever.mp3 file was created, the snifferlog-1.dat file was moved to the directory in block group 113. After it was moved, the goldfinger.mp3 file was created, and it overwrote the directory entry and took the next available inode. The M-time and C-time of the inode 32577 directory are the same as those for the goldfinger.mp3 file, which are both after the times for the snifferlog-1.dat file. We can see this relationship in Figure 14.12 where the directory entry in group 113 points to the inode in block group 2. We still do not know how the file was moved and if it always had that name or if it had an MP3 name. Analyzing the executable may shed light on those answers.

In this scenario, we have tied a file back to its original directory using its inode address. If the file were moved within the same block group or to a different file system, then this technique would not work. But it does illustrate how knowing the allocation algorithms can help when these minor details are useful.

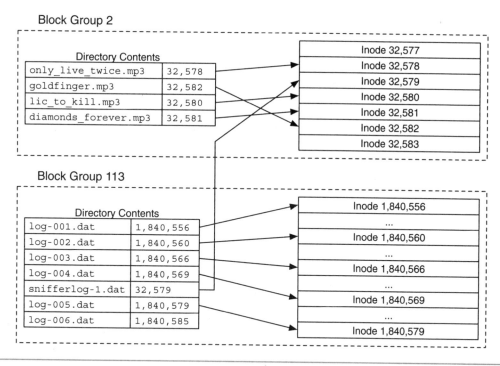

Block Group 2

Block Group 113

**Figure 14.12** Scenario where the `snifferlog-1.dat` file was moved from a directory in block group 2.

## File Deletion Order

While investigating a Linux system, we find a directory named `/usr/local/.oops/`. This is not typical in a Linux system, and we look at its contents. It contains eight deleted file names, and all of the corresponding inodes have been reallocated to new files, so file recovery will not be trivial. We are curious about how the files were deleted, though, and we parse the directory entries to determine the values given in Table 14.3. The names are listed in the order in which they exist in the directory.

**Table 14.3** Values in unallocated directory entry structures for scenario.

| Byte Location | Name | Record Length | Needed Length |
|---|---|---|---|
| 12 | .. | 1,012 | 12 |
| 24 | config.dat | 20 | 20 |
| 44 | readme.txt | 104 | 20 |

*continues*

435

**Table 14.3**    Values in unallocated directory entry structures for scenario (Continued).

| Byte Location | Name | Record Length | Needed Length |
|---|---|---|---|
| 64 | allfiles.tar | 20 | 20 |
| 84 | random.dat | 64 | 20 |
| 104 | mytools.zip | 44 | 20 |
| 124 | delete-files.sh | 24 | 24 |
| 148 | sniffer | 876 | 16 |
| 164 | passwords.txt | 860 | 860 |

We can make some general observations from this output. If the record length of an unallocated directory entry is the actual size that it needs (based on the length of its name), the next directory entry was deleted after it was. For example, config.dat was deleted before readme.txt was deleted because if readme.txt was deleted before config.dat, the length of the config.dat file would have been increased by 20 to cover up readme.txt. Therefore, we know that config.dat was deleted before readme.txt, allfiles.tar was deleted before random.dat, and delete-files.sh was deleted before sniffer.

We also can observe that mytools.zip was deleted after delete-files.sh but before sniffer was deleted. We know this because the length of mytools.zip was increased to 44 to account for delete-files-sh being deleted. If sniffer had been deleted before mytools.zip, the length of mytools.zip would have been increased to account for it. We also can see that passwords.txt was deleted before sniffer was and that random.dat was deleted after mytools.zip. We also see that readme.txt was deleted before sniffer because the record length for readme.txt points to sniffer.

If we spend some more time determining the relative order of these deletions, we conclude that the files may have been deleted in alphabetical order. We do not know the order in which allfiles.tar, config.dat, and delete-files.sh were deleted, but we do know they were before the other files and they are the first three files when the names are sorted. Therefore, these files might have been deleted when they were shown in a window sorted by name or by a command, such as rm *. The rm tool deletes files, and my tests show that the command deletes files in alphabetical order. With these results, it is likely that the files were not individually deleted one by one and that maybe a script was used or a file manager window. Note that the results are more difficult to interpret when there were file creations in between the file deletions.

## APPLICATION CATEGORY

Ext3 has only one application-level feature, which is the file system journal. Ext2 does not have the journal, and other application category features, such as quotas, are implemented with normal user files.

### FILE SYSTEM JOURNALING

Ext3 includes a file system journal, which was discussed in Chapter 8. A file system journal records updates to the file system so that the file system can be recovered more quickly after a crash. This section describes the Ext3 journal and how to analyze it.

#### Overview

The Ext3 journal typically uses inode 8 although its location is specified in the superblock and can exist anywhere. The journal is considered a compatible file system feature, and the corresponding value in the superblock is set when it is used. The superblock also has an incompatible feature for a journal device. When this is set, the file system is using an external journal and not saving the data to a local file. The location of the device is given in the superblock.

The journal records what block updates will occur, and after the update it identifies that the update is finished. There are two modes within which the journal can operate. In one mode, only metadata updates are recorded in the journal, and in the other mode, all updates, including data blocks, are recorded in the journal. The first version of the journal used the latter approach, but the current version gives an option and by default records only the metadata changes.

Journaling in Ext3 is done at a block level, which means that if one bit of one inode is updated, the entire file system block in which the inode is located will be saved to the journal. This is in comparison to a record level approach that would save only the inode data and not the full block. The first block in the journal is for its superblock and contains general information. The other blocks are used for the journal entries, and the journal wraps around to the start when it reaches the end. The size of a journal block should be the same size as a file system block.

Updates are done in transactions, and each transaction has a sequence number. Blocks in the journal contain either transaction administrative data or file system update data. Each transaction starts with a descriptor block that contains the transaction sequence number and a list of what file system blocks are being updated. Following the descriptor block are the updated blocks that were described in the descriptor. When the updates have been written to disk, a commit block exists with the same sequence number. The descriptor for a new transaction may exist after the commit block. We can see an example of this in Figure 14.13.

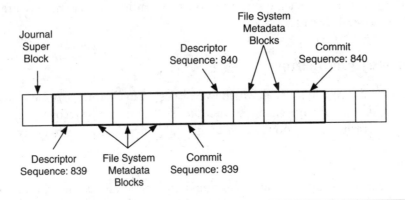

**Figure 14.13**   An Ext3 journal with two transactions.

The superblock identifies where the first descriptor block is located and its sequence number. If a descriptor block becomes full, a new one is allocated with the same sequence number for the remaining entries. A file system block that was added to the journal can be revoked so that the change is not applied during a recovery. This is done using a revoke block, which contains a sequence number and a list of blocks that were revoked. During recovery, any block that is listed in the revoke block and whose sequence number is less than the sequence number of the revoke block, will not be restored.

The data structures for the journal and a sample journal are given in Chapter 15. The `jls` tool in TSK will list the contents of a journal. Here is the output from a file system image:

```
# jls -f linux-ext3 /dev/hdb2
JBlk     Descriptrion
0:       Superblock (seq: 0)
1:       Allocated Descriptor Block (seq: 295)
2:       Allocated FS Block 4
3:       Allocated FS Block 2
4:       Allocated FS Block 14
5:       Allocated FS Block 5
6:       Allocated FS Block 163
7:       Allocated FS Block 3
```

```
8:       Allocated Commit Block (seq: 295)
9:       Unallocated FS Block Unknown
[REMOVED]
```

This output shows us the superblock, descriptor, and commit blocks. Transaction 295 starts in journal block 1 and ends in block 8. We also see the file system blocks to which each journal block corresponds. We can extract the journal blocks from the journal using the jcat tool in TSK.

### Analysis Techniques

We analyze a file system journal in order to obtain additional information about recent events. To do this, we simply locate the log using the address given in the file system superblock and process the journal superblock. This tells us where the first valid transaction exists. We then process the descriptor block to determine which file system blocks are being updated in this transaction.

If we are looking for a specific block, we can examine all the descriptor blocks for the one that describes the block in question. If we are looking for a specific keyword or value, we can search the entire file for it and then backtrack to the group descriptor where we can learn from what block it comes. We might be able to recover files if we can find a block from an inode table that has the block pointers before an inode was deleted. We also may be able to get time information from the journal if we can find a block with an inode or other file system data structure that contains a temporal value.

### Analysis Considerations

The journal can be useful for investigations that involve recent events. As time progresses, the log cycles and the data from an incident are overwritten. Linux starts the journal from the start every time the file system is mounted.

It can be difficult to intelligently analyze the unused journal blocks. To identify where a given journal block belongs in the file system; its descriptor block must be located. In some cases, you can go backwards until you find one, but sometimes the descriptor might have been overwritten by a later transaction.

By default, only metadata data is logged, so you cannot recover deleted file content. The superblock and directory contents will be recorded, though, so you could theoretically monitor when files were added and deleted by using the superblock values, and you can watch the file names in the directories. The amount of benefit from the journal will greatly depend on how much system activity occurred between the incident and the investigation.

## ANALYSIS SCENARIO

In this scenario, we are investigating a Linux system that has been compromised. It was imaged on the same day as the compromise, so there could be information in the journal from the compromise. As part of the investigation, we find a directory with various attack tools. We also find a deleted file named passwords.txt. This interests us, and we want to recover the file but do not want to sift through the strings output of the block group. Therefore, we turn to the journal.

We know that the deleted file allocated inode 488,650, which is located in block group 30. The first inode in the block group is 488,641, the inode table starts in block 983,044, and each block is 4,096 bytes. Therefore, our inode of interest is entry 10 of the group's inode table and is in the first block of the table.

We run jls on the journal and look for an entry for file system block 983,044.

```
# jls -f linux-ext3 ext3-8.dd 8
[REMOVED]
2293:    Unallocated Descriptor Block (seq: 136723)
2294:    Unallocated FS Block 983041
2295:    Unallocated FS Block 1
2296:    Unallocated FS Block 0
2297:    Unallocated FS Block 983044
2298:    Unallocated FS Block 983568
2299:    Unallocated FS Block 983040
2300:    Unallocated Commit Block (seq: 136723)
[REMOVED]
```

There are several references to block 983,044, and we analyze each of them by comparing what their differences are. The previous entries are for the creation of a file at inode 488,650. We see the inode table being updated, as well as the superblock, group descriptors, parent directory, and block bitmap. We extract the inode table from journal block 2297 and use dd to skip ahead to the tenth inode in the table:

```
# jcat -f linux-ext3 ext3-8.dd 8 2297 | dd bs=128 skip=9 count=1 | xxd
0000000: a481 0000 041f 0000 8880 3741 3780 3741  .....  ....7A7.7A
0000016: 3780 3741 0000 0000 0000 0100 1000 0000  7.7A...........
0000032: 0000 0000 0000 0000 1102 0f00 1202 0f00  ...............
0000048: 0000 0000 0000 0000 0000 0000 0000 0000  ...............
[REMOVED]
```

This is the data that was once inode 488,650; its size is given in bytes 4 to 7, and it is 7,940 bytes (0x1f04). The two direct block pointers are given in bytes 40 to 43 and 44 to

47. We see that it allocated blocks 983,569 and 983,570. When we view the contents of those blocks, we find a list of passwords for various systems that our attacker had compromised.

In this scenario, the journal allowed us to find a previous copy of an inode. The file was recently created, and its inode was still in the journal. We are not 100% sure that the inode in the journal is the last valid data for the file, but the contents matched the name.

## THE BIG PICTURE

Now that we have seen each individual component of a file and directory, we will put all the information together with some examples. We will allocate and then delete the /dir1/file1.dat file. The file size is 6,000 bytes, and the block size of the Ext3 file system is 1,024 bytes.

### FILE ALLOCATION EXAMPLE

The high-level process for creating the /dir1/file1.dat file is to locate the dir1 directory, create a directory entry, allocate an inode, and then allocate blocks for the file content. The exact ordering of allocating the different data structures may vary by OS, and the order presented here may not reflect an actual system.

1. We read the superblock data structure, which is 1,024 bytes in size and is located 1,024 bytes into the file system. From processing this, we learn that the block and fragment sizes are 1,024 bytes. Each block group has 8,192 blocks and 2,016 inodes. There are no reserved blocks before the start of the first block group.
2. We read the group descriptor table, which is located in blocks 2 and 3 of the file system. This tells us the layout of each block group.
3. We need to locate the dir1 directory in the root directory, so we process inode 2. Using the number of inodes per group, we determine that inode 2 is in block group 0. We use the group descriptor table entry for group 0 and determine that the inode table starts in block 6.
4. We read the inode table from block 6 and process the second entry. The inode for inode 2 shows that the directory entry structures for the root directory are located in block 258.
5. We read the root directory contents from block 258 and process the contents as a list of directory entries. The first two entries are for '.' and '..'. We advance ahead using the reported record length of each entry (we don't care about deleted files) and find the

entry whose name is dir1. It has an inode value of 5,033. The A-time of the root directory is updated to reflect the directory being opened.

6.  We determine where inode 5,033 is located by dividing it by the number of inodes per group and determine that it is in block group 2. Using the group descriptor entry for group 2, we determine that its inode table starts in block 16,390.

7.  We read the inode table from block 16,390 and process entry 1,001, which is the relative location of inode 5,033. The inode contents show us that the contents of dir1 are located in block 18,431.

8.  We read the dir1 contents from block 18,431 and process the contents as a list of directory entries. We are looking for unused space in the directory. The file1.dat name is eight characters long, so the directory entry requires 16 bytes. The name is added between two allocated names, and the M-and C-times of the directory are updated. The directory content changes are recorded in the journal.

9.  We need to allocate an inode for the file, and it will be allocated in the same group as the parent, which is block group 2. We locate the inode bitmap for group 2 in block 16,386 using the group descriptor. We use a first available search and identify that inode 5,110 is not allocated. Its corresponding bit in the bitmap is set to 1, the free inode count in the group descriptor table is decremented, and the free inode count in the superblock is decremented. The inode address is added to the file1.dat directory entry. The bitmap, group descriptor, and superblock changes are recorded in the journal.

10. We fill in the contents of inode 5,110 by locating it in the group 2 inode table and initializing the inode values. The time values are set to the current time, and the link value is set to 1 to correspond to the directory entry link. The inode table changes are recorded in the journal.

11. We need to allocate six blocks to store the file content, so we process the block bitmap, which is located in block 16,385. We use a first-available algorithm to search block group 2 for available blocks and find blocks 20,002 to 20,003 and 20,114, to 20,117. The bit for each of these blocks is set and the addresses are added to the direct pointers in inode 5,110. The free block counts in the group descriptor, and the superblock is also updated. The modified and changed times in the inode are updated to reflect the changes. The inode, group descriptor, superblock and bitmap changes are recorded in the journal.

12. The file content of file1.dat is written to the allocated blocks.

The final state of the system can be found in Figure 14.14.

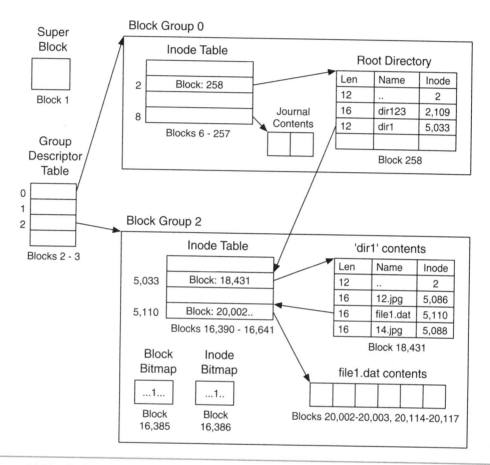

**Figure 14.14**  Final state after adding the 'dir1/file1.dat' file.

## FILE DELETION EXAMPLE

We will now delete the /dir1/file1.dat file. As mentioned in the previous section, the order of unallocating the data structures might vary by OS, and the order presented here may not be the same as an actual OS.

1.  We read the superblock data structure, which is 1,024 bytes in size and is located 1,024 bytes into the file system. From processing this, we learn that the block and

fragment sizes are 1,024 bytes. Each block group has 8,192 blocks and 2,016 inodes. There are no reserved blocks before the start of the first block group.

2.  We read the group descriptor table, which is located in blocks 2 and 3 of the file system. This tells us the layout of each block group.

3.  We need to locate the dir1 directory in the root directory, so we process inode 2. Using the number of inodes per group, we determine that inode 2 is in block group 0. We use the group descriptor table entry for group 0 and determine that the inode table starts in block 6.

4.  We read the inode table from block 6 and process the second entry. The inode for inode 2 shows that the directory entry structures for the root directory are located in block 258.

5.  We read the root directory contents from block 258 and process the contents as a list of directory entries. The first two entries are for '.' and '..'. We advance ahead using the reported record length of each entry (we don't care about deleted files) and find the entry whose name is dir1. It has an inode value of 5,033. The A-time of the root directory is updated to reflect the directory being opened.

6.  We determine where inode 5,033 is located by dividing it by the number of inodes per group and determine that it is in block group 2. Using the group descriptor entry for group 2, we determine that its inode table starts in block 16,390.

7.  We read the inode table for group 2, which is in block 16,390 and process entry 1,001, which is the relative location of inode 5,033. The inode contents show us that the contents of dir1 are located in block 18,431.

8.  We read the dir1 contents from block 18,431 and process the contents as a list of directory entries. We are looking for an entry for the 'file1.dat' file. We find its entry and observe that it has allocated inode 5,110. The directory entry is unallocated by adding its record length to the record length field in the previous directory entry, which belongs to the 12.jpg file. The M-, A-, and C-times are updated as a result of this process. The changes are recorded in the journal.

9.  We process the contents of inode 5,110 from the group 2 inode table and decrement the link count by one to account for the name being deleted. The link count becomes 0, which means that the inode must be deallocated. To deallocate the inode, the corresponding bit in the inode bitmap is set to 0, and we update the free inode counts in the group descriptor and superblock. The changes are recorded in the journal.

10. We also need to deallocate the six blocks that the file has allocated. For each block, the corresponding bit in the block bitmap is set to 0, and the block pointer in the inode is cleared. The file size is decremented each time a block is deallocated, and it eventually reaches 0. The M-time, C-time, and D-times are updated to reflect the inode changes. The free block counts are updated in the group descriptor and superblock. The changes are added to the journal.

The final state of the file system can be seen in Figure 14.15. The bolded lines and values represent the changes to the file system because of the deletion.

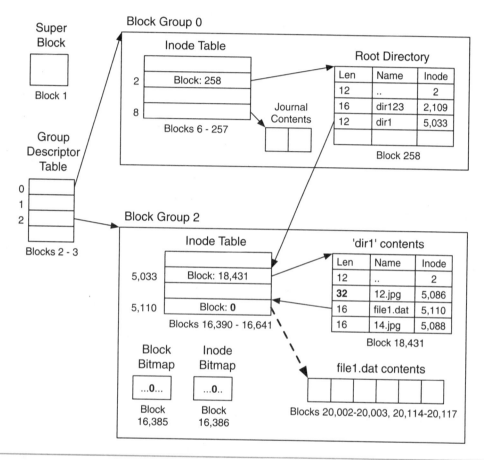

**Figure 14.15**  Final state after deleting the '/dir1/file1.dat' file.

## OTHER TOPICS

This section looks at ExtX deleted file recovery and file system consistency checks. Both of these topics are outside the scope of a specific data category.

## FILE RECOVERY

With standard Linux systems, recovering files from Ext3 is not easy, but it can be from Ext2. With Ext2, the inode values are not wiped when the file is deleted, so the block pointers will still exist. The time values also are updated when the file is deleted so you will know when the deletion occurred. The link between the directory entry and the inode is wiped, though, so you will have to recover files by searching the unallocated inode entries. When viewing the contents of a deleted Ext2 file, keep in mind that indirect block pointers could have been reallocated before the inode entry was, so the block no longer contains block addresses.

With Ext3, the pointer between the file name and inode still exists, but the block pointers are wiped. To recover the data, you will need to use data carving techniques. You can use the group information to your advantage when carving out a specific file because you can restrict yourself to the blocks in that group. Most OSes will allocate blocks in the same group as the inode, and therefore you can focus on a smaller area. The OS could have allocated blocks elsewhere, though, and a full carving might need to occur.

When carving data, keep in mind that the indirect block pointers may exist in the middle of the data. Even in the ideal situation where consecutive blocks were allocated for the deleted file, the thirteenth block will be the first indirect block pointer. You can calculate when the next indirect block pointer will be based on the block size. For a deleted file, they will be all zeros, and you should remove these from a carved file.

Finally, with an Ext3 file system, you may want to look in the journal for an older copy of the inode if the file was recently deleted. The journal may contain a copy of the inode's block when the inode had all its block pointers and a copy of the indirect block pointers.

## CONSISTENCY CHECK

Consistency checks are used in an investigation to find invalid values in file system data structures that could be used to hide data, and it looks at unused areas to identify if they are being used to hide data. We will start in the file system category and examine the superblock. Most of the 1,024 bytes in the superblock are not used and could be used to hide data. The group descriptors are more efficient with their storage, and the backup copies of the group descriptors and superblocks could be used to detect any changes that were manually performed by the perpetrator.

The number of bits in a block typically defines the size of block groups, and the block bitmap will typically be fully used. On the other hand, the last bytes of the inode bitmap might not be fully used because there are typically fewer inodes per group than there are blocks per group, so the block allocated to the inode bitmap may not be fully used. The final block group may have unused bits in the block bitmap.

Every allocated block must have one and only one allocated inode entry pointing to it unless it is one of the administrative blocks that stores the group descriptor table, inode table, block bitmap, inode bitmap, or superblock.

Most of the data in each inode are used, and not much data could be hidden in each, although there could be unused bytes at the end of each inode table. All blocks that an allocated inode entry has in its block pointers also must be allocated. Inodes for special file types may not need to allocate blocks and therefore they should not have any allocated to them. The first 10 inodes are reserved, but many are not used. These could be used to hide data [grugq 2002]. The unused space in extended attributes also could be used to hide data.

With the exception of the reserved and orphan inodes, all allocated inode entries should have a file name pointing to them. Orphan files should be listed in the superblock. The number of names should be equal to the link count. If you acquired the system while it was running, there could be orphan files for those that were open by running processes. All allocated file names must point to an allocated inode entry. The space at the end of a directory could be used to hide data.

## SUMMARY

Ext2 and Ext3 are two of the dominant Linux file systems and can be found in many servers and some desktop systems. The file system uses simple data structures, but it is made slightly more complex because everything is divided into block groups. File recovery is very difficult with Ext3 because all block pointers are cleared when a file is deleted.

Perhaps the most challenging problem with ExtX is how it evolves. FAT has had a few evolutions, and NTFS has had changes with each major release of Windows, but there are several "experimental" variations of ExtX that any user can install or enable. In this chapter, I have outlined the technology as it currently exists. At any time, new features can be added to ExtX, but that does not mean that every instance of ExtX will have all these features. The kernel and system configuration of the suspect system should be investigated to identify what features were enabled.

## BIBLIOGRAPHY

Card, Rémy, Theodore Ts'o, and Stephen Tweedie. "Design and Implementation of the Second Extended Filesystem." In *Proceedings of the First Dutch International Symposium on Linux*, ed. Frank B. Brokken et al, Amsterdam, December 1994. http://web.mit.edu/tytso/www/linux/ext2intro.html.

Carrier, Brian. "EXT3FS Keyword Search Test #1." *Digital Forensic Tool Testing*, November 2003. http://dftt.sourceforge.net.

Crane, Aaron. "Linux Ext2fs Undeletion mini-HOWTO." *The Linux Documentation Project*, February 1999. http://en.tldp.org/HOWTO/Ext2fs-Undeletion.html.

Dubeau, Louis-Dominique. "Analysis of the Ext2fs Structure." *The Operating System Resource Center*, 1994. http://www.nondot.org/sabre/os/files/FileSystems/ext2fs/.

Red Hat, Inc. *Ext3 Users Mailing List*, n.d. https://listman.redhat.com/mailman/listinfo/ext3-users/.

Heavner, Scott D. *Linux Disk Editor*, n.d. http://lde.sourceforge.net/.

Garfinkel, Simson, Gene Spafford, and Alan Schwartz. *Practical Unix and Internet Security*. 3rd ed. Sebastopol: O'Reilly, 2003.

Gleditsch, Arne Georg, and Per Kristian Gjermshus. *Linux Source Code*, n.d. http://lxr.linux.no/source/.

grugq. "Defeating Forensic Analysis on Unix." *Phrack, Issue 15*, July 28, 2002. http://www.phrack.org/show.php?p=59&a=6.

Honeynet Project. "The Forensic Challenge." January 15, 2001. http://www.honeynet.org/challenge/index.html.

McKusick, Marshall, Keith Bostic, Michael Karels, and John Quarterman. *The Design and Implementation of the 4.4 BSD Operating System*. Boston: Addison-Wesley, 1996.

Phillips, Daniel. "A Directory Index for Ext2." *Proceedings of the Usenix Fifth Annual Linux Showcase and Conference*, 2001.

Poirier, Dave. "Second Extended File System: Internal Layout." 2002. http://www.nongnu.org/ext2-doc/.

Ts'o, Theodore. "E2fsprogs." *Sourceforge*, n.d. http://e2fsprogs.sourceforge.net/.

Ts'o, Theodore, and Stephen Tweedie. "Planned Extensions to the Linux Ext2/Ext3 Filesystem." *Proceedings of the 2002 Usenix Technical Conference FREENIX Track*, 2002.

Tweedie, Stephen. "EXT3, Journaling Filesystem." *Sourceforge*, July 20, 2000. http://olstrans.sourceforge.net/release/OLS2000-ext3/OLS2000-ext3.html.

# Ext2 and Ext3 Data Structures

The previous chapter outlined the concepts behind the design of ExtX, and this chapter describes the various data structures that make up an ExtX file system. It is assumed that you have either read the previous chapter or are reading it in parallel with this one. If you are not interested in learning about the data structures and layout, you can safely skip this chapter.

## SUPERBLOCK

ExtX uses the superblock to store the basic file system category data. It is located 1,024 bytes from the start of the file system and has 1,024 bytes allocated to it. It has the fields given in Table 15.1.

**Table 15.1**   Data structure for the ExtX superblock.

| Byte Range | Description | Essential |
|---|---|---|
| 0–3 | Number of inodes in file system | Yes |
| 4–7 | Number of blocks in file system | Yes |
| 8–11 | Number of blocks reserved to prevent file system from filling up | No |
| 12–15 | Number of unallocated blocks | No |

*continues*

**Table 15.1**   Data structure for the ExtX superblock (Continued).

| Byte Range | Description | Essential |
|---|---|---|
| 16–19 | Number of unallocated inodes | No |
| 20–23 | Block where block group 0 starts | Yes |
| 24–27 | Block size (saved as the number of places to shift 1,024 to the left) | Yes |
| 28–31 | Fragment size (saved as the number of bits to shift 1,024 to the left) | Yes |
| 32–35 | Number of blocks in each block group | Yes |
| 36–39 | Number of fragments in each block group | Yes |
| 40–43 | Number of inodes in each block group | Yes |
| 44–47 | Last mount time | No |
| 48–51 | Last written time | No |
| 52–53 | Current mount count | No |
| 54–55 | Maximum mount count | No |
| 56–57 | Signature (0xef53) | No |
| 58–59 | File system state (see Table 15.2) | No |
| 60–61 | Error handling method (see Table 15.3) | No |
| 62–63 | Minor version | No |
| 64–67 | Last consistency check time | No |
| 68–71 | Interval between forced consistency checks | No |
| 72–75 | Creator OS (see Table 15.4) | No |
| 76–79 | Major version (see Table 15.5) | Yes |
| 80–81 | UID that can use reserved blocks | No |
| 82–83 | GID that can use reserved blocks | No |
| 84–87 | First non-reserved inode in file system | No |
| 88–89 | Size of each inode structure | Yes |
| 90–91 | Block group that this superblock is part of (if backup copy) | No |

| Byte Range | Description | Essential |
|---|---|---|
| 92–95 | Compatible feature flags (see Table 15.6) | No |
| 96–99 | Incompatible feature flags (see Table 15.7) | Yes |
| 100–103 | Read only feature flags (see Table 15.8) | No |
| 104–119 | File system ID | No |
| 120–135 | Volume name | No |
| 136–199 | Path where last mounted on | No |
| 200–203 | Algorithm usage bitmap | No |
| 204–204 | Number of blocks to preallocate for files | No |
| 205–205 | Number of blocks to preallocate for directories | No |
| 206–207 | Unused | No |
| 208–223 | Journal ID | No |
| 224–227 | Journal inode | No |
| 228–231 | Journal device | No |
| 232–235 | Head of orphan inode list | No |
| 236–1023 | Unused | No |

Bytes 58 to 59 contain a flag for the state of the file system, and the flag can have the bits shown in Table 15.2 set.

**Table 15.2** Flags for the file system state in the superblock.

| Flag Value | Description | Essential |
|---|---|---|
| 0x0001 | File system is clean | No |
| 0x0002 | File system has errors | No |
| 0x0004 | Orphan inodes are being recovered | No |

The error handling method in bytes 60 to 61 identifies what the OS should do when it encounters a file system error. These values can be configured when the file system is created. It has one of the three values given in Table 15.3.

**Table 15.3**   Values for the error-handling field of the superblock.

| Value | Description | Essential |
|---|---|---|
| 1 | Continue | No |
| 2 | Remount file system as read only | No |
| 3 | Panic | No |

The creator OS value in bytes 72 to 75 identifies the OS that might have created the file system. Many Linux tools that create the file system allow the user to specify this value. The five values given in Table 15.4 are defined.

**Table 15.4**   Values for the OS creator field in the superblock.

| Value | Description | Essential |
|---|---|---|
| 0 | Linux | No |
| 1 | GNU Hurd | No |
| 2 | Masix | No |
| 3 | FreeBSD | No |
| 4 | Lites | No |

The major version level in bytes 76 to 79 can have one of the values defined in Table 15.5.

**Table 15.5**   Values for the major version field in the superblock.

| Value | Description | Essential |
|---|---|---|
| 0 | Original version | Yes |
| 1 | "Dynamic" version | Yes |

If the major version is not set to the dynamic version, the values from bytes 84 onward might not be accurate. The dynamic in the version name refers to the fact that each inode can be a dynamic size, and the exact size is given in the superblock in bytes 88 to 89. The current Linux kernel does not support dynamic-sized inodes but uses the dynamic version so that it can use the feature set fields.

The concept of compatible, read only compatible, and incompatible features was discussed in Chapter 14, "Ext2 and Ext3 Concepts and Analysis." A field for each type exists in the superblock. It should be noted that some of the flags have been defined but are never used in the Linux code. Therefore, not all of these are in a standard Linux system. The compatible features can have the values given in Table 15.6; the incompatible features are given in Table 15.7; and the read only compatible features are given in Table 15.8.

**Table 15.6** Flag values for the compatible features in the superblock.

| Flag Value | Description | Essential |
|---|---|---|
| 0x0001 | Preallocate directory blocks to reduce fragmentation | No |
| 0x0002 | AFS server inodes exist | No |
| 0x0004 | File system has a journal (Ext3) | No |
| 0x0008 | Inodes have extended attributes | No |
| 0x0010 | File system can resize itself for larger partitions | No |
| 0x0020 | Directories use hash index | No |

**Table 15.7** Flag values for the incompatible features in the superblock.

| Flag Value | Description | Essential |
|---|---|---|
| 0x0001 | Compression (not yet supported) | Yes |
| 0x0002 | Directory entries contain a file type field | Yes |
| 0x0004 | File system needs recovery | No |
| 0x0008 | File system uses a journal device | No |

**Table 15.8** Flag values for the read only compatible features in the superblock.

| Flag Value | Description | Essential |
|---|---|---|
| 0x0001 | Sparse superblocks and group descriptor tables | No |
| 0x0002 | File system contains a large file | No |
| 0x0004 | Directories use B-Trees (not implemented) | No |

Now that we have given the data structures and all the flags, let's look at an actual Ext3 superblock. We will use dd and extract out 1,024 bytes starting at offset 1,024.

```
# dd if=ext3.dd bs=1024 skip=1 count=1 | xxd
0000000: c053 1d00 ff9d 3a00 4cee 0200 4708 0b00   .S....:.L...G...
0000016: 6745 1d00 0000 0000 0200 0000 0200 0000   gE..............
0000032: 0080 0000 0080 0000 a03f 0000 c9fd 1141   .........?.....A
0000048: c9fd 1141 3601 2500 53ef 0100 0100 0000   ...A6.%.S.......
0000064: da9d e83e 004e ed00 0000 0000 0100 0000   ...>.N..........
0000080: 0000 0000 0b00 0000 8000 0000 0400 0000   ................
0000096: 0600 0000 0300 0000 077a 06a5 1795 486e   .........z....Hn
0000112: 9485 ecc4 486f 63e4 0000 0000 0000 0000   ....Hoc.........
0000128: 0000 0000 0000 0000 0000 0000 0000 0000   ................
[REMOVED]
0000224: 0800 0000 0000 0000 0000 0000 0000 0000   ................
[REMOVED]
0001008: 0000 0000 0000 0000 0000 0000 0000 0000   ................
```

Bytes 0 to 3 show us that there are 1,921,984 (0x001d53c0) inodes, and bytes 4 to 7 show that there are 3,841,535 (0x003a9dff) blocks. Bytes 20 to 23 show that block 0 is where block group 0 starts. Bytes 24 to 27 and 28 to 31 contain the number of bits to shift the number 1,024 (0x0400) in order to calculate the block and fragment sizes. Both values are 2, which means that the block and fragments are 4,096 (0x1000) bytes. Bytes 32 to 35 show that there are 32,768 (0x8000) blocks in each block group, and bytes 40 to 43 show that there are 16,288 (0x3fa0) inodes per group. With this information, we know the total size of the file system, where each block group starts, and how many inodes are allocated to each block group.

Bytes 76 to 79 show that we have the dynamic version of ExtX, so the bytes following offset 84 should be valid. We see in bytes 88 to 91 that the size of each inode is 128 (0x80) bytes. Bytes 92 to 95 have the compatible feature flags, and the flag for the journal (0x0004) is set, so we have an Ext3 file system. Bytes 96 to 99 have the incompatible feature flag value of 0x0006, which means that recovery should be done during the next boot (0x0004) and the special directory entries are being used (0x0002). Bytes 100 to 103 contain the read only compatibility features and they are set to 0x0003, which means that there are files that are larger than 32-bits (0x0002) and that not every block group has a backup copy of the superblock (0x0001). Bytes 224 to 227 show that the journal is located in inode 8.

There are many other values in the superblock that were not discussed. Their purposes will be discussed in the appropriate section, and you can extract them from the fsstat output given in the "File System Category" section of Chapter 14.

## GROUP DESCRIPTOR TABLES

The group descriptor table is a list of group descriptor data structures that is located in the file system block following the superblock. The table has an entry for every block group in the file system, and each entry contains information about that group. Each entry is only 32 bytes and has the fields given in Table 15.9.

**Table 15.9**  Data structure for the group descriptor table entries.

| Byte Range | Description | Essential |
|---|---|---|
| 0–3 | Starting block address of block bitmap | Yes |
| 4–7 | Starting block address of inode bitmap | Yes |
| 8–11 | Starting block address of inode table | Yes |
| 12–13 | Number of unallocated blocks in group | No |
| 14–15 | Number of unallocated inodes in group | No |
| 16–17 | Number of directories in group | No |
| 18–31 | Unused | No |

To view the contents of the primary group descriptor table, we extract the block following the superblock. In our image, each block is 4,096 bytes, the superblock is located inside block 0, and the group descriptor table is, therefore, in block 1. Note that when the block size is 1,024 bytes, the superblock is in block 1 and the group descriptor table starts in block 2.

We extract the table with dcat:

```
# dcat -f linux-ext3 ext3.dd 1 | xxd
0000000: 0200 0000 0300 0000 0400 0000 d610 7b3f  .............{?
0000016: 0a00 0000 0000 0000 0000 0000 0000 0000  ...............
0000032: 0280 0000 0380 0000 0480 0000 0000 8e3f  ...............?
0000048: 0100 0000 0000 0000 0000 0000 0000 0000  ...............
  [REMOVED]
```

This output shows two of the group descriptor entries. Bytes 0 to 3 show that the block bitmap is located in block 2, and bytes 4 to 7 show that the inode bitmap is located in block 3. According to bytes 8 to 11, the inode table starts in block 4. This image has 32,768 blocks per block group, which means that the block bitmap will need 4,096 bytes and, therefore, one block. There are 16,288 inodes per group, so the inode bitmap will need 2,036 bytes. The inode table will have 16,288 entries that are 128 bytes each, which totals 2,084,864 bytes. With a 4,096-byte block size, the inode table will need 509 blocks and extend from block 4 to 512.

The table entry for group 1 starts at byte 32. We see in bytes 32 to 35 that the block bitmap is in block 32,770 (0x8002). This is intuitive because we know that group 1 will start in block 32,768 and that a backup superblock and backup group descriptor table will use the first two blocks. When a block group does not have a backup superblock and group descriptor, the block bitmap is located in the first block of the group.

## BLOCK BITMAP

File and directory content is stored in blocks, and the allocation status of each block is stored in a block bitmap. Every block group has a bitmap for its blocks. The starting location of the bitmap is given in the group descriptor, and it is allocated at least one block.

Like other bitmaps we have seen in this book, it is organized into bytes, and the least-significant bit corresponds to the block after the most-significant bit of the previous byte. In other words, when we read the bytes we go left to right, but inside each byte we read right to left.

When we analyzed the contents of the group descriptor in our example image, we saw that the block bitmap for group 0 started in block 2. We can extract the contents of that block with dcat (or dd):

```
# dcat -f linux-ext3 ext3.dd 2 | xxd
0000000: ffff ffff ffff ffff ffff ffff ffff ffff  ................
[REMOVED]
0001168: ff01 fcff ffff 0ffe ffff ffff 03fe ffff  ...............
```

The rows of all 'f' values show that there are many allocated blocks in the beginning of block group 0. At byte 1,169 we see the value 0x01. Byte 1,169 corresponds with blocks 9,352 to 9,359. The value 0x01 shows us that block 9,352 is allocated, but blocks 9,353 to 9,359 are not.

# INODES

The inode data structure is used to store the metadata for a file or directory. Inodes are located in inode tables, which are located in each of the block groups. The starting location of the inode table is defined in the group descriptor, and the number of inodes per group is defined in the superblock.

The basic inode data structure is 128 bytes in size. If the file system is a "dynamic" version, as defined in the superblock, the inode can be a dynamic size, which is given in the superblock. Larger inodes are not supported in the current Linux kernel, but the first 128 bytes will have the same fields as the standard inode [Ts'o and Tweedie 2002]. The basic inode has the fields given in Table 15.10.

**Table 15.10**   Data structure for an inode.

| Byte Range | Description | Essential |
|---|---|---|
| 0–1 | File mode (type and permissions) (see Tables 15.11, 15.12, and 15.13) | Yes |
| 2–3 | Lower 16 bits of user ID | No |
| 4–7 | Lower 32 bits of size in bytes | Yes |
| 8–11 | Access Time | No |
| 12–15 | Change Time | No |
| 16–19 | Modification time | No |
| 20–23 | Deletion time | No |
| 24–25 | Lower 16 bits of group ID | No |
| 26–27 | Link count | No |
| 28–31 | Sector count | No |
| 32–35 | Flags (see Table 15.14) | No |
| 36–39 | Unused | No |
| 40–87 | 12 direct block pointers | Yes |
| 88–91 | 1 single indirect block pointer | Yes |
| 92–95 | 1 double indirect block pointer | Yes |

*continues*

**Table 15.10**   Data structure for an inode (Continued).

| Byte Range | Description | Essential |
|---|---|---|
| 96–99 | 1 triple indirect block pointer | Yes |
| 100–103 | Generation number (NFS) | No |
| 104–107 | Extended attribute block (File ACL) | No |
| 108–111 | Upper 32 bits of size / Directory ACL | Yes / No |
| 112–115 | Block address of fragment | No |
| 116–116 | Fragment index in block | No |
| 117–117 | Fragment size | No |
| 118–119 | Unused | No |
| 120–121 | Upper 16 bits of user ID | No |
| 122–123 | Upper 16 bits of group ID | No |
| 124–127 | Unused | No |

As was mentioned in the overview, the size was originally only 32 bits, but it was made into a 64-bit value by using the directory ACL value at bytes 108 to 111. There should be a read only compatible feature set in the superblock if any file uses a 64-bit size.

The 16-bit file mode value is broken up into three sections. In the lower 9 bits are the permissions flags, and each bit corresponds to a permission. The permissions use the notion of user, group, and world where user is the user ID in the inode, group is the group ID in the inode, and world is all other users. Each of these collections of users can have read, write, or execute permissions. The flags for each of these permissions are given in Table 15.11.

**Table 15.11**   Permission flags for bits 0 to 8 of the file mode field.

| Permission Flag | Description |
|---|---|
| 0x001 | Other—execute permission |
| 0x002 | Other—write permission |
| 0x004 | Other—read permission |
| 0x008 | Group—execute permission |

| Permission Flag | Description |
| --- | --- |
| 0x010 | Group—write permission |
| 0x020 | Group—read permission |
| 0x040 | User—execute permission |
| 0x080 | User—write permission |
| 0x100 | User—read permission |

The next three bits are for executable files and directories. If any of these are set, an executable will behave differently when it is run, or files in a directory will have special properties. These flags are given in Table 15.12.

**Table 15.12** Flags for bits 9 to 11 of the file mode field.

| Flag Value | Description |
| --- | --- |
| 0x200 | Sticky bit |
| 0x400 | Set group ID |
| 0x800 | Set user ID |

Refer to the "Metadata Category" section in Chapter 14 for a description of these flags. Lastly, bits 12 to 15 identify the type of the file that the inode is for. These are values and not flags, so only one should be set. They are given in Table 15.13.

**Table 15.13** Type flags for bits 12 to 15 of the file mode field.

| Type Value | Description |
| --- | --- |
| 0x1000 | FIFO |
| 0x2000 | Character device |
| 0x4000 | Directory |
| 0x6000 | Block device |
| 0x8000 | Regular file |
| 0xA000 | Symbolic link |
| 0xC000 | Unix socket |

The four time values are each stored as the number of seconds since January 1, 1970 UTC, which will stop working in January 2038 because the value is only 32 bits. The flags field identifies the attributes that are set for the file. Recall from the previous section that not every OS supports some of these flag values. The values included in Table 15.14 are either discussed in the manual pages or are used in the current kernel source code.

**Table 15.14**   Flag values for the inode flag field.

| Flag Value | Description |
| --- | --- |
| 0x00000001 | Secure deletion (not used) |
| 0x00000002 | Keep a copy of data when deleted (not used) |
| 0x00000004 | File compression (not used) |
| 0x00000008 | Synchronous updates—new data is written immediately to disk |
| 0x00000010 | Immutable file—content cannot be changed |
| 0x00000020 | Append only |
| 0x00000040 | File is not included in 'dump' command |
| 0x00000080 | A-time is not updated |
| 0x00001000 | Hash indexed directory |
| 0x00002000 | File data is journaled with Ext3 |

Let's look at inode entry 16 from the previous image. The first step is to identify the group of which it is a part. We know that each group has 16,288 inodes per group, which means that we need group 0. The starting address of the inode table is given in the group descriptor, and we previously saw that it starts in block 4, and each block is 4,096 bytes. To extract the data, we will use dd with a block size of 4096 to skip ahead to the inode table and then use dd with a block size of 128 to skip ahead to inode 16. The first inode is number 1, so we need to subtract 1 from our skip value.

```
# dd if=ext3.dd bs=4096 skip=4 | dd bs=128 skip=15 count=1 | xxd
0000000: a481 f401 0040 9c00 6d09 2a3f f607 2a3f  .....@..m.*?..*?
0000016: 8107 2a3f 0000 0000 f401 0100 404e 0000  ..*?........@N..
0000032: 0000 0000 0000 0000 2c38 0000 2d38 0000  ........,8..-8..
0000048: 2e38 0000 2f38 0000 3038 0000 3138 0000  .8../8..08..18..
0000064: 3238 0000 3338 0000 3438 0000 3538 0000  28..38..48..58..
```

```
0000080: 3638 0000 3738 0000 3838 0000 393c 0000  68..78..88..9<..
0000096: 0000 0000 ba94 ea0b 0000 0000 0000 0000  ................
0000112: 0000 0000 0000 0000 0000 0000 0000 0000  ................
```

Bytes 0 to 1 show the mode, which is 0x81a4. These bits show us that everyone can read this file (0x004), the group can read (0x020), the user can write (0x080), and the user can read (0x100). The upper four bits show that it is a regular file (0x8000). Bytes 4 to 7 show that the size of the file is 10,240,000 bytes (0x009c4000). Bytes 8 to 11 show the A-time as 0x3f2a096d, which translates to August 1, 2003 at 06:32:13 UTC. Bytes 26 to 27 show the link count is 1, which means that there is a file name pointing to it. Bytes 32 to 35 show that there are no special flags or attributes set.

Bytes 40 to 43 are for the first direct block pointer, and they are for block 14,380 (0x0000382c). Bytes 44 to 47 are for the second direct pointer, and they are for block 14,381 (0x0000382d). Bytes 88 to 91 contain the address of a single indirect block pointer, which is in block 14,392 (0x00003838). Bytes 92 to 95 also show a double indirect block pointer in block 15,417 (0x00003c39). The contents of both of these blocks will be a list of 4-byte addresses. The single indirect block pointer contains a list of addresses where file content is stored:

```
# dcat -f linux-ext3 ext3.dd 14392 | xxd
0000000: 3938 0000 3a38 0000 3b38 0000 3c38 0000  98..:8..;8..<8..
0000016: 3d38 0000 3e38 0000 3f38 0000 4038 0000  =8..>8..?8..@8..
0000032: 4138 0000 4238 0000 4338 0000 4438 0000  A8..B8..C8..D8..
[REMOVED]
```

The allocation status of an inode is stored in the inode bitmap, which is located in the same group as the inode. The group descriptor contains the block address of the inode bitmap, and our example image has its bitmap in block 3, whose contents are shown here:

```
# dcat -f linux-ext3 ext3.dd 3 | xxd
0000000: fff7 fcff 1f00 0000 00c8 0000 0000 0000  ................
```

To determine the correct byte, we subtract 1 to account for the first inode of the group and divide by 8.

```
(16 - 1) / 8 = 1 remainder 7
```

The bit for inode 16 is the most significant bit in byte 1 (0xf7), which is a 1, so it is allocated.

We can get all the inode details from the istat command, and they are listed here for the inode that we just examined:

```
# istat -f linux-ext3 ext3.dd 16
inode: 16
Allocated
Group: 0
Generation Id: 199922874
uid / gid: 500 / 500
mode: -rw-r--r--
size: 10240000
num of links: 1

Inode Times:
Accessed:       Fri Aug  1 06:32:13 2003
File Modified:  Fri Aug  1 06:24:01 2003
Inode Modified: Fri Aug  1 06:25:58 2003

Direct Blocks:
14380 14381 14382 14383 14384 14385 14386 14387
14388 14389 14390 14391 14393 14394 14395 14396
[REMOVED]
16880 16881 16882 16883

Indirect Blocks:
14392 15417 15418 16443
```

## EXTENDED ATTRIBUTES

A file or directory can have extended attributes, which are name and value pairs. If a file or directory has extended attributes, its inode will contain the block address where they are stored.

The extended attributes block has three sections to it. The first 32 bytes are used by the header, and following the header is the second section with a list of attribute name entries. The third section starts at the end of the block and works its way up. It contains the values for each of the attribute pairs, and they may not be in the same order as the name entries were. We can see this in Figure 15.1.

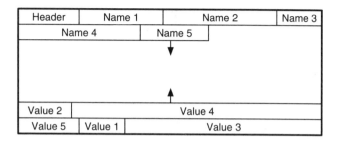

**Figure 15.1**    The extended attributes block has the name at the top and value at the bottom. They grow towards the middle.

The extended attribute header starts at byte 0 of the block and is 32-bytes long. It has the fields given in Table 15.15.

**Table 15.15**    Data structure for the extended attribute header.

| Byte Range | Description | Essential |
|------------|-------------|-----------|
| 0–3 | Signature (0xEA020000) | No |
| 4–7 | Reference count | No |
| 8–11 | Number of blocks | Yes |
| 12–15 | Hash | No |
| 16–31 | Reserved | No |

The reference count refers to how many files are using this block because files with the same extended attributes will share an extended attribute block. Linux currently does not support attribute lists with more than one block, but other OSes could in the future. The hash value is the hash for the attributes so that the OS can easily determine if two files have the same attributes.

The name entries start after the header, and each has the data structure given in Table 15.16.

**Table 15.16**   Data structure for the extended attribute name entries.

| Byte Range | Description | Essential |
|---|---|---|
| 0–0 | Length of name | Yes |
| 1–1 | Attribute type (see Table 15.17) | Yes |
| 2–3 | Offset to value | Yes |
| 4–7 | Block location of value | Yes |
| 8–11 | Size of value | Yes |
| 12–15 | Hash of value | No |
| 16+ | Name in ASCII | Yes |

The offset value is the byte offset in the block specified. For current Linux systems, there is only one block, and the block field is not set. The size value is the number of bytes in the value. The length of the name determines the length of the entry, and the next entry starts at the next 4-byte boundary. The entry type value can have one of the six values given in Table 15.17.

**Table 15.17**   Values for the type field in the extended attribute name entry.

| Type Value | Description |
|---|---|
| 1 | User space attribute |
| 2 | POSIX ACL |
| 3 | POSIX ACL Default (directories only) |
| 4 | Trusted space attribute |
| 5 | LUSTRE (not currently used by Linux) |
| 6 | Security space attribute |

If the type of the attribute is a user, trusted, or security space attribute, the value at the end of the block will simply be the value part of the attribute pair. If the type is one of the POSIX ACL types, the value has its own set of data structures.

The value part of a POSIX ACL attribute starts with a header and then a list of entries. The header data structure has only one field and is given in Table 15.18. The data structure for the ACL entries is given in Table 15.19.

**Table 15.18**  Data structure for the POSIX ACL header.

| Byte Range | Description | Essential |
|---|---|---|
| 0–3 | Version (1) | Yes |

**Table 15.19**  Data structure for the POSIX ACL entries.

| Byte Range | Description | Essential |
|---|---|---|
| 0–1 | Type (tag) (see Table 15.20) | Yes |
| 2–3 | Permissions (see Table 15.21) | Yes |
| 4–7 | User / Group ID (not included for some types) | Yes |

The type field in the ACL entry identifies the type of permission that the entry is for. The values given in Table 15.20 are defined.

**Table 15.20**  Values defined for the POSIX ACL entry type field.

| Type | Description |
|---|---|
| 0x01 | User—specified in inode |
| 0x04 | Group—specified in inode |
| 0x20 | Other—all other users |
| 0x10 | Effective rights mask |
| 0x02 | User—specified in attribute |
| 0x08 | Group—specified in attribute |

The first three types apply to the same owner, group, and "world" set of users that are normally used with ExtX inodes. In other words, the information in these entries should duplicate the information found in the inode. An entry that has one of these types is only four bytes in size because it does not use the ID field in bytes 4 to 7. The other types need to specify the user or group to which the permissions apply.

The permissions field in the entry has the flags in Table 15.21 defined.

Table 15.21   Flag values for the POSIX ACL entry permissions field.

| Permission Flag | Description |
| --- | --- |
| 0x01 | Execute |
| 0x02 | Write |
| 0x04 | Read |

Let's take a look at a block that contains some extended attributes.

```
# dcat -f linux-ext3 ext3-2.dd 1238
0000000: 0000 02ea 0100 0000 0100 0000 7447 05e8   ...........tG..
0000016: 0000 0000 0000 0000 0000 0000 0000 0000   ...............
0000032: 0601 c003 0000 0000 1900 0000 a8e9 5147   ..............QG
0000048: 736f 7572 6365 0000 0002 dc03 0000 0000   source.........
0000064: 2400 0000 2500 ad01 0000 0000 0000 0000   $...%..........
[REMOVED]
0000944: 0000 0000 0000 0000 0000 0000 0000 0000   ...............
0000960: 7777 772e 6469 6774 6974 616c 2d65 7669   www.digtital-evi
0000976: 6465 6e63 652e 6f72 6700 0000 0100 0000   dence.org.......
0000992: 0100 0600 0200 0400 4a00 0000 0200 0600   ........J.......
0001008: f401 0000 0400 0400 1000 0600 2000 0400   ............ ...
```

The first four bytes show the signature value, bytes 4 to 7 shows a reference count of 1, and bytes 8 to 11 show a block count of 1. Byte 32 is where the first entry starts, and we see that its name length is 6. Its type is 1, which is user space attribute, and bytes 2 to 3 show that the value is located at byte offset 960 (0x03c0). Bytes 40 to 43 show the size of the value is 25 bytes, and byte 48 is the start of the name, which is "source." The name ends in byte 53, and the entries are on 4-byte boundaries, so we advance to byte 56 for the next attribute. The value for the first attribute can be found in bytes 960 to 984, and the value is "www.digital-evidence.org."

There is a second attribute in the block, and it is for an ACL. It starts at byte 988 and extends until byte 1023. The header is at byte 988 to 991, and the first entry is at byte 992 to 993. It has a type of 1, which is for the permissions of the user ID specified in the inode. The permission is given in bytes 994 to 995, and it is 0x06, so we know the owner has read and write permissions. The second entry starts at byte 996 and has a type of 2. It gives read permissions to the user with an ID of 74 (0x4a). The remaining permissions are left as an exercise, but here is the relevant output from running istat on the file:

```
# istat -f linux-ext3 ext3-2.dd 70
[REMOVED]
Extended Attributes  (Block: 1238)
user.source=www.digtital-evidence.org
POSIX Access Control List Entries:
  uid: 0: Read, Write
  uid: 74: Read
  uid: 500: Read, Write
  gid: 0: Read
  mask: Read, Write
  other: Read
[REMOVED]
```

## DIRECTORY ENTRY

Directory entries are used to store the name of a file or directory. They are located in the blocks allocated to a directory, and they contain the address of the inode that the file or directory has allocated.

The directory entry structure comes in two formats, but both are the same size. The second format makes better use of the available space. The incompatible features value in the superblock will identify which version is being used. The original format is not the default in current systems, but it has the fields given in Table 15.22.

**Table 15.22**  Data structure for the original directory entry.

| Byte Range | Description | Essential |
|---|---|---|
| 0–3 | Inode value | Yes |
| 4–5 | Length of this entry | Yes |
| 6–7 | Name length | Yes |
| 8+ | Name in ASCII | Yes |

This is a very basic data structure where all the fields are essential. One structure exists for each name in a directory, and the structure points to the inode where the metadata can be found. The name is not null terminated, so the name length field is needed. Linux aligns these data structures on 4-byte boundaries.

The second version of these data structures makes better use of the name length field. The maximum number of characters in a file name is 255, so only one byte is needed. The second version of the directory entry uses the other byte to store the file type, which also can be found in the inode. It has the fields given in Table 15.23.

**Table 15.23**  Data structure for the second version of the directory entry.

| Byte Range | Description | Essential |
|---|---|---|
| 0–3 | Inode value | Yes |
| 4–5 | Length of this entry | Yes |
| 6–6 | Name length | Yes |
| 7–7 | File type (see Table 15.24) | No |
| 8+ | Name in ASCII | Yes |

The file type value is not an essential value, and it can have one of the values given in table 15.24.

**Table 15.24**  Values for the directory entry type field.

| | Description |
|---|---|
| 0 | Unknown type |
| 1 | Regular file |
| 2 | Directory |
| 3 | Character device |
| 4 | Block device |
| 5 | FIFO |
| 6 | Unix Socket |
| 7 | Symbolic link |

To look at the raw contents of a directory, we can use the `icat` command. Our test image uses the new version 2 directory entries, and inode 69,457 corresponds to a directory:

```
# icat -f linux-ext3 ext3.dd 69457 | xxd
0000000: 510f 0100 0c00 0102 2e00 0000 00d0 0000   Q...............
0000016: 0c00 0202 2e2e 0000 520f 0100 2800 0b01   ........R...(...
0000032: 6162 6364 6566 672e 7478 7400 530f 0100   abcdefg.txt.S...
0000048: 1400 0c01 6669 6c65 2074 776f 2e64 6174   ....file two.dat
0000064: 540f 0100 1000 0702 7375 6264 6972 3100   T.......subdir1.
0000080: 550f 0100 b003 0801 5253 5455 5657 5859   U.......RSTUVWXY
0000096: 0000 0000 0000 0000 0000 0000 0000 0000   ................
[REMOVED]
```

We see in bytes 0 to 3 that the inode corresponding to the first entry is 64,457 (0x010f51), and bytes 4 to 5 show that the directory entry is 12 bytes (0x0c). Byte 6 shows that the name is 1 byte long, and byte 7 shows that the entry is for a directory (0x02). The name is given in byte 8 and we see that it is '.'. This corresponds to the directory entry for the current directory. We can do a sanity check by comparing the inode in the entry with the inode value we used with `icat` to display the contents, and we see that they are both 64,457.

To find the second entry, we add the length of the first entry to its start, which means that the second entry will start in byte 12. We see in bytes 16 to 17 that the length of this entry is also 12 bytes, and it is for the '..' directory.

To find the third entry, we add the length of the second entry to its start and get byte 24. We see in bytes 28 to 29 that the entry length is 40 bytes (0x28). Byte 30 shows the name length is 11 (0x0b). The name starts at byte 32 and extends until byte 42, and it contains the string `abcdefg.txt`.

If we jump ahead from the start of the previous entry at byte 24 to the next entry, we get to byte 64. You might notice that the last entry ended in byte 42, so there are 20 unused bytes in between. The space in between contains a deleted file name, and its entry starts in byte 42 with a name of `file two.dat`.

The rest of the data is left for you to parse if you would like. We can see the output of running the `fls` tool on the same directory:

```
# fls -f linux-ext3 -a ext3.dd 69457
d/d 69457:      .
d/d 53248:      ..
r/r 69458:      abcdefg.txt
```

```
r/r * 69459:      file two.dat
d/d 69460:        subdir1
r/r 69461:        RSTUVWXY
```

## SYMBOLIC LINK

Symbolic links are special files that point to another file or directory. The "content" of the file is the target of the link. Therefore, they do not require any new data structures. If the path of the destination file or directory is less than 60 characters long, it is stored in the 60 bytes in the inode that are used for the 12 direct and 3 indirect block pointers. If the path is longer than 60 characters, a block is allocated, and the block contains the destination path. The file size corresponds to the path length of the destination.

We can see an example with icat. icat shows the contents of a file, and it shows the full path because it does not process it as a symbolic link. It processes it as a normal file.

```
# fls -f linux-ext3 ext3-3.dd
[REMOVED]
1/1 26: file1.txt
# icat -f linux-ext3 ext3-3.dd 26
/dir1/dir2/dir3/dir4/dir5/dir6/dir7/dir8/dir9/dir10/dir11/dir12/dir13/dir14/dir15/
file1.txt
```

The size reported in the inode is 90, and we see in the fls output that it has the type of 'l,' which is for link.

## HASH TREES

Instead of having directory entries in an unsorted order, a hash tree can be used to sort some of the entries. Each block in the directory corresponds to a node in the tree. The non-leaf nodes have data structures that point to the next layer. In a smaller directory, there are two layers, and the first block is the only node at the top layer.

To show which blocks correspond to the nodes in the next layer, there are node descriptor data structures. Before the node descriptors is a header data structure, and it starts following the '.' directory entry. The node descriptor header has the fields given in Table 15.25.

**Table 15.25** Data structure for the hash tree node descriptor header.

| Byte Range | Description | Essential |
|---|---|---|
| 0–3 | Unused | No |
| 4–4 | Hash version | Yes |
| 5–5 | Length of this structure | Yes |
| 6–6 | Levels of leaves | No |
| 7–7 | Unused | No |

Following the header is a list of node descriptors that identifies what hash values are in each block. Each entry in the list has the data structure given in Table 15.26.

**Table 15.26** Data structure for the hash tree node descriptor entries.

| Byte Range | Description | Essential |
|---|---|---|
| 0 – 3 | Minimum hash value in node | Yes |
| 4 – 7 | Block address | Yes |

Each entry contains the smallest hash value and the directory block of the node. The first node descriptor does not need a minimum because it should be 0. Therefore, those four bytes are used for another purpose. They store the current number of node descriptors and the maximum number of node descriptors that can fit in the block. Therefore, the first node descriptor has the fields given in Table 15.27.

**Table 15.27** Data structure for the first node descriptor entry.

| Byte Range | Description | Essential |
|---|---|---|
| 0–1 | Maximum number of node descriptors | No |
| 2–3 | Current number of node descriptors | Yes |
| 4–7 | Block address of first node | Yes |

The remainder of the block after the last node descriptor typically contains data from previous directory entries.

Here we see the contents of the first block in a large directory using a hash index:

```
# icat -f linux-ext3 ext3-3.dd 16
0000000: 1000 0000 0c00 0100 2e00 0000 0200 0000   ................
0000016: f403 0200 2e2e 0000 0000 0000 0208 0000   ................
0000032: 7c00 0400 0100 0000 3295 6541 0400 0000   |.......2.eA....
0000048: 88d5 fa92 0200 0000 86e7 50be 0300 0000   ..........P.....
0000064: 3738 3930 2e31 3233 3400 0000 1200 0000   7890.1234.......
```

In this output, bytes 0 to 9 are for the '.' directory entry, and bytes 12 to 23 are for the '..' entry. Notice that the record length field of the '..' entry in bytes 16 to 17 is 1,012 bytes (0x03f4). That points to the end of the 1,024-byte block.

The hash index header starts at byte 24, and the first four bytes are unused. Byte 28 shows us that hash version 2 is being used, and byte 29 shows us that the structure is eight bytes long. The first node descriptor is in bytes 32 to 39. Bytes 32 to 33 show that it can have 124 (0x7c) descriptors in the block, but bytes 34 to 35 show that only 4 are used. Bytes 36 to 39 show that block 1 of the directory contains the first node.

The second node descriptor starts in byte 40. We see that this node contains files with a file name hash greater than 0x41659532, and the names are located in block 4 of the directory. To find the upper bound of the hashes in this node, we look at the entry for the next node, which starts in byte 48, and see that its hash value is 0x92fad588. The entry for the fourth node starts in byte 63.

## JOURNAL DATA STRUCTURES

The journal records metadata updates so that a file system crash can be more quickly recovered from. There are four data structures in the Ext3 journal. One is for the journal superblock, which is located in the first block of the journal. The others are for the Descriptor, Commit, and Revoke blocks. Each data structure has a signature value, and it is essential because it is used to distinguish between normal journal blocks and journal administrative blocks. The journal data is all written in big-endian ordering, which is the opposite of what we have seen in the other ExtX data structures.

All four data structures start off with the same header, which is given in Table 15.28.

**Table 15.28**  Data structure for the standard header of the journal data structures.

| Byte Range | Description | Essential |
|---|---|---|
| 0–3 | Signature (0xC03B3998) | Yes |
| 4–7 | Block type (see Table 15.29) | Yes |
| 8–11 | Sequence Number | Yes |

The block type is used to distinguish between the four data structures. It has the values given in Table 15.29.

**Table 15.29**  Values for the type field in the journal header fields.

| Value | Description |
|---|---|
| 1 | Descriptor block |
| 2 | Commit block |
| 3 | Superblock version 1 |
| 4 | Superblock version 2 |
| 5 | Revoke block |

The default action of the first version of the journal is to record all data updates, and the second version records only metadata updates. A mount option can force a second version journal to record all data updates. The superblock has the fields given in Table 15.30.

**Table 15.30**  Data structure for version 1 and 2 of the journal superblock.

| Byte Range | Description | Essential |
|---|---|---|
| 0–11 | Standard header (see Table 15.28) | Yes |
| 12–15 | Journal block size | Yes |
| 16–19 | Number of journal blocks | Yes |

*continues*

**Table 15.30**   Data structure for version 1 and 2 of the journal superblock (Continued).

| Byte Range | Description | Essential |
| --- | --- | --- |
| 20–23 | Journal block where the journal actually starts | Yes |
| 24–27 | Sequence number of first transaction | Yes |
| 28–31 | Journal block of first transaction | Yes |
| 32–35 | Error number | No |

If the superblock is a version 1 superblock, only the first 36 bytes are used. If it is a version 2 superblock, the fields given in Table 15.31 are also used.

**Table 15.31**   Data structure for the remainder of the version 2 journal superblock.

| Byte Range | Description | Essential |
| --- | --- | --- |
| 36–39 | Compatible Features | No |
| 40–43 | Incompatible Features | No |
| 44–47 | Read only compatible Features | No |
| 48–63 | Journal UUID | No |
| 64–67 | Number of file systems using journal | No |
| 68–71 | Location of superblock copy | No |
| 72–75 | Max journal blocks per transaction | No |
| 76–79 | Max file system blocks per transaction | No |
| 80–255 | Unused | No |
| 256–1023 | 16-byte IDs of file systems using the journal | No |

At the time of this writing, the only feature available is the revoke feature. It is an incompatible feature, and its flag value is 0x00000001.

The descriptor block contains the standard header data structure that was previously given in Table 15.28, and it occupies bytes 0 to 11. Starting with byte 12 are descriptor entries, which have the fields given in Table 15.32.

**Table 15.32**  Data structures for the journal descriptor block entries.

| Byte Range | Description | Essential |
|---|---|---|
| 0–3 | File system block | Yes |
| 4–7 | Entry flags (see Table 15.33) | Yes |
| 8–23 | UUID (does not exist if the SAME_UUID flag is set) | No |

Each of these entries identifies with which file system block a given journal block corresponds. For example, the first journal block after the descriptor block corresponds to the file system block that is described in the first descriptor entry. The flags field has the values given in Table 15.33.

**Table 15.33**  Flag values for the journal descriptor entry flag field.

| Flag Values | Description |
|---|---|
| 0x01 | Journal block has been escaped |
| 0x02 | Entry has the same UUID as the previous (SAME_UUID) |
| 0x04 | Block was deleted by this transaction (currently not used) |
| 0x08 | Last entry in descriptor block |

The escape flag is used when a file system block has the same four bytes as the signature value in the header data structure. In this situation, the four bytes are cleared when it is written to the journal.

The Commit block has only the standard header. The header contains the block type and sequence number needed to identify its type and which transaction it is committing.

The Revoke block has the standard header and a list of file system blocks that have been revoked. It has the fields given in Table 15.34.

**Table 15.34**  Data structure for the journal revoke block.

| Byte Range | Description | Essential |
|---|---|---|
| 0–11 | Standard header (see Table 15.28) | Yes |
| 12–15 | Size in bytes of revoke data | Yes |
| 16–SIZE | List of 4-byte file system block addresses | Yes |

A revoke applies to transactions whose sequence number is equal to or less than the sequence number of the revoke record.

Let's look at a journal from a file system. We can view the contents using icat and running it on inode 8:

```
# icat -f linux-ext3 /dev/hdb2 8 | xxd
0000000: c03b 3998 0000 0004 0000 0000 0000 0400  .;9.............
0000016: 0000 0400 0000 0001 0000 0126 0000 0000  ...........&....
0000032: 0000 0000 0000 0000 0000 0000 0000 0000  ................
0000048: a34c 4be5 c222 460b b76f d45b 518b 083c  .LK.."F..o.[Q..<
0000064: 0000 0001 0000 0000 0000 0000 0000 0000  ................
0000080: 0000 0000 0000 0000 0000 0000 0000 0000  ................
```

We see the signature in bytes 0 to 3, and bytes 4 to 7 show that this block has a type of 4, which is the version 2 superblock. Bytes 8 to 11 show the sequence is 0, and bytes 12 to 15 show the journal block size is 1,024 bytes (0x0400). Bytes 16 to 19 show that there is 1,024 blocks in the journal, and 20 to 23 show that the journal entries start in journal block 1. To identify the first transaction in the journal, we refer to bytes 24 to 27 to see that the first sequence number is 294 (0x0126), and bytes 28 to 31 show that it is in block 0. We already saw that the journal entries start in block 1. The reason that the first transaction is in block 0 is because the file system was cleanly unmounted and all transactions are complete.

We mount the file system and create a file in the root directory. The superblock now contains the following:

```
# icat -f linux-ext3 /dev/hdb2 8 | xxd
0000000: c03b 3998 0000 0004 0000 0000 0000 0400 .;9.............
0000016: 0000 0400 0000 0001 0000 0127 0000 0001 ...........'....
```

The difference from the previous output is that starting sequence number has increased to 295 (0x0124), and the corresponding journal block is now set to block 1 because there are valid transactions in the journal.

We now examine the contents of journal block 1. Keep in mind that this is not file system block 1; this is the block inside the journal file. We can view this block by piping the icat output into dd with a block size of 1024, or we can use the jcat tool in TSK. We will use jcat here:

```
# jcat -f linux-ext3 /dev/hdb2 1 | xxd
0000000: c03b 3998 0000 0001 0000 0127 0000 0004  .;9........'....
0000016: 0000 0000 0000 0000 0000 0000 0000 0000  ................
```

```
0000032: 0000 0000 0000 0002 0000 0002 0000 000e   ...............
0000048: 0000 0002 0000 0005 0000 0002 0000 00a3   ...............
0000064: 0000 0002 0000 0003 0000 000a 0000 0000   ...............
```

We see from the type value in bytes 4 to 7 that this is a descriptor block, and its sequence is 295 (0x0127). The first descriptor entry starts at byte 12, and it is for file system block 4. The flags field in bytes 16 to 19 is 0, which means that the UUID field exists in the next 16 bytes. This entry shows that the block following the descriptor block corresponds to file system block 4. Block 4 is the inode bitmap, and it was updated when the new inode was allocated.

The second entry starts at byte 36, and bytes 36 to 39 show that it is for file system block 2 and its flag values are 2, which means that there is no UUID field. This entry shows that the second block after the descriptor block is for file system block 2, which is the group descriptor table. By parsing the rest of the block, we can see that block 14 was updated because it is in the inode table and contains the inode that was allocated for the new file; block 5 was updated because it contains the inode for the root directory; block 163 was updated because it is where the root directory stores its directory entries; and block 3 was updated because it contains the block bitmap. If our journal also recorded content updates, there would be another entry for the new file content.

There were six entries in the descriptor table, so we can examine journal block 8 for the commit block. We can see it here:

```
# jcat -f linux-ext3 /dev/hdb2 8 | xxd
0000000: c03b 3998 0000 0002 0000 0127 0000 0000   .;9........'....
0000016: 0000 0000 0000 0000 0000 0000 0000 0000   ...............
```

Bytes 4 to 7 show us that it is a commit block (0x02), and bytes 8 to 11 show us that it is for sequence 295 (0x127). As a final example, the descriptor block shows that journal block 6 contains the file system block for the root directory. We can see the updated block with the new-file.txt entry by viewing block 6:

```
# jcat -f linux-ext3 /dev/hdb2 6 | xxd
0000000: 0200 0000 0c00 0100 2e00 0000 0200 0000   ...............
0000016: 0c00 0200 2e2e 0000 0b00 0000 e803 0c00   ...............
0000032: 6e65 772d 6669 6c65 2e74 7874 0c00 0000   new-file.txt....
[REMOVED]
```

This could allow you to determine which files were recently created and deleted from the system. The `jls` tool in TSK will display the contents of the journal. Here is the output from the previous example:

```
# jls -f linux-ext3 /dev/hdb2
JBlk       Descriptrion
0:         Superblock (seq: 0)
1:         Allocated Descriptor Block (seq: 295)
2:         Allocated FS Block 4
3:         Allocated FS Block 2
4:         Allocated FS Block 14
5:         Allocated FS Block 5
6:         Allocated FS Block 163
7:         Allocated FS Block 3
8:         Allocated Commit Block (seq: 295)
9:         Unallocated FS Block Unknown
[REMOVED]
```

## SUMMARY

This chapter has shown the data structures for the Ext2 and Ext3 file systems. There are a small number of core data structures, and they all have a specific purpose. Some of the data structures and flag options described in this chapter will be found only in non-standard systems. The ExtX data structures are similar to those that we will later see for UFS, but they are a little simpler.

## BIBLIOGRAPHY

Ts'o, Theodore, and Stephen Tweedie. "Planned Extensions to the Linux Ext2/Ext3 Filesystem." *Proceedings of the 2002 Usenix Technical Conference FREENIX Track*, 2002.

Refer to the Bibliography section of Chapter 14.

# UFS1 and UFS2 Concepts and Analysis

The *Unix File System* (UFS) comes in several variations and can be found in many types of UNIX systems, including FreeBSD, HP-UX, NetBSD, OpenBSD, Apple OS X, and Sun Solaris. Many OSes have modified one or more data structures over the years to suit their needs, but they all have the same concepts. Currently, the two major variations are UFS1 and UFS2. UFS2 supports larger disks and larger time stamps. I will use the term UFS to refer to both file systems. An investigator might encounter a UFS file system when investigating a Unix system, typically a server. Ext2 and Ext3 are based on UFS, and because they were already discussed in detail, this chapter will be briefer and assume that you understand the concepts from Chapter 14, "Ext2 and Ext3 Concepts and Analysis." This chapter covers the concepts and analysis techniques of a UFS file system, and Chapter 17, "UFS1 and UFS2 Data Structures," covers the data structures. The next chapter can be read in parallel with this chapter or in series.

## INTRODUCTION

UFS is related to the Berkeley *Fast File System* (FFS) and was designed to be fast and reliable. Copies of important data structures are stored throughout the file system, and data are localized so that the hard disk heads do not need to travel much when reading a file. A UFS is organized into sections, called *cylinder groups*, and the size of each group is based on the geometry of the hard disk. These are similar to the ExtX block groups.

UFS has a superblock data structure in the beginning of the file system that contains the basic layout information. The content of each file is saved to a block, which is a group of consecutive sectors. Blocks also can be broken up into fragments, which are used to store the final bytes of a file instead of allocating a full block. The metadata for each file and directory is stored in an inode data structure. The names of files are stored in directory entry structures, which are located in the blocks allocated to directories. Directory entry structures are basic data structures that contain the name of the file and a pointer to the file's inode entry. The relationship between these data structures can be seen in Figure 16.1. Each cylinder group contains its own inode table, bitmaps for the allocation status of fragments, and copies of the superblock.

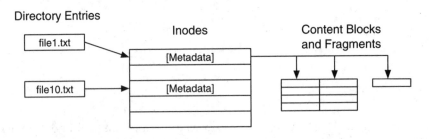

**Figure 16.1**   Relationship between UFS directory entries, inodes, and data blocks that are used to store file content.

All variants of UFS have the basic concepts that I just described, and it should be obvious that they are the same concepts that we saw for ExtX. The differences among the UFS-based variants are in how each of the data structures is organized and what additional features are included. There are fewer experimental features in UFS than in ExtX that affect the on-disk data.

The UFS1 file system is the default file system of OpenBSD and Solaris. It used to be the default file system of FreeBSD and NetBSD until FreeBSD 5.0 and NetBSD 2.0 included UFS2. UFS2 adds support for larger files and disks and other advanced features. At the time of this writing, only FreeBSD and NetBSD support UFS2. Apple OS X and Linux also support UFS1, but it is not their default file system. Solaris also has a version of UFS to support large files and disks. Note that Sun has not published the data structures for its version of UFS, but tools developed using the essential data in the data structures published by FreeBSD work on a Solaris file system. The non-essential data may be different, though.

In the rest of this chapter, we will examine the five-category data model with respect to the variants of UFS. Each section will discuss the basic properties of the category and the differences in each variant. I will refer to FreeBSD, NetBSD, and OpenBSD as BSD systems.

# FILE SYSTEM CATEGORY

The file system category of data includes the general layout and size information of the file system. This section covers where the data are located in UFS and how they can be analyzed.

## OVERVIEW

UFS has three types of data structures that store the file system category of data: the superblock, the cylinder group summary, and the group descriptor. The superblock is located in the beginning of the file system and contains the basic size and configuration information. The superblock references an area of the file system called the cylinder group summary area, which gives a summary of the cylinder group usage. Each cylinder group has a group descriptor data structure that provides details the group. We will now examine each of these data structures in more detail.

### Superblock

The UFS superblock contains basic information, such as the size of each fragment and the number of fragments in each block. It is here that we will also learn how big each cylinder group is and where the various data structures are inside each group. With these values, we can determine the layout of the file system. The superblock also might contain a volume label and the time that the file system was last mounted. The UFS superblock plays the same role as the superblock in ExtX, but the layout and non-essential data are different.

The UFS superblock is located somewhere in the start of the file system. With removable media, it could start in the first sector. A UFS1 superblock is typically located 8 KB from the start of the file system, and a UFS2 superblock is typically located 64 KB from the start. It is also possible for the UFS2 superblock to exist at 256 KB from the start of the file system, but this is not the default. Backup copies of the superblock can be found in each of the cylinder groups.

UFS1 and UFS2 use slightly different data structures, but both are over 1 KB in size and contain nearly 100 fields. The difference between the UFS1 and UFS2 superblocks is that the UFS2 version includes 64-bit versions of the size and date fields, which were added to the end of the data structure. The unused 32-bit fields are ignored and not reused.

General bookkeeping information is also stored in the superblock, such as the total number of free inodes, fragments, and blocks. From the superblock, we can find the location of the cylinder group summary area. This area contains a table with an entry for each cylinder group and the entry documents the number of free blocks, fragments, and inodes. As we will later see, this information also exists in the group descriptor of each group.

The superblock contains disk geometry information that was used to most efficiently organize and optimize a file system. It also contains many variations of a single value so that the OS does not have to compute the variation every time. For example, the size of a block is given in both bytes and in fragments. Further, the bitwise mask and shift values are also given so that a byte address can be converted to its block address and vice versa. Theoretically, only one of these values needs to exist and the others can be calculated. Many of the fields are non-essential, and in this section I will focus on the essential data and the non-essential data that could contain evidence.

The details of the data structures can be found in Chapter 17. Both UFS1 and UFS2 superblocks are given with an example file system image.

### Cylinder Group Descriptor

As previously stated, the file system is organized into cylinder groups. All the groups, except for maybe the last, are the same size, and each contains a group descriptor data structure that describes the group. The first group starts at the beginning of the file system, and the number of fragments in each group is given in the superblock. In addition to the group descriptor, each group also contains an inode table and a backup copy of the superblock.

The UFS group descriptor is much larger than its ExtX counter part, although much of it is non-essential data. The group descriptor is allocated a full block and has a combination of standard fields and a wide-open area that can be used for various tables. The standard fields provide bookkeeping information and describe how the latter part of the block is organized. Bookkeeping information exists to make the allocation of files more efficient, such as the location of the last allocated block, fragment, and inode. Summary information about the number of free blocks, fragments, and inodes is also given, but it should be the same as the values in the cylinder group summary area. The group descriptor also contains the time of the last write to the group.

The latter part of the group descriptor contains bitmaps for the inodes, blocks, and fragments in the group. It also contains tables that help find consecutive fragments and blocks of a given size. The starting location of each of these data structures is given as a byte offset that is relative to the start of the group descriptor, and the size of the data structure must typically be calculated. Figure 16.2 shows how a group descriptor could be laid out. The specific data structures and layout are given in the next chapter.

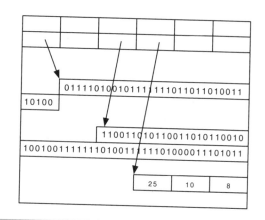

**Figure 16.2** Layout of group descriptor with the standard fields and then bitmaps and other tables in a wide-open area.

With ExtX, we saw that the second block of each group always had a table of group descriptors. With UFS, the location of the group descriptor, inode table, and backup superblock is specific to each file system, and the offsets are given in the superblock. For example, the inode table could start 32 fragments from the start and the group descriptor 16 fragments from the start. UFS1 adds an additional twist because the offsets are relative to a base location that changes for each cylinder group. For example, if the inode table has an offset of 32 fragments, it could be 32 fragments from the start of group 0, 64 fragments from the start of group 1, and 96 fragments from the start of group 2. The reason the data are staggered is to reduce the impact of physical damage to a platter in older disks.

Cylinder groups are so named because they were aligned on cylinder boundaries. Older hard disks had the same number of sectors per track, which meant that the first sector of every group was on the same platter. To reduce the effect of a hard disk error, the administrative data are staggered so that not every copy of the superblock is on the same platter. Newer hard disks do not have the same number of sectors in each cylinder, so this is not an issue, and UFS2 no longer staggers the data.

The "base" location for each group is calculated using two values from the superblock. The superblock defines a cycle value $c$ and a delta value $d$. The base increases by $d$ for every group and returns to the beginning after $c$ groups. For example, the base might increase by 32 fragments for every group and then start at an offset of 0 after 16 groups.

Figure 16.3 shows an example of a UFS1 and a UFS2 file system. The UFS1 file system has administrative data with a cycle of 3 and the UFS2 file system has the data at a constant offset for each group. The fragments before and after the administrative data can be used to store file content.

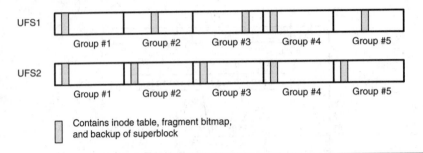

**Figure 16.3** UFS1 with five groups and staggering administrative data and UFS2 with five groups and administrative data at a constant offset.

Figure 16.4 shows an example layout of a group. Its base address is located several blocks inside the group, and the backup superblock, group descriptor, and inode table all follow in consecutive order. Inside the group descriptor are bitmaps and the standard data structure fields. All other fragments are for file and directory content.

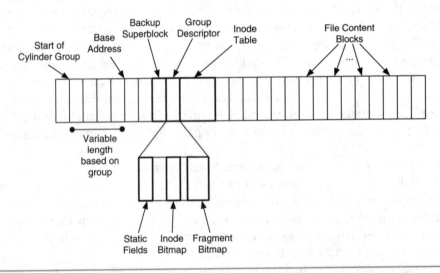

**Figure 16.4** An example layout of a UFS1 cylinder group. The base address is a variable number of blocks from the start of the group, and the bitmaps are a static distance from the base.

## Boot Code

If a UFS file system contains the OS kernel, it needs boot code. The boot code is located in the first sector of the file system and can continue until the superblock or disk label data structure. To fully understand the layout of UFS, it might be helpful to refer back to Chapter 6, "Server-based Partitions."

BSD and Solaris systems have their own partitioning systems. An IA32 (i.e., x86/i386) BSD system will have one DOS partition and one or more BSD partitions inside of it. The BSD partition locations are defined by the disk label structure, which is located in sector 1 of the DOS partition. The boot code is located in sector 0 and then in sectors 2 to 15. If the file system is UFS1, the superblock will be in sector 16, and if the file system is UFS2, the superblock will be in sector 128. If the file system is UFS2, the boot code might also occupy additional sectors.

An i386 Solaris system is similar where it will have two DOS partitions. One is small and contains only boot code. The other contains the file systems and has a *Volume Table of Contents* (VTOC) data structure in sector 0. A disk for a Sparc Solaris system has a VTOC in sector 0 of the disk and the boot code in sectors 1 to 15. Newer Sparc Solaris systems might use an EFI partition table instead of a VTOC.

File systems that do not contain boot code will not use the sectors before the superblock. Figure 16.5(A) shows an example IA32 FreeBSD disk and Figure 16.5(B) shows an example Sparc Solaris disk.

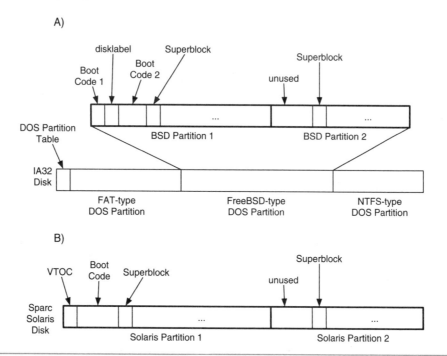

**Figure 16.5**  Examples of A) an IA32 system with three DOS partitions and two BSD partitions inside the FreeBSD partition and B) a Sparc Solaris disk with two Solaris partitions in it.

## Example Image

To close this section, I will run the `fsstat` tool from *The Sleuth Kit* (TSK) on the UFS1 image. We will be using this example image later in this chapter, and it is used for the manual analysis in the next chapter. The `fsstat` output is much larger that what is shown here because it details every cylinder group, but the relevant parts are shown.

```
# fsstat -f openbsd openbsd.dd
FILE SYSTEM INFORMATION
--------------------------------------------
File System Type: UFS 1
Last Written: Tue Aug 3 09:14:52 2004
Last Mount Point: /mnt

METADATA INFORMATION
--------------------------------------------
Inode Range: 0 - 3839
Root Directory: 2
Num of Avail Inodes: 3813
Num of Directories: 4

CONTENT INFORMATION
--------------------------------------------
Fragment Range: 0 - 9999
Block Size: 8192
Fragment Size: 1024
Num of Avail Full Blocks: 1022
Num of Avail Fragments: 16

CYLINDER GROUP INFORMATION
--------------------------------------------
Number of Cylinder Groups: 2
Inodes per group: 1920
Fragments per group: 8064

Group 0:
  Last Written: Tue Aug  3 09:14:33 2004
  Inode Range: 0 - 1919
  Fragment Range: 0 - 8063
    Boot Block: 0 - 7
    Super Block: 8 - 15
    Super Block: 16 - 23
    Group Desc: 24 - 31
    Inode Table: 32 - 271
    Data Fragments: 272 - 8063
```

```
Global Summary (from the superblock summary area):
  Num of Dirs: 2
  Num of Avail Blocks: 815
  Num of Avail Inodes: 1912
  Num of Avail Frags: 11
Local Summary (from the group descriptor):
  Num of Dirs: 2
  Num of Avail Blocks: 815
  Num of Avail Inodes: 1912
  Num of Avail Frags: 11
  Last Block Allocated: 392
  Last Fragment Allocated: 272
  Last Inode Allocated: 7
[REMOVED]
```

This output shows us the general information, such as block size, fragment size, and number of inodes. We also get a breakdown of each cylinder group with respect to what fragments are in each group and which resources were last allocated. This output merges the data from the superblock, the cylinder group summary area, and the group descriptors. For example, if we are given a block address, we can determine to which group it belongs. We also can identify where the inode table and group descriptor for each group are located. This is important for UFS1 where they are located at different offsets for each group.

Notice that there are two superblocks in the first group. The first one is because there is always a superblock in sector 16 (which is block 8 in this file system). The second one is because every cylinder group has a backup copy located at an offset of 16 fragments.

## ANALYSIS TECHNIQUES

Analysis of the file system category involves locating and processing the general file system information so that additional analysis techniques can be applied. With a UFS file system, the first step is to locate the superblock at one of the standard locations. Using the data in the superblock, we can find the locations of each cylinder group and data block. Backup copies of the superblock can be found in each cylinder group.

To locate the group descriptor for a specific group, we need to use the offset location given in the superblock and add it to the group's base address. The base address for a UFS2 group is the start of the group, but it staggers for a UFS1 cylinder group. The starting location can be calculated using the delta and cycle values in the superblock. We will use the group descriptor when determining the allocation status of the group's resources.

The last relevant data structure is located in the cylinder group summary area. Its address is given in the superblock, and it contains a table of usage information for each cylinder group. We can use this to get basic information about a group.

## ANALYSIS CONSIDERATIONS

The file system category of data will not typically include much evidence of an incident. With UFS, there is a lot of non-essential data in this category, and detecting hidden data is further complicated because the essential and non-essential data are intertwined. There also could be unused space at the end of the block allocated to a superblock, cylinder group summary area, or group descriptor. Compare the size of the file system with the size of the volume to find volume slack.

There is a lot of bookkeeping information in the superblock, group descriptors, and cylinder group summary area. If an incident occurred very recently, you might be able to draw conclusions about where files were deleted from and which file was last allocated. Having multiple copies of this data also allows them to be compared if tampering is suspected. Backup copies of the superblock can be found in each cylinder group. You can search for the backup copies using the data structure's signature value.

## CONTENT CATEGORY

The content category includes the file and directory content data. This section describes where UFS stores file and directory content and how to analyze it.

### OVERVIEW

UFS uses fragments and blocks to store file and directory content. A *fragment* is a group of consecutive sectors, and a *block* is a group of consecutive fragments. Every fragment has an address, starting with 0. A block is addressed using the address of the first fragment in the block. The first block and fragment start with the first sector of the file system. The minimum size of a UFS block is 4,096 bytes, and the maximum number of fragments per block is eight. An example of the block and fragment relationship is shown in Figure 16.6 where block 64, which contains fragments 64 to 71, is fully allocated to a file, and fragments 74 and 75 in block 72 are allocated to a file. The other fragments in block 72 can be allocated to other files.

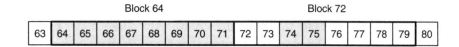

**Figure 16.6** Two UFS blocks with 8 fragments in each. One block is allocated, and two fragments of the other are allocated to a file.

The motivation for having two types of data units is to allow files to allocate large amounts of consecutive data while not wasting space in the last block. Investigators frequently utilize the large amounts of wasted slack space at the end of a file, but UFS tries to minimize the amount of wasted space.

With UFS, if a file can fill an entire block, it will be allocated a full block. When the final data are being written, only enough fragments for the data are allocated. When the file grows in size and can fill an entire block, it will be moved to one if needed.

Consider an example file system with 8,192 byte blocks and 1,024 byte fragments. A file that is 20,000 bytes in size will need 2 blocks and 4 fragments. This can be seen in Figure 16.7 where the two blocks start in fragments 584 and 592. This can store 16,384 bytes of the file, and the remaining 3,616 bytes are stored in fragments 610 to 613. The first two fragments in this block are used by another file.

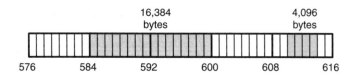

**Figure 16.7** A 20,000-byte file is stored in two 8,192-byte blocks and four 1,024 byte fragments.

The allocation status of a block or fragment is determined using one of two bitmaps. One has a bit for each fragment, and the other has a bit for each block, and they should contain nearly the same information, but the block bitmap allows the system to more quickly find consecutive blocks when allocating a large file. The UFS bitmaps are opposite of normal bitmaps because they are "free" bitmaps. Therefore, when the bit is 1, the block or fragment is available. If the bit is a 0, the block or fragment is being used.

The bitmaps are stored inside of a cylinder group's group descriptor data structure, which we previously examined. Therefore, before we determine the allocation status of a block, we will need to determine in which group it is located. This is easy because all we need to do is divide the fragment address by the number of fragments per cylinder group.

To determine the bit in the bitmap for a specific block, we calculate the starting block address of the group and subtract that value from our block address. Refer to Chapter 14 for an example of this. The UFS block and fragment bitmaps are discussed in more detail in Chapter 17.

The dstat tool in TSK shows us the allocation status of a UFS fragment and gives us the cylinder group that it is a part of. An example from our UFS1 image is shown here:

```
# dstat -f openbsd openbsd.dd 288
Fragment: 288
Allocated
Group: 0
```

## ALLOCATION ALGORITHMS

The designers of UFS have spent a lot of time researching allocation strategies and have focused on making block allocation efficient. Similar work has likely occurred with the commercial file systems, but the work has not been published, and my basic testing might not have shown the full extent of their algorithms. In this section, I will give an overview of the documented BSD allocation strategies but would recommend the *Design and Implementation of the 4.4 BSD Operating System* or *Design and Implementation of the FreeBSD Operating System* books for anyone who wants more details. While there is a documented allocation strategy, there is no requirement that an OS must follow it. They are free to allocate in any method they want.

The first consideration when allocating a block or fragment is the cylinder group. If the OS is allocating blocks for a new file and there are available blocks in the cylinder group of the inode, blocks from that cylinder group are used. If it is an existing file, restrictions might be placed on how many blocks any file can have in a single group, so a new group might need to be selected. For example, many of the OSes will restrict how many blocks a file or directory can allocate in a single group. The restriction is typically placed at 25% or 33% of the total number of blocks. When that value is reached, a new group is selected. Solaris has a similar strategy where it allocates the first 12 blocks (i.e., the direct blocks in the inode) for a file in one cylinder group and then allocates the remaining blocks in other groups.

After the cylinder group has been selected, the OS will allocate blocks based on how many data are being written. If the size of the file is unknown or if it slowly increases, blocks will be added one by one using a next-available strategy. This has historically involved taking the rotational delay of the disk into consideration to find the optimal location for the next block, but now the next consecutive block is used. If the size is known, the data are broken up into chunks, which are typically the size of 16 blocks. Blocks are allocated for each of these chunks using a first-available strategy. Therefore, if you have an 8,192-byte block size, each chunk will be 128 KB. This value can be configured in the file system and is set in the superblock.

For the final data in the file, fragments will be allocated instead of a full block. The OS will look for consecutive fragments that have enough space for the data. The consecutive fragments cannot cross a block boundary, and the bookkeeping information in the file system provides a list of where fragments of a given length can be found. A first-available strategy is used when allocating the final fragments.

When a file is extended and it already has fragments, the OS first tries to extend the existing fragments. If this is not possible, a new set of fragments or a full block is allocated and the data are moved. If the file has 12 full blocks, fragments are generally no longer used. Full blocks are allocated when the file is extended.

The superblock defines how many blocks should remain free at any given time. The free blocks are reserved so that a system administrator can login and clean up the file system, but an OS might choose to not enforce the limit.

The BSD and Solaris systems that I tested will all wipe the unused sectors in a fragment. Therefore, there will not be any data from a deleted file in the slack space of an allocated fragment.

## ANALYSIS TECHNIQUES

We analyze data in the content category by locating a block or fragment, viewing the contents, and identifying its allocation status. To locate the data, we need its fragment or block address. The sizes of a block and fragment are given in the superblock, and we simply advance from the start of the file system until we reach the specific address. The block address corresponds to the address of the first fragment in the block.

To determine the allocation status of any fragment, we must first determine the cylinder group in which it is located. This is done by dividing the block address by the number of fragments in a group. The group descriptor for the group is located using the offset value from the superblock and adding it to the base address for the group. The group descriptor will contain the fragment bitmap.

To extract all unallocated fragments in the file system, we cycle through each group and examine each fragment bitmap. Any fragment that is not allocated is extracted for analysis. Fragments and blocks that are used to store superblocks, inode tables, group descriptors, and the cylinder group summary area are considered allocated even though they are not allocated to a file.

## ANALYSIS CONSIDERATIONS

The design and allocation strategies of UFS provide some benefit and challenges for investigators. On the plus side, blocks should be localized to their inode, which could make file recovery easier, and if deleted data are in a group that has little activity, it could exist for longer than deleted data in other groups. Also on the plus side is that clusters of consecutive blocks are allocated when possible so that fragmentation is reduced, which could help carving tools.

One of the down sides of UFS is the final fragment. It is common for the final data in a file to exist in some other part of the cylinder group because it needed only one fragment. This can make carving more difficult. On the other hand, the fragments might allow more data to be recovered than with ExtX, which wiped all bytes in a block. UFS will wipe only the fragments allocated, so parts of a block will still exist after some of it has been reallocated.

Very large files that need to be recovered, such as a large e-mail file, could be difficult because they might have taken up more than 25% of the cylinder group and the remainder moved to another group. Further, Solaris uses a new cylinder group after allocating the first 12 blocks of the file, which prevents carving tools from working. Of course, the OS that created the file system might not have been following every rule of UFS and did not use these allocation principles.

## METADATA CATEGORY

The metadata category of data contains the descriptive data for a file or directory. This section describes where UFS stores the data and how we can analyze them.

### OVERVIEW

Like ExtX, UFS uses inode data structures to store file and directory metadata. UFS2 also has extended attributes to store additional descriptive data about a file. We will examine each of these data structures separately.

#### Inodes

Inodes in UFS have the same basic concept as we saw with ExtX. Each cylinder group has an inode table, whose relative location is given in the superblock. With UFS1, all inodes are initialized when the file system is created. UFS2 has dynamic inodes where they are initialized when they are needed, and the space in the inode table can be used for file content if all other blocks in the file system have been used. Each file and directory uses one inode, and it contains the address of the blocks that a file has allocated, the file size, and temporal information.

UFS inodes have 12 direct block pointers, one indirect block pointer, one double indirect block pointer, and one triple indirect block pointer. The address in each block pointer is for a full block, except for the final pointer, which could be for one or more fragments. The file size is used to determine how many fragments are being used. The block pointers are 32-bit values in UFS1 and 64-bit values in UFS2.

UFS supports sparse files, which were discussed in Chapter 8, "File System Analysis." If a file has not defined the contents of part of a file or if the block is all zeros, the OS will probably not allocate a block. Instead, it will place a 0 in the block pointer and output a block of zeros when that part of the file is read.

The same file types and permissions are used with UFS as we saw with ExtX. An inode has a last modified, last accessed, and last changed time values, but it does not have a deleted time value. Although UFS2 added a create time value to the inode. The times are saved as the number of seconds since January 1, 1970 12:00 GMT, and the number of nanoseconds also is given for finer resolution. The time values in UFS1 are 32 bits and 64 bits in UFS2.

Each inode is given an address, starting with 0. Note that this is different from ExtX, which started with inode 1. Inodes 0 and 1 are reserved, but not used for anything. Inode 1 used to be used for bad blocks. Inode 2 is reserved for the root directory. The allocation status of any inode is determined using the inode bitmap, which is located in the group descriptor. To determine which group an inode is in, its address is divided by the number of inodes per group, which can be found in the superblock. The UFS1 and UFS2 inode data structures are described with file system images in the next chapter.

### Extended Attributes

Extended attributes were added to UFS2, and they provide an additional location to store descriptive data about a file or directory. Extended attributes are a name value pair, and there are currently two "types": user name space and system name space. Any user that can read the file's contents can read the file's user name space attributes. Although only privileged users can read the file's system name space attributes.

The UFS2 inode has three fields for the extended attributes. One is a size value, and the other two are block addresses where the attributes are stored. The blocks are filled with variable length data structures that contain a header and the attribute value. A user can set the attributes with the `setextattr` command, and applications can set them with special system calls. The extended attribute data structure is shown in Chapter 17.

## Example Image

Here is the output from running istat on our example file system image. This inode is manually processed in Chapter 17 and is included here as a reference about what data exist.

```
# istat -f openbsd -z UTC openbsd.dd 3
inode: 3
Allocated
Group: 0
uid / gid: 0 / 0
mode: -rw-r-r-
size: 1274880
num of links: 1

Inode Times:
Accessed:       Tue Aug  3 14:12:56 2004
File Modified:  Tue Aug  3 14:13:14 2004
Inode Modified: Tue Aug  3 14:13:14 2004

Direct Blocks:
288 289 290 291 292 293 294 295
296 297 298 299 300 301 302 303
304 305 306 307 308 309 310 311
[REMOVED]
1568 1569 1570 1571 1572 1573 1574 1575
1576 1577 1578 1579 1580
Indirect Blocks:
384 385 386 387 388 389 390 391
```

We can see that this file is 1,247,880 bytes, so it needs more than 12 of the 8KB blocks. The bottom of the istat output lists each fragment that the file has allocated. Recall that only the block address is given in the inode, but istat will give the addresses of all fragments in the block. The last line of the 'Direct Blocks' section shows that only five of the eight fragments in block 1576 are being used. Therefore, fragments 1581 to 1583 could be used by another file. Also notice that block 384 is being used as an indirect block pointer.

## ALLOCATION ALGORITHMS

The documented allocation method of UFS inodes is the same that we saw for ExtX. An OS can choose any algorithm, but the typical policy is to allocate an inode for a directory in a new cylinder group that has a less than average number of directories and a greater than average number of available blocks. The inode for a file is allocated in the same cylinder group as the parent directory, if space exists. When looking for a free inode in a cylinder group, a first-available strategy is used.

When the inode is allocated, its contents are cleared and the M-time, A-time, C-time, and Create-time (for UFS2) are set to the current time. The link count is set to 1 for files and 2 for directories to account for the '.' name inside of the directory.

When a file is deleted, BSD systems and Solaris will clear the block pointers inside the inode, clear the size, and clear the mode. Therefore, the full size, content location, and type of file will not be known. The contents of the indirect block pointers are not cleared, though, so searching for a block of indirect block pointers could help during recovery. A special tool would likely be needed to find a block full of 32-bit or 64-bit addresses. Note that the differences between the deletion routines with this and what we saw with Linux and ExtX is that Linux did not clear the mode field, but it did clear the contents of the Ext3 indirect block pointers.

The time updating for OpenBSD 3, FreeBSD 5, and Sun Solaris 9 systems are the same as reported in ExtX for Fedora Core 2. Namely, when a file is created, all times are set to the current time. The M- and C-times of the parent directory are also updated. When a file is moved, the new file has an updated C-time, but the M- and A-times remain the same. When a file is copied, the A-time on the source file is updated, and the destination file has all new M-, A-, and C-times. When a file is deleted, its M- and C-times are updated.

## ANALYSIS TECHNIQUES

When we analyze the metadata category of data, we are looking for descriptive data about a file so that we can sort it and obtain more information. To do this, we need to be able to locate the inodes, determine their allocation status, and process the extended attributes that might exist.

To locate a specific inode, we need to first identify its group, and we can do that by dividing the inode address by the number of inodes per group. Next, we need to locate the inode table by using the starting fragment of the group and the inode table offset, which is given in the superblock. With UFS1 we also will need to calculate what the staggering offset for the group is. Lastly, we locate the specific inode in the table by subtracting the inode address from the address of the first inode in the group.

Processing an inode is fairly straightforward. The mode field and time values are encoded and must be processed before sense can be made of them. To locate the content, the addresses given in the 12 direct block pointers are used. If the file is larger, the indirect blocks must be read and their contents processed as a list of block addresses. Any pointer with a value of 0 is a sparse block and corresponds to a block of all zeros. For the final block pointer, consider the total size of the file and process only that amount. The final block could be a fragment, and the next fragment might be used by another file.

To determine the allocation status of an inode, we use the inode bitmap for the group, which is located in the group descriptor. The group descriptor is located using the starting address of the group and offset values from the superblock. If the inode's bit is set to 1, it is allocated.

It is sometimes useful to examine all the unallocated inode entries because they might contain temporal or other information from deleted files. We can do this by searching the bitmaps for inodes whose bits are 0 and processing inodes that are non-zero. Inodes that are all zeros are typically ones that have not been used and are still in an initialized state.

The extended attributes also might have evidence or hidden data and should be examined. We do this by reading the blocks that are listed in the inode and processing each entry. The user can assign the name and value pairs.

## ANALYSIS CONSIDERATIONS

Most of the analysis considerations of ExtX metadata apply to UFS. Deleted files have the block pointers, size, and mode cleared from the inode, but UFS preserves the state of the indirect block pointers. Therefore, recovery could try to locate an indirect block pointer and reconstruct the file. The M- and C-time in an unallocated inode entry might reflect the time that the corresponding file was deleted. The allocation strategies can be used when carving data by focusing attention on only a specific group instead of the entire file system.

As we saw with ExtX, the touch command can be used to modify the M- and A-times of any file. Therefore, it is best to have a second source of temporal data to help determine the reliability of the time values. The C-time of the file is updated when the touch command is used. The time values are stored in UTC, so your analysis tool will need to convert that to the time zone where the computer was actually located so that the displayed time values are correct.

The BSD systems that I tested wrote 0s for the unused bytes in the final fragment of a file, also called slack space. Therefore, the only place to find data from deleted files is in the unallocated fragments. Fortunately, only the minimum number of fragments are allocated and wiped. Therefore, a block still might contain deleted data in the fragments that have not been reallocated. Slack space might contain hidden data, though.

The extended attributes of a UFS2 file system could be used to hide small amounts of data. They are limited to two blocks in size, but test if your analysis tools will show you this content and if they include the content in a keyword search.

The dynamic UFS2 inode tables also allow another area for data hiding. The OS does not initialize a block of inode entries in the inode table until it is needed. Therefore, data could be placed in the unused areas without being noticed until the OS reclaims the area and erases the data.

## FILE NAME CATEGORY

The file name category of data includes the data that assigns human readable names to inodes and other metadata. This section describes where UFS stores the data and how we can analyze them.

### OVERVIEW

UFS1 and UFS2 use the same file name data structure that ExtX does, so this section is only a review of the key ideas that were already described in the "File Name Category" section of Chapter 14. The *directory entry* data structure stores the file's name, inode address, and type value. The length of the structure is based on the name length, which has a maximum file length of 255 characters. The name is stored in ASCII and is null terminated, although an ExtX name is not null terminated.

The directory entry structures are located in the blocks allocated to a directory. Directories are like normal files except that their type is set to directory in the mode field. The first two entries in a directory should be for the '.' and '..' directories. Each entry has a length value that points to the next entry, and the length of the final entry points to the end of the block. When a file is deleted, the length of the previous entry is increased so that it points to the entry after the deleted entry. Refer to Chapter 14 for diagrams of this. The root directory is always located in inode 2. Chapter 17 contains the directory entry data structure and an example from a file system image. Here is the output of running fls on our example file system image that is processed in the next chapter.

```
# fls -f openbsd -a openbsd.dd 1921
d/d 1921:       .
d/d 2:          ..
r/r 1932:       file1.txt
r/r 1933:       file8.txt
r/r 1934:       file7.txt
r/- * 1935:     file6.txt
[REMOVED]
```

The entry with a "*" next to it is a deleted file. The first column contains the file type as reported in the directory entry and then in the inode. We can see that UFS clears the file type value in the inode because the deleted file name does not have a type in its inode column.

UFS supports both hard and soft links so that multiple names can be used for a single file or directory. Hard links are a second name for a file or directory in the same file system. When a hard link is created, a new directory entry is allocated, and it points to the inode of the original file. The link count in the inode is incremented to account for the new name. Soft links are created using symbolic links. A symbolic link stores the path of the destination file in either a fragment or in the 60 bytes usually used for block pointers. UFS2 has 64-bit pointers instead of 32-bit pointers, so it has 120 bytes in which to store the path. Chapter 14 has figures of hard and soft links.

Note that directories in Unix are used as both a place to store file names and as mounting points for other file systems. Refer to Chapter 14 for examples where you might not find a name you are looking for in a directory because there was another volume mounted there. Although not enabled by default, many BSD systems support a *union mount*, where the files in the directory that are being used as a mounting point will still be visible. The OS merges the files from the mount directory and the root directory of the volume so that they appear as one.

## ALLOCATION ALGORITHMS

With BSD and Solaris systems, directory entries are allocated on a first available strategy. The OS scans each of the directory entries and compares the reported entry length with the length that is actually needed based on the file name length. If the reported length is larger and the new file can fit inside that space, it is placed there. The directory blocks are wiped with zeros when they are allocated. Directory entry structures will not cross a block boundary.

When a file is deleted, the reported length of the previous entry is increased to point to the entry after the deleted file. BSD systems do not wipe the type or inode fields, although Solaris does. This means that you can get temporal data about the file name from a BSD system, but its direct block pointers will likely have been wiped. Other OSes could choose other techniques and wipe the name.

## ANALYSIS TECHNIQUES

Analysis of the file name category involves listing the files and subdirectories in a given directory and looking for some pattern and specific name. To do this, we generally need to first locate the root directory. The root directory is always located at inode 2, so we can locate its content using the same techniques that we saw in the section titled, "Metadata Category." After the contents of a directory have been located, we need to process them as a list of directory entries.

When processing the directory contents, the next allocated entry can be found by using the pointer in the current entry. To find deleted entries, the space in between the end of the file name of the one allocated entry and the start of the next allocated entry is examined. If any data there meets the format of a directory entry, it was probably there from a deleted file. When we locate a file or directory that we are interested in, we can get more details about it by identifying its corresponding inode address and processing it. Many tools do this automatically and list the time information with the name information. Refer to Chapter 14 for a figure and scenario on how the sequence of file deletions might be determined.

When a directory is deleted, the link between its inode and blocks will likely be deleted. To search for the contents of a deleted directory, we can look for the . and .. entries. Directory entries do not cross block segments, and therefore each block should start with a new entry.

## ANALYSIS CONSIDERATIONS

The design of the directory entry and the implementation in most systems allows deleted file names to be easily located, and the inode value is not cleared in BSD systems so the file metadata can also be found. Solaris wipes this value, so no additional data can be found. If a deleted directory entry is found and its inode value exists, it can be difficult to determine if the inode contents correspond to the file name or if the inode was reallocated and the contents correspond to a different file. A basic test for this is to determine if the inode is currently allocated. If it is, the inode could have been reallocated or the file could have been moved within the same file system and you are looking at the original location. Many OSes clear the mode field in a UFS inode, so the file type cannot be compared with the type in the directory entry.

It could be possible for data to be hidden in directory entry structures. The space between the last directory entry and the end of the block is unused and could contain data. However, this is a dangerous hiding technique because the OS could overwrite it when a new file name is created.

# THE BIG PICTURE

To conclude the discussion on UFS, we will step through an example where we allocate and then delete a /dir1/file1.dat file, which is 25,000 bytes in size, from a UFS2 file system.

## FILE ALLOCATION EXAMPLE

The high-level process for creating the /dir1/file1.dat file is to locate the dir1 directory, create a directory entry, allocate an inode, and then allocate blocks for the file content. The exact ordering of allocating the different data structures might vary by OS, and the order presented here might not reflect an actual system. There are several data structures that keep lists of available fragment sizes and clusters that are ignored for simplicity in this example.

1.  We read the superblock data structure, which is 2 KB in size and is located 64 KB into the file system. From processing this, we learn that the block size is 16KB and fragment size is 2KB. Each cylinder group has 32,776 fragments and 8,256 inodes. We also learn that the group descriptor is located 40 fragments, and the inode table is located 56 fragments into each cylinder group.
2.  We need to locate the dir1 directory in the root directory, so we process inode 2. Using the number of inodes per group, we determine that inode 2 is in cylinder group 0. Therefore, the inode table for inode 2 will start in block 56.
3.  We read the inode table from block 56 and process the third entry (the first entry is inode 0). The data in inode 2 shows that the directory entry structures for the root directory are located in block 1,096.
4.  We read the root directory contents from block 1096 and process the contents as a list of directory entries. We advance ahead by using the reported record length of each entry (we don't care about deleted files) and find the entry named dir1. It has an inode value of 16,549. The A-time of the root directory is updated.
5.  We determine where inode 16,549 is located by dividing it by the number of inodes per group and determine that it is in cylinder group 2. Group 2 starts in block 65,552, so its inode table starts in block 65,608. (If we were using a UFS1 file system, we would also need to calculate the base address for the group.)
6.  We read the inode table from block 65,608 and process entry 37, which is the relative location of inode 16,549. The inode contents show us that the contents of dir1 are located in block 66,816.

7. We read the `dir1` contents from block 66,816 and process the contents as a list of directory entries. We are looking for unused space in the directory. The `file1.dat` name is eight characters long and therefore the directory entry will require 16 bytes. We find space in between two allocated names, and the M- and C-times of the directory are updated. The space we took had been used by a deleted file.

8. We need to allocate an inode for the file, and it will be allocated in the same cylinder group as the parent directory, which is group 2. To locate the inode bitmap, we must first locate the group descriptor, which is 48 fragments from the start of the group. The group descriptor turns out to be in block 65,600, and it shows us that the inode bitmap is located 168 bytes into the group descriptor. The group descriptor also tells us that the last allocated inode entry was 16,650. We check the status of inode 16,651 and find it to be unallocated. We set its bit in the bitmap, update the last allocated inode value in the group descriptor, and decrement the number of free inodes value in the group descriptor and cylinder group summary area. The inode address is added to the `file1.dat` directory entry.

9. We locate inode 139 in the inode table, which is the relative location of inode 16,651, and initialize its values. The time values are set to the current time and the link value is set to 1. We also set the UID, GID, and mode fields.

10. The size of the file is 25,000 bytes, so we need to allocate one block and five fragments. We first need to process the group descriptor to find the offset of the fragment bitmap, which is located at byte offset 1,200. The group descriptor identifies block 67,896 as the last block allocated. We examine block 67,904 in the free fragment bitmap and determine that it is not allocated. The bit for this block is set to 0 to show that it is no longer free, and the count of available blocks is decremented. The last allocated pointer is also updated. The five available fragments are found using the bitmap (or one of the bookkeeping lists), and they are located in 74,242 to 74,246. Their bits are set to 0, and the proper bookkeeping values are updated. The address of the block and the starting fragment are added to the inode.

11. The file content of `file1.dat` is written to the allocated block and fragments.

The final state of the system can be found in Figure 16.8.

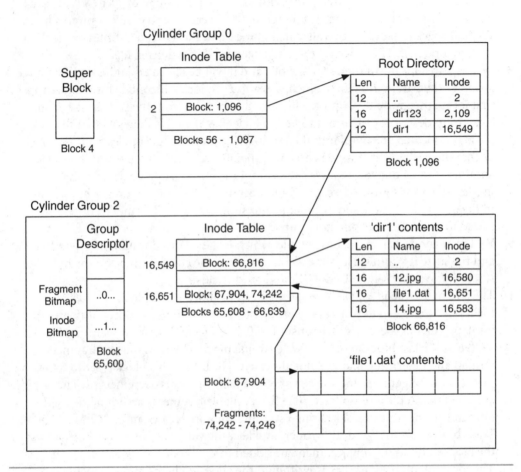

**Figure 16.8**    Final state after adding the 'dir1/file1.dat' file.

## FILE DELETION EXAMPLE

We will now delete the /dir1/file1.dat file using BSD-type methods. As mentioned in the previous section, the order of unallocating the data structures might vary by OS and the order presented here might not be the same as an actual OS.

1.  We read the superblock data structure, which is 2 KB in size and is located 64 KB into the file system. From processing this, we learn that the block size is 16 KB and fragment size is 2 KB. Each cylinder group has 32,776 fragments and 8,256 inodes. We

also learn that the group descriptor is located 40 fragments, and the inode table is located 56 fragments into each cylinder group.

2. We need to locate the dir1 directory in the root directory, so we process inode 2. Using the number of inodes per group, we determine that inode 2 is in cylinder group 0. Therefore, the inode table for inode 2 will start in block 56.

3. We read the inode table from block 56 and process the third entry (the first entry is inode 0). The data in inode 2 shows that the directory entry structures for the root directory are located in block 1,096.

4. We read the root directory contents from block 1,096 and process the contents as a list of directory entries. We advance ahead using the reported record length of each entry (we don't care about deleted files) and find the entry whose name is dir1. It has an inode value of 16,549. The A-time for the root directory is updated.

5. We determine where inode 16,549 is located by dividing it by the number of inodes per group and determine that it is in cylinder group 2. Group 2 starts in block 65,552, so its inode table starts in block 65,608.

6. We read the inode table from block 65,608 and process entry 37, which is the relative location of inode 16,549. The inode contents show us that the contents of dir1 are located in block 66,816.

7. We read the dir1 contents from block 66,816 and process the contents as a list of directory entries. We are looking the entry for the file1.dat file. We find its entry and observe that it has allocated inode entry 16,651. The directory entry is unallocated by adding its record length to the record length field in the previous directory entry, which belongs to the 12.jpg file. If the system were a Solaris system, the inode pointer would also be cleared. The M-time, A-time, and C-time are updated for dir1.

8. We process the contents of inode 16,651 from the group 2 inode table and decrement the link count by 1 to account for the name being deleted. The link count becomes 0, which means that the inode must be deallocated. To deallocate the inode, the corresponding bit in the inode bitmap is set to 0, and we update the free inode counts in the group descriptor and cylinder group summary area. The mode value in the inode is cleared.

9. We also need to deallocate the one block and five fragments that the file has allocated. For each block and fragment, the corresponding bit in the block and fragment bitmaps are set to 1, and the block pointer in the inode is cleared. The file size is decremented each time a block is deallocated, and it eventually reaches 0. The M-time and C-time are updated to reflect the inode changes. The free block and fragment counts are updated in the group descriptor and cylinder group summary area.

The final state of the file system can be seen in Figure 16.9. The bold lines and values represent the changes to the file system because of the deletion.

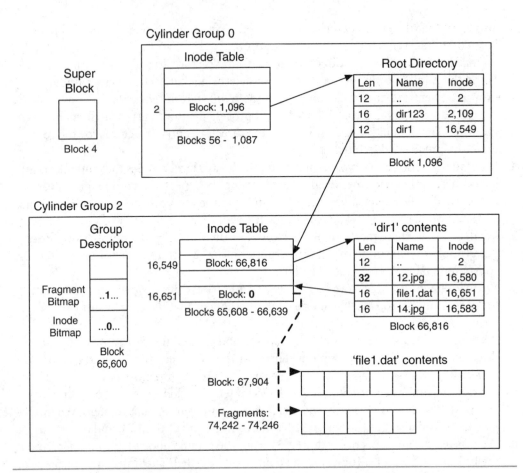

**Figure 16.9**   Final state after deleting the '/dir1/file1.dat' file.

## OTHER TOPICS

We will now discuss two analysis topics that apply to multiple data categories. In this section we discuss file recovery and file system consistency checks.

### FILE RECOVERY

Recovery of UFS files that were deleted by one of the standard OSes is not an easy task. The difficulty of recovery is similar to what we saw with ExtX, but it is even worse with Solaris because the link between the directory entry and the inode is wiped. The direct block pointers are wiped with BSD systems, so recovery will depend on application-level carving techniques. It is highly likely that the final data will be in a set of fragments and, therefore, might not be in the next consecutive block, even if the rest of the file was in consecutive blocks.

Many of the BSD systems allocate files in chunks of 64KB or 128KB consecutive blocks. This could be beneficial because there might be more data in consecutive blocks instead of randomly arranged from a first-available strategy. On the other hand, this is not as beneficial as a best-fit strategy that might place the entire file in consecutive blocks. Further, because some systems will limit the number of blocks that a file can allocate in any single group, large files will be fragmented even if the file could have been saved in consecutive blocks. Solaris changes cylinder groups after allocating the first 12 blocks, so carving those files will be very difficult. The contents of an indirect block pointer are not wiped in BSD or Solaris systems, so that might provide insight about recovery if it can be found.

## CONSISTENCY CHECK

Consistency checks are used in an investigation to find invalid values in the file system data structures and to find data that the suspect might have hidden. We will start in the file system category and examine the superblock. Most of the 2,048 bytes in the superblock are not used and could be used to hide data. It is difficult to determine which values are and are not used by a given OS because many are redundant and not as necessary with modern systems. These redundant values could be used for sanity checks, though, if tampering is suspected. In addition, there are unused sectors before the superblock that could be used for boot code and disk labels but are unused for non-root file systems. The superblock will be allocated a full block, so the unused fragments in the block also could be used to hide data.

The group descriptors also could be used for data hiding. The start of the data structure has structure, but the rest of it is wide open, and one could take advantage of this. A check for this is to compare where the bitmap structures start and how much space they actually need.

Every allocated inode entry should be examined and verified that the blocks and fragments that it points to are allocated. Care must be taken when considering the number of fragments that are needed for the final fragment run. All allocated blocks must either be used for cylinder group administrative data structures or pointed to by an inode. The end of the inode table also could have unused bytes.

Every allocated directory entry should point to an allocated inode entry. Inodes 0, 1, and 2 will be allocated but will not have file names pointing to them because they are reserved. The space at the end of a directory could contain hidden data, but this is more difficult for an attacker to control because the OS could overwrite it.

## SUMMARY

The UFS can be found in many server environments. It has a long history and has been designed for speed and efficiency, which also means that some parts of it are confusing. There are many structures that I did not discuss in this chapter that exist to help with the allocation of blocks and fragments. There are also many values in the superblock that can be calculated from other known values. This makes the superblock and similar file system category data structures larger than what we have previously seen.

The most difficult part of analyzing a UFS file system from one of the standard OSes is any type of deleted file recovery. The block pointers are wiped, and Solaris even wipes the pointer between the name and the inode. Therefore, application-level recovery techniques are needed, but the carving could be hampered by the block allocation routines, which try to prevent any one file from dominating a cylinder group. Although the structure and deletion methods of a UFS file system are much different from a FAT or NTFS file system, the same basic analysis techniques can be applied.

## BIBLIOGRAPHY

FreeBSD Source Code. 2004. http://fxr.watson.org/fxr/source/.

Garfinkel, Simson, Gene Spafford, and Alan Schwartz. *Practical Unix and Internet Security*. 3rd ed. Sebastopol: O'Reilly, 2003.

Mauro, Jim, and Richard McDougall. *Solaris Internals: Core Kernel Architecture*. Upper Saddle River: Sun Microsystems Press, 2001.

McKusick, Marshall K. "Enhancements to the Fast File System to Support Multi-Terabyte Storage Systems." *Proceedings of USENIX BSDCON '03 Conference*, September 2003.

McKusick, Marshall, Keith Bostic, Michael Karels, and John Quarterman. *The Design and Implementation of the 4.4 BSD Operating System*. Boston: Addison-Wesley, 1996.

McKusick, Marshall K., William N. Joy, Samuel J. Leffler, and Robert S. Fabry. "A Fast File System for Unix." *ACM Transactions on Computer Systems* 2(3): 181-197, August 1984.

McKusick, Marshall, and George Neville-Neil. *The Design and Implementation of the FreeBSD Operating System*. Boston: Addison-Wesley, 2004.

OpenBSD Source Code. 2004. `http://fxr.watson.org/fxr/source/?v=OPENBSD`.

Smith, Keith A. and Margo Seltzer. "A Comparison of FFS Disk Allocation Algorithms." *Proceedings of the 1996 Usenix Annual Technical Conference*, 1996.

# UFS1 and UFS2 Data Structures

This chapter describes the data structures that make up a UFS1 or UFS2 file system. The general concepts and analysis techniques for UFS were discussed in the previous chapter, and this chapter shows the layout of the data structures and where they are located in an example file system image. It is assumed that you are reading this chapter in parallel with the previous chapter or that you have already read it. As mentioned in the previous chapter, the UFS data structures contain multiple fields to store a single value in different formats. For example, the size of a block is stored both as a number of fragments and as a number of bytes. The different formats prevent the OS from having to calculate the different values each time. Although some OSes may require that both be set to equivalent values, it is not essential that both of them be set. Yet it is not trivial to identify which of the formats is essential. One OS could determine the block size based only on the byte size, and another could determine the block sized based only on the fragment size. It is essential to know the block size, but it is not essential which format to use. In this chapter, I have identified one of the formats as essential, but it may not apply to all tools or OSes.

## UFS1 SUPERBLOCK

The superblock contains the basic file system category of data in a UFS file system and UFS1 and UFS2 use different data structures. The UFS1 superblock is located in sector 16 and is allocated 2,048 bytes, but most of it is not essential or is zero. I am going to discuss only the essential data, but all the fields are included in the following table, if only to show how many non-essential values there are. The fields in the UFS1 superblock that are used by FreeBSD, NetBSD, and OpenBSD are shown in Table 17.1.

**Table 17.1** Data structure for the UFS1 superblock.

| Byte Range | Description | Essential |
| --- | --- | --- |
| 0–7 | Unused | No |
| 8–11 | Offset to backup superblock in cylinder group relative to a "base" | Yes |
| 12–15 | Offset to group descriptor in cylinder group relative to a "base" | Yes |
| 16–19 | Offset to inode table in cylinder group relative to a "base" | Yes |
| 20–23 | Offset to first data block in cylinder group relative to a "base" | No |
| 24–27 | Delta value for calculating staggering offset in cylinder group | Yes |
| 28–31 | Mask for calculating staggering offset (cycle value) in cylinder group | Yes |
| 32–35 | Last written time | No |
| 36–39 | Number of fragments in file system | Yes |
| 40–43 | Number of fragments that can store file data | No |
| 44–47 | Number of cylinder groups in file system | Yes |
| 48–51 | Size of a block in bytes | Yes |
| 52–55 | Size of a fragment in bytes | Yes |
| 56–59 | Size of a block in fragments | No |
| 60–63 | Minimum percent of free blocks | No |
| 64–67 | Milliseconds of rotation for next block | No |
| 68–71 | Disk RPMs | No |
| 72–75 | Mask used to calculate the address for a block | No |
| 76–79 | Mask used to calculate the address for a fragment | No |
| 80–83 | Shift used to calculate the byte address for a block | No |
| 84–87 | Shift used to calculate the byte address for a fragment | No |
| 88–91 | Maximum number of contiguous blocks to allocate | No |

| Byte Range | Description | Essential |
|---|---|---|
| 92–95 | Maximum number of blocks per cylinder group per file | No |
| 96–99 | Number of bits to convert between a block address and a fragment address | No |
| 100–103 | Number of bits to convert between a fragment address and a sector address | No |
| 104–107 | Size of superblock | No |
| 108–111 | Offset to cylinder summary area (no longer used) | No |
| 112–115 | Size of cylinder summary area (no longer used) | No |
| 116–119 | Number of indirect addresses per fragment | No |
| 120–123 | Number of inodes per block in inode table | No |
| 124–127 | Number of sectors per fragment | No |
| 128–131 | Optimization technique | No |
| 132–135 | Sectors per track | No |
| 136–139 | Hard disk sector interleave | No |
| 140–143 | Hard disk track skew | No |
| 144–151 | File System ID | No |
| 152–155 | Fragment address of cylinder group summary area | No |
| 156–159 | Size of cylinder group summary area in bytes | No |
| 160–163 | Size of cylinder group descriptor in bytes | No |
| 164–167 | Hard disk tracks per cylinder | No |
| 168–171 | Hard disk sectors per track | No |
| 172–175 | Hard disk sectors per cylinder | No |
| 176–179 | Cylinders in file system | No |
| 180–183 | Cylinders per cylinder group | No |
| 184–187 | Inodes per cylinder group | Yes |
| 188–191 | Fragments per cylinder group | Yes |

*continues*

**Table 17.1**   Data structure for the UFS1 superblock (Continued).

| Byte Range | Description | Essential |
|---|---|---|
| 192–195 | Number of directories | No |
| 196–199 | Number of free blocks | No |
| 200–203 | Number of free inodes | No |
| 204–207 | Number of free fragments | No |
| 208–208 | Super block modified flag | No |
| 209–209 | FS was clean when it was mounted | No |
| 210–210 | Mounted read only flag (set to 1 if read only) | No |
| 211–211 | General flags (see Table 17.2) | No |
| 212–723 | Last mount point | No |
| 724–727 | Last cylinder group searched | No |
| 728–1115 | Unused | No |
| 1116–1195 | Array inode addresses for snap shot inodes | No |
| 1196–1199 | Expected average file size | No |
| 1200–1203 | Expected number of files per directory | No |
| 1204–1311 | Unused | No |
| 1312–1315 | Last time fsck was run | No |
| 1316– 1319 | Size of cluster summary array in group descriptors | No |
| 1320–1323 | Maximum length of internal symbolic link | Yes |
| 1324–1327 | Format of inodes | Yes |
| 1328–1335 | Maximum file size | No |
| 1336–1343 | Mask used to calculate the offset in a block for an address | No |
| 1344–1351 | Mask used to calculate the offset in a fragment for an address | No |
| 1352–1355 | File system state | No |
| 1356–1359 | Format of positional layout tables | No |

| Byte Range | Description | Essential |
|---|---|---|
| 1360–1363 | Number of rotational positions | No |
| 1364–1367 | Rotational block list head | No |
| 1368–1371 | Blocks for each rotation | No |
| 1372–1375 | Signature value (0x011954) | Yes |

The first fields give the offsets that are used to locate data structures inside each cylinder group. We also can see the delta and cycle values that are used to calculate the base address for each cylinder group in UFS1. The standard total number of blocks, fragments, and cylinder groups is given, sometimes in multiple formats. The number of inodes and fragments per cylinder group is given later in the superblock.

Byte 128 has a field for the block allocation optimization technique. There are currently two values for this field. If set to 0, the OS should try to save time when allocating new blocks, which might cause wasted space and fragmentation as the file system fills up. If set to 1, the OS should try to save space when allocating new blocks and find an ideal-sized location. This might take more time though when creating files. Knowing this might help during file recovery.

There are several flags starting at byte 208. The first flag is set when the superblock has been modified and is cleared when mounted. The flag in byte 209 is set to 0 if the file system was clean when it was mounted. The flag in byte 210 is set to 1 if the file system was mounted read only. Lastly, the flag in byte 211 is a general flag and can contain any of the values given in Table 17.2.

**Table 17.2**   Flag values for the superblock general flag field.

| Flag Value | Description | Essential |
|---|---|---|
| 0x01 | Unclean—set when file system is mounted | No |
| 0x02 | Soft dependencies are being used | No |
| 0x04 | Needs consistency check next time it is mounted | No |
| 0x08 | Directories are indexed using hashtree or B-Tree | No |
| 0x10 | Access Control Lists are being used | No |
| 0x20 | TrustedBSD Mandatory Access Control multi-labels are being used | No |
| 0x80 | Flags have been moved (used by UFS2 in the "old" field) | No |

There is also a field at byte 1234 to 1237 that identifies which type of inode is used to store file metadata. If the field is 2, it is the 4.4BSD inode, and if it is 0xffffffff, it is the 4.2BSD inode. The other data in the superblock are non-essential and might or might not contain valid data.

Let's take a look at an OpenBSD system. The superblock is in sector 16 and is allocated four sectors, so we use the following dd command:

```
# dd if=openbsd1.dd bs=512 skip=16 count=4 | xxd
0000000: 0000 0000 0000 0000 1000 0000 1800 0000   ..............
0000016: 2000 0000 1001 0000 2000 0000 f0ff ffff    .......  .......
0000032: dc9d 0f41 1027 0000 ff24 0000 0200 0000   ...A.'...$......
0000048: 0020 0000 0004 0000 0800 0000 0500 0000   . .............
0000064: 0000 0000 3c00 0000 00e0 ffff 00fc ffff   ....<.........
0000080: 0d00 0000 0a00 0000 0700 0000 0008 0000   ..............
0000096: 0300 0000 0100 0000 0008 0000 00fe ffff   ..............
0000112: 0900 0000 0008 0000 4000 0000 0200 0000   ........@.......
0000128: 0000 0000 3f00 0000 0100 0000 0000 0000   ....?..........
0000144: 2c9d 0f41 8f5a 19a2 1001 0000 0004 0000   ,..A.Z.........
0000160: 0008 0000 1000 0000 3f00 0000 f003 0000   ........?.......
0000176: 1400 0000 1000 0000 8007 0000 801f 0000   ..............
0000192: 0400 0000 fe03 0000 e50e 0000 1000 0000   ..............
0000208: 0001 0000 2f6d 6e74 0000 0000 0000 0000   ..../mnt........
0000224: 0000 0000 0000 0000 0000 0000 0000 0000   ..............
[REMOVED]
0000832: 0000 0000 0000 0000 0000 0000 00e6 d2d0   ..............
0000848: 0038 d3d0 003c d3d0 0100 0000 0000 0000   .8...<.........
[REMOVED]
0001184: 0000 0000 0000 0000 0000 0000 0040 0000   ............@..
0001200: 4000 0000 0000 0000 0000 0000 0000 0000   @..............
[REMOVED]
0001312: 0000 0000 0700 0000 3c00 0000 0200 0000   ........<.......
0001328: ff7f 0101 0840 0000 ff1f 0000 0000 0000   .....@.........
0001344: ff03 0000 0000 0000 0000 0000 0100 0000   ..............
0001360: 0100 0000 6005 0000 6205 0000 5419 0100   ....`...b...T...
0001376: 0000 0101 0101 0101 0101 0101 0101 0101   ..............
```

This file system is from an IA32 system, so the bytes are in a little-endian ordering. If the file system were from a big-endian system, such as a Sparc system, the bytes in each numeric field would be reversed.

Bytes 8 to 11 show that the backup superblocks are located at an offset of 16 fragments (0x10) from the base of each cylinder group. Bytes 12 to 15 show that the group descriptor is located at an offset of 24 fragments (0x18) from the base, and bytes 16 to 19 show that the inode table starts 32 fragments (0x20) from the base.

To calculate the base of a UFS1 cylinder group, we start with bytes 24 to 27, which shows the delta value as 32 (0x20). This means that group 0 will have its base at fragment 0, and group 1 will have its base at fragment 32. Bytes 28 to 31 in the superblock show that the cycle mask is 0xfffffff0, which means that we care only about the final four bits of the group number. Therefore, after every 16 groups, we cycle back to the beginning and the base offset returns to fragment 0. In this case, group 15 will have a base offset of fragment 480, and group 16 will have a base offset of fragment 0.

Bytes 32 to 35 is the time that this was last written to, and the format is the number of seconds since January 1, 1970 GMT. Bytes 36 to 39 show that there are 10,000 (0x2710) fragments in the file system, and bytes 44 to 47 show that there are only two cylinder groups in this file system. The size of each block is given in bytes 48 to 51, and we see that it is 8,192 bytes (0x2000). The fragment size is in bytes 52 to 55, and it is 1,024 bytes (0x0400). To ensure you don't have to divide these two numbers, the number of fragments per block is given in bytes 56 to 59, which is 8.

Bytes 104 to 107 show that the superblock is 2,048 bytes (0x0800). Bytes 152 to 155 give the location of the cylinder group summary area, and it is located in fragment 272 of this file system. Its size is given in bytes 156 to 159, and we see that it is 1,024 bytes, or one fragment. Bytes 184 to 187 give the number of inodes per cylinder group, and there are 1,920 (0x0780) in this file system. The number of fragments per cylinder group is in bytes 188 to 191, and there are 8064 (0x1f80).

The flags start at byte 208 and the first byte is 0, which means that the superblock has been written after the last modification. Byte 209 shows that soft dependencies are used, and the flags in 210 and 211 are in their default state. Byte 212 starts the location of the last mount point, and this file system claims to have been last mounted at /mnt/. The remaining fields are left for you to enjoy processing. The fsstat tool output for this image was previously given in the "File System Category" section of Chapter 16.

## UFS2 SUPERBLOCK

The UFS 2 superblock stores the same basic information as the UFS1 version, but it has removed many of the unused fields and is a little simpler. It has many of the same fields but has replaced the essential fields that were only 32 bits with 64 bit versions. It is typically located in sector 128, and the version that is used by FreeBSD and NetBSD has the fields shown in Table 17.3.

**Table 17.3**   Data structure for the UFS2 superblock.

| Byte Range | Description | Essential |
|------------|-------------|-----------|
| 0–7 | Unused | No |
| 8–11 | Offset to backup superblock in cylinder group relative to a "base" | Yes |
| 12–15 | Offset to group descriptor in cylinder group relative to a "base" | Yes |
| 16–19 | Offset to inode table in cylinder group relative to a "base" | Yes |
| 20–23 | Offset to first data block in cylinder group relative to a "base" | No |
| 24–43 | Unused | No |
| 44–47 | Number of cylinder groups in file system | Yes |
| 48–51 | Size of a block in bytes | Yes |
| 52–55 | Size of a fragment in bytes | Yes |
| 56–59 | Size of a block in fragments | No |
| 60–63 | Minimum % of free blocks | No |
| 64–71 | Unused | No |
| 72–75 | Mask used to calculate the address for a block | No |
| 76–79 | Mask used to calculate the address for a fragment | No |
| 80–83 | Shift used to calculate the byte address for a block | No |
| 84–87 | Shift used to calculate the byte address for a fragment | No |
| 88–91 | Maximum number of contiguous blocks to allocate | No |
| 92–95 | Maximum number of blocks per cylinder group | No |
| 96–99 | Number of bits to convert between a block address and a fragment address | No |
| 100–103 | Number of bits to convert between a fragment address and a sector address | No |
| 104–107 | Size of superblock | No |
| 108–115 | Unused | No |
| 116–119 | Number of indirect addresses per fragment | No |

| Byte Range | Description | Essential |
|---|---|---|
| 120–123 | Number of inodes per block in inode table | No |
| 124–127 | Unused | No |
| 128–131 | Optimization technique | No |
| 132–143 | Unused | No |
| 144–151 | File System Id | No |
| 152–155 | Unused | No |
| 156–159 | Size of cylinder group summary area in bytes | No |
| 160–163 | Size of cylinder group descriptor in bytes | No |
| 164–183 | Unused | No |
| 184–187 | Inodes per cylinder group | Yes |
| 188–191 | Fragments per cylinder group | Yes |
| 192–207 | Unused | No |
| 208–208 | Super block modified flag | No |
| 209–209 | FS was clean when it was mounted | No |
| 210–210 | Mounted read only flag (set to 1 if read only) | No |
| 211–211 | Unused | No |
| 212–679 | Last mount point | No |
| 680–711 | Volume name | No |
| 712–719 | System UID | No |
| 720–723 | Unused | No |
| 724–727 | Last cylinder group searched | No |
| 728–999 | Unused | No |
| 1000–1007 | Location of superblock | No |
| 1008–1015 | Number of directories | No |
| 1016–1023 | Number of free blocks | No |

*continues*

**Table 17.3** Data structure for the UFS2 superblock (Continued).

| Byte Range | Description | Essential |
|---|---|---|
| 1024–1031 | Number of free inodes | No |
| 1032–1039 | Number of free fragments | No |
| 1040–1047 | Number of free clusters | No |
| 1048–1071 | Unused | No |
| 1072–1079 | Last written time | No |
| 1080–1087 | Number of fragments in file system | Yes |
| 1088–1095 | Number of fragments that can store file data | No |
| 1096–1103 | Fragment address of cylinder group summary area | No |
| 1104–1111 | Blocks in process of being freed | No |
| 1112–1115 | Inodes in process of being freed | No |
| 1116–1195 | Array inode addresses for snap inodes | No |
| 1196–1199 | Expected average file size | No |
| 1200–1203 | Expected number of files per directory | No |
| 1204–1311 | Unused | No |
| 1312–1315 | Flags (see Table 17.2) | No |
| 1316– 1319 | Size of cluster summary array in group descriptors | No |
| 1320–1323 | Maximum length of internal symbolic link | Yes |
| 1324–1327 | Format of inodes | Yes |
| 1328–1335 | Maximum file size | No |
| 1336–1343 | Mask used to calculate the offset in a block for an address | No |
| 1344–1351 | Mask used to calculate the offset in a fragment for an address | No |
| 1352–1355 | File system state | No |
| 1356–1371 | Unused | No |
| 1372–1375 | Signature value (0x19540119) | Yes |

You might notice that fields have moved around. The only changes that could be of interest are that the mount point is shorter and there is now a volume label field. The flags field is four bytes instead of only one, but the same flag values given in Table 17.2 are used. Also note that the magic value is different, which is how we can differentiate between UFS1 and UFS2.

Here are the contents of a UFS2 file system from a FreeBSD 5 system:

```
# dd if=freebsd5.dd skip=128 count=4 | xxd
0000000: 0000 0000 0000 0000 2800 0000 3000 0000  ........(...0...
0000016: 3800 0000 d800 0000 0000 0000 0000 0000  8...............
0000032: 0000 0000 0000 0000 0000 0000 0400 0000  ................
0000048: 0040 0000 0008 0000 0800 0000 0800 0000  .@..............
0000064: 0000 0000 0000 0000 00c0 ffff 00f8 ffff  ................
0000080: 0e00 0000 0b00 0000 0800 0000 0008 0000  ................
0000096: 0300 0000 0200 0000 0008 0000 0000 0000  ................
0000112: 0000 0000 0008 0000 4000 0000 0000 0000  ........@.......
0000128: 0000 0000 0000 0000 0000 0000 0000 0000  ................
0000144: adb2 0f41 fd01 4a17 0000 0000 0008 0000  ...A..J.........
0000160: 0008 0000 0000 0000 0000 0000 0000 0000  ................
0000176: 0000 0000 0000 0000 0005 0000 b813 0000  ................
0000192: 0000 0000 0000 0000 0000 0000 0000 0000  ................
0000208: 0000 0080 2f6d 6e74 0000 0000 0000 0000  ..../mnt........
[REMOVED]
0000672: 0000 0000 0000 0000 5546 5332 0000 0000  ........UFS2....
[REMOVED]
0000832: 0000 0000 0000 0000 1038 66c3 0030 66c3  .........8f..0f.
0000848: 0038 66c3 0000 0000 0000 0000 0040 0000  .8f..........@..
[REMOVED]
0000992: 0000 0000 0000 0000 0000 0100 0000 0000  ................
0001008: 0400 0000 0000 0000 f308 0000 0000 0000  ................
0001024: e213 0000 0000 0000 1800 0000 0000 0000  ................
[REMOVED]
0001072: bdb4 0f41 0000 0000 c04e 0000 0000 0000  ...A.....N......
0001088: d74b 0000 0000 0000 d800 0000 0000 0000  .K..............
[REMOVED]
0001184: 0000 0000 0000 0000 0000 0000 0040 0000  .............@..
0001200: 4000 0000 0000 0000 0000 0000 0000 0000  @...............
[REMOVED]
0001312: 0000 0000 0800 0000 7800 0000 0000 0000  ........x.......
0001328: ffff 0202 1080 0000 ff3f 0000 0000 0000  .........?......
0001344: ff07 0000 0000 0000 0000 0000 0000 0000  ................
0001360: 0000 0000 0000 0000 0000 0000 1901 5419  ..............T.
```

We see in bytes 8 to 11, 12 to 15, and 16 to 19 that the superblock is located 40 fragments (0x28) from the start of each cylinder group, the group descriptor is 48 fragments (0x30) from the start, and the inode table is 56 fragments (0x38) from the start. Bytes 44 to 47 show that there are four cylinder groups.

The size of a block is given in bytes 48 to 51, and we see that it is 16,384 bytes (0x4000), and the size of each fragment is in bytes 52 to 55, which is 2,048 bytes (0x0800). Bytes 184 to 187 show that there are 1,280 (0x0500) inodes per cylinder group, and bytes 188 to 191 show that there are 5,048 (0x13b8) fragments per group. The total number of fragments is given in bytes 1080 to 1087, and this small file system has only 20,160.

Here is the relevant output from running fsstat on the UFS2 image:

```
# fsstat -f freebsd freebsd5.dd
FILE SYSTEM INFORMATION
--------------------------------------------
File System Type: UFS 2
Last Written: Tue Aug  3 10:52:29 2004
Last Mount Point: /mnt
Volume Name: UFS2
System UID: 0

METADATA INFORMATION
--------------------------------------------
Inode Range: 0 - 5119
Root Directory: 2
Num of Avail Inodes: 5090
Num of Directories: 4

CONTENT INFORMATION
--------------------------------------------
Fragment Range: 0 - 20159
Block Size: 16384
Fragment Size: 2048
Num of Avail Full Blocks: 2291
Num of Avail Fragments: 24
[REMOVED]
```

## CYLINDER GROUP SUMMARY

Both UFS1 and UFS2 have one or more fragments that contain the cylinder group summary data structures. These data structures are the same in both versions of UFS, and they contain statistical information about each cylinder group. They are organized as a table, and each entry in the table corresponds to a cylinder group. The address and size of the area are given in the superblock. Each table entry has the fields given in Table 17.4.

**Table 17.4**   Data structure for cylinder group summary area entries.

| Byte Range | Description | Essential |
|---|---|---|
| 0–3 | Number of directories | No |
| 4–7 | Number of free blocks (full set of fragments) | No |
| 8–11 | Number of free inodes | No |
| 12–15 | Number of free fragments (partial blocks) | No |

As we will see in the next section, these data also can be found in each of the cylinder group descriptors. This information is used when allocating new inodes and blocks.

In our example UFS1 file system image, we saw that the cylinder group summary area was in block 272 and that it was allocated 1,024 bytes. The contents of that fragment are shown here:

```
# dcat -f openbsd openbsd.dd 272 | xxd
0000000: 0200 0000 2f03 0000 7807 0000 0b00 0000   ..../...x.......
0000016: 0200 0000 cf00 0000 6d07 0000 0500 0000   ........m.......
[REMOVED]
```

The table entry for group 0 is the first line, and we can see that it has two directories and 815 (0x032f) free blocks. Bytes 8 to 11 show that it has 1,912 (0x0778) free inodes, and bytes 12 to 15 show it has 11 (0x0b) free fragments in partial blocks. The second row is for the second group.

The fsstat tool in TSK will show the cylinder group information when run on a UFS image. The "File System Category" section of Chapter 16 has the fsstat output for our example image. The output contains the cylinder group information from the superblock, from the cylinder group summary area, and from the group descriptors.

# UFS1 GROUP DESCRIPTOR

Group descriptor data structures contain the configuration information for a specific cylinder group. One data structure is located in each cylinder group. Its offset from the base is given in the superblock, and UFS1 and UFS2 use different data structures. This section will describe the data structure that is used in UFS1.

The location of the UFS1 group descriptor staggers in each cylinder group, although its distance from a base value is always the same. The methods for calculating the base were discussed in the previous chapter and in the previous superblock section. The descriptor is typically allocated a full block, even if it does not need it. Many of the values are non-essential and are used to more efficiently allocate resources.

The fields for the UFS1 group descriptor are given in Table 17.5.

**Table 17.5**   Data structure for the UFS1 group descriptor.

| Byte Range | Description | Essential |
|------------|-------------|-----------|
| 0–3 | Unused | No |
| 4–7 | Magic signature (0x090255) | No |
| 8–11 | Last written time | No |
| 12–15 | Group number | No |
| 16–17 | Number of cylinders in group | No |
| 18–19 | Number of inodes in group | No |
| 20–23 | Number of fragments in group | No |
| 24–27 | Number of directories | No |
| 28–31 | Number of free blocks | No |
| 32–35 | Number of free inodes | No |
| 36–39 | Number of free fragments (partial blocks) | No |
| 40–43 | Last block allocated | No |
| 44–47 | Last fragment allocated | No |
| 48–51 | Last inode allocated | No |
| 52–83 | Summary of available fragments | No |
| 84–87 | Number of free blocks in each cylinder (byte offset) | No |
| 88–91 | Free block positions table (byte offset) | No |
| 92–95 | Inode bitmap (byte offset) | Yes |

| Byte Range | Description | Essential |
|---|---|---|
| 96–99 | Fragment bitmap (byte offset) | Yes |
| 100–103 | Next available space in descriptor (byte offset) | No |
| 104–107 | Counts of available clusters (consecutive blocks) (byte offset) | No |
| 108–111 | Block bitmap (byte offset) | No |
| 112–115 | Number of blocks in group | No |
| 116–167 | Unused | No |
| 168+ | Bitmaps, and so on | Yes |

Starting at byte 168 are bytes that can be used for a variety of purposes, including bitmaps and tables. The group descriptor gives the byte offset for the various bitmaps relative to the start of the group descriptor block. There are several other tables and bitmaps in the space following these fields, but most are non-essential. They exist for efficiency when allocating new blocks. For example, the block bitmap, also called the cluster bitmap, is a reduced version of the fragment bitmap, and a bit corresponds to a block, and it is set to 1 if all the corresponding fragments for the block have a 1 in the fragment bitmap.

To examine the group descriptor for the first group of our OpenBSD UFS1 system, we need to determine where it is located. It is the first group, so its base offset is fragment 0. We saw in the superblock that the group descriptor is 24 fragments from the base, so we examine fragment 24 using dcat:

```
# dcat -f openbsd openbsd.dd 24
0000000: 0000 0000 5502 0900 c99d 0f41 0000 0000   ....U......A....
0000016: 1000 8007 801f 0000 0200 0000 2f03 0000   ............/...
0000032: 7807 0000 0b00 0000 8801 0000 1001 0000   x...............
0000048: 0700 0000 0000 0000 0000 0000 0000 0000   ................
0000064: 0000 0000 0100 0000 0000 0000 0000 0000   ................
0000080: 0100 0000 a800 0000 e800 0000 0801 0000   ................
0000096: f801 0000 8206 0000 e405 0000 0406 0000   ................
0000112: f003 0000 0000 0000 0000 0000 0000 0000   ................
[REMOVED]
```

We see the magic value in bytes 4 to 7, and byte 24 starts the information about the number of available inodes and blocks, which we previously saw in the cylinder group summary area. There is also allocation information, and bytes 40 to 43 show that the last block allocated was block 392 (0x0188) and bytes 44 to 47 show that the last fragment (partial block) allocated was 272 (0x0110). The last allocated inode entry is listed in bytes 48 to 51, and it is for inode 7.

The byte offset for the inode bitmap is located in bytes 92 to 95, and we see that it is located 264 bytes (0x0108) bytes from the start of the group descriptor. The location of the fragment bitmap is given in bytes 96 to 99, and we see that it is located 504 bytes (0x01f8) from the start of the group descriptor. The block bitmap is given in bytes 108 to 111, and it is located 1,540 bytes (0x0604) from the start of the descriptor.

## UFS2 GROUP DESCRIPTOR

The UFS2 group descriptor has the same basic concepts as the UFS1 version, but some of its fields are larger. Its location relative to the start of the cylinder group is given in the superblock, and its location does not stagger like the UFS1 group descriptor does. The UFS2 version has the fields given in Table 17.6.

Table 17.6   Data structure for the UFS2 group descriptor.

| Byte Range | Description | Essential |
| --- | --- | --- |
| 0–3 | Unused | No |
| 4–7 | Magic signature (0x090255) | No |
| 8–11 | Unused | No |
| 12–15 | Group number | No |
| 16–19 | Unused | No |
| 20–23 | Number of fragments in group | No |
| 24–27 | Number of directories | No |
| 28–31 | Number of free blocks | No |
| 32–35 | Number of free inodes | No |
| 36–39 | Number of free fragments (partial blocks) | No |
| 40–43 | Last block allocated | No |
| 44–47 | Last fragment allocated | No |
| 48–51 | Last inode allocated | No |

| Byte Range | Description | Essential |
|---|---|---|
| 52–83 | Summary of available fragments | No |
| 84–91 | Unused | No |
| 92–95 | Inode bitmap (byte offset) | Yes |
| 96–99 | Fragment bitmap (byte offset) | Yes |
| 100–103 | Next available space in descriptor (byte offset) | No |
| 104–107 | Counts of available clusters (consecutive blocks) (byte offset) | No |
| 108–111 | Block bitmap (byte offset) | No |
| 112–115 | Number of blocks in group | No |
| 116–119 | Number of inodes in group | No |
| 120- 123 | Last initialized inode | No |
| 124–135 | Unused | No |
| 136–143 | Last written time | No |
| 144–167 | Unused | No |
| 168+ | Bitmaps and so on | Yes |

Notice that in both versions, the only essential information is the offsets to the inode and fragment bitmaps. The bitmaps are located after byte 168, but still inside the block allocated to the group descriptor.

## BLOCK AND FRAGMENT BITMAPS

The allocation status of blocks and fragments is determined by a bitmap. In fact, there are two bitmaps for every block in UFS because there is a fragment bitmap and a block bitmap. You will notice that these bitmaps are opposite from what we typically find. These bitmaps are "free bitmaps" and are set to 1 when the object is unallocated and set to 0 when it is allocated.

We will first examine the fragment bitmap. Each cylinder group has a fragment bitmap located inside its group descriptor. The bitmap's byte offset is given in the group descriptor, and its size can be determined based on the number of fragments in the group. To find the bit for a specific fragment, we determine its address relative to the start of the cylinder group by subtracting the address of the first fragment in the group.

If a fragment is the fiftieth in a group, its allocation status is given in the fiftieth bit, which is the second bit in byte 6.

In the UFS1 file system that we previously dissected, the group descriptor was located in block 24, and the fragment bitmap had an offset of 504 bytes. We view that with dcat and supply the 8 to show all eight fragments in the block:

```
# dcat -f openbsd openbsd.dd 24 8 | xxd
[REMOVED]
0000496: 0000 0000 0000 0000 0000 0000 0000 0000    ................
0000512: 0000 0000 0000 0000 0000 0000 0000 0000    ................
0000528: 0000 0000 0000 0000 0000 f0fe 0000 0000    ................
0000544: 0000 0000 ffff ffff 00ff 0000 0000 0000    ................
0000560: 0000 0000 0000 0000 0000 0000 0000 0000    ................
0000576: 0000 0000 0000 0000 0000 0000 0000 0000    ................
[REMOVED]
```

Byte 504 is the first byte in the fragment bitmap, and we see that it is 0, which means that the first eight fragments are allocated. We do not see any free fragments until byte 538, which is byte 34 in the bitmap. The four upper bits of the byte are set to 1, which means that fragments that are 276 to 279 are available. Because this is the first group, this is also their actual address; otherwise, we would have to add the starting address of the group. Notice that these four unallocated fragments do not represent a full block because each block has eight fragments in it. In this case, the first four fragments of a block are allocated and the final four are not.

Bytes 548 to 551 show a span of 32 consecutive fragments that are not allocated. Byte 548 corresponds to byte 44 of the bitmap, so the first bit is for fragment 352.

The fragment bitmap is not efficient for allocating blocks or large groups of consecutive blocks, so the block bitmap also exists. This bitmap duplicates the information that can be found in the fragment bitmap, but it uses 1 bit for each block. Because each bit corresponds to a block, we need to address the blocks differently. Therefore, we assign each block a consecutive address. For example, if we have eight fragments per block, instead of having block 0, 8, 16, 24, and so on, we would have block 0, 1, 2, 3, and so on. To calculate the block address, simply divide the fragment-based address by the number of fragments per block. If the corresponding bit is set to 1, the block is available.

In our UFS1 system, we saw that the block bitmap was located at offset 1,540 within the group descriptor:

```
# dcat -f openbsd openbsd.dd 24 8 | xxd
[REMOVED]
0001536: 0100 0000 0000 0000 00f0 0200 0000 0000    ................
```

```
0001552: 0000 0000 0000 0000 0000 0000 c0ff ffff   ...............
0001568: ffff ffff ffff ffff ffff ffff ffff ffff   ...............
[REMOVED]
```

We see that byte 1,540 is 0, and we do not see any bits set until byte 1,545, which has the upper four bits set. This is byte 5 in the bitmap, which means that its bits correspond to relative blocks 40 to 47, and the bits for relative blocks 44 to 47 are set to 1. If we convert these addresses to their fragment address, we get fragments 352 to 383, which we saw in the fragment bitmap as a collection of free consecutive fragments.

## UFS1 INODES

Inode data structures store the metadata for each file and directory. Again, UFS1 and UFS2 use different data structures because UFS2 has larger fields. Inodes are divided among the different cylinder groups, and the number of inodes per group is given in the superblock. Each cylinder group has its own inode table, with its location given in the superblock. The starting location of a UFS1 inode table will stagger with each cylinder group, but UFS2 inode tables are always at the same offset relative to the start of the group.

The UFS1 inode is 128 bytes in size and has the fields given in Table 17.7.

**Table 17.7**   Data structure for the UFS1 inode.

| Byte Range | Description | Essential |
| --- | --- | --- |
| 0–1 | File mode (Type and permissions) (see "Inode" section in Chapter 15) | Yes |
| 2–3 | Link count | Yes |
| 4–7 | Unused | No |
| 8–15 | Size | Yes |
| 16–19 | Access time | No |
| 20–23 | Access time (nanoseconds) | No |
| 24–27 | Modified time | No |
| 28–31 | Modified time (nanoseconds) | No |
| 32–35 | Change time | No |

*continues*

**Table 17.7**   Data structure for the UFS1 inode (Continued).

| Byte Range | Description | Essential |
| --- | --- | --- |
| 36–39 | Change time (nanoseconds) | No |
| 40–87 | 12 Direct block pointers | Yes |
| 88–91 | 1 Indirect block pointer | Yes |
| 92–95 | 1 Double indirect block pointer | Yes |
| 96–99 | 1 Triple indirect block pointer | Yes |
| 100–103 | Status flags | No |
| 104–107 | Blocks Held | No |
| 108–111 | Generation number (NFS) | No |
| 112–115 | User ID | No |
| 116–119 | Group ID | No |
| 120–127 | Unused | No |

The mode field has the same values as were given for ExtX. The link serves the same purpose as we previously saw with ExtX, and it is incremented for every file name pointing to it. Refer to Chapter 15 for more details.

Let's look at an inode in our UFS1 image. We saw in the beginning of the chapter that the superblock showed the inode table as being 32 fragments from the group base, and because this is group 0, we know it is in fragment 32. The first usable inode in the file system is number 3, so we extract it with dcat and dd:

```
# dcat -f openbsd openbsd.dd 32 | dd bs=128 skip=3 count=1 | xxd
0000000: a481 0100 0000 0000 0074 1300 0000 0000  .........t......
0000016: 689d 0f41 8033 023b 7a9d 0f41 0057 a616  h..A.3.;z..A.W..
0000032: 7a9d 0f41 0057 a616 2001 0000 2801 0000  z..A.W.. ...(...
0000048: 3001 0000 3801 0000 4001 0000 4801 0000  0...8...@...H...
0000064: 5001 0000 5801 0000 9001 0000 9801 0000  P...X...........
0000080: a001 0000 a801 0000 8001 0000 0000 0000  ................
0000096: 0000 0000 0000 0000 d009 0000 5ade 19ac  ............Z...
00000112: 0000 0000 0000 0000 0000 0000 0000 0000  ................
```

The first four bytes are the mode, and we parsed one of UFS2 these in the "Inodes" section of Chapter 15, so we will skip that process in this chapter. We can see the 8 in bits

12 to 15, though, so we know that is a regular file. The size is given in bytes 8 to 15, and we see that it is 1,274,880 bytes (0x00137400). The A-time is given in bytes 16 to 19, and when converted to a human readable format results in Tue Aug 3 14:12:56 2004 UTC.

The address of the first block is in bytes 40 to 43, and it is 288 (0x0120). The second block is 296 (0x0128). Note that these are consecutive blocks because the file system has eight fragments per block. We see in bytes 88 to 91 that there is an indirect block pointer being used, and it is located in block 384.

The istat output of this file is as follows:

```
# istat -f openbsd -z UTC openbsd.dd 3
inode: 3
Allocated
Group: 0
uid / gid: 0 / 0
mode: -rw-r--r--
size: 1274880
num of links: 1

Inode Times:
Accessed:       Tue Aug  3 14:12:56 2004
File Modified:  Tue Aug  3 14:13:14 2004
Inode Modified: Tue Aug  3 14:13:14 2004

Direct Blocks:
288 289 290 291 292 293 294 295
296 297 298 299 300 301 302 303
304 305 306 307 308 309 310 311
[REMOVED]
1568 1569 1570 1571 1572 1573 1574 1575
1576 1577 1578 1579 1580
Indirect Blocks:
384 385 386 387 388 389 390 391
```

Notice that the output of istat lists every fragment allocated and that the final line has only five fragments.

The allocation status of an inode is stored in an inode bitmap. Each cylinder group has an inode bitmap, and it is located inside of the group descriptor. We saw in the UFS1 group descriptor that the inode table started at a byte offset of 264. We can see it here:

```
# dcat -f openbsd openbsd.dd 24 8 | xxd
[REMOVED]
```

```
0000256: 3f00 3f00 3f00 3f00 ff00 0000 0000 0000   ?.?.?.?.........
0000272: 0000 0000 0000 0000 0000 0000 0000 0000   ................
[REMOVED]
```

Byte 264 is set to 0xff, which means that inodes 0 to 7 are allocated. We previously analyzed inode 3, which we can see is allocated. Inodes 8 and beyond are unallocated in this cylinder group.

## UFS2 INODES

The UFS2 inode is 128 bytes larger than its UFS1 counterpart, and it has many 64-bit fields instead of 32-bit fields. It, too, is located in an inode table, which has its offset location given in the superblock. The UFS2 inode table does not stagger, however, like a UFS1 does. The UFS2 inode has the fields given in Table 17.8.

**Table 17.8**  Data structure for the UFS2 inode.

| Byte Range | Description | Essential |
|---|---|---|
| 0–1 | File mode (type and permissions) (see "Inodes" section in Chapter 15) | Yes |
| 2–3 | Link count | Yes |
| 4–7 | User ID | No |
| 8–11 | Group ID | No |
| 12–15 | Inode block size | No |
| 16–23 | Size | Yes |
| 24–31 | Bytes held | No |
| 32–39 | Access time | No |
| 40–47 | Modified time | No |
| 48–55 | Change time | No |
| 56–63 | Create time | No |
| 64–67 | Modified time (nanoseconds) | No |
| 68–71 | Access time (nanoseconds) | No |

| Byte Range | Description | Essential |
|---|---|---|
| 72–75 | Change time (nanoseconds) | No |
| 76–79 | Create time (nanoseconds) | No |
| 80–83 | Generation number (NFS) | No |
| 84–87 | Kernel flags | No |
| 88–91 | Status flags | No |
| 92–95 | Extended attributes size | No |
| 96–111 | 2 Direct extended attribute block pointers | No |
| 112–207 | 12 Direct block pointers | Yes |
| 208–215 | 1 Indirect block pointer | Yes |
| 216–223 | 1 Double indirect block pointer | Yes |
| 224–231 | 1 Triple indirect block pointer | Yes |
| 232–255 | Unused | No |

The most noticeable difference between the UFS1 and UFS2 versions is the block pointers are 64 bits, and the time values are 64 bits. The address values in the indirect blocks are also 64 bits.

We saw in our UFS2 image that the inode table starts in fragment 56. We view inode 5 as follows:

```
% dcat -f freebsd freebsd.dd 56 8 | dd bs=256 skip=5 count=1 | xxd
0000000: a481 0100 0000 0000 0000 0000 0000 0000  ................
0000016: 0000 2000 0000 0000 2010 0000 0000 0000  .. ..... ........
0000032: b5b3 0f41 0000 0000 b6b3 0f41 0000 0000  ...A.......A....
0000048: b6b3 0f41 0000 0000 b5b3 0f41 0000 0000  ...A.......A....
0000064: 0000 0000 0000 0000 0000 0000 0000 0000  ................
0000080: 11fe 8458 0000 0000 0000 0000 0000 0000  ...X............
0000096: 0000 0000 0000 0000 0000 0000 0000 0000  ................
0000112: e800 0000 0000 0000 f000 0000 0000 0000  ................
0000128: f800 0000 0000 0000 0001 0000 0000 0000  ................
0000144: 0801 0000 0000 0000 1001 0000 0000 0000  ................
0000160: 1801 0000 0000 0000 2001 0000 0000 0000  ........ .......
0000176: 5801 0000 0000 0000 6001 0000 0000 0000  X.......`.......
0000192: 6801 0000 0000 0000 7001 0000 0000 0000  h.......p.......
```

```
0000208: 4801 0000 0000 0000 0000 0000 0000 0000   H...............
0000224: 0000 0000 0000 0000 0000 0000 0000 0000   ................
0000230: 0000 0000 0000 0000 0000 0000 0000 0000   ................
```

In bytes 0 to 1 we see the mode, and the 8 shows that it is a regular file. Bytes 16 to 23 show that the file size is 2,097,152 bytes (0x00200000). The 8-byte A-time is given in bytes 32 to 39, and it translates to Tue Aug 3 15:48:05 2004 UTC.

Bytes 112 to 119 are the first direct block pointer, and we see that it is for block 232 (0xe8). The second block pointer is for block 240 (0xf0), and the block size of this image is 8 fragments per block. Bytes 208 to 215 are for the first indirect block pointer, and we see that it has allocated block 328 (0x0148) for this purpose.

The istat output for this inode is as follows:

```
# istat -f freebsd -z UTC freebsd.dd 5
inode: 5
Allocated
Group: 0
uid / gid: 0 / 0
mode: -rw-r--r--
size: 2097152
num of links: 1

Inode Times:
Accessed:       Tue Aug  3 15:48:05 2004
File Modified:  Tue Aug  3 15:48:06 2004
Inode Modified: Tue Aug  3 15:48:06 2004

Direct Blocks:
232 233 234 235 236 237 238 239
240 241 242 243 244 245 246 247
[REMOVED]
1296 1297 1298 1299 1300 1301 1302 1303
Indirect Blocks:
328 329 330 331 332 333 334 335
```

## UFS2 EXTENDED ATTRIBUTES

UFS2 files and directories can have extended attributes, which are user or system assigned name and value pairs. Extended attributes are stored in normal data blocks, and the block addresses are given in the inode. Each block contains a list of variable length data structures that have the fields shown in Table 17.9.

**Table 17.9**  Data structure for the UFS2 extended attribute entry.

| Byte Range | Description | Essential |
|---|---|---|
| 0–3 | Record length | Yes |
| 4–4 | Namespace (see Table 17.10) | No |
| 5–5 | Content padding | Yes |
| 6–6 | Name length | Yes |
| 7–(7 + name length) | Name | Yes |
| (After name and padded to 8-byte boundary) | Value | Yes |

The name is padded so that the value starts on an 8-byte boundary. The value also is padded so that the next entry starts on an 8-byte boundary. The amount of padding for the name can be calculated using the name length and the amount of padding for the value is given in byte 5. The namespace value can take on one of the values given in Table 17.10.

**Table 17.10**  Values for the extended attribute name space field.

| Value | Description |
|---|---|
| 1 | User |
| 2 | System |

Here we see the contents of an extended attribute block with two attributes:

```
0000000:  3000 0000 0107 0673 6f75 7263 6500 0000   0......source...
0000016:  7777 7777 2e64 6967 6974 616c 2d65 7669   wwww.digital-evi
0000032:  6465 6e63 652e 6f72 6700 0000 0000 0000   dence.org.......
0000048:  2000 0000 0104 0464 6174 6500 0000 0000    ......date.....
0000064:  4175 6720 3132 2c20 3230 3034 0000 0000   Aug 12, 2004....
0000080:  0000 0000 0000 0000 0000 0000 0000 0000   ...............
```

Bytes 0 to 3 show the record length as 48 bytes (0x30). Byte 4 shows the namespace as 1, which means it is a user attribute. We see that there are seven bytes of padding in the content, the name length is six bytes, and that the name is "source." The name ends in byte 12, so the next 8-byte boundary is byte 16. To find the ending location of the value, we subtract the starting byte from the record length and the padding length (48–16–7 = 25). The value is the string "www.digital-evidence.org."

## DIRECTORY ENTRIES

Directory entry data structures store the names of files and directories. They are located in the blocks that have been allocated to a directory. Each data structure contains the name of the file and the inode address where the metadata can be found. The directory entry data structure for UFS1 and UFS2 has the fields given in Table 17.11.

**Table 17.11**   Data structure for UFS1 and UFS2 directory entry.

| Byte Range | Description | Essential |
|---|---|---|
| 0–3 | Inode value | Yes |
| 4–5 | Directory entry length | Yes |
| 6–6 | Name length | Yes |
| 7–7 | File type (see Table 17.12) | No |
| 8+ | Name in ASCII | Yes |

The file type flag can have one of the values from Table 17.12.

**Table 17.12**   Values for the directory entry type field.

| Type Value | Description |
|---|---|
| 0 | Unknown type |
| 1 | FIFO |
| 2 | Character device |
| 4 | Directory |
| 6 | Block device |
| 8 | Regular file |
| 10 | Symbolic Link |

| Type Value | Description |
| --- | --- |
| 12 | Socket |
| 14 | Whiteout |

The flags have the same names as we saw with ExtX, except for the whiteout type. It is used when a file system has been mounted with the union option and there exist two files with the same name. The whiteout type is used as a flag for the duplicate file, and the OS will not show it to the user (like applying whiteout to a typo).

The directory entry length field is used to locate the next allocated directory entry, and the name length field is used to both determine where the name ends and determine how long the entry needs to be. Refer to the "File Name Category" section of Chapter 14 for details on how directory entries are allocated and unallocated.

Here are the contents of a UFS1 directory from our image:

```
# icat -f openbsd openbsd.dd 1921 | xxd
0000000: 8107 0000 0c00 0401 2e00 0000 0200 0000   ...............
0000016: 0c00 0402 2e2e 0000 8c07 0000 1400 0809   ...............
0000032: 6669 6c65 312e 7478 7400 93e7 8d07 0000   file1.txt.......
0000048: 1400 0809 6669 6c65 382e 7478 7400 93e7   ....file8.txt...
0000064: 8e07 0000 2800 0809 6669 6c65 372e 7478   ....(...file7.tx
0000080: 7400 93e7 8f07 0000 1400 0809 6669 6c65   t..........file
0000096: 362e 7478 7400 93e7 9007 0000 1400 0809   6.txt..........
0000112: 6669 6c65 352e 7478 7400 93e7 9107 0000   file5.txt.......
0000128: 2800 0809 6669 6c65 342e 7478 7400 93e7   (...file4.txt...
0000144: 9207 0000 1400 0809 6669 6c65 332e 7478   ........file3.tx
[REMOVED]
```

We dissected a directory in the ExtX Data Structures chapter, so I will show only some of the highlights of this output. The first four bytes show the inode of the '.' entry, which we can verify is inode 1921 (0x0781). Bytes 24 to 27 are the inode field of the first file entry, which is file1.txt and at inode 1,932 (0x078c). Bytes 68 to 69 are for the length field for the file7.txt file, and it is 40 bytes (0x28), but the name is only nine bytes long. The next entry, for file6.txt, has been deleted, and the length field for file7.txt file points to the entry after file6.txt.

The directory listing for this directory is as follows:

```
# fls -f openbsd -a openbsd.dd 1921
d/d 1921:       .
d/d 2:          ..
r/r 1932:       file1.txt
```

```
r/r  1933:      file8.txt
r/r  1934:      file7.txt
r/- * 1935:     file6.txt
r/r  1936:      file5.txt
r/r  1937:      file4.txt
r/- * 1938:     file3.txt
r/r  1939:      file2.txt
r/- * 1940:     file10.txt
r/r  1941:      file9.txt
```

## SUMMARY

This chapter has shown the data structures associated with UFS1 and UFS2 file systems. In comparison to the ones we saw for ExtX, these are typically larger and contain more non-essential data, but the data exists to make the normal operation of the file system more efficient.

## BIBLIOGRAPHY

Refer to the Bibliography section in Chapter 16.

# The Sleuth Kit and Autopsy

The Sleuth Kit (TSK) and the Autopsy Forensic Browser are open source Unix-based tools that I first released (in some form) in early 2001. TSK is a collection of over 20 command line tools that can analyze disk and file system images for evidence. To make the analysis easier, the Autopsy Forensic Browser can be used. Autopsy is a front end to the TSK tools and provides a point-and-click type of interface.

This appendix gives more details about TSK and Autopsy. TSK is used throughout this book in the examples, but this is the only place that describes how you can use it. Both Autopsy and TSK can be downloaded for free from http://www.sleuthkit.org.

The Web site also contains information about e-mail lists for tool users and developers and the bi-monthly "Sleuth Kit Informer" newsletter, which contains articles on using TSK, Autopsy, and other open source investigation tools.

## THE SLEUTH KIT

TSK contains over 20 command line tools, which are organized into groups. The groups include disk tools, volume tools, file system tools, and searching tools. The file system tools are further organized into the data categories that we discussed in Chapter 8, "File System Analysis." Each tool name has two parts, where the first part identifies its group and the second part identifies its function. For example, fls is a file name category tool (the f) that lists (the ls), and the istat tool is in the metadata category (the i) that displays statistics (the stat).

This section gives an overview to each of the tools in TSK. At the time of this writing, the current version is 1.73, but there are plans for big changes in a 2.00 release. Those changes are not included in this description, but 2.00 could be available by the time you read this. We will start from the bottom and work our way up. Not all option flags are listed here. Refer to the man pages or the website for more details.

## DISK TOOLS

There is only one disk tool in TSK, which is the diskstat tool. diskstat currently runs only on Linux, and it gives the statistics about an ATA hard disk. diskstat was used in Chapter 3, "Hard Disk Acquisition," when we looked for Host Protected Areas (HPA) before acquiring a disk. The tool displays the total number of sectors and the user-accessible sectors, which show if an HPA exists. Refer to "A Case Study Using dd" in Chapter 3 for a specific example.

## VOLUME SYSTEM TOOLS

The contents of a disk are organized into volumes, and TSK includes one tool that will list the partition layout of a volume. The mmls was used in Chapters 5, "PC-based Partitions," and 6, "Server-based Partitions," of this book, and it supports DOS (dos), Apple (mac), BSD (bsd), Sun (sun), and GPT (gpt) partitions. The type of partition table can be specified on the command line using the -t argument and the type, which are given in this paragraph in parentheses.

The output of mmls is sorted by the starting address of the partition, regardless of where it is located in the table. It also shows you which sectors in the volume are not allocated to a partition. Refer to any of the specific partition types in Chapters 5 and 6 for examples.

## FILE SYSTEM TOOLS

Inside most volumes is a file system, and the bulk of TSK is in the file system layer. The file system tools in TSK are based on the tools from The Coroner's Toolkit (TCT) (http://www.porcupine.org), which is by Dan Farmer and Wietse Venema. There are currently 13 tools in the file system layer tools, and they are organized into five categories. The tools currently require a raw partition image as input, but version 2.00 will support disk images.

The file system tools support Ext2/3 (linux-ext2, linux-ext3), FAT (fat, fat12, fat16, fat32), NTFS (ntfs), and UFS1/2 (freebsd, netbsd, openbsd, solaris) file system formats. They also support raw and swap images to view individual pages. The file system type must be specified with the -f flag and one of the types given previously in parentheses.

## File System Category

The file system category of data includes the data that describes the layout and general information about a file system. This data can be displayed by using the fsstat tool, which will read the boot sector or superblock and other data structures that are specific to the different types of file systems. The type of data in the output of fsstat is different for each file system because different types of data are available. Refer to the "File System Category" sections of Chapters 9, "FAT Concepts and Analysis," 12, "NTFS Analysis," 14, "Ext2 and Ext3 Concepts and Analysis," and 16, "UFS1 and UFS2 Concepts and Analysis," for specific outputs.

## Content Category

The content category of data includes the file and directory content. Typically, the content category includes equal-sized data units that are allocated for files and directories. All TSK tools in this category start with the letter d.

The dls tool lists the contents of data units, and by default it outputs the contents of all unallocated data units. The -e flag can be used to output all data units, which is the same as using dd on the image. You also can use the -l flag to list the allocation status instead of outputting the actual contents. For example, the next example lists the allocation status of each data unit in an NTFS image:

```
# dls -f ntfs -e -l ntfs-10.dd
addr|alloc
0|a
1|a
[REMOVED]
13423|a
13424|f
```

The 'a' after each address signals that the data unit is allocated, and an 'f' signals that it is unallocated. The next example will extract all unallocated space of the NTFS image:

```
# dls -f ntfs ntfs-10.dd > ntfs-10.dls
```

The resulting file will have no structure to it because it simply contains random data units from the file system. If you search the file and find evidence, you can determine from where it originally came by using the dcalc tool. dcalc will calculate the original data unit address by using the data unit address from the unallocated data. For example, if our NTFS file system had 4,096-byte clusters and we found evidence in the 123rd cluster in the unallocated data file, we would supply 123 with the -u flag:

```
# dcalc -f ntfs -u 123 ntfs-10.dd
15945
```

We also can determine the allocation status of a specific data unit by using the dstat tool. dstat also will display the block or cylinder group information for UFS and Ext2/3 file systems.

```
# dstat -f linux-ext3 ext3-5.dd 23456
Block: 23456
Not Allocated
Group: 2
```

Lastly, we can view the contents of any data unit using the dcat tool. For example, we can view the contents of data unit 23,456 in our Ext3 image by using the following:

```
# dcat -f linux-ext3 ext3-5.dd 23456
```

## Metadata Category

The metadata category includes the data that describe a file. Here you will find the data unit addresses that a file has allocated, the size of the file, and temporal information. The types of data in this category vary depending on the file system type. There are four TSK tools in this category, and the names all start with i.

We can get the details about a specific metadata entry by using the istat tool. The output will show the size and temporal data as well as any permissions fields. The addresses of all allocated data units also will be shown. When run on an NTFS image, it will show all the file's attributes. Example output of this tool was given in Chapters 9, 12, 14, and 16.

We also can list the details of several metadata structures by using the ils tool. By default, ils will show only unallocated metadata entries, but all of them can be shown with -e. Listing the unallocated entries is useful to find the entries from deleted files where the file name has been reallocated.

```
# ils -f ntfs -e ntfs10.dd
0|a|0|0|1089795287|1089795287|1089795287|100555|1|24755200|0|0
1|a|0|0|1089795287|1089795287|1089795287|100555|1|4096|0|0
[REMOVED]
255|a|256|0|998568000|1100132856|1089795731|100777|1|15360|0|0
256|f|256|0|1100132871|1100132871|1100132871|100777|1|256|0|0
```

The output was designed so that it can be processed by another tool, and it is frequently used with the mactime tool to make timelines of file activity. If we find a data unit with interesting evidence, we can search all the metadata entries using the ifind tool with the -d flag. Similarly, if we want to find the metadata entry that a specific file name points to, we can use ifind with the -n flag. In the following example, we find that NTFS cluster 3,456 has been allocated by the $DATA attribute of MFT entry 18,080.

```
# ifind -f ntfs -d 3456 ntfs10.dd
18080-128-3
```

Lastly, we can view the contents of any file based on its metadata address instead of its file name using the icat tool. This is useful for unallocated files that no longer have a name pointing to their metadata entry. We used this command in the NTFS chapters because it stores all data in files.

```
 # icat -f ntfs ntfs10.dd 18080
```

## File Name Category

The file name category of data includes the data that associates a name with a metadata entry. Most file systems separate the name and metadata, and the name is located inside of the data units allocated to a directory. There are two TSK tools that operate at the file name layer, and their names start with f.

fls will list the file names in a given directory. It takes the metadata address of the directory as an argument and will list both allocated and unallocated names. The -r flag will cause the tool to recursively analyze directories, and the -l flag will look up the metadata and list the temporal data along with the file name. Examples of this were given in each of the previous file system chapters. Here is an Ext3 image with a directory in inode 69457, which contains a deleted file named file two.dat.

```
# fls -f linux-ext3 ext3.dd 69457
r/r 69458:      abcdefg.txt
r/r * 69459:    file two.dat
d/d 69460:      subdir1
r/r 69461:      RSTUVWXY
```

If we want to know which file name corresponds to a given metadata address, the ffind tool can be used. For example:

```
# ffind -f linux-ext3 ext3.dd 69458
/dir1/abcdefg.txt
```

## Application Category

The application category of data includes the data that are included in a file system because it is more efficient using normal system files. In TSK, this includes only two tools, which are for the journal in Ext3. The journal records what updates are going to be made to the file system metadata so that a crash can be more quickly recovered from. This was discussed in Chapters 8 and 14.

The jls tool will list the contents of the journal and show which file system blocks are saved in the journal blocks. The contents of a specific journal block can be viewed by using the jcat tool. Here is an example:

```
# jls -f linux-ext3 ext3-6.dd
JBlk      Descriptrion
0:        Superblock (seq: 0)
1:        Unallocated Descriptor Block (seq: 41012)
2:        Unallocated FS Block 98313
3:        Unallocated FS Block 1376258
[REMOVED]
```

If we are interested in file system block 98,313, we can view the contents of journal block 2 using jcat.

```
# jcat -f linux-ext3 ext3-6.dd 2
```

## Multiple Category

There are a few tools that combine the data from the various categories to produce the data sorted in a different order. The first tool is `mactime`, and it takes temporal data from `fls` and `ils` to produce a timeline of file activity. Each line in the output corresponds to a file being accessed or changed somehow, which we discussed in Chapter 8. Here is an example output (which has been reduced so that it will fit the width of the book):

```
Wed Aug 11 2004 19:31:58     34528 .a. /system32/ntio804.sys
                             35392 .a. /system32/ntio412.sys
[REMOVED]
Wed Aug 11 2004 19:33:27      2048 mac /bootstat.dat
                             1024 mac /system32/config/default.LOG
                             1024 mac /system32/config/software.LOG
Wed Aug 11 2004 19:33:28    262144 ma. /system32/config/SECURITY
                            262144 ma. /system32/config/default
```

Another tool that reorders data is the `sorter` tool, which sorts files based on their content type. The tool runs the `file` command on each tool and saves the file to a category based on a set of rules. The `fls`, `ils`, and `icat` tools are used to extract the files from the image.

Lastly, there is a hash database tool named `hfind`, that allows you to quickly lookup a MD5 or SHA-1 hash value from the NIST NSRL or one that you made using `md5sum`.

```
# hfind NSRLFile.txt FBF4C1B7ECC0DB33515B00DB987C0474EC3F4B62
FBF4C1B7ECC0DB33515B00DB987C0474EC3F4B62        MOVELIT.GIF
```

## SEARCHING TOOLS

The last major category of tools in TSK is searching tools. This area will be expanded in the 2.00 release. The current version has the `sigfind` tool, which searches for binary values. This was used in several of the scenarios in Part 3, "File System Analysis," of the book.

Paul Bakker has been working on adding indexed searches to TSK and Autopsy, and that feature will be part of the 2.00 release (http://www.brainspark.nl/). The indexing process makes a tree of the strings in an image so that you can more quickly find the occurrences of specific strings. A more detailed description can be found in "The Sleuth Kit Informer, Issue 16" [Bakker 2004].

## AUTOPSY

Theoretically, you could do an entire investigation using the command line, but it would not be fun. Autopsy was developed to automate the investigation process when TSK is being used, but it does not limit what an investigator can do. You can still use the command line when you need to do something that the interface does not allow.

Autopsy is HTML-based and is basically a Web server that knows how to run tools from TSK and how to parse the output. It does not know anything about file systems or disks, only TSK does. Autopsy can be used for both dead and live analysis.

For a dead analysis, Autopsy provides case management so that you can have multiple hosts per case and each host can have its own time zone and hash database. All actions are logged so that you can keep track of what you analyzed. You also can make notes about evidence that is found. Because Autopsy uses HTTP, you can connect to it from any computer. When you run Autopsy, you provide the IP address of your computer, and it allows you to remotely connect to it. This allows a central repository of images to exist.

For a live analysis, you will need to compile Autopsy and TSK and then burn them to a CD. The CD can be placed in a Unix system that is suspected of being in an incident, and you can analyze the file system contents by connecting to Autopsy from your laptop or other computer. There are several benefits of running Autopsy and TSK during a live analysis, including that they will show files that are hidden by most rootkits and will not modify the A-times of files and directories when you are looking at their contents. As with all types of live analysis, this process relies on the OS for data, which can lie if it has been modified by an attacker.

### ANALYSIS MODES

Autopsy is organized into analysis modes, which are similar to the organization of the TSK tools. The File Analysis mode allows you to list the files and directories in the image and view file contents. The Metadata mode shows all the metadata associated with a specific entry and allows you to view any data unit allocated to the file. The Data Unit mode allows you to view any data unit, similar to a hex editor, and the Keyword Search mode allows you to search for ASCII or Unicode strings. The keyword searching is done as a logical volume search and not a logical file search. Refer to Chapter 8 for more details on the search type differences.

Autopsy also allows you to sort all files based on type and make HTML pages of thumbnails of all pictures. Timelines of file activity can be created, and notes can be added when evidence is found. The notes allow you to more easily return to where the evidence exists. Lastly, there is an event sequencer that allows you to make notes based on temporal data from the evidence, and it sorts the data. For example, you can make event notes for the creation times of evidence files and Intrusion Detection System (IDS) alerts. The notes will be sorted and will help during the Event Reconstruction Phase of the investigation.

An example screen shot of the File Analysis mode is given in Figure A.1.

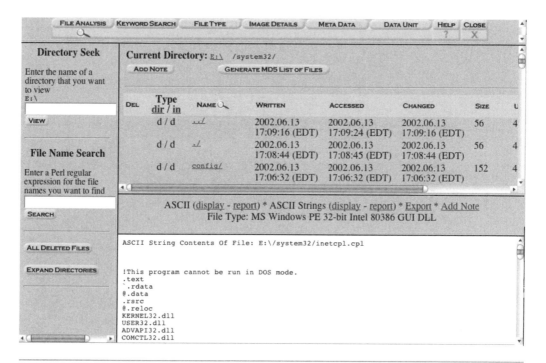

**Figure A.1**   Screen shot of Autopsy in File Analysis mode.

## BIBLIOGRAPHY

Bakker, Paul. "SearchTools, Indexed Searching in Forensic Images." *Sleuth Kit Informer* #16, September 2004. http://www.sleuthkit.org/informer/sleuthkit-informer-16.html#search.

# Index

## Symbols

## M

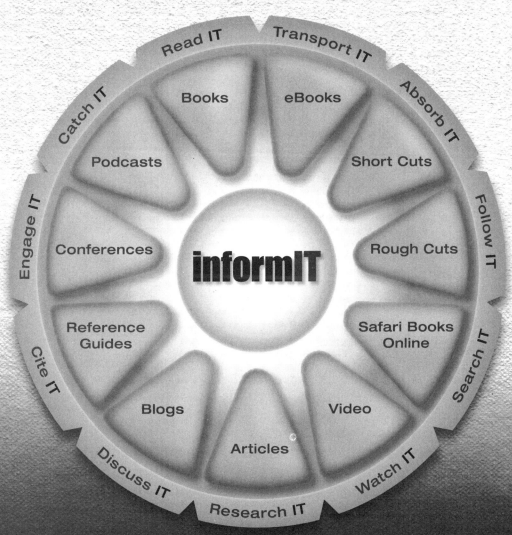